# THE NATURE OF ROMAN COMEDY

# THE NATURE
# OF ROMAN COMEDY

## A STUDY IN
## POPULAR ENTERTAINMENT

BY

GEORGE E. DUCKWORTH

PRINCETON, NEW JERSEY

PRINCETON UNIVERSITY PRESS

1952

Printed in the United States of America by
Princeton University Press, Princeton, New Jersey

# PREFACE

THE study of Roman comedy is primarily a study of the work of two comic poets, Titus Maccius Plautus (c. 254-184 B.C.) and Publius Terentius Afer (c. 195-159 B.C.). Since the comedies of their contemporaries and successors have survived only in fragmentary form, the twenty extant plays of Plautus and the six composed by Terence form our *corpus* of Roman comedy and are of great value and significance to students of both ancient and modern drama.

For the classical scholar, the twenty-six comedies provide an invaluable storehouse of material on the nature of the language, style, meter, and prosody of the second century B.C.; here is the Latin language as it was spoken and written in the age between the second and third Punic wars. Short fragments survive of the other literary works of the period (chiefly epics and tragedies) but there is nothing to rival in importance the linguistic and metrical information to be derived from these plays. The ancient historian, furthermore, can find in the comedies of Plautus numerous references to Roman life and customs, to Roman and Italian localities, and occasionally to Roman personages and events. The plays of Terence contain few Roman allusions, but his prologues are rich in biographical details and throw considerable light on the literary methods and literary feuds of the period.

But it is as drama that these plays have their greatest significance, not only to students of Greek and Roman comedy, but to all who are interested in the history and development of the drama in general. The value of the plays may be considered to be threefold. In the first place, almost all of Greek New Comedy is lost, and the works of Plautus and Terence, adapted from Greek originals, are helpful in giving at least a general idea of the themes, structure, and roles of the later Greek comedy. Second, many of the plays are well-constructed and amusing comedies or farces which have often been produced in modern times and are still presented on the stage. Such plays well deserve attention and study for their plot construction, their delineation of character, and the nature of their humor. The third aspect is even more important for students of the drama; the plays of Plautus and Terence provided models for the Renaissance dramatists, and playwrights in Italy, France, England, and elsewhere translated and imitated the Roman plays, adapting their plots and characters to new and original creations. Ariosto, Molière, Shakespeare, and Ben Jonson are among the many dramatists who came under the Roman influence.

It is a surprising fact that no full and adequate work on the nature of Roman comedy has ever appeared in English. General books on Plautus are available in French, i.e., G. Michaut, *Plaute* (1920) and P. Lejay, *Plaute* (1925), in Dutch, i.e., P. J. Enk, *Handboek der Latijnse Letterkunde*, II (1937), and in Italian on both Plautus and

Terence, i.e., F. Arnaldi, *Da Plauto a Terenzio* (2 vols., 1946-47). Numerous German books, such as F. Leo, *Plautinische Forschungen* (2nd ed., 1912), E. Fraenkel, *Plautinisches im Plautus* (1922), and G. Jachmann, *Plautinisches und Attisches* (1931), are written primarily for the Plautine specialist. In English good summaries of Plautus and Terence may be found in handbooks of Latin literature, e.g., J. W. Duff, *A Literary History of Rome From the Origins to the Close of the Golden Age* (1909), but such accounts are out of date in many respects. G. Norwood's book, *The Art of Terence* (1923), contains much useful material, but his *Plautus and Terence* (1932) is both inadequate and misleading, especially in its treatment of Plautus. A more recent work, P. W. Harsh's *A Handbook of Classical Drama* (1944), contains brief analyses and discussions of each of the twenty-six Roman comedies.

Worthy of mention also is *The New Greek Comedy* (1917), a translation into English by J. Loeb of P. E. Legrand's *Daos. Tableau de la comédie grecque pendant la période dite nouvelle* (1910). In this work are lengthy discussions of many aspects of the plays of Plautus and Terence, but the purpose of the book is chiefly to give a complete picture of Greek New Comedy, and the description of Roman comedy is incidental to the author's main plan. This same tendency has been carried to an extreme by many later scholars who have used the Roman playwrights as a quarry for the reconstruction of Greek comedy. Much of their work is based upon questionable premises, such as the assumed perfection of the Greek originals or the belief in a rigid and mechanical plot structure on the part of the Greek playwrights. Their conclusions about the originality of Plautus and Terence are often most unconvincing, for they maintain that the Roman elements can be detected largely by means of real or imagined flaws and inconsistencies, and they likewise do no service to Greek comedy by their attempted separation of Greek and Roman elements and their fanciful theories about the nature of the non-existent Greek originals. Results far more helpful for an understanding of the technique and originality of Plautus and Terence have been achieved in recent years by many American and British scholars. The contributions of Prescott, Flickinger, Hough, Harsh, Beare, and others have done much to advance and correct earlier views about Roman comedy. This material at present is largely unknown except to the classical scholar who has access to professional journals, but must be considered in any attempted evaluation of the work of the Roman playwrights.

This book is not written for the specialist in Roman comedy; it is directed primarily to classical students, to those who are interested in classical literature in a more general way, and to all readers of ancient and modern comedy. I have endeavored to include in one volume the background and history of Roman comedy, the staging and presentation of the plays, the nature of the comedies (with attention to stage conventions, the structure of the plots, suspense and irony, the delineation of character, the moral tone of the plays, the humor in situation, character, and language), the difficult problem of the originality of Plautus and Terence and their relation to the Greek originals, and finally some consideration of their extensive influence on later comedy. The lack of any such book in English has been a prime factor in my desire to undertake so comprehensive a treatment of the subject, and it has been my aim to incorporate in the work the results of the most recent scholarly investigations, wherever such results seem sound and useful for a better comprehension of the achievements of Plautus and Terence. I have sought to avoid unnecessary documentation, and have cited sparingly from works other than English, for the general reader does not desire such references and the classical student will have no trouble locating them in the works cited. The general bibliography and the bibliographies for each chapter serve the double purpose of providing a selected list of works for supplementary reading and making possible briefer citations in the footnotes.

I have not outlined in detail the plots of the twenty-six comedies; a brief summary of each play appears in Chapter 6 under its appropriate classification, and somewhat fuller analyses of the comedies may be found in Harsh, *A Handbook of Classical Drama*, and in my introductions to the plays in *The Complete Roman Drama* (1942). Technical discussions of the structure and composition of the plays are in general omitted as of interest only to the specialist in Plautus and Terence. Those who wish to pursue further such investigations will find the necessary bibliographical material in the volumes of Marouzeau, *L'année philologique*, and (for each of Plautus' plays) in Enk's *Handboek*, II, a useful work even for those who read no Dutch. General bibliographies covering many aspects of Roman comedy appear in Enk, II, 2, pp. 293-322, and in my edition of the *Epidicus* of Plautus (1940), pp. 429-453.

The dilemma which an author faces in writing a book of this nature is obvious: some readers will possibly prefer an even more general treatment and fewer references to scholarly problems; others may desire more detailed discussions and perhaps lament the omission of certain topics. No one will regret more than does the author himself that many subjects have not been treated more thoroughly, but to have done so would have required minutiae of detail and a mass of documentation impossible in a single volume. I have tried, therefore, to steer a middle course by including the material which seemed of greatest importance and broadest interest and, working directly from the contents of the plays, I have endeavored to present the most striking illustrations of the many features of Roman comic technique. I trust that the many topics and problems treated in this volume will make for better understanding and greater enjoyment when the plays themselves are read or reread.

Many of the so-called difficulties which some critics find in the comedies of Plautus and Terence emerge only upon minute and scholarly examination of the comedies, and I wish at the outset to stress the fact that neither Greek nor Roman comedy was composed for such a purpose. The plays were written for single productions before audiences which desired entertainment and which viewed the plays far less critically than does the modern scholar who tests each comedy by strict laws of logic and often searches for flaws to prove some hypothesis concerning its origin. It is highly important for all readers of ancient comedy to visualize as fully as possible the presentation of the plays on the stage. The manner of delivery, the use of gestures and asides, the limitations of the stage setting, the acceptance of many conventions which are not the conventions of the modern stage—all these are important for our understanding of the comedies. Too often a scholar views each comedy as a kind of artistic unit in a vacuum, so to speak, and then complains that the play does not fulfill his expectation. The fault lies with the critic himself because he fails to look upon ancient comedy as popular entertainment and so ignores the very essence of its being.

In citing from the Greek and Roman comedies I have used the following texts: T. Kock, *Comicorum Atticorum Fragmenta* (3 vols., Leipzig, 1880-88) ; C. Jensen, *Menandri Reliquiae in Papyris et Membranis Servatae* (Berlin, 1929) ; O. Ribbeck, *Scaenicae Romanorum Poesis Fragmenta*, Vol. II (3rd ed., Leipzig, 1898) ; W. M. Lindsay, *T. Macci Plauti Comoediae* (2 vols., Oxford, 1910) ; R. Kauer and W. M. Lindsay, *P. Terenti Afri Comoediae* (Oxford, 1926). For Donatus I have used the text of P. Wessner, *Aeli Donati quod fertur Commentum Terenti* (3 vols., Leipzig, 1902-08). All translations from Plautus and Terence are my own unless otherwise specified.

I wish to express my thanks to the many friends who have read all or part of this book in manuscript and have given me helpful advice and criticism; these include Professors Allan C. Johnson, Whitney J. Oates, Paul R. Coleman-Norton, Samuel D. Atkins, and Frank C. Bourne, of Princeton University; Professor John N. Hough, of the University of Colorado; and Mr. George A. Kennedy, now a graduate student at Harvard University. To Professor Antony E. Raubitschek, of Princeton University, and to Professor Charles T. Murphy, of Oberlin College, I am also grateful for ideas and suggestions of value. I have profited much from Professor Hough's own researches in the field of Roman comedy, as well as from those of other friends, notably Professor P. W. Harsh, of Stanford University, Professor P. J. Enk, of the University of Groningen, and Professor W. Beare, of the University of Bristol. Professor Beare's many valuable and stimulating theories about the history and staging of Roman drama are now available in *The Roman Stage* (1950), which reached me just as *The Nature of Roman Comedy* was going to press.

I am deeply indebted to the authorities of the Princeton University Press, and especially to Mr. Datus C. Smith, Jr., its Director, for kind and helpful cooperation in the publication of this volume. The illustrations have been taken from L. W. Jones and C. R. Morey, *The Miniatures of the Manuscripts of Terence*, published by the Princeton University Press.

GEORGE E. DUCKWORTH

*November* 1, 1951

# CONTENTS

# ILLUSTRATIONS

# THE NATURE OF ROMAN COMEDY

# CHAPTER 1

## *EARLY ITALIAN POPULAR COMEDY*

THE traditional date of the founding of Rome was 753 B.C. and more than five hundred years elapsed before a Greek named Livius Andronicus adapted a Greek tragedy and a Greek comedy for presentation on the Roman stage. This date, 240 B.C., is important, for it marks not only the appearance of Greek drama at Rome but also the beginning of formal Latin literature. Latin prose and verse had appeared earlier in primitive form (e.g., laws, maxims, religious songs, dirges, epitaphs) and had been slowly developing throughout the centuries; the linguistic medium was being prepared for the time when a sudden impetus would make literary creation inevitable.

In the early days of the Republic the Romans were too busily engaged in the mastery of their environment to give much thought to cultural pursuits. Gradually they consolidated their position as the ruling people of the Italian peninsula and in so doing came into closer contact with the Greeks of southern Italy. The first Punic war (264-241 B.C.) gave the Romans a knowledge of Greek life and culture in Sicily, and their victory over Carthage, which marked the beginning of their expansion as a world power, may have brought to them a self-consciousness, a realization of their own cultural deficiencies and what would be expected of them as a great nation. Certainly it is no accident that the regular production of tragedies and comedies at Rome began in 240 B.C., one year after the conclusion of the war. The necessary stimulus to literary activity had arrived. Whether the dramatic presentations were primarily to satisfy the desires of soldiers who had seen Greek tragedies and comedies at Syracuse and elsewhere or whether the plays reflected a more general realization that the cultural development of the Romans had not kept pace with their political prestige is difficult to decide. The fact that Livius Andronicus also translated the *Odyssey* into Latin for use in schools reveals an increasing concern for better educational methods. From this time on for the next hundred years epic and drama remained the chief concern of the Roman poets.

The beginnings of Roman literature are sometimes criticized as imitation and translation but it is worth recalling that the Greeks by the third century B.C. had already invented, developed, and brought to a state of perfection almost every conceivable literary form—epic, drama (both tragedy and comedy), lyric, elegy, epigram, pastoral, history, oratory, philosophical dialogue and treatise. The literature of ancient Greece is the one truly original European literature and in a broad sense all later literatures of western Europe are and must be imitative in that they are all indebted to Greece, directly or indirectly, for their literary forms. The Romans had nothing of their own that deserved the name of literature and so, when they came into contact with Greek culture and Greek literature, they were naturally eager to imitate and adapt the Greek masterpieces. The Romans may have lost some strength and realism by their generous use of Greek writers but they doubtless saved much time by entering quickly on their heritage, and early writers like Naevius and Plautus brought vigor and originality to the literary types taken over from the Greeks.

It is well to remember that of all the peoples of the period who came into contact with the Greeks only the Romans had the maturity and the imagination to assimilate and carry on the culture of their Greek neighbors. The very beginnings of Roman literature were audacious and merit our admiration. A new art was developed—the art of translation. To transfer a literary work from one language to another was in itself a new idea and a bold undertaking at a time when the Latin tongue had not yet attained a truly poetic expression. Livius Andronicus and his successors, Naevius, Plautus, and Ennius, did much to make Latin a more flexible and melodious medium. They mark the beginnings of a development in the language which did not reach its culmination until the days of Cicero and Vergil.

Although 240 B.C. is the all important date for the beginning of Roman literature, we must believe that the ground had already been prepared for the introduction of formal drama. The very fact that there were theatrical performances and a theater-going public in 240 B.C. implies that some form of dramatic activity existed prior to this date. Our first concern will be to describe the nature of this drama, as accurately as can be determined, and to discover what influence, if any, this primitive, non-literary drama may have had upon Roman comedy of the second century B.C.

## Horace and Livy on Early Drama

The ancient Romans, like the modern Italians, had a fondness for gesticulation and mimicry, and it is difficult to conceive of primitive festivals without some form of song and dance in which the mimetic element played a part. The poet Horace in a famous passage (*Epistles* II, I, 139-163) describes the farmers resting from their toil and making sacrifices to their gods in a rural harvest festival, on which occasion they uttered rustic jests of an abusive nature in alternate verse, and Horace refers to this practice as *Fescennina licentia*.[1] These Fescennine verses, he says, developed into so scurrilous a form (*iam saevus apertam in rabiem verti iocus*) that they were restrained by law, after which they again lapsed into a form of harmless entertainment (*ad bene dicendum*

[1] 145 f.: *Fescennina per hunc inventa licentia morem versibus alternis opprobria rustica fudit.*

*delectandumque redacti*). Then Horace utters the famous sentence: "Conquered Greece took captive her fierce conqueror and brought the arts to rustic Latium,"[2] and states that after the Punic wars the Romans turned to the pages of the Greeks and began to search for the useful matter to be found in Sophocles, Thespis, and Aeschylus. He admits, however, that traces of the earlier rustic verses (*vestigia ruris*) have survived to his own day.

Horace thus ascribes to rural festivals the origin of a crude form of dramatic dialogue in verse, and gives also a brief history of its development prior to the importation of Greek drama. He does not mention the name of Livius Andronicus, and the references to Greek drama seem to be entirely to tragedy.

Much more is learned about the early history of drama at Rome from an important and much discussed passage in Livy's *History of Rome* (VII, 2), which gives a very different account. Livy describes the various stages of the development as follows. (1) During a plague at Rome in 364 B.C., as one means of appeasing the wrath of the gods, performers were brought from Etruria to dance to the music of the flute. (2) This Etruscan dance was taken over by Roman youth who added rough dialogue and appropriate gestures; the form became popular, and native professionals (*vernaculi artifices*) received the name of *histriones*, from *ister*, the Etruscan word for performer. These early productions, containing repartee and impromptu verse, are considered by Livy to be similar to the Fescennine verses, but apparently are not to be identified with them.

(3) A more elaborate performance followed, a kind of musical medley, no longer improvised but with song and dance now arranged for accompaniment by the flute; to this performance Livy applies the term *satura*.[3] This medley of song, dance, and dialogue had no real plot and was easily displaced by (4) plays with a plot (*argumentum*) which were first introduced by Livius Andronicus. Livy fails to mention that the plays of Livius Andronicus were Greek plays translated and adapted for the Roman stage, but refers to him as an actor in his own compositions and tells the story that once, when Livius had strained his voice from taking too many encores, he employed a boy to sing and he himself merely acted out the song with gestures; from this, says Livy, arose a distinction between songs (*cantica*) and dialogue verse (*diverbia*), and

[2] 156 f.: *Graecia capta ferum victorem cepit et artis intulit agresti Latio.* The phrase *Graecia capta*, if specific, refers to the subjugation of the Greek cities of southern Italy in the third century B.C., not to the final conquest of Greece in 146 B.C. But Horace is probably thinking of the contrast between the earlier, crude Latin verses and the more artistic Greek drama without intending a precise chronological sequence. On the problem of the chronology involved and the attempt to connect Horace's account with the mistaken chronology of Accius, see Knapp, *TAPhA* 43 (1912), pp. 125 ff.

[3] *impletas modis saturas descripto iam ad tibicinem cantu motuque congruenti peragebant.*

the *histriones* confined themselves to dialogue and accompanied with gestures the songs when sung by others.

(5) The final stage in Livy's account marks a reaction from the highly developed drama[4] of the professionals; the Roman youth left to the *histriones* the acting of little plays[5] and returned to the responsive songs and jests of the earlier period, that is, of the second stage; these were later called *exodia* or afterpieces, and were attached to the *fabula Atellana*, a type of comedy that had been developed by the Oscans in Campania.[6] Since the Atellan plays were acted by Roman youth, they were kept free from any degrading association with professional actors; hence the custom remained that the amateur performers retained membership in their tribes and served in the army. Livy concludes his discussion with these words: "In my account of the small beginnings of other institutions it seemed advisable to include also the origin of stage performances, in order to show how from a wholesome beginning they have developed into a craze which can scarcely be supported by wealthy kingdoms."

A passage in Valerius Maximus (II, 4, 4) gives a history of the early drama that in most respects resembles Livy's account. Valerius Maximus mentions the development of an early song and dance into the metrical *saturae*, the introduction of plays with plots by Livius, the story about Livius losing his voice and acting out songs in pantomime, the coming in of Atellan farces from Campania, and the fact that the performer of such plays was allowed to retain both membership in his tribe and the right of serving in the army. All this closely parallels the details given by Livy; the chief difference is the assignment to Roman youths of the earliest song and dance, after which a dancer was summoned from Etruria. It seems unlikely that Valerius Maximus took his material from Livy, but the close resemblance shows that the two accounts at least came from the same source.[7]

---

[4] Livy says: *ludus in artem paulatim verterat; ars* here is usually taken as describing an aesthetic advance in the drama, but it may well mean "profession," i.e., Livy may be referring to a social decline in the drama, since his purpose is to show that drama, from an innocent beginning, has become in his own day a great social evil; cf. Beare, *Ha* 54 (1939), p. 35.

[5] Livy here uses the word *fabella*, "playlet," although the play with a plot introduced by Livius Andronicus is called *fabula*. There is no indication here that the Roman youth had ever taken part in the production of the regular *fabulae*. Beare (*Ha* 54, 1939, p. 38) suggests (a) that *fabellae* may be a contemptuous equivalent of *fabulae* and Livy may mean that the young men decided to set up in opposition to the professionals by reviving the Fescennine-like performances, or (b) that the young men had been in the habit of performing playlets, possibly akin to the mime, and that they now abandoned these because of the growth of professionalism.

[6] It is probable that the Atellan farces were also used as *exodia* after presentation of regular dramas; that is, the *Atellanae* were *exodia*, but not all *exodia* were *Atellanae*; see Michaut, *Sur les tréteaux latins*, pp. 74 ff. Ullman (*CPh* 9, 1914, p. 12) thinks that the *exodia* presented by the amateurs were *Atellanae*.

[7] Ullman, however, considers that Valerius Maximus is paraphrasing Livy; cf. *CPh* 9 (1914), p. 8, n. 5; *SPhNC* 17 (1920), p. 395.

Horace and Livy in the Augustan age and Valerius Maximus in the early Empire wrote centuries after the events they were attempting to describe, and it is quite possible that they or their sources may on occasion have been guilty of theorizing and guesswork. For instance, the popularity of the mime and the pantomime in the later Republic perhaps led to the theory of the separation of the actors from the singers—an incredible procedure for comedy in the age of Plautus.[8] Again, the status of actors in the late Republic when manumitted slaves were employed on the stage may have been responsible for the theories in Livy and Valerius Maximus that a stigma was attached to the profession of acting in the earlier period with the exception of the performers in the Atellan plays. But if Livy is correct in stating that all regular actors of Roman birth were removed from army service and from membership in their tribes, the procedure was a mark of disgrace; it could hardly, as Frank suggests,[9] have resulted from a scarcity of actors and been originally intended as an honorable exemption, which was misunderstood when the theater deteriorated and ex-slaves entered the profession.

In other respects also it is possible that the accounts of Livy and Valerius Maximus are untrustworthy, and that they have been in part invented to produce a history of early Roman drama where none really existed. We shall return to this point later in the chapter. As to the various types of the pre-literary drama, Horace, Livy, and Valerius Maximus provide us with the following names: the Fescennine verses, the dramatic *satura*, the *fabula Atellana*; to these must be added the mime, whose existence in Italy is well attested for the early period. What can be determined about the nature of these four forms? With the exception of the *satura*, all survived and flourished in the classical period; fragments of the later mime and *Atellana* are extant, as well as numerous references to them, and certain inferences may reasonably be drawn from this information concerning their nature in the third century B.C.

## The Fescennine Verses

There were in antiquity two explanations of the word "Fescennine"; either the name of the verses came from the Etruscan town Fescennium, or they were so called because they were thought to ward off witchcraft (*fascinum*).[10] Most modern scholars accept the former derivation; just

[8] Cf. Beare, *Ha* 54 (1939), pp. 51 f. See below, "*Diverbium* and *Canticum*" in chap. 13.

[9] *CPh* 26 (1931), pp. 19 f.; *Life and Literature in the Roman Republic*, pp. 95 ff. But cf. Green, *CPh* 28 (1933), pp. 301 ff., who argues against Frank and thinks that the censorial stigma "may have been more strictly applied when the drama was still regarded as a Greek innovation than in the late Republic, when Rome was more tolerant."

[10] Festus (*ap.* Paul) 76, Lindsay: *Fescennini versus, qui canebantur in nuptiis, ex urbe Fescennina dicuntur allati, sive ideo dicti, quia fascinum putabantur arcere*; cf. Servius, *ad Aen.* VII, 695: *Fescenninum oppidum est ubi nuptialia inventa sunt carmina.*

as the *fabula Atellana* was named for Atella, a town in Campania, so these crude verses received their name from the town of their origin; also, there are linguistic difficulties in deriving *Fescennine* from *fascinum*.[11]

There is no evidence that the Fescennine verses were dramatic in the classical period. They were used chiefly at weddings and are referred to as *nuptialia carmina*. Numerous citations in Catullus, Seneca, and later authors attest to this practice. They were apparently also employed for invective; Macrobius (*Sat. 2, 4, 21*) refers to *Fescennini* written by the emperor Augustus attacking Asinius Pollio, and quotes Pollio's witty answer with its play upon *scribere* and *proscribere*:

> I am silent; for it is not easy to inscribe verses against a person who has the power to proscribe.

The general character of the earlier Fescennine verses seems clear; they were jesting, abusive, and doubtless obscene, and were especially associated with weddings and harvest festivals. There can be little doubt that they were dramatic in a crude fashion, since they were improvised and responsive, and they were probably accompanied by dramatic gestures. As to the verse form, it is most likely that they were composed in the native Saturnian meter although the trochaic septenarius, so frequently employed by Plautus and Terence, seems to have been a native Latin meter well known in the early period.

## The Problem of the Dramatic *Satura*

From a dance with gestures and dramatic dialogue, which, according to Livy, resembled the Fescennine verses, it would be only a step to a more elaborate musical performance. To this more developed stage of drama both Livy and Valerius Maximus gave the name of *satura*, but little is known of its nature; that it was a kind of musical medley is implied by Livy's phraseology (*impletas modis saturas*; cf. Valerius Maximus: *saturarum modos*) and it apparently had little plot, since it was sharply distinguished from the play with a plot introduced by Livius Andronicus. The word *satura* itself indicated a mixture, or medley; cf. the phrase *lanx satura*, "a platter filled with mixed foods"; the word also occurred in legal terminology to refer to an omnibus law (e.g., *imperium per saturam dare, sententias per saturam exquirere*) and was used by Ennius as a title for his collection of miscellaneous poems.

Many modern scholars have rejected outright the tradition of an

[11] Cf., however, Michaut, *Sur les tréteaux latins*, pp. 42 ff., who favors the derivation from *fascinum*, and explains the Fescennine verses as songs originally used to invoke the protection of the god Fascinus (phallus, or male organ), considered as a powerful force against magic. He suggests that the town was so named because the god Fascinus was held in special honor there.

early dramatic *satura*. Hendrickson and Leo,[12] in particular, maintain that the account of Livy and Valerius Maximus is completely untrustworthy. Briefly, the arguments against the existence of the *satura* are these : the tradition of the *satura* goes back to a pre-Varronian Roman grammarian, who, having no facts about drama in the pre-literary period, wrote up a history of Roman comedy based upon Aristotle's account of Greek comedy (*Poetics* 1449a, 10 ff., 1449b, 7 ff.). Hendrickson believes that both Livy (VII, 2) and Horace (*Epist.* II, 1, 139 ff.) go back to this source. Horace's rustic festival and Livy's city ritual correspond to Aristotle's origin of comedy in phallic verses; the scurrility (*aperta rabies*) of the Fescennine verses in Horace's account and the *satura* of Livy are a parallel to the lampooning and abuse (ἰαμβικὴ ἰδέα) of Old Attic Comedy, while the introduction of Greek plays (Horace) and the introduction of plays with plots by Livius Andronicus (Livy) correspond to Aristotle's description of Crates as giving up lampooning and introducing plays with plots. On the basis of this supposed dependence on Aristotle the Roman account could have no validity; the dramatic *satura* had never existed but was invented to provide a parallel to Aristotle's second stage, the ἰαμβικὴ ἰδέα of Old Comedy. Leo believes that the term *satura* was invented to correspond to the Greek satyr play, and he denies that Horace and Livy go back to the same source,[13] but he too thinks that the accounts reflect the attempts of Roman scholars to write a history of Roman drama using Greek methods and Greek material.

This sceptical assault on the Roman tradition aroused much controversy and considerable opposition.[14] The use of Greek methods by Roman grammarians cannot be denied but it does not follow that the tradition of dramatic performances at Rome prior to Livius Andronicus must be rejected in its entirety. Hendrickson pressed too far the assumed parallels with Aristotle. There can be little doubt about the early existence of the Fescennine verses,[15] and Livius Andronicus is an historical person who actually did introduce a new kind of drama at Rome. It is difficult to see how the parallelism could have been avoided on these two points. Is it not probable that a more advanced kind of musical performance may also have existed? Furthermore, there is no trace in

[12] Hendrickson, *AJPh* 15 (1894), pp. 1-30; 19 (1898), pp. 285-311; Leo, *H* 39 (1904), pp. 63-77.

[13] E.g., Horace's description is largely rural and stresses the Greek influence; Livy's account is urban and fails to mention the Greek influence. See Knapp, *PAPhA* 40 (1909), pp. liii f.; Michaut, *Sur les tréteaux latins*, pp. 102 f.

[14] Cf. especially the defense of the *satura* by Knapp, *PAPhA* 40 (1909), pp. lii-lvi; *AJPh* 33 (1912), pp. 125-148; *TAPhA* 43 (1912), pp. 125-142.

[15] Cf. however G. Wissowa (*RE*, VI, 1909, cols. 2222 f.), who, either misunderstanding Hendrickson and Leo, or extending their methods, maintains that the accounts in Livy and Horace of the early dramatic Fescennine verses are an invention to parallel Aristotle's phallic verses.

Livy's *satura* of an element of abuse and invective to correspond to Horace's *aperta rabies* and Aristotle's ἰαμβικὴ ἰδέα. The very weakness of the parallelism here argues against Hendrickson's theory and strengthens the view that there was some such musical medley.

That this dramatic form had the name *satura*, however, seems most unlikely. The term was probably used by Livy and Valerius Maximus (or their source) to denote the hodgepodge, medley-like character of this stage of drama, and the term *impletae modis saturae* served to stress its musical character and to distinguish it from other forms of *saturae*, such as the miscellaneous poems of Ennius. Ullman reflects the opinion of conservative scholars when he denies any rigid adherence to Aristotelian theory in the formation of Livy's account and considers *satura* a descriptive term "used to suggest the miscellaneous character of the performance."[16] In other words, the dramatic *satura* as such perhaps did not exist, but Livy's version does describe a definite stage in the development of the drama. It is inconceivable that the early Romans would not have favored some such musical performance in the days before Livius Andronicus. Little, who accepts the *satura* as the name of this dramatic form, points out that it "has the hall-marks of popular drama . . . it combined libretto, musical accompaniments and gestures suited to the action. It was marked by broad humor and tomfoolery; it lacked consecutive plot; it could hardly be dignified by the title of art . . . the *Satura* relied upon its music to heighten the liveliness of its performance."[17]

## The *fabula Atellana*

The *fabula Atellana* was a type of farce which had been developed by the Oscans in Campania and taken over by the Latins at an early date, although even in the classical period performances were occasionally given in Oscan. The name was derived from Atella, a town between Naples and Capua. The *Atellana* had a long history in Rome and was exceedingly popular in the early part of the first century B.C. when it became a literary form at the hands of Pomponius and Novius. No complete farces are extant from this later period, merely titles and short fragments, but enough has survived to give some indication of its nature.

The plays dealt mostly with life in the country or the small town; there is a definite note of rusticity in titles such as *Bubulcus* ("The Cowherd"), *Vindemiatores* ("The Vine-dressers"), *Pappus Agricola* ("Daddy the Farmer"), *Rusticus* ("The Yokel"), *Capella* ("The Kid"), *Verres Aegrotus* ("The Sick Boar"). Some titles are derived

[16] Ullman, *CPh* 9 (1914), p. 18; cf. Beare, *The Roman Stage*, p. 14.

[17] Little, *HSCPh* 49 (1938), pp. 216 f. See also Lejay, *Histoire de la littérature latine*, pp. 177 ff.; Boyancé, *REA* 34 (1932), pp. 11 ff.

from festivals (e.g., *Kalendae Martiae*) and from districts (*Campani, Galli Transalpini*), and occasional mythological titles such as *Andromacha, Hercules Coactor* ("Hercules the Tax-Collector"), and *Armorum Iudicium* ("The Award of Arms") imply a parody of tragedy. A few titles resemble those of regular comedy, e.g., *Adelphi* ("The Brothers"), *Hetaera* ("The Courtesan"), *Citharista* ("The Music-girl"). By the first century the *Atellana* had become assimilated to some extent with the *fabula palliata* (the regular Roman comedy adapted from the Greek) and the *fabula togata* (the comedy with Latin settings and characters). In the earlier period the rustic element was doubtless more pronounced.

The plays were short, perhaps about three or four hundred verses, since they were used as *exodia*. Little is known about the plot, but farcical situations were frequent, and cheating and trickery and general tomfoolery played a large part. The presence of obscenity seems highly probable in popular comedy of this type, and there is some evidence of a fondness for riddles and *double entendres*.[18] The meters of the later *Atellana* are the regular meters of Roman comedy, but in this respect the pre-literary form must have differed, for it was limited to the Saturnian meter and possibly the trochaic septenarius. Music and song played an important part, as is apparent from references to *cantica* in the time of Hadrian, when the *Atellana* again flourished for a time.[19]

The most interesting feature of the *Atellana* was the fixed characters (*personae Oscae*). The actors regularly wore masks, which facilitated the representation of stock characters. These were four in number: (1) Maccus was the fool, the stupid clown, whose name is usually related to the Greek verb μακκοᾶν, "to be stupid." (2) Bucco was the glutton or braggart. Beare says: "It is usually taken for granted that Bucco is connected with *bucca*, and that the characteristic feature of this type would be the large cheeks—whether these denote stupidity, talkativeness or gluttony."[20] In Plautus, *Bacch.* 1088, *buccones* clearly means "stupid fools" (cf. the synonyms *stulti, stolidi, fatui, fungi, bardi, blenni*). (3) Pappus was the foolish old man, the old dotard who was easily deceived. The name is probably Greek in origin, and Varro informs us that the Oscan name was *casnar*. (4) Dossennus is usually considered the cunning swindler, the glutton,[21] perhaps the clever hunchback; the idea of his deformity comes from the common derivation of his name from *dorsum*, "back," but there is no other indication that he was abnormal in appearance; also there is almost no evidence to show that he

[18] Quintilian (VI, 3, 47) is often cited to support the existence of obscenity: *illa obscaena, quae Atellani e more captant*; but *obscaena* is an emendation; cf. Beare, *CR* 44 (1930), p. 167, who accepts the reading of the MSS: *obscura*, i.e., "riddles." See also Beare's discussion of the passage in *CR* 51 (1937), pp. 213 ff.

[19] Cf. Suetonius, *Nero*, 39, *Galba* 13.     [20] *Ha* 54 (1939), p. 46.

[21] Cf. Horace's reference to Plautus in *Epist.* II, I, 173: *quantus sit Dossennus edacibus in parasitis*.

was cunning, a "wise man" among fools. Accordingly Beare suggests[22] that the name might come from a derivative of *dorsum*, i.e., *dossuarius*, "the backbearer," and so signify stupidity. The difficulty with this explanation is that a type of farce with trickery and stupid characters like Maccus, Bucco, and Pappus would need a character with a certain degree of cunning to engineer the deception; the most logical character for this purpose is Dossennus.

Attempts have been made to add other characters to this list of four *personae Oscae*. Horace (*Serm.* 1, 5, 51-70) relates an incident during the trip to Brundisium when a verbal battle ensued between Sarmentus, a buffoon (*scurra*) and an Oscan named Messius, to whom the epithet Cicirrus was added. The conjecture that Cicirrus, the Oscan name for gamecock, was a regular character in the *Atellana*[23] has not been generally accepted. A more likely candidate for inclusion is Manducus, the character who was represented as constantly eating or champing his jaws in a grotesque manner. In Plautus' *Rudens* (535 f.) the shivering slavedealer suggests hiring himself out at the games as a Manducus, because his teeth are chattering. Manducus has been identified with Dossennus solely on the authority of an emended citation from Varro,[24] but most scholars accept the identification. Beare says that "nothing is certain about Dossennus-Manducus except the chattering jaws."[25] It is worth noting that the characters Maccus, Bucco, Pappus, and Dossennus all appear in titles (e.g., *Maccus Virgo, Maccus Copo, Maccus Miles, Bucco Adoptatus, Bucco Auctoratus, Pappus Agricola, Pappus Praeteritus, Duo Dossenni*); the fact that Manducus does not occur as a name in a title perhaps indicates that he was not a separate character, if indeed we are correct in assuming that he belongs in the *Atellana* at all.

No fragments have survived of the early Atellan farces; there is no indication that they were written out and preserved. A prearranged comic situation may have been worked out with considerable improvisation; each actor knew his role and made many jokes on the spur of the moment. In many respects the plays in situation and characters were not unlike Punch and Judy shows, or those of the Italian *commedia dell' arte*.[26] There is no reason to doubt the antiquity of the four stock characters; masks were worn and feminine roles were played by men. The early plays doubtless dealt more largely with country life, and in theme (e.g., cheating and obscenity) and style they were much cruder

[22] *Ha* 54 (1939), p. 49.

[23] Dieterich, *Pulcinella*, pp. 94 f. Nicoll (*Masks Mimes and Miracles*, p. 74) accepts Dieterich's theory and lists Cicirrus as a fifth Atellan character.

[24] *De ling Lat.* VII, 95: *unde manducari, a quo in Atellanis Dossennum vocant Manducum.* But *Dossennum* is Mueller's emendation for the reading of the MSS: *ad obsenum* or *ad obscenum.*

[25] *Ha* 54 (1939), p. 49; cf. also Nicoll, *Masks Mimes and Miracles*, pp. 70 ff.

[26] Cf. Michaut, *Sur les tréteaux latins*, pp. 269 ff.

than the later literary *Atellana*. They were essentially Italian, but even before 240 B.C. they had been subjected to Greek influences.

Greek farces resembling the *Atellana* had long existed in southern Italy. These plays, known as *phlyakes*, had masked actors and portrayed scenes from everyday life. Rhinthon of Tarentum, writing at the end of the fourth century B.C., was especially famed for a type of *phlyax* play known as *hilarotragodia*, a burlesque of mythology; fortunately, numerous vase paintings have survived to show us how these mythological travesties were put on the stage; the paintings depict Heracles, Odysseus, and even Zeus in many farcical situations and give an excellent idea of the masks and costumes employed.[27]

It is unwise to identify the *fabula Atellana* with the *phlyakes*, as some scholars have done, but the Greek plays had a decided effect upon the Italian farces at an early date. The area around Naples, only a few miles from Atella, had been Greek for centuries. The use of names such as Maccus and Pappus for stock characters indicates an early Greek influence, and the presence of mythological titles in the literary *Atellana* may be accounted for by the popularity of Rhinthon's mythological burlesques. As Little says, "it is not altogether fanciful, although in no way capable of proof, to see the influence of the South Italian playlets in the title Pappus, to trace perhaps the survival of the Dorian Herakles in the greedy Bucco, of his parasite in Maccus, of the wily Odysseus in Dossennus."[28]

## The Mime

The Italian mime is said to have reached Rome not later than 211 B.C., since we know of the presence of a mimic actor in the city at that time. A well-known anecdote preserved by Festus (436 ff., L.) and Servius (*ad Aen.* VIII, 110) relates that, during a celebration of the games of Apollo in 211 B.C., news came that Hannibal was approaching the city; the spectators rushed to their arms and later, when they returned to the theater victorious but worried about the interruption of the festival, they discovered that an aged mimic actor named Pomponius was still dancing to the flute. The ritual had not been interrupted and there was no need of repetition. From this episode came the famous proverb: "All is well; the old man is dancing" (*salva res est; saltat senex*).

Mimes were regularly presented at the *Floralia*, which became an annual festival in 173 B.C. The story of the *mimus* in 211 B.C. has been doubted since the details do not square with the historical account of Hannibal's activity in that year,[29] but the *Floralia* was first celebrated

27 See Nicoll, *Masks Mimes and Miracles*, pp. 51-58; Bieber, *The History of the Greek and Roman Theater*, pp. 258-300.

28 *HSCPh* 49 (1938), p. 216.    29 See Reynolds, *Ha* 61 (1943), pp. 56 ff.

in 238 B.C. and there is nothing inherently improbable in the presentation of mimic performances long before 173 B.C., perhaps even earlier than 211 B.C.

This fourth type of Roman popular comedy received literary form at the hands of Decimus Laberius and Publilius Syrus in the late Republic and throughout the Empire remained the most popular form of comedy. The word *mimus* was Greek, from μιμεῖσθαι, "to imitate," and referred both to the play and the actor; a common Latin word for mimic actor was *planipes*, "with bare feet," the implication being that the actor of the mime was distinguished from other actors because he wore neither the *cothurnus* ("buskin") of tragedy nor the *soccus* ("slipper") of comedy. The *planipes* was a performer who wore no shoes in order to have greater freedom of movement. A less likely explanation of *planipes* is that the actors of the mimes performed, not on the stage, but on the level of the orchestra. Even if this were likely for the early period when the mimes were presented as *exodia*, it would hardly be true in the Empire when the mime had largely supplanted not merely tragedy and comedy but the *Atellana* as well.

The mime was a type of farce in which mimetic action—dancing, gesticulation, and facial expression—played a large part. Masks were apparently not worn[30] and female roles were played by women. Defined in antiquity as "an imitation of speech and action without reverence, the lascivious imitation of shameful deeds and words,"[31] the mime was regarded as the imitative art *par excellence*; it sought to imitate life in all its aspects. Aristotle in the *Poetics* (1448a) had said that comedy represented people as worse than they are, tragedy represented people as better; the mime had no such purpose; its attitude toward life was completely unmoral.

The fragments and titles of the mimes of Laberius and Publilius Syrus give us little information about the nature of the plays. Publilius Syrus was especially famed for his clever *sententiae* which were collected and edited separately. Some of Laberius' titles resemble those of the *fabula palliata*, e.g., *Gemelli* ("The Twins"), *Aulularia* ("The Pot of Gold"), the latter being the title of one of Plautus' plays; other titles had already appeared in Greek New Comedy, e.g., *Colax* ("The Flatterer"), *Phasma* ("The Ghost"). Such titles imply that in the Ciceronian period the mime had encroached upon other forms of comedy and had taken over themes from both the regular comedy and the *Atellana*. Titles like *Aquae Caldae* ("Hot Baths"), *Aries* ("The

[30] See, however, Nicoll (*Masks Mimes and Miracles*, p. 91), who thinks that some actors may have worn masks.

[31] Diomedes, in Keil, *Grammatici Latini*, I, p. 491: *mimus est sermonis cuius libet (imitatio et) motus sine reverentia, vel factorum et (dictorum) turpium cum lascivia imitatio*. But cf. Kroll-Skutsch, *Teuffels Geschichte der römischen Literatur* (6th ed., Leipzig, 1916), I, p. 8, who read *vel factorum (et honestorum) et turpium cum lascivia imitatio*, "the lascivious imitation of deeds both decent and indecent."

Ram"), *Hetaera* ("The Mistress"), *Piscator* ("The Fisherman"), *Sorores* ("The Sisters") would serve equally well as titles of the *Atellanae*. But unlike the Atellan farces, the mime preferred urban scenes to those of country life.

The plays presented farcical and often indecent situations, acted out by two or three persons. Usually the mime was short, corresponding to a modern vaudeville or burlesque sketch, but in some cases it might have a fairly lengthy *hypothesis*, or plot. Adultery was a popular theme from the first century on, and it was the fat and stupid husband who was mocked and ridiculed when he returned home to find his wife with a lover.[32] Many writers of the Empire, especially the early Christians, condemned the plays for their obscenity and indecency, and some of their comments sound surprisingly modern. But not all mimes dealt with such subjects; many were on more serious themes and it is interesting to find that Seneca, discussing the vices of the age in his essay *De Brevitate Vitae* (12, 8), accuses the mimes of neglect because they omit and fail to put on the stage so many incredible vices. The mime, as an imitation of life, sought to make everything ridiculous, and as such it may have had a certain social value.

The pre-literary Italian mime was indubitably much cruder than the later form. How far it can claim to be original is difficult to determine. The theory of Reich[33] that the Italian mime had no originality and was merely a Greek importation represents an extreme view that has not received general acceptance. The fondness of the ancient Italians for song and dance, for gesticulation and mimicry, makes it difficult to think of early Italian life without some type of mimic performance. But such performances at an early date were blended with the Greek mime from southern Italy and Sicily, where it had flourished for centuries. Epicharmus, the earliest writer of Greek comedy, had composed at Syracuse short plays, some of which were realistic scenes from everyday life while others were mythological parodies.[34] It seems unwise to term these plays mimes, as do some writers, but at least from this western Dorian comedy the later Greek mime developed. The prose mime of Sophron in the fifth century B.C. continued the themes from mythology and real life, and the influence of this form upon the *phlyakes* and the plays of Rhinthon cannot be doubted. The mime, along with other forms of popular comedy, flourished in Sicily and Magna Graecia from the fifth century to the time of Plautus. The threads of the Greek and the Italian mime are so closely interwoven that it is best to refer to it as the Graeco-Roman mime.

[32] See Nicoll, *Masks Mimes and Miracles*, pp. 119 f.; Reynolds, *CQ* 40 (1946), pp. 77 ff.
[33] *Der Mimus*, p. 558.
[34] See "Epicharmus" in chap. 2.

## The Influence of Pre-literary Comedy

When Livius Andronicus and his successors began to translate and adapt Greek comedies for Roman audiences, there were thus several well developed dramatic types already existent: (1) the Fescennine verses, containing jesting and abuse; (2) a more elaborate medley, with dialogue and gestures set to a musical accompaniment; (3) the Atellan plays, noted for their stock characters and slapstick farce; and (4) the Graeco-Roman mime, with its emphasis upon gesticulation and fooling. These forms of popular comedy had much in common; they portrayed broadly humorous situations of a universal appeal; they parodied serious themes, presented the characters as exaggerated and ridiculous, cared less for a coherent plot than for liveliness and irrelevance, and did not shrink from indecency and filth. Through all these forms ran a fondness for song and dance.

We must of course be cautious lest we hold too high an opinion of this early popular comedy. It was coarse and crude, and was easily supplanted by the superior comedy imported from Greece. We may well ask whether these pre-literary forms had any influence upon Roman comedy and especially upon Plautus. A detailed answer is possible only after we have looked at the nature of Greek comedy and have analyzed with care the characteristics of the plays of Plautus and Terence. But a few preliminary remarks may not be out of place at this point.

It will perhaps never be possible to say with certainty that a particular passage in a Roman play is based on a definite type of popular comedy although such attempts have been made. The farcical conclusion of Plautus' *Casina* has been considered indebted either to a *phlyax* play or to the *Atellana*,[35] and passages of abuse and invective such as occur in the *Mostellaria* (1 ff.) and in the *Pseudolus* (360 ff.) may give some idea of the raillery for which the Fescennine verses were noted. The large amount of song and dance in many of Plautus' comedies has been believed by some to be an inheritance from the earlier musical medley.[36] One such play, the *Stichus*, abnormal in its complete lack of plot, has been explained as the result of Plautus' dependence on popular forms of Hellenistic drama; this view assumes that Plautus produced from a Menandrian original a series of scenes on the theme of homecoming in the style of the Hellenistic mime.[37]

Actually, two possible lines of influence seem indicated: (1) if we

[35] Cf. Duckworth, *CPh* 33 (1938), pp. 279 ff. Beare (*CR* 44, 1930, pp. 165 ff.) finds elements from the *Atellana* in Plautus' *Rudens* 515-539, a passage which he suggests might be named *Duo Dossenni*.

[36] So Lejay, *Plaute*, p. 31, who accepts the ancient tradition and uses the term *satura*; for other theories concerning the origin of the Plautine *cantica*, see below, "The Origin of the Lyrical *Cantica*" in chap. 13.

[37] Such is the view of Immisch, *SHAW* 14 (1923), Abh. 7, pp. 25-28; cf., however, Sedgwick, *CR* 39 (1925), pp. 59 f. See below, pp. 146, 206.

find that Roman comedy contains a larger musical element than seems to have existed in the Greek comedy from which the Roman plays were adapted, it is at least a reasonable inference that the fondness of the Italians for song and dance may have led the playwrights to follow the example of earlier popular comedy; (2) likewise, if Greek comedy is sentimental rather than farcical, concerned with love affairs rather than with trickery, and if many Roman comedies are largely devoted to deception and impersonation, it seems not unlikely that early popular comedy with its predilection for slapstick comedy, farcical deception, and coarse jests may have had an influence in this respect also. If the early popular comedy had never existed, would Roman comedy have developed along different lines? A question such as this, which concerns the originality of Plautus and Terence, must be reserved for later discussion.

# CHAPTER 2

## *GREEK COMEDY*

Long before the rudimentary forms of drama described above appeared at Rome, comedy in Greece had already reached a state of artistic perfection. We have seen that a purely native form of Roman comedy was impossible, for the early dramatic forms such as the *fabula Atellana* and the mime had been subjected to Greek influences in Italy even in the pre-literary period, i.e., prior to 240 B.C. Roman comedy, as we find it in Plautus and Terence, is avowedly an adaptation of Greek comedy; the plays are *fabulae palliatae*, comedies in Greek dress, i.e., comedies which preserve the themes, characters, costumes, and stage-settings of the Greek originals. An adequate understanding of the nature and development of Roman comedy is therefore impossible without first looking at the various stages of Greek comedy and attempting to gain as clear a picture as possible (considering the gaps in our knowledge) of the type of comedy which the Romans chose for adaptation and imitation. A survey of Greek comedy, however incomplete, will help to answer some of the important questions which will arise later; e.g., why did the Romans choose for models comedies of the Hellenistic period rather than those of the fifth century? What light does the nature of the Greek comedies throw upon the originality of Plautus and Terence? Can the differences in the comic technique of the two Roman playwrights be explained by their choice of Greek originals, or is the explanation of these differences to be sought elsewhere?

## Epicharmus

Epicharmus, the earliest of the Greek comic playwrights, was a Sicilian who flourished at Syracuse in the early part of the fifth century. Numerous writers in antiquity referred to him both as a philosopher and as a dramatist, but so few fragments remain that it is difficult to form a reliable estimate of his work. His comedies apparently included mythological travesties, plays presenting conflicts between non-human abstractions or personifications, and more realistic social comedies about contemporary life.[1] The travesties of mythology, a subject popular in later Athenian comedy, dealt largely with humorous versions of the adventures of Odysseus and Heracles. A few fragments are extant of *Hebe's Wedding* (which celebrated the marriage-feast of Hebe and Heracles), *Heracles and the Girdle*, *Odysseus the Deserter*, and *Odysseus Shipwrecked*. The conflict of abstractions is represented by the

---

[1] Norwood (*Greek Comedy*, p. 97) suggests that "these different types of comedy were addressed to different kinds of audience." On the general character of Epicharmus' comedy, see Pickard-Cambridge, *Dithyramb Tragedy and Comedy*, pp. 402 ff.

title *Earth and Sea* and by a curiously named play, *Logos and Logina* ("Male and Female Argument"?).

The fact that Epicharmus composed also a type of social comedy is of especial interest to all students of later Greek and Roman comedy, and it is believed by some that the so-called Comedy of Manners first made its appearance in Sicily in the works of Epicharmus. Plays like *The Megarian Woman* and *The Rustic* may have been character studies. One sizable fragment of fifteen verses from *Hope or Wealth* is important, for it describes the man who goes out to dinner and entertains the host with his wit:

I dine out with the man who wishes, he need only invite me; and the one who doesn't wish need not invite me. And while there I'm witty and arouse much laughter and praise my host. And if anyone wishes to speak against him, I insult the fellow and take the quarrel on myself. And then, when I've had a lot to eat and drink, I go away. . . .[2]

The character who describes himself in this amusing fashion sounds much like the parasite who appears so frequently in later comedy, the man who lives by his wits and hopes to gain free meals either by flattery (cf. Artotrogus in Plautus' *Miles Gloriosus*, Gnatho in Terence's *Eunuchus*) or by a ready supply of jokes (cf. Gelasimus and his joke-books in Plautus' *Stichus*). To Epicharmus, therefore, we are evidently indebted for the earliest parasite in dramatic literature. It has also been suggested that he invented the type of swaggering soldier found in Plautus (e.g., Therapontigonus in the *Curculio*, Pyrgopolynices in the *Miles Gloriosus*, Antamoenides in the *Poenulus*), but there are no fragments that would indicate this; the professional soldier did, however, exist in Sicily in the time of Epicharmus, but was unknown in early fifth-century Athens.

Concerning the plot and structure of Epicharmus' plays almost nothing is known, and even the authenticity of many of the fragments has been questioned. The plays were written in Doric Greek verse, in simple dialogue meters (iambic trimeter and trochaic tetrameter) and there are no indications of a chorus or a choral leader. Both external and internal evidence suggest that the plays were short, perhaps about four hundred lines (roughly the length of a later mime). His work was undoubtedly primitive, but he deserves to be considered the first real comic poet of antiquity; Plato in the *Theaetetus* (152e) calls him the best of comic poets, and Aristotle in his *Poetics* (1448a) mentions him in connection with the claim of the Dorians to have originated comedy, and later says (1449b) that the making of plots came originally from Sicily.

There can be little doubt of Epicharmus' influence upon later comedy at Athens, and also upon the Greek mime, as developed by Sophron of Syracuse at the end of the fifth century. But his works were not used

[2] *Athenaeus*, VI, 235f-236b.

directly by the comic playwrights of Rome. Horace's statement that "Plautus is said to hurry along on the model of Sicilian Epicharmus"[3] does not mean that Plautus imitated the Sicilian poet, but that the two playwrights were alike in the liveliness of their dialogue or the rapid action of their plots. Indirectly, however, Epicharmus did influence Plautus, and not merely through Greek comedy. Plautus preserved in his plays features of Italian popular drama, and many of the elements of the Atellan farces and the Graeco-Roman mime were undoubtedly derived from western Dorian comedy.[4] As Norwood says, "the modern world owes to this earliest master, through Aristophanes and Menander, through Plautus and the *commedia dell' arte*, a great deal more than it dreams."[5]

## Old Comedy (486-404 B.C.)

Comedy at Athens developed from the worship of Dionysus, god of the vine. Aristotle states that comedy originated with the leader of the phallic processions,[6] i.e., processions carrying a pole on which was a representation of the phallus (the male sex organ). Attic Comedy at its origin was undoubtedly connected with the *komos*, or revel, but probably not with a phallic revel. The phallic element in Old Comedy, and especially the garb of the actor, appears to be derived from the non-choral Dorian farce or mime. The fact that so many choruses of fifth-century Attic Comedy were disguised as animals implies that the animal-masquerade lies at the very basis of Old Comedy. In other respects also the nature of early comedy is best explained by an origin in a procession of revelers, often masquerading as animals, who danced and sang and uttered impromptu lampoons against bystanders or important public characters. Such a revel doubtless concluded with a song, in part satirical and jesting, addressed to those standing by. These performances were essentially choral, and after a time were no longer improvised; poets wrote more elaborate songs and touched upon serious themes of literature and politics in the final address to the audience, or *parabasis*, which became a regular feature of Old Comedy.

The next step was the introduction of an actor, partly under the influence of tragedy, but even more under the influence of Dorian farce; this actor wore a costume which included the phallus and padding of stomach and buttocks—the same garb worn by attendants of Dionysus among the Dorian Greeks and also by actors of Greek farces in southern Italy (the *phlyakes*). The part of the actor was at first clowning with

---

[3] *Epistles*, II, I, 58; cf. Norwood, *Greek Comedy*, p. 109, n. 3, for a discussion of this passage.

[4] Cf. Little, *HSCPh* 49 (1938), pp. 212, 227 f.      [5] *Greek Comedy*, p. 113.

[6] *Poetics*, 1449a. For the brief summary of the origin of comedy which follows, I am indebted in part to Norwood, *Greek Comedy*, pp. 5-13; cf. also Pickard-Cambridge, *Dithyramb Tragedy and Comedy*, pp. 225 ff.

the chorus after the *parabasis*, but a second actor was provided and dramatic action was now possible in the early part of the performance also. The successive playwrights developed more elaborate plots, treated mythological, social, or political themes, and composed lyrics of great beauty. This plausible origin of comedy leads directly to the plays as we find them in the latter part of the fifth century.

The first official presentation of comedy in Athens was at the Great Dionysia in 486 B.C. The earliest writers, Chionides, Magnes, Ecphantides, are little more than names. The three greatest comic playwrights of the century were Cratinus, Eupolis, and Aristophanes. Mythological travesties were popular (e.g., the *Dionysalexandros* and the *Odysses* of Cratinus); this type of comedy had been written by Epicharmus, and was favored later by playwrights of Middle Comedy, as well as by Rhinthon, the writer of *phlyax*-plays.[7] Fantasy, the unfettered play of the imagination, provided themes for comedies, as did the politics of the day with its outstanding personalities who could be attacked and satirized with impunity.

Of the many comedies produced in this period, none has survived[8] with the exception of eleven plays of Aristophanes (and the last two, the *Ecclesiazusae* and the *Plutus*, are in form and content more suggestive of Middle than of Old Comedy). Aristophanes (c. 445-388 B.C.) is one of the great comic and poetic geniuses of all time. His plays deal with themes drawn from literature (the *Frogs* and the *Thesmophoriazusae*, both parodying the tragic art of Euripides), philosophy (the *Clouds*, which ridicules Socrates and his "thinking-shop"), and politics (e.g., the *Acharnians*, the *Peace*, and *Lysistrata*, all highly amusing comedies in favor of peace). His most fantastic comedy is the *Birds*, which portrays a political Utopia known as Cloud-Cuckoo-Land. As a playwright Aristophanes combined beauty and brilliance with broad humor and a frankness that was characteristically Greek but hardly obscene in the modern sense. His plays were intensely local, scurrilous, and filled with parody, but underlying his farce and vulgarity were a depth of thought and a seriousness of purpose, for which we look in vain in later comedy.

Structurally his plays were in certain respects similar to fifth-century tragedy, with an expository scene (*prologos*) preceding the *parodos*, or entrance of the chorus, which was often fantastically garbed as birds, or clouds, or wasps, or frogs.[9] Lyric measures of great beauty and complexity abounded and made possible elaborate song and dance. The

---

[7] See above, p. 13.

[8] There are extant numerous short fragments of Eupolis, Pherecrates, Cratinus, and others; cf. T. Kock, *Comicorum Atticorum Fragmenta*, I (Leipzig, 1880), III (Leipzig, 1888), pp. 397-418. The oft-quoted fragment, "He is either dead or a schoolteacher," which Norwood (*Greek Comedy*, p. 69) cites as a fragment of New Comedy is listed by Kock as from Old Comedy (III, p. 401, fr. 20).

[9] For the origin of the famous cheer, "Brekekekex koax koax," cf. the song of the chorus in Aristophanes' *Frogs*, 209 ff.

main problem of the play, often with an *agon* or debate between two characters, was usually treated in the first half of the play. Both the *agon* and the *parabasis* (address to the audience in the middle of the play) were peculiar to Old Comedy. After the *parabasis* the results of the main theme were displayed in a series of loosely connected scenes of a farcical nature separated by choral odes. A feast or a wedding sometimes occurred at the close.

Comedies of this type were difficult to compose and expensive to produce, and depended upon freedom of speech. With the defeat of Athens at the end of the Peloponnesian War (404 B.C.) it was no longer possible to present fantastic comedies filled with personal and political invective. Freedom of speech was now restricted, and the impoverishment of Athens made the former productions with their elaborate choruses far too expensive. It is possible also that changing ideals of dramatic art were in part responsible for the shift to social comedy at this time. At any rate, 404 B.C. seems the appropriate year for marking the end of Old Comedy, rather than 388 B.C., the date of Aristophanes' last play. His last two comedies display less imagination, less song and dance, choruses more commonplace and less essential to the action, more attention to construction of plot. We stand here at the beginning of the transition.

The fact that only eleven plays of Aristophanes have survived out of hundreds composed by various playwrights gives us an inaccurate picture of Old Comedy; we tend to think of all fifth-century comedy as Aristophanic, having the same qualities of fantasy and satire, beauty and indecency, that are found in such profusion in the extant plays. We forget that mythological travesty was popular among other playwrights (especially Cratinus), and we forget also that contemporary with Aristophanes was a type of social comedy which gave more attention to a smoothly constructed plot. Historically, perhaps, the most significant of Old Comedy playwrights was Crates, who, according to Aristotle (*Poetics*, 1449b), "was the first to give up the lampooning form and to compose dialogue and plots of a general nature." The social comedy developed by Crates (probably under the influence of Epicharmus) was continued by other fifth-century dramatists (Phrynichus, Pherecrates, and Plato the Comedian), and is important in that it is the forerunner of Middle and New Comedy. Some of the fragments present scenes from ordinary life, portray drunken persons, and hint at the love-intrigue so frequently found in later comedy.

## Middle Comedy (404-336 B.C.)

Middle Comedy was essentially a period of transition. Plays of fantasy and invective continued for a time, but more and more they were supplanted by mythological travesty and social comedy. Unlike tragedy, which after the fifth century became mediocre and conventional, comedy continued to develop and change; it remained extremely popular at Athens throughout the fourth and third centuries. Hundreds of plays were produced in the Middle period, between the fall of Athens (404 B.C.) and the accession of Alexander (336 B.C.). Athenaeus (VIII, 336d), writing in the third century A.D., claimed to have read more than eight hundred comedies. But, if we exclude the last two plays of Aristophanes which chronologically fall into the Middle period and show the beginning of the transition, of these hundreds of comedies not a single play, not even a single complete scene, has survived; what we have consists of several hundred short fragments cited by later anthologists and grammarians. No plot can be restored and it is precarious to attempt a discussion of the nature of the comedy in any detail. A few broad generalizations nevertheless are possible.

The chorus became less prominent, and the *parabasis* gradually disappeared. The language was more that of everyday speech, and especial care was devoted to the construction of plots. Plays on mythological themes were popular, but more and more the action dealt with everyday life and often centered about a love story and its complications. As to characters, in addition to family types (husbands, wives, sons, slaves), the parasite, the soldier, the courtesan appeared more frequently. Titles like *The Perfumer, The Doll-maker, The Jeweler, The Twins, The Sister, The Miser, The Misanthrope* reveal clearly the increasing trend toward social types and themes.

The outstanding poets of Middle Comedy were Antiphanes and Alexis, whose combined output was said to exceed five hundred comedies. The description of the Pythagoreans in a fragment by Alexis is famous:

. . . no dinner, no soap, no fire, no conversation, no fun, and no bath.[10]

More than three hundred fragments of Antiphanes have been preserved, and while it is obviously unsafe to draw conclusions from fragments out of their context, it cannot be denied that several sound as if Antiphanes were something of a misogynist:

Only one thing can be believed of a woman—her mortality. (251)

A blind man suffers many evils, but he has one blessing—he can't see a woman. (252)

What's this you say? You tell something to a woman when you want to keep it a secret? You might as well announce it to all the heralds in the marketplace. (253)

Marriage is the worst of evils. (292)

What's this you tell me? He is married? Why, the last time I saw him he was alive and walking about. (221)

[10] The translation by Norwood (*Greek Comedy*, p. 47) of fr. 197.

But such criticisms of marriage and women are frequently uttered by married men in the Roman plays of Plautus and Terence; it is a common theme in ancient comedy and does not necessarily express the character or the personal opinion of the playwright himself.

If any extant comedies of the Roman playwrights had been adapted from plays of Middle Comedy, it might be possible to gain a more satisfactory conception of a typical play of this period, but unfortunately there is no clear evidence of the use of Middle Comedy by the Romans. It has been suggested that two of Plautus' comedies, the *Amphitruo* and the *Persa*, were derived from originals of this period; the *Amphitruo* is a play on a mythological theme (the only Roman comedy of the type extant) and may show how Middle Comedy treated such legends; others have considered that the *Amphitruo* might be indebted to a parody of a tragic theme such as was composed by Rhinthon in Tarentum. Actually, however, the technique and structure of the play, the comic devices, the delineation of character, are all so similar to what we find in the other Roman comedies that there seems no reason to deny here the influence of New Comedy. The *Persa*, a coarse slave-controlled farce, which involves the tricking of a slavedealer and ends in a scene of riotous revelry, has been thought by many to be based upon a Greek original of Middle Comedy, partly because of its theme and structure but chiefly because of a reference in the play (506) to the Persians. Such a reference would seem to place the Greek original in the Middle period, before the overthrow of Persia by Alexander the Great. But it is unlikely that this is a definite allusion to contemporary history for the statement occurs in a purely fictitious letter about a fabulous "Goldtown." Moreover, the supposedly peculiar features of structure and character-treatment do not require a fourth-century original; some of the elements, e.g., the part played by the parasite's daughter, are the direct result of the plot;[11] some appear in other Plautine comedies, and, if not an inheritance from New Comedy, may well be Plautus' own addition, modeled possibly upon earlier Italian farces.[12] At any rate, there seems no valid reason for assuming that either the *Persa* or the *Amphitruo* were necessarily adapted from Greek comedies of the Middle period. It is particularly foolhardy for scholars to compare the plot and characters of the *Persa* with those of other Plautine comedies, and from such a comparison to draw conclusions about the similarity of Middle and New Comedy.[13]

We must be careful not to make too sharp a distinction between the plays of Middle and New Comedy. The division is a purely arbitrary

[11] Cf. Prescott, *CPh* 11 (1916), pp. 128 ff.
[12] Cf. Little, *HSCPh* 49 (1938), pp. 219 ff.
[13] As does Legrand; cf. *The New Greek Comedy* (translated by Loeb), pp. 228 ff. I shall regularly refer to Loeb's translation rather than to the original, for two reasons: the translation is more available, and it has a lengthy index which makes it more convenient to use.

one, and some modern scholars, favoring a twofold classification, speak merely of Old and New Comedy. That Aristophanes and Menander represent entirely different phases in the development of comic drama cannot be doubted. There was apparently a sharp break at the end of the fifth century in both form and content, but the work of Antiphanes and his contemporaries developed into that of the following period without any violent change. Dramatists like Eubulus and Alexis bridged the transition and lived also in the period of New Comedy. But the three-fold division has become traditional, and seems justified, inasmuch as a typical play of Antiphanes probably differed considerably from a typical comedy by Philemon or Menander.

## New Comedy (336-c. 250 B.C.)

The writers of New Comedy lived in a changing world. Athens had lost her freedom and was under Macedonian domination. The conquests of Alexander had opened up large portions of the world to the Greeks, and the Athenians developed a more cosmopolitan outlook. The break-down of local patriotism and the lack of civic duties led many to the pursuit of wealth and pleasure, while others sought spiritual values in philosophical creeds which enabled them to rise above externals and achieve mastery of themselves by the use of reason or the pursuit of virtue. But it was a world in which wars, sudden reversals of fortune, the enslavement of men and women, the separation and reunions of families, were frequent. It was inevitable that the playwrights would find in such a period rich material for drama and would reflect in their plays the society and the spirit of the times.

The names of sixty-four writers of New Comedy are known. Of these the most important were Diphilus, Philemon, and Menander, each of whom was said to have composed about one hundred plays. Other active playwrights were Philippides, Demophilus, Posidippus, Apollodorus of Carystus, and Theognetus. The total number of comedies produced in this period is believed to have been about fourteen hundred, but not a single complete play survived the downfall of the Graeco-Roman civilization. It is an appalling thought that so large a body of dramatic literature vanished, and until the end of the nineteenth century it was believed to have vanished completely except for hundreds of short fragments which vary in length from a single word or a single verse to a few passages of forty or fifty lines. From such fragments it was impossible to derive much information about the structure or content of the plays, and the Roman adaptations by Plautus and Terence were used as our main source of information about the works of New Comedy—a dangerous procedure, as the criteria for separating the Greek elements from the Roman were often extremely subjective.

The fragments quoted by ancient grammarians and anthologists are often interesting and some of them are famous. Kock's edition of the fragments contains two hundred forty-seven from Philemon, one hundred and thirty-eight from Diphilus, but over eleven hundred from Menander—an eloquent testimony of Menander's fame in antiquity and the extent to which he was valued over his contemporaries. Among the more familiar of the Menander quotations are the following:

> We live not as we wish but as we can. (50)[14]
> He whom the gods love dies young. (125)[15]
> A man's character is known from his talk. (143)[16]
> Evil communications corrupt good manners. (218)[17]

It is difficult in a single day to remove folly of long standing. (262; cf. 504, 726)

If one faces the truth, marriage is an evil, but a necessary evil. (651)

Some fragments breathe an air of resignation and melancholy:

> The bravest man is he who knows how to suffer the most injuries with patience. (95)
> What stings you is the lightest of all ills, poverty. (282)

It is impossible to find anyone whose life is free from trouble. (411)

Since you are a mortal, do not pray to the gods to be free from grief, but pray for endurance; to be forever free from grief you must be either immortal or a corpse. (549)

Of the longer passages one frequently quoted is fr. 481, which, according to Murray, gives "the true savour of Menander:"[18]

>                     I count it happiness,
> Ere we go quickly thither whence we came,
> To gaze ungrieving on these majesties,
> The world-wide sun, the stars, water and clouds,
> And fire. Live, Parmeno, a hundred years
> Or a few months, these you will always see,
> And never, never, any greater things.
> Think of this life-time as a festival
> Or visit to a strange city, full of noise,
> Buying and selling, thieving, dicing stalls
> And joy-parks. If you leave it early, friend,
> Why, think you have gone to find a better inn;
> You have paid your fare and leave no enemies.

[14] This is from the *Andria*; cf. Caecilius 177: *uiuas ut possis, quando nec quis ut uelis*; Terence, *Andria*, 805: *ut quimus, aiunt, quando ut uolumus non licet.*

[15] This is from the *Dis Exapaton*, the original of Plautus' *Bacchides*; cf. *Bacch.* 816 f.: *quem di diligunt adulescens moritur.*

[16] From the *Heauton Timoroumenos*; cf. Terence, *Heaut.* 384; *nam mihi quale ingenium haberes fuit indicio oratio.*

[17] This fragment is quoted by St. Paul in *First Epistle to the Corinthians*, 15, 33.

[18] *Aristophanes*, p. 223; the verse translation is by Murray.

A few fragments of the other playwrights deserve quoting, some serious, some in a lighter vein:

> Love of money is the root of all evil. (Apollodorus of Gela, 4)
>
> A just man is not he who does no wrong, but one who does not wish to do wrong when he has the power. (Philemon, 94)
>
> Believe in God and reverence Him, do not seek to know whether or not He exists. (Philemon, 118 ab)
>
> Do not find fault with an old man when he makes an error; it is difficult to transplant an old tree. (Philemon, 147)
>
> It's better to bury a woman than to marry her. (Philemon, 236)
>
> Nothing is more fortunate than a poor man, for he expects nothing worse. (Diphilus, 104)

A longer fragment by Phoenicides (4) gives an amusing picture of the life of a courtesan:

> By Aphrodite, I can't endure to be a courtesan any longer, Pythias. Enough of it. Not a word. I was a failure. It's not for me. I want to end it. My first lover was a soldier; the fellow always kept talking about his battles, and as he talked he showed me his wounds, but he never brought in any money. He said that he was going to receive a gift from the King, and he was always talking about it; because of this gift the rascal had me as a gift for a year. I got rid of him and took another man, a doctor. He kept bringing in a lot of patients, and cut and cauterized them, but never made a cent. He seemed to me more dangerous than the other; the soldier merely talked about killing, but the doctor produced the corpses. My third lover happened to be a philosopher, all beard, gown, and talk; there I met with the trouble I should have anticipated, for he gave me nothing. If I asked for anything, he said that money was an evil. "Suppose it is," I said, "then throw it away, but throw it toward me." He didn't do it.

In 1905 the famous discovery of the papyrus fragments of Menander was made at the site of ancient Aphroditopolis, and New Comedy was born again for the modern world. This collection, known as the Cairo papyrus, contains portions of five comedies, and enough is preserved of three plays so that continuous scenes may be read and the nature of the plot inferred in considerable detail. These are the *Epitrepontes* ("The Arbitration"), a comedy praised in antiquity as one of Menander's masterpieces, the *Perikeiromene* ("The Shearing of Glycera"), and the *Samia* ("The Girl from Samos"); of the *Epitrepontes*, we have about eight hundred verses, or approximately two-thirds of the play, of the other two rather less than half is extant. Shorter fragments exist of *The Hero* and an unidentified play. Since the discovery of the Cairo papyrus additional fragments from several other plays have been found. The amount of labor that has been expended upon the reconstruction of the fragments can hardly be imagined. The united scholarship of the world has, as Norwood says, "toiled with microscope and photographic camera, with limitless patience, immense ingenuity and learning, to build up a trustworthy text of these lightly-written comedies."[19]

It is still true that no complete play of New Comedy is in existence but we are now in a position to discuss the nature of Menandrian comedy in far more detail and with far greater accuracy than was possible prior to 1905. I use the term "Menandrian" advisedly, for we have no assurance that Diphilus, Philemon, and the other playwrights of the period handled their themes and portrayed their characters in the delicate and refined manner characteristic of Menander. Philemon, who often defeated his famous contemporary in competition, may have been more farcical; Diphilus may have placed more emphasis upon plots of trickery and deception;[20] of this we cannot be certain but we do see clearly that Menander cared little for farce and intrigue. The fragmentary plays are all cut from a similar pattern but a pattern which allowed considerable ingenuity and novelty.

The basis of each play is a love story,[21] and portrays the love of a young man for his neighbor's daughter or for a mistress whose true identity is later revealed; in the *Epitrepontes*, the couple in love is already married and separated through a series of misunderstandings. The main characters are the usual family types—husbands, wives, sons, daughters, but all are sympathetically portrayed as individuals, e.g., Demeas (in the *Samia*) who drives Chrysis in wrath from his house, or Charisius (in the *Epitrepontes*) who bitterly reproaches himself for his harshness to his wife. The slave takes part in the action but is not the intriguing slave of Plautine comedy; he is faithful, sometimes a bit stupid, and on occasion causes trouble inadvertently (e.g., Onesimus in the *Epitrepontes*). Soldiers, parasites, slavedealers, courtesans, cooks appear in the plays—they too are treated as human beings and not as caricatures. Polemon, the soldier in the *Perikeiromene*, is far less the braggart warrior than a jealous, lovesick youth. Much of the action in the plays develops from the characters themselves, but chance plays an important role. Certain features recur in the plots with amazing frequency—the violation of maidens, the birth and exposure of children who are saved and reared as foundlings, the numerous misunderstandings which result before the recognition scene or scenes solve the complications.

The plays are rich in comic irony, for the audience knows far more

---

[19] *Greek Comedy*, p. 318.

[20] The evidence from Plautus does not necessarily support this; his *Mercator* and *Trinummus*, both adapted from Philemon, are less farcical than many other Plautine comedies. The *Casina*, adapted from Diphilus, has a coarse intrigue which may be due largely to Plautus and the influence of Italian farces (see "Guileful Deception: *Casina*" in chap. 6). The *Rudens*, also from Diphilus, is rich in action and humor, but is not a comedy of deception.

[21] Cf. Ovid, *Trist.* II, 369: *fabula iucundi nulla est sine amore Menandri*; cf. Beare, *Ha* 56 (1940), p. 35, who wrongly assigns the verse to Horace.

than the characters. Menander favors the expository prologue (some-times deferred, as in the *Perikeiromene*),[22] which explains the truth about the foundlings and the mistaken identities. The goddess *Agnoia* (Misapprehension) who speaks the prologue of the *Perikeiromene* might well be considered a motivating factor in all the extant plays of Menander. In the *Perikeiromene*, Polemon wrongly thinks that his sweetheart Glycera is in love with the youth next door (who is really her brother); in the *Samia*, considered Menander's comedy of errors, Demeas' son has violated the daughter of a neighbor and when the baby is born, it is concealed with Chrysis, Demeas' common-law wife, with the result that Demeas wrongly believes that Chrysis has had an affair with his son; in the *Epitrepontes*, Smicrines arbitrates in a dispute be-tween two slaves over a foundling, not realizing that the baby is his own grandchild; Charisius leaves his wife Pamphila, thinking that she has given birth to a child by another, and Pamphila thinks Abrotonon has presented Charisius with a son, whereas the baby in question is really her own. Such complicated plots demanded great dexterity on the part of the playwright, and a clear understanding of the truth was necessary for the spectators if they were to appreciate the irony of each situation.

The language of Menander has been highly praised for its natural-ness, clarity, and simplicity. It is colloquial, but at the same time dra-matic and suited to the characters. Almost all the fragments are written in iambic meter, and lyrical measures are practically non-existent. The chorus, which lost its importance in the Middle period, had now ceased to be an integral part of the play. That there was an inorganic chorus which sang and perhaps danced during pauses in the action is known from the Cairo papyrus, which occasionally indicates the presence of a chorus by the word χοροῦ;[23] the fact that no songs are preserved implies that the chorus had become a mere musical interlude and had no con-nection with the action of the play.

The plays of Menander are comedy only in a broad sense of the term. The jealousies, misunderstandings, and wrong conclusions of the char-acters lead to serious situations which are solved only by the happy end-ing. A genial and tolerant sympathy for human weakness pervades the plays, and slaves and cooks provide some good-natured banter, but jokes are few. In the *Samia* (68 ff.), Parmeno tells the cook:

> I don't know why you carry knives about; you can chop every-
> thing up with your chatter.

Later in the same play (244 ff.), Demeas, whose son has wronged the daughter of Niceratus, says that Zeus once came through the roof to

---

[22] So also in Plautus' *Cistellaria* and *Miles Gloriosus*.

[23] *Heros*, 54; *Epitrepontes*, 35, 201, 584; *Samia*, 270; *Perikeiromene*, 76; cf. Flick-inger, *The Greek Theater and its Drama*, pp. 145-149.

Danaë in a shower of gold and suggests that Niceratus had better see if his own roof is leaking.

If Menander is at all typical of New Comedy, then we must conclude that Greek comedy in the Hellenistic period developed into a type of social drama, the purpose of which was not merely amusement but rather the delineation of human weaknesses and the presentation of complicated problems of everyday life. That this comedy was taken over by the Romans is easily explained. The Romans naturally found their models for tragedy in the masterpieces of the fifth century, especially those of Euripides, but fifth-century comedy, as we see it in Aristophanes, did not readily lend itself to imitation; with its fantastic themes and colorful choruses, it was too difficult to reproduce on the Roman stage, and it was too filled with personal and political invective to be intelligible to the Romans. Furthermore, the Roman state would not have tolerated political satire such as that of Aristophanes. New Comedy, on the contrary, was the current modern drama and was at the height of its popularity when the Romans turned to the writing of plays. It was easy to adapt because its themes were of universal interest, and the realistic portrayal of human relationships could be transferred to the the Roman stage with little or no change.

Greek New Comedy—the culmination of centuries of literary effort by a people of great artistic and aesthetic endowments, "the final manifestation of genuine creative power in Attic literature,"[24]—was adapted by the Romans in their literary infancy and produced before audiences less racially gifted for literature and lacking the necessary background for the appreciation of subtleties and refinements in drama. It is hardly probable that Plautus, or even Terence, could take over New Comedy without many changes. Hence the question arises: What is Greek and what is Roman in Plautus and Terence? Since our knowledge of New Comedy is based primarily upon Menander, it is easy for critics to equate Menander with New Comedy and set up a standard of perfection which the Roman playwrights fail to meet. This standard is raised to still higher levels by the insistence of these same critics that New Comedy is not really comedy but a fusion of earlier comedy and Euripidean tragedy. Before we turn to an examination of the work of Plautus and Terence, a final consideration of Menander and his relation to Euripides will therefore be of value.

## The Significance of Menander

Menander (c. 342-291 B.C.) was the most quoted of the writers of New Comedy, and his fame in later antiquity surpassed that of all classical poets with the exception of Homer and Vergil.[25] He was con-

---

[24] J. W. White, in Legrand-Loeb, *The New Greek Comedy*, p. xii.
[25] Cf. Norwood, *Greek Comedy*, pp. 314-317.

sidered not only a comic dramatist of unsurpassed power but also a mirror of the life of the times, the life of Hellenistic Athens at the end of the third century B.C. Such was the estimate of Quintilian in the first century A.D., and the remark of the Alexandrian critic, Aristophanes of Byzantium, is famous: "O Menander, O Life, which of you imitated the other?"

Many modern critics are less inclined to accept Menander's work as a mirror of life. Admitting his realism and psychological truth, they point out that his world is too limited, too concerned with the problems of love and money; his picture of life is unreal, for it "knows only seduced girls and frivolous youths, crafty slaves, depraved procurers, stupid fathers and so on."[26] But *frivolous, crafty, depraved, stupid* are hardly the correct adjectives to apply to Menander's characters. Menander portrayed the society with which he was familiar, the life of the upper middle class; he dealt with universal emotions, the loves, hopes, and fears of ordinary men and women. Nor should the term "universal" be denied to Menander because the actions and emotions of his characters "are not interrupted and complicated by the necessities of a full day's work."[27] On the other hand, few would maintain that Menander gives a complete representation of the life of the *bourgeois* class as a whole; Allinson seems correct in saying that Menander "holds his mirror to contemporary life but contrives to reflect far more of good than of evil."[28]

The criticisms of modern scholars result in part from the narrow range of Menander's plots. Even in antiquity the poets of New Comedy were accused of repetition and lack of invention. Modern writers echo this criticism and speak of the wearisome repetition of the same devices and details. But to the audiences these plays were not monotonous; we forget the different generations of spectators who saw the plays and we forget also the short memories of people who go to the theater. Ancient critics who could read and compare plays written for different audiences might be impressed by the similarity of plots; the same would be true if modern movie scenarios were studied and evaluated, but the average movie audience is far less conscious of repetition and monotony. Moreover, the limited number of motives in New Comedy—the betrayed maiden, the foundling, the love affair, the recognition scene—fails to give a true impression of the diversity to be found in the plays. Many of these repeated motives provide the background of the play, not the dramatic action itself, and it was here that the playwright showed his skill. Furthermore, a survey of the titles of Menander's lost plays reveals

[26] Ehrenberg, *The People of Aristophanes*, p. 29.

[27] Dunkin, *Post-Aristophanic Comedy*, p. 52 n. But Dunkin accepts the view that Menander's work was a mirror of life, in spite of his belief that the dramatist's primary purpose was a sympathetic portrayal of the rich man. Menander, however, "depicted with sympathy all classes, not merely High Society" (Post, *TAPhA* 65, 1934, p. 34).

[28] *Menander*, p. 7.

his wide range and the variety and flexibility of his composition. But, in general, ancient writers did not value originality as highly as do many moderns; they realized that originality of theme was often impossible and, accepting the subjects of their predecessors, sought for originality of treatment. To illustrate from tragedy, the manner in which Aeschylus, Sophocles, and Euripides treated the story of Electra and Orestes shows the tendency of successive dramatists to treat the same plot in different ways. So in comedy, the stereotyped motives were merely the frame within which the inventive genius of the playwright could display its ingenuity.

Menandrian comedy is often referred to as a comedy of manners;[29] but, as Post points out,[30] the term "comedy of manners" implies the absence of sincerity, simplicity, universality and emotion—the very qualities for which Menander has been noted. The comedy of manners, more interested in a society than in individuals as such, presents stereotyped characters, and Menander is famed for portraying characters that are true to life. On one point all scholars seem to agree: although there is considerable humor in the misunderstandings in which the various characters find themselves involved, the plays of Menander are not comedy in the modern sense of the term. Even in antiquity New Comedy was described as disregarding laughter and tending toward the serious,[31] and this is assuredly true of the extant plays of Menander, whose chief excellence is considered his delineation of character. Even those who criticize New Comedy for its use of stock characters admit that Menander's characters have personality and that the motivation of the action rests upon subtle psychological analysis.[32]

The discovery of the Cairo papyrus in 1905 led not only to intensive study of the text of the plays but to numerous attempts to evaluate anew Menander's position in Greek literature. Estimates vary widely: to some he is "a good second-rate author,"[33] a writer whose plots seem "monotonous, sordid, and artificial."[34] At the other end of the scale are critics who, like Post, have studied Menander with great care and devotion and who find him a great genius; Post ranks Menander "with the greatest of the ancient Greek writers" and does not hesitate to accept the opinion of Aristophanes of Byzantium who placed him second only to Homer.[35] Such praise is excessive; those who read Menander may

[29] E.g., Norwood, *Greek Comedy*, p. 357; cf. Little, *HSCPh* 49 (1938), p. 205: "It is, in effect, a comedy of manners with a distinctly limited range."

[30] *TAPhA* 65 (1934), pp. 13 ff.

[31] *Tract. Cois.* 10; cf. L. Cooper, *An Aristotelian Theory of Comedy*, p. 226.

[32] Cf. C. R. Post, *HSCPh* 24 (1913), pp. 112, 145.

[33] Rose, *Handbook of Greek Literature*, p. 246.

[34] F. A. Wright, *A History of Later Greek Literature* (London, 1932), p. 28. For an even more damning estimate of New Comedy, cf. Adams, *UTQ* 7 (1937-38), pp. 518 ff.

[35] Post, *TAPhA* 62 (1931), pp. 203, 211, 234; cf. *TAPhA* 69 (1938), p. 42: "Purely as a dramatist, Menander is unsurpassed."

not find the richness and vitality which his admirers claim for him, but neither will they find him second-rate, sordid, and monotonous. Menander understood the human heart and delineated his characters with vigor and charm. It is a great loss to world literature that so little of his drama has been preserved.

## The Problem of Euripidean Influence

Most modern discussions of Greek comedy stress heavily the influence of Euripides and his tragic art upon the comedy of the Hellenistic age. Many of the later plays of Euripides with their melodramatic themes, their realism, their recognition scenes and happy endings, apparently did not differ much from comedy as it developed more and more in the direction of a serious social drama. Euripides above all was famed for his understanding of human nature, and this quality could not fail to appeal to the later comic playwrights. In the fourth and third centuries B.C. Euripides was the most popular of the tragic poets, and there can be no doubt of the admiration and esteem in which he was held by the chief poets of New Comedy—Menander, Diphilus, and Philemon. In a well-known fragment (130) Philemon has a character state that "if the dead had consciousness, he would have hanged himself in order to see Euripides," and Quintilian, the famous Roman teacher, rhetorician, and literary critic of the first century A.D., says that Menander often testified to his great admiration for Euripides and followed him, although in a different type of work.[36]

The problem, for it is a problem, deserves a careful examination; if the theory of the influence of Euripides is sound, New Comedy may be said to have a double ancestry: (1) from Old through Middle Comedy; (2) from Euripides partly through Middle Comedy, partly direct. But the proponents of the modern theory of Euripidean influence are not content with this; they assert as an incontrovertible fact that comedy took over the themes and structure of Euripidean tragedy; they go even further and maintain that the artistic unity of Roman comedy and much of its content are inherited from Euripides by way of Hellenistic comedy. The danger of such a theory is obvious; if Euripidean art was so dominant an influence upon the development of Greek comedy, then that comedy acquired an artistic form of such regularity that flaws were impossible; if any flaws or defects appeared in the Roman adaptations, those flaws must inevitably be due to the faulty workmanship of the Roman playwrights. Thus the theory of Euripidean influence has led to a method of interpreting Roman comedy which gives a false picture of Roman comedy and of New Comedy as well.

[36] x, 1, 69: *hunc et admiratus maxime est, ut saepe testatur, et secutus, quamquam in opere diverso, Menander.* Note that Quintilian does not represent Menander as testifying to his imitation of Euripides.

The scholars who insisted upon the influence of Euripides (e.g., Wilamowitz, Leo) and referred to Greek comedy as "the daughter" or "the true heiress" of Euripidean tragedy may have meant merely that the comic playwrights unconsciously carried on a development begun by Euripides rather than that they purposely imitated or adapted Euripidean tragedy. But the theory, once accepted, has produced many rash statements, e.g.: "Though the framework is directly inherited from Old Comedy, Middle writers are more indebted for their subjects to Euripides than to any comic dramatist";[37] "New Comedy is a social drama which comes directly from Euripidean drama, with a few comic characters which stem from earlier comedy";[38] "New Comedy is hardly comedy at all, but rather the bourgeois rehabilitation of tragedy."[39] Such statements give to the reader the unfortunate impression that both Middle and New Comedy are indebted to Euripides rather than to earlier comedy. But wherein is the indebtedness said to lie? Here the proponents of the Euripidean theory present a formidable list of topics dealing with both the form and content of comedy: the love theme, plots of mistaken identity (e.g., violations of maidens, exposure of children, recognition scenes), plots of intrigue, details of character portrayal, the serious nature of New Comedy, its critical attitude toward life, the general structure of the plays, the use of monologue and especially the expository prologue.[40] If these can be shown to be taken from Euripides, then surely Hellenistic comedy becomes a form of Euripidean tragedy with a few additions from the comic tradition. But let us subject this list to a brief examination.

(1) The love theme is more prominent in Euripides than in Aeschylus and Sophocles, but this does not mean that the playwrights of New Comedy imitated Euripides in their realistic treatment of love. There is a great difference between the illicit love of a Phaedra and the premarital frailty of respectable women. And surely love affairs with courtesans were not unknown in real life! Love becomes an important theme in nearly all types of Hellenistic poetry, and it is highly probable that actual life, not literary tradition, was responsible for the use of love as a dramatic motive. Prescott seems correct when he states: "As a mere theme love is inevitable in comedy of the later period. In this development Euripides is simply in advance of his time."[41]

(2) On plays of mistaken identity there is ancient evidence. Satyrus, in his biography of Euripides, refers to the relations of domestic characters, husband and wife, father and son, slave and master, and to motives

---

[37] Norwood, *Greek Comedy*, p. 38.          [38] See Dieterich, *Pulcinella*, pp. 52 f.
[39] Little, *HSCPh* 49 (1938), p. 206. Cf. also Mendell, *Our Seneca*, p. 76.
[40] For an excellent discussion of these supposedly Euripidean features in comedy, see Prescott, *CPh* 12 (1917), pp. 405-425, 13 (1918), pp. 113-137, 14 (1919), 108-135. Prescott's approach seems very sane and has been accepted in the discussion which follows. See also Kolář, *PhW* 41 (1921), cols. 688-696.
[41] *CPh* 13 (1918), p. 118.

used in reversals of fortune, i.e., violations of maidens, substitutions of children, recognitions by means of rings and necklaces. "For," he says, "these are the things which comprise the New Comedy, and they were brought to perfection by Euripides."[42] It is very possible that many of these motives came into New Comedy from tragedy, either directly or by way of mythological travesty in Old and Middle Comedy. Satyrus also points out that recognition scenes go back to Homer; they may well have come into both tragedy and comedy from epic poetry. The recognition "seems to have been almost as integral a part of the Greek comic tradition as the legends were of tragedy."[43] But if we accept the influence of tragedy here, it still proves less than many realize; these motives do not give us the comic plot but provide merely the initial stages of the complication and the final solution; in between is the action of the play itself which derives not from tragic sources but from earlier comedy or contemporary life. The betrayal of maidens, the exposure of children, the later discovery of their identity, occurred in real life with considerable frequency.[44] Perhaps in this respect literary tradition and actual life went hand in hand as contributing factors.

(3) The presence of trickery in so many of Plautus' plays indicates that plots of intrigue were frequent in New Comedy. On this point the fragmentary plays of Menander, being free from trickery and deception, may well give a distorted picture; it is possible that many of the lost plays of Menander, especially those of his youth, contained deception, and this is implied by such a title as *Dis Exapaton*, "The Double Deceiver," the original of Plautus' *Bacchides*,[45] and by a slave in the *Perinthia* who refers to cheating an easy-going, stupid master.[46] But Menander must not be equated with New Comedy. It is folly to assume that dozens of dramatists, writing hundreds of plays, resembled Menander in form and content as closely as is often assumed. However much they were interested in depicting character and portraying contemporary life, there can be little doubt that Diphilus, Philemon, and many others wrote comedies in which intrigue played its part.[47] But does this intrigue stem from Euripides? Leo cites as a decisive bit of evidence the similarity between the intrigue in Euripides' *Helen* and Plautus'

---

[42] *Oxyrhynchus Papyri*, IX (London, 1912), n. 1176, fr. 39, col. vii.

[43] Lumb, "The New Menander," p. 93.

[44] Babies were still being exposed and reared as foundlings in slavery throughout the eastern Roman provinces in the early second century A.D.; cf. Pliny, *Epist. ad Traianum*, LXV f.

[45] Cf. Dunkin, *Post-Aristophanic Comedy*, pp. 24, 34, 50. Dunkin makes the unconvincing suggestion that the original of the *Bacchides* "was a philosophical study of the reaction of the Rich Man to luxury" (p. 34).

[46] Fr. 393; cf. Allinson, *Menander*, pp. 422 ff.

[47] Plautus, favoring plots of trickery, apparently made deception and intrigue far more prominent. In this he was probably influenced by early Italian popular drama; cf. Wieand, *Deception in Plautus*, pp. 187 ff.; Little, *HSCPh* 49 (1938), pp. 217 ff. See below p. 168.

*Miles Gloriosus.*[48] Cheating and intrigue, however, are elements of popular comedy and as such could hardly be expected to develop out of a highly artistic form such as tragedy. It is far more likely that Euripides in his plays of intrigue drew upon devices already existent in fifth-century comedy. Many points of resemblance between Aristophanes and Plautus in the use of trickery, lies, and impersonation may be seen, and there is actually less a break in the continuity between Old and New Comedy than is often realized.

(4) The proponents of the Euripidean theory admit that the characters of comedy come from real life; they seek, nevertheless, for traces of Euripides in the details of character portrayal, e.g., the philosophizing slave, the noble courtesan, the use of the confidant and messenger. But such characters or roles are necessary in all drama, are often used for dramatic convenience, and are far from unrealistic. A good courtesan may be idealized but need not be less realistic than a bad courtesan. Certainly the speeches of comic messengers, in their directness and brevity, have far more realism than the long and detailed speeches of messengers in tragedy.

(5) The essentially serious nature of New Comedy (as we see it in Menander) need not be explained as an inheritance from Euripidean tragedy. The plot determines the difficulties, the generally pathetic situations, in which the characters find themselves. If the plot, i.e., the sequence of events within the play itself, does not come from tragedy, neither does the serious nature of the play. Plots and situations drawn largely from life can provide serious emotional comedy. (6) A critical attitude toward life and society can be found in Euripides, but it also exists in Aristophanes. Perhaps the presence of such an attitude in New Comedy is to be explained by the influence of earlier drama; it can also be derived from contemporary life and thought.

(7) The arguments from the structure of New Comedy likewise seem far from conclusive. The divisions of the play, with sections of dialogue set off by choral song, may reflect the structure of tragedy, or they may result from a gradual decrease in the importance of the chorus in Middle and New Comedy. In Aristophanes the chorus was never as organic in the second part of the play as in the first. (8) In spirit and content the monologues of comedy do not seem Euripidean, with the exception of the expository prologue; this, most critics agree, is evidence of a close relationship between Euripides and Hellenistic Comedy. But if we grant that the detachable prologue which narrates the antecedents of the plot shows Euripidean technique, there is also much in the prologues (as we find them in Plautus) which recalls Aristophanes, e.g., extreme informality and direct address to the spectators.

---

[48] *Plautinische Forschungen,* pp. 165 f.

What then of the Euripidean influence on comedy in general? Certain details of plot may perhaps be accepted, such as the violation of maidens and the exposure and rearing of children as foundlings—the basic elements which create confusion of identity and make possible the later recognition scenes; also certain features of structure, and chief among them the expository prologue. But the themes of the plays, the main action, the characters, the outlook upon life, do not seem Euripidean; on the contrary, they either reflect contemporary life or can be explained from earlier comedy. Prescott states: "The material of the comic plots is almost entirely independent of tragedy."[49] Many features of New Comedy, furthermore, are sometimes cited to show its close relationship to Old Comedy: the similarity of titles and characters, the frequent appearance of weddings and other festivities at the conclusion of the plays, traces of the *agon*, or debate, between slaves or other characters, the suppression of dramatic probability in character or situation for the purpose of comic effect, appeals to the audience for favor and the breaking of the dramatic illusion, the use of a creaking door to announce the entrance of a character on the stage. These details appear in Aristophanes, and occur either in Menander or in Roman plays adapted from New Comedy. To argue from their presence in Plautus is admittedly dangerous, for such features as festal conclusions and direct addresses to the spectators could come from early Italian farces as well; but there is also the possibility that they could go back through New Comedy to the comedies of Aristophanes and his contemporaries. Cicero (*De Off.* 1, 29, 104) considered that Plautus and the writers of Old Attic Comedy had much in common in their use of jests that were refined, polite, clever, and witty (*elegans, urbanum, ingeniosum, facetum*).[50]

The safest course here is to admit our lack of adequate knowledge; we are hampered on all sides by ignorance—ignorance of Epicharmus, of much of Old Comedy, of Middle Comedy, of most of New Comedy. In view of the enormous amount of comic drama that has been lost, we cannot be certain about the background of New Comedy, or even about the nature of much of New Comedy itself. I am fully convinced that Euripides, who was so admired by the writers of New Comedy, did influence their dramatic output in more than one respect. There are numerous resemblances in thought and phrasing between Euripides and Menander, and lines are occasionally borrowed from Euripides with very little change. But the works of Menander and his contemporaries must be considered a complex phenomenon—a form of drama that is indebted to real life, to tragedy, to Aristophanic comedy, to the social drama of Crates and indirectly to Epicharmus. There is no justification

[49] *CPh* 14 (1919), p. 109.
[50] For Cicero's other references to Plautus, see Wright, *Cicero and the Theater*, pp. 62 ff.

for looking upon New Comedy merely as a kind of Euripidean tragedy
with a few comic additions.[51]

[51] Menander's indebtedness to earlier Greek drama has recently been re-examined
by Webster in *Studies in Menander*, pp. 153 ff. This book reached me too late to be
used in my discussion of Euripides' influence upon Menander but I find that Webster's
view is essentially the same as mine. He says (p. 184) : "Thus in plot-construction,
as in scenes and situations, we can see three main influences on Menander—Classical
Tragedy, Middle Comedy, and Peripatetic theory"; cf. his conclusion (p. 194) :
"Menander did not imitate Sophocles and Euripides, but used their methods to build
his new character drama on the foundations of Middle Comedy."

# CHAPTER 3

# *THE GOLDEN AGE OF DRAMA AT ROME*

ROMAN literature in the first century B.C. attained heights in both poetry (epic, lyric, satire, elegy) and prose (oratory, philosophy, history) that well justify the term "Golden Age." In the field of drama, however, the best work was done a century and a half earlier, in the hundred-year period ushered in by Livius Andronicus in 240 B.C., and it seems not inappropriate to call this period "The Golden Age of Drama." A brief account of the historical development of drama at Rome from its beginning will provide the necessary background for biographical sketches of Plautus and Terence and help to clarify their relations with their predecessors and their contemporaries. To complete the picture of the dramatic activity of the Romans, I shall describe briefly the later decline of tragedy and comedy and the nature of the dramatic forms which survived to the late Empire.

## Livius Andronicus and Naevius

Little has survived from the dramas of Livius Andronicus. The titles of three comedies (*Gladiolus, Ludius*, and *Verpus* or *Virgo*) and nine tragedies (several of which, e.g., *Achilles, Aiax Mastigophorus, Equos Troianus*, had themes connected with the Trojan cycle) are known, and about fifty lines of fragments are extant. But even these fragments, as scanty as they are, suffice to show that Andronicus was more than a mere translator,[1] and his historical importance as the founder of Roman drama, as the first to make Greek poetry available to the Romans, is not lessened by the fact that his plays seemed crude and archaic to the Romans of the classical period. Cicero's estimate (*Brutus*, 18, 71) that they were not worth a second reading was doubtless colored by later achievements in drama.

Although in his translation of the *Odyssey* Andronicus wrote in the primitive Saturnian meter, in his dramas he used iambic and trochaic lines, and occasionally lyric meters such as cretics. He thus established the basic meters of Roman tragedy and comedy for later dramatists. Since he treated the Greek iambic trimeter with freedom by admitting spondees in the second and fourth feet, he must be considered the inventor of the iambic senarius. One comic fragment in iambic meter (8):

> lepus tute es: pulpamentum quaeris?
> You're a hare yourself; do you hunt game?

[1] Cf. Sanford, *CJ* 18 (1922-23), pp. 274 f.

is a proverbial expression which appears later in Terence, *Eun.* 426.

The details of Andronicus' life present several difficulties. Certain facts about his career seem trustworthy: he first presented drama at Rome in 240 B.C.; his tragedies were adaptations from fifth-century Greek plays of Sophocles and Euripides, while his comedies, being based upon plots and characters from Greek New Comedy, initiated the *fabula palliata* at Rome; in 207 B.C. Andronicus was commissioned to compose a hymn to propitiate the gods before the battle of Sena; shortly after, an association of poets and actors (*scribae et histriones*) was formed and he was honored by being recognized as the head of this poets' guild (*collegium poetarum*). We are also told that Andronicus was a Greek slave, who, brought from Tarentum as a child and later manumitted by his master, taught school for a number of years. Even in antiquity the accounts were inaccurate, for the dramatist Accius believed that Andronicus had been captured at Tarentum and brought to Rome in 209 B.C. and had produced a play (his first?) in 198 B.C. Cicero (*Brutus*, 18, 72 f.) took pains to correct this obviously mistaken chronology, and modern scholars, believing that Accius confused two captures of Tarentum, state that Andronicus had really been taken prisoner in 272 B.C. But since Andronicus was still active sixty-five years later, he could hardly have been more than a child at the time and would not have had the necessary knowledge of Greek drama and the Greek theater. Accius was doubtless wrong not only in his chronology but also in stating that Andronicus was captured at Tarentum. This city was a center of dramatic activity in Magna Graecia, and it is far more probable that Andronicus was an expert actor and dramatist brought from Tarentum to Rome in 240 B.C. or shortly before for the express purpose of writing and producing Roman versions of Greek plays. The story that he was a slave and later a schoolmaster may be a bit of agreeable fiction that has been accepted uncritically by most historians of Latin literature.[2] But that he had some connection with the Livian *gens* is implied by the name Livius.

Gnaeus Naevius (c. 270-c. 201 B.C.), the first native dramatist, was a man of great independence and originality. He served in the first Punic war, and later wrote a national epic, *Bellum Punicum*, in which he traced the foundations of Rome back to the time of Aeneas. Of his tragedies six titles and about sixty verses survive; that he too was interested in themes from the Trojan cycle is shown by titles such as *Equos Troianus, Hector Proficiscens, Iphigenia*. Naevius' originality and strong national feeling displayed themselves in drama as in epic, for he composed plays on themes from Roman history; he is thus the inventor of the *fabula praetexta*, or Roman historical play.[3] His *Romulus*

---

[2] For a good discussion of the problem, see Beare, *CQ* 34 (1940), pp. 11-19; cf. also his remarks in *The Roman Stage*, pp. 16 ff.

[3] These plays were probably not tragedies, although the one surviving example of

dealt with the legendary beginnings of Rome, and the *Clastidium* re-counted the victory of Marcellus over the Insubrians in 222 B.C.

Naevius was active in the field of comedy. About one hundred and thirty lines of fragments and more than thirty titles imply that he found the writing of *palliatae* far more congenial than that of tragedy. A fragment in trochaics (75-79) from the *Tarentilla* ("The Girl of Tarentum") reveals Naevius' style with its fondness for anaphora, alliteration, asyndeton, and parataxis, and displays a certain liveliness and charm in spite of the monotony of expression:

> Quase in choro ludens datatim dat se et communem facit.
> Alii adnutat, alii adnictat, alium amat, alium tenet.
> Alibi manus est occupata, alii percellit pedem,
> Anulum dat alii spectandum, a labris alium inuocat,
> Cum alio cantat, at tamen alii suo dat digito litteras.

A translation in the same meter follows:

> Like a dancer in a ring she gives herself to each in turn,
> Nodding here and winking there, embracing this one, loving that,
> Giving now her hand to one, and pressing hard another's foot,
> Giving a ring for one to view, enticing others with her lips,
> Singing with one, and to another beckoning coyly all the while.

Other fragments are of interest because of their similarity to passages in Plautus; 26: "He stands when he eats"; cf. the words of the parasite in *Men.* 102 f.: "he heaps up such piles of dishes that you have to stand on your couch if you want something from the top"; 53: "Tell me, which is better, to marry a maid or a widow?" cf. *Stich.* 118 f., where Antipho asks his daughters the same question; 82: "Look out, don't fall, I beg of you!" This recalls the words of Delphium to the drunken Callidamates in *Most.* 324; 95: "I pray the gods to take away both my father and mother"; cf. the unfilial sentiment of Philolaches in *Most.* 233.[4] In 36 ff. a jest is found on the phrase *amare efflictim*, "to love desperately," "to love to death"; a youth says: "I don't want to love her to death; I want her to live to give me pleasure"; cf. Phaedromus in *Curc.* 47 f.: "I don't want to return her love . . . because I want it for always." The same phrase (*ecflictim amare*) occurs in Plautus (*Amph.* 517, *Cas.* 49),[5] and there are numerous other parallels in diction which reveal a close similarity between Naevius and his successor.[6]

---

the *praetexta*, the *Octavia* of the age of Seneca, is a tragedy dealing with the divorce and unhappy fate of Nero's wife. For a detailed treatment of the fragments of the early historical plays, see Pasculli, *Studio sulla Fabula Praetexta*; cf. also Beare, *The Roman Stage*, pp. 31 ff.

[4] In Terence, *Ad.* 519 f., Ctesipho merely desires that his father be unable to rise from bed for three days; cf. Donatus, *ad Ad.* 521.

[5] Cf. also *ecflictim perire* in *Merc.* 444, *Poen.* 96, 1095.

[6] E.g., 43: *utinam nasum abstulisset mordicus*, cf. *Men.* 195: *oportebat nasum*

The fragments of Naevius' comedies are too short to enable us to reconstruct the plots of the plays, and titles such as *Ariolus* ("The Soothsayer"), *Carbonaria* ("The Charcoal Woman"), *Colax* ("The Flatterer"), *Dementes* ("The Crazy Persons"), *Quadrigemini* ("The Quadruplets") afford almost no clue. Parasites, braggart warriors, slaves, masters, and sweethearts appeared in the plays, just as they were later to appear in the comedies of Plautus and Terence.[7] The scene of the *Ariolus* was apparently laid in Italy, which implies that Naevius anticipated the comedy with Roman characters, the *fabula togata*, later developed by Titinius and Afranius.[8]

Naevius was outspoken and evidently had a fondness for political criticism not unlike that of the poets of Greek Old Comedy. Unfortunately, there was less freedom of speech in Rome than in fifth-century Athens. His famous attack on the Metelli and their consulship, perhaps a verse from one of his comedies,

> Fato Metelli Romae fiunt consules,
> By Fate the Metelli are made consuls at Rome,

with its ambiguous word *fato*, "by chance" or "to the misfortune (of Rome)," was answered by Metellus, consul of 206 B.C.:

> Dabunt malum Metelli Naevio poetae.
> The Metelli will give misfortune to the poet Naevius.

The misfortune threatened by Metellus occurred and Naevius was thrown into prison.[9] Plautus refers in the *Miles Gloriosus* (211 f.) to a *barbarus* (i.e., Roman) *poeta* who rests head on hand and is watched constantly by two prison guards, obviously an allusion to Naevius. The date of the imprisonment was apparently between 206 and 204 B.C. and almost all scholars accept 205 B.C. as the date of the *Miles*.[10] Aulus Gellius in his *Attic Nights* (III, 3, 15) relates that Naevius wrote two plays in prison, the *Ariolus* and the *Leo*, and was released when he had apologized for his offensive language. But he was soon in trouble again, and went into exile at Utica, where he died about 201 B.C.

---

*abreptum mordicus*; 47: *caue uerbum faxis*, cf. *Asin.* 625: *uerbum caue faxis*; see Fraenkel, "Naevius" in *RE* Supplb. VI (1935), cols. 628-631.

[7] Cf. 60 for mention of a parasite; see also Terence, *Eun.* 25 f., which refers to the roles of soldier and parasite in Naevius' *Colax* ("The Flatterer").

[8] See below, "The Decline of the *Palliata*."

[9] Frank (*AJPh* 48, 1927, pp. 109 f.) doubts that the charge was slander, since ridicule of people high and low occurred throughout the Republic, and suggests that the imprisonment was due to a temporary censorship resulting from "the severe strain of war-nervousness" during the last four years of the Punic war. See Robinson, *CJ* 42 (1946-47), pp. 147 ff., who points out that censorship of the theater did exist at Rome in the last two centuries of the Republic.

[10] Cf. West, *AJPh* 8 (1887), pp. 15-33; Buck, *A Chronology of the Plays of Plautus*, pp. 79-84.

## Tragedy: Ennius, Pacuvius, Accius

Livius Andronicus and Naevius had devoted themselves to both tragedy and comedy. The playwrights who followed them specialized in a particular genre, and in tragedy the outstanding dramatists were three in number—Ennius, Pacuvius, and Accius; at their hands tragic drama reached its highest development at Rome.

Quintus Ennius (239-169 B.C.) was the most versatile poet of the age. Born in southern Italy, he had absorbed much of the Hellenistic culture of Magna Graecia; after fighting in the second Punic war he was brought to Rome by Cato in 204 B.C., and there he earned a living by teaching and writing. He composed miscellaneous poems (*Saturae*), and was renowned for his historical epic, the *Annales*, which remained the great national poem of the Romans until it was superseded by Vergil's *Aeneid* a century and a half later. Ennius substituted for the Saturnian meter of earlier Latin epic the quantitative dactylic hexameter of Greek epic; this innovation gave to his poem a flexibility and a poetic power that Andronicus and Naevius had never attained, and the importance of Ennius' influence upon the meter and style of Lucretius and Vergil can hardly be overestimated, however rugged and archaic his work may seem when contrasted with that of the later poets.

Two comedies (*Caupuncula, Pancratiastes*) and two *praetextae* (*Ambracia, Sabinae*) are ascribed to Ennius, but his fame in drama rests upon his achievements in tragedy. Twenty titles and about four hundred lines of fragments have survived. Increasing interest in the legend of Aeneas which linked together Trojans and Latins at an early date doubtless accounts for many plays dealing with the Trojan cycle, e.g., *Achilles, Ajax, Alexander, Andromacha Aechmalotis* ("Andromacha the Captive"), *Hectoris Lutra* ("The Ransoming of Hector"), *Hecuba*. One of the most effective fragments (75-88) expresses the despair of Andromacha at the fall of Troy and her farewell to the city of her fathers; a lyric *canticum*, shifting from cretics to trochees and then to anapaests, it begins as follows:

> Quid petam praesidi aut exequar? quoue nunc
> Auxilio exili aut fugae freta sim?
> Arce et urbe orba sum. quo accedam? quo applicem?
> What resource should I seek, should I beg? To what aid,
> Either flight or exile, can I turn for relief?
> City, home I have lost. Whither kneel? Where appeal?

In another fragment (91-93) she laments the death of husband and son:

> I saw what grieved me Oh! most bitterly to see:
> 'Twas Hector dragged behind the four-horse chariot,
> 'Twas Hector's son I saw hurled cruelly from the wall.

Ennius' humanity and his interest in Greek ideas led him to adapt many tragedies from Euripides. Of the *Medea Exul* ("Medea in Exile") fewer than forty lines are extant but these are sufficient to show that in this play he is closely following the famous original; e.g., Medea says (222 f.) :

> For thrice I would prefer to stake my life in battle
> Than once to give birth to a child.

This is an exact translation of Euripides, *Medea*, 250 f. But not all passages are such close renderings; there are numerous indications of originality and imagination, and a truly Roman flavor pervades the fragments.

Marcus Pacuvius (c. 220-c. 130 B.C.) was the nephew of Ennius and his successor in tragic drama. The titles of thirteen tragedies are known, one of which was a historical play, *Paulus*; the others (e.g., *Antiope, Atalanta, Chryses, Hermiona, Pentheus*) were based upon Greek originals by Sophocles and Euripides. Pacuvius' recondite themes and his tragic diction earned for him in antiquity the reputation of being "learned,"[11] and several of the fragments which present philosophical sentiments (cf. 87-93 and 366-375) support this ancient judgment. Perhaps the most effective fragment is the one describing a storm at sea as the Greeks set sail from Troy on their homeward journey (409-416). The excellent translation by Duff[12] in the trochaic meter of the original preserves much of the alliteration and assonance of the Latin:

> Happy when their fleet left harbour, they could watch the fish at play,
> They were never weary watching, though they watched the livelong day.
> Meanwhile when it turned to sundown, rough and rougher grew the main,
> Darkness doubled, blinding blackness came with night and clouds of rain,
> Flame flashed out athwart the welkin, thunder made the heavens rock,
> Hail, with plenteous sleet commingled, sudden fell with headlong shock.
> Everywhere the gales broke prison, cruel whirling winds arose,
> And the ocean boiled in fury. . . .

Lucius Accius (170-c. 86 B.C.), literary critic and grammarian, was also Rome's most prolific writer of tragedy. About forty-five titles and seven hundred lines of fragments imply that his dramatic output perhaps equaled that of Ennius and Pacuvius combined. Among his plays

[11] Cf. Horace, *Epist.* II, 1, 56; Quintilian, *Instit. orat.* X, 1, 97.

[12] *A Literary History of Rome*, pp. 226 f. This fragment is quoted by Cicero (*De div.* I, 14, 24), who preserves for us many such passages of literary merit. The majority of the fragments of the early dramatists has been found in the writings of Roman grammarians who were chiefly interested in illustrating some peculiarity of syntax or spelling. This accounts both for the brevity of the fragments and for their lack of literary worth.

were well-known titles such as *Aegisthus, Atreus, Clutemestra, Bacchae, Prometheus, Medea, Alcestis,* and also, as was to be expected, many dealing with the Trojan war, e.g., *Achilles, Armorum Iudicium* ("The Award of Arms"), *Neoptolemus, Philocteta, Deiphobus, Troades* ("The Trojan Women"), *Hecuba, Astyanax.* In addition to the plays based upon Greek tragedies, Accius composed at least two historical plays on Roman themes, *Brutus* and *Decius* or *Aeneadae.* Accius was praised for the dignity and the elevation of his style, and for the rhetorical skill with which he gave utterance to sentiments of heroism and moral courage. Ajax says to his son in the *Armorum Iudicium* (156):

> Virtuti sis par, dispar fortunis patris.
> In valor be like your father, his fortune far excel.[13]

A similar tone pervades many other fragments:

> . . . nam si a me regnum Fortuna atque opes
> Eripere quiuit, at virtutem nec quiit. (619 f.)
> If Fortune snatched my kingdom and my wealth,
> My honesty she could not snatch away.

> Vt nunc, cum animatus iero, satis armatus sum. (308)
> When forth I go with courage, armored well am I.

The last fragment is especially effective with its play upon *animatus* and *armatus.* The words of Atreus (203 f.): *oderint, dum metuant* ("Let them hate me, provided they fear") became famous and were quoted by Cicero, Seneca, and others. According to Suetonius (*Calig.* 30) these words were very dear to the heart of the emperor Caligula.

Ancient critics were divided in their estimates of the three playwrights. Velleius Paterculus (1, 17, 1) gave Accius the highest place in tragedy, while Cicero considered Pacuvius Rome's greatest tragic poet.[14] Many modern critics believe that in sheer poetic power Ennius was superior to both his successors, and perhaps of all the tragic writers of the period the loss of his plays is most to be regretted. All three dramatists wrote with deep feeling and their tragedies were characterized by dignity and moral earnestness. The plays were Roman in spirit in spite of their dependence upon Greek stories, and it would be inaccurate to call them merely translations (cf. Cicero, *Acad. post.* 1, 3, 10). The Greek legends by the second century B.C. had become the common stock of all educated Romans, and there is little doubt that the playwrights handled the themes with considerable freedom.[15]

---

[13] This is a translation from Sophocles, *Ajax,* 550 f.; cf. Vergil, *Aeneid,* XII, 435 f.: *disce, puer, uirtutem ex me uerumque laborem, fortunam ex aliis.*

[14] *De opt. gen. orat.* 1, 2; Cicero gives the palm in epic to Ennius, and in comedy perhaps (*fortasse*) to Caecilius.

[15] Cf. Steuart, *AJPh* 47 (1926), pp. 272 ff. Miss Steuart's theory of direct Homeric influence seems most unlikely. On the musical innovations of Ennius and his successors, see Coppola, *Il Teatro Tragico,* pp. 59 ff., 66 ff.

Accius, who died when Cicero was a young man, brings to an end the Golden Age of Roman drama. The tragedies of Ennius, Pacuvius, and Accius were produced on the stage in the first century B.C., and new tragedies were occasionally written, but the only other important tragic playwright was Seneca, who lived in the time of Nero, and whose works will be briefly mentioned later in this chapter.

## Comedy: Plautus, Caecilius, Terence

Just as tragedy was represented in the second century B.C. by three outstanding playwrights, so comedy after Naevius flourished at the hands of three dramatists who devoted themselves entirely to the composition of *fabulae palliatae*. These three in chronological order were Plautus, Caecilius, and Terence. There were, however, several other comic playwrights active in this period. Aulus Gellius (xv, 24) quotes the curious canon of Volcacius Sedigitus who, at the end of the century, gave in verse a rating to ten writers of comedy; the order was as follows: Caecilius, Plautus, Naevius, Licinius, Atilius, Terence, Turpilius, Trabea, Luscius, and Ennius, who was included at the end of the list *causa antiquitatis*. The basis of Volcacius' judgment is not known, but it is surprising that the works of Caecilius, to whom first place was given, have survived only in fragmentary form (some forty titles and about three hundred lines), while Terence, whose six plays are extant, rated only sixth place, after the almost unknown Licinius and Atilius. Perhaps the hostility of Luscius Lanuvinus and other dramatists of the *collegium poetarum*, the hostility about which we learn so many details from Terence's prologues, contributed to a later dislike of Terence and his plays which was reflected in the canon of Volcacius Sedigitus.[16] But there can be no doubt that Caecilius was a most able and successful dramatist who, if less popular than Plautus during the latter's lifetime, became the leading comic dramatist of Rome after Plautus' death. Since Caecilius was a younger contemporary of Plautus, it will hardly distort the chronological sequence to give a brief account of Caecilius at this point before turning to a more detailed consideration of the lives and works of Plautus and Terence.

Caecilius Statius (c. 219-168 B.C.) was an Insubrian Gaul who was brought to Rome as a slave and later freed.[17] A friend of Ennius, he apparently aimed at a more Hellenic type of comedy than had Naevius and Plautus; the majority of his titles are Greek, more than half being identical with titles of Menander's plays, and the extant fragments are free from Roman allusions. That Caecilius' comedies at first were not

[16] Cf. Sihler, *AJPh* 26 (1905), pp. 9 ff.

[17] The name Statius was given to slaves (Aulus Gellius, IV, 20), but was also used as a *cognomen*, and Beare (*Ha* 59, 1942, p. 26; cf. *The Roman Stage*, p. 76) suggests that Caecilius may have been wrongly considered a slave because he bore the name Statius. See also Robson, *AJPh* 59 (1938), pp. 301 ff.

favorably received and that he suffered from the criticism of rival poets is evident from the words of Ambivius Turpio in the prologue of Terence's *Hecyra* (14-23). Caecilius' ultimate success implies that he was able to combine his desire for artistic purity with the grosser demands of the Roman public.

The fragments of his comedies contain references to pregnancies and the birth of (illegitimate?) children, to the rearing of sons and the cheating of fathers. In one interesting passage (199-209) a young man says that it's nice to have a stingy father to cheat when one is in love and without money, but a generous father is a disadvantage and spoils the trickery. The contrast here between two types of parent is not unlike that which Terence made the basic theme of his *Adelphoe*. In another fragment (243 f.) the speaker says that he has been deceived more than all the stupid old fools of comedy, a reference to the stock character of the *stultus senex* found frequently in Plautus' comedies. Slaves, parasites, and courtesans appear in the fragments, but there are indications that the treatment of these characters was occasionally somewhat unconventional:

Capital crimes are being committed in the State; for a courtesan doesn't want to take a cent from her lovesick sweetheart. (213 f.)

By far the most significant fragments are those of the *Plocium* ("The Little Necklace"), quoted by Aulus Gellius (II, 23) with the parallel passages from Menander. The plot is typically Menandrian, with its misunderstandings and recognition scene; it has been restored in part as follows: a youth seduced a young girl one night and later became betrothed to her without either recognizing the other; the father of the young man was suspected by his rich but ugly wife of having the girl as his mistress; the birth of the baby postponed the wedding, but by means of a necklace the girl and the young man recognized each other as the parents of the child. Gellius quotes the passages (143-162, 169-172) to prove how superior Menander was in expression and wit, in description of emotion, in truthfulness to life; read by itself, Caecilius' play was not displeasing, but it could not be compared with the Greek original. But Gellius is perhaps unjust to Caecilius and fails to appreciate the greater vigor and realism of the Latin versions.[18] It is significant that Gellius criticizes Caecilius for departing from the original and not reproducing faithfully the words of Menander. If Caecilius as a translator follows the Greek text more closely than did Naevius and Plautus, he is still far from being what we should consider a literal translator; he omits or adds ideas, introduces new jests, transforms a passage of iambic trimeter into a lyrical *canticum*, and in general seems to adapt the original to the tastes of his audience. The passages display the rhythmic effects and the vivacity that had made the comedies of Plautus so suc-

18 Cf. Argenio, *MC* 7 (1937), pp. 359 ff.

cessful, and reveal the liberties that a Roman dramatist might take with the Greek original.

And yet we must assume that Caecilius was in general more serious and less boisterous than his predecessors. He was praised by Horace for his *gravitas*, by Varro for his excellence in plot-construction (*in argumentis*); others commented upon his portrayal of emotion. The extent to which he influenced the dramatic art of Terence cannot be fully determined; the younger dramatist doubtless followed his example in using Menander as a chief model and in continuing the transition to a more refined, more Hellenic type of Roman comedy. It is possible that Caecilius made several contributions to the development of the *palliata*; Oppermann suggests[19] that he may have been the first to maintain that a Latin playwright should not "contaminate," i.e., he should follow only one Greek original and not add part of a second original to his play; and also that Caecilius may have introduced the rule that a Roman comedy must be taken from a Greek play not previously translated into Latin. As to the first suggestion, Terence (*And.* 18 f.) states that Naevius, Plautus, and Ennius had "contaminated," and does not mention Caecilius. There is no other evidence in ancient literature to support the theory that any of Terence's predecessors used this method of composition, and it is surely an *argumentum ex silentio* to attempt to show Caecilius' attitude on this matter. As to the second possibility, we do not know when the rule about plagiarism first originated; the fact that the same titles (*Carbonaria, Colax, Nervolaria*) appear in the lists of the comedies of Plautus and Naevius could imply that the rule did not exist in the earlier period of the *palliata*, and Terence (*Eun.* 25 ff.) makes it clear that the *Colax* of Naevius and Plautus went back to the same original. And if Caecilius' *Synaristosae* was based upon Menander's play, which Plautus had previously adapted in his *Cistellaria*, Caecilius could hardly have introduced such a rule with a clear conscience.

If Caecilius employed the prologues of his plays to set forth his theories of comic drama, he perhaps anticipated Terence in the elimination of exposition from the prologue. This would give some support to Frank's theory that Caecilius was responsible for Terence's development in his comedies of the elements of suspense and surprise;[20] Frank argues from the fact that Terence in composing his plays had had the advice of Caecilius, but the only evidence for this is the anecdote that Terence read his *Andria* to Caecilius shortly before the latter's death and, as we shall see, there are strong reasons for rejecting the story as apocryphal.

[19] *H* 74 (1939), pp. 119, 124 ff.

[20] *Life and Literature in the Roman Republic*, pp. 104, 122 f. The omission of the narrative prologue made it easier for the dramatist to introduce surprise, but it does not follow that suspense and surprise were lacking in Plautine comedy; see below, "Devices to Arouse Suspense" and "Surprise in Plautus and Terence" in chap. 8.

In spite of our uncertainty about the extent of his contributions to Roman comedy, there can be no doubt that Caecilius was an important transitional figure between the more lively and robust comedies of Plautus and the more restrained work of Terence. Indebted to Plautus in many respects, he apparently initiated the type of comedy which Terence favored and developed.[21] The loss of his comedies should not blind us to the fact that the consensus of later Roman writers looked upon him as the equal, if not the superior, of the two playwrights whose comedies have survived.

## Plautus' Life

Little is actually known about the life of Plautus, and the meager accounts found in handbooks have been pieced together from random remarks made by Cicero, Aulus Gellius (who quotes Varro), Jerome, and others. The authenticity of many of the so-called facts has been denied by some modern scholars who reject as fiction the more picturesque details of the tradition.

The dates given for Plautus' birth and death are 254 and 184 B.C. The year of his death is stated by Cicero (*Brutus*, 15, 60), and this is doubtless approximately correct, although it may be an inference from the latest mention of the presentation of his plays. Two other dates are definitely known from didascalic notices—the production of the *Stichus* in 200 B.C. and that of the *Pseudolus* in 191 B.C. Cicero says (*De sen.* 14, 50) that Plautus as an old man took great delight in his *Truculentus* and his *Pseudolus*; the assumption that Plautus was at least sixty in 191 B.C. is responsible for the birth year of 254 B.C., which generously assigns to him a full three score and ten years. The statement of Jerome that Plautus died in 200 B.C. is clearly an error since not merely the *Pseudolus* but by far the majority of his extant plays are believed to have been produced after that date.

Plautus' name appeared in later antiquity as T. Maccius Plautus. In the Middle Ages his *nomen* was wrongly divided, and all editions of Plautus prior to 1845 gave the playwright's name as M. Accius Plautus. Ritschl examined the Ambrosian Palimpsest, which, dating from the fourth century A.D., is centuries older than the other manuscripts of the plays, and found several instances of the complete name in the genitive: T. MACCI PLAVTI. There can be no doubt that the correct name in antiquity was Titus Maccius Plautus, but many scholars have not been so positive that Plautus in his own day had all three names.

Leo, whose essay on Plautus' life[22] has been the most significant

---

21 Cf. Faider, *MB* 13 (1909), pp. 33 ff., who opposes the view of Caecilius as a transitional figure between Plautus and Terence, and believes that his work was similar in most respects to that of the younger dramatist. See also Lana, *RFC* 25 (1947), pp. 155 ff.

22 *Plautinische Forschungen*, pp. 63-86.

treatment of the problem since Ritschl's work a half century earlier, points out that nowhere in the prologues or the early references are all three names found together, and that only Roman nobles had three names prior to 150 B.C. Plautus was an Umbrian from the town of Sarsina (mentioned in *Most.* 770, which contains also a pun upon *umbra*, "shade" and "Umbrian woman"), and Leo thinks that the system of three names would not have been in use there in the third century B.C. He assumes, therefore, that the playwright as a boy was named Titus by his father and that Plotus (later Plautus) was his Umbrian nickname, which signified, according to ancient writers, either "Flatfoot" or "Dog-eared." When he came to Rome he acted on the stage in Atellan farces as a clown and from such acting was called Maccus; this is supported by the prologue of the *Asinaria* (11: *Maccus uortit barbare*) ;[23] later, when three names were regularly used, Maccus was changed to the ordinary *nomen* Maccius.

Other scholars have argued that the Roman system of nomenclature did not apply to Umbria and assume that Plautus had all three names before coming to Rome; if true, the use of Maccus (*Asin.* 11) could be a mere jest on the similarity of names. In either case, it is very probable that Plautus began his career by acting the part of the clown in Atellan farces; Beare[24] goes even further and makes the rather unlikely suggestion that Plautus acted also in mimes; he finds support for this in the *cognomen* Plautus; if the word Plautus meant "Flatfoot," *planis pedibus*, it is perhaps an alternate term for *planipes*, the Latin word for the bare-footed actor of the mime. According to this view, Maccus and Plotus (Plautus) are both stage names which the poet bore at different periods and which were combined and modified by a later generation. The exact source of the playwright's name will probably never be known but his close knowledge of the theater and his wide range of comic devices make it extremely likely that he had personal experience on the stage as an actor before he turned to the writing of plays based upon Greek models.

Our knowledge about Plautus' life at Rome is slight indeed. Aulus Gellius, in an interesting paragraph (III, 3, 14) based upon Varro and others, relates that Plautus made money in theatrical work (*in operis artificum scaenicorum*), lost the money in trade (*in mercatibus*), returned to Rome penniless and earned his living for a time by working in a mill; while thus employed he wrote the *Saturio, Addictus*, and a third play. This short account has been the subject of considerable controversy. Leo and others who were conversant with the methods of ancient biographers considered much of the story pure inference from

[23] Cf. also *Merc.* 10: *eadem Latine Mercator Macci Titi.* Curcio (*Storia della Letteratura Latina*, p. 158) reads *Marcus* in *Asin.* 11 and seeks to prove that the correct form of the name was M. Accius Plautus, but his arguments are not convincing.
[24] *CR* 53 (1939), pp. 115 f.; *The Roman Stage*, p. 143.

the plays themselves, augmented by conventional topics from Greek biography. The story about Plautus' unfortunate venture in business was reminiscent of the foreign trade of numerous characters in the comedies, and the anecdote about the mill was a conventional motif which had appeared earlier in Greek biographical accounts.[25] The statement that Naevius had composed two plays in prison was similar. Somewhere in the three Plautine comedies mentioned by Aulus Gellius were contexts into which autobiographical allusions could be read.

Other critics have accepted the ancient account as reliable, believing that the incidents concerning trade, resultant impoverishment, and work in the mill really occurred and perhaps were mentioned in the prologue of one or more plays now lost. This unfortunately cannot be proved, and the well-established fact that ancient biographers did make wrong inferences from an author's works weakens one's confidence in the dependability of the tradition.

On the other hand, the statement that Plautus was engaged *in operis artificum scaenicorum* has been generally accepted,[26] but there has been disagreement about the exact meaning of the phrase; it has been interpreted as stage-hand, as carpenter,[27] as writer of comedies, as actor. Those who, like Buck,[28] accept the tradition about the trade and the work in the mill argue that he could not have made enough money as a stage-hand to have invested in a business venture, and, if he had earlier been a successful dramatist, it would have been unnecessary for him to earn his living by working in a mill. Moreover, the words of Gellius are believed to imply that he wrote plays for the first time while thus engaged in manual labor. But even if we reject the mill-story as fanciful, the interpretation of Plautus' theatrical work as that of actor still remains the most attractive; it accounts for the possible confusion between his name and that of the clown in the *fabula Atellana*, and helps to explain his mastery of stage-craft and farcical effects. That Plautus had considerable knowledge of the theater before turning to the career of playwright cannot be doubted. When and how this Umbrian from Sarsina learned Greek, and familiarized himself with the masterpieces of New Comedy, and likewise how he achieved the supreme control of the Latin tongue which he displays in his comedies is one of the puzzles of ancient literature. As Duff says, "no amount of detail could lessen or explain the mystery of genius, to which the plays, rather than disputed items of biography, are the best testimony."[29]

[25] Cf. Stuart, "Authors' Lives," p. 296.

[26] Frank (*AJPh* 58, 1937, p. 348) wrongly implies that Leo rejected this statement also as based on Greek literary gossip; see Leo, *Plautinische Forschungen*, pp. 74 f., 84 f.

[27] Cf. Forbes, *CW* 39 (1945-46), pp. 44 f., who points out the large number of metaphors from carpentry and the building trades in the text of Plautus.

[28] *A Chronology of the Plays of Plautus*, pp. 2-4, 22 f.

[29] *A Literary History of Rome*, p. 161.

## The Plays of Plautus

There was great uncertainty among ancient critics concerning the number of plays written by Plautus, and estimates ranged as high as one hundred and thirty. Lists of genuine plays were drawn up by various scholars and, according to Aulus Gellius (III, 3), Varro examined these lists and found that twenty-one had been accepted as Plautine *consensu omnium*; these were henceforth known as the *fabulae Varronianae* and are probably identical with the plays in our modern editions (twenty plays and the fragmentary *Vidularia*). Varro, however, selected other comedies also as Plautine on the basis of their style and humor; how many in all he attributed to Plautus is not known. In addition to the twenty-one comedies which have survived in our manuscripts, the titles of more than thirty others are known from ancient citations, among them the *Saturio* and the *Addictus*, both of which were said to have been written while Plautus was working in a mill, and the *Colax* and the *Commorientes*, to which Terence referred as Plautine (*Eun. 25, Ad. 7*). We have too little information about the lost plays to determine with certainty how many, if any, are spurious and have been wrongly ascribed to Plautus, or whether the additional thirty odd titles are genuine. In a recent examination of the citations[30] Miss Clift concludes that fourteen of the lost plays are probably Plautine and thirteen others possibly so. In this case we would have a total of forty-eight comedies which Plautus wrote during his career as a dramatist, and of which less than half have survived.

The following list gives the twenty extant plays, the titles in English translation,[31] and, wherever known, the author and title of the Greek original:

| | | | |
|---|---|---|---|
| *Amphitruo* | "Amphitryon" | | |
| *Asinaria* | "The Comedy of Asses" | Demophilus | *Onagos* |
| *Aulularia* | "The Pot of Gold" | Menander(?) | |
| *Bacchides* | "The Two Bacchides" | Menander | *Dis Exapaton* |
| *Captivi* | "The Captives" | | |
| *Casina* | "Casina" | Diphilus | *Cleroumenoe* |
| *Cistellaria* | "The Casket" | Menander | *Synaristosae* |
| *Curculio* | "Curculio" | | |
| *Epidicus* | "Epidicus" | | |
| *Menaechmi* | "The Twin Menaechmi" | | |
| *Mercator* | "The Merchant" | Philemon | *Emporos* |
| *Miles Gloriosus* | "The Braggart Warrior" | | *Alazon* |
| *Mostellaria* | "The Haunted House" | Philemon(?) | *Phasma* |
| *Persa* | "The Girl from Persia" | | |
| *Poenulus* | "The Carthaginian" | Menander(?) | *Carchedonios* |
| *Pseudolus* | "Pseudolus" | | |

[30] *Latin Pseudepigrapha*, pp. 40-78.

[31] For the sake of uniformity, I give the English titles as they appear in Duckworth, *The Complete Roman Drama*, and in Harsh, *A Handbook of Classical Drama*.

| | | | |
|---|---|---|---|
| *Rudens* | "The Rope" | Diphilus | *Pera*(?) |
| *Stichus* | "Stichus" | Menander | *Adelphoe* |
| *Trinummus* | "The Three Penny Day" | Philemon | *Thesauros* |
| *Truculentus* | "Truculentus" | | |

The Greek original of the *Vidularia*, "The Traveling Bag," the twenty-first comedy, of which fewer than one hundred lines are extant, was entitled *Schedia* (cf. *Vid.* 6), and the only known author of a comedy of this name is Diphilus.

In the list of the twenty plays the Greek dramatists are definitely known for only eight; from information given in the prologues we learn that one (*Asinaria*) was based upon a comedy by a minor Greek playwright named Demophilus, that Diphilus provided the originals for the *Casina* and the *Rudens*, Philemon for the *Mercator* and the *Trinummus*. Three comedies were based upon works of Menander; these were the *Bacchides*, the *Cistellaria*, and the *Stichus*. The last-named play, according to the didascalic notice, was adapted from an *Adelphoe*; this was certainly not the Menandrian original of Terence's *Adelphoe*; and there is ancient evidence that Menander composed two plays with the same title; Norwood was ill-advised to argue that Plautus and Terence used the same Greek comedy and that both introduced striking innovations.[32] The two Roman plays have nothing in common and could not under any circumstances be ascribed to the same Greek comedy. The case of the *Cistellaria* is equally interesting; it was long suspected that the original was by Menander,[33] but only recently has the name of the original been learned. An ancient reference by Festus to *Cist.* 408 as *in Syr* or *in Sym* led to the erroneous theory that *Syra* was the name of a character or an alternate title of the play. The recent discovery in a medieval letter of a reference to the same passage with the words "Plautus in Sinaristosis" clears away all uncertainty, and the Roman comedy is now known to be an adaptation from Menander's *Synaristosae*.[34]

There can be little certainty about the Greek originals of the other plays. The *Poenulus* and the *Aulularia* may be based upon comedies of Menander, and the *Mostellaria* upon a *Phasma* by Philemon, but both Menander and Theognetus wrote comedies with the same title.[35] The *Amphitruo* and the *Persa* have been assigned to originals of Middle

---

[32] *The Art of Terence*, p. 10.

[33] *Cist.* 89 ff. was considered a translation of Menander, fr. 558. The nature of the play is Menandrian, with its love theme, misunderstandings, recognition scene, and lack of farcical humor.

[34] See Duckworth, *CPh* 33 (1938), p. 276 and n. 46.

[35] Plautus did not adapt the *Mostellaria* from Menander's *Phasma*, as this was later translated by Luscius Lanuvinus, and very badly, according to Terence (*Eun.* 9). If the reference to Diphilus and Philemon in *Most.* 1149 is taken over from the Greek, the author was probably Theognetus. But Plautus in this passage may be asserting that he has improved upon his original, in which case the author of the *Phasma* could be Philemon. See Knorr, *Das griechische Vorbild der Mostellaria*, p. 60.

Comedy, but the evidence for this is far from convincing.[36] Many ingenious suggestions have been offered for some of the other plays, but the Greek sources of about half of Plautus' comedies still remain unidentified.

There have been numerous attempts to establish the chronology of the twenty extant comedies. If we knew the dates of the plays, it would be possible to see more clearly the development of Plautus' dramatic art, his increasing use of certain comic devices and his rejection of others; such information would be invaluable for an understanding of Plautus' originality. But we have definite dates for only two plays, the *Stichus* (200 B.C.) and the *Pseudolus* (191 B.C.). References to contemporary personages and events provide approximate dates for others, e.g., the allusion to Naevius in *Mil. Gl.* 211 f. dates the production about 205 B.C., and the mention of the Punic war in *Cist.* 197-202 implies a time not later than 202 B.C. That both the *Cistellaria* and the *Miles Gloriosus* are relatively early plays seems highly probable; the *Cistellaria* in plot and character is extremely Menandrian and lacks Plautus' usual humor and vivacity; the *Miles* contains almost no lyrical *cantica* and this seems also an indication of an early date. Another comedy which has a dearth of song and dance is the *Asinaria*, and this too is considered an early play on the basis of 123 f., a possible reference to Scipio which scholars date either in 212 or 207 B.C. On the other hand, the *Casina*, usually placed in 185 or 184 B.C. by a reference to the *senatusconsultum de Bacchanalibus* of 186 B.C. (cf. *Cas.* 980) has an unusually large amount of lyric and is very probably one of Plautus' latest plays.[37]

The two main criteria used to establish a relative chronology of the plays are thus (1) references to contemporary persons and events, and (2) the quantity of song and dance in the various comedies. If, as Sedgwick believes,[38] Plautus gradually increased the proportion of lyrics as his technique improved and as he departed more and more from his Greek models, we have a helpful means of checking the dates established by historical references, which by themselves are often far from conclusive. Many scholars unfortunately read contemporary allusions into passages where none really exists; a passage which appears to contain a Roman reference may often be a reflection in Roman language of a similar passage in the Greek original.[39] Both Enk and Buck

[36] See "Middle Comedy" in chap. 2.
[37] Mattingly and Robinson (*CR* 47, 1933, pp. 52 ff.) attempt on numismatic evidence to date the revival of the *Casina* shortly after Plautus' death; this would make the time of the original production about 210 B.C. This theory has not been accepted; see Frank, *AJPh* 54 (1933), pp. 368-372; Beare, *CR* 48 (1934), pp. 123 f.; Buck, *A Chronology of the Plays of Plautus*, pp. 54-61.
[38] *CR* 39 (1925), pp. 55 ff.; *CQ* 24 (1930), pp. 102 ff.; cf. his later remarks in *AJPh* 70 (1949), pp. 376 ff.
[39] Cf. Hough, *TAPhA* 71 (1940), pp. 194 ff.

use the historical method as the basis of their chronologies and, as I
have shown elsewhere,[40] although they agree upon some plays, there
are many instances of wide divergency, e.g., the *Menaechmi*, dated by
Enk about 215 B.C. on the basis of a reference to Hiero, king of Syracuse (*Men.* 412), is dated by Buck in 186 B.C., almost thirty years later,
because of a supposed reference to Scipio (*Men.* 196); neither argument
is convincing but the complicated metrical structure of the comedy
strongly favors a later rather than an earlier period.

In recent years, many other criteria have been suggested, especially
by Hough who, although unwilling to assign definite years to most
plays, believes that it is possible to establish a classification of the comedies as early, middle, and late. Among the criteria he uses are the increasingly artistic employment of Greek words, more dexterous plot
construction, a more subtle handling of intrigue, a less mechanical use
of link monologues, greater originality in his methods of achieving
humorous effects.[41] When these various tests check with the results
gained independently through the presence of Roman allusions and the
quantity of lyrical *cantica*, such agreement cannot be considered mere
coincidence. Hough's work is of value, not only for establishing a general chronological trend, but also for showing how Plautus' art may
have developed during his career, and therefore must be considered
in any discussion of the originality of Plautus.

The various chronological lists agree on the relative dating of the
following plays:

Early period: *Asinaria, Mercator, Miles Gloriosus* (c. 205 B.C.), *Cis-
tellaria* (before 201 B.C.)
Middle period: *Stichus* (200 B.C.), *Aulularia, Curculio*
Late period: *Pseudolus* (191 B.C.), *Bacchides, Casina* (185 or 184 B.C.)

For the remaining plays there is less agreement. The *Epidicus* must be
dated before the *Bacchides* (cf. *Bacch.* 214 f.), and the *Truculentus*
belongs to the same period as the *Pseudolus*. For certain comedies the
historical method seems particularly unsatisfactory, unless verified by
the use of additional criteria; e.g., Enk considers the *Menaechmi,
Rudens,* and *Amphitruo* all as early plays (between 215 and 206 B.C.)
while Buck, also working from Roman allusions, dates these same plays
as late (189-186 B.C.). The work of Sedgwick and Hough is more convincing; they agree in considering the *Poenulus* an early play, in placing
the *Amphitruo, Captivi, Rudens,* and *Trinummus* in the middle period,
and in assigning the *Persa* and the *Truculentus* to the latest period. But
even these results must be considered tentative.[42]

[40] *AJPh* 64 (1943), pp. 348 ff.
[41] Cf. Hough, *AJPh* 55 (1934), pp. 346-364; *CPh* 30 (1935), pp. 43-57; *AJPh* 60
(1939), pp. 422-435; *TAPhA* 70 (1939), pp. 231-241; 71 (1940), pp. 186-198; 73
(1942), pp. 108-118.
[42] Cf. Sedgwick's revised chronology in *AJPh* 70 (1949), p. 382; he now dates the

When Plautus first began to compose comedies is likewise not known. The extant plays apparently all date from the last twenty or twenty-five years of his life. Even if fifty or more comedies are to be ascribed to him, all could have been written within this same period, for several might have been produced in a single year. Buck assigns eleven plays to a six-year period (191-186 B.C.), and believes that none of the extant plays was produced in the period between 200 and 194 B.C.—a curious phenomenon, if his chronology is accepted.[43] Perhaps some of the plays which failed to find a place among the *fabulae Varronianae* were produced during this period. But it is unnecessary to compress Plautus' dramatic career to the last two decades of his life. He could have acquired fame as an actor and then have begun to compose plays at the age of thirty-five or forty, in other words, about the beginning of the second Punic war.[44] The fact that the earlier comedies have not survived need cause no surprise, for if they were close translations from the Greek and lacked the gaiety and spontaneity which later endeared him to his audiences, they would be less likely to be selected as characteristically Plautine by Roman critics of a later generation.

## The Life and Works of Terence

Although our information about Plautus' life is meager and uncertain, we seem, at first sight, to be much more fortunate in our knowledge of Terence's career. Here we have two important sources—Terence's own prologues, which paint a picture of the literary rivalries of the period and present his defense against adverse criticism, and the interesting *Life of Terence*, written by Suetonius and preserved by Donatus in his commentary on Terence. Modern accounts of the life of Terence are derived largely from the latter source, and usually agree upon the following facts. Publius Terentius Afer was born in Carthage and brought to Rome as a slave at an early age; he was educated by his master, the Roman senator Terentius Lucanus, and manumitted. Terence became an intimate friend of Scipio and Laelius and thus a member of the Scipionic circle. Their friendship and patronage led to jealous accusations from other playwrights that Scipio and Laelius had written his plays or at least had aided him in their composition. Terence read his first comedy, the *Andria*, to the aged Caecilius and received the latter's enthusiastic approval. His six plays were performed during the years 166-160 B.C., after which he went to Greece, where he died the

---

*Poenulus* in 191 B.C., the *Rudens* and the *Captivi* in 189 B.C., and the *Amphitruo* in 188 B.C.

[43] Enk, however, places the *Epidicus, Persa, Aulularia*, and perhaps the *Mostellaria* in the years 200-194 B.C. On the date of the *Epidicus*, cf. Duckworth, *T. Macci Plauti Epidicus*, pp. 239 f.

[44] Cf. Buck, *A Chronology of the Plays of Plautus*, p. 23. Ritschl's date of 224 B.C. seems unnecessarily early.

following year on his way home with new translations of Menander's plays. He left a small estate on the Appian Way, and was survived by a daughter who later married a Roman knight.

These are, in general, the "facts" of his life which most writers accept. As Norwood says, "they seem to provide small help toward explaining his achievement in dramatic composition, or the notable circumstance that this African stripling, who learned Latin as a foreign tongue, could use it with an elegance and purity which quickened the coarse-grained Roman language with Attic elasticity and charm."[45] Such a sketch of his life not only fails to explain his achievements in drama, but it over-looks the fact that the Suetonian *Life* is filled with innumerable con-flicting statements. Suetonius' biographical method, as is well known, was not only to procure information from all possible earlier sources but also to fill out his *Lives* with certain stock themes and anecdotes, and especially to derive material from an author's own works. In his *Life of Vergil*, for instance, Suetonius follows normal biographical procedure when he recounts omens and prodigies connected with Vergil's birth and gives aspersions on his moral character, and when he describes the loss and restoration of Vergil's farm by inference from *Bucolics* I and IX. Likewise, in his *Life of Terence*, Suetonius may be making ill-founded guesses from Terence's own works, or repeating earlier statements which are also mere conjectures. Basically, the prob-lem is very similar to that provided by the ancient accounts about Plautus; what is fact and what is mere invention or inference from the poet's own work?

We cannot be certain about the date of Terence's birth. Some manu-scripts of Suetonius' *Life* state that he had not yet entered his twenty-fifth year when he left Rome in 160 B.C.; others read "thirty-fifth." It seems hardly plausible that Terence began his dramatic career at the age of eighteen, or younger, and it is very likely that the age of twenty-five was invented to make him the same age as Scipio (born in 185 B.C.) and Laelius (born in 186 B.C.); although Suetonius quotes Nepos to the effect that the three were contemporaries (*aequales*), he cites also the conflicting view of Fenestella that Terence was older than either Scipio or Laelius. The year 195 B.C. seems a likely date for the birth of Ter-ence,[46] but there is no real evidence to prove it, apart from the variant reading in the Suetonian *Life*.

But if Terence was several years older than Scipio and Laelius, what of their supposed patronage and collaboration? Twice in his prologues (*Heaut.* 22-24 and *Ad.* 15-21) he mentions without denial the charge

---

[45] *The Art of Terence*, p. 132.
[46] Cf. Dziatzko-Hauler, *Phormio*, p. 12; Terzaghi, *Prolegomeni a Terenzio*, pp. 27 f. The usual view that Terence was of Libyan parentage is rejected by Frank, *AJPh* 54 (1933), pp. 269 ff., who suggests that his mother may have been one of Hannibal's captives from southern Italy and therefore of Italian or Greek stock.

that he has been aided in the writing of his plays by friends, and in
*Ad.* 19 ff. he refers to these friends as nobles

who are pleasing to all of you and to the public at large, whose services
each one of you has used unreservedly at his convenience in war, in peace,
in private affairs.

This passage hardly sounds as if it could refer to young men of twenty-
five, and when the *Heauton* was produced in 163 B.C. Scipio was only
twenty-two. Terence does not give the names of his friends and, although later writers (Cicero, Quintilian, Donatus) identified them with
Scipio and Laelius, it is worth noting that Suetonius quotes Santra to
the effect that Terence might have had the aid of Sulpicius Gallus (consul in 166 B.C.), Fabius Labeo, or M. Popillius; that these were the
men "whose services the people had used in war, in peace, and in private
affairs." At the same time, Suetonius cites the verses of Porcius concerning Terence's improper relations with Scipio and Laelius and his
later departure to Greece in poverty and disgrace. This might be a
reasonably true picture of the facts but it sounds like the usual moral
aspersions so dear to ancient biographers. We have in the Suetonian
*Life* a mass of contradictions and actually, as Beare points out,[47] the
only real evidence connecting Terence and Scipio is the production of
the *Hecyra* and the *Adelphoe* at the funeral games for Scipio's father,
L. Aemilius Paulus. Is then Terence's supposed friendship with Scipio
to be rejected as a myth? Probably not. Terence's devotion to Menander
and his desire to compose more artistic comedy would naturally com-
mend him to the young nobles whose literary interests paralleled those
of the dramatist. It is not impossible that the prologues of the *Heauton*
and the *Adelphoe* refer to Scipio and his group although there are too
many uncertainties and contradictions in the tradition to assert it as
an incontrovertible fact.[48]

There is difficulty also about the story of Terence and Caecilius. The
*Andria* was produced in 166 B.C., but Caecilius, according to Jerome,
died in 168 B.C. If Terence at the request of the aediles read his play
to Caecilius during dinner, it was presumably shortly before its production. To resolve the conflict it has seemed necessary either to change the
date of Caecilius' death to 166 B.C., as do many historians, or to assume
that the performance of the *Andria* was a second presentation and that
the comedy was read to Caecilius in 168 B.C. and produced soon after
without success.[49] Such attempts to preserve the anecdote as authentic

---

[47] *Ha* 59 (1942), p. 25; *The Roman Stage*, p. 85.

[48] Flickinger (*PhQ* 6, 1927, pp. 245 f., 265 ff.) accepts Gallus as the friend who
helped Terence get the *Andria* produced in 166 B.C., but believes that the friendship
with Laelius and Scipio began about 163 B.C. and that Terence referred to them in
*Heaut.* 24 and *Ad.* 17 ff. He suggests that the story in the *Life* about Laelius revising
the *Heauton* confirms the beginning of the friendship. See Brown, *A Study of the
Scipionic Circle*, pp. 55 ff.

[49] Cf. Terzaghi, *Prolegomeni a Terenzio*, pp. 35 f. But see Flickinger, *PhQ* 6

are ingenious, but seem unnecessary in the light of ancient biographical method. Both Greek and Roman biographers delighted in stories connecting different writers of a particular genre, e.g., the anecdote of Accius reading his *Atreus* to Pacuvius, as related by Aulus Gellius (XIII, 2, 2) and the statement in Suetonius' *Life of Vergil* that Lucretius died on the very day that Vergil assumed the *toga virilis*. The frequency of these stories makes the supposed meeting of Terence and Caecilius look suspiciously like a later invention.

Perhaps the most extreme of modern scholars is Beare, who regards Suetonius' account of Terence as "based entirely on the evidence of the plays and prologues, on notes in the manuscripts concerning first and later performances, on inferences sound or unsound from such evidence, and on pure invention."[50] But Beare seems far too sceptical when he suggests that the story of Terence's birth in Africa and his slavery and manumission may be pure inference from the name Afer, and he leaves the Suetonian *Life* in shreds when he concludes that nothing was really known of Terence after the sudden ending of his career in 160 B.C. and that later Roman biographers may have taken the idea of the voyage from such a passage as *Ad.* 703: "He's perished, he's departed, he's gone on board ship." It is unfortunately true that there are many conflicting statements in Suetonius about Terence's departure from Rome and his death. But even if it cannot be proved, a voyage to Greece seems highly plausible; the number of Greek comedies already translated by Naevius, Plautus, Caecilius, and others doubtless totaled hundreds; can we assume so large a supply of Greek comedies available at Rome in the middle of the second century B.C.? A trip to Greece to procure more Menandrian models and to make new adaptations of his favorite author would be natural under the circumstances, all the more so since he had been accused of using scenes from plays already translated by Roman playwrights (cf. *Eun.* 22-34, *Ad.* 4-14). Love of Greece and a desire to study Greek culture at first hand may also have been contributing factors.

When we turn to the comedies themselves and the dates of their presentation, we are on more solid ground, for the didascalic notices have been preserved for all six plays. Four were adapted from Menander, *Andria* ("The Woman of Andros"), *Heauton Timorumenos* ("The Self-Tormentor"), *Eunuchus* ("The Eunuch") and *Adelphoe* ("The Brothers"); the two remaining comedies, *Phormio* and *Hecyra* ("The Mother-in-law"), were based upon Greek originals (*Epidikazomenos*

---

(1927), pp. 236 ff., who argues against the theory that the *Andria* prologue was intended for a second presentation; he thinks that the *Andria* was read to Caecilius in 168 B.C., but that the death of Caecilius and the hostility of Terence's detractors prevented the production of the play until 166 B.C.

[50] *Ha* 59 (1942), p. 26; cf. *The Roman Stage*, pp. 82 ff. See also Leo, *Plautinische Forschungen*, pp. 64 f., who regards the *Life* as a fabrication on Greek models.

and *Hekyra*) by Apollodorus of Carystus. In three of the Menandrian plays, Terence, as we learn from the prologues, practiced what is called "contamination," usually defined as the process of interweaving parts of two or more Greek comedies to form one Latin play. In his *Andria*, based upon Menander's *Andria*, he used additional material from Menander's *Perinthia*, a comedy with a very similar plot (*And.* 11), and he admits that his *Eunuchus*, adapted from Menander's play of the same title, contains a parasite and a soldier taken from Menander's *Colax*; in the *Adelphoe* a scene is added from the *Synapothnescontes* of Diphilus. In each case the additions from the second original were of a minor nature, and so Terence adopted as the title of his Latin play the title of the Greek original from which the plot and characters were chiefly drawn.

The prologues of the *Hecyra* refer to two unsuccessful productions; at the first presentation, the audience was distracted by a rope-dancer or boxer (*Hec.* 4, 33-35) and a second attempt fared no better, since the audience was stampeded by the rumor of a gladiatorial exhibition (*Hec.* 39-42). The following chronology of the six plays, including the two unsuccessful attempts with the *Hecyra*, is generally accepted:

| | | |
|---|---|---|
| *Andria* | 166 B.C. | *Ludi Megalenses* |
| *Hecyra* I | 165 B.C. | *Ludi Megalenses* (first failure) |
| *Heauton* | 163 B.C. | *Ludi Megalenses* |
| *Eunuchus* | 161 B.C. | *Ludi Megalenses* |
| *Phormio* | 161 B.C. | *Ludi Romani* |
| *Adelphoe* | 160 B.C. | *Ludi funebres* (for Paulus) |
| *Hecyra* II | 160 B.C. | *Ludi funebres* (for Paulus) (second failure) |
| *Hecyra* III | 160 B.C. | *Ludi Romani* |

Yet, even here, minor contradictions between the *didascaliae* and statements of Donatus have led to various alternative theories, e.g., that the *Eunuchus* preceded the *Heauton* and was first produced in 166 B.C., being repeated in 161 B.C.,[51] and that the *Adelphoe* was written after the *Andria* and either produced or scheduled for production in 166 or 165 B.C.[52]

One difficulty is that Terence in the prologue of the *Heauton* (16-18) refers to the accusation that he has "contaminated" many Greek plays while writing a few Latin plays. But of the plays already produced only the *Andria* had been adapted from two Greek originals; in neither the *Hecyra* nor the *Heauton* itself had contamination been employed. Could Terence in 163 B.C. have said that he had contaminated many Greek plays to make a few Latin plays, if he had used only four Greek originals to compose three comedies? Hence Terzaghi assumes that the *Adelphoe*,

[51] Cf. Fabia, *Les Prologues de Térence*, pp. 33-43.

[52] Terzaghi, *Prolegomeni a Terenzio*, p. 33. For other theories involving more radical changes in the usual chronology, cf. Gestri, *SIFC* 13 (1936), pp. 61-105; Blum, *SIFC* 13 (1936), pp. 106-116; their views are rejected by Arnaldi, *Da Plauto a Terenzio*, II, pp. 109 ff.

based on a Menandrian original with a scene added from *Diphilus*, preceded the *Heauton*, and further assumes that between 165 and 163 B.C. Terence had composed other comedies, using the same method of *contaminatio*, but had not succeeded in having them produced.[53] Such a theory is possible but not very probable. The charge as stated in the prologue was undoubtedly an exaggeration; Terence's enemies may have overstated the facts or Terence may have sought to weaken their criticism by expressing it as he did. Moreover, Terence's comedies display careful craftsmanship and it is not likely that he composed rapidly. The voice of antiquity is united in ascribing six and only six plays to Terence, and the superior artistry of the *Adelphoe* makes it most probably the last of Terence's comedies.

## Terence and Lanuvinus

In his use of the prologue Terence differed strikingly from Plautus and earlier comic dramatists, both Greek and Roman. The prologue, which originally, as Aristotle states in his *Poetics* (1452b), was that part of the play preceding the entrance of the chorus, had been utilized by Euripides and the playwrights of Middle and New Comedy chiefly for the exposition of the plot (*argumentum*); this did not mean necessarily a description of the action of the play itself, but rather of the antecedents of the action, in order to make the situation at the beginning of the play more intelligible. A portion of the prologue was often given over to an appeal to the audience for good will (*captatio benevolentiae*). Plautus in several of his comedies had dispensed with the expository prologue and had begun naturally with the dialogue of the characters (e.g., *Curculio, Epidicus, Mostellaria, Persa, Stichus*), and in the prologue of the *Trinummus* (16 f.) Luxury tells the audience not to expect the plot of the comedy, for the old men who will come upon the stage will explain the situation:

> sed de argumento ne exspectetis fabulae:
> senes qui huc uenient, i rem uobis aperient.

Terence obviously had this passage in mind when he wrote in the prologue of the *Adelphoe* (22 ff.):

> dehinc ne exspectetis argumentum fabulae:
> senes qui primi uenient, i partem aperient,
> in agendo partem ostendent.

What had been the exception with Plautus became Terence's normal procedure. He achieved the final stage in the evolution of the prologue by his suppression of the *argumentum*; the prologue was now entirely divorced from the drama. Terence's omission of the expository prologue

---

[53] *Prolegomeni a Terenzio*, p. 34; he suggests also (p. 37) that between 163 and 161 B.C. Terence wrote other comedies that were lost without a trace.

is considered by many scholars as a most important innovation, one which had far-reaching effects upon the irony and suspense in his plays. This aspect of his work will be considered later;[54] the important point now is the use he made of the prologues from which he had excluded all references to the plots of the comedies.

Although Terence was favored and encouraged by influential friends, he incurred throughout his career the hostility and jealousy of other playwrights, and one in particular, whom he calls (*And.* 6 f., *Heaut.* 22) a "spiteful old poet" (*maliuolus uetus poeta*). This poet, we learn from Donatus, was the dramatist Luscius Lanuvinus, and the charges and accusations which Lanuvinus advanced against Terence and his work made it necessary for the younger poet to defend himself and even attack his adversary in return. It is very possible, as Fabia suggests,[55] that Terence originally intended to omit the prologue altogether, since it was less an innovation to present comedies without prologues than to write prologues without some discussion of the *argumentum*. But the attacks of Lanuvinus and his colleagues could not be passed over in silence and Terence found the prologue a convenient means of replying to unfavorable criticisms (cf. *And.* 5-7). It is possible also that the accusations of Lanuvinus had been expressed in prologues and that Terence was using the same means in defending himself. At any rate, we have in the Terentian plays a new form of prologue: the *argumentum* has disappeared, and the appeal to the audience no longer contains the jests and pleasantries of the Plautine *captatio benevolentiae*. When Ambivius Turpio, the chief actor and stage manager of Terence's comedies, delivered the prologues of the *Heauton* and the *Hecyra* (at its third production), he stated that he came before the spectators as an *orator*, not as a *prologus* (*Heaut.* 11, *Hec.* 9). In its use of polemic the Terentian prologue somewhat resembles the *parabasis* of Old Comedy. Whereas the prologues of Menander and Plautus were a part of the play and could be used for repeated performances, Terence's prologues were composed for one particular production. From these prologues we gain an interesting insight into the literary quarrels of the period, and we learn much about the poetic ideals and character of Terence, and of his opponent Lanuvinus as well.

Luscius Lanuvinus, though rated by Volcacius Sedigitus as ninth in his canon of comic playwrights, may well have been the most influential dramatist in the *collegium poetarum* after the death of Caecilius, and as such probably viewed with undisguised hostility the sudden appearance of a young writer of great promise. The fact that Terence had well-to-do friends may have led Lanuvinus and his fellow playwrights

---

[54] See "Surprise in Plautus and Terence" and "Suspense and Irony" in chap. 8.
[55] *Les Prologues de Térence*, p. 100.

to view the competition as unfair;[56] there seems to have been a con-
certed effort to drive Terence from his career as a dramatist.

The accusations made against Terence, to which he refers in his
prologues, were four in number. (1) The first charge was that "plays
ought not to be contaminated" (*And.* 16); i.e., the mingling of two
Greek comedies to form one Latin play was in a sense a "spoiling" of
the Greek original.[57] Terence admits adding to his *Andria* material from
Menander's *Perinthia*, but he defends this practice by appealing to the
example of Naevius, Plautus, and Ennius, whose *neclegentia* he would
rather imitate than the *obscura diligentia* of his critics (*And.* 9-21; cf.
*Heaut.* 16-21).[58] His failure to include Caecilius in the list of earlier
"contaminators" leads some scholars to assume that Caecilius anticipated Lanuvinus in his attitude toward contamination.

(2) A more serious accusation was that of plagiarism. In an age
when literary originality consisted in translating or adapting from the
Greek, it came to be considered plagiarism to rework what had already
been translated. Terence wished to enliven his *Eunuchus* by adding the
characters of the soldier and the parasite from Menander's *Colax*. This
was theft, maintained his opponent, since the *Colax* was an old play of
Naevius and Plautus (*Eun.* 23-25).[59] Terence admits that he had
transferred to his *Eunuchus* the parasite and soldier, but maintains that
he did not know that they had been used earlier in a Latin play. This as
a defense seems at first sight so clumsy that critics have not hesitated
to call it a downright lie,[60] but we must remember that many years had
elapsed since the earlier plays had been produced and the manuscripts
were not readily available for consultation. Terence may well have been
telling the truth. There is, however, considerable sophistry in his statement (*Eun.* 35-40) that the parasite and the soldier were stock characters, to be used like running slaves, virtuous matrons, evil courtesans,

---

[56] Cf. Dunkin, *Post-Aristophanic Comedy*, p. 130; it does not follow, however, that
Terence always scorned the *populus stupidus* and was primarily interested in presenting "philosophical studies of wealthy men" (p. 133); cf. Duckworth, *AJPh* 68 (1947),
pp. 421 ff.

[57] On the meaning of *contaminatio*, see "The Problem of *Contaminatio*" in chap. 7.

[58] But why bother to defend himself against the charge if the earlier poets had
regularly practised *contaminatio*? Beare (*CR* 51, 1937, p. 108) thinks that Terence's
statement in *And.* 18 is an outright lie which would not be detected by the spectators.
See also *RPh* 66 (1940), pp. 34 ff., where Beare suggests that Terence was purposely
confusing his audience by combining his procedure (use of a second original) with
Plautus' free invention (*neclegentia*). See below, pp. 204 f.

[59] Whether Plautus had revised the *Colax* of Naevius or written a second play from
the same Menandrian original cannot be determined. Terzaghi's theory ("Una scena
di Plauto ed una di Terenzio," *Mélanges Paul Thomas*, Bruges, 1930, pp. 650-660),
that the soldier and the parasite in Plautus, *Miles*, Act 1, were taken from Menander's
*Colax*, is not convincing.

[60] Cf. Fabia, *Les Prologues de Térence*, p. 225; Norwood, *The Art of Terence*,
p. 138, n. 3. Flickinger (*PhQ* 6, 1927, pp. 259 f.) accepts the emendation *asciuisse* for
*scisse sese* in *Eun.* 34; with this reading Terence says merely that his borrowing was
from the Greek rather than from the Latin. Such a defense, however, seems weaker
than his plea of *inprudentia*.

and the like; this was not the point at issue. He had not been accused of adding a parasite and a soldier to the *Eunuchus* but of adding particular scenes from a Greek play which had already been translated into Latin. When Terence wrote his *Adelphoe* and added a scene from a comedy of Diphilus previously Latinized by Plautus, he was again accused of theft (*furtum*), but in this case his defense was more successful; he was not guilty of plagiarism since Plautus in using the comedy of Diphilus had omitted that particular scene (*Ad.* 6-14). This defense perhaps rests upon a technicality, but the assurance of his manner shows that he now felt his position as a dramatist to be secure. It is interesting to note that his adversaries were no longer accusing him of contamination although he was guilty of this procedure in both the *Eunuchus* and the *Adelphoe*.

(3) From the prologues of the *Heauton* (22-27) and the *Adelphoe* (15-21) it is evident that Lanuvinus and his colleagues attacked Terence with the charge that he was aided by his friends, that he relied upon their genius rather than his own ability:

> amicum ingenio fretum, haud natura sua (*Heaut.* 24).

Terence neither affirms nor denies the accusation, but expresses pride in the friendship. The charge of collaboration was not surprising under the circumstances; Terence was young, he had arisen suddenly to prominence as a playwright, he had wealthy and aristocratic friends, he displayed a purity and elegance of style surprising in a former slave of African birth. There can be little doubt that Terence received advice and encouragement from his friends; there is no evidence, apart from the hostile attacks of his adversaries, that they assisted him in the writing of his plays. The rumors lived on long after his death and took the form that Scipio or Laelius had written his plays for him. These later versions were known to Cicero and Quintilian but were not accepted by them.

(4) The prologue of the *Phormio* (1-5) states that the earlier *maledicta* of Lanuvinus had been unsuccessful in driving Terence from the stage, and so the *uetus poeta* had now attacked the stylistic qualities of his rival, saying that the content of Terence's plays was thin and their expression feeble:

> tenui esse oratione et scriptura leui.

This implied that both his thought and expression were lacking in elevation and strength. Of all the accusations hurled against Terence, this was perhaps the one which to his contemporaries seemed most justified, and the estimates of later antiquity have been interpreted as confirming it.[61] Terence did not attempt to answer the charge, but turned quickly to a criticism of Lanuvinus' own work.

---

[61] Cf. Fabia, *Les Prologues de Térence*, pp. 252 ff., who refers to the comments of Cicero (*sedatis motibus*) and Caesar (*lenibus scriptis*), quoted in the Suetonian *Life*.

In his attacks upon his critic, Terence's most enlightening comment is perhaps the following: "Lanuvinus, by translating literally and writing badly, produced poor Latin plays from good Greek ones."

> qui bene uortendo et easdem scribendo male
> ex Graecis bonis Latinas fecit non bonas. (*Eun.* 7 f.)

It is evident also (*Heaut.* 35-40) that Lanuvinus favored comedies with more vigorous action and the usual stock characters (running slave, hungry parasite, greedy slavedealer, etc.). From these and other passages we can derive the following picture of Lanuvinus as a dramatist: he believed in literal translation, and this led him to disapprove of the process of contamination as employed by Terence. We have no evidence that Caecilius contaminated, but it is possible that Caecilius' adversaries, to whom Ambivius refers in *Hec.* 22, included Lanuvinus, for the fragments of the *Plocium* proved that Caecilius was far from being a literal translator of Menander. Lanuvinus, if he followed the Greek originals closely, must have selected his models with care, for he opposed calm and sedate comedies and attempted to present his characters in lively fashion. His theory of comic drama differed from Terence's in many respects, but his hostility is not to be explained merely by disinterested principles of dramatic art; he was undoubtedly *maliuolus* and was motivated by bitterness and jealousy. The jealousy may not have been entirely personal; the fact that the assault began at the outset of Terence's career and continued to its end implies that at the bottom of the whole affair was the corporate jealousy of the poets' guild.[62]

However feeble some of Terence's rejoinders seem to be, and however pointless some of his attacks, there can be no doubt about his ultimate victory. Lanuvinus had all the advantage at the beginning and Terence was powerless to stop the series of hostile accusations. Driven to defend himself, he struck back with all the means at his disposal. Both dramatists were at times guilty of bad faith, but Terence had more of the right on his side. His plays survive and his fame increases with the years; almost all that we know of Lanuvinus and his work comes as a result of his futile effort to keep Terence from a successful career.

## The Plautine Revival and *Retractatio*

The popularity of Plautus' comedies led to a demand for the revival of certain plays after his death. The best evidence for this revival period is the prologue of the *Casina* (5-20), which refers to the desire of the spectators to see old plays,

---

But these phrases are perhaps less unfavorable than Fabia believes; see below, chap. 14, n. 4.

[62] Minar (*PAPhA* 76, 1945, p. xxxvii) suggests also that "political opposition to the nobles who were Terence's friends and sponsors may have played a part." Lana (*RFC* 25, 1947, pp. 53 ff.) believes that the hostility resulted from opposition to Terence's philhellenism, his desire to portray Greek life in a more favorable light.

For the new comedies which are produced today are much more worthless than new coins. (9 f.)

The play about to be produced, the speaker continues, was approved formerly by those of advanced age (*in senioribus*), but the younger men (*iuniores*) do not know the play. At the time of its first production there lived a group of outstanding dramatists (*flos poetarum*) who since have died. We learn also (*Cas.* 31 ff.) that the original title of the Latin play was *Sortientes*, "The Men Who Draw Lots," an exact translation of the name of Diphilus' play (*Cleroumenoe*). *Casina* is therefore the revival title which has supplanted the Plautine title.

When did this Plautine revival take place and what is meant by the *flos poetarum*? The second production of the *Casina* is clearly a generation, i.e., twenty-five or thirty years, later than the original presentation. Mattingly and Robinson attempt to date the revival shortly after Plautus' death by the reference to *novi nummi*, which they believe indicates a particular issue of coins,[63] but this places the first production of the *Casina* (under the title *Sortientes*) about 210 B.C., and, as we have seen, such a date runs counter to all the evidence about the *Casina*; also the *flos poetarum* would then exclude outstanding poets like Caecilius and Ennius who were alive for fifteen years after Plautus' death. It is highly probable that the *Casina* was originally produced about 185 or 184 B.C. and that the revival period began between 160 and 150 B.C. Beare suggests[64] that the revival of the *Casina* occurred during Terence's lifetime, and that his are the "worthless new plays" to which the speaker of the prologue referred; according to this view, the "flower of poets" included Plautus, Caecilius, and Ennius, but not Terence and his contemporaries. But Terence, in spite of the attacks of Luscius Lanuvinus, produced most of his plays with success, and the *Eunuchus* (161 B.C.) received such acclaim that it was twice presented on the same day and brought to the playwright the unheard-of sum of eight thousand sesterces. To exclude Terence from the *flos poetarum* seems unwise, and we can therefore assume that the revival of Plautus' plays took place after Terence's death, beginning perhaps about 155 B.C. That Terence's plays were also revived in this later period is indicated by the second ending of the *Andria*, and this is an additional argument against Beare's desire to include Terence among the writers of the "worthless new plays."

We do not know how long the revival period lasted or how many comedies of Plautus were presented again on the stage. During this period changes were doubtless introduced into the texts of the plays; passages were expanded or abbreviated, jokes may have been added, and lines substituted for others. This process of reworking is known

[63] *CR* 47 (1933), pp. 52 ff.; see above, n. 37.
[64] *CR* 48 (1934), pp. 123 f.; *The Roman Stage*, p. 75.

as *retractatio*. It is a curious fact that the *Casina*, apart from the prologue, shows no signs of such reworking, but there are traces in other
plays; e.g., the *Poenulus* with its double ending displays more extensive
alteration than any other Plautine comedy, and *Patruos*, "The Uncle,"
(*Poen.* 54) has been suggested as the original Plautine title; if this is
true, our present title *Poenulus*, a translation of the Greek *Carchedonios*,
goes back only to the revival era, as is the case with the title *Casina*.

During the latter part of the nineteenth century, scholars found in
*retractatio* a most convenient solution for the many flaws, contradictions, and repetitions which they saw in Plautus' comedies; variant
lines, alternate passages, omissions and additions—all were ascribed to
the work of *retractatores*.[65] If a play, e.g., the *Epidicus*,[66] was short and
lacking in clarity, it had been cut down for a revival production; if a
play was long and repetitious, it had been expanded by the addition of
jokes or through the desire to smooth out passages which had seemed
too brief or too awkward.

While it is very possible that the text of Plautus' plays was exposed
to changes of this sort in the revival era, it is not probable that widespread alterations such as many scholars have assumed were made at
that time. Repetition and redundancy are characteristic of Plautus'
style, and there is no need to ascribe a passage to the revival period
merely because it echoes the thought or expression of an earlier passage;
e.g., in *Most.* 208 ff. Scapha gives Philematium almost the same advice
she has expressed in 186 ff.; this has been viewed as an alternate version,[67] but the development of the thought in the second passage depends
upon the first (cf. 209 f. with 204) and there seems little justification
for the theory that 208-223 is a substitute for 186-207. On the other
hand, *Stich.* 48-57, which are missing in the Ambrosian Palimpsest,
repeat in dialogue meter the substance of the previous *canticum* and are
usually considered a variant for the lyrical passage.

Although *retractatio* for a time proved a most convenient means of
explaining Plautine contradictions and repetitions, the more recent
tendency has been to reject it as a significant factor in Plautine criticism.
As Miss Coulter says, "on the whole, the *retractatores* made no very
important contributions to our text,"[68] and modern editors are far more
conservative in their retention of the text as Plautine than were their
nineteenth-century predecessors. The scholarly pendulum swings, and
what seemed of vital significance in 1875 was hardly noticed in 1925,

[65] Cf. Coulter, *Retractatio in the Ambrosian and Palatine Recensions*, pp. 13-26,
for a brief mention of the earlier work of Goetz, Langen, and others; for a discussion
of many disputed passages, see Coulter, pp. 27 ff., and Thierfelder, *De rationibus
interpolationum Plautinarum*.

[66] Cf. Wheeler, *AJPh* 38 (1917), pp. 263 f.

[67] Cf. Leo, *Geschichte der römischen Literatur*, I, p. 114, n. 1; but see Langen,
*Plautinische Studien*, p. 331.

[68] *Retractatio in the Ambrosian and Palatine Recensions*, p. 109.

when scholars, working with the same or similar repetitions and dis-
crepancies, found their answers in *contaminatio* and careless workmanship on Plautus' part rather than in the reworking of comedies in the
revival period. That the newer theories were equally extreme and just
as unreliable is maintained by many critics today. The importance of
*retractatio* was exaggerated in the nineteenth century, but the reaction
to it in the early twentieth century went too far; as a possible explanation for variant lines and dittographies, awkwardly inserted jests, and
passages that lack Plautus' style and expression, it still deserves consideration. It is very probable, however, that far fewer Plautine comedies
were produced on the stage in the revival period than was formerly
believed, and most of the passages that were assigned to *retractatio* are
undoubtedly the work of Plautus himself.

## The Decline of the *Palliata*

About the time of Terence's death and the revival of Plautus' plays
there developed a more purely native comedy, the *fabula togata*, or
comedy in Roman dress, which dealt with lower-class life in Rome or in
nearby country towns. This type of comedy, stressing as it did the everyday life of humble folk, was also called *tabernaria*, from *tabernae*, the
homes of poor people.[69] We have already seen that Naevius invented
a type of Roman historical drama, the *fabula praetexta*, and apparently
composed comedies with Italian settings which at least foreshadowed
the later *togata*. Both the native tragedy and comedy received a stamp
of approval from Horace (*Epist.* ii, 3, 286-288):

Our poets deserve great praise for daring to forsake the footsteps of the
Greeks and to celebrate national deeds, both those who produced *praetextae*
and those who produced *togatae*.

The *palliata* is often regarded as becoming too Greek for popular
taste in the time of Terence and his contemporaries, most of whom (e.g.,
Atilius and Trabea) are little more than names. Turpilius, the last
writer of comedies in Greek dress, died in 103 B.C.; that the *palliata*
was increasingly more Greek in tone in the latter part of the second
century is implied by the frequency of Greek titles and by the fact that
the fragments of Turpilius sound like close translations from the Greek.
The theory that the Roman spectators wearied of the *palliata* as it became more thoroughly Hellenized has been used to explain not only the
popularity of Plautine revivals, but also the rise to favor of the *togata*
and the later decay of the *palliata*.

But the *palliata* was still popular in the time of Cicero, when comedies
of Plautus, Terence, and Turpilius were performed on the stage. The

---

[69] Cf. Horace, *Odes* i, 4, 13: *pauperum tabernas; Epist.* ii, 3, 229: *migret in
obscuras humili sermone tabernas.* The term "tavern-play" is misleading.

three chief writers of the *togata* were Titinius, L. Afranius, and Quinctius Atta. Titinius, usually considered the founder of the *togata* and the earliest poet to specialize in this form of comedy, lived in the time of Terence, or earlier; Afranius seems to have been active in the latter part of the second century, while Atta, the latest of the three playwrights, died in 77 B.C. There is no real evidence that the *togata* was invented to satisfy the demands of spectators who had tired of the *palliata*, and Beare seems correct in attributing the rise of the *togata* to differentiation rather than to reaction.[70] .The earlier *palliata*, that of Naevius and Plautus, had contained both Greek and Roman elements; as the later *palliata* became more Greek, the Roman element was developed by the writers of the *togata*. Comedies from the Greek and comedies with Roman settings flourished side by side in the second half of the second century B.C.

The *togata* differed from the *palliata* not merely in setting and costume; women played a far larger part and the plays portrayed more normal family relationships than was possible in the adaptations from Greek comedies where only wives or courtesans or slave-girls (later discovered to be free-born) could appear. There are frequent references in the fragments to love affairs between young people of respectable families. Donatus (*ad. Eun.* 57) is authority for the statement that in the *togata* slaves were not allowed to appear cleverer than their masters. Trickery and deceit, such as the Romans permitted in the case of slaves in Greek plays, were frowned upon when the slaves were Roman. Slaves were present in the *togata* but apparently played a relatively minor role. This is perhaps to be explained also by the fact that the characters were mostly poor people—tradesmen, country folk, and the like. But characters such as the slavedealer and the parasite, so frequent in the *palliata*, are mentioned in the fragments of the *togata*.[71]

About sixty titles of the *togata* and more than six hundred lines of fragments have survived, but it is impossible to reconstruct the plot of a single play; trickery, love affairs, betrothal and marriage doubtless furnished the material for many plots. Paederasty, which does not appear in either New Comedy or the *palliata* as a dramatic theme, is found in Afranius, and Quintilian (x, 1, 100) expresses the wish that Afranius had not stained his plots *puerorum foedis amoribus*. But Afranius, the most productive of the writers of the *togata*, approximated the *palliata* in his language and his poetic style, and sought to give artistic polish to his plays. In a fragment from the prologue of the *Compitalia*, a passage in which he is defending himself against criticism in Terentian fashion, Afranius expressed his indebtedness to Menander, to whom he evidently felt himself more closely related than to Naevius

[70] *Ha* 55 (1940), pp. 38 f.; cf. *The Roman Stage*, p. 121.
[71] Cf. Titinius, 45; Afranius, 367; Atta, 24.

and Plautus.[72] There is, however, no reason for doubting the strongly Italian flavor of the *togata*.

By the end of the second century B.C. the great creative period of Roman drama was at an end. Atellan farces flourished at the hands of Pomponius and Novius in the age of Sulla and by the end of the Republic the mime was in the ascendancy, having been brought to a high degree of artistry by Laberius and Publilius Syrus. But the popularity of the *Atellana* and the mime does not mean that the demand for the regular comedy and tragedy had disappeared. In the case of tragedy, the decline has been attributed to a lack of interest on the part of the audience or to a lack of vitality in the tragedies themselves; it has been suggested also that the available myths had all been utilized and the dramatists had exhausted their material.[73] In the case of comedy likewise, it might be argued that the writers of the *palliata* and the *togata* had presented almost all the available plots and characters. Even in the middle of the previous century Terence in his prologue to the *Eunuchus* (41) had lamented that "nothing is said that has not been said earlier." Given the social conventions of the period, more realistic plots were not possible, and the audiences gradually turned to forms of drama which, although cruder, were at the same time more sensational.[74]

In the age of Cicero, however, the older tragedy and comedy remained extremely popular, and to this period belong two of Rome's greatest actors. Aesopus, called *summus artifex* by Cicero (*Pro Sest.* 56, 120), specialized in tragic drama, appearing in tragedies of Ennius and Pacuvius, while Roscius, "one of the most famous actors of all time,"[75] played the part of Ballio (the slavedealer in Plautus' *Pseudolus*), acted in comedies of Turpilius, and also appeared in tragedies (e.g., Ennius' *Telephus*) since, as Cicero says (*Orator* 31, 109), actors in this period did not confine themselves to one department of drama. Aesopus and Roscius both acquired fortunes from their acting.

There are references also to actors of tragedy and comedy in the early Empire.[76] The *Incendium* of Afranius was presented at a festival given by the emperor Nero; the chief actor, Demetrius, was skilled in portraying gods, young men, good fathers and slaves, and wives; his contemporary Stratocles was famed for his portrayal of parasites, procurers, and cunning slaves, according to Quintilian (XI, 3, 178-180), who sounds as if he is referring to the *palliata* rather than to the *togata*. New tragedies were composed on occasion, e.g., Varius' *Thyestes* and Ovid's

---

[72] Cf. Horace, *Epist.* II, I, 57: *dicitur Afrani toga conuenisse Menandro.*

[73] Cf. Frank, *CJ* 12 (1916-17), pp. 176-187.

[74] See Beare, *The Roman Stage*, p. 109, who attributes the decline of the *palliata* also to "a change in the social status of dramatic composers." His explanation of the decline of tragedy (*ibid.*, pp. 118 f.) is similar.

[75] Henry, *SPhNC* 16 (1919), p. 343. Cf. also Wright, *Cicero and the Theater*, pp. 16 ff.

[76] Cf. Henry, *SPhNC* 16 (1919), pp. 370-373.

*Medea* in the Augustan age, but the only great name in tragedy after Accius is L. Annaeus Seneca.

Ten tragedies have come down under Seneca's name. One of these, the *Octavia*, a tragedy about Nero and his youthful wife, is probably not by Seneca, but is of interest in that it is the one surviving example of the *fabula praetexta*. The other nine tragedies deal with Greek characters and legends which, with one exception (*Thyestes*), are found in extant tragedies of Aeschylus, Sophocles, and Euripides. Seneca took many liberties with the Greek originals, suppressed characters and scenes, and added others. Since one of his chief interests was human psychology, his most successful plays were those modeled upon Euripides (e.g., *The Trojan Women, Mad Hercules, Medea, Phaedra*). There is no evidence that Seneca's tragedies were presented on the stage, and many critics maintain that they were composed solely for recitation; but the plays conform to the technical requirements of stage production and it seems likely that they were at least written with an eye to presentation.[77] The philosophical moralizing, the rhetorical elements, the ghost scenes and scenes of horror, often cited as undramatic features, could hardly have failed to appeal to spectators of the age of Nero. This is not the occasion to describe either the nature or the influence of Senecan tragedy, but it seems rather ironical that the doubtless superior tragedies of Ennius, Pacuvius, and Accius were lost and that the Italian, French, and English dramatists of the Renaissance and after found in Seneca the very qualities they desired and could use to create a drama greater than their model. It is very possible that Seneca's plays appealed far more to the Renaissance playwrights than the less sensational and less rhetorical tragedy of the early republic would have done, had it survived to modern times.[78]

In the field of comedy, the *fabula Atellana* and the mime, both of which had developed into a more literary form by the end of the Republic, continued in popularity during the earlier Empire. There are references to Atellan farces in the age of Hadrian but in the later Empire the mime reigned supreme. As Miss Bieber states, "it enjoyed the greatest popularity of all, because of its lack of masks, its sketching of ordinary life, and its frequent use of current themes and political sat-

---

[77] Cf. L. Herrmann, *Le Théâtre de Sénèque* (Paris, 1924), pp. 153-232. Miss Bieber (*The History of the Greek and Roman Theater*, p. 397) believes that the tragedies were produced on the stage. For typical expressions of the opposite view, that the plays were intended only for recitation, cf. Mendell, *Our Seneca*, p. 88; Beare, *The Roman Stage*, pp. 226 f.

[78] On the influence of Seneca upon later tragedy, see J. W. Cunliffe, *The Influence of Seneca on Elizabethan Tragedy* (London, 1893); L. E. Kastner and H. B. Charlton, *The Poetical Works of Sir William Alexander, Earl of Stirling*, 1 (Edinburgh, 1921), pp. xvii-clxxxvi; F. L. Lucas, *Seneca and Elizabethan Tragedy* (Cambridge, 1922); T. S. Eliot, *Selected Essays 1917-1932* (New York, 1932), pp. 51-88, 107-120; Mendell, *Our Seneca*, pp. 189-200; Duckworth, *The Complete Roman Drama*, 1, pp. xli-xlvi.

ire."[79] Another type of dramatic performance, dating from the age of Augustus and remaining popular throughout the Empire, was the pantomime—acting and dancing in dumb show. The pantomime actor sang and danced individual roles, changing masks and costume as he portrayed different characters. The themes were usually chosen from mythology and history. Both the mime and the pantomime gradually degenerated and were bitterly attacked by the Christian writers.

Although the *palliata* was no longer written and seldom produced on the stage, the comedies of Plautus and Terence were read and studied; numerous editions and commentaries on the plays were composed. In the fourth century A.D. originated the Ambrosian Palimpsest of Plautus, the Codex Bembinus of Terence, and Donatus' commentary on the plays of Terence. To the following century belongs the archetype of the famous illustrated manuscripts of Terence. Thus the comedies of Plautus and Terence lived on into the Middle Ages.[80]

It is worth mentioning that, in addition to the twenty-six comedies of Plautus and Terence which have survived to modern times, there is also a twenty-seventh comedy extant, *Querolus* or *The Pot of Gold*, probably composed in the early fifth century A.D., perhaps for production at a private banquet. This play, indebted to Plautus but by no means an adaptation from his *Aulularia*, is a curious mixture of classical and medieval elements; it has scenes of dialogue that are witty and amusing, while others are long discourses on religious and philosophical themes.[81] The comedy is wholly characteristic of the age in which it was written and brings to a conclusion the history of Greek and Roman comedy in antiquity.

[79] *The History of the Greek and Roman Theater*, p. 420. In the time of Cicero verses from the regular tragedy and comedy had been applied to contemporary politics; cf. Abbott, *TAPhA* 38 (1907), pp. 49 ff.

[80] For a brief account of the manuscripts of Plautus and Terence, see Appendix.

[81] The *Querolus* is translated into English by Duckworth, *The Complete Roman Drama*, II, pp. 896-949. On the plot of the *Querolus*, see Lockwood, *TAPhA* 44 (1913), pp. 215 ff.

# CHAPTER 4

## PRESENTATION AND STAGING

MODERN forms of entertainment such as the motion picture, the radio, and television prove that scientific advancement and creative genius do not necessarily go hand in hand and that more efficient techniques of production serve often to provide audiences with mediocre forms of drama. So in ancient Rome the development of engineering and architectural skills made possible the construction of spacious theaters with ornately decorated stage-buildings, but such luxurious theaters were not erected until long after the creative period of Roman drama had passed.[1] Not until a century after Terence's death, and a generation after the death of Accius, was the first permanent theater of stone erected at Rome, in a period when serious drama was represented largely by revivals of the masterpieces of a previous age. In the Empire, as the theaters and the stage-buildings became even more elaborate, tragedy and comedy were pushed into the background by the mime and the pantomime; greater splendor was accompanied by triviality of content. In the earlier period, when the best Roman plays were being written, the productions were given in much simpler and far less ornate surroundings.

### From Poet to Producer

The production of Roman comedies in the second century B.C. was in the hands of a *dominus gregis*, the manager of a *grex*, or company of actors. This producer himself was usually the chief actor of the troupe. Although Livy (VII, 2) refers to Livius Andronicus as both playwright and actor, there is no evidence that Plautus, Caecilius Statius, or Terence ever performed in their own comedies. The *actor* and *dominus gregis* of Terence's comedies was the aged L. Ambivius Turpio, who had also acted in Caecilius' comedies (*Hec.* 14 f.), and the chief actor of Plautus' *Stichus* and *Epidicus* was T. Publilius Pellio, upon whose ability Chrysalus in the *Bacchides* (214 f.) makes the following unfavorable comment:

> Though I love the *Epidicus* like my own self, there's no play I so hate to see, if Pellio acts it.[2]

[1] Cf., e.g., the reconstructions of the theaters at Ostia (Augustan Age) and at Aspendos (age of Marcus Aurelius) in Bieber, *The History of the Greek and Roman Theater*, p. 358, fig. 463; p. 378, fig. 497.

[2] Did Plautus insert this passage into the *Bacchides* because of a quarrel with Pellio? I see no justification for Buck's assumption (*A Chronology of the Plays of Plautus*, p. 4, n. 11; p. 32, n. 9; p. 66, n. 1) that Plautus played the part of Chrysalus and that the lines were an interpolation which found their way into the written text.

But in spite of this seemingly adverse criticism, Pellio was later listed (Symmachus, x, 2) among Rome's great actors, along with Turpio, Roscius, and Aesopus.

The comedies were usually produced at public games, and the officials (aediles or praetors) in charge of the games doubtless supplemented the senatorial appropriation by liberal contributions of their own; there was no other source of income to pay for the games, since admission was free. From the money thus available all the expenses of the theatrical performances (*ludi scaenici*) had to be paid; these included money for playwright, actors, costumes, and other production costs.

The procedure seems to have been as follows: the officials in charge of the games made a contract with the *dominus gregis*, who either himself bought the play from the poet or recommended its purchase by the officials,[3] hired the actors, and made all necessary arrangements for the rehearsals and the production. It was his task also to arrange with a musician for the musical accompaniment,[4] and to procure costumes, masks (if worn at this time), and stage properties (*ornamenta*). The costumes and other equipment were later assigned to the actors by the *choragus*, or property manager (cf. *Curc.* 464 f., *Pers.* 159 f., *Trin.* 857 ff.), who perhaps also supervised the staging of the plays (cf. Don. *ad Eun.* 967).

The dramatist had no control over the play after it left his hands, and received nothing but the original purchase price, even though the play might be produced more than once. Terence's *Hecyra* was apparently an exception; it did not receive a hearing at its first presentation in 165 B.C. and therefore could be sold again and produced as a substitute for a new play (*Hec.* 5-7). After the performance of a play the text remained in the possession of the *dominus gregis*. If a play had an unfavorable reception, the playwright suffered no direct financial loss,[5] although his chances of having other comedies accepted for production might be lessened. The *dominus gregis* ran all the risk, since the amount of money he received from the aediles depended on the success of the production (Don. *ad Hec.* 57).

The prologues of Plautus' plays frequently contain an appeal to the

---

[3] Cf. *Hec.* 57: *pretio emptas meo*; but see *Eun.* 20: *postquam aediles emerunt* and Don. *ad Hec.* 57; possibly Terence's close relationship with the nobility made it possible for him on occasion to deal directly with the curule aediles; cf. Dziatzko-Hauler, *Phormio*, p. 39, n. 2.

[4] Michaut (*Sur les tréteaux latins*, p. 364) suggests also the possibility that the musician was no other than the flute-player in the troupe.

[5] This perhaps is the significance of Horace, *Epist.* II, I, 175 f.: "For he (Plautus) is eager to drop a coin in his purse, and afterwards he doesn't care whether the play fails or succeeds." It can hardly mean (as Wickham, *ad loc.* implies) that Plautus is in such a hurry "that he does not stay to finish his work." But if his object was, as all agree, to provide the greatest amusement for the spectators, he could hardly have been indifferent to the success of his plays.

audience for favor (*captatio benevolentiae*). Of such a nature are the words of Mercury in *Amph.* 13 ff.:

If you wish me to approve your undertakings and strive that you always have everlasting profit, listen in silence to this company and be fair and impartial judges.

The Prologus of the *Menaechmi* (3 f.) speaks in somewhat lighter vein:

I bring you Plautus—by word, not by hand; I beg you to welcome him with kindly ears.

The Prologus of the *Asinaria* mentions the troupe of actors, the manager, and the officials (1-3):

Pay attention, if you please, spectators, and may good fortune attend me and you, this company, the managers,[6] and the contractors.

The plea of the Prologus in Terence's *Andria* (24): "Show favor and listen with impartial mind" appears in various forms in the other Terentian prologues,[7] and it is obvious that both Plautus and Terence were eager to have their plays approved by the theater-going public. Although the part of the Prologus was usually assigned to one of the younger actors (*Heaut.* 2), in two plays, at least, the *Heauton* and *Hecyra* II, Ambivius Turpio, the *dominus gregis* and now an old man, spoke the prologues to give added weight to Terence's plea for a just hearing.

The statement is made by most historians that the *dominus gregis* was a freedman who owned most of the actors. That the actors were slaves liable to punishment for poor performances has been inferred from *Cist.* 785:

He who has made a mistake will be beaten; he who hasn't will receive a drink.

It seems unwise to stress a jesting passage unduly, and modern scholars point out that the honors accorded to members of the *collegium poetarum*, composed of actors as well as playwrights, indicate that they did not lack civil rights.[8] The available number of good actors in the early second century was apparently limited; this implies not only that the profession was still comparatively young and offered little in the way of financial inducements but also that there were probably few slave actors to draw upon. It has been suggested that the small number of days each year devoted to the production of plays at Rome would hardly have made it worth while to train slaves for such an occupation but, as we

[6] The plural *dominis* (*Asin.* 3) has been changed to *domino* by some editors but it is not impossible that troupes were occasionally headed by two *domini gregis*. The didascalic notices of Terence's plays (*Andria, Eunuchus, Phormio, Adelphoe*) list both Ambivius Turpio and Hatilius Praenestinus although the latter has been suggested as belonging to a later performance.

[7] Cf. *Heaut.* 28, 41, *Eun.* 44, *Phorm.* 30, *Hec.* 28, 55.

[8] E.g., Kurrelmeyer, *The Economy of Actors in Plautus*, p. 8; see also Beare, *The Roman Stage*, pp. 158 f.

shall see, there were frequent repetitions (*instaurationes*) of the games, and it is also very possible that the managers, to augment their earnings, took their companies out on the road.[9] If the statements of Livy (VII, 2) and Valerius Maximus (II, 4) that professional actors were barred from military service is accepted for the early period of drama,[10] this fact also indicates that some of the actors, at least, were not slaves. It is probable that at this time they were mostly aliens or freedmen.

The size of the troupes is not known; they may have been limited in number, perhaps to five or six actors, depending upon the needs of the individual play. There are indications in the comedies themselves that two or more parts may often have been assigned to the same actor. Female roles were acted by men. Perhaps the later attacks on the mime and the pantomime for their immorality were partly due to the fact that women took part in them. But Donatus implies (*ad And.* 716) that in his day female roles were taken by women even in the *palliata*.

## Roman Festivals

The regular Roman festivals at which the *palliatae* were produced in the time of Plautus and Terence were at least four in number:

(1) The *ludi Romani* in honor of *Iuppiter Optimus Maximus* were given in September under the direction of the curule aediles. These games originally consisted of *ludi circenses* but *ludi scaenici* were introduced in 364 B.C. At the *ludi Romani* in 240 B.C. the first regular tragedy and comedy, translated from the Greek by Livius Andronicus, were presented. By 214 B.C. four days were devoted to dramatic performances at this festival (Livy, XXIV, 43). Terence's *Phormio* and *Hecyra* (third presentation) were later performed at the *ludi Romani*.

(2) The *ludi plebeii* were given in November under the plebeian aediles, also in honor of Jupiter. These were instituted not later than 220 B.C., and perhaps earlier. It was at the plebeian games that Plautus' *Stichus* was performed in 200 B.C. At least three days were set aside for dramatic performances at this festival in the second century.

(3) The *ludi Apollinares*, given in July under the direction of the city praetor, were first celebrated in 212 B.C. The institution of this and other festivals after the beginning of the second Punic war has been explained as the result of the popularity of Roman drama and a growing demand for more *ludi scaenici*.[11] At the *ludi Apollinares* there were at least two days of dramatic performances. The fact that in 179 B.C. a contract was let for a theater near the temple of Apollo (Livy, XL, 51) shows that drama played an important part at the festival.

---

[9] Cf. Taylor, *TAPhA* 68 (1937), pp. 303 f., who says that such an assumption explains "the rapid development of professional acting which took place in the period of Plautus' dramatic activity."

[10] See above, p. 7.        [11] Cf. Taylor, *TAPhA* 68 (1937), pp. 288 f.

(4) The *ludi Megalenses* in honor of the Great Mother (*Magna Mater*) were first celebrated in April, 204 B.C. and became a regular annual festival under the curule aediles in 194 B.C. In April, 191 B.C., when the temple of *Magna Mater* was dedicated, special games were held, and we learn from the didascalic notice of the *Pseudolus*, presented on that occasion, that these games were under the direction of the urban praetor. At the end of the play, Pseudolus says (1334):

If you wish to applaud and approve this troupe of ours (*hunc gregem*), I'll invite you to a play tomorrow also.

This passage indicates that the dramatic performances lasted more than one day, and it is possible that from 191 B.C. on six days were given over to drama, as was the case in the age of Augustus. Four of Terence's plays, the *Andria, Hecyra* (first presentation), *Heauton,* and *Eunuchus,* were presented at this festival.

There is no evidence that in the second century dramas were a part of the *ludi Cereales,* which had been fully established by 202 B.C., but in the Augustan age seven days were allotted to dramatic performances at the *Cereales,* and Miss Taylor believes that at least two days were devoted to *ludi scaenici* in the earlier period.[12] The *ludi Florales* became a regular festival in 173 B.C. but the dramatic performances at these games were chiefly mimes.

The number of days each year devoted to drama at the regular festivals by 200 B.C. may thus be estimated at about eleven, after 191 B.C. perhaps as many as seventeen. By the time of Augustus the number had increased to forty-three, but how much of this growth took place in the second century cannot be determined. In addition to the regular festivals, there were special games to celebrate triumphs, dedications, and funerals, and dramatic performances might be given at these. Both Terence's *Adelphoe* and his *Hecyra* (second failure) were presented in 160 B.C. at the funeral games in honor of L. Aemilius Paulus. Also special votive games to Jupiter (usually called *ludi magni*) were celebrated from time to time, and these festivals too may have been partly theatrical.

It is impossible, therefore, to estimate the number of days in a given year that might be allotted to dramatic productions. The problem is complicated still further by the practice of *instauratio,* or repetition of a festival. Livy enumerates many instances of *instauratio* at the *ludi Romani* and *ludi plebeii* during the years 216 to 179 B.C.,[13] and it is amazing how regularly the games were repeated; in the fifteen years between 214 and 200 B.C., for instance, the Roman games were *in-*

---

[12] *TAPhA* 68 (1937), pp. 286, 291. Miss Taylor points out (p. 286, n. 3) that "the only evidence for *ludi scaenici* at the Plebeii before the empire is provided by the chance preservation of the *Didascalia* of the *Stichus.*"

[13] Cf. Taylor, *TAPhA* 68 (1937), p. 292; Buck, *A Chronology of the Plays of Plautus,* pp. 13 ff.

*staurati* in eleven years, the plebeian games in nine. What is the explanation of this?

*Instauratio*, the repetition of a festival because of some impropriety in its observance, was primarily a religious matter. But it is extremely difficult to account for almost yearly repetitions as the result of accidental improprieties in the observance of the rites. Moreover, the games in some years were repeated not once but three or four times and, in two cases for the *ludi plebeii*, seven times; these occurred in 205 and 197 B.C. It seems very probable that the large number of *instaurationes* during the latter years of the second Punic war is related to the success of the dramatic productions in this period; the popularity of Plautus' plays may have been a chief factor, and the audience or the performers could always create an interruption or a disturbance which would necessitate the repetition of the festival.[14] Buck makes the attractive suggestion[15] that the popularity of the *Miles Gloriosus*, usually dated about 205 B.C., accounts for the fact that in that year the plebeian games were given eight times in all.

*Instauratio* materially increased the total number of days which were allotted to theatrical performances, and perhaps on an average there were six or seven extra days each year. The regular festivals and their repetitions would thus provide a minimum of perhaps twenty to twenty-five days, to which special festivals might add a few more on occasion. Actually, as Miss Taylor points out,[16] Plautus, even at the beginning of his career, had more opportunities to present his plays than did the great dramatists of fifth-century Athens, but the honors paid to the playwrights and actors at Athens compensated for the infrequent performances. There may have been contests for actors in the time of Plautus; references to the awarding of the *palma* to a successful actor occur (*Amph.* 69, *Poen.* 37, *Trin.* 706; cf. *Phorm.* 16 f.), but the chief incentive for the actor was undoubtedly financial, even though the inducement was not large.

Where the performances of the plays took place is not definitely known. The *ludi Romani* were presented in the Circus Maximus, the *ludi plebeii* in the Circus Flaminius, but it does not necessarily follow that the theatrical performances were also given in the Circus. The words of Milphidippa in *Mil.* 991:

Now the circus is in front of the house, where my tricks (*ludi*) must be performed,

[14] Cicero says (*De Har. Resp.* 11, 23): "If the dancer has stopped, or the flute-player suddenly become silent, . . . the games have not been correctly performed"; cf. Green, *CW* 26 (1933), pp. 156 f.

[15] *A Chronology of the Plays of Plautus*, p. 16. Did a play of Plautus also account for the seven *instaurationes* at the *ludi plebeii* in 197 B.C.? Perhaps so, in which case Buck is unwise in refusing to date any Plautine plays between 200 and 194 B.C.

[16] *TAPhA* 68 (1937), p. 302.

are usually adduced as evidence, but such an announcement proves nothing about the site of the stage. It is equally possible, as Miss Saunders suggests,[17] that the early plays were given near the Capitoline temple of Jupiter, i.e., in the forum. The *ludi Apollinares* were celebrated in the Circus Maximus, but the theater begun in 179 B.C. was located by the temple of Apollo near the Circus Flaminius, which implies that the scenic part of the festival was given there for a time, at least. Performances at the *ludi Megalenses* were held in the open space in front of the temple of the goddess on the Palatine hill. Plays given in connection with funeral games were evidently presented in the forum. The sites of the dramatic performances thus varied for different festivals and also for different periods.

## The Theater and the Stage

Public spectacles such as circus games and gladiatorial shows went back to the very beginnings of Roman history, and were doubtless first introduced by the Etruscans or under Etruscan influence. Livy (I, 35) speaks of stands erected for the senators and equites at the circus (later called Maximus) in the reign of Tarquinius Priscus; there were special areas where they were to provide seats for themselves (*ubi spectacula sibi quisque facerent*), and Livy describes the seats as resting on forked poles twelve feet high and the show (*ludicrum*) as consisting of horses and boxers brought from Etruria.

In the earliest days of the Roman theater, temporary stages were constructed of wood for each performance. The spectators at first probably stood or sat on the hillside or brought stools; later, wooden stands were provided. In the year 195 B.C., according to Livy (XXXIV, 44), special seats were assigned to the senators at the Roman games (*ludi Romani*) that they might be separated from the *populus*. Soon after, in 179 B.C., there was an attempt to construct a permanent theater-building of stone near the temple of Apollo, evidently for the *ludi Apollinares*; Livy (XL, 51) calls it a *theatrum et proscaenium*, i.e., an auditorium with seats (*cavea*) and a stage (*scaena*);[18] we have no additional information concerning the structure but it was apparently not completed. There is a reference (Livy, XLI, 27) to a stage building constructed under the censors of 174 B.C. for the use of the aediles and the praetors at the various *ludi*. Again our information is tantalizingly scanty and we

[17] *TAPhA* 44 (1913), p. 90.
[18] Bauer (*Quaestiones scaenicae Plautinae*, pp. 36 ff.) shows that *theatrum* regularly signifies *cavea* and *proscaenium* refers to the stage (cf. *Amph.* 91, *Truc.* 10); *Poen.* 17 f. (*scortum exoletum ne quis in proscaenio sedeat*) might seem to imply that *proscaenium* here refers to seats in the *cavea*, but the passage probably means that "prostitutes are cautioned not to seat themselves on the stage itself" (Beare, *The Roman Stage*, p. 166).

know nothing of the fate of the building. Miss Bieber assumes[19] that the foundations of these buildings had been demolished.

Twenty years later, in 154 B.C., the censors Cassius Longinus and Valerius Messala began the erection of a stone theater; Livy (Epit. XLVIII) and Valerius Maximus (II, 4, 2) inform us that the consul P. Scipio Nasica stopped its construction and had the material sold, and the senate passed a decree that seats should not be used at theatrical productions as harmful to public morals. For a few years, therefore, the Roman populace viewed plays standing until in 145 B.C. L. Mummius is said to have erected a wooden theater with seats for the plays presented in connection with his triumphs.[20] The first permanent stone theater at Rome was that built by Pompey in 55 B.C.

Throughout the second century there was thus a constantly growing demand for larger and more permanent theaters, and along with this demand there seems to have existed an undisguised hostility to theatrical shows and to structures which might encourage such shows. The reaction of 154 B.C. came at a time when the great writers of comedy were dead but some, at least, of the plays of Plautus were being revived, and in tragedy Pacuvius was at the peak of his career. If the hostility of the senate to the theater was one aspect of a general opposition to the influx of Greek culture, it is somewhat surprising that the *senatusconsultum* was passed at the very time when the more Roman comedies of Plautus were appearing once again on the stage and the more native *togata* was being developed by Titinius.

The decree of 154 B.C. implies that there had been seats in the Roman theater prior to that date. Ritschl, however, interpreted the passage differently; he believed that the auditorium with rows of seats had not existed earlier, and that in the age of Plautus and Terence the spectators had either stood or brought their own stools. This theory created difficulties, for there are references in the text of Plautus to the *cavea*, to seats (*subsellia*), and to seated spectators:

. . . that detectives go from seat to seat (*singula in subsellia*) among the spectators throughout the entire *cavea*. (*Amph.* 65 f.)

That fellow in the rear says he doesn't understand the plot, by Jove. Come up front. If you don't find room to sit down, you can find room to walk. (*Capt.* 11 f.)

Let no worn-out harlot sit on the stage itself (*in praescaenio*) and . . . let no usher roam about in front of the people or show anyone to a seat while the actor is on the stage. . . . Keep slaves from occupying the seats, so there will be room for free men. (*Poen.* 17 ff.)

These references are all found in prologues, and Ritschl solved the problem by assuming that the prologues of the *Amphitruo, Captivi,* and

---

[19] *The History of the Greek and Roman Theater,* p. 327.

[20] That Mummius actually constructed a theater for his spectacle has been doubted; cf. Knapp, *AJPh* 35 (1914), p. 25, n. 1. The statement of Tacitus (*Ann.* XIV, 21) is unfortunately vague.

Plate I. Typical slaves with scarves
*Phorm.* 51-152 (ms C: folio 78)

Plate II. *Aedicula* with masks
*Hecyra* (MS C: folio 65)

*Poenulus*, among others,[21] were post-Plautine and written in the revival era, i.e., after 145 B.C., when Mummius had erected a theater with fixed seats.

But there are other references in the comedies to seats. Occasionally a play closes with the exhortation:

> Give your applause and farewell; stretch your legs and rise,
> (*Epid.* 733; cf. *Truc.* 968)

and the two-line prologue of the *Pseudolus* says:

> You'd better get up and stretch your legs; a long play by Plautus is coming on the stage.

Similarly, seats are mentioned in the body of the plays:

> Make it brief; the audience (*qui sedent*, "those who are seated") is getting thirsty. (*Poen.* 1224)

> What's the matter? Why do you laugh? I know all of you, I know there are thieves here, plenty of them, who disguise themselves and sit still like honest men. (*Aul.* 718 f.)

> If he doesn't wish to listen, let him rise and leave, so that there will be a seat for one who does wish to listen. (*Mil.* 81 f.)

A passage such as the last can hardly refer to a standing audience or even to spectators who brought their own stools. Again, when Acanthio in *Merc.* 160 asks

> Are you afraid you'll awaken the sleeping spectators?

we can hardly assume that Plautus thought of the audience as standing. Actually, there is nothing either in the early history of the theater or in the plays of Plautus that would make the use of wooden seats in the theater impossible from the early second or even the late third century, and scholars today are almost unanimous in rejecting Ritschl's theory.[22] We can safely assume that the spectators of Plautus' plays had seats, and that the prologues formerly considered non-Plautine derive almost entirely from Plautus' own hand.

The prologues of Terence, as we have already seen, give us an interesting insight into the nature of the audience which viewed Roman comedy in the second century B.C. The playwright's constant plea for silence and a fair hearing implies that the spectators were a noisy and unruly lot, and if a play had less appeal than some nearby attraction,

---

[21] Ritschl considered that the prologues to the *Asinaria, Casina, Menaechmi, Pseudolus, Trinummus,* and *Truculentus* were also written for revivals after Plautus' death, because the name of the playwright (Plautus or Maccus) was mentioned; this theory is still accepted by Buck, *A Chronology of the Plays of Plautus,* p. 7. But *Cas.* 5-20 is the only passage of any size which definitely dates from a later period; cf. Hornstein, *WS* 36 (1914), pp. 120 f.

[22] Cf. Fabia, *RPh* 21 (1897), pp. 11-25; Bauer, *Quaestiones scaenicae Plautinae,* pp. 31-35; Beare, *CR* 53 (1939), pp. 51-55 (= *The Roman Stage,* pp. 233-239); cf. also *The Roman Stage,* pp. 163 f.

such as a boxing match or a gladiatorial combat, they might rush from the theater, as in fact happened in the case of the first two presentations of the *Hecyra*. A more amusing picture of the spectators of the time is given by the Prologus of Plautus' *Poenulus*. After the reference to harlots and slaves (quoted above), the speaker continues:

Nurses should keep tiny children at home and not bring them to see the play, lest the nurses themselves get thirsty and the children die of hunger or cry for food like young goats. Married women should view the play in silence, laugh in silence, and refrain from their constant chatter; they should take home their gossip, so as not to annoy their husbands both here and at home. (*Poen.* 28-35)

Dignified senators and unruly populace, harlots and slaves, crying infants and gossiping women—these made up the *spectatores* of Roman comedy, and among them were undoubtedly claqueurs to lead the applause. Mercury says that actors should win by merit and not by hired applause, and devotes a portion of the prologue of the *Amphitruo* (64-85) to the request that detectives (*conquistores*) seek out such individuals and prevent them from giving an unfair advantage to certain actors; he demands also the punishment of actors and aediles who have been guilty of unfair practices.

The actors performed on a long narrow stage which represented in most plays a city street; in the extant comedies the scene was usually laid in Athens, but we find in Plautus several exceptions: Thebes (*Amphitruo*), a city in Aetolia (*Captivi*), Sicyon (*Cistellaria*), Epidaurus (*Curculio*), Epidamnus (*Menaechmi*), Ephesus (*Miles*), Calydon (*Poenulus*), the seacoast near Cyrene (*Rudens*). The normal background consisted of boards painted to resemble the fronts of one, two, or three houses, with doors providing a means of entrance to the stage from the houses. It is generally believed that there were regularly three doors facing the stage and, if less than three houses were represented, two (or even three) doors might belong to one house. The doors were probably recessed to provide small vestibules; Varro (*De ling. Lat.* VII, 81), referring to *Pseud.* 955, speaks of a *uestibulum quod est ante domum*, and Tranio (*Most.* 817) asks his master if he sees the *uestibulum ante aedes*. The reference to cleaning cobwebs from the columns (*Asin.* 425; cf. *Stich.* 347-355) probably applies also to the vestibule (cf. Plautus, fr. inc. 27). Aulus Gellius (XVI, 5, 3) calls it the open space in front of the door and says that the door itself was set back at a distance from the street. Such a space would be convenient for eavesdropping (cf. *Aul.* 666, *Merc.* 477).

Actors entered the stage not only through the doors but also from either wing, and the length of the stage (believed to be as much as sixty yards) made the numerous soliloquies and asides, the instances of eavesdropping, and the failure to see other characters on the stage, far more natural than is possible on the modern stage which is usually smaller and often represents indoor scenes.

The number of dwellings on the stage varied according to the needs of the play.[23] The action of many comedies requires two houses, e.g., the homes of Menaechmus I and Erotium in the *Menaechmi*, of Simo and Theopropides in the *Mostellaria*, of Micio and Sostrata in the *Adelphoe*. The prologue-speaker or one of the characters often announces who lives in the house; cf. *Cas.* 35 f.:

An old man who is married lives here; he has a son who lives with his father in this house (*in illisce aedibus*).

Two plays need only one dwelling; the *Captivi* (that of Hegio) and the *Amphitruo* (that of Amphitryon) ; in the latter case the dwelling might be considered a palace since the play is a *tragicomoedia*, but Plautus refers to it as *aedes*, the word which he regularly uses for the homes of ordinary citizens: cf. 97 f.: *in illisce habitat aedibus Amphitruo*. Several plays require either three houses (e.g., *Pseudolus, Stichus, Phormio, Hecyra*, perhaps also *Trinummus* and *Truculentus*) or two houses and a shrine or temple; the stage-setting of the *Aulularia* has the houses of Euclio and Megadorus and a temple of Faith (*Fides*), while the scene of the *Curculio*, laid in Epidaurus, needs, in addition to the houses of Phaedromus and Cappadox, a shrine of Aesculapius. The setting of the *Rudens* is most unusual; it is not the normal city street but a stretch of seashore near Cyrene in North Africa, and in the background are the cottage (*uilla*) of Daemones and the temple of Venus, where dwells a priestess. Arcturus, the speaker of the prologue, announces the stage-setting:

Daemones dwells here in a villa on a farm near the sea (33 f.) . . . and here is the shrine (*fanum*) of Venus (61).

Much of the romantic charm which readers find in the *Rudens* comes from the fact that its setting is so different from that of the usual Roman comedy, and also that a storm at sea and a shipwreck are included in the action. Terence in the *Heauton* departs slightly from the normal setting by placing the two houses[24] on a country road outside Athens.

On the stage in front of one of the houses stood an altar (*ara*), usually the altar of Apollo, although altars to Diana (*Mil.* 411 f.), to Lucina (*Truc.* 476), and to Venus (*Curc.* 71 f.; *Rud.* 688 ff.) are also

[23] For a summary of the stage settings in Plautus and Terence, cf. Johnston, *Exits and Entrances in Roman Comedy*, pp. 20-33. Her analysis is at times faulty; e.g., in the *Curculio* the house of Cappadox, not that of Lyco, is represented on the stage; in the *Bacchides* there is no need to have a shrine of Apollo in the background; *Bacch.* 172 f. refers merely to an altar in front of the neighbor's house.

[24] There are three if, in addition to the houses of Chremes and Menedemus, that of Phania is on the stage; Chremes refers to Phania as "this neighbor of mine" (*hunc uicinum*, 170), the usual term for a person who lives *in aedibus scaenicis*; but Phania does not appear in the play and is not mentioned elsewhere.

mentioned. Returning travelers invoke the god, e.g., Chrysalus in *Bacch.* 172 f.:

> I greet you, neighbor Apollo, who dwell next door to us.

Euclio (*Aul.* 394) prays to Apollo for aid, and in *Merc.* 675 ff. Dorippa asks Syra for laurel to place on the altar and then prays to Apollo for the welfare of her son and the household. The altar mentioned in *And.* 726 is probably that of Apollo also (cf. Don. *ad loc.*). Some scholars have assumed that the altar on the stage was always Apollo's and that sacrifices to other divinities (e.g., to Diana in *Mil.* 411 f.) were made on this altar but it seems improbable that the altar of one god would be applied to the use of another. The older view (based on *De comoedia*, VIII, 3) that there were two altars on the stage, one to Liber, the other to the god in whose honor the *ludi* were being celebrated, is no longer accepted.[25]

In two comedies of Plautus the altar plays a prominent part. In the *Rudens* (664 ff.) Palaestra and Ampelisca flee from the temple of Venus to escape Labrax and (688 ff.) seek refuge at the altar; Labrax, though prevented by Daemones' slaves from approaching the girls, declares he will bring Vulcan, who is opposed to Venus (761), and threatens to make a big fire and burn the girls alive; Daemones replies (769 f.):

> By gad, I'll seize you by the beard and throw you into the fire, and when you're half-cooked I'll give you to the vultures to eat.

In the *Mostellaria* (1094 ff.) Tranio takes refuge on an altar to escape punishment at the hands of his angry master, who likewise threatens to heap firewood about the altar and set fire to it. Tranio, impudent as ever, retorts (1115):

> Don't do it, for I'm usually sweeter boiled than roasted.

Terence perhaps has such a passage in mind when in *Heaut.* 975 f. Chremes says to his slave:

> No one's accusing you, Syrus; you don't need an altar (for sanctuary) or an intercessor (to plead your case).

In the later Roman theater there was a curtain (*aulaeum*) which was lowered to reveal the stage at the beginning of the performance and raised at the close (cf. Cic., *Pro Cael.* 27, 65), but there is no evidence for the use of such a curtain in the theater in the days of Plautus and Terence. In the Empire, as theatrical performances increased in splendor, elaborately embroidered curtains were used, and they worked like modern curtains, being raised at the beginning of the performance and lowered at the end (*Amm. Marc.* XVI, 6, 3; XXVIII, 6, 29). Donatus says (*ad Eun. praef.* 1, 5):

---

[25] Cf. Saunders, *TAPhA* 42 (1911), pp. 91 ff.

Terence avoids pauses between the five acts lest . . . the spectator might grow weary and leave his seat before the curtain rose.

Beare sees here an allusion to the use of a drop curtain of the modern type between the acts;[26] but Donatus seems to imply, not that the spectator might leave before the curtain rose at the beginning of the next act, but rather that he might leave before the end of the play, when the curtain rose. At any rate, Donatus is wrongly ascribing the use of a curtain to the age of Terence; according to *De comoedia* (VIII, 8) embroidered *aulaea* were first introduced at Rome *ab Attalica regia*, i.e., in 133 B.C., and it is perhaps unwise to assume the use of a curtain before this date.

## Wing-Entrances and the *Angiportum*

If one wishes to visualize the staging of Roman comedy, he must understand clearly the ancient convention concerning the entrances and exits of the characters. The entrances from a house or temple fronting the stage create no difficulty, but the significance of the wing-entrances has been the subject of extensive controversy.[27] The ancient tradition as found in Vitruvius (v, 6, 8) is that one entrance leads from the forum (*a foro*), the other from foreign parts (*a peregre*), but Vitruvius does not specify which entrance is on the right and which is on the left. Pollux (*Onomasticon*, IV, 126) locates the city and harbor off the same side of the stage, opposite the entrance from the country (*rure*), but it is agreed that Pollux has in mind the theater of Dionysus at Athens, where to the spectator's right lie the Piraeus and the city, to his left the open country. One would normally assume that the Roman playwrights, as they adapted Greek comedies, would preserve the Greek convention concerning wing-entrances, but only one Roman comedy, the *Rudens*, locates city and harbor off the same side of the stage (cf. *Rud.* 856), and the *Rudens*, as we have seen, does not have a normal stage-setting.

An examination of the other twenty-five comedies reveals that forum and harbor entrances, when mentioned, are on opposite sides of the stage,[28] thus confirming the statement of Vitruvius. Furthermore, the entrance on the spectator's right leads from the forum, and that on his left from the harbor and foreign parts. For this, Plautus' *Menaechmi* is decisive. Menaechmus II, coming from abroad, always uses the entrance *a peregre*, his brother the entrance *a foro*; in 466 Menaechmus II enters from Erotium's house and says (555 f.), facing the audience:

I'll take off this wreath and throw it to my left, so if they follow me they'll think I've gone this way.

[26] *Ha* 58 (1941), p. 112 (= *The Roman Stage*, p. 264).
[27] For a summary of the earlier discussions, see Johnston, *Exits and Entrances in Roman Comedy*, pp. 1-12.
[28] Cf. Rambo, *CPh* 10 (1915), pp. 429 f., Johnston, *Exits and Entrances in Roman Comedy*, pp. 104 f.

He throws the wreath to his left (the spectator's right) and leaves the stage in the opposite direction to find Messenio at the harbor. Peniculus and the wife of Menaechmus I find the wreath and assume it was dropped by Menaechmus I, whom they see returning from the forum. Thus the harbor exit is on the spectator's left, the entrance from the forum on his right. Similarly, in *Amph.* 333 Mercury refers to a voice on his right, the voice of Sosia who has entered from the harbor. As Mercury is facing the audience, Sosia thus enters from the audience's left. The *Rudens* is perhaps less an exception to the general rule than at first appears; in the other comedies the forum is the center of local activity off-stage, while the events at the harbor are more remote; in the *Rudens*, the off-stage local activity takes place on the beach at the spectator's right, and the site of the more remote activity (in this case, both city and harbor) is on the left; in other words, when we make allowance for the abnormal stage-setting of the *Rudens*, we realize that the playwright is following usual Roman procedure as closely as possible.

Miss Johnston is unable to account for the change from the Greek to the Roman convention, for the shift of the harbor entrance from the spectator's right (Greek theater) to his left (Roman theater). It is possible that to the Romans the country and the harbor would seem most naturally located in one direction opposite the forum and the city. But the Romans would accept all statements by actors about trips to and from the harbor as part of the Greek element in the plays, since the harbor at Rome in the republic was Puteoli near Naples and involved a long journey overland. Beare suggests[29] that our conception of Greek procedure has been faulty; he points out that the exit to the country is used far less than either the harbor or the forum exit; to accept the Greek convention would mean that the originals of Plautus and Terence would be staged in a most awkward fashion, for the characters, instead of passing naturally across the stage from harbor to forum, would often enter and then, after a short speech, depart by the same side-entrance. He cites as an illustration the *Captivi*, where Ergasilus enters from the forum (461), delivers a monologue, and leaves for the harbor (497).[30] Since opposition of harbor and forum in the Greek plays would make possible a more reasonable use of both wing-entrances, Beare believes that the Greek convention was the same as the Roman; in other words,

---

[29] *CQ* 32 (1938), pp. 205-210 (= *The Roman Stage*, pp. 240-247).

[30] Beare's illustration is somewhat unfortunate, since Ergasilus is possibly an addition by Plautus and may not have existed in the Greek original; cf. Hough, *AJPh* 63 (1942), pp. 26-37. But Beare's point in general is sound; the Greek originals would use one wing very little if harbor and forum were placed at the same entrance. The Roman plays which need only one side-entrance have been considered extremely awkward to stage, since overcrowding of the one entrance results; cf. Kemble, *PAPhA* 61 (1930), p. xl. Such plays, however, are very few.

the Roman dramatists took over the use of side-entrances which they found in vogue in the Greek theaters of southern Italy.

Thus far I have purposely avoided all mention of the *angiportum*, defined in most books as an alleyway leading back between the houses fronting the stage. Miss Rambo had considered the *angiportum* a possible exit to the country; "*rus*, then, is reached, not by the exit *peregre*, but by one of the exits *ad forum*, either the right wing or the *angiportum*";[31] according to this view, the *angiportum* also served as a means of reaching the forum. Miss Johnston, though accepting the traditional definition of the *angiportum*, says: "No entrances are made through an *angiportum* at any time, so far as our material shows. In most passages where the *angiportum* is referred to at all it is mentioned in accounting for movements of the characters when they are unseen and off the stage."[32] Miss Johnston locates the exit to the country on the spectator's left, i.e., the forum and the city lie to the right, everything else—country, harbor, foreign ports—lies in the opposite direction.

The *angiportum* has always been considered of great assistance to the staging of the plays. A typical expression of the older view is this: "At right angles to the main street a lane, known as an *angiportum*, sometimes, if not always, ran back between the houses. By this *angiportum* access was had to the back or garden part of the houses, or to the country (the *rus* that figures so largely in the Roman comedies); by the *angiportum*, again, an actor might leave the stage and return to it by a roundabout route, as Davus does so cleverly in Terence, *And.* 732-746. The *angiportum*, finally, was a favorite place for eavesdroppers."[33] All this sounds so plausible and so attractive and yet, according to the most recent investigations,[34] can no longer be accepted. *Angiportum* does not mean "alley"; on the contrary, it means "street," sometimes the very thoroughfare in which the characters stand. Simia says (*Pseud.* 960 f.):

I've kept careful count; this is the sixth street (*angiportum*) from the gate, and he told me to turn in at this street.

Here there can be no doubt that *angiportum* refers to the street where the action takes place. In other instances it may be a street in the rear and parallel to the stage, from which a character can reach his house through a garden (*per hortum*; cf. *Asin.* 741 f., *Pers.* 678 f.); it may be described as lonely (*angiportum desertum*, *Eun.* 845) or as dead-end (*angiportum non peruium*, *Ad.* 578) but in all cases it refers to a street, and usually to a street off-stage. There is no evidence that it was ever an alley between two houses at right angles to the stage. The one pas-

---

[31] *CPh* 10 (1915), p. 431.     [32] *Exits and Entrances in Roman Comedy*, p. 37.
[33] Knapp, *A & A* 1 (1915), p. 196.
[34] Cf. Dalman, *De aedibus scaenicis comoediae novae*, pp. 66 ff.; Harsh, *CPh* 32 (1937), pp. 44 ff.; Beare, *Ha* 53 (1939), pp. 88 ff. (= *The Roman Stage*, pp. 248 ff.). Miss Haight, however, believes in the existence of narrow alleyways between the houses; cf. *The Symbolism of the House Door*, pp. 73, 77 f.

sage which looks as if it might support the traditional theory (*Phorm.* 891: "I'll withdraw into this nearest street") perhaps actually disproves it; Phormio steps into the right-hand wing-entrance and then appears as if coming from the forum; an entry from an alley in such a case would be highly suspicious.

Thus the *angiportum* is no longer available to serve as an exit to the country, as a means of reaching the rear of a house from the stage, as a convenient hangout for eavesdroppers. Occasionally, two houses might have a common wall, as in the *Miles* where a hole was dug through the wall to enable Philocomasium to visit her lover next door. In most plays a common wall is not required but we need not assume that the houses were separated and the intervening space used as a means of entrance or exit. The stage directions in editions and translations of Roman comedy are therefore often faulty and need careful revision. To the best of our knowledge, the only means of entrance and exit were the two wing-entrances and the doors of the houses opening on the stage.

## Costume and Mask

The costumes worn by the actors of the *palliata* were modeled upon those of New Comedy, the regular costumes of the ordinary Greek citizens and slaves portrayed in the plays. Our evidence for the nature of these costumes is in part literary (the plays of Plautus and Terence, the commentary of Donatus, and scattered references in Greek and Roman writers) and in part artistic (the illustrated manuscripts of Terence, Pompeian wall-paintings, Campanian reliefs, statuettes and terra-cottas). The late date of Donatus and the Terentian miniatures weakens the value of their testimony; the drawings in the manuscripts were made by artists who were copying from an archetype costumes they did not understand, and this accounts for some of the peculiarities and difficulties in their treatment of the dress of certain characters.[35] If the illustrations originated in the fifth century A.D., as the best evidence indicates, they can hardly depend on actual stage productions but they perhaps vaguely reflect earlier traditions about the costumes and masks of the *palliata*.[36]

The terms most frequently used in Plautus and Terence for clothing

[35] Cf. Saunders, *Costume in Roman Comedy*, pp. 13 ff. Miss Saunders' book is a convenient collection of the pertinent material. For the Terentian illustrations, see Weston, *HSCPh* 14 (1903), pp. 37 ff. and Plates 1-96; Jones and Morey, *The Miniatures of the Manuscripts of Terence*. For statuettes, etc., illustrating the costumes and masks of Greek and Roman comedy, see Bieber, *The History of the Greek and Roman Theater*, figs. 225-290, 408-416.

[36] Cf. Jones and Morey, *The Miniatures of the Manuscripts of Terence*, p. 204: "they are the product of literary rather than theatrical usage." Miss Bieber (*The History of the Greek and Roman Theater*, p. 400, n. 17) objects: "I cannot see, however, how a purely literary creation could give to all characters the right theatrical masks, garments and outfit." But the characters do not all have the correct garments.

are *uestis, uestitus*, and *uestimentum*. Although *uestimentum* usually signifies "garments" in general, the *palla* of the wife of Menaechmus I is called *uestimentum muliebre* (*Men.* 167, 659). There are numerous instances where a woman's jewelry and clothing (*aurum et uestis*) are mentioned together.[37] In the *Miles* (981, 1147, cf. 1127) Palaestrio keeps reminding the soldier that Philocomasium should be allowed to keep the *aurum atque ornamenta* which she has received; here, however, *ornamenta* may mean merely "outfit"—jewelry and trinkets as well as clothing—since later, in a similar passage (1302), Palaestrio mentions *aurum, ornamenta, uestis. Ornamenta*, though used of stage properties and of jewelry in particular (cf. *Most.* 248, 294) refers also (in Plautus) to clothing; the swindler in *Trin.* 857 f. says that the man who hired him to disguise himself "borrowed the costume (*ornamenta*) from the property man (*choragus*) at his own risk." *Ornamenta* and *ornatus* are both employed in the sense of "garb," "attire," but *ornamenta* regularly occurs when there is mention of the *choragus* and seems to be the more technical term for theatrical costume.

The nature of the *ornamenta* seems to have been as follows: the characters all wore an undergarment, *tunica* (Gr. *chiton*), over which was a mantle, the Greek *himation*, called *pallium* by the Romans; that worn by women characters was termed *palla*. Since the mantle of free persons was long, a shorter cloak (*chlamys*) was used by soldiers and sometimes by young men. All characters used the thin sandal or slipper (*soccus*), which was as distinctive a feature of comedy as was the *cothurnus*, or buskin, of tragedy. The plays mention frequently the use of *socci* or *soleae*; in *Epid.* 725, Periphanes promises to give his slave *soccos, tunicam, pallium*. When Philolaches' party is thrown into confusion by the imminent arrival of his father, Callidamates, who has taken off his slippers at the beginning of the banquet, is finally aroused from his drunken stupor (*Most.* 383 f.):

PH.: Wake up, won't you? My father will soon be here, I say.
CA.: What's that you say, your father? Give me my slippers (*soleas*), so that I can arm myself. Damn it, I'll kill that father of yours.

Wigs of different colors were used, white for old men, black for young, and red for slaves, but there seems no good authority for the statement that slaves always wore red wigs. Leonida (*Asin.* 400), Pseudolus (*Pseud.* 1218), and Phormio (*Phorm.* 51) are the only slaves described as red-haired in the extant plays.[38]

The term *senex* could be applied to a man from the age of forty upwards but often in comedy he is to be thought of as sixty or more. He is described as white-haired (*cano capite, albicapillus*), occasion-

---

[37] Cf. *Cist.* 487, *Curc.* 344, 435, 488, *Mil.* 1099, *Pseud.* 182, *Heaut.* 248, 252, 452, etc.
[38] Philocrates (*Capt.* 648), though a young man (*adulescens*), is described by his countryman as having somewhat reddish hair (*subrufus aliquantum*); perhaps this was necessary inasmuch as he had been disguised as a slave earlier in the play.

ally bearded (*barbatus*), toothless (*edentulus*), quivering (*tremulus*), feeble (*decrepitus*). He is often portrayed with a staff and sometimes with a purse. The undergarment, long-sleeved and reaching almost to the ankles, is a bluish-white in the colored miniatures of the Vatican manuscript, the *pallium* yellow or yellow-brown; from *De comoedia* (VIII, 6), however, we learn that the clothing of the *senes* was white. The artist has portrayed Menedemus in the *Heauton* with the usual garb of a *senex*, but Varro (*De re rust*. II, 11) says that men in comedies who engaged *in rustico opere*, like Menedemus, wore jackets made of goatskins. How one *senex* appeared on the stage may be visualized from *Merc*. 639 f., where Lysimachus is unsympathetically described as

Gray-haired, knock-kneed, pot-bellied, big-mouthed, stubby-shaped, black-eyed, slanting-jawed, splay-footed.

"That's no man you're describing," replies Charinus, "it's a treasure-house of atrocities."

The young man (*adulescens*) might have a *pallium* of rich material and bright colors (e.g., crimson); he is portrayed as wearing over the long-sleeved tunic either the *pallium* or a *chlamys*-like mantle. In *Merc*. 851 ff. Charinus, a young man, plans to go on an expedition to find his sweetheart and dons the *chlamys*; hearing his love is found (910 ff.), he calls for his *pallium* and takes off the *chlamys*; when told he can't see her, he comically reverses his garb a third time (921 ff.). The *chlamys* is regularly assigned to the soldier (*miles*) whose outfit is summed up in *Mil*. 1423:

Don't have any hopes about your tunic and your *chlamys* and your sword (*machaera*); you won't get them back.

The Terentian miniatures provide the soldier with a peculiar headgear, a high cylindrical Oriental-like cap, which appears in art not before the fourth century A.D. and which certainly was not worn by soldiers on the early Roman stage. Plautus apparently thought of the *petasus*, or travel-ing-hat, as the proper headgear for the soldier; cf. *Amph*. 145, where Jupiter in the guise of Amphitruo has the *petasus*, and *Pseud*. 735, where *chlamys, machaera*, and *petasus* are mentioned as the garb needed for a disguise.

The slave (*seruus*), so common in the plays of Plautus and Terence, often appeared as a grotesque character. The description of Pseudolus (1218 ff.) is perhaps typical:

A red-headed fellow, pot-bellied, with thick legs, dark complexion, big head, sharp eyes, red face, and very big feet.
Ballio replies:

You ruined me when you mentioned the feet. It was Pseudolus himself.

Perhaps large feet were as frequent as red wigs among slaves on the stage. As to garb, the tunic was often short, and the sleeves were tight and reached to the wrist; in some cases a wide oversleeve came to the elbow. The miniatures either show no *pallium* or a *pallium* piled high on his back; but regularly they portray the slave grasping with the left hand a scarf which hangs from his left shoulder. This scarf is believed to be a conventionalized form of the *pallium collectum*, the *pallium* thrown over the shoulder to enable slaves to bustle about more energetically.[39] In *Capt.* 778 f. Ergasilus says:

I'll throw my cloak over my shoulder just as slaves in comedies usually do.

There are similar references to the *pallium* on the shoulder in *Epid.* 194 f., fr. inc. 56, and *Phorm.* 844 f.

The various female characters (wives, maidservants, courtesans) all wore a long flowing garment; the miniatures show a set of tight sleeves reaching to the wrist and often a second set of flaring sleeves to the elbow, and portray a mantle over the left shoulder. That both wives (*matronae*) and courtesans (*meretrices*) wore the *palla* is clear from such passages as *Men.* 130, *Most.* 282, *Truc.* 536; much of the action of the *Menaechmi* revolves about the fate of the *palla* which Menaechmus I stole from his wife and gave to his mistress Erotium. The courtesans' mantle was said to be saffron-colored because of her greed (*ob auaritiam luteum, De com.* VIII, 6). The courtesans are praised for their beauty, and both they and the maidservants devoted much attention to their appearance; cf. *Most.* 157 ff., in which Scapha helps Philematium bedeck herself with the aid of cosmetics and jewelry. The maid Astaphium (*Truc.* 287 ff.) has curled her hair and made a liberal use of cosmetics and perfume. The *ancillae* give us the impression of being young and beautiful but sometimes the maidservant is an old woman (*anus*); Syra, Dorippa's maid, is eighty-four (*Merc.* 673), and Scapha is certainly no longer young (cf. *Most.* 199 ff.)

Concerning the other characters little needs to be added. Cooks are pictured as wearing short tunics girded at the waist and carrying a spoon or articles of food (birds, fish, etc.). Parasites wear a long-sleeved undergarment and a *chlamys*-like mantle, although in the miniatures Phormio is portrayed with a *pallium* and bearded. Gelasimus is a poor parasite who owns nothing but the *pallium* he is wearing (*Stich.* 257, 350). The slavedealer is apparently unpleasant in appearance; he is sometimes bearded, carries a staff, and often a purse. The nature of his garb is apparent from *Rud.* 549 f.; Labrax has been shipwrecked and his luggage lost at sea:

[39] For the conventional scarf of the *seruus* in the miniatures, see Plate I. Cf. *De com.* VIII, 6: *serui comici amictu exiguo teguntur paupertatis antiquae gratia uel quo expeditiores agant.* Beare believes that the costume of the slave did not differ greatly from that of his master; cf. *CQ* 43 (1949), pp. 30 f.; *The Roman Stage*, pp. 179 ff.

Oh, dear! Now I'm reduced to this one little tunic and this wretched *pallium*; I'm completely ruined.

Fabia believed that the speaker of the prologue wore the costume of the *adulescens* and carried an olive branch to indicate that he was a suppliant beseeching the favor of the audience. The evidence for this is slight, and Miss Saunders rejects the theory, concluding that the branch was not always used, and that the *prologus* was made up as any man young in years, either slave or free; his function was always clear to the spectators without the aid of special insignia.[40] The contrast between *senex* and *adulescens* in the words of Ambivius Turpio (*Heaut.* 1 f.), when he enters to speak the prologue, seems to emphasize a difference in age rather than in role and costume.

In the days of Greek New Comedy the actors wore masks (*personae*) when they appeared on the stage, and masks were used at Rome in the first century B.C. One would naturally assume that the Romans, in adapting the Greek plays and preserving the settings and costumes of the originals, would likewise have taken over the convention of masks. The traditional view, however, and the one found in almost all handbooks and literary histories states that masks were not introduced at Rome until after the death of Terence; according to this theory, the plays of Plautus and Terence were presented during their lifetime by actors who used make-up to depict the various roles. The ancient evidence on the subject of masks at Rome is confused and contradictory and modern scholars fail to agree in their interpretation of this material.[41] The Terentian miniatures give no help on the problem; they portray the characters with masks but the illustrations prove only that the original artist (fifth century A.D.) realized that masks had earlier been worn. Furthermore, whereas Pollux (*Onomasticon*, IV, 143-154) lists forty-four masks used by New Comedy, the miniatures show only two broad classes—the grotesque, big-mouthed type for slaves, parasites, old men, and comic characters in general, and more natural masks for women and young men.

In general, apart from troublesome details, the ancient evidence is as follows: (1) Roscius wore a mask (Cicero, *De orat.* III, 59, 221) and introduced its use to conceal a squint (Diomedes, p. 489 K); (2) Cincius Faliscus was the first to use masks in comedy, Minucius Prothymus the first in tragedy (*De com.* VI, 3); (3) Minucius Prothymus and Ambivius Turpio used masks at the productions of the *Eunuchus* and the *Adelphoe* (Don. *ad Eun.* praef. 1, 6; *ad Ad.* praef 1, 6); (4) a certain play of Naevius, entitled *Personata*, was thought by some to be

---

[40] *Costume in Roman Comedy*, pp. 28 ff.

[41] Cf. Saunders, *AJPh* 32 (1911), pp. 58-73, who supports the traditional view; both Gow (*JRS*, 2, 1912, pp. 65-77) and Beare (*CQ* 33, 1939, pp. 139-146) conclude that masks may have been worn at Rome from the beginnings of the drama; see also Beare, *The Roman Stage*, pp. 184 ff.

presented by masked actors (Festus, p. 238 L).[42] Festus objects on the ground that masks were not used until a later date, and suggests that the play was so called because it was acted by *Atellani* who did not have to remove their masks as did other actors (at the end of the performance, presumably). Thus Festus, without realizing it, confirms the view that at an early period there were other actors besides the *Atellani* who wore masks.

The traditional view attempts to reconcile the contradictions by saying that the accounts have confused two productions, those of Ambivius Turpio without masks in the time of Terence, and those of Minucius Prothymus with masks, perhaps about 130 B.C. or later. The suggestion is made also that Minucius may have been a Greek *dominus gregis* who introduced masks at Rome and that Roscius, perhaps acting under his supervision, was the first Roman to use them. Miss Saunders favors a date after 130 B.C.; rejecting the evidence of Festus, she maintains that there are several traditions about the introduction of masks between Terence and Cicero but none earlier, and she is convinced also that there are no situations in Plautus and Terence which demand masks, whereas *Phorm.* 209 ff., in which Antipho gradually changes his expression, implies that he did not wear a mask.

Both Gow and Beare accept Festus as an authority for the existence of a masked performance as far back as the time of Naevius. Also, as Beare asserts,[43] the fact that Festus does not believe the statement and tries to explain it away is strong evidence in favor of its being genuine. Gow stresses the fact that the use of masks is a convention with which we are unfamiliar, and says that references to changes of expression, such as occur in Terence, are very similar to those in Greek drama, where masks were worn; such references were directed to the imagination of the spectators. The remarks in Donatus' commentary about the expression (*uultus*) of the characters were obviously intended for readers, not for actors.

Comedies with pairs of characters of similar appearance (e.g., *Amphitruo, Menaechmi*) could be produced far more easily by the use of masks than with the aid of cosmetics, and the minute descriptions of many characters in both Plautus and Terence imply masks as much as make-up. There are passages in Plautus, furthermore, which refer to the use of masks, e.g., *Amph.* 458 f., in which Sosia, gazing at his double, says:

[42] The passage is corrupt and reads *Personata fabula quaedam ne ut inscribitur.* Mueller's emendation *Naeui* is accepted by most scholars, including Lindsay, but not by Saunders, *AJPh* 32 (1911), pp. 64 f. The fact that Festus seems puzzled by the early mention of the use of masks argues in favor of the emendation, and it is difficult to accept Miss Saunders' view that the reading *Naeui*, if it could be trusted, might turn the scales "in favor of a later date" (p. 64). Gow (*JRS* 2, 1912, p. 69) interpreted the passage as meaning that the play was the first to be acted with masks; cf. Beare, *CQ* 33 (1939), p. 141.

[43] *CQ* 33 (1939), p. 141.

This fellow has my complete mask (*imago*). I'm having done for me while I'm alive what no one will ever do for me when I'm dead.

There is a play here upon the type of *imago* used at funerals; cf. *Capt.* 39, where the prologue-speaker states that Philocrates and Tyndarus wear each other's *imago*. The word *persona* itself is known to Plautus in the sense of "personage" (*Pers.* 783)[44] and to Terence in the sense of "stage-character" (*Eun.* 26, 32, 35). This implies that the word for mask had already had a long usage on the stage.[45]

Thus the evidence for the late introduction of masks in Roman comedy is weak. Latin grammarians, perhaps eager to point out as many differences between Greek and Roman usage as possible, developed conflicting theories as to who made the innovation. The problem may never be solved but the probabilities favor their use from the earliest period of Roman drama. Such a view explains the passage in Festus, accounts for the presence of the word *persona* in Plautus and Terence, and best accords with the history and nature of Roman comedy.[46]

## The Doubling of Roles

The number of characters in the comedies of Plautus and Terence, excluding silent roles, ranges from seven (*Amphitruo*) to fourteen (*Eunuchus*), with most plays requiring ten to twelve roles. Many scholars today believe that the plays were produced by troupes, which by the doubling of roles could produce the plays with a maximum of five or six actors.[47] The only reference in the comedies themselves to doubling the roles occurs in *Poen.* 123, 126 (one of which is probably the work of a *retractator*);[48] the speaker of the prologue announces that he will depart to assume another role. The fact that the part of the prologue could be doubled with that of one of the characters is of course no proof that roles within the play proper were likewise combined but it does argue in favor of such a procedure. The problem is related to the use of masks; if masks were not worn in the days of Plautus and Terence, the doubling

---

[44] Dordalus says: "May all the gods damn that Persian and all other Persians and all other persons, too." *Persona* here cannot mean "disguise," as Beare (*CQ* 33, 1939, p. 146) suggests. In *Curc.* 192 the diminutive *persolla* occurs; Palinurus calls his master's sweetheart a "tipsy little fright" (*ebriola persolla*).

[45] Beare (*CQ* 33, 1939, p. 143) bases the early use of the mask (*persona*) in part upon its derivation from the Etruscan *φersu*.

[46] Michaut (*Sur les tréteaux latins*, pp. 419 ff.) mentions both the advantages and disadvantages arising from the use of masks. The disadvantages would not seem significant to Roman playwrights adapting dramatic forms for which the mask was an accepted convention.

[47] The opposite view is given by Schanz-Hosius (*Geschichte der römischen Literatur*, I, p. 146), who state that the number of actors was not limited in any way and that the producer could assign each role to a single actor. This would mean companies of ten to fourteen actors exclusive of silent roles, and seems most uneconomical.

[48] Lindsay rejects 123 (*ego ibo, ornabor*) and considers 126 (*ibo, alius nunc fieri uolo*) genuine. Goetz-Schoell retain 123 and reject 126.

of roles would be far more difficult, and more time would be required for changes of make-up. But if masks were used (as seems more likely), the changes of role would be greatly facilitated, and one actor could play several parts without danger of recognition.[49] The question whether vacant stages mark pauses in the action (to be discussed below) is also important in this connection, for such pauses would allow time for changing roles, as did the choral interlude in Greek New Comedy. That the Greek comedies did not use more than four or five actors is generally assumed.[50]

Any three-actor law, such as was formerly accepted for Greek tragedy,[51] is of course impossible for comedy, where four and five characters are often on the stage together; cf. e.g., *Rud.* 839 ff., where in addition to the two girls at the altar (silent throughout the scene), Labrax, the overseers (*lorarii*), Plesidippus, and Trachalio are on the stage and during the scene Charmides enters from the temple; later, in the recognition scene (1045 ff.), Daemones, the two girls, Trachalio, and Labrax are on the stage together. In the *Eunuchus* (771 ff.), when Thraso makes his famous attack on the house of Thais, there are apparently eight characters on the stage, although three members of the "army" (Simalio, Donax, Syriscus) remain silent. There is no good reason to assume, as do many editors, that Chremes and Thais go inside after 770 and speak their lines to Thraso and Gnatho from an upper window.[52] But even in scenes of four and five characters it should be noted that seldom do more than three persons speak at a time; when a fourth

---

[49] Miss Kurrelmeyer, who attempts to limit the size of the troupe by combining roles wherever possible, nevertheless rejects the use of masks; cf. *The Economy of Actors in Plautus*, pp. 3 f.

[50] Cf. Rees, *CPh* 5 (1910), pp. 291-302.

[51] Cf. Rees, *The So-Called Rule of Three Actors*, pp. 42 ff., who points out the difficulties of applying such a law.

[52] This use of an upper window was believed likely by Ashmore and Sargeaunt, and I accepted it in *The Complete Roman Drama*, II, p. 288. I no longer consider it probable; there are no parallels in the extant comedies, with the possible exception of Mercury on the roof of Amphitruo's house (*Amph.* 1021 ff., cf. 1008). Thais and Chremes probably remain at the door and watch the approach of Thraso and his cronies; cf. Legrand-Loeb, *The New Greek Comedy*, p. 344. Chremes' suggestion to Thais that they go in and lock the door (763, cf. 784) was apparently disregarded, for Gnatho's desire that they be put to flight (787) is more meaningful if they are present on the stage. Donatus (*ad Eun.* 773) refers to Thais as being outside the house. It is worth noting that the Terentian miniatures of MSS C, P, and O portray Thais and Chremes on the stage viewing with consternation the approach of the others; in the miniature of MS F Thais and Chremes are behind the portal apparently unconcerned by the presence of the "army" outside (see Plates III, IV); cf. Watson, *HSCPh* 14 (1903), pp. 86 ff.; Jones and Morey, *The Miniatures of the Manuscripts of Terence*, Text, pp. 108 ff.; 196. Jones and Morey think that F rather than CPO reflects the archetype, one argument being that it shows the portal necessary to the scene; they admit, however, that the arrangement of the characters in F is faulty and has been corrected in the original of CPO. Possibly the elimination of the portal in CPO should also be viewed as a correction. (On the illustrated MSS of Terence, see Appendix.)

character enters the conversation, one of the three ceases to speak. A conversation of four or five actors would be confused and difficult to follow;[53] sometimes, with four characters speaking, we have actually two dialogues, e.g., in *Poen.* 210-330, where Agorastocles and Milphio listen to the speeches of the two sisters and make numerous amusing comments.

The advantages from the standpoint of economy in presenting a play of ten or twelve characters with a company of five or six actors are readily apparent, and such a limitation would be particularly desirable at a time when actors were scarce. But can such a doubling be shown to have existed? The best evidence would be the presence of passages in the plays themselves which seem to have no other function but that of facilitating a change of role. The problem is complicated by the fact that passages which present structural peculiarities of any sort are apt to be used by scholars to support theories of *retractatio* or *contaminatio* in a given play. But Prescott believes[54] that there are at least three scenes in Plautus, all spoken by a boy (*puer*), which do not contribute to the action or provide humor and seem to serve no purpose other than that of aiding the distribution of roles. These are *Mil.* IV, 9 (1378-1393), which provides a lapse of time for the actors of IV, 8 to assume new roles for V, 1; *Capt.* IV, 4 (909-921), in which the monologue of the *puer* enables Ergasilus to change to one of the characters in V, 1; *Pseud.* III, 1 (767-789), also a *puer*-monologue, which permits the actor who played the part of Pseudolus in the preceding scene to change to the role of the cook.[55] That the cook and Pseudolus could be played by the same actor is confirmed by the fact that Ballio's monologue at the end of III, 2 (892-904) provides time for the cook to retire and appear in the next scene as Pseudolus. Prescott points out that these three *puer*-scenes are short (from thirteen to twenty-three verses) and do not advance the action, and they are followed by scenes requiring from three to five actors; they were apparently inserted to facilitate the distribution of roles, and so argue strongly for production by a small cast of actors.

Additional evidence may be found in other monologues (e.g., *Rud.* 892-905), and in the large number of early exits and late entrances, especially if they are unmotivated; these too indicate that an actor needed time to change his garb for another role.[56] Such passages doubt-

---

[53] Cf. Legrand-Loeb, *The New Greek Comedy*, pp. 295 f. Donatus (*ad Eun.* 454) comments on the skill with which Terence avoids confusion in a scene with four speaking parts.

[54] *HSCPh* 21 (1910), pp. 31-50; cf. *CPh* 18 (1923), pp. 29 ff.

[55] The *puer* of III, 1 is not to be identified with the *puer* of III, 2, who returns with Ballio from the market and is the same boy that attended him in I, 2 and I, 3 as a mute character; cf. Prescott, *HSCPh* 21 (1910), pp. 41 f. Miss Kurrelmeyer (*The Economy of Actors in Plautus*, pp. 76 f.) lists only one *puer* and distributes the characters among four actors.

[56] Cf. Prescott, *HSCPh* 21 (1910), pp. 47 ff.; *CPh* 18 (1923), pp. 25 ff.; *TAPhA* 63 (1932), pp. 121 ff.; Kurrelmeyer, *The Economy of Actors in Plautus*, pp. 17 ff.

Plate III. Thraso attacks the house of Thais

*Eun.* 771-816 (MS C: folio 29 verso) (see Chap. 4, n. 52)

Plate IV. Thraso attacks the house of Thais

*Eun.* 771-816 (MS F: folio 10) (see Chap. 4. n. 52)

less reveal Roman workmanship, since in the Greek originals the difficulties of operating with a limited cast were lessened by the use of a
choral interlude; it will be noted that all three *puer*-scenes, as well as
*Pseud.* 892-904, *Rud.* 892-905, and other monologues occur either before or after vacant stages and (modern) act-divisions; many such
Plautine monologues are probably substitutes for the choral interludes
of the original.

I thus accept as plausible the theory that Roman comedies were
produced by small companies, but I am very sceptical about suggested
methods of distributing the roles in the various plays. It is folly to assume that the roles were so divided that each comedy could be produced
with the smallest possible number of actors. Miss Kurrelmeyer, for
instance, believes that no play of Plautus required more than five
actors (plus supernumeraries), and that some (*Amphitruo, Cistellaria,
Stichus*) needed only three. Such a limitation is possible only if the
same role is sometimes divided between two actors (Sosia in the *Amphitruo,* Menaechmus II in the *Menaechmi*), and if actors are frequently loaded with as many as four parts, often of an extremely varied
and incongruous nature. Even more difficult to accept is the necessary
assumption that a character suddenly departs from the stage and is
replaced by a silent actor; Miss Kurrelmeyer thinks that Philematium
in *Most.* 348 ff. is a mute substitute and that the actor who earlier appeared as Philematium now plays the part of Tranio; similarly, at *Rud.*
705 Palaestra and Ampelisca must slip behind the scenes to change
their garb while mute substitutes take their place at the altar for the next
few scenes. Such substitutions by mute actors seem most improbable.[57]

The attempts of various scholars to assign the parts in a given play
seldom agree,[58] and we have little assurance that any hypothetical distribution indicates the manner in which the roles were actually assigned
on the Roman stage. To argue, as Miss Kurrelmeyer does,[59] that the
very small number of actors made it necessary for the playwright to
omit important scenes which otherwise he would have added (e.g., the
reunion of parents and daughter in the *Epidicus*, the presence of the
*senex*, wife, and Erotium at the recognition of the twin brothers in the
*Menaechmi*, the reappearance of Philolaches at the end of the *Mostellaria*) is highly subjective and extremely foolhardy; too many other
factors are involved, including the purpose and wishes of the playwright himself. There is strong evidence that the comedies were composed for production by small companies and that roles were often

[57] Cf. Prescott, *CPh* 32 (1937), pp. 205 f., who believes that the silence of the two
girls in *Rud.* 706-885 is no indication that supernumeraries slipped in and the regular
actors disappeared in some mysterious fashion. These same two characters are also
silent for a long period in 1045 ff.

[58] Cf. Duckworth, *T. Macci Plauti Epidicus*, pp. 367 f.

[59] *The Economy of Actors in Plautus*, pp. 88 ff.; see Prescott, *CPh* 29 (1934),
pp. 350 f., who points out many errors and omissions in Miss Kurrelmeyer's work.

doubled; there is no evidence that the companies were so limited in number that the plays could be staged only with a maximum of awkwardness and confusion.

## Act-Divisions and Continuity of Action

The plays of Plautus and Terence in almost all modern editions are each divided into five acts, and each act into several scenes. That any such division was known to the playwrights is very unlikely. The scene-divisions appear in the manuscripts of the plays, including the Ambrosian Palimpsest of Plautus and the Bembinus of Terence, each dating from about the fourth century A.D.; the entrance of one or more characters on the stage was regularly indicated by a scene-heading, which gave the names and usually the roles of the characters in that scene; such scenes might vary in length from eight or ten lines to two hundred or more.[60] The famous five-act law had been established by the time of Horace (*Epist.* II, 3, 189 f.),[61] and Donatus and other commentators tried to fit the comedies of Terence into a scheme of five acts even though they apparently realized that the Roman comic poets wrote their plays for continuous presentation; they admitted also that a division into five acts was difficult.[62] That act-divisions of Terence's plays went back to a much earlier period, to the time of Varro, is also stated by Donatus (*ad Hec.* praef. III, 6; cf. *ad And.* praef. III, 6). The plays of Plautus were not divided into acts until 1500, in the edition of J. B. Pius, and his divisions have been followed with modifications by most later editors.

The chief criterion for any division into acts is of course the vacant stage, which may or may not indicate a significant pause in the action; e.g., the *Rudens* has ten empty stages, but no one would attempt to divide the play into eleven acts; many of the empty stages do not indicate a lapse of dramatic time.[63] Other comedies have an insufficient

[60] The exit of a character was sometimes indicated by a new scene-heading, but more often not; cf. Watson, HSCPh 14 (1903), pp. 137 f.

[61] We must keep in mind that Horace is speaking of tragedy and probably thinking of prologue, three episodes, and exode, the parts being separated by choral song.

[62] Cf. Evanthius, III, 1; Donatus, *ad Ad.* praef. I, 4, *ad And.* praef. II, 3, *ad Eun.* praef. I, 5. See Beare, Ha 67 (1946), pp. 52 ff.; in Ha 72 (1948), pp. 44 ff., Beare has discussed the problem at length, and concludes (p. 69) that "the five-act rule, as applied to Terence, appears to be the product of Roman pedantry." (This article reappears in a slightly modified form in *The Roman Stage*, pp. 188-210.) See also Baldwin, *Shakspere's Five-Act Structure*, pp. 1-52, for a detailed discussion both of the act-structure of Terence's plays and of Donatus' comments on act-divisions. Baldwin believes (pp. 9, 12, 22, 27, 31 f.) that Terence constructed each of his comedies in five clearly demarcated plot stages; these divisions, however, are not to be looked upon as units of staging.

[63] This is particularly true of *Rud.* 184, for Sceparnio (162 ff.) has already seen the plight of the two girls; also of 457 and 484; cf. 450 ff., in which Ampelisca announces the approach of Labrax and Charmides who enter in 485; Sceparnio's return at 457

number of vacant stages; the *Mostellaria* has only two, but editors provide five acts instead of three by indicating act-divisions at 347 and 531 (the first empty stage occurs at 857). Act-divisions without an empty stage occur in modern editions of at least half of the twenty-six extant comedies,[64] and this fact indicates that the criterion of the vacant stage and significant lapse of time is faulty, or that the plays were never intended for such a division. Modern scholars who have attempted to correct the traditional divisions have failed to agree in many instances; Weissinger cites[65] their complete disagreement concerning Plautus' *Rudens* and Terence's *Adelphoe*, but these cases are perhaps extreme; there is less dissent concerning other plays, e.g., the *Epidicus*, where the traditional division at 525 has been rejected in favor of 381.[66] But to what extent is it advisable to divide the plays into acts? Are there any indications in the comedies that imaginary pauses required by the off-stage action were represented on the stage by real pauses?

That the plays of Greek New Comedy were divided into sections by choral interludes is known from the presence of the word χοροῦ in the papyrus fragments of Menander. These sections (μέρη) were apparently integral, coherent parts of the play but we have no assurance that there were in each comedy four interludes and five *mere*; they may have ranged from three or four to seven or eight.[67] The Roman dramatists in their adaptation of the Greek comedies were undoubtedly conscious of these divisions, though they made no attempt to preserve them; they dispensed with the chorus, bridged the resultant gaps by monologues or monodies, and often reworked the dialogue meters of the originals into lyric *cantica*.

Is it possible that there are still traces of the original pauses and even the choral interludes in the Roman comedies? The following passages are cited as noteworthy:

Someone's coming here to create a disturbance. Let's depart. (*Bacch.* 107)

I'm going inside, but I won't delay you long; meanwhile the flute-player here will entertain you. (*Pseud.* 573-573a)

The second passage clearly refers to a brief musical interlude before the monody of Pseudolus,[68] and the former has been believed to refer to a

---

is expected (cf. 439). See Conrad, *The Technique of Continuous Action*, p. 48; on pp. 64 f. he argues for continuity of action at 592 (end of Act II).

[64] Cf. Weissinger, *A Study of Act Divisions*, p. 71.

[65] *A Study of Act Divisions*, pp. 73 ff.

[66] Cf. Duckworth, *T. Macci Plauti Epidicus*, pp. 206 f., 309.

[67] Cf. Flickinger, *The Greek Theater and its Drama*, p. 195. See, however, Legrand-Loeb, *The New Greek Comedy*, pp. 383 ff.; Legrand believes that five would be the most natural, and therefore the normal, number; he suggests that the rule of five acts might well be called "the rule of four *entr'actes*," since the number of *mere* was determined by the number of choral interludes.

[68] Cf. the references to the *tibicen* in *Cas.* 798, *Stich.* 715 ff., 757 ff. Beare (*Ha* 55, 1940, p. 115) points out that Pseudolus has been on the stage continuously for 573

chorus of revelers which had no relation to the characters and resembled the inorganic chorus of Greek New Comedy.[69] Flickinger believes that there was an intermission at *Heaut.* 170 filled by a group of banqueters,[70] and other scholars have seen vestigial survivals of a more organic chorus in the *piscatores* of the *Rudens* (290 ff.), the *aduocati* of the *Poenulus* (515 ff.), in the bands of cooks, slaves, courtesans, and the like, which so often appear in the Roman plays as supernumeraries. The existence of *entr'actes* as postulated by Mlle. Freté[71] depends largely upon the length of the intervals needed off-stage for errands, banquets, and the like, but the time required for such action is often highly compressed,[72] and covered also by song and dance or by monologue. In all such studies there seems to be a regrettable confusion between imaginary dramatic time and actual time of stage-presentation.

In a recent survey of the problem, Weissinger admits that some Roman comedies may have been presented continuously; he believes, however, not only that we have traces of the original choruses and divisions of the Greek comedies, but that many of the empty stages represent real pauses and act-divisions in the plays as originally produced at Rome; this means that Plautus and Terence consciously made such divisions as they wrote their plays.[73] This view in one sense goes far beyond that of other scholars who merely try to discover in the Roman comedies the vacant stages and significant pauses which indicate the five *mere* of the Greek originals; in another sense Weissinger is less extreme, for he thinks that the number of acts in the Roman plays probably varied originally from three to six or seven, and that these divisions were lost when a standardized five-act rule was applied to the plays in the first century B.C. Weissinger stresses one argument which seems particularly weak: the comedies of Plautus and Terence close with an appeal for applause (e.g., *plaudite, plausum date, ualete et plaudite*); "this *clausula*," he says, "would not have been needed if there had been no pauses in the course of the action until the end."[74] Surely, the conventional farewell and request for applause were inevitable at the

---

lines and returns for almost 200 more, "a period of duty unequalled in Latin comedy"; cf. also *The Roman Stage*, pp. 204 f.

[69] *Bacch.* 107 has been considered corrupt and different emendations have been proposed; cf. Conrad, *The Technique of Continuous Action*, pp. 72 ff.; Weissinger, *A Study of Act Divisions*, p. 68, n. 23. Conrad sees no reference to a chorus in *Bacch.* 107; the crowd referred to could be the slaves with Pistoclerus (*tanta pompa*, 114).

[70] *CPh* 7 (1912), pp. 24 ff. Kauer and Lindsay have inserted *Saltatio Conviuarum* into their Oxford text at this point but give the credit for the discovery to Skutsch; see Weissinger, *A Study of Act Divisions*, p. 64, n. 8; Beare, *The Roman Stage*, pp. 201 f. The theory of an intermission at this point is far less probable if Phania's house is on the stage; see above, n. 24, and cf. Beare, *Ha* 55 (1940), p. 115, 74 (1949), pp. 26 ff.

[71] *REL* 7 (1929), pp. 291 ff.     [72] See "Off-Stage Action" in chap. 5.

[73] *A Study of Act Divisions*, pp. 82, 97 ff.

[74] *A Study of Act Divisions*, p. 70.

end of the play and prove nothing concerning the manner of presentation.

The earlier conclusions of Conrad are far more acceptable; admitting the existence of an occasional choral or musical interlude, he maintains that most vacant stages mark only momentary, insignificant pauses which have no relation to act-divisions, and he believes that the Latin playwrights provided for continuous action.[75] Added support for this view may be found in the evidence cited above concerning the doubling of roles. The use of *puer*-scenes and other monologues to provide time for actors to change their parts seems clearly established; but these monologues usually stand in the text where act-divisions are indicated.[76] Divisions into acts and provisions for distributing roles are thus mutually exclusive; if the plays were produced with pauses, such monologues were absolutely unnecessary as devices to fill time; the very fact that these passages are necessary confirms the view that the Roman comedies had no pauses and that the dramatic action was continuous throughout.

In summary, we may conclude that neither Plautus nor Terence applied any rule of act-division to their comedies, and that the plays were usually produced on the stage with complete continuity of action. Such pauses or interludes as may be detected are relics of Greek structure and prove nothing about the presentation of the Roman adaptations (with the exception of *Pseud.* 573a). If act-divisions are to be retained in modern editions, the errors of Donatus as well as those of Pius and more modern editors should be corrected wherever necessary. The ideal situation would perhaps be to have new editions of the comedies with no divisions whatsoever but a tradition of almost two thousand years cannot lightly be cast aside. It is, however, very misleading for the student to read plays divided into acts and scenes unless he realizes clearly that such divisions have no meaning for the presentation of Roman comedy in the second century B.C.[77]

[75] *Continuous Action in Roman Comedy*, pp. 46, 70, 82 ff.; cf. Flickinger, *CW* 10 (1916-17), p. 151, who is convinced that essential pauses were not infrequent, but admits that many comedies were presented continuously or comparatively so.

[76] Cf. also *Epid.* 158-165, 306-319, 382-393; see Prescott, *CPh* 36 (1941), pp. 284 f.; *CPh* 37 (1942), pp. 20 f.

[77] A statement seems necessary, since my discussion of act-divisions (*T. Macci Plauti Epidicus*, pp. 206 f., 309, 372) did not sufficiently clarify my own position (cf. Prescott, *CPh* 36, 1941, p. 284). Imaginary time needed for off-stage action (*Epid.* 381, 606) seemed a convenient aid for determining the divisions according to the modern convention; but my use of the word "pause" was perhaps unfortunate; I did not mean to imply that parts of the play were separated by actual stage-pauses at the time of production. I am in complete agreement with Prescott that the problem of act-divisions cannot be handled apart from the evidence for the distribution of roles.

# CHAPTER 5

## STAGE CONVENTIONS AND TECHNIQUES

THE first four chapters have presented a survey of the background, history, and staging of Roman comedy, and much of the information on these topics was inevitably drawn from external sources rather than from the comedies. For the remainder of the book (with the exception of a final chapter on the influence of Roman comedy) the extant plays themselves provide a rich storehouse of material from which I shall endeavor to cull the most significant classifications and illustrations. Plautus and Terence will be discussed together in the chapters which follow; this does not, however, indicate "some kind of partnership,"[1] for the two dramatists often differ strikingly in their handling of plot and character, in their use of suspense, in their comic devices, in their linguistic and metrical effects. Every effort will be made to point out the dissimilarities as well as the similarities. Only in this way can an unbiased estimate of the two playwrights be reached. All too often Plautus and Terence have been lumped together as a kind of dim reflection of Greek comedy and used as a quarry for the restoration of the supposedly flawless Greek originals, and this has been done in spite of the obvious differences between the two poets; on the other hand, the likenesses between the two have often been disregarded and unfair evaluations of Plautus and Terence have been the result. How narrow the passage between Scylla and Charybdis!

The nature of the stage conventions must be considered at the outset, for they differ in many respects from those of the modern theater; the student of Greek and Roman drama must realize that many features which are frowned upon today, such as asides, soliloquies, chance meetings, failure to see eavesdroppers, secrets discussed in public, were all accepted devices of the ancient comic writers[2] and were used without hesitation by Plautus and Terence, but not all to the same extent nor in the same way. Other techniques favored by Plautus were practically ignored by Terence. An analysis of stage conventions and techniques, therefore, not only will be helpful for a comprehension of the nature of Roman comedy but will provide a preliminary study of some of the characteristic differences between the two playwrights. Many of these

[1] Cf. Norwood, *Plautus and Terence*, p. 3, who says that "the work of Terence is high comedy, that of Plautus mostly farce." Norwood, however, exaggerates the differences between the two playwrights and gives a misleading impression of Plautus' work.

[2] In spite of the small amount of New Comedy preserved, it is possible to see in the fragments of Menander and his contemporaries most of the devices and conventions to be discussed in this chapter.

conventions, e.g., monologues (especially those uttered by a running slave), asides, the protatic character, the breaking of the dramatic illusion, will necessarily be mentioned again in later chapters, where the value of these devices for exposition, characterization, or comedy can be treated more profitably and additional distinctions drawn between the dramatic technique of Plautus and Terence.

## The Function of the Monologue[3]

Drama naturally presupposes dramatic dialogue, and in the plays of Plautus and Terence the action develops largely by means of dialogue. But monologues were an accepted convention in all ancient drama, both Greek and Roman, and the existence of numerous monologues in Roman comedy need cause the modern reader no surprise. In the plays of Plautus the average amount of monologue is seventeen per cent of the total number of verses, in those of Terence only twelve; Terence thus favored dramatic dialogue slightly more than Plautus, but the latter utilized the monologue for a greater variety of purposes.[4]

The use of monologues in ancient comedy is often condemned as artificial and unrealistic, and by modern standards the criticism is perhaps justified; but we must not judge by modern standards, since ancient playwrights were not troubled by the convention. We can, however, distinguish between the true soliloquy and monologues which are mere addresses to the audience. A true soliloquy is one in which a character, believing himself to be alone, talks aloud under the stress of strong emotion;[5] many illustrations of this type can be found in both Plautus and Terence. In *Cist.* 203 ff. the unhappy Alcesimarchus, beset by the pangs of love, addresses himself in the following maudlin fashion:

I do believe that Love was the first to invent torture for mankind. I can make this surmise from my own experience at home, without looking elsewhere, for I surpass, I excel all men in torturability of soul! I'm tossed, tormented, driven, goaded, whirled on the wheel of love, made lifeless in my misery! I'm torn, distorted, distracted, distressed, my mind is so beclouded! Where I am, there I'm not; where I'm not, there my thoughts are. . . . My father kept me at his villa in the country for six whole days and I haven't had a chance to see my sweetheart once. . . .

[3] In this section I use the term "monologue" regularly for ordinary solo speeches, restricting the term "soliloquy" to more emotional self-addresses. Some writers, e.g., Bickford, call all solo speeches soliloquies. I include under monologues many passages which are composed in lyric meters to be sung and which should more properly be termed monodies.

[4] Cf. Bickford, *Soliloquy in Ancient Comedy*, pp. 60, 62; the amount of monologue in individual plays ranges, for Plautus, from two per cent (*Asin.*) to thirty-one (*Merc.*); for Terence, from seven per cent (*Heaut.*) to eighteen (*Ad.*).

[5] Some monologues take the form of an address to a god (cf. *Most.* 431 ff., *Trin.* 820 ff.) or an apostrophe to one's door (*Merc.* 830 ff.). Cf. *Merc.* 3 ff.: "I'll not do what other love-smitten characters do, when they tell their troubles to Night or Day, to Sun or Moon." Philemon in the original was doubtless parodying tragedy (cf. Euripides, *Medea*, 57 f.). See Flickinger, *The Greek Theater and its Drama*, pp. 307 ff.

Less ridiculous and more effective are the words of the unhappy Aeschinus (*Ad.* 610 ff.), when he is wrongly accused of deserting Pamphila for a music girl:

I'm in terrible distress; that such a disaster should have come upon me so unexpectedly! I don't know what to do or how to act. My limbs are weak with fear; my mind is dazed with terror. My heart can form no plan. How can I get myself out of this mess? Such a terrible suspicion about me, and on good grounds, too! Sostrata thinks I bought the music girl for myself. The old woman just told me this. . . . What am I to do now? Say the girl is for my brother? That secret must not be revealed to anyone. . . .

The lament of the shipwrecked Palaestra (*Rud.* 185 ff.) as she reaches land wet and exhausted is exceedingly natural under the circumstances:

Ah, how much more unkind is Fate than what men say about it! Was it the will of the gods that, garbed like this, in terror, I should be cast up on an unknown shore? Was I born for this fate? Is this my reward for an upright life? If I had sinned in the sight of the gods or my parents, I would have deserved this suffering; but if I have been careful to commit no wrong, then, immortals, you have treated me unjustly and unfairly. If in this way you treat the innocent, how will you repay sinners hereafter? I should have less pity for myself if either my parents or I were to blame. But it's my villainous master and his wrongdoing that have brought this trouble to me. Well, he's lost his ship and everything in the sea; I'm all that remains of his fortune. Even the girl that was with me on the boat is gone. I'm all alone. If only she were left, life wouldn't be so difficult. What hope or help or advice can I find now? Here I am in a lonely spot, all rocks and sea, and no one to come to my aid. . . .

There are many soliloquies of this type in which the characters express perplexity, indignation, anger, remorse, anxiety. The distress of Lydus at the behavior of the youth he has trained (*Bacch.* 368 ff.), the grief of Pamphilus when he is told that he must give up Glycerium and marry the girl of his father's choice (*And.* 236 ff.), the anxiety of Micio about his adopted son (*Ad.* 26 ff.), are among the most realistic soliloquies to be found in Roman comedy.[6] When Gripus returns from a night of fishing with a chest which gives him delusions of wealth and grandeur (he even thinks of founding a city and calling it Gripusburg), he expresses his hopes and ambitions in a monologue (*Rud.* 906 ff.), which portrays his character and provides considerable humor. One of the most emotional of all soliloquies is that in which Euclio pours forth his rage and despair at the discovery that his pot of gold has been stolen (*Aul.* 713 ff.), but this frantic speech is not a true soliloquy for much of it is addressed to the spectators.

In reality, all soliloquies are spoken for the benefit of the audience, but the true soliloquy, uttered under emotional stress, does not violate dramatic probability. Many monologues in both Plautus and Terence,

---

[6] Cf. Harsh, *A Handbook of Classical Drama*, pp. 396 ff., who points out that there are three true soliloquies in the *Adelphoe*, at 26 ff., 610 ff., 855 ff.

however, are frankly directed to the spectators; speeches of this type have been criticized for their lack of dramatic fitness, since the excessive amount of narrative serves primarily to enlighten the audience about the development of the plot,[7] and in some instances the speakers blurt out confidential matters, even though other characters are near and may overhear them;[8] this is true even of so excellent a soliloquy as that of Pamphilus in *And.* 236 ff., which is overheard by Mysis. Norwood condemns *Aul.* 608 ff., in which Euclio tells where he has concealed his gold and the secret is heard by an eavesdropping slave, as "the silliest piece of stage-writing in the world," and says that "here Plautus may be seen murdering dramatic art."[9] It is perhaps true that Euclio's betrayal of his secret is foolish and exceeds the limits of psychological probability, but we must remember that solo speech was a racial characteristic of the Greeks and the Romans and that the use of monologue in comedy was doubtless far more realistic to the ancient audience than it seems to modern critics.[10] At any rate, Norwood's rash statements give an entirely erroneous impression of the normal use of the convention; such speeches need not be inaudible to other persons on the stage. In both Plautus and Terence monologues could be overheard or not, as it suited the convenience of the playwright.

The monologues of Roman comedy serve a variety of purposes: (1) they are used for exposition, i.e., for the development or the explanation of the plot throughout the play and for the description of what has already happened off stage; (2) they announce what will take place either on the stage or behind the scenes; (3) they comment upon action that is already known to the audience; these, numerically the most frequent, do not advance the plot, but often contribute to the irony or suspense felt by the audience by revealing either the misplaced confidence of dupes (e.g., *Pers.* 470 ff., *Pseud.* 1052 ff.) or the fears and forebodings of intriguing slaves (e.g., *Pseud.* 394 ff., *And.* 599 ff.). By far the majority of the monologues of Roman comedy are those of development, announcement, and comment. Monologues are used also (4) for deliberation on a possible course of action, (5) for delineation of character, (6) for moralizing on a topic suggested by the situation in the play, and (7) for comic effect. An additional type is the topical-rhetorical monologue, such as Philolaches' comparison of the training of a young man to the building of a house (*Most.* 84 ff.), and Chrysalus'

---

[7] E.g., *Aul.* 371 ff., *Capt.* 498 ff., *Most.* 1041 ff., *Eun.* 615 ff., 840 ff., *Hec.* 361 ff.; cf. Legrand-Loeb, *The New Greek Comedy*, pp. 426 ff., and see Menander, *Sam.* 1 ff., 113 ff.

[8] E.g., *Aul.* 475 ff., 608 ff., 667 ff., *Cas.* 217 ff., 563 ff., *Trin.* 843 ff.; see Legrand-Loeb, *The New Greek Comedy*, pp. 329 f.

[9] *Plautus and Terence*, p. 81. In his treatment of this and other conventions Norwood gives a false picture in his attempt to prove that Plautus is "the worst of all writers who have ever won permanent repute" (p. 4). See Duckworth, *CW* 41 (1947-48), pp. 87 f.

[10] Cf. Hiatt, *Eavesdropping in Roman Comedy*, p. 5, n. 1.

comparison of his exploits to the siege of Troy (*Bacch.* 925 ff.). The
types overlap and one monologue may combine several elements; e.g.,
*Rud.* 906 ff., mentioned above, contains explanation, characterization,
moralizing, and comedy.[11] From the standpoint of the plot, monologues
of exposition and announcement are functionally the most useful but
many of the others (e.g., those of comment, characterization, and comedy) are dramatically more effective.

In Plautus monologues are delivered most frequently by slaves (44
per cent), old men (25 per cent), young men (11 per cent); Terence
reverses the order: young men (33 per cent), old men (27 per cent),
slaves (23 per cent); this is not surprising since many of the slave monologues are devoted to moralizing and comedy, types which are numerous
in Plautus but extremely rare in Terence. We have an indication here
of Terence's desire to eliminate comic effect and use monologues primarily for development of the plot and announcement of future action.

A special kind of monologue is delivered by a character (usually a
slave, sometimes a parasite) who, often breathless from haste and excitement, hurries on the stage with news of great importance (good or
bad); he fails at first to see the very person he is seeking and, when he
does meet him, he indulges in buffoonery and delays the delivery of his
message. Such monologues are partly for comic effect, partly to develop
the action and create suspense by retarding the delivery of the news.
Acanthio in *Merc.* 111 ff. begins his soliloquy as follows:

Use all your strength and every ounce of energy to save your young
master; come now, Acanthio, drive away your weariness, don't yield to
idleness. (*Panting loudly.*) This shortness of breath will be the death of me,
I'm utterly winded, confound it! And at the same time the streets are full
of people in my way; hit 'em, shove 'em aside, throw 'em in the street.
What a disgusting custom they have here: when a fellow's running and in
a hurry, not a person has the decency to get out of his way. So when you've
started one thing, you have to do three things all at once—run, and fight,
and argue all along the street. . . .

Fifteen verses later Acanthio sees his master, who has been on the stage
and has uttered occasional asides, but fifty verses of dialogue ensue
before the perplexed Charinus learns the nature of the bad tidings.

There are thirteen scenes in Roman comedy in which the running
slave (*seruus currens*) plays a part, eight in Plautus, five in Terence.[12]

---

[11] Cf. Bickford, *Soliloquy in Ancient Comedy*, pp. 53 ff., for a classification of the
monologues of Plautus and Terence according to content. Certain monologues in
Plautus defy classification, e.g., the words of the *choragus* (*Curc.* 462 ff.) which have
no connection with the plot of the play, and the dreams of the *senes* (*Merc.* 225 ff.,
*Rud.* 593 ff.) which foreshadow the action in the two plays; see Bickford, pp. 14, 44.

[12] E.g., *Asin.* 267 ff., *Capt.* 768 ff., *Curc.* 280 ff., *And.* 338 ff., *Ad.* 299 ff. Cf. Duckworth, "Dramatic Function of the *seruus currens*," pp. 93 ff., and bibliography there
cited. I do not include as true running slave scenes either *Amph.* 984 ff., a humorous
parody on the usual monologue, or *Epid.* 192 ff., in which Epidicus pretends to be a
*seruus currens* with important news for Periphanes.

The younger dramatist thus employs the device relatively more often than does Plautus but he uses it in a different way; he reduces the comic effect and arouses irony since the knowledge brought by the running slave is usually known to the spectators in advance; Plautus in most instances keeps his audience in uncertainty as to the nature of the information to be divulged.[13] That Plautus' treatment of the running slave scenes is a Roman development cannot be proved but it seems highly probable; at any rate, the difference between Plautus and Terence in this respect is very striking and it seems likely that Terence more closely reflects the use of the running slave in the Greek originals.

The structural function of the monologue deserves a brief mention; there are three types: (1) entrance monologues, delivered by a character who comes in on an empty stage and speaks before the arrival of other persons; (2) exit monologues, spoken by a character who remains on the stage after the departure of one or more persons and delivers a speech before he too leaves the stage;[14] and (3) link monologues, in which the person left alone on the stage speaks but does not depart, and one or more characters come on the stage immediately after the conclusion of his words. The characteristic function of the entrance monologue is to narrate off-stage action. It is significant also that many of the entrance speeches, emotional in content and composed in lyric measures, are actually monodies; of this type are *Cist.* 203 ff., *Rud.* 185 ff., 906 ff., *And.* 236 ff., all mentioned above as true soliloquies. Song does not occur in link or exit monologues, except in *Epid.* 81 ff., where the link monologue concludes a longer passage in lyric measures, and in *Truc.* 209 ff. All other monodies are sung by entering characters. Both the exit and the link monologue provide time for off-stage action and for change of role, and both permit reflection on past events and deliberation on future action. The exit monologue, however, clears the stage for future developments, while the link monologue continues the stream of the action.[15] The speaker of a link monologue usually announces the oncoming character (or characters) and remains on the

[13] See "Devices to Arouse Suspense" in chap. 8. Norwood (*Plautus and Terence*, p. 83) says that Plautus is "shelving the play proper so as to amuse his hearers precisely by ludicrous time-wasting at a crisis." The scenes are often expanded but not merely for comic effect; the so-called padding serves also to heighten the suspense. It is interesting to note that the *Mercator*, which Norwood considers the one comedy of Plautus closely translated from the Greek, contains a long running slave scene (111 ff.) which is typically Plautine.

[14] A monologue may be both an entrance and exit monologue if a character comes on an empty stage, speaks a few lines, and then departs; cf., e.g., *Rud.* 892 ff., which prepares the audience for the arrival of Gripus. Monologues of this type are rare, and in most instances (e.g., *Capt.* 909 ff., *Pseud.* 767 ff.) help to facilitate the doubling of roles; see Prescott, *TAPhA* 63 (1932), pp. 121 ff., and cf. above, p. 96.

[15] See Prescott, *CPh* 34 (1939), pp. 1 ff., 116 ff.; 37 (1942), pp. 1 ff. Hough (*TAPhA* 70, 1939, pp. 231 ff.) believes that Plautus increased the number of link monologues in his later plays, reducing some to bare essentials and expanding others so that they become an integral part of the action.

stage, often unseen; he is thus in an excellent position to serve as an eavesdropper.

Occasionally both Plautus and Terence avoid a long narrative monologue at the opening of the play by bringing in a "protatic" character, i.e., a character who is introduced to make exposition possible by means of dialogue and who then disappears from the scene, never to reappear.[16] But if the protatic character is a mere interlocutor who contributes nothing to the dialogue, the scene differs little from a monologue. Norwood criticizes Plautus for the "fault of sending out for exposition-purposes people who will not appear again,"[17] and admits that Sosia in Terence's *Andria* is "a thoroughly amateurish device for helping to convey information to the audience," a character "who interjects 'Hum!' 'Ha!' and the like at intervals, thereafter disappearing with entire abruptness from the play."[18] But a distinction must be drawn here between Plautus and Terence in their use of the protatic character. Sosia (*Andria*), Davus (*Phormio*), Philotis and Syra (*Hecyra*) are mere interlocutors who ask occasional questions and listen to a long narrative giving the situation at the beginning of each play. Philotis tells Parmeno (*Hec.* 110 f.) that he is more eager to confide in her than she is to listen and he admits sadly that talkativeness is his greatest vice. Donatus (*ad Hec.* 58) states that Philotis and Syra have no part in the *argumentum fabulae* and says that Terence preferred this to the use of an expository prologue. In *Eun.* 539 ff. Antipho is introduced to enable Chaerea to describe his off-stage escapade to a character on the stage rather than in a monologue to the audience, as in the Menandrian original (cf. Donatus, *ad Eun.* 539), and Antipho thus serves a purpose very similar to that of the protatic character.

Terence deserves praise for the laudable desire to substitute dramatic dialogue for the monologue of the Greek original but he has not been entirely successful with his protatic characters; there is no harm in the fact that they do not appear later in the play; the fault is that they are colorless and have no personality; they contribute nothing to the scene and are, as Donatus says, *extra argumentum*. Such scenes are not really dialogues but monologues which pretend to be dramatic.[19]

When we turn to the comedies of Plautus which contain protatic characters, we find a decided difference; although he uses the protatic

---

[16] Donatus defines the protatic character as one *quae semel inducta in principio fabulae in nullis deinceps fabulae partibus adhibetur* (*ad And.* praef. 1, 8), a *persona extra argumentum* to whom the events are narrated (*ad Phorm.* 35). In *Mil.* 948 f. the soldier explains why his parasite does not return.

[17] *Plautus and Terence*, p. 72.

[18] *The Art of Terence*, p. 32. We know from Donatus (*ad And.* 14) that the opening scene of Menander's *Andria* was a monologue; in the *Perinthia* the *senex* conversed with his wife.

[19] Cf. Gomme, *Essays in Greek History and Literature*, p. 269.

character proportionately less often than Terence,[20] he has succeeded in making the scenes dramatic. Grumio (*Mostellaria*) and Artotrogus (*Miles*) are valuable in delineating the characters of Tranio and Pyrgopolynices and they provide much incidental comedy. Thesprio (*Epidicus*) and Acanthio (*Mercator*), both running slaves as well as protatic characters, contribute much humorous banter and both bring important tidings which start the action of the play; this is an interesting deviation from the normal function of the character as a listener. Plautus must be credited with handling the protatic character far more skilfully than did Terence; or should we say that the true protatic character, defined by Donatus as a person *extra argumentum* to whom events are narrated, does not actually occur in Plautus?

## Eavesdropping and Asides

Eavesdropping as a stage device occurs not once but several times in each play of Plautus and Terence; the frequency of eavesdropping results from the fact that the action is continuous and the characters who utter link monologues remain on the stage and listen to an entrance monologue or dialogue before engaging in conversation with the newcomers.[21] In many instances the eavesdropper does not hear anything of importance to himself, but he has the opportunity to indulge in asides, usually of a comic nature. In other cases eavesdropping is essential to the success of the plot, and the hearer gains information of vital significance; e.g., when Pseudolus (*Pseud.* 594 ff.) overhears Harpax, he knows at once how to trick the *leno* and get the girl for his young master; he utters an exultant aside (600 ff.):

Hush, quiet! This fellow is my game, unless all gods and mortals desert me. Now I need a new plan; a new trick has suddenly occurred to me. I'll turn to this to begin with. Away with all those plans I started to carry out.

Similarly, the eavesdropping scene in *Bacch.* 842 ff. makes it possible for Chrysalus to carry out his second deception of his master, and the information about the plans of Lysidamus which Chalinus overhears (*Cas.* 437 ff.) enables Lysidamus' wife to plan a counter-intrigue.

Often eavesdropping scenes which contribute to the plot deviate from the normal pattern in that the characters who enter and are overheard

[20] Four comedies (*Epidicus, Mercator, Miles,* and *Mostellaria*) contain protatic characters, i.e., twenty per cent of his plays as against fifty per cent of Terence's (exclusive of Antipho in *Eun.* 539 ff.). Norwood (*Plautus* and *Terence*, p. 72) omits the *Miles* and wrongly includes the *Curculio* and the *Cistellaria*. The last named play is perhaps doubtful because of the corrupt state of the text but Gymnasium appears later in the action, and probably the *lena* also (cf. 374 ff.).

[21] Cf. Prescott, *CPh* 34 (1939), pp. 13 ff.; Hiatt, *Eavesdropping in Roman Comedy*, pp. 4 ff. Hiatt has made a useful study of the device in relation to the plot. Eavesdropping scenes are relatively much more frequent in Terence than in Plautus, occurring on an average about nine times in each of Plautus' plays, over fourteen times in Terence's.

depart from the stage without discovering the presence of the eaves-dropper, or the entering character eavesdrops on the conversation of men already on the stage. Plautus' technique in the *Epidicus* is interest-ing; at 181 Epidicus enters with a short monody, overhears a few words between Apoecides and Periphanes which give him an idea for a trick, then pretends to come in as a running slave, making a speech which he wants the two men to overhear.[22]

The eavesdropper often states at the conclusion of a link monologue that a certain character is coming and that he intends to withdraw and listen to the words of the other. So Epidicus, as he sees his master and a friend approaching (*Epid.* 101 ff.), says:

Look, there he is! Dejected, too. He's coming along with his friend Chaeribulus. I'll step back here where I can easily overhear their conver-sation.[23]

Such statements of intention to eavesdrop are more frequent in Plautus than in Terence. Entering characters at times take pains to avoid being overheard. Palaestrio says (*Mil.* 596 ff.) :

You stay inside for a while, Pleusicles; let me look around first to make sure there's no ambush for the meeting which we wish to hold. We need a safe place where no enemy can plunder our plans.

In this and similar passages[24] there is usually no other person on the stage. The situation is somewhat different, however, when Chaerea in *Eun.* 549 comes out and says:

There's no one here, is there? Not a one. And no one following me out? Not a person.

Antipho is on the stage at the time and listens to Chaerea's expression of delight before accosting him. Gomme states that the convention of overhearing a monologue or dialogue is acceptable enough, provided attention is not drawn to it, and he criticizes Terence for straining dramatic probability in *Eun.* 549 ff.[25] I doubt if the lack of verisimili-tude in this passage is as great as Gomme maintains. The Roman au-dience, accustomed to numerous eavesdropping scenes, would be no more conscious of dramatic improbability here than are modern au-diences of the numerous improbabilities which constantly occur in radio and movie programs. Moreover, the *Eunuchus* is Terence's most farci-

---

[22] See Duckworth, *T. Macci Plauti Epidicus*, p. 219; Hiatt, *Eavesdropping in Roman Comedy*, pp. 18, 34.

[23] Cf. the similar statements in *Aul.* 665 f., *Bacch.* 403 f., 610 f., *Cas.* 434 ff., *Most.* 429, *Pseud.* 410 ff., *Stich.* 197, *Trin.* 622 ff., *And.* 234 f., *Heaut.* 173 f., *Eun.* 545 ff.; see also Menander, *Sam.* 153. Two characters sometimes withdraw to listen to an entrance speech, e.g., *Men.* 570; Menander, *Georg.* 31 ff.

[24] See also *Mil.* 955 f., 1137, *Most.* 472 ff., *Stich.* 102, *Trin.* 146 f.

[25] *Essays in Greek History and Literature*, p. 256. Gomme believes that Menander avoided calling attention to conventions in this fashion and that the opening of the scene is Terence's own.

cal comedy and the humorous effect of Chaerea's mistaken belief that he
is alone should not be overlooked.

Scenes of eavesdropping, even if they do not contribute to the development of the plot, provide valuable incidental effects. Often emotions
of fear or joy, anxiety or confidence are momentarily aroused; this
happens especially when a *seruus currens* monologue is overheard, for
the slave is the bearer of important news and his delay in divulging the
information develops considerable suspense and anxiety. The attitude
and gestures of the eavesdropper would amuse the audience, as would
the side remarks which break the monotony of his silence (e.g., *Eun.*
232 ff., 391 ff.). An unusually lengthy case of eavesdropping occurs in
*Most.* 157-292, the famous dressing scene in which the conversation
of Scapha and Philematium is overheard by the lovesick Philolaches
who utters twenty amusing asides of approval or disapproval; e.g.,
228 ff.:

PHILEM.: If I keep my good name, I'll be rich enough.
PHILOL. (*aside*): If my father has to be sold, he'll be sold before I ever
   permit you to be in need or go begging while I'm alive.
SC.: What will become of the other men who love you?
PHILEM.: They'll love me all the more when they see that I'm grateful
   to my benefactor.
PHILOL. (*aside*): I wish the news of my father's death would be announced
   to me; I'd disinherit myself and make her my heir.
SC.: His property will soon be used up. Day and night, nothing but eating
   and drinking, and no one shows any thrift; it's outright stuffing.
PHILOL. (*aside*): By heaven, I'll begin by being thrifty with you; you won't
   have anything to eat or drink at my house for the next ten days.

In *And.* 236 ff., the asides of Mysis as she overhears the excited soliloquy of Pamphilus are much shorter and serve to portray her fears and
distress at the words of the other:

What's all this? (237)
Oh, dear me, what's this I hear? (240)
These words of his frighten me to death. (251)

Her final aside (264 ff.), much longer than the others, is overheard by
Pamphilus, who accosts her and the two then engage in conversation.
Such short asides are far more natural than the longer interruptions of
Philolaches but do not have the same comic value.

Asides are spoken not only by eavesdroppers but also by characters
engaged in conversation with others. Here the danger of improbability
is greater, especially if the aside is of any length, for it causes an unnatural interruption in the conversation. In this respect Terence is better
than Plautus, for his asides are usually limited to one or two verses,
though it is probable that many of Plautus' longer asides contain expansions for comic effect.[26] Conversational asides which refer to the

[26] Cf. Hiatt, *Eavesdropping in Roman Comedy*, pp. 25, n. 3.

tricking of the other person have been severely condemned. In *Cas.*
685 ff., Pardalisca, after arousing the fears of Lysidamus by the false
yarn about Casina's threats with a sword, says in an aside:

I'm deceiving him cleverly, for all the happenings I described to him are
false.

"Pardalisca's aside," says Norwood, "would provoke comment in a
madhouse."[27] But the aside in this instance is necessary since the deception has been planned off stage and the audience might otherwise
believe Pardalisca's tale to be true. It seems unwise to criticize ancient
practice by modern standards and asides referring to the progress of
trickery or deception are not uncommon in Roman comedy. Terence
makes very effective use of them in the *Adelphoe*:

I'm laughing at him; he says he's the first to know, and he's the only one
who doesn't know everything. (548)

I'm cutting his throat with his own sword. (958)

The aside by dramatic convention is audible to the spectators, but
usually not to the characters on the stage even when they stand near the
speaker.[28] At times, however, the aside is heard by other actors; at
least they realize that something has been said, even if they do not understand the words. Pamphilus, at the end of Mysis' aside, says (*And.*
267): "Who's speaking here?"[29] The overhearing of asides seems a
regular part of the ancient convention and should not be criticized as
unnatural. Plautus puts this feature of the aside to excellent use in *Mil.*
1348, where Palaestrio expresses his fear that the deception will be
discovered; when the soldier overhears his words, Palaestrio quick-
wittedly completes the thought in a different vein.

When an actor enters from the forum or harbor and fails to see another person on the stage, the latter is in a favorable position to eavesdrop and make comments on the side; cf. the asides of Hegio in the
*Captivi* when the parasite Ergasilus rushes in, threatening the imaginary people in his way:

This fellow's beginning a boxing match. (793)

What in the world do these threats mean? I can't understand it. (799)

This fellow must have got his confidence from a well-filled belly; I pity
the poor chap whose food has made him so boastful. (805 f.)

What's this joy that he's so happy to hand over to me? (829)[30]

---

[27] *Plautus and Terence*, p. 79.

[28] For the effectiveness of such asides for comedy, compare e.g., *Men.* 204, 206,
*Mil.* 33 ff., *Most.* 662 ff., *Poen.* 647 ff., 653 ff. (both of which refer to the deception of
Lycus), *And.* 746. In *Mil.* 20 ff., an aside of five lines, Artotrogus apparently walks
away from the soldier as he speaks; cf. 25: *ubi tu es?*

[29] Cf. *quis hic loquitur?* (*Capt.* 133, *Pseud.* 445, *And.* 783, *Heaut.* 517); *quis loquitur
prope?* (*Bacch.* 773), *quid illic solus secum loquitur?* (*Pseud.* 615), *quem ego hic
audiui loqui?* (*Hec.* 453).

[30] Cf. also the asides in the *seruus currens* scenes in *Asin.* 267 ff., *Merc.* 111 ff.,

One of the most amusing series of asides in Roman comedy is found in the *Amphitruo*; Mercury, watching the approach of Sosia, speaks aloud for the benefit of the slave, who overhears and comments on the words as he draws near the house; cf. 302 ff.:

ME.: Come, fists, it's a long time since you've had food. Yesterday seems ages ago when you put four men to sleep and stole their clothes.

SO. *(aside)*: I'm afraid that I'll change my name here and become Quintus instead of Sosia. He says he's put four men to sleep. I fear I'll increase the number.

ME.: There now, that's what I want.

SO. *(aside)*: He's girding himself; he's certainly getting ready.

ME.: He won't get away without a beating.

SO. *(aside)*: What man does he mean?

ME.: Whoever comes here shall eat my fists.

SO. *(aside)*: Get out! I don't care to eat at this time of night; I've just dined. If you're smart, you'll give that meal of yours to people who are hungry.

ME.: Not a bad weight to this fist!

SO *(aside)*: I'm done for; he's weighing his fists.

ME.: What if I just stroke him gently and put him to sleep?

SO. *(aside)*: You'll save my life, for I haven't slept for three whole nights. . . .

ME.: Someone is certainly talking near me.

SO. *(aside)*: I'm safe, he doesn't see me. He says that "someone" is talking; and my name is certainly Sosia.

In dialogue we occasionally find what may be termed "the double aside"; two persons eavesdrop on a conversation and make amusing comments on what they overhear. Just as Philolaches in *Most.* 157 ff. listens to the conversation of his sweetheart and her maid, so in *Poen.* 210 ff. Agorastocles and his slave Milphio overhear the words of Adelphasium and her sister; e.g., Adelphasium says (304 ff.):

A courtesan should garb herself with modesty rather than with purple; it's better for a girl to have modesty than gold. A dirty character soils a lovely dress worse than mud, while a dainty character makes even an ugly dress acceptable.

This trite moralizing calls forth the following offside conversation:

AG.: Hey, you, do you want to do a dainty and darling deed?

MI.: Of course.

AG.: Can you obey me?

MI.: I can.

AG.: Then go home and hang yourself.

MI.: Why?

AG.: Because you'll never again hear so many words as sweet as these.

---

*Stich.* 274 ff., *Trin.* 1008 ff., *And.* 338 ff., *Eun.* 643 ff., *Phorm.* 179 ff., *Ad.* 299 ff. In some instances the slave's monologue is not interrupted by asides; cf. *Curc.* 280 ff., *Most.* 348 ff.

In a situation such as this we are obviously to think of the two separate dialogues as simultaneous. As to the value of such asides, Prescott says, "the dialogue between the two girls would be a dull affair without the interspersed comments of the lovesick young man and the dry cynicism of the unsympathetic slave."[31] Perhaps it would be more appropriate to say that much of the conversation between the two girls has no other purpose than to make possible the amusing comments of the two eavesdroppers.

## Entrance and Exit Announcements

The emphasis upon plot in Roman comedy demanded clarity in situation and character. The identity of the actors is usually made known at their first entrance, or shortly before. The name may be mentioned casually in a conversation prior to a person's appearance (e.g., *Men.* 173), or in an announcement of his approach (e.g., *Most.* 311). Such announcements are often made by a character at the end of a monologue (usually a link monologue),[32] and are presented in a somewhat artificial and conventional form, e.g., the statement of Peniculus in *Men.* 108:

> There he is. I see Menaechmus, he's coming outside.

Stereotyped phrases such as *eccum uideo; uenit (adest, incedit,* or *egreditur)* are common; they helped to keep the thread of the action clear to the audience,[33] and were doubtless of great value also to the actors; we are, I believe, justified in looking upon such formulas as helpful cues to aid the actors in their entries. Occasionally introductions by means of monologues are handled somewhat crudely; in *Rud.* 892 ff. Daemones comes from his house, tells that his wife is suspicious of his attitude toward the two girls he has befriended, and says (897 f.):

> I wonder what my slave Gripus is doing, who left last night to do some deep-sea fishing.

Then Daemones returns to his house for lunch. Both his entrance and his exit are weakly motivated, and the scene obviously serves to provide a mechanical introduction of Gripus, who appears in 906. But, as we have seen, the monologue is useful also for the doubling of roles.[34]

---

[31] *CPh* 34 (1939), p. 23. For other examples of the "double aside," cf. *Pers.* 551 ff., *Poen.* 1187 ff., *Pseud.* 193 ff., *Heaut.* 397 ff., *Eun.* 1053 ff.

[32] For mention of a character by name at the end of an exit monologue, cf. *And.* 226; in *Most.* 82, Grumio refers in an exit monologue to the approach of his master's son, who appears immediately after; we do not learn the youth's name until it is mentioned by Philematium in 167. Some characters in the comedies of Plautus are left unnamed; these are usually minor roles, but not always; e.g., the *matrona* and the *senex* in the *Menaechmi* have no names, and the *senex* in the *Casina,* named Lysidamus in the scene-headings of the Ambrosian Palimpsest, is nowhere mentioned by name in the play; cf. Duckworth, *CPh* 33 (1938), pp. 267 ff.

[33] Cf. Key, *The Introduction of Characters by Name,* pp. 45 ff., 56 f.

[34] See above, n. 14.

When two characters meet and converse, either may call the other by name at some point in their talk; this is a far more natural method of introduction and occurs frequently in both Plautus and Terence. Another realistic device for bringing out the name of a character is for a person to ask the question directly, but this method is rare in Plautus and does not appear in Terence at all; e.g., Pseudolus meets the servant of the soldier (*Pseud.* 604) and after fifty verses of verbal fencing learns his name (653 f.) :

PS.: But what *is* your name?
HA.: Harpax.
PS.: Get out of here, Harpax. I don't like your name. You won't get inside the house, by heaven! We want no Harpies here.[35]

Just as the majority of the characters were named at their first entrance, so to a somewhat less degree they were named when they made subsequent entries. Both Plautus and Terence were careful to differentiate the characters throughout the course of the action.

The formulaic expression already mentioned (e.g., "There he is; I see him coming from the house") often involves the idea of an opportune meeting. By dramatic convention, characters are on the stage or enter just when they are needed. So, frequently, the formula is not merely *eccum uideo* or *eccum egreditur*, but such phrases as *in tempore, per tempus, optume,* or *opportune* are added.[36] Plautus and Terence seem conscious of the element of chance in such meetings; e.g.:

You've both come at the most opportune moment (*optuma opportunitate, Merc.* 964, cf. *And.* 345).

You couldn't have come at a more fitting time (*per tempus, Men.* 139).

You meet me at an excellent and opportune moment (*bene opportuneque, Mil.* 898, cf. *Pers.* 101).

You're the very person I was looking for. (*Ad.* 461, cf. *Pers.* 300 f.)

In *Mil.* 1132 ff. Palaestrio says:

Now I need to have Acroteleutium appear, or her maid, or Pleusicles. Jupiter! How old Nick-of-Time (*Commoditas*) aids me in every respect. I see the very ones I wanted, all coming out of the house next door.

Gomme, who rightly states that Plautus handles comic conventions with a gayer spirit than Terence, cites this passage as an illustration of the manner in which the older poet laughed at "the conventions which he did not understand, or the value of which he did not appreciate."[37] It

---

[35] See also *Curc.* 419 f., *Merc.* 474, 516; cf. Key, *The Introduction of Characters by Name*, pp. 34 ff.

[36] E.g., *in tempore* (*Capt.* 836, *Poen.* 1138, *And.* 532, *Phorm.* 464) ; *per tempus* (*Bacch.* 844, *Hec.* 622) ; *optume*, very frequent in Plautus (*Pers.* 543, *Rud.* 705, 1209, *Hec.* 246, *Heaut.* 757) ; *opportune* (*Pers.* 101, *And.* 345). *Commodum* and *commode* are similarly used; cf. *Mil.* 1198, *Rud.* 309, *Trin.* 400 f.

[37] *Essays in Greek History and Literature*, p. 258. Norwood (*Plautus and Terence*, pp. 92 f.) is less sympathetic; he cites Palaestrio's remark as an example of construction that is "childishly obvious."

is very likely that Plautus is ridiculing the "opportune meeting" convention in *Mil.* 1132 ff., but there is no evidence that he did not understand its value. In general, he handles the entrance formulas with more variety and flexibility than does Terence who, Gomme believes, "cannot handle these entrances naturally."

Often coupled with the entrance formula described above is another, frequent in both Greek and Roman comedy; this may be called "the convention of the creaking door." The following illustrations are typical:

I'll stop talking; the door creaked; there he is, he's coming out. . . .
(*Amph.* 496 f.; cf. *Aul.* 665, *Phorm.* 840, *Ad.* 264)

But our door creaked; who in the world is coming out? (*Bacch.* 234; cf. *Pers.* 404, *Heaut.* 173 f.)

But my next-door neighbor's door creaked. I'll hush. (*Mil.* 410; cf. *Curc.* 486, *Poen.* 741)

The usual expression is *crepuit* (or *concrepuit*) *ostium* (or *foris*). Plautus sometimes varies it by saying "the door is opening" (e.g., *Amph.* 955, *Mil.* 1198, *Pers.* 80, 300) and "the door made a noise" (*Mil.* 1377). These passages doubtless provided a helpful cue to the actors on the stage that another character was about to enter from one of the houses.

Norwood's comment upon the convention is most amusing: "Nothing is more frequent than the warning: 'But hush! The door is rattling. Someone is coming out!' In fact, this same 'Ostium' is a leading Plautine character: small wonder that Phaedromus in *Curculio* (16) inquires after its health! Had it succumbed to the fever, Plautine Comedy would have shared its funeral pyre."[38] Norwood's facetious wit and unsympathetic attitude towards Plautus have seldom been displayed to better advantage, but his words are most misleading to the general reader unacquainted with the facts. Two remarks are in order: (1) The passage in the *Curculio* has nothing to do with the convention; Phaedromus' greeting to the door, ridiculed by Palinurus in the next speech, is the beginning of his attempt to meet Planesium; he pours wine on the *fores* to make them favorably disposed to him (80, 87 ff.) and finally sings a song to the doors, begging them to send out his sweetheart (147 ff.); this is the earliest paraclausithyron, or serenade to the closed door, in Latin literature. (2) The *ostium* can scarcely be called a "Plautine character"; the formula of the creaking door appears in every play

---

[38] *Plautus and Terence*, p. 82. Miss Haight also looks upon the door as a character in the plays of Plautus (*The Symbolism of the House Door*, pp. 69 ff.) but she analyzes (pp. 77 ff.) its structural value in the plots of the comedies with far greater understanding, and says (p. 87): "These emotional reactions to the old house door show how it takes on personality, indeed, has become one of the characters on the stage." It is difficult, however, to accept her conclusion (p. 91) that Plautus' "tremendous *vis comica* centers in the house door."

of Terence, and frequently in Menander as well.[39] Norwood is here blaming Plautus for a convention that was accepted by Greek and Roman dramatists alike. Actually, as was true of the protatic character, Plautus is more at ease with the convention than is Terence, for he uses it to assist in trickery (*Mil.* 328 f., *Most.* 507 ff.) and for comic effect; e.g., *Pseud.* 130 f.:

CA.: The slavedealer's door cracked.
PS.: I only wish it had been his legs.

For other jokes on the convention, see *Poen.* 609 f., *Pseud.* 952 f.

In everyday life the Greeks and Romans knocked before entering another's house; on the stage, knocking was a convenient method of summoning a person from a house. An actor states: "I'll knock at the door" (*foris pultabo*) and the character desired appears with the words: "Who is knocking?" or "Why do you knock?" or "Who is breaking down the door?" Sometimes the person wanted is already outside, but the other either does not know it (e.g., *Merc.* 130 ff.) or pretends not to know (*Mil.* 1250 ff.). Colloquial formulas of this sort are frequent in Aristophanes and later Greek comedy, as well as in Plautus, but are rare in Terence (cf. *Heaut.* 410 ff., *Ad.* 632 ff.). Boisterous scenes of knocking gave Plautus an opportunity to increase the farcical effect of a scene, e.g., *Bacch.* 578 ff.:

PARASITE (*to* SLAVE): You know which house it is; knock. Go right up to the door. (SLAVE *knocks gently.*) Come back from there. How the rascal knocks! You can eat a loaf of bread three feet wide, but you don't know how to knock on doors. (PARASITE *pounds furiously.*) Is anyone in the house? Hallo, anyone here? Is there anyone to open this door? Anyone coming out?
PISTOCLERUS (*comes angrily from house*): What goes on here? What's this pounding? What the devil do you mean by using up your strength on another person's door in this manner? You almost smashed the panels! What do you want?

Colloquial greetings reflect everyday speech and give an air of naturalness to the action on the stage. Among the various greetings used by Plautus and Terence, those appearing most frequently are "Good day" (*salue, saluos sis*), "I'm glad you've arrived safely" (*saluom uenisse gaudeo*), "How's your health?" (*ut uales?*), "How goes it?" (*quid fit? quid agitur?*) "How do you do?" (*quid agis?*). To such greetings the usual response is "The gods bless you" (*di te ament*), "The gods grant your wishes" (*di dent quae uelis*, etc.), or merely

---

[39] Cf. Duckworth, *CW* 41 (1947-48), p. 90, n. 45. Mooney (*The House-Door on the Ancient Stage*, pp. 34 ff.) gives the examples in Plautus and Terence of *crepuit* and *concrepuit*. Even in the fragmentary *Samia* of Menander there are five references to the door creaking or being opened noisily (85 f., 151 f., 210, 222, 324). See Beare, *The Roman Stage*, pp. 279 ff., who argues convincingly that the doors on the stage opened inward rather than outward, as maintained by Mooney and others.

*salue* (very common in Terence). At times a greeting is not answered; this seems to be the regular procedure when a slave or servant greets his master (e.g., *Epid.* 126 ff., *Merc.* 809). In *Phorm.* 286 f. Demipho replies to the greeting of the slave (*salue: saluom te aduenisse gaudeo*) with the following ironical response:

Oh, excellent guardian, good day, true pillar of the household, to whom I entrusted my son upon my departure!

There is similar irony in *And.* 846. In the *Adelphoe* Demea's failure to return the greeting of Micio (80 ff.) serves to portray his rudeness and the distressed state of his mind.[40] The greeting *quid agis?* does not appear in Terence but is common in Plautus, often with a jest on the literal meaning of the phrase ("What are you doing?"); cf. the answer of the parasite in *Men.* 138: "I'm holding my good genius by the hand"; cf. *Most.* 719, *Truc.* 126. In general Terence used fewer formulas of greeting than did Plautus and in this respect probably reflected more closely the practice of the Greek playwrights.

Colloquial expressions of departure include "Farewell" (*uale, ualeas*), "Good luck" (*bene sit tibi*), "Have a good walk" (*bene ambula*), "Nothing else, is there?" (*numquid uis? numquid me uis? numquid aliud?*). This last is at times a mere leave-taking formula, but in many cases it is not limited to this function alone but (1) paves the way for witty replies and jests, or (2), taken as a real question, motivates the addition of instructions or information of value to the dramatic structure of the play. This employment of the formula is found more often in Plautus than in Terence, and in many instances the additional material is undoubtedly a Plautine insertion; this seems especially likely when there is rather pointless jesting after the formula, and the passage closes with a second *numquid uis* (e.g., *Pers.* 692-709). In other words, Plautus uses the *numquid uis* formula as one means of delaying a departure and providing an opportunity for the introduction of supplementary matter.[41]

Not only did the Roman playwrights keep the identity of their characters clear throughout the action, but they took pains also to make the whereabouts of the actors known to the audience when they were absent from the stage and to motivate their entrances and exits. The con-

---

[40] Donatus (*ad Ad.* 81) points out that in the Greek original Demea did reply to the greeting; Terence's change here is an improvement; cf. 883, where Demea, testing out his new way of life, says to the slave Syrus: *O Syre noster, salue! quid fit? quid agitur?*

[41] Delayed exits are numerous in Plautus and often the material introduced is obviously a Roman addition to the thread of the Greek plot; such insertions consist of humorous matter and explanations of the plot which may have been necessitated by changes in adaptation. Delayed exits followed by insertions of this type do not appear in Terence. For a discussion of Plautus' treatment of delayed exits and the function of the *numquid uis* formula in Roman comedy, see Hough, *CPh* 35 (1940), pp. 39 ff.; *AJPh* 66 (1945), pp. 282 ff.

ventional significance of the wing-entrances was a valuable aid in this respect, for a person going off the stage to the right of the spectators would be assumed to be going to the forum, in the opposite direction, to the harbor or the country. But characters frequently say as they leave the stage where they are going and why; e.g., Tranio in *Most.* 66 f. announces:

I want to go to the Piraeus to get some fish for supper.

And Demipho says in *Phorm.* 311 ff.:

I'll go into the house and pay my respects to the household gods; then I'll go to the forum and ask some friends of mine to aid me in this matter so that I'll be prepared when Phormio comes.

It was a fixed convention that if a character returned to the stage after an absence he must return by the door through which he had departed, or else he must explain why he appeared at a different entrance. In the passage cited above from the *Phormio*, the audience knows that Demipho has gone from his house to the forum, presumably by a rear exit, and therefore is not puzzled when he returns from the forum with his three friends (348 ff.).[42] Characters often explain their off-stage movements, e.g., Tranio (*Most.* 928 ff.) tells Theopropides that he will go to the country, but in an aside to the audience says that he will go around by the back door (*per posticum*) and join his cronies; when he appears later (1041) he explains that he entered the house through the garden and led the others forth to safety.[43]

There are a few violations of the re-entry rule in both Plautus and Terence, and these have been used to support theories of *retractatio* or *contaminatio*, to show the changes introduced by the Roman playwrights into the Greek originals, or to illustrate their carelessness in not giving sufficient information. These views assume that the Greek orginals were flawless in their handling of entrances and exits—a hypothesis that cannot be substantiated. At times the violation may not exist, but may result from a failure to visualize the action on the stage. *Curc.* 524 ff. is perhaps an instance of this type; Curculio is said to leave with Planesium *peregre*, but in 591 ff. they enter from Phaedromus' house. Such a violation is not confusing to the spectators, who know that Curculio was conducting the girl to Phaedromus;[44] the actors could leave the stage and then enter the house from the rear; actually, even this assumption is unnecessary, for Curculio and Planesium might pretend to depart and then dart quickly into Phaedromus' house from

---

[42] It is hardly likely that a musical interlude took place after 314 during which Demipho came out of his house in silence and departed in the direction of the forum; this is the suggestion of Johnston, *Exits and Entrances in Roman Comedy*, p. 112.

[43] Cf. the references to movements *per hortum*, e.g., *Cas.* 613 f., *Epid.* 660, *Pers.* 445 f., *Stich.* 437 f., 451 f., 614.

[44] Cf. Conrad, *UCCPh* 2 (1916), p. 300.

the stage when the slavedealer and the banker were engaged in conversation. Another apparent violation of the convention occurs in *Stich.*
143; Antipho says he will go and inform his friends of the resolution
of his daughters; such a statement usually implies that a person goes
to the forum (cf. *Men.* 700, *Phorm.* 312 ff.), but since much of Antipho's conversation with his daughters was pretense to confuse them
(cf. 84 ff.), and the friends were doubtless imaginary, we may assume
that he actually left, not by the forum, but by the harbor exit. At 402
Epignomus enters from the harbor, having already met Antipho, and
Antipho himself comes from the harbor in 505 with Pamphilippus, the
other son-in-law. Neither these nor other such violations of the re-entry
convention are sufficiently serious to perplex the audience.[45]

The entrances and exits are in general adequately motivated. As
Legrand points out,[46] complete motivation is hardly necessary. In both
Athens and Rome people were in the habit of strolling about the streets
and gazing at the shops. Since the stage represents a street, people may
come and go as in real life, without clearly defined aims. When two characters enter together engaged in conversation, it is customary for motivation of entrance to be omitted; it would seem unnatural to interrupt
the conversation for such a purpose. Also, we can hardly expect a character to account for his appearance every time he comes from his house
(e.g., *Epid.* 382, 675, where no reasons are given for the entrance).
Gomme believes that it is much better not to call attention to the exits
and entrances and prefers Menander's frequent lack of motivation to
Terence's attempt to explain the movements of his characters.[47] But
Terence in general has less motivation than Plautus.

In several passages Terence's handling of entrances and exits lacks
clarity, and editors and critics fail to agree on the staging of the scenes.
Does Simo leave the stage at *And.* 171 (cf. his words: "You go ahead,
I'll follow") and return, or does the arrival of Davus postpone Simo's
departure until 205 (cf. Donatus, *ad And.* 173)?[48] Does Pamphilus

---

[45] Cf. *Bacch.* 348, where Nicobulus departs to the forum; in 770 he enters from his
house; in *Asin.* 248 Argyrippus goes to the forum (cf. 245) and at 591 enters from
Cleareta's house (cf. Hough, *AJPh* 58, 1937, pp. 25 ff., who explains the violation as
resulting from Plautus' use of two Greek originals); in *Ad.* 354 Canthara departs to
summon a midwife; are the two women in the house at 486, when the baby is born?
Conrad (*UCCPh* 2, 1916, p. 300) says: "Terence's mastery of dramatic technique is
exhibited in the omission of the unessential scene of Canthara's return." Is this the
reason why Hegio does not reappear after *Ad.* 609, when he enters Sostrata's house
with Micio?

[46] Cf. Legrand-Loeb, *The New Greek Comedy*, p. 365. Bennett (*The Motivation of
Exits*, pp. 39 ff.) finds the exits all adequately motivated with the exception of a few
passages suspected of contamination or later corruption; cf., however, Clifford, *CJ*
26 (1930-31), p. 608. For a few instances in which motivation of entrance is inadequate or lacking, cf. Fields, *The Technique of Exposition*, pp. 189 ff.

[47] *Essays in Greek History and Literature*, pp. 254 f.

[48] Cf. Harsh, *CW* 28 (1934-35), p. 163, who calls this "an abandoned exit-motivation."
There is nothing objectionable about a change of mind; in *Mil.* 582 ff. (a passage

make his exit at *And.* 300 and return at 311, or does he remain on the stage?[49] In the *Eunuchus*, do Parmeno and Phaedria go indoors before Thais' speech (197-206) and return after her exit (as modern editors assume), or do they start toward Phaedria's house and resume their conversation at 207 (as Donatus, *ad Eun.* 197, implies)?[50] Does Dorias in *Eun.* 628 go in with the jewelry? Probably not, for in 656 she seems ignorant of the event indoors and later is ordered to take in the casket of jewels (726). In the *Adelphoe*, where does Demea go at 140? Presumably to the forum (cf. 355 ff.), but the reason for his departure is not clear. And at 854 does he go in as Micio suggests and return at 855, thereby leaving the stage momentarily vacant, or does he disregard Micio's words and remain on the stage to give expression to his sudden decision to follow Micio's example? Such a change in his philosophy, even though pretended (cf. *Ad.* 877 f., 958, 968 ff.; see also Donatus, *ad Ad.* 992), could scarcely have occurred instantaneously, and this perhaps implies that Demea entered and returned from Micio's house,[51] but many scholars believe that he did not leave the stage.

In all these cases, the difficulty seems to lie, not with the motivation of entrances and exits as such, but with Terence's failure to visualize the stage business as successfully as Plautus had done.[52] Perhaps it would be more accurate to say that he had less inclination than Plautus to write into the text announcements which might be helpful as stage directions to the actors (and to the modern reader). In whatever manner the problems mentioned above were handled in actual presentation, there would be little in their staging to perplex the Roman audience.

## Problems of Outdoor Staging

Since the stage of Greek and Roman comedy regularly represented a street in front of two or three houses and there were no changes of scenery, it was necessary for all action to take place out of doors and in

---

often used as an argument for contamination) Sceledrus contemplates flight and then decides to return home; cf. Harsh, *Studies in Dramatic "Preparation,"* p. 67, n. 9.

[49] Sargeaunt (Loeb translation), Bennett (*The Motivation of Exits*, p. 53), Norwood (*Art of Terence*, p. 19) all believe that Pamphilus entered the house at 300; cf. also Duckworth, *The Complete Roman Drama*, II, p. 153. But there is no mention of any departure and it seems more likely that Pamphilus remains on the stage, where he is seen by Charinus in 311; cf. Harsh, *CW* 28 (1934-35), p. 162.

[50] The commands of Phaedria in 207 f. repeat those of 189 and there seems no reason for the assumed exit and re-entry. Phaedria says (187) that he will go to the country and leaves in the next scene (224).

[51] Cf. Clifford, *CJ* 26 (1930-31), pp. 617 ff., who suggests that in the original there may have been a chorus (possibly composed of wedding guests) which bridged a pause at this point; see Harsh, *CW* 28 (1934-35), p. 163, n. 20.

[52] Miss Clifford (*CJ* 26, 1930-31, pp. 609 ff.) criticizes also the aimless movements of Charinus and Byrria in the *Andria* and of Thraso and Gnatho in the *Eunuchus*, and believes that these weaknesses occur in passages where Terence is making changes in the Greek originals; see, however, Harsh, *CW* 28 (1934-35), pp. 161 ff., who suggests that so-called "blunders" of this sort may have existed in the Greek originals.

one particular location. Many situations arose which to the modern reader, accustomed to indoor scenes and frequent shifting of scenery, seem often unrealistic and improbable. That the ancient playwrights themselves were not unconscious of the limitations of the setting is shown by the various devices which they used to bring on the stage both action and conversation which normally would take place elsewhere.

In some respects, the setting would seem far more natural to the ancient audiences than to us. Both the Greeks and the Romans were accustomed to spending much time out of doors. If the setting made it necessary for characters to come from their houses and talk over confidential matters in the street, it is very possible that the street offered more privacy for such discussion than was afforded by their houses, where a remark in one room might easily be overheard in another room by slaves or other inquisitive persons.[53]

It seems rather improbable, at first sight, that the characters in the plays have so little knowledge of their neighbors next door (e.g., the *Miles*),[54] or are able to engage in amorous activities in the adjoining house with so little fear of detection; in many instances a young man falls in love with a girl next door, either a courtesan (*Asinaria, Bacchides, Truculentus, Eunuchus, Phormio, Hecyra*)[55] or a pseudo-courtesan whose parentage is later revealed (*Curculio, Poenulus, Andria*), or he seduces a girl of good family who lives next door (*Adelphoe*). Lecherous old reprobates like Lysidamus (*Casina*) and Demipho (*Mercator*) plan to hide their lady-loves next door to the house where their wives dwell; the wife and the mistress of Menaechmus likewise live in adjoining houses. Such proximity was required by the stage-setting, but the nature of the ancient house, with rooms opening on interior courts, made for greater seclusion than is possible today in most residential streets. The ancient convention thus is less lacking in realism than is often believed.

Furthermore, we are justified in looking upon the scene represented by the stage not merely as the space in front of two or three houses, but as a much larger area, a street of indefinite length.[56] Thus the numerous

---

[53] Cf. Flickinger, *The Greek Theater and its Drama*, pp. 237 ff.; Johnston, *Exits and Entrances in Roman Comedy*, p. 17. For an instance of eavesdropping inside the house, cf. *Phorm.* 866 ff.; Geta hurries from the house excited by the news he has overheard. It is not unnatural for characters to rush from the house under the stress of emotion; cf. Legrand-Loeb, *The New Greek Comedy*, pp. 363 f.

[54] The fact that Pyrgopolynices in the *Miles* does not know that Periplectomenus is a bachelor makes possible the second deception of the play, in which the supposed wife of Periplectomenus pretends to be madly in love with the soldier.

[55] Donatus (*ad Eun.* 359) says that in Terence courtesans are often made neighbors to young men "that this may be the first enticement of love" (*ut haec prima sit amoris illecebra*); the real reason is undoubtedly the stage-setting.

[56] Cf. Legrand-Loeb, *The New Greek Comedy*, p. 366: "the area in which the actors move about is an epitome, so to speak, of a much larger space."

instances of eavesdropping and asides and the failure to see or overhear other characters become less improbable. If we keep in mind that the street scene is elastic, passages which have caused confusion among critics and have given rise to various conflicting theories of composition will present less difficulty. For instance, in *Amph.* 551 ff., Amphitruo arrives with Sosia and scolds his slave for the fantastic yarn about a second Sosia; Alcumena comes out and delivers a monody (633-653), which they apparently do not hear, for they continue their conversation before they see and accost her. Certainly there is no reason to believe that we have two versions of Amphitruo's arrival at home, clumsily joined together by the process of contamination. Amphitruo and Sosia in 551 ff. are not in front of the house (cf. *hic* and *domi*, 562, 593), but on the contrary are making their way along the street from the harbor to their home, and are still some distance from the house.[57]

Other passages are to be interpreted in a similar fashion; in *Stich.* 150 ff., Panegyris calls out Crocotium and tells her to summon Gelasimus, the parasite. Gelasimus appears and speaks a long and amusing monologue on his famished condition (155-195), after which Crocotium says:

Here's that parasite I'm supposed to bring back. I'll listen to what he's saying before I speak to him.

She listens to the rest of his monologue and accosts him in 239. But apparently she did not see or hear him during the first forty lines of his monologue when he was coming along the street. Nixon suggests[58] as stage business that she was chatting with another slave at the doorway of Antipho's house; this is possible but hardly necessary, and the assumption of others that she left the stage at 154 and returned in 196 is even less attractive; such silences are not unusual while a monologue or dialogue is being spoken elsewhere on the stage; cf. *Men.* 753-808, where Menaechmus II stands apart and apparently does not hear the song of the *senex* and the dialogue of the *senex* and the *matrona* which follows. In like manner, Theopropides in *Most.* 566-609 and 684-784 is silent and remote from Tranio, who converses first with the moneylender and then with Simo; in neither case does Theopropides overhear the conversation and, as Prescott says, "it is probable that a stage manager faced a difficult problem in keeping Theopropides plausibly occupied during this long period of complete aloofness from the action."[59]

---

[57] Cf. E. T. M(errill), *CPh* 11 (1916), pp. 340 f., who believes that the dialogue of Amphitruo and Sosia and the song of Alcumena are to be thought of as taking place simultaneously. Prescott (*CPh* 8, 1913, pp. 18 ff.) suggests that the scene shifts to the harbor at 551, but such a change of scene would be without parallel in Roman comedy.

[58] *Plautus*, v, p. 25.

[59] *CPh* 32 (1937), p. 207. Such silences are easier to handle when the actor is an attentive listener and can relieve the silence by occasional byplay; cf. e.g., *Capt.*

There is no indication that Phaniscus and Pinacium overhear the conversation of Theopropides and Tranio in *Most.* 904-932, but they are busily engaged in knocking at the door and perhaps pretending to converse *sotto voce*. So in *Amph.* 633 ff. (mentioned above), Amphitruo and Sosia could feign a conversation during Alcumena's monody as they draw near the house.

The playwrights met the limitations of the stage-setting by presenting on the stage various types of off-stage conversation and action: (1) Two characters enter, usually from a side entrance, and their opening words make clear that the dialogue heard by the audience is the continuation or the conclusion of one begun before their appearance; e.g., Stratippocles says:

> I've told you the whole story, Chaeribulus, and I've given you a complete account of my passions and my pains. (*Epid.* 104 f.; cf. *Aul.* 682, *Cist.* 631, *Mil.* 874 f.)

Commands and questions likewise enable the spectators to pick up the thread of the earlier discourse:

> Be sure to remember my instructions. (*Mil.* 354)
> Do you say he ran off because he was afraid of his father? (*Phorm.* 315)

Terence usually begins these dialogues with a question[60] rather than with a statement about the nature of the earlier discussion and his procedure seems the more effective. Often such conversations are brought before the audience with great naturalness; cf. the words of Hegio (*Ad.* 447):

> Immortal gods, Geta, what disgraceful conduct you relate to me!

The audience knows at once the nature of the conversation already held and is spared a repetition of the information which it has already acquired from the earlier stage action (cf. Donatus, *ad loc.*).

At times the characters on entering make statements or ask questions which have obviously been postponed for the benefit of the spectators (e.g., *Men.* 230 ff., *Phorm.* 567 ff.) [61] and Plautus sometimes finds it necessary, when the details of a deception are unusually involved, to repeat the instructions even though the audience knows them already and the characters have been informed off stage, e.g., the coaching of the conspirators in *Mil.* 874-946, where Periplectomenus begins the conversation by saying "I've explained the whole matter to you in detail."[62] In *Rud.* 1265 ff. Plesidippus asks questions which belong more

---

649-696, in which Aristophontes listens in silence while Hegio threatens Tyndarus, and *Phorm.* 348-446, where the attentive listening of the three *aduocati* and their nods of approval or disapproval would be effective during their long silence.

[60] Cf. *And.* 301, *Eun.* 391, *Phorm.* 348, *Hec.* 415, 451, *Ad.* 517.

[61] Cf. Legrand-Loeb, *The New Greek Comedy*, pp. 366 f.

[62] Cf. also *Poen.* 547 ff., and see Hough, *AJPh* 60 (1939), pp. 422 ff. There is often considerable humor in the repeated coaching of persons on the stage.

properly to the off-stage conversation but he is excited and eager to hear again the good news:

Tell me everything again, my darling Trachalio, my freedman, my patron rather, nay, my father. Has Palaestra really discovered her father and her mother?

His series of questions makes possible the amusing repetition of *censeo* in Trachalio's replies.

(2) Another method of bringing on the stage conversations which belong elsewhere is to have an actor, as he comes out of the house, talk to other characters who remain inside. The words spoken at the doorway usually take the form of instructions or advice or threats or statements of intention. This device helps to bring about closer communication between the street and indoors. The one-sided conversations in their normal form are as follows:

I'll come back inside, if I find out what I want from these fellows. (*Capt.* 251 f.; cf. *Merc.* 962 f., *Poen.* 615)

Take care of everything inside. I'll soon be home again. (*Pers.* 405)

Wherever he is, I'll find him and bring him to you. Don't worry, my dear. (*And.* 684 f.; cf. *Ad.* 209, 636 f.)

Everything is ready at our house, as I told you, Sostrata. (*Ad.* 787 f.)[63]

If the old man asks for me, say that I've gone to the harbor to inquire about Pamphilus' arrival. Do you hear what I say, Scirtus? Tell him if he asks, but if he doesn't don't say a word so I'll have this excuse to use some other time. (*Hec.* 76 ff.)

These speeches are often expanded by Plautus for comic effect; cf. Menaechmus' instructions to his wife (*Men.* 110-124), those of Periplectomenus to his servants (*Mil.* 156-165), of Antipho to his slaves (*Stich.* 58-67), and occasionally a surprise turn is given to a speech when the door closes and the actor utters his real intention:

Yes, you've done your part; now I must do mine. As far as the money is concerned, you can rest easy (*the door closes*) for it's gone already. (*Epid.* 337 f.; cf. *Trin.* 39 ff.)

Terence, although using this convention with relatively greater frequency than Plautus, omits humorous material (with the exception of *Hec.* 76 ff.) and makes the one-sided conversation more natural by keeping it short, usually only two or three verses, sometimes less (cf. *Phorm.* 51).[64] Only occasionally does such a speech exceed the limits of probability, e.g., when Phidippus calls to his daughter inside the house just before the birth of the baby (*Hec.* 243 ff.) and just after (623 ff.).

[63] Donatus (*ad loc.*) comments on the convention as follows: "The poet wishes to show from the words of Micio as he departs the conversation which he had inside with Sostrata."

[64] The longest are *And.* 481-485, *Hec.* 76-80, *Ad.* 511-516. The *Andria* passage falls in a special category, for Terence is here treating the convention in an unusual manner; this will be discussed at the end of the chapter.

Variations on the usual one-sided speeches occur when a character already on the stage goes to a door and calls to someone inside (e.g., *Aul.* 268 ff., *Mil.* 522 ff., *Rud.* 1205 ff.), and when the words of a character indoors are heard by those on the stage (cf. *Aul.* 390 ff., *Most.* 515, *Ad.* 543); to the latter category belong the cries of suffering, the labor pains of those who are supposed to give birth to babies behind the scenes (*Aul.* 691 f., *And.* 473, *Ad.* 486 f.; cf. *Hec.* 318), and here the existence of an artificial stage convention is most readily apparent.

(3) The strict observance of the unity of place made it impossible for the comic playwrights to change the stage-setting in the course of a play, but Plautus did not hesitate to portray on the stage certain scenes which to us today seem more appropriate as indoor scenes. These are episodes of banqueting and festivity which are rich in comic values: *Asin.* 828-941, in which Demaenetus, dining with his son and Philaenium, is discovered by his wife and a parasite and dragged home ignominiously; *Pers.* 757-858, scenes of drinking and dancing which complete the discomfiture of the *leno* Dordalus; *Stich.* 683-775, scenes of wine, women, and song which have no structural value, but which conclude the play with a farcical orgy unparalleled in Roman comedy. The most amusing series of scenes of this type is found in the *Mostellaria*: here Plautus presents a dressing scene (157 ff.) in which Scapha helps Philematium adorn herself with cosmetics and jewelry for her lover Philolaches, who eavesdrops on the conversation and utters numerous asides; finally he accosts her (293), and a banquet is prepared (308 ff.); his friend Callidamates, already intoxicated, arrives with a girl, falls asleep immediately (344 ff.), while the others continue their party until Tranio approaches with the news that the father of Philolaches has disembarked and is on his way home; a scene of laughable confusion ensues as they hurry to move the banquet indoors, while Tranio stands on guard outside to keep the *senex* from entering the house. This combination of dressing and banquet scenes perhaps exceeds the liberty which Plautus elsewhere takes in putting indoor scenes on the stage, but it enlivens the comedy with passages of unforgettable gaiety.

There can be no doubt that these banquets were enacted on the stage in front of the house, as instructions are given to slaves to bring out food and drink and arrange the tables and couches; characters later speak of going indoors.[65] It is important to note that Terence, striving

---

[65] Cf. e.g., *Asin.* 828 f., 940 f., *Most.* 308 f., 391, *Pers.* 757 ff., *Stich.* 683, 774. Some editors and translators have wrongly considered *Asin.* 828 ff. a real indoor scene, visible to the spectators through the open door; so also Legrand-Loeb, *The New Greek Comedy*, pp. 347, 354 f. Rees (*CPh* 10, 1915, pp. 117 ff.) believes that all these indoor scenes were presented in the *uestibulum*; he says (p. 121): "Plautus consistently uses the expressions, *ante aedes, ante ianuam*, to designate a part of the stage separate and distinct from the street." This is possible, but *Most.* 326 does not prove

for greater realism, did not present such banquets out of doors, and Plautus has been accused of a willingness to disregard verisimilitude and present any indoor scene on the stage.[66] This, however, is an exaggeration; in addition to the dressing scene and the four banquet scenes described above, Plautus only once brings on the stage an indoor scene: *Truc.* 448 ff., where Phronesium rests on a couch in front of her house after her pretended confinement; this can hardly be condemned as unrealistic since it is part of her deception of the soldier, e.g.:

Kiss me please, here. Ah! I can't lift my hand, it pains me so, and I haven't yet the strength to walk by myself. (525 ff.)

Such a little gift for all those terrible labor pains? (537)

When real confinements are supposed to occur during the course of the action, they invariably take place behind the scenes, even though, as we have seen, the cries of the women in labor are heard by the audience. As to the banquets on the stage, if the ancient Roman spectator lived outdoors and dined and entertained friends in the street as much as many modern Italians do,[67] he would hardly be troubled by the lack of verisimilitude in such scenes. Plautus may have followed the example of Greek dramatists in presenting on the stage scenes of festivity,[68] but the large amount of song and dance (as in the conclusions of the *Persa* and the *Stichus*) may well be an inheritance from earlier native comedy which he chose to develop in his own exuberant manner. Such scenes were effective, and it is surprising that Plautus did not use them more often. Although he has been criticized for bringing such action on the stage, both he and Terence keep off the stage many scenes which are important for the complication or the resolution of the plot.

## Off-stage Action and Lapse of Dramatic Time

The passages cited above have shown the various means by which the playwrights enriched the action on the stage and informed the audience of the conversations which had been held either in the houses or elsewhere in the city. In fact, the action of each comedy takes place only in part on the stage, and the activity of the characters off stage is constantly kept before the spectators; as Riedel says, "in reality, the scene of action is no longer the fronts of three houses, but the entire

---

the distinction; it seems more probable that the space *ante aedes* refers not only to the vestibule but also to that part of the street directly in front of the house.

[66] Cf. Stuart, *The Development of Dramatic Art*, p. 147.

[67] See Flickinger, *CJ* 34 (1938-39), pp. 538 ff.; cf. also *The Greek Theater and Its Drama*, p. 239.

[68] For the extent to which banquets were presented on the stage in Greek comedy, see Prehn, *Quaestiones Plautinae*, pp. 8 ff., who concludes (p. 24) that episodes of drinking, singing, and dancing had been popular in Old and Middle Comedy, and in the plays of Diphilus, but that Philemon and Menander (at least in his later comedies) had avoided such scenes.

city."[69] Most of the off-stage action is essential to the plot in both Plautus and Terence and is regularly reported to the actors on the stage, partly by monologue, often more naturally by dialogue.

Among the most important and most frequent types of off-stage action are (1) meetings and interviews which result in a revelation of significance to one or more of the characters; sometimes a slave makes a discovery which provides the basis for the plot of the play (e.g., *Merc.* 180 ff., *Most.* 353); (2) off-stage activity that is necessary to bring a deception to a successful conclusion; sometimes the details are made known to the other characters (and the audience) before the off-stage action is carried out,[70] and at times the details are announced only upon their completion;[71] (3) discoveries of the truth (e.g., *Cas.* 875 ff., 937 ff.) and recognition scenes, usually between parents and children; these latter are placed behind the scenes with surprising frequency.[72]

Other off-stage events described or mentioned on the stage include a shipwreck off shore (*Rud.* 148 ff.), a seduction (*Eun.* 568 ff.), betrothals (cf. *And.* 980, *Eun.* 1036 ff.), births (e.g., *Amph.* 1053 ff., *Hec.* 373 ff.), and banquets. In spite of Plautus' fondness for putting banquet scenes on the stage, those which offer less material for comedy are not presented to view, e.g., the banquet of the husbands and the wives in the *Stichus* (cf. 663 ff.), held indoors while the slaves carouse outside; cf. also the banquets mentioned in *Bacch.* 754 ff., *Men.* 473 ff., *Pseud.* 1051, 1252 ff. Terence has off-stage banquets in the *Heauton* (cf. 455 ff.) and in the *Eunuchus* (cf. 615 ff.); the latter would have provided material for a delightful episode if it had been presented on the stage in Plautine fashion; unfortunately, the soldier's house did not front the stage, and Terence did not wish to portray indoor scenes on the street.

[69] *CW* II (1917-18), p. 28. For a summary of off-stage action classified by location (port, country, forum, etc.), see Johnston, *Exits and Entrances in Roman Comedy*, pp. 127 ff.

[70] E.g., *Epid.* 364 ff.; on the complicated nature of the off-stage action involved in the deception, cf. Duckworth, *T. Macci Plauti Epidicus*, pp. 303 ff.

[71] E.g., the second letter in the *Bacchides*, composed off stage and read aloud by Nicobulus (997 ff.). There is an interesting variation in the handling of the two letters, for the first was dictated on the stage (731 ff.), but not read aloud; cf. Harsh, *Studies in Dramatic "Preparation,"* p. 59, n. 1.

[72] In the *Cistellaria, Epidicus, Rudens, Stichus, Andria, Heauton, Eunuchus, Phormio,* and *Hecyra*; cf. the passages cited by Johnston, *Exits and Entrances in Roman Comedy*, pp. 144 f., who suggests that recognition scenes frequently take place within the house "because they commonly involve women and girls"; this is true of Terence's plays (*Andria, Eunuchus, Phormio, Hecyra*) where the girls concerned do not take part in the action; in the other comedies listed above, the girls or women have active parts in the plays. In the *Epidicus* the real recognition between parents and daughter is not represented, but Plautus puts on the stage the amusing meetings between Philippa and the girl posing as her daughter, and between the soldier and the girl supposed to be his sweetheart; such abortive recognitions were rich in comic effect. On off-stage discoveries in general, cf. Smith, *The Technique of Solution*, pp. 72 ff., 76, n. 2.

Since off-stage action usually contributes to the development or resolution of the plot, humorous scenes seldom happen *post scaenam*; the description of the havoc wrought by Ergasilus in the kitchen (*Capt.* 909 ff.) would fall into this category, as would Lurcio's description of the events in the wine-cellar (*Mil.* 818 ff.) and Olympio's discovery of the truth about the pretended bride (*Cas.* 875 ff.), a scene which, because of its ribald nature, obviously could not be presented on the stage. Pardalisca's fantastic tale about the madness of the bride (*Cas.* 649 ff.) is fictitious and part of the deception of the *senex*, a deception which has been planned off stage (cf. 685 ff.). Other tales of off-stage action which are concocted to deceive characters on the stage are Geta's description of his meeting with Phormio (*Phorm.* 615 ff.), an excellent scene, since he not only deceives the *senes* but confuses Antipho who overhears the conversation, and Pythias' story to Parmeno (*Eun.* 943 ff.), in which the supposed treatment of Chaerea indoors is related for the purpose of deceiving the slave.[73]

Terence has been criticized for the omission of essential action, for a tendency to place important situations behind the scenes. Stuart says: "In comparison with modern plays, Terentian comedy seems to reach the spectator indirectly. . . . If the plays of Terence were produced on a revolving stage with the action taking place in the interiors as well as in the street, and if the stage were revolved halfway, we would witness the scenes which a modern dramatist would naturally place before our eyes; and we would only hear about the scenes which Terence placed before the Roman audience."[74] Stuart's view gains some support from the fact that the heroine and the recognition scene are often banished from the stage in Terence's comedies, but Plautus' use of off-stage action resembles Terence's far more than Stuart is willing to admit. As important as the off-stage action is to the development of the plot, it need not be witnessed by the spectators, if they gain a clear conception of what is happening elsewhere either by preliminary statement or by later announcement. Recognition scenes between parents and children are not obligatory when the audience has already learned the facts, and both playwrights are less interested in the emotional values of such reunions than in the misunderstandings and comic complications which lead up to these happy endings.

Both Plautus and Terence make clear to the audience that they are putting action off stage to avoid repetition or to save time:

Go on in and have water heated for her. I'll explain everything else to you later, when there's more time. (*Epid.* 655 f.)

[73] Cf. also *Ad.* 404 ff., in which Syrus delights Demea with a false yarn about Ctesipho's upright actions, and 645 ff., Micio's story about the non-existent friend who will marry Pamphila.

[74] *The Development of Dramatic Art*, p. 150.

Your father said that you were to be married today and a lot more that I haven't time now to tell you. (*And.* 353 f.) [75]

Plautus at times breaks the dramatic illusion and mentions frankly his desire to avoid repetition; e.g., the words of Milphio to the audience in *Poen.* 920 ff.:

I'll go in and inform my master of this. It would be sheer stupidity to call him out in front of the house and repeat here again what you've just heard. I'd rather be a nuisance to one man inside than to all of you out here. (cf. also *Pseud.* 720 f.)

In *Merc.* 1005 ff. Eutychus says:

Let's go in; this place isn't suitable. While we're talking, the people who pass by can learn all about your business.

Demipho replies:

That's a good idea, and at the same time the play will be shorter.

In *Pseud.* 387 f. the slave says:

I'll see that you learn in good time. I don't want to tell it twice; these plays are long enough as it is.

But in this instance (as in *Phorm.* 566), the information is postponed and the audience is kept in suspense as to the manner of the deception.

The large amount of off-stage action in the comedies of Plautus and Terence is evidence that the playwrights were presenting on the stage a world of three dimensions. However much critics may find fault with certain scenes which they think should have been placed before the eyes of the spectators, it is clear that the dramatists in general realized the importance of off-stage action in accompanying and supporting the development of the plot that was worked out on the stage. The limitations of the stage-setting did not prevent them from giving a well-rounded and realistic picture of the activity of the characters when they were absent from the stage; at the same time both playwrights avoided unnecessary repetition by putting off stage scenes which they considered unnecessary and uninteresting.

The time required for the off-stage action is often much greater than that which passes on the stage. I mentioned above that the stage is somewhat elastic and includes a larger area of street than that in front of the houses. Elasticity of dramatic time is even more an accepted convention of Roman comedy. The plays observe in general the unity of time (with the exception of the *Heauton*, where the passing of a night is mentioned in 410; the action of the *Amphitruo* and the *Curculio* begins before day-

[75] Cf. also *Aul.* 800 ff., *Cist.* 782 f., *Most.* 1039 f., *Trin.* 1101 f., *Phorm.* 818 f. See Johnston, *Exits and Entrances in Roman Comedy*, pp. 145 ff. *Phorm.* 566, cited by Miss Johnston (p. 134) as an instance of information put off stage to avoid repetition, has a somewhat different function, for it keeps the audience in suspense concerning the manner in which money will be procured for Phaedria.

break and continues on through the morning), but there is often little correlation between the time required for the action seen by the spectators and the lapse of imaginary time behind the scenes. The failure to understand or the unwillingness to accept this convention has led many critics (e.g., Freté, Johnston, Weissinger) to theories of musical interludes or act-divisions, since they considered that pauses were necessary at various points in each play to indicate a lapse of time.[76]

In numerous instances the playwrights provide adequately for the off-stage action by the use of monologues which serve to fill time during the absence of a character from the stage.[77] Often an exit monologue is followed by an entrance monologue; since both provide a means of filling time, the vacant stage between exit and entrance is meaningless from the standpoint of dramatic time, e.g., in the *Mercator*, the exit monologue of Syra (817-829) and the entrance speech of Charinus (830-841) provide ample time for the absence of Eutychus; similarly, in the *Menaechmi*, Messenio's exit speech (441-445) and the entrance monologue of Peniculus (446-465) fill the interval while Menaechmus II dines with Erotium; in this instance, the off-stage action seems hurried, but Peniculus implies that he has been delayed in the forum and expresses disgust, but not surprise, that the meal is over. In general, any monologue, even if short, may fill in a period of indefinite time.

Since continuity of action on the stage is hardly compatible with the passing of dramatic time, the playwrights often take pains to point out that there has been a considerable lapse of time off stage; e.g., Lysidamus complains that he has wasted the entire day in the forum (*Cas.* 563 ff.) although he has been absent from the stage during only one short scene (531-562); Menaechmus I returns from the forum and likewise tells how a client has ruined his day (*Men.* 595 ff.) but, in his case, a longer absence (216-570) makes the statement less implausible.[78] Terence inserts similar comments to denote the passing of time off stage; Parmeno, sent with a message for Callidemides in *Hec.* 443, returns in 799 and says he has wasted the whole day hunting for a non-existent person; Demea complains that he has looked for his brother over the whole town during his absence from the stage (*Ad.* 587-712).

In other instances, the off-stage time is even more compressed. Menaechmus' father-in-law goes for the doctor in *Men.* 875, and returns almost immediately (882), saying that he is exhausted from waiting for the doctor. Here again Plautus apparently tries to reconcile dramatic time and stage action but in other cases he makes no such attempt. After Lysidamus enters his house (*Cas.* 758), Pardalisca comes out

[76] See "Act-Divisions" in chap. 4.
[77] Cf. Prescott, *CPh* 34 (1939), pp. 116 ff.; 37 (1942), pp. 11 ff.
[78] Cf. Hough, *CPh* 31 (1936), pp. 244 ff., who cites many other illustrations from Plautus.

and relates (759 ff.) what took place indoors after Lysidamus' arrival; in *Cist.* 629 f., Melaenis goes in to get Selenium and returns in 631, saying "I've told you the whole story"; in *Cist.* 774 the father arrives from the forum saying that everyone is talking about his newly found daughter, and this in spite of the fact that the discovery of the girl's identity was made only in the preceding scene. Passages such as these are eagerly seized upon by proponents of the theory of act-divisions, but actually they are extreme examples of the poet's desire to describe off-stage events without slowing up the action on the stage. The momentarily vacant stages at *Cas.* 758, *Cist.* 630, and *Cist.* 773 may represent a lapse of time even though there is no real pause in the action. Perhaps the most striking example of the lapse of dramatic time occurs in the *Captivi*, where between 452 and 922 Philocrates journeys from Aetolia to Elis and back again, a trip which in real life would require several days. This recalls the trip of Amphitheus to Sparta and back to Athens in Aristophanes' *Acharnians*, all in less than fifty verses (cf. 130 ff., 175).

But dramatic time off stage is not always compressed; it may be expanded, if the playwright finds it convenient to keep a character off the stage. Lydus accompanies Pistoclerus into the house of Bacchis in *Bacch.* 169; in 368 ff., two hundred verses later, he rushes from the house, appalled at the situation he has found inside:

As soon as I had seen this I straightway betook myself to flight. (374)

His words give the impression of a very short stay inside. So, too, the absences of Messenio (*Men.* 446-965) and Parmeno (*Hec.* 444-798), although dramatically justified, are unusually long because their return earlier in the play would have interfered with the development of the action.

## The Violation of the Dramatic Illusion

One of the most effective means by which writers of comedy create a sudden laugh is to break the dramatic illusion by having characters either speak directly to the audience or refer to the action as merely a play and to themselves as actors playing a part. A familiarity with the spectators is frequently found in farce and low comedy today, and actors do not hesitate to speak out of character (*ex persona*) and to jest upon the part they are playing. The late John Barrymore once delighted his audience by saying, as he poured a drink and lifted the glass to his lips: "I wish to heaven that this were a real highball." Stage and radio comedians regularly joke about each other's idiosyncrasies, even when they are playing a part; they ridicule the dramatic machinery, and make no pretense of preserving the dramatic illusion. Blancké cites[79]

[79] *The Dramatic Values in Plautus*, p. 65.

the vaudeville actor who comments as he dances: "I hate to do this, but it's the only way I can earn a living."

Plautus has been condemned for the frequency with which his characters speak to the spectators and comment on the stage machinery; in many cases he is laughing at the stage machinery, and the effect of the *ex persona* speeches is highly amusing. Terence has more regard for realism; he seeks to preserve the dramatic illusion, and for this he has been praised by critics both ancient and modern. Evanthius (*De fabula*, III, 8) commends Terence because "his characters do not speak to the audience *extra comoediam*, which is a most common fault of Plautus (*uitium Plauti frequentissimum*)," and modern writers repeatedly state that Terence improved upon earlier comedy and made a great advance in dramatic realism by eliminating direct address to the audience.[80] This in general is true, but needs to be qualified, since the distinction between Plautus and Terence in this respect is not as great as Evanthius and modern critics have maintained.[81]

By direct address to the audience I do not mean narrative monologues, such as those described above, the primary purpose of which was to inform the audience about the action of the play. Such monologues do not break the dramatic illusion as long as there is no reference to the spectators. Direct address occurs when an actor speaks to the audience in the second person, but the extent to which dramatic propriety is violated depends upon the nature of the passage. The address to the spectators in the *parabasis* was a regular feature of Aristophanes' comedies, and the playwright did not hesitate to refer to the audience, the stage, the play, and the actors (e.g., *Peace*, 729 ff., *Birds*, 753 ff.); there are occasional addresses to the spectators in the extant fragments of Menander,[82] but these are mostly parenthetical vocatives which could be omitted without altering the nature of the monologue in which they occur. Plautus' familiarity with the audience resembles somewhat Aristophanes' method, but probably goes back to earlier Italian farces. The extent to which the writers of New Comedy were willing to break the dramatic illusion cannot be determined; certain passages in Plautus may reflect the Greek original, but the majority are doubtless Plautus' own additions which he inserted for their comic effect.[83]

Before analyzing the nature of the *ex persona* speeches in Plautus and Terence (who uses them rarely), I wish to refer to a group of passages which are considered border-line cases; the words uttered are

---

[80] Cf. e.g., Leo, *Plautinische Forschungen*, p. 112, n. 3; Harsh, *A Handbook of Classical Drama*, p. 380; Enk, *Mn* 13 (1947), p. 82.

[81] Cf. Kraus, *WS* 52 (1934), p. 69, n. 5.

[82] *Epitrep*. 503, *Sam*. 54 ff., 114, 338; cf. Hough, *TAPhA* 71 (1940), p. 194; Duckworth, *CW* 41 (1947-48), p. 91, n. 47.

[83] Plautus seems to have used *ex persona* speeches with greater frequency toward the close of his career; cf. Hough, *TAPhA* 71 (1940), pp. 192 ff.

not inappropriate to real life but they make a comparison with some theatrical production or technique:

I'll throw my *pallium* over my shoulder just as slaves in comedies usually do. (*Capt.* 778 f.)

No comic poet ever contrived a cleverer plot than this which we've concocted. (*Cas.* 860 f.)

I don't want this to be done as in comedies, where everyone finds out everything. (*Hec.* 866 f.)[84]

These passages might even be said to strengthen the dramatic illusion. In modern detective novels the situation is presumably made more real when a character says, "This proves that worse things happen in real life than in detective stories"; so Palaestra says (*Rud.* 185 f.):

Ah, how much more unkind is Fate than what men say about it!

But when Simo says in *Pseud.* 1239 f.:

Now I've determined to lay a trap for Pseudolus—but not the kind that they set in other comedies,

the border-line has been crossed; the presence of the word "other" shatters the dramatic illusion.

Appeals to the audience for favor have already been mentioned as a regular feature of the prologues, and in Plautus the speaker of the prologue frequently jests with the spectators as a means of putting them in a receptive mood for the play (e.g., *Capt.* 10 ff., *Men.* 51 ff., *Poen.* 79 ff.). Also, as we have seen, both Plautus and Terence end their plays with a request for applause. In the analysis of *ex persona* speeches which follows, I omit the prologues and the formulaic endings of the plays; normal asides also are excluded, since the aside, an accepted convention, was not considered a speech out of character. The passages to be reviewed are those which occur during the course of the action, where a realistic presentation demanded that the dramatic illusion be preserved—but where Plautus preferred to sacrifice realism to humor.

(1) Frequently the speaker of a monologue either addresses the spectators directly or makes a statement to show that he is conscious of their presence:

He'll be tricked in fine shape, spectators, as you look on. (*Amph.* 997 f.)

Pay attention now, while I repeat my exploits; it's well worth your listening, so ridiculous to hear and to repeat are the mishaps I encountered inside. (*Cas.* 879 f.)

Spectators, don't expect me to praise my prowess. (*Truc.* 482)

I can't find a proper starting-point, I can't begin to tell the troubles which have come to me unexpectedly. (*Hec.* 361 f.)

[84] Cf. also *Amph.* 986 f., *Asin.* 173 ff., *Most.* 1149 ff., *Pers.* 465 f., *Poen.* 581, *Pseud.* 1081 f., *Rud.* 1249 f., *Truc.* 931.

Passages such as these are an extension of the narrative monologue; the normal function of the audience as listener is made more specific. The closest parallel in Menander is *Sam.* 54 ff.:

I won't tell you my suspicions, men, but I'll reveal the fact and what I myself have heard.

In Terence characters address the audience in *And.* 231 and 980 f., and elsewhere show a realization of its presence (as in *Hec.* 361 f., cited above; cf. also *And.* 217, 957 f., *Phorm.* 1026, *Ad.* 862); but Terence nowhere uses the vocative *spectatores*, and in these passages the dramatic illusion is perhaps cracked, but hardly broken. Plautus addresses the audience as such with much greater freedom[85] but the words are appropriate for the spectators in their capacity as listeners.

(2) At times the audience is requested to participate more actively in the situation on the stage:

Please, all of you, if the old man returns, don't tell him which way I fled. (*Men.* 879 f.; cf. *Mil.* 861 f.)

The famous monody of Euclio, when he discovers the theft of his gold (*Aul.* 713 ff.), best illustrates this type of appeal:

I'm done for, dead, destroyed! Where should I run? Where should I not run? Stop him, stop him! Whom? I don't know, I see nothing, I'm blind, nor can I say where to go or where I am or who I am. (*To audience*) I beg, beseech, entreat you to aid me and point out the man who stole it. What's that you say? I'm determined to trust you for I know from your expression that you're an honest man. What's that? Why do you laugh? I know all of you, I know that there are thieves here, plenty of them, who disguise themselves and sit still like honest men. What, none of these has it? Tell me then, who has it? You don't know? Alas, poor me, I'm completely ruined![86]

There are no passages of this type in Terence's comedies.

(3) In the passages cited above the references to the spectators tend to break the dramatic illusion but the speakers say what is natural under the circumstances. The situation is very different when the characters frankly refer to themselves as actors and joke about stage conventions and stage machinery. Neither in the extant fragments of Menander nor in Terence is there anything resembling the liberty which Plautus takes in this respect. All pretense of drama is for the moment discarded. To this category belong the passages mentioned earlier in which an actor puts conversation or action off stage to avoid repetition and

---

[85] Cf. *Bacch.* 1072 f., *Merc.* 267, 851, *Mil.* 1130 f., *Most.* 280 f., 708 f., *Pseud.* 584, 1234, *Stich.* 446 ff., 579, 673 f., *Truc.* 105, 463.

[86] Cf. also *Cas.* 951 f., *Cist.* 678 f. Kraus (*WS* 52, 1934, p. 73) lists in this group passages such as *Most.* 280 f.: "Most of you fellows know this, you who have old wives who won you with their dowry"; also *Most.* 708 f., *Pseud.* 584, *Truc.* 105; but these passages do not require active participation by the audience and belong rather in Group 1.

"make the play shorter."[87] Pseudolus refers (*Pseud.* 562 ff.) to his promise to entertain the audience with amazing feats as he acts out the *fabula* (cf. *Amph.* 868), and the *aduocati* mention stage money in *Poen.* 597; but the most striking allusion to the staging of the plays occurs when the same characters say (550 ff.) :

> We know this already, if the spectators know it; it's for the benefit of these spectators that this play is now being acted here. You'd better instruct them, so that they'll know what you're doing when you do it. Don't bother about us; we know the whole plan, since we learned it along with you, so as to be able to make our responses.

(4) Plautus permits his characters to say what no Greek citizen in a Greek city would ever say. He introduces allusions to persons, places, and events in Rome and in Italy which make the plays more truly native in spirit, but in so doing he fails to preserve the Greek atmosphere of the original. In most instances such references do not violate the dramatic illusion as much as they shatter the Greek illusion. Certainly it is misleading to say, as Blancké does,[88] that this procedure is an "item of careless composition" and that Plautus is forgetful of his Greek environment; the playwright undoubtedly realized that references to familiar places would have a strong popular appeal.

Of such a nature are the mention of Apulia (*Mil.* 648), Capua (*Rud.* 631), Etruria (*Cist.* 562), Praeneste (*Bacch.* fr. VIII, *Trin.* 609, *Truc.* 691), Sarsina and Umbria (*Most.* 770). Characters speak of the *Capitolium* (*Curc.* 269, *Trin.* 84), the *Velabrum* (*Capt.* 489), the *porta Trigemina* (*Capt.* 90). The monologue of the *choragus* in *Curc.* 462-486 is virtually a miniature guidebook to the streets of Rome.[89] Occasionally the actions of the characters are described as "playing the Greek" (*pergraecari*) when the idea of extravagance and wanton living is involved (*Bacch.* 813, *Most.* 22, 64, 960, *Poen.* 603, *Truc.* 88), and the adjective *barbarus* is frequently applied to things Roman; Naevius is a *poeta barbarus* (*Mil.* 211), Italian cities are *barbaricae urbes* (*Capt.* 884), native dancers are *ludii barbari* (*Curc.* 150), and Italy itself is called *barbaria* (*Poen.* 598). All such Roman references represent one important aspect of Plautus' originality. Terence, eager to maintain the Greek environment, avoids all mention of Roman places and events, except in his prologues, and to this extent follows his models with greater fidelity. It is hardly accurate to say that Terence eliminated direct address to the audience but he did seek to preserve the dramatic illusion, and nowhere does he jest upon the dramatic machinery.

---

[87] Cf. *Cas.* 1006, *Merc.* 1007, *Poen.* 1224, *Pseud.* 388, 720 f.; cf. *Poen.* 920.

[88] *The Dramatic Values in Plautus,* p. 63.

[89] For other passages, see Westaway, *The Original Element in Plautus,* pp. 16 ff.; Kraus, *WS* 52 (1934), pp. 81 ff.; Hough, *TAPhA* 71 (1940), pp. 194 ff. It is often difficult to distinguish truly Roman passages from those which merely express a Greek idea in Latin; cf. the criticism of Westaway by Hough, *ibid.,* p. 196, n. 18.

## Summary: Convention and Revolt

The conventions of Roman comedy were inherited from Greek comedy—monologues and asides, the announcement of entrances (e.g., the creaking door), the description of off-stage action, direct address to the audience. Plautus, a master of stagecraft, accepted the normal conventions and used them with gusto but he went far beyond his predecessors in his willingness to sacrifice realism for comic effect. He presented banquets and other indoor scenes on the stage, expanded the farcical possibilities inherent in many devices (e.g., the running slave episodes), and developed the address to the spectators into a frank admission that it was all a play. Roman allusions gave his comedies a more popular appeal. Many of the passages cited above have shown the gaiety and the ease with which he made fun of different conventions (e.g., the running slave, opportune meetings, the creaking door).[90] He preferred laughter to dramatic verisimilitude although the improbabilities in his plays are neither so crude nor so numerous as is often believed.

Terence, striving to write a higher type of comedy that was devoid of farce and slapstick, took pains to avoid improbabilities of various kinds (Roman references, indoor scenes on the stage, buffoonery in connection with running slaves, violation of the dramatic illusion), and he aimed at a more realistic treatment of conversation and action; he was more restrained in his use of monologues and asides, and his handling of entrances and exits was usually very natural, but sometimes vague or mechanical, since he lacked the flexibility of Plautus' technique. Both Plautus and Terence appear to have been conscious of the limitations of ancient methods of staging; but whereas Plautus made fun of the conventions and developed their comic possibilities, Terence sought rather for new variations on old themes; there is often an implied criticism of the normal procedure in his desire to present an accepted convention in a new manner.

In the *Andria*, Mysis goes indoors with the midwife and at once the cries of Glycerum are heard from within. Simo, who believes that the birth of the child is being faked for his benefit, says (474 f.) :

What, so soon? Absurd! As soon as she heard I was here in front of the door, she makes haste to be in labor. Davus, you haven't arranged the timing of your incidents at all well.

Terence here calls attention to the manner in which off-stage action is frequently compressed. In *Eun.* 359, Chaerea expresses surprise that Thais is living next door and, in *Phorm.* 818, Chremes says that the stage is not a safe place for talking about the discovery of his daughter's identity; is this merely the normal way of avoiding repetition of some-

90 Cf. Knapp, *CPh* 14 (1919), pp. 48 ff.; Gomme, *Essays in Greek History and Literature*, pp. 258 ff.

thing already known to the audience (cf. *Merc.* 1005 f.), or is Terence expressing his disapproval of the discussion of intimate matters in the street?

Perhaps the most interesting illustration of Terence's unusual treatment of a convention which he himself used repeatedly is *And.* 481 ff.: the midwife comes out, giving directions to Archilis inside about the care of Glycerium. Simo says (490 ff.):

She didn't give her orders to the servant face to face about the mother, but waited until she was outside and then shouted from the street to those inside. Oh, Davus, do you think so little of me? Do I seem to you a fit subject for so obvious a trick as this?

Terence here seems to criticize the usual conversation to persons indoors, although he makes excellent use of the convention by having it contribute to the self-deception of Simo. Norwood says that the words of the *senex* "are the poet's own trenchant satire on a mortifying stage convention."[91] But Terence is not laughing at the convention as Plautus so often does; he is rather putting it to a new and unconventional use. Norwood praises as a "charming feat of artistry" the passage in the *Hecyra* (866 ff.) "where Bacchis and Pamphilus agree to outrage all comic convention, and, instead of summoning the whole cast to hear the explanation, keep it to themselves."[92] We have seen that neither Plautus nor Terence summons the cast to hear such explanations; on the contrary, they regularly put these explanations off stage when the details are already known to the audience; Terence's procedure here is unusual in that the other characters, including the bewildered Parmeno, are to be kept in the dark.

Thus Terence on occasion expressed his dissatisfaction with certain conventions and attempted to present them with innovations which would be both interesting and amusing to spectators accustomed to the normal technique. Were such innovations his own contribution, or did he find them in his Greek originals? A definite answer is hardly possible. If these unconventional touches were Greek, Terence's employment of them still gives us an insight into his interests and technique, just as Plautus' handling of the conventions throws light upon his dramatic aims. But if we find that Terence in his treatment of plot and character likewise deviated from what seems to have been normal procedure on the Greek and Roman stage, we shall have added justification for assuming that such innovations are, in great part, at least, a sign of Terence's originality.

[91] *The Art of Terence*, p. 30; cf. Gomme, *Essays in Greek History and Literature*, p. 260, n. 1. Both Norwood and Gomme speak here of the convention that private matters are discussed in the open street; it is rather the device of bringing off-stage conversation before the audience.

[92] *The Art of Terence*, p. 105.

# CHAPTER 6
## *THEME AND TREATMENT*

Our limited knowledge of Greek New Comedy makes it impossible to determine with exactitude the nature of the lost originals from which Plautus and Terence took the themes of their comedies.[1] The extant fragments and fragmentary plays of Menander contain almost no deception and trickery. Love affairs, mistaken identity, misunderstandings arising from ignorance, a fortunate discovery which clears up the confusion and brings about a happy ending—these are the elements which are prominent in the plays of Menander as we have them. Many comedies of Plautus and Terence follow this pattern, but others do not. The wider range of the Plautine plot indicates both that the poets of New Comedy were much more versatile than is often believed and also that the Roman playwright made numerous changes and innovations to enliven his plays and increase their comic power. Terence reveals far less variety in his choice of theme, but he apparently has also introduced subtle changes and refinements to heighten the effectiveness of his creations.

To determine with any degree of accuracy what is basically Greek and what is Plautine or Terentian in the plays is one of the most difficult and most controversial problems in the study of Roman comedy. We know that in general the plots of the Roman plays are the plots of the Greek originals; if, however, we find that Plautus and Terence differ strikingly from each other in choice of subject and in treatment of theme, such differences cannot be explained merely by the nature of the originals which each adapted. Not only did the two playwrights select from the available Greek plays those which appealed to them as having suitable comic material but they must have remodeled the originals, each in accordance with his own conception of effective comedy. To this extent the plays, however Greek in subject matter, necessarily reflect the interests and techniques of the two playwrights. We must remember, however, that the audiences of the second century B.C. who viewed the dramatic productions of the *ludi* were not concerned, as are modern critics, with the problem of Roman originality; to such audiences the plays were popular entertainment, and they neither knew nor cared whether the comedies were close translations from the Greek or were

---

[1] Ingenious efforts have been made by Kuiper to restore in outline form the Greek originals of Terence's six comedies and Plautus' *Aulularia, Bacchides, Cistellaria, Epidicus,* and *Rudens.* (With the exception of *Two Comedies by Apollodorus of Carystus* and *The Greek Aulularia,* his works are in Dutch, with English summaries.) Unfortunately, the similarity of these outlines with their mechanical regularity of structure and their many additional recognition scenes, usually between half-brother and half-sister, makes their acceptance very difficult; cf. Post, *AJPh* 59 (1938), pp. 367 ff.; Hough, *AJPh* 62 (1941), pp. 237 ff.; Duckworth, *CPh* 35 (1940), pp. 86 ff., 201 ff.; *CW* 34 (1940-41), pp. 260 f.

more original productions built upon Greek themes. What the spectators demanded were ingenious plots, amusing characters, and an abundance of laughter.

## The Importance of Being Mistaken

It is not my desire at this point to analyze ancient theories of comedy,[2] but any discussion of the nature of the plays of Plautus and Terence should begin with the one feature which they have in common. This feature I believe to be mental error, or misapprehension. Aristotle in his treatment of tragedy (*Poet.* 1452a) comments upon the importance to the plot of *anagnorisis*, or discovery, the transition from ignorance to knowledge, and of *peripeteia*, or reversal of fortune, the transition from happiness to misery (or the reverse). The discovery may be either the recognition of individuals or the revelation of hitherto unknown facts; the change from ignorance (*agnoia*) to knowledge often coincides with the reversal of situation and leads directly to the tragic conclusion. Ignorance or misapprehension seems equally to be the basis of the complications in the plots of New Comedy. In Menander's *Perikeiromene*, the prologue is spoken by the goddess Agnoia (Misapprehension) who considers herself the controlling force in the action of the play and admits that she is responsible for the jealous rage of the soldier. I said above[3] that Agnoia might well be considered a motivating factor in the extant plays of Menander and this statement must now be broadened to include almost all extant Roman comedy.

This does not mean that all Roman comedies deal with mistaken identities, or that the ignorance of the characters concerning the real state of affairs is always brought to an end by a conventional recognition scene. Many misleading statements are made about the plots of Roman comedy. It is said, for instance that Plautus and Terence "both treat as a rule the same theme. Their methods of handling it differ immensely, but their starting-point in most of the twenty-six comedies varies only in detail."[4] Then a "composite photograph" of the plots of the plays is presented to the unsuspecting reader; this typical plot includes a young Athenian in love with a girl who is in the power of a *leno*; he is unable through lack of funds to purchase her as his mistress, so his slave schemes to defraud the hero's father of the needed money or the slavedealer of the girl; the deception is discovered, but the heroine is revealed to be of Athenian birth (kidnaped or lost in babyhood) and

[2] For a brief treatment of the nature and function of comedy, see "Ancient and Modern Theories of Comedy" in chap. 11.

[3] Cf. p. 29.

[4] Norwood, *Plautus and Terence*, pp. 11 f. See also Wieand, *Deception in Plautus*, p. 51, who says: "The plays accordingly are very much alike. In fact it would almost seem as if Plautus used the same stock scenes and motives for his plays."

can marry the hero.[5] It is, of course, true that ignorance of the heroine's real identity, the love affair in which the unhappy youth finds himself in seemingly hopeless difficulties, trickery either to provide money or free the courtesan from her master, the recognition scene which solves the complications and brings about the happy ending, are features frequently found in the plots of the Roman plays, but such a "composite photograph" bears little relation to the themes of many other comedies (e.g., *Amphitruo, Aulularia, Captivi, Menaechmi, Stichus, Truculentus, Hecyra*), and combines the elements of mistaken identity and trickery in a manner seldom seen in the comedies themselves.

We cannot say, therefore, as is said of the extant plays of Menander, that the basis of each play is a love story although love in one form or another appears in the majority of the plays; nor can we state that deception is the chief interest in spite of the fact that few comedies lack some type of trickery. A general atmosphere of misapprehension seems by far the most essential factor in developing the action and producing the complications in comedy. Donatus in his commentary on Terence makes many references to the errors which create danger (*periculum*) for the characters; the complication (*nodus*) is finally disentangled by the discovery (*cognitio*) and the reversal of the action from unhappiness to happiness (*catastrophe*).[6] In the *Andria*, for example, the basic misapprehension (*error fabulae*) which controls the action of the comedy is the ignorance of the characters regarding the identity of Glycerium, and this misapprehension is cleared up with the arrival of Crito.[7] The conflicts and misunderstandings in the *Hecyra* arise from Philumena's return to her parents' home—the result of her ignorance that the man who violated her before her marriage was Pamphilus, now her husband. In the *Mostellaria*, considered below as primarily a comedy of trickery, the basic error is Theopropides' ignorance of the true situation in his household when he returns home unexpectedly. In the *Adelphoe*, a psychological study dealing with the education of youth, the complications arise from the fact that the other characters do not realize that Aeschinus has stolen a music girl for his brother rather than for himself. In all these plays the *error fabulae* usually produces numerous minor misapprehensions. Other complicating factors are the mistakes and confusions which develop from the tricks and deceptions concocted by one or more

[5] Cf. Norwood, *Plautus and Terence*, p. 12. How such typical plots fail to bring out the diversity in Plautus' plays has been shown by Kent, *PhQ* 2 (1923), pp. 164 ff.

[6] Evanthius (*De fab.* IV, 5) defines *catastrophe* as "the transition of events to a happy outcome after the discovery of the facts has been revealed to all." There are numerous references in Donatus to *catastrophe* and "happy ending."

[7] Cf. Donatus, *ad And.* Praef. II, 1; 221, 404, 796, 904. For other references to *error* in Donatus, see Prescott, *CPh* 24 (1929), pp. 35 ff.; cf. also Baldwin, *Shakspere's Five-Act Structure*, pp. 34 ff., who says of Donatus "the motive force for the plot he finds in 'error'" (p. 52).

intriguing characters and, in a broader sense, the term *error* may be applied to ignorance of this type also; in other words, *error* may arise not merely from circumstances for which no person is responsible but also as the result of deliberate intention.

Prescott states that misapprehension or error is the primary force in developing the complication of the comic plot and that the turning-point in the action comes when the true facts are discovered,[8] but both he and Miss Smith who, writing under his direction, classifies the Roman comedies as *error*-plays and plays of intrigue,[9] fail to include as examples of *error* the misapprehensions arising from trickery and impersonation; the broader conception of *error* provides a more satisfactory starting-point for the analysis of the comedies of Plautus and Terence. When Cooper said of New Comedy that it "must have been full of incidents turning upon both innocent mistakes and guileful deceptions with regard to identity,"[10] he was actually summarizing the themes of the extant Roman comedies, with the exception of the *Stichus*, a play *sui generis* (and even here mistaken assumptions and frustrated hopes play a part in the action). Innocent mistakes, guileful deceptions —these, either separately or in combination, produce the errors and misapprehensions to be found in all the plays.

To classify the plots of the twenty-six comedies is far from easy. Many plays can properly be considered comedies of mistaken identity, or comedies of deception; others combine both elements, using trickery to provide the dramatic action but making the solution depend upon a fortunate discovery. There are others in which the elements of trickery or mistaken identity play a minor role and the major emphasis of the playwright appears to be the portrayal of character or customs.[11] Some plays contain a large amount of song and dance and have a festal conclusion; these are lyrical dramas, or "festival plays," and are sometimes listed separately as musical comedies, or "opéras comiques à divertissement final."[12] The following classifications can at best be only tentative but will, I trust, serve to reveal the richness and variety to be found in the plots of the Roman comedies.

[8] *CPh* 24 (1929), p. 36. Prescott believes that the many references to *error* in Donatus reflect a Hellenistic theory of comedy which goes back to Aristotle; see also Pack, *CPh* 33 (1938), pp. 405 ff.; Smith, *The Technique of Solution*, pp. 1 ff.

[9] *The Technique of Solution*, pp. 12 ff.

[10] *An Aristotelian Theory of Comedy*, p. 305.

[11] See, for Plautus, Michaut, *Plaute*, I, pp. 146 ff.; Lejay, *Plaute*, pp. 107 ff., 131 ff. Lejay includes in this category many comedies (e.g., *Amphitruo, Cistellaria, Miles, Poenulus, Rudens*) for which I suggest a different listing.

[12] Lejay (*Plaute*, pp. 37 ff.) includes in this category the *Asinaria, Bacchides, Casina, Persa, Pseudolus*, and *Stichus*, but his classifications seem faulty as they are based in part on subject matter, in part on form. The comedies which he lists as comic operas are, with the exception of the *Stichus*, more properly included under comedies of deception.

## Portrayal of Character and Customs

In this category I include five comedies, Plautus' *Aulularia, Stichus, Trinummus, Truculentus*, and the *Adelphoe* of Terence. The *Aulularia* and the *Adelphoe* are primarily plays of character, and the chief purpose of the other three appears to be the humorous portrayal of certain aspects of ancient life although these too contain much psychological interest. These five comedies differ strikingly from one another in plot and treatment, and prove at the outset, if such proof be needed, that the plays of Roman comedy do not follow a set pattern.

(1) The *Aulularia* ("The Pot of Gold"), one of Plautus' most famous comedies, has as its central interest the character of Euclio. Euclio is a poor man who has carried thrift to the point of meanness. Strobilus says (300 ff.) with comic exaggeration:

> He shouts to heaven and earth that he is bankrupt and ruined if a puff of smoke comes from his chimney. When he goes to bed he puts a bag over his mouth so he won't lose any breath while he's asleep. . . . It grieves him to throw away the water when he's had a bath.

But Euclio is not really a miser; after the household god has revealed to him a pot of gold, he is unable to adjust himself to the change in his fortunes; he attempts to hide the gold and is suspicious of everyone; there is delightful comedy in his frantic attempts to keep his treasure safe, but he is at the same time a pathetic figure and when the gold is stolen he is overcome with anguish and despair. Woven into the main action is the story of Euclio's daughter who has been violated by Lyconides. The ending of the play is lost but Lyconides apparently restored the treasure to Euclio, who gave him his daughter in marriage and presented her with the gold as a dowry—not the act of a miser overcome by insatiable greed.[13] The play is the best example of a comedy of character to be found in Plautus but, as Michaut points out,[14] the love complications do not result from Euclio's character, nor is Plautus primarily interested in making a study of avarice; he is rather more concerned in presenting the comic situations created by Euclio's unfounded suspicions of his household and of his neighbors.

(2) The *Adelphoe* ("The Brothers") is undoubtedly Terence's

---

[13] Beare (*The Roman Stage*, p. 48) says that Euclio is "fundamentally a decent old fellow, crazed by the sudden acquisition of wealth; he is not a Shylock or a Harpagon, though these famous characters owe much to him." But Euclio is often spoken of as a miser; cf. e.g., Harsh, *A Handbook of Classical Drama*, pp. 343 f.; see also Legrand-Loeb, *The New Greek Comedy*, pp. 168 f.; Kuiper, *The Greek Aulularia*, pp. 12 ff. I am unable to understand how Kuiper can refer to the character of Euclio as a "point of minor importance" (*ibid.*, p. 6). Webster (*Studies in Menander*, p. 121), who regards Menander's *Apistos* as the original of the *Aulularia*, says: "Menander's chief object is the portrayal of Euclio."

[14] *Plaute*, I, p. 150. Norwood (*Plautus and Terence*, p. 56) considers the characterization of Euclio excellent but says of the *Aulularia*, "a character-sketch is not a play" (*ibid.*, p. 98).

finest play. Norwood with justification calls it "a perfect masterpiece of high comedy."[15] More than any other Roman comedy, the *Adelphoe* is a play with a purpose and deals with the ever-important problem of the proper education for young men. The two sons of Demea are both in love, Ctesipho with a music girl. Aeschinus with Sostrata's daughter, Pamphila, whom he has wronged. Aeschinus has been adopted by Micio, Demea's brother, and has been reared with tolerance and understanding, while Demea has used harshness and restraint in the upbringing of Ctesipho. The amusing complications and misunderstandings of the plot are the logical outcome of the virtues and weaknesses of the characters themselves. Donatus calls the play one of *multiplex error* (Praef. II, I); the ignorance of the fathers concerning the love affairs of the young men and, in particular, the mistaken belief that Aeschinus has stolen a music girl for himself initiate the action of the comedy; deception plays a minor role, for Syrus attempts to keep Demea in ignorance of the true state of affairs. The two love stories do not, however, provide the main theme; they serve rather to illustrate the center of interest—the problem of education and the clash between the older brothers. The characters of Demea and Micio are portrayed with great skill; "neither is perfectly right, but each has a good deal of human sentiment and experience on his side."[16] Although both educational methods fail, Micio's system is at first presented with far more sympathy and his relations with Aeschinus are preferable to the lack of understanding between Demea and Ctesipho.[17] The delightful and astonishing conclusion, when Demea fully realizes the result of his sternness and pretends to go to the other extreme,[18] points up the basic flaw in Micio's method and reveals how the latter's character has been undermined by his generosity and indulgence. The ideal system propounded by Demea includes a moderate amount of restraint but is a wise and sympathetic treatment of youth which avoids the weaknesses of either extreme (986 ff.).

(3) Plautus' *Trinummus* ("The Three Penny Day") is a quiet play of family life. Like the *Captivi*, it lacks female roles, and the characters are far more serious and dignified than is usually the case in Plautus' comedies. Although we find a spendthrift youth, an absent father returning unexpectedly, a hidden treasure, the plot is still far from stereotyped. Callicles' desire to preserve for his absent friend Charmides the latter's treasure leads to misunderstandings when Lesbonicus sells his father's house, ignorant of the existence of the hoard. A friendly deception which Callicles and a friend devise to provide Les-

---

[15] *Plautus and Terence*, p. 176; cf. Norwood's excellent analysis of the play in *The Art of Terence*, pp. 110 ff. See also Enk, *Mn* 13 (1947), pp. 86 ff.

[16] Norwood, *The Art of Terence*, p. 127.

[17] Cf. the words of Aeschinus in 629 ff., 707 ff., with Ctesipho's attitude towards his father in 518 ff.

[18] Cf. above, p. 121.

bonicus with money for his sister's dowry is discovered by Charmides on his return, at which time it is no longer necessary. But ignorance and deception are minor elements in the plot; the major problem concerns the honor of Lesbonicus and his unwillingness to have his sister marry without a dowry since the lack of a dowry meant a sacrifice of social prestige; Lysiteles is not only willing but eager to marry the sister without a dowry, and the conflict between the two youths constitutes the main action of the drama. The play contains much moralizing on virtue and vice, some of it rather tedious, and lacks the broad humor in which Plautus so often indulged although the attempts of Stasimus to help Lesbonicus and the meeting of the Swindler (Trinummus) and Charmides provide considerable amusement. Harsh finds in the first part of the play "excellent scenes of high comedy," but considers its conclusion rather farcical, and regrets that "the serious moral dilemma of the young men is not exploited in a more satisfactory manner."[19]

(4) The *Truculentus*, unlike the *Trinummus*, may be called an "unpleasant" play. It is primarily concerned with the delineation of characters who are unattractive and unsympathetic, and presents a serious and rather sordid picture of the life of a courtesan and her treatment of three foolish rivals for her favor. Although Miss Smith considers the *Truculentus* a comedy of intrigue,[20] there is actually very little plot. Phronesium pretends to have given birth to a baby in order to enrich herself at the expense of the soldier Stratophanes; she persuades Diniarchus, another suitor (who has wronged Callicles' daughter and is discovered to be the father of the child), to allow her to keep the baby until she has succeeded in swindling the soldier, and at the end of the play she promises to divide her favors between Stratophanes and a third lover as long as both bring her money. Astaphium, the courtesan's maid, sums up the situation (950):

A fool and a madman are competing for their own ruin. It's fine for us.

The depressing nature of the play and its low moral tone have led to much adverse criticism, but more modern writers consider it a masterpiece, one of Plautus' cleverest plays, a satiric comedy in which Plautus portrays with bitter cynicism an unpleasant aspect of ancient society.[21] Harsh calls the *Truculentus* "one of the most remarkable pieces of stark realism in classical drama."[22] It is perhaps significant that the play was one of Plautus' favorites; Cicero (*De sen.* 14, 50) relates that the playwright as an old man took great delight in both the *Pseudolus* and the *Truculentus*.

---

19 *A Handbook of Classical Drama*, pp. 370, 372.
20 *The Technique of Solution*, pp. 50 f.
21 Cf. Duckworth, *The Complete Roman Drama*, II, pp. 93 f.
22 *A Handbook of Classical Drama*, p. 373.

(5) The *Stichus*, adapted from an *Adelphoe* by Menander, almost defies classification; there is nothing quite like it in Roman comedy. Two sisters yearn for the return of their husbands and oppose their father's desire for divorce; the husbands (who are brothers) arrive, are reconciled with their father-in-law, and resist the attempts of a jolly parasite to cadge a free meal; the reunion and banquet of husbands and wives takes place off stage, and the play ends in a drunken revel of slaves which doubtless parodies the more restrained festivities of their masters indoors. The *Stichus* is hardly a drama; there is no real plot, and complication and denouement of the usual sort are lacking. The scenes fall into three groups: these might be called "The Abandoned Wives" (1-401), "The Homecoming, or the Disappointed Parasite" (402-640), and "The Carousal of the Slaves" (641-775); the center of interest shifts from one group of characters to another, and the action proceeds from serious comedy through farce to the festal conclusion of song and dance; many of the scenes are highly amusing, e.g., the parasite's excitement at the arrival of the brothers and the frustration of his hopes, and the desire of the father-in-law for a music girl. The play as a whole is a very merry one, but in its complete lack of a conventional dramatic plot it stands alone among the comedies of Plautus and Terence. As a social document it provides an interesting and humorous portrayal of certain aspects of ancient society, and depicts in particular the gaiety and freedom of the life of the slaves.

Character studies as such are rare in Roman comedy. In many plays, however, even when the plot seems motivated largely by coincidence or trickery, the characters have a decisive influence upon the course of the action; e.g., in the *Miles*, the pretense that Periplectomenus has a wife madly in love with the soldier succeeds only because the soldier has a conceited and lecherous nature. The exchange of roles in the *Captivi* is the direct result of the loyalty and devotion of master and slave, and the action of the *Hecyra* depends to no little degree upon the noble characters of the mother-in-law and the courtesan. The fact that only two comedies are listed as plays of character does not imply that character and plot are not intimately related in many other instances also.[23] But there is no reason to believe that Plautus, or even Terence, was able to delineate character with the subtlety or the psychological truth for which Menander is so often praised.

## Innocent Mistakes

The five plays which follow best display the dramatic complications caused by the working of *error*; the ignorance of the true identity of one or more individuals leads to misunderstandings for which no one is to blame, and the solution comes with the recognition or discovery of

[23] Cf. Legrand-Loeb, *The New Greek Comedy*, pp. 325 ff.

the truth. Chance, or coincidence, is an important factor in plays of this sort, and the excessive use of chance as a motivating force is sometimes condemned. However, the part played by chance usually concerns the antecedents of the comedy, not the action of the play itself; e.g., the fact that Pamphilus in the *Hecyra* married the very girl he had earlier violated at a festival, where neither had learned the identity of the other, is responsible for the numerous misunderstandings—but both the rape of Philumena and the subsequent marriage occurred months before the opening of the drama. In other words, chance prepares matters in advance and then allows the actors to play their parts with but little interference until the discovery of the truth which extricates them from their difficulties.

More will be said later about the use and importance of coincidence but it should be noted that in the *Rudens* the events are brought about by the god Arcturus, while in the *Amphitruo* the confusion arising from double identity is caused by Jupiter and Mercury who disguise themselves as Amphitruo and Sosia; in the latter instance the misapprehension in one sense is the result of deception, but from the viewpoint of the human characters the *errores* are just as incomprehensible as those which occur when Menaechmus II arrives in the city where his twin brother lives.

In most comedies of mistaken identity love plays an important part, and in many instances the denouement results from a series of stereotyped events—premarital violation of maidens, exposure and rescue of unwanted babies, kidnaping of children, the use of rings and tokens to establish their identity. These have been the ingredients of sentimental fiction in every age. Miss Macmullen, speaking of certain popular novels of the early twentieth century, says that "the fairy tale happy ending, the cheerful moral lesson, the salt of sex were combined in a perfect formula";[24] this formula was already old when it was taken over from Greek comedy by the Roman dramatists.

(6) The *Cistellaria* takes its name from the casket (*cistella*) of trinkets, whose discovery brings about the recognition of the heroine's identity. Alcesimarchus is madly in love with Selenium, his mistress, who believes herself to be the daughter of Melaenis. The complications begin when the father of Alcesimarchus insists that his son marry the daughter of Demipho, a situation very similar to that in Terence's *Andria*. The misunderstandings are brought to an end by the revelation that Selenium is also Demipho's daughter, a fact that had been made known to the audience early in the play (156 ff.). Demipho years before, after violating a maiden, had fled to Lemnos and married, leaving

---

[24] M. Macmullen, "Love's Old Sweetish Song," *Harper's Magazine*, 195 (1947), pp. 378 f. For examples of mistaken identity and recognition, cf. her analysis (pp. 376 f.) of the plots of *Freckles* (Gene Stratton Porter) and *The Eyes of the World* (Harold Bell Wright).

the girl to give birth to a baby which was abandoned but picked up by a woman who gave it to Melaenis to rear; after the death of his Lemnian wife, Demipho returned to Athens and married the mother of the lost baby, and together they instituted a search for the woman who had found the child. This unlikely series of events is typical of the means whereby Menander and his contemporaries accounted for the mistaken identities in their plays. That the very girl Demipho and his wife desired to find was living next door with Alcesimarchus is the type of coincidence which the stage-setting of Greek and Roman comedy made inevitable. The text of the central portion of the *Cistellaria* is badly mutilated, but in its present form there is little farce and buffoonery in the action; the play is a sentimental comedy in a serious vein—Alcesimarchus even toys with the idea of suicide (639 ff.)—and it is undoubtedly the most Menandrian of Plautus' comedies.

(7) The *Rudens* ("The Rope"), usually considered Plautus' masterpiece, is rich in both character and dramatic action. Its unusual setting—a stretch of seacoast after a storm and a shipwreck—gives it an atmosphere of romance quite unlike the other Roman comedies. Labrax, a slavedealer, had promised to sell Palaestra to Plesidippus but broke his word and set sail for Sicily. The intervention of the god Arcturus was responsible for the shipwreck of the *leno* at the very spot where he had agreed to meet Plesidippus and, moreover, where lived the aged Daemones, who discovers Palaestra to be his long-lost daughter. Again the recognition is made possible by tokens (*crepundia*) in a *cistella* but is effected in a natural manner. Gripus, who had gone fishing the night of the storm, found in the sea a trunk belonging to the *leno*, and it was Palaestra's attempt to claim her property that led to the revelation of her identity. The *Rudens* is an excellent example of the recognition play; much of the action is in a serious vein, e.g., the pathetic plight of the two shipwrecked girls, but this is relieved by many scenes of excellent comedy—the love scene of Sceparnio and Ampelisca, the arrival of the drenched and shivering Labrax and his crony, Trachalio's altercation with Gripus concerning the ownership of the trunk. Harsh says of the *Rudens* that it "is noteworthy not only for its romantic atmosphere but also for its unsurpassed vivacity, its irrepressible and sometimes sardonic humor, its dramatic irony, and its melodramatic pulsation of emotions."[25]

(8) Not only in the *Cistellaria* and the *Rudens*, but in most plays of mistaken identity, the recognition scene restores the heroine to her parents and makes possible her marriage to the youthful lover. Terence's *Hecyra* ("The Mother-in-law"), however, is unlike most Roman comedies in that it is a serious play of married life.[26] The numerous

---

[25] *A Handbook of Classical Drama*, p. 365. Cf. Post, *TAPhA* 69 (1938), p. 32: "There is more atmosphere in the *Rudens* of Plautus than in the whole of Terence."
[26] In other respects also, the comedy is most unconventional; cf. Duckworth, *The*

misunderstandings result from Philumena's action in leaving her husband's home during his absence. The separation is at first blamed upon Sostrata, Philumena's mother-in-law, and later upon the possibility that Pamphilus, the husband, has renewed his pre-marital affection for a courtesan. The real reason is that Philumena was violated before her marriage (although neither she nor her assailant learned the identity of the other) and is about to give birth to a child who, she thinks, is not her husband's. The fortunate discovery, brought about by the good services of the courtesan, that Pamphilus himself is the culprit and the father of the child solves all the difficulties and brings about the happy conclusion—the reunion of husband and wife. Although based upon a Greek original by Apollodorus, the *Hecyra* is remarkably similar to Menander's *Epitrepontes*, which apparently served Apollodorus as a model. Norwood considers the Terentian adaptation "the purest and most perfect example of classical high comedy, strictly so called, which dramatic literature can offer from any age or any nation,"[27] but few critics rate the play thus highly. Terence, using stock themes and motives in an unconventional manner, has made a courageous attempt to portray the development of character and emotional experience after marriage, but the play lacks both humor and dramatic action; the playwright's departure from the more normal technique of Roman comedy undoubtedly accounts for the failure of the comedy at its first two presentations.

(9) The *Menaechmi* is Plautus' most successful comedy of errors; pure farce, but skilfully constructed and rapidly moving, it has remained a favorite among later adapters and imitators. Menaechmus of Syracuse, searching for his long-lost twin brother, comes at last to Epidamnus, where the brother resides. The fun is fast and furious when he is mistaken for his brother by the latter's mistress, wife, parasite, father-in-law, and others. The basic implausibility that the newcomer and his slave Messenio should not realize they have reached the goal of their search is somewhat lessened by Messenio's warning that Epidamnus is filled with sharpers and seductive women on the watch for strangers. As Menaechmus grows more confused and angry, he is less apt to think of the true solution and, in any case, the continuance of the dramatic action depends upon his failure to realize the truth. The best scenes are those in which Menaechmus of Epidamnus returns from the forum to find a series of complications for which he naturally has no explanation. Plautus manipulates the numerous misunderstandings with great skill and takes unusual pains to make the identity of each brother clear whenever he enters. After the recognition scene, unduly prolonged but limited to Messenio and the two brothers, Menaechmus of Epidamnus decides

---

*Complete Roman Drama*, II, pp. 363 ff., and see below, "Surprise in Plautus and Terence" in chap. 8; "Female Roles" in chap. 9.

[27] *The Art of Terence*, p. 90; cf. Flickinger, *PhQ* 7 (1928), pp. 110 ff.

to sell his property at auction and return to Syracuse with his brother; Messenio, as he announces the auction, remarks cynically (1160):

His wife will be sold too, if any buyer can be found for her.

(10) The *Amphitruo*, considered one of Plautus' most successful plays, and the only mythological travesty extant, is a delightful comedy of errors involving two pairs of doublets. Much of the action is pure farce, as in the *Menaechmi*, but serious elements are present as well; the play is a *tragicomoedia*, as Mercury states in the prologue (cf. 50 ff.). The theme is the familiar legend of the birth of Hercules. Jupiter and Mercury, disguised as Amphitruo and his slave Sosia, have visited Amphitruo's house during the latter's absence, and Jupiter has made Alcumena pregnant. The play opens months later when Jupiter is again visiting Alcumena for a night of love-making. The conversion of the "long night" of generation into a night of dalliance enables the comedy of errors to conclude with the birth of Hercules and the subsequent miracles. The arrival of Sosia to announce his master's return leads to an amusing low comedy scene in which the slave is almost convinced by Mercury that he has lost his identity. There is excellent irony when Sosia swears by Jupiter that he is really Sosia, and Mercury replies (436 f.):

I swear by Mercury that Jupiter doesn't believe you; he'll believe me without an oath, I know, more than you on your oath.

When Amphitruo enters and finds Alcumena pregnant, the situation becomes tragic, for he suspects his wife of unfaithfulness. In a sense we have here the theme of an adulterous wife and a duped husband—a theme not elsewhere found in the extant *palliata*—but Alcumena is morally innocent of wrongdoing. Actually, she is a devoted wife and a person of honor and dignity; she is the noblest woman character in Plautine comedy, and deserves to rank with Sostrata, the unselfish and misunderstood mother-in-law of Terence's *Hecyra*. Bromia, Alcumena's maidservant, and Jupiter himself as *deus ex machina* reveal the truth and vouch for Alcumena's fidelity.

These five plays, although very dissimilar, have been grouped together inasmuch as the dramatic action depends upon the "innocent mistakes" of the characters. If the true identity of Selenium in the *Cistellaria*, or of Palaestra in the *Rudens*, had been known at the beginning of the play, the complications and difficulties into which the characters are plunged would never have occurred; nor would Philumena in the *Hecyra* have left her husband's house and returned to her own home, thus disrupting both households, if she had known her assailant to be her own husband. In the *Amphitruo* and the *Menaechmi*, comedies of error in the true sense of the word, confusion from double identity controls the entire action of the play; in the *Menaechmi* the confusion is accidental and is initiated by Menaechmus' search for his lost twin, while the confusion in the *Amphitruo* is the direct result of divine intrigue.

## Mistaken Identity and Deception

We pass now to a group of eight plays in which confusions arising from mistaken identity play an important part, but only a part, in the dramatic action. These comedies are more complicated in their structure and much of the action is motivated by deception rather than by *error* in the narrower sense. The theme of mistaken identity provides the framework of the comedy and contributes significantly to the denouement. If the intrigue is successful (as in the *Poenulus*), the discovery of the heroine's free birth supplements the completion of the intrigue and enables the hero to marry her; often, however, the trickery does not succeed, and the discovery of the deception complicates the action to a point where a revelation of identity is necessary to save the trickster from punishment, as in the *Captivi* and the *Epidicus*.[28] At times the recognition scene fails to have its usual function. It may lead to a change of plan or purpose (*Curculio, Epidicus*) or interfere with a deception already under way (*Heauton, Phormio*). The comic poets reveal great ingenuity in the manner in which they weave together the elements of trickery and recognition.

(11) The *Captivi*, like the *Trinummus*, is a quiet comedy but is rich in humor and pathos and irony. The play is unusual in that, as the prologue states (55 ff.) :

It is not composed in the hackneyed style of other comedies; there are in it no filthy lines that cannot be repeated, nor does it contain a perjured pimp, or evil courtesan, or braggart warrior.

The epilogue (1029 ff.) likewise stresses the fact that there is no love affair, no getting money by trickery, no young lover freeing a harlot without his father's knowledge; "few such comedies are written to make the good still better." The theme of the *Captivi* is the loyalty and devotion of master and slave; in the words of Michaut, it is a play of "graves événements et dangers tragiques, beau dévouement et noble fidélité, tristesse et joies paternelles, reconnaissances émouvantes."[29] Hegio has lost two sons; one, Paegnium, was stolen by a slave when a child; the other, Philopolemus, has recently been captured by the Eleans, and, to recover Philopolemus, Hegio begins to buy Elean captives, among whom are Philocrates and his slave Tyndarus (in reality the

---

[28] Cf. Smith, *The Technique of Solution*, p. 78 and n. 1.

[29] *Plaute*, 1, pp. 157 f. Michaut lists the play under Comedy of Manners and Portrayal of Everyday Life, and Lejay (*Plaute*, p. 131) considers it a psychological comedy. Although I include it among comedies of mistaken identity and deception, the extent to which it differs from the other plays in this category will be readily apparent.

lost Paegnium). The two prisoners exchange roles so that, when the slave is sent to arrange for the return of Philopolemus, it is really Philocrates who escapes. When another Elean captive (Aristophontes) convinces Hegio that he has been victimized, Tyndarus is punished for the deception, but Philocrates returns with Philopolemus and the kidnaping slave, and the recognition of Tyndarus' identity solves all difficulties. The intrigue has been criticized as contributing little to the solution of the plot, but the combination of trickery and mistaken identity provides excellent dramatic irony; the words of the master and slave in their assumed roles are most effective. Tyndarus (as Philocrates) says to Hegio:

> Formerly I was just as free as your own son. (310)
> My father misses me just as you miss your own son. (316)

Here Tyndarus intends to lie, but Hegio, thinking Tyndarus is Philocrates, believes he is telling the truth, while "the audience know that Tyndarus is really saying what is true because he is the son of Hegio."[30] This is actually a rare instance of triple irony, in which the words have one meaning to the speaker, another to the hearer, and a third to the spectators, who know the truth about Tyndarus' parentage. The unusually serious tone of the play is relieved by the comic character of the parasite Ergasilus. His role has been considered unnecessary,[31] but he is useful in providing an emotional foil for Hegio. Critical estimates of the *Captivi* have varied widely. Lessing, believing that comedy should have an ethical purpose, considered it the finest play ever produced. Modern scholars point to many weaknesses, e.g., the uselessness of the exchange of roles, and the excessive credulity of Hegio,[32] but these are less serious than is often believed. The intrigue, in fact, would have succeeded in providing for Philocrates' freedom, had not Philopolemus been found; and Hegio's credulity does not seem excessive in view of the cleverness with which the captives play their parts.

(12) The *Curculio* is a short play (about half the length of the *Miles* or the *Rudens*) and one of the less popular of Plautus' comedies, but it is fast moving and contains several amusing scenes. The plot lacks originality: Phaedromus is in love with Planesium, who is in the power of a *leno* (Cappadox) and about to be given over to a soldier (Thera-

[30] Harsh, *A Handbook of Classical Drama*, p. 349. Cf. Moulton, *The Ancient Classical Drama*, pp. 418 f. For other examples of dramatic irony in Roman comedy, see below, "Suspense and Irony" in chap. 8.

[31] Cf. Michaut, *Plaute*, 1, p. 158. Hough (*AJPh* 63, 1942, pp. 26 ff.) believes that Ergasilus was added by Plautus from a second Greek original.

[32] Cf. e.g., Lejay, *Plaute*, p. 133. Norwood is unusually violent in his denunciation of the play; cf. *Plautus and Terence*, p. 63 ("sheer blockheadedness"), p. 89 ("gulf of ineptitude"), p. 91 ("crass nonsense"). Norwood believes that Hegio's original plan to buy up prisoners was absurd but this, like so many improbabilities and coincidences in ancient comedy, lies outside the dramatic action of the play. On Lessing's opinion of the *Captivi*, see Agnew, *CW* 39 (1945-46), pp. 66 ff.

pontigonus), who has already deposited the money for her with a banker. By means of a deception, engineered by the parasite Curculio, Phaedromus secures the girl. The soldier arrives in anger, but discovers to his surprise (and to that of the audience) that Planesium is his sister. Cappadox now becomes the victim; he must reimburse the soldier since he has guaranteed that Planesium was not of free birth. The elements of deception and recognition are well combined, for the stolen ring of the soldier is instrumental both in getting Planesium from Cappadox and in bringing about the revelation of her identity. The play, in spite of its brevity, contains a large number of the conventional character types—young lover, sweetheart, impudent slave, drunken old woman, parasite, pimp, cook, braggart soldier—but they are portrayed with humor and originality. Among the interesting features of the comedy are Phaedromus' serenade to his sweetheart's door (cf. 147 ff.), the address of the *choragus* to the spectators (462 ff.), and the rather unusual setting; the scene is laid in Epidaurus, and on the stage is the temple of Aesculapius, to which Cappadox has gone to cure himself of his many ailments.

(13) The *Epidicus*, although, like the *Curculio*, a short play, has a much more intricate plot, involving, in addition to the recognition, two deceptions of a *senex* by an intriguing slave, one of which is completed when the comedy begins. During the absence of Stratippocles, Epidicus has persuaded Stratippocles' father (Periphanes) to accept his son's sweetheart (Acropolistis) as his long-lost daughter (Telestis, Stratippocles' half-sister). Unfortunately, Stratippocles has fallen in love with another girl, a captive, and on his return from war wishes Epidicus to provide money for his new love. An ingenious and elaborate deception follows. Epidicus, one of the best of Plautus' intriguing slaves, gets money from Periphanes by pretending to buy Stratippocles' sweetheart (i.e., Acropolistis) in order to sell her to a soldier. Actually he hires a music girl to pose as Acropolistis.[33] Amusing scenes follow: the soldier comes for Acropolistis and indignantly rejects the music girl; Philippa, the mother of Telestis, is heartbroken when she discovers that the supposed daughter is not Telestis. Epidicus is saved from the consequences of his knavery by his fortunate discovery that Stratippocles' new love is in reality Telestis, his youthful master's half-sister, but for Stratippocles the recognition does not bring a happy ending; the only reference to his later fate is the suggestion of Epidicus (653) that he, Stratippocles, return to Acropolistis, his first love. The unsatisfactory nature of the conclusion has led many scholars to the belief that Plautus has changed the ending of the Greek original; whereas marriages between half-brother and half-sister—children of the same father but of different mothers—were legal in Athens, they were looked upon as incest

---

[33] The trickery here is unusually involved; see Duckworth, *T. Macci Plauti Epidicus*, pp. 277 ff., and bibliography there cited.

by the Romans. But if Telestis lacked Athenian citizenship, as seems probable, her marriage to Stratippocles in the Greek original would have been equally impossible.[34]

(14) In the *Poenulus* ("The Carthaginian"), one of the least successful of Plautus' comedies, an elaborate deception is directed by Milphio against Lycus, who has in his possession two sisters, the elder of whom is beloved by Milphio's master, Agorastocles. This trick, which involves impersonation and the use of witnesses (*aduocati*), will embroil the *leno* in a lawsuit for accepting stolen money from a slave, and will result in his losing his property, including the girls. The intrigue is successful but before the lawsuit takes place Milphio learns that the girls are of free birth and devises a second plan,[35] in which Hanno, a newly arrived Carthaginian, is to claim the girls as his daughters. By an amazing coincidence the fiction proves to be fact, and Hanno not only discovers his daughters but recognizes Agorastocles as his brother's son.

(15) The basic error in Terence's *Andria* arises from ignorance of the heroine's identity, and the situation is not unlike that in the *Cistellaria* of Plautus. Simo wishes his son Pamphilus to marry the daughter of Chremes (Philumena), but Pamphilus has fallen in love with Glycerium, a girl from Andros, and Chremes quite properly refuses to permit the marriage. The complications begin when Simo, in order to test his son's feelings, pretends that the marriage will take place, and hopes, if Pamphilus consents, to persuade Chremes to agree. Davus, the unscrupulous slave, suspects Simo of trickery and advises Pamphilus to fall in with his father's suggestion since, as he thinks, there will be no marriage. Pamphilus' friend, Charinus, who is in love with Philumena, suspects that Pamphilus has really transferred his affections to Chremes' daughter, and Pamphilus finds himself in danger of marrying the wrong girl. The misapprehensions and fears of the characters are multiplied and the result is, in the words of Donatus, an *elegans perturbatio* in which Simo, Davus, Pamphilus, Charinus, and Chremes are all at odds with one another (*ad And.* 625). Davus is an amusing character; unlike the typical intriguing slave of Plautus, his suggestions and plans increase Pamphilus' difficulties; cf. 669 ff.:

[34] Cf. Keyes, *TAPhA* 71 (1940), pp. 217 ff. For a summary of the older views, see Duckworth, *T. Macci Plauti Epidicus*, pp. 394 ff. There is little support in the *Epidicus* for Kuiper's belief that many Greek originals of Plautus and Terence concluded with marriages between half-brothers and half-sisters; cf. Keyes, *ibid.*, p. 229, who refers to this "plague of half-sisters," and suggests that "the restorers of Greek comedies might do better to omit them from their reconstructions."

[35] Cf. Wieand, *Deception in Plautus*, p. 119, who says of the first deception: "the whole trick is purposeless"; rather, it is rendered unnecessary by Milphio's information about the girls' birth and the subsequent recognition scene. The difficulties in the *Poenulus*, like those in the *Miles* and other comedies, have often been attributed to *contaminatio*; see below, pp. 199, 201, 206.

DA.: I've been fooled, but I'm not finished.

PA.: I understand.

DA.: This method didn't work, but we'll try another, unless you think one failure means that things can't now be straightened out.

PA.: On the contrary. I'm sure that, if you put your mind to it, you'll land me into two marriages instead of one.

Equally entertaining are the scenes in which Davus tells the truth and Simo's suspicions of his slave lead him into self-deception. Terence has introduced into his first comedy a number of new and interesting variations of the usual stock themes and devices, but the solution depends upon coincidence in its crudest form. The opportune and unexpected arrival of Crito leads to the revelation that Glycerium is also the daughter of Chremes. Pamphilus is thus able to fulfill his promise to his father and at the same time marry the girl he loves, and the love affair of Charinus (who, with his slave, has been added by Terence to the original plot) is by this same discovery brought to a happy conclusion.

(16) Terence's *Heauton Timorumenos* ("The Self-Tormentor") has a dual plot—two young men in love, two sweethearts, two fathers. Menedemus repents of his former harshness towards his son Clinia but, not wishing to appear too generous, is willing to be cheated out of the money which he thinks Clinia needs for his sweetheart. Menedemus' friend and neighbor, Chremes, aids and abets Syrus in the supposed deception of Menedemus, not realizing that he is the real victim. Chremes' own son, Clitipho, is in love with Bacchis, a mercenary courtesan. When Bacchis and Antiphila (Clinia's virtuous ladylove) come to Chremes' house, Bacchis poses as the mistress of Clinia, at the suggestion of Syrus, and this deception—coupled with the ignorance of the characters that Antiphila is really Chremes' daughter—is responsible for the misunderstandings in the play. The recognition occurs early in the dramatic action and provides additional complications since the solution of Clinia's problem threatens the exposure of Clitipho's love affair. Mistaken identity and trickery are thus closely interwoven. Syrus' new deception of Chremes is extremely intricate, and depends as much upon the use of truth as of falsehood; as Norwood says, "Menedemus is to know that he is not being fooled as Chremes thinks he is, and is to tell Chremes, so as to fool him, that he is not being fooled as he intended to allow himself to be. The stalwart sons of Romulus must have found this trying."[36] In spite of its complexity the trick is rather pointless, and Chremes learns that his own son's escapades have been far more serious than Clinia's. The contrast between the two fathers and their theories of education anticipates the theme of the *Adelphoe* but is less successfully developed. Chremes, a busybody, always interested in the affairs of others,[37] is generous with his advice to Menedemus about

---

[36] *Plautus and Terence*, p. 150.

[37] Cf. 77: *homo sum: humani nil a me alienum puto.* This famous verse, often

the value of confidence and understanding between father and son. He does not, however, practice his own philosophy and in the end it is Menedemus who rebukes him for his stern treatment of his son (cf. 922 ff.). Chremes pardons Clitipho, on the condition that he give up Bacchis and accept as wife a girl of his father's choice—one of the few instances in Roman comedy where a love affair does not have a happy ending.

(17) The *Eunuchus* is rich in character and action; more Plautine in its farcical humor than his other comedies, it was Terence's most successful play financially and, in the opinion of many modern critics, one of his best.[38] Again trickery and mistaken identity are fused together into a unified whole. Again we have a double plot with the love complications of two young men. But in addition there is an amusing subplot with the characters of a boastful soldier (Thraso) and his parasite (Gnatho); these two characters have been added by Terence from a second Menandrian original and, though condemned as unnecessary, they provide much comedy (e.g., the attack of Thraso and his "army" upon Thais' house, 771 ff.) and are admirably integrated in the action. Phaedria, in love with Thais, a courtesan, consents to retire until his sweetheart has procured from Thraso a young girl (Pamphila) whom she suspects of being freeborn. Chaerea, Phaedria's brother, falls in love with Pamphila and, impersonating a eunuch (Phaedria's gift to Thais), gains admission to the courtesan's house where he takes full advantage of his opportunity and violates the maiden; boasting of his deed to Antipho, Chaerea says (604 ff.):

Was I to lose such an opportunity, so brief, so eagerly desired, so unexpected? If I had, I would certainly have been what I pretended to be.

The discovery of the outrage arouses the anger of the household, but Chaerea is saved from the consequences of his act by the opportune arrival of his father and the recognition of Pamphila as the sister of Chremes, a young man whom Thraso has wrongly suspected of being his rival. The final arrangement between Phaedria and Thraso, even if merely financial, is somewhat reminiscent of Plautus' *Truculentus*, as is Phaedria's situation at the opening of the play. But Thais is a much finer character than Phronesium: wise, generous, and sympathetic, she is one of Terence's most attractive women and has much in common with Bacchis in the *Hecyra*.

(18) In Terence's *Phormio*, love affairs, deception, mistaken identity, and recognition are blended with an expert hand. Structurally perhaps the best of Roman comedies, it makes effective use of suspense and surprise, and is deservedly praised for brilliance of dialogue and

---

quoted in antiquity, has been used as an illustration of Terence's belief in the common brotherhood of man. See below, p. 304 and n. 66.

[38] Cf. Rand. *TAPhA* 63 (1932), pp. 54 f.

liveliness of action. Although the *Phormio* lacks the serious content and the psychological interest of the *Adelphoe*, it is fully its equal in entertainment value. Phormio, the parasite, an impudent rogue who controls the action from beginning to end, is one of the cleverest scoundrels in ancient comedy. When Antipho, son of Demipho, fell in love with a poor but respectable girl (Phanium), Phormio engineered the marriage by making the fictitious claim that Antipho was her nearest relative and according to law must marry her. Phaedria, son of Chremes (Demipho's brother), is devoted to a music girl but has no money to purchase her. This is the situation at the beginning of the play: Antipho is married but dreads the danger of being separated from his wife; Phaedria is in love and fears he cannot procure his sweetheart. The return of the *senes* leads to numerous complications; Chremes, who has had a second wife in Lemnos, is eager to marry his Lemnian daughter to Antipho. He and his brother plan to break up the present marriage, and so persuade Phormio to take Phanium off Antipho's hands for a sum of money—the very amount needed by Phaedria to purchase his sweetheart. The recognition scene causes an amusing reversal in their plans, for Chremes discovers that his daughter is already Antipho's wife. "What? Does he have two wives?" Chremes asks in amazement (754), evidently attributing to his nephew his own loose morality. But to the surprise of all, including the audience, Phormio's fiction has turned into reality and Chremes, in terror that his own secret life will be revealed, is now anxious to halt the projected divorce. Phormio, discovering Chremes' secret, uses it to excellent advantage; his revelation to Chremes' wife of her husband's second marriage provides satisfactorily for Phaedria. Chremes has no answer to his wife's question (1040 f.):

Do you think it's so disgraceful for your son, a young man, to have one mistress, when you have two wives?

The *Phormio* brings to an end the list of plays which employ the conventional themes of mistaken identity and recognition. It will be noted that the introduction of trickery into a framework of general misapprehension produces plots of greater complexity, and that in most instances the solution of the plot depends upon the *anagnorisis*, not upon the successful outcome of the deception. In the comedies of Terence (with the exception of the *Hecyra*), the situation is unusually involved, for the themes of mistaken identity and intrigue are blended into a double plot portraying the fears and misapprehensions of two sets of characters. This duality method is so important an aspect of Terence's dramatic technique that it will be treated more fully in the next chapter; from the standpoint of the *anagnorisis*, however, it is significant that Terence, when he presents two love affairs, limits the recognition in each play to one of the heroines. The true identity of Glycerium (*Andria*), Antiphila (*Heauton*), Pamphila (*Eunuchus*), and Phanium (*Phormio*) is revealed, but the second love affair, if with a music girl or courtesan, usually results in an illicit union (*Eunuchus, Phormio, Adelphoe*). Bacchis in the *Heauton* is so hardened and mercenary a creature that Clitipho is forced to give her up for a decent girl of his father's choice. In the *Andria* the second love affair is unusual; Charinus' love for a respectable girl whose virtue is still intact has been considered an anticipation of a more modern attitude towards love and sex. More frequently in Plautus and Terence the heroine, if of respectable parentage, has been violated before the opening of the drama (*Aulularia, Adelphoe*), or she is a foreigner, a courtesan, or a slave girl. When the virtue of such a maiden is stressed, it is, of course, a foreshadowing of her later recognition as an Attic citizen.

In all comedies involving mistaken identity and *anagnorisis* the element of chance is necessarily prominent. It is somewhat startling to discover that Phormio's supposedly false claim about the relationship of Antipho and Phanium proves to be the truth. Milphio's attempted deception in the *Poenulus* about the parentage of the two Carthaginian sisters likewise turns into fact and, although this recognition was announced to the audience in the prologue, the coincidence is hardly less striking. Still, as I said above, the use of chance should not in most instances be too severely criticized. It seems at first sight highly improbable that, in the *Andria*, Glycerium, whom Pamphilus' father wished him to discard for the daughter of Chremes, should (as in the *Cistellaria*) prove to be the daughter of the very man desired as a father-in-law, and that in the *Epidicus* the very girl whom Stratippocles purchased as a prospective mistress should turn out to be his lost half-sister. But such discoveries are the result of a long chain of events; certainly no ancient audience would have been critical about incidents which had happened long before the play began, in comedy far less than in tragedy, where even in a masterpiece such as the *Oedipus Rex* of Sophocles the antecedents of the action are not free of improbabilities (Aristotle, *Poet.* 1454b).

A more important question remains: are we justified in condemning the use of chance in comic drama, if such apparently improbable happenings occur in real life? In 1937, while engaged upon a critical edition of the *Epidicus*, I read in the *New York Herald Tribune* the following two items, which deserve to be quoted in full:

"Alessandria, Italy, March 4.—For most of the thirty-one years of his foundling life Michele Debiago yearned to find his relatives. Recently he moved here from a neighboring town and met twenty-nine-year-old Maria Debiago, also a foundling, to whom he became greatly attached. Today they compared identical halves of a silver medal they wore around their necks and found they were brother and sister."

"Warrensburg, Mo., Nov. 1.—Ben Ipock and Mary Lee Williams settled down to life as brother and sister under the same roof today.

The marriage was annulled last week when they learned of their true relationship. Their father and mother died within a year almost twenty years ago and they were taken to the orphanage at Jefferson City. Mr. and Mrs. Ben Williams, of Chilhowee, adopted Mary Lee. Mr. and Mrs. Sod Yocum, of Mountain Grove, adopted Ben. Six months ago Ben found farm work at the Williams home. He fell in love with Mary Lee, who thought the Williamses were her true parents. A month ago Mary Lee accompanied Ben on a visit to his foster parents, and en route they were married. Meanwhile, Mrs. Williams, not knowing of the secret marriage, discovered that the couple were brother and sister. Ben decided to remain here with his former wife's parents."

The similarity of these stories to the situation in the *Epidicus* proves that fact, if not stranger than fiction, deals with happenings of equal unlikelihood. Stratippocles' falling in love with and buying his own sister is "a highly improbable coincidence," as Harsh states,[39] but the highly improbable does sometimes happen. That such a coincidence is typical of New Comedy is of course true. Syriscus says in Menander's *Epitrepontes* (124 ff.) :

A youth about to marry his sister was restrained by the discovery of tokens; one found and saved a mother, another a brother.

But such events do occur even in modern times; in antiquity exposure of children, kidnapings, shipwrecks, forced separations, the discovery of foundlings, were relatively far more frequent, and their appearance in comedy merely means that New Comedy in this respect mirrored the life of the period and developed what sometimes happened in real life into themes that became conventional and stereotyped.

The use of chance is more reprehensible when an external character is mechanically introduced to motivate the recognition. In the *Captivi*, Stalagmus, the runaway slave, is brought in at the end to reveal the identity of Tyndarus. He is essential if the *anagnorisis* is to take place, but his arrival is unexpected and unmotivated. Similarly, in the *Andria*, Crito arrives without warning to disclose that Glycerium is Chremes' daughter; he is, as Donatus says, a *persona ad catastropham machinata*, whose sole purpose is to reveal the *error fabulae* (cf. *ad And*. 796, 904). There are many characters in Roman comedy whose primary function is to serve as "discovering agents" (e.g., Sophrona in the *Phormio*, Bacchis in the *Hecyra*), but such characters are usually bound neatly to the plot of the play;[40] Stalagmus and Crito are introduced far more crudely than is the regular practice of the ancient drama-

---

[39] *A Handbook of Classical Drama*, p. 355.

[40] Cf. Smith, *The Technique of Solution*, pp. 63 f., and, on the abrupt appearance of Crito and Stalagmus, p. 64, n. 2; see also Hough, *AJPh* 63 (1942), pp. 31 f. Norwood (*The Art of Terence*, pp. 30 f.) attempts to justify the entrance of Crito by saying that "the very fact which has made Crito necessary has also brought him"; on this, see Gomme, *Essays in Greek History and Literature*, p. 271.

tists. That Terence himself was conscious of the awkwardness of Crito's entrance is evident and he put it to excellent use when Simo refused to believe Davus' story of Crito's arrival (855 ff.) and said later to Chremes (915 ff.) :

> This fellow an honest citizen? When he arrived so opportunely on the very day of the wedding, and never came here before? (*ironically*) He is to be believed, of course.

The conventional recognition scene was, at best, a rather mechanical device which in most comedies of mistaken identity (e.g., *Cistellaria, Menaechmi, Poenulus, Andria*) solved the difficulties of the characters and brought the comedy to an end. A few plays show a refreshing variation from the usual technique. In Plautus' *Rudens* the main complication is solved when Palaestra is restored to her parents, but the minor threads concerning Labrax and Gripus provide scenes of delightful humor at the end of the play. The tricking of the soldier in the *Curculio* ends suddenly with the discovery that he is the heroine's brother, and the *anagnorisis* in the *Epidicus* separates the *adulescens* from the girl with whom he is enamored. But the most interesting treatment of the recognition scene occurs in two comedies of Terence (*Heauton, Phormio*), where the revelation of identity complicates the action and increases the fears of the characters.

## Guileful Deception

The remaining eight comedies, all by Plautus, are plays of trickery only, in which the misapprehensions and confusions are created by willful lies and impersonations by one or more characters. The element of chance sometimes helps the plot, but is much less prominent than in comedies of mistaken identity. In the *Miles*, Palaestrio before the play begins has fallen into the hands of the very man who has possession of his master's sweetheart. Occasionally the opportune entrance of a character suggests to an intriguing slave the nature of his deception, e.g., the arrival of Cleomachus in *Bacch*. 842, of Harpax in *Pseud*. 594, and in each instance the slave comments upon the fact that he has been aided by chance (*Bacch*. 884, *Pseud*. 667 ff.).

In six of the eight plays the deception is engineered by wily slaves, but some are much cleverer and more resourceful than others, and their victims are completely overthrown and have no possible redress. The trickery when successful does not result in marriage (as in recognition plays where the heroine is found to be of free birth) but in the illicit union of the youthful lovers. Actually, in plays of this type, the love affair is often of secondary importance and serves primarily as a pretext for the trickery—to give the intriguing slave a justification for indulging in the knavery so dear to his heart (and to that of the audience). In the *Pseudolus* and the *Mostellaria*, for instance, the interest of the spectators throughout the greater part of the dramatic action is directed far less to the lovers and their problems than to the success or failure of the deception and the manner in which the impudent slave extricates himself from his difficulties.

Among the plays in this group are some of Plautus' most farcical and best known comedies: *Bacchides, Miles, Mostellaria,* and *Pseudolus.* They lack the serious tone, the richness and variety, to be found in some of his other works (e.g., the *Amphitruo, Aulularia, Captivi,* and *Rudens*) but they are conspicuous for their brilliance and rapidity of dialogue, the gaiety and insolence of the tricksters, the cleverness and ingenuity with which the tricks are conceived and carried out.

(19) The *Miles Gloriosus* ("The Braggart Warrior"), a long comedy with two delightful deceptions, has as a central character the boastful soldier, Pyrgopolynices, whose stupid conceit and lustful desires motivate the greater part of the action. Philocomasium, the sweetheart of Pleusicles, has fallen into the hands of the soldier, as has Palaestrio, formerly the slave of Pleusicles. After summoning Pleusicles to the home of Periplectomenus next door, Palaestrio makes it possible for the lovers to meet by digging a secret passage between the dividing wall of the two houses. If this deed, which has been completed before the opening of the play, be considered a separate trick, the comedy actually contains three deceptions,[41] but the hole in the wall is usually considered a necessary preliminary to the fooling of Sceledrus, who discovers Philocomasium's presence next door. With the capable assistance of the heroine Palaestrio finally persuades the slave that he has seen Philocomasium's twin sister (who is, of course, a product of Palaestrio's fertile imagination). For the lovers to have employed the secret passage as a means of escape would have provided a dangerous and unsatisfactory solution, and Palaestrio now develops a more elaborate and amusing intrigue in which five helpers are needed to assist the *architectus*— Philocomasium, Pleusicles, Periplectomenus, a courtesan (Acroteleutium) and her maid. Acroteleutium, pretending to be the neighbor's wife, so appeals to Pyrgopolynices' vanity and lust that he willingly sends away Philocomasium with gifts (including Palaestrio, to whom he is grateful for the slave's supposedly kind services). The soldier's discomfiture is thus complete, and he is only too happy to escape the dire consequences of his attempted adultery. The *Miles* has often been condemned for clumsy construction, long and irrelevant scenes, and structural flaws which have been attributed to the process of *contaminatio,*[42] but many of the scenes are Plautine farce at its best, and Pyrgopolynices, as he exults in his prowess as man-killer and lady-killer, is by far the best of the braggart warriors in Roman comedy.

---

[41] Cf. Wieand, *Deception in Plautus,* p. 102; Smith, *The Technique of Solution,* p. 45.

[42] See below, pp. 199, 200, 201, 206.

Another feature of unusual interest is the trick of the secret passage and the pretended twin sister—one version of a famous story which has appeared in numerous forms throughout the Near East and Europe.[43]

(20) The *Persa* is a light farce in which the characters represent the lowest strata of ancient society—slaves, a *leno*, a parasite and his daughter. Toxilus borrows funds from his friend Sagaristio to procure the freedom of his sweetheart, and then gets the money back from Dordalus, a slavedealer, by a clever trick; Sagaristio, posing as a Persian, sells to the *leno* Saturio's daughter (disguised as a Persian captive). Dordalus' greed is such that he is willing to buy the girl without guarantee of title, and he loses his money when Saturio claims the girl as his daughter. The play ends in a scene of riotous revelry in which additional abuse and ridicule are heaped upon Dordalus' head. The comedy contains much buffoonery and coarse humor, amid which the moralizing of Saturio's virtuous and idealistic daughter strikes an amusingly incongruous note; in its emphasis on the low life of slaves and in the final slave-banquet, more suggestive of comic opera or burlesque than of straight farce, the play has much in common with the *Stichus*.

(21) The *Pseudolus*, one of Plautus' most amusing plays of intrigue, has in its title role a slave who in shrewdness and self-confidence is fully the equal of Epidicus and Palaestrio. The usual motive of a young master (Calidorus) in love with a girl who is about to be sold to a soldier motivates a deception against the slavedealer which, as in the *Persa*, is completely successful. Plautus devotes much attention to the portrayal of Ballio, undoubtedly the most villainous and repulsive *leno* in Roman comedy. The intrigue is complicated by the suspicions of Simo, father of the *adulescens*, that Pseudolus will attempt to get the needed twenty minae from him. Pseudolus warns Simo to be on his guard:

You yourself will give me the money, I swear; I'll get it out of you. (508 f., cf. 517 f.)

Then Pseudolus says that he will first swindle Ballio, and Simo promises, if the slave accomplishes these tricks, to give him twenty minae of his own free will. The deception of Ballio involves a double impersonation—Pseudolus pretends to be Ballio's slave when the soldier's messenger (Harpax) arrives, and procures an assistant to pose as Harpax. Ballio, completing the financial transaction (as he thinks), bets Simo twenty minae that Pseudolus' trickery won't succeed. Their meeting with the real Harpax (whom they take at first to be Pseudolus' assistant) brings about the discovery of the truth. Simo collects from Ballio and pays Pseudolus who says (1314):

You said you wouldn't give it to me, but you're paying it just the same.

[43] Cf. Brotherton, *TAPhA* 55 (1924), pp. 128 ff.

The confusing wagers and financial transactions have led some scholars to believe that Plautus has omitted from the *Pseudolus* a deception of Simo which existed in the Greek original, possibly in a second Greek original, in which case the difficulties are the result of *contaminatio*. But Pseudolus speaks in 1314 as if he has made good his threat to get money from Simo. Possibly Simo's promise to pay is the very means Pseudolus had in mind when he made the wager. Certainly it is extremely doubtful if the Roman audience would have noticed the logical inconsistency, for the comedy is fast-moving and full of fun. Especially noteworthy is the low comedy of the concluding scenes, in which the drunken Pseudolus gloats over his victory, returns ten minae to Simo, and invites him to join his son's celebration.

(22) In the *Mostellaria* ("The Haunted House"), the victim of the deception is the father but, as in the *Epidicus*, the knavery is discovered and the intriguing slave narrowly escapes a severe penalty for his misdeeds. The opening scenes of the comedy are excellent. A long exposition provides a careful delineation of Tranio, his master Philolaches, and the latter's mistress Philematium; the dressing scene in which Philolaches eavesdrops on Philematium and her maid, the arrival of Delphium and the drunken Callidamates, and the banquet which is interrupted by Tranio's announcement of the father's return add unusual richness and variety to the theme of intrigue and are deservedly popular. With the arrival of Theopropides, the love affair is pushed into the background—indoors, to be more exact—and the center of interest shifts to Tranio's attempt to keep the *senex* from learning the true state of affairs in his household. Tranio's series of lies, developed one from another on the spur of the moment, are entertaining and full of surprises. The house is haunted, so Philolaches has moved away. But why did he borrow money from the *danista*? To buy another house. Where? The house of Simo next door. When Theopropides wants to examine the house, Tranio deceives Simo also, and even delights in ridiculing the two men to their face; cf. 832 ff.:

Do you see the picture of a crow making fools of two old vultures? . . . The crow is standing between the vultures and pecking at each in turn.

Deception of this nature can have only a temporary success but, even when Tranio's castle of falsehoods crumbles and Theopropides threatens him with punishment, the slave's insolence is in no way lessened; cf. 1116 ff.:

TH.: I'll make an example of you, I will!
TR.: You'll use me as an example because you approve of me, eh?
TH.: Tell me, what kind of a son did I leave here when I went away?
TR.: The usual kind—one with feet, hands, fingers, ears, eyes, lips.
TH. (*enraged*): I'm asking you a different question.
TR.: Well, I'm giving you a different answer.

When Callidamates intercedes in the slave's behalf, Tranio adds (1178 f.):

> Why not consent? As if I wouldn't commit another crime tomorrow, and then you can punish me for both.

(23) The *Bacchides* combines two deceptions in a comedy that has many surprising developments and unexpected reversals. The plot is complex, with a dualism of structure rare in Plautus—two young men (Mnesilochus and Pistoclerus), two love affairs, two courtesans (sisters, both named Bacchis), and two fathers (Nicobulus and Philoxenus). The love affair of Pistoclerus is of secondary importance but the two sets of characters are closely interwoven. The ingenious lies of Chrysalus have enabled Mnesilochus to use as his own the money which he had brought for Nicobulus, his father, but the *adulescens* learns of Pistoclerus' love for Bacchis and, being ignorant of the existence of a sister of the same name and convinced that his friend has betrayed him, reveals the deception to his father and returns the money. A second intrigue is now necessary, and Chrysalus' task is doubly difficult since the *senex* is on his guard. But the trickster is equal to the occasion; the second trick involves the pretense that Mnesilochus' rival, a soldier, is actually the husband of Bacchis; two letters from Mnesilochus (composed by Chrysalus) and the pretended reluctance of the slave to participate in the action (cf. 1061 ff.) make the second tricking of the *senex* both plausible and amusing. Nicobulus pays out to the soldier and to Chrysalus (for Mnesilochus) only to discover that he has been duped a second time (1090; cf. 1128).[44] Both he and Philoxenus are distressed at the love affairs of their sons, but, won over by the blandishments of the two courtesans, they consent to join their sons at a banquet.

In the plays of intrigue already mentioned, when the trickery has been directed against a soldier (*Miles*) or a *leno* (*Curculio, Persa, Poenulus, Pseudolus*),[45] the victory of the intriguing slave is complete and the dupe has no means of recovering either money or girl, even when he discovers the nature of the fraud. The situation is different when the victim is the father of the *adulescens*; in such cases the deception is revealed and the trickster narrowly escapes punishment, being saved by a chance discovery (*Epidicus*) or by the intercession of other characters (*Bacchides, Mostellaria*). Deception in Terence, as we shall see below,

---

[44] Some critics find in the *Bacchides* three deceptions and believe that Plautus has added an intrigue to the two tricks of the Menandrian original (*Dis Exapaton*); cf. Smith, *The Technique of Solution*, p. 88, n. 2. For an analysis of the trickery in the *Bacchides*, see Wieand, *Deception in Plautus*, pp. 16 ff., who points out that the third attempt to get money "is really a second application of the second trick" (p. 25). Nicobulus is still under the misapprehension that Bacchis is the wife of the soldier, and he is eager to free his son from her clutches.

[45] In the *Curculio* the soldier appears at first to be the victim since he has already deposited the necessary money for Planesium, but the discovery that he is her brother makes the *leno* the real dupe, as he must refund the amount received.

does not follow a fixed pattern. Chremes' attitude towards Syrus is most unusual (cf. *Heaut.* 975 ff.) and the two *senes* in the *Phormio* are helpless in the hands of the parasite. In Plautine comedy, when a soldier or a *leno* is the victim, he is presented in a grotesque manner, and is mocked and ridiculed by the other characters. This is not true of the father as a dupe; he may be portrayed as almost unbelievably stupid and gullible, but he is less grossly caricatured and retains a modicum of sympathy. When, however, the *senes* in Plautus cease to be merely dupes and become either accomplices or rivals of their sons, they are no longer merely the victims of trickery; instead, they have the role of chief intriguer, but their deceptions fail; they become the object of mockery and are punished for their lechery, at least to a degree.[46] There is no character in Roman comedy more repulsive than an amorous old man who attempts to conceal his lustful desires from his wife or son. We have seen that the *senes* yielded to the seductive entreaties of the courtesans in the concluding scenes of the *Bacchides*. The three remaining comedies are plays of trickery which depart from the usual pattern in both the nature of the intrigue and the role of the *senes*.

(24) In the *Asinaria* ("The Comedy of Asses"), Demaenetus aids his son Argyrippus in gaining possession of Philaenium, whom the youth loves desperately. Neither father nor son has money although Artemona, wife of Demaenetus, is rich. A deception, engineered by two slaves with the assistance of Demaenetus, provides the needed amount. The trick involves the impersonation of Artemona's overseer to whom a merchant comes to pay money; Demaenetus' wife is thus indirectly the victim of the intrigue. The trickery itself is somewhat stereotyped, but the comedy is abnormal in that the *senex* not only works in his son's behalf but even demands as his reward to share in the favors of Philaenium (cf. 735 ff.). Although the deception succeeds in securing for Argyrippus the girl he desires, the outcome for Demaenetus is less happy. Artemona learns of her husband's duplicity from the parasite of a defeated rival, finds her amorous husband banqueting with Argyrippus and Philaenium, and angrily drags him home in disgrace. The *Asinaria* has many scenes of broad humor and buffoonery but is not considered one of Plautus' more successful plays. Norwood says of the conclusion that "Plautus carries bad taste to the pitch of infamy,"[47] but the moral tone is perhaps higher than in the two comedies in which fathers are avowedly the rivals of their sons.

(25) The *Casina*, a hilarious musical farce on a low and indecent level, portrays the desire of the aged Lysidamus, the most lecherous old rascal in Roman comedy, to spend a night with his wife's maid. This he hopes to achieve by arranging a marriage between the girl and his slave

---

[46] For the rivalry of father and son, see Wehrli, *Motivstudien zur griechischen Komödie*, pp. 56 ff.

[47] *Plautus and Terence*, p. 66.

Olympio. Another slave, Chalinus, wishes to marry Casina in the interests of Lysidamus' son, who does not appear in the action of the play. The conflict between the two slaves, which reflects the basic rivalry of father and son, is decided by lot. Lysidamus betrays his own eagerness to Cleustrata, his wife (363 ff.) :

LY.: Place the urn here and give me the lots. Pay attention. And yet I did think, wife, that I could persuade you to have Casina married to me, and I still think so.
CL.: Married to you?
LY.: Yes, to me—oh, I didn't mean to say that; when I said "to him," I meant "to me," and while I'm so eager for myself—God! Now I've got all mixed up.
CL.: You certainly have, and you still are.

The lottery favors Olympio, and Lysidamus delightedly arranges for a night with the bride at his neighbor's house. Cleustrata and Chalinus plan a counter-intrigue, which produces frustration after frustration for the old man. The false yarn of Casina's madness, the impersonation of the bride by Chalinus, the double-crossing of the *senex* by his own helper—these lead to a vulgar and uproarious conclusion and the utter disgrace of Lysidamus. The prologue and the epilogue of the play refer to Casina as a foundling who will be revealed as the daughter of the neighbor and married to the son of Lysidamus. But the recognition scene and the marriage of the lovers are unessential; the play as it stands is a well-knit, swift-moving farce in which the goal of the dramatic action is the complete discomfiture of the lecherous *senex*. That it was Plautus rather than Diphilus who suppressed the recognition scene seems probable;[48] whether the impersonation of the bride and the burlesque ending are Plautine additions is less certain since they seem the logical result of the theme of the Greek original. The *Casina* is one of the comedies which, many critics believe, is strongly indebted to the earlier Italian farces but there is little agreement as to the extent of the Plautine innovations.[49]

(26) In the *Mercator* ("The Merchant") rivalry between father and son, which in the *Casina* was partially subordinated to the contest of the slaves, provides the basis of the action. Charinus arrives at the harbor with his mistress but pretends that the girl is a maid for his mother. Demipho, Charinus' father, sees the girl and falls madly in love with her. He persuades his neighbor Lysimachus to get the girl and hide her next door during the absence of Dorippa, Lysimachus' wife, where a banquet is planned. The inopportune return of Dorippa pro-

[48] Cf. *Cas.* 64 ff.: "The son won't return to the city today in this comedy, don't expect it; Plautus didn't wish it, and broke down the bridge that was on his route." Cf., however, Harsh, *A Handbook of Classical Drama*, p. 484, n. 34, who suggests that "Plautus" here may signify merely "the author."
[49] Cf. the bibliography cited by Duckworth, *CPh* 33 (1938), p. 281, n. 57, and by Smith, *The Technique of Solution*, p. 106, n. 1.

duces a situation rich in misapprehensions. Dorippa suspects that the girl is Lysimachus' mistress and accuses him of disgraceful conduct while the caterer thinks Dorippa herself is the mistress of Lysimachus. When Charinus, frantic over the disappearance of his sweetheart and about to leave home, learns that she is next door, the ridiculous passion of the aged Demipho is exposed and, like Chremes in the *Phormio*, he cannot object to the fact that his son has a mistress. The *Mercator* is an unusual play in that there is very little intrigue and none by a deceitful slave; the attempt of Demipho to possess his son's sweetheart causes greater embarrassment to his friend than to himself, and he is forgiven at the end without suffering the ignominious treatment accorded to Demaenetus (*Asinaria*) and to Lysidamus (*Casina*). Demipho is even permitted to keep the escapade a secret from his wife (1004). He is a more decent old rascal than Lysidamus for he sincerely believed that Charinus had brought the girl as a maid; cf. 993 f.:

> By Jove, if I'd only known, or if he'd told me even in jest that he loved her, I'd never have taken her away from him.

Many critics have rated the comedy as one of Plautus' poorest productions. It has, however, many scenes of sparkling wit (e.g., the attempt of father and son to buy the girl for imaginary "clients," the portrayal of Pasicompsa as a pert and amusing courtesan, the caterer's mistaken belief about Dorippa), and on the whole must be considered a highly entertaining farce.[50]

## Methods of Trickery

The importance of deception in developing the errors and complications of the comic plot is now evident: it provides the main interest in eight comedies (of Plautus), contributes significantly to the action of eight more (four by Plautus, four by Terence), and appears also in others, e.g., the *Trinummus* (Callicles' attempt to provide Lesbonicus' sister with a dowry) and the *Adelphoe* (Syrus' amusing lies to keep Demea from learning the truth). In other words, trickery plays a promi-

---

[50] Norwood regards the *Mercator* as Plautus' best play, a "sparkling, sophisticated, immoral light comedy" (*Plautus and Terence*, p. 36), which has been closely translated from the Greek; see his analysis of the play, *ibid.*, pp. 29 ff. Charinus' farewell (830 ff.) and the mad scene which follows are highly praised as "a marvellous blend of beauty, pathos, and absurdity" (*ibid.*, p. 52); though undoubtedly effective as a parody of tragedy, the passage seems puerile and pointless when compared with the scene of pretended madness in the *Menaechmi*. The play has many features which Norwood condemns severely in other Plautine comedies, e.g., the protatic character, the prolonged running-slave scene, lack of characterization. Much of the humor, especially the delineation of Demipho as an amorous old rascal, seems definitely Plautine, and the comedy probably reflects its Greek original less closely than do the *Cistellaria* and the *Trinummus*. I am unable to agree with Beare (*The Roman Stage*, pp. 37, 39, 57) that the *Mercator* is different in style from the other plays and possibly not the work of Plautus.

nent role in at least two thirds of the extant comedies. This seems an amazing proportion when one looks at the fragmentary plays of Menander where no intrigue of this type can be found. But there can be little doubt that Diphilus and Philemon (and also Menander in his lost comedies, e.g., the *Dis Exapaton*) composed comedies of more farcical deception. We cannot be sure, however, that the sentimental love theme was ever suppressed as in Plautus where in many instances the plight of the young lover serves merely to motivate the activity of the intriguing slave. Trickery and impersonation, the ludicrous fooling of one person by another, are characteristic of low comedy and existed, as we have seen, in the pre-literary Italian farces. Plautus, adapting his originals to the tastes of his audience, may have increased the farcical elements of fooling and trickery under the influence of the native comic forms, at the same time subordinating the love element. Certainly, in comedies like the *Pseudolus*, the *Persa*, and the *Mostellaria*, the *adulescens* and his problems cease to be the center of interest as soon as the deceitful lies of the *callidus seruus* get under way.[51] In Terence, on the contrary, the trickery seems always secondary to the difficulties of the young lovers; recognition scenes and happy endings to the love affairs are never suppressed. In this respect Terence perhaps reflects more closely the sentimental tone of the Greek originals, and possibly expresses his own disapproval of the cruder and more boisterous deceptions employed by his predecessor. Just as Terence differed from Plautus in his use of stage conventions, so in his treatment of deception we find a striking deviation from the practice of the older dramatist.

Intrigue in Plautus follows in general definitely fixed patterns. Except in plays of rivalry between father and son, the tricks are always invented and developed by the slave of the *adulescens* or by a parasite working in his behalf. Some tricksters lack farsightedness and devise their plans on a moment's notice, e.g., when Theopropides asks Tranio whose house his son has purchased, the slave says in an aside (*Most.* 662 ff.):

> What am I to do now? Better pass it off on the neighbor next door and say he bought Simo's house. I've heard that a lie right off the fire is best. Whatever the gods suggest, that's what I've decided to say.

Other slaves like Chrysalus (*Bacchides*) and Palaestrio (*Miles*) invent their stratagems with calm deliberation and, undaunted by difficulties and setbacks, carry them through to a glorious conclusion; cf. Chrysalus' words of exultation in *Bacch.* 640 ff., 925 ff., 1067 ff. Usually the object of the intrigue is to procure money for the *adulescens* so that he can buy the object of his affection from a slavedealer; at times it enables the youth to gain direct possession of the girl (*Curculio*, second trick of

---

[51] This does not imply that the lover is completely disregarded in the latter part of the play. The trick, when successful, solves the youth's problems (*Asinaria, Miles, Persa, Pseudolus*), or an eloquent intercessor persuades the *senex* to forgive his son (*Bacchides, Mostellaria*).

the *Miles*; cf. also the first deception of the *Poenulus*). Less stereotyped trickery occurs in the *Mostellaria*, where Tranio attempts to prevent Theopropides from learning the truth (cf. the fooling of Sceledrus in the *Miles*), and in the *Captivi*, where the exchange of roles permits the master to escape.

The most common method of deception is impersonation, which appears in half of Plautus' plays;[52] e.g., in the *Epidicus* the slave pretends that Acropolistis is Stratippocles' half-sister and hires a music girl to take the place of Acropolistis; the *Miles* contains three impersonations: Philocomasium poses as her own twin sister, a *meretrix* plays the part of the neighbor's wife, and Pleusicles pretends to be a ship captain. The fantastic schemes in which characters impersonate imaginary individuals (*Miles, Persa, Poenulus*) are invariably successful. Less effective are the imitations of real persons, for sooner or later the false identity is disclosed; when in the *Epidicus* the soldier comes for Acropolistis and Philippa meets her "daughter," revelation of the double imposture is inevitable. The meeting of the real Harpax with Ballio and Simo leads to the discovery of the impersonation but, in this case, the *leno* can only admit defeat; the scene is highly amusing, since Ballio, who has been forewarned of Pseudolus' intentions, is convinced that Harpax is the slave's emissary (cf. *Pseud.* 1124 f., 1160 ff., 1191 ff.) although he has earlier been completely hoodwinked by the false Harpax.

The dupes in Plautus are of three types: (1) those who fall innocently into the trap but still pride themselves on their astuteness, e.g., Theopropides completely swallows Tranio's falsehoods; cf. *Most.* 924 ff.:

TH.: Would I dare not be on my guard in trusting anything to you?
TR.: What? Have I ever cheated you in any way since I've been your slave?
TH.: No; I've always been too careful for that.[53]

(2) Even more amusing is the dupe who has been forewarned and is on his guard. Mnesilochus through an unfortunate misunderstanding reveals to his father Chrysalus' first deception and returns the money; realizing his mistake he appeals to Chrysalus to deceive Nicobulus a second time; cf. *Bacch.* 695 ff.:

CH.: It hardly seems possible.
MN.: Keep on, and you'll do it easily.
CH.: How the deuce easily, when he just caught me in an open falsehood? If I told him to put no trust in me, he wouldn't believe me.

---

[52] Cf. Wieand, *Deception in Plautus*, pp. 55 f. This type of deception is found also in Terence; in the *Heauton* Bacchis poses as Clinia's mistress, and in the *Eunuchus* Chaerea disguises himself as Dorus, the eunuch, in order to have access to Pamphila.

[53] Likewise, in Terence's *Adelphoe*, Demea accepts without question Syrus' tales about Ctesipho's virtue, but boasts that he would know of any misbehavior six months before it began; cf. *Ad.* 396 ff.

MN.: You should have heard what he told me about you.
CH.: What did he say?
MN.: If you told him the sun was the sun, he'd believe it was the moon, and
that the day was really night.

Chrysalus increases Nicobulus' attitude of suspicion and distrust by the
first letter, ostensibly from Mnesilochus, which warns the *senex* of the
slave's intentions (cf. 739 ff.). Chrysalus' ultimate victory reflects great
credit upon his ingenuity and cunning. In the *Pseudolus* Ballio was
warned by Simo to be on his guard against the schemes of Pseudolus
(cf. 896 ff.) but the warning served merely to make him suspicious at
the wrong time. (3) Most delightful of all is the duping of a character
who thinks that the intriguing slave is working in his behalf. Pyrgopolynices in the *Miles* believes that Palaestrio is aiding him in his affair
with the neighbor's "wife"; Dordalus is at first grateful to Toxilus for
enabling him to make what seems a profitable purchase (cf. *Pers.*
719 ff., 734); and Lycus falls into Milphio's trap just when he thinks
he is about to plunder an unsuspecting stranger (cf. *Poen.* 660 ff.).
Periphanes persuades Epidicus to devise a plan to get rid of his son's
*meretrix*, not knowing that he is playing into the hands of his slave.
The bitterness of the dupes is all the greater when they discover the full
extent of the slave's deceitfulness since their own schemes are at the
same time brought to a sudden and unsuccessful conclusion.

There are several interesting passages in Plautus' comedies where
the playwright handles the theme of deception in a new and refreshing
manner. In the *Trinummus* the intrigue is planned by a *senex* and the
purpose of the fake messenger is to bring money, not to cheat another
person; the device fails, since he meets the very man he is supposed to
represent. Other plays contain tricks that are contrived by fathers
against their sons, e.g., the *Epidicus* and the two plays in which *pater*
and *filius* are in love with the same maiden (*Casina, Mercator*). The
*Casina* has an effective counter-trick by Lysidamus' wife—Chalinus'
impersonation of the bride. Even when the intrigue is directed against
the father of the youth in the traditional fashion, occasionally the slave
or the youthful master expresses reluctance; cf. the soliloquy of Libanus
in *Asin.* 256 ff.:

Protect your master; don't do the same thing that other slaves usually do,
who bring all their cunning and skill to the cheating of their master.

In *Pseud.* 288 ff. Calidorus opposes the suggestion of Ballio to steal
money from his father, and gives two reasons: the old man is too shrewd
and, besides, it isn't right to do so. It is worth noting that in both plays
the father differs from the usual *iratus senex*; Demaenetus is willing to
be tricked (*Asin.* 76 ff., 91, 96) although the suggestion is a safe one
since he has no money; he does, however, tell Libanus to devise some
scheme and get the needed amount for his son (101 ff.). Simo is

delighted with the successful cheating of Ballio, and says (*Pseud.* 1239 ff.) :

> I've decided to set an ambush for Pseudolus—but not the kind they set in other comedies, where they lie in wait for their slaves with goads and whips. I'm going in to get the twenty minae I promised him.

Sometimes, in carrying out their plans, the slaves employ a clever admixture of truth and falsehood. When Nicobulus himself sees Bacchis and Mnesilochus dining together (*Bacch.* 834 ff.) he is all the more willing, in spite of his distrust of Chrysalus, to credit the slave's story that she is the soldier's wife. Palaestrio, in convincing Sceledrus that the girl seen next door is Philocomasium's twin sister, cunningly agrees with him that it is really Philocomasium (*Mil.* 417 ff., 457 f., 462) but Sceledrus finds his master's concubine indoors and believes that both he and Palaestrio have been mistaken. The more intricate deception of Periphanes and his friend in the *Epidicus* also involves the use of truth: the *senes* accept as true what is false (the purchase of the music girl) and consider false what is really true (that she has been hired).[54]

Such deviations from the Plautine norm are amusing and anticipate many of Terence's methods of handling intrigue. In general, however, it must be admitted that in Plautus the devices of the slaves—their fantastic falsehoods and ingenious impersonations—resemble each other rather closely, as do the reactions of their dupes—the willingness of slavedealers and parents, in spite of their professed shrewdness, to accept as truth the most amazing fictions. Such a treatment of deception provides broad farcical humor but lacks subtlety and variety. Terence employs the theme of deception in a much less conventional fashion. Whether he should be praised more for his choice of Greek originals or for the freedom with which he adapted those originals is difficult to determine; certainly to a more sophisticated audience sated with the traditional presentation of trickery his plays would present variations of refreshing novelty. It is perhaps doubtful if the Roman spectators of his day were ready for such innovations, and it is significant that in this respect Terence departs more from tradition in his earlier comedies than in his two last (and best) productions.

The unconventional elements in Terence's handling of deception may best be presented under three headings: (1) the role of the *senex*. The father is regularly a more sensible and reasonable parent than in Plautus, and usually much less gullible.[55] Demea is deceived in the *Adelphoe* because he has implicit faith in his son's virtue, and Syrus reveals a sound knowledge of psychology in the fanciful yarns he tells

---

[54] Cf. Duckworth, *T. Macci Plauti Epidicus*, pp. 277 ff.

[55] Donatus (*ad Ad.* 141) points out that Terence appears to favor *lenissimi patres*, and says later (*ad Ad.* 578) that it is Terence's practice to have those who are deceived display some wisdom; cf. also *ad Ad.* 540, 560. On Simo's cleverness in the *Andria*, see below.

of Ctesipho's reaction to Aeschinus' supposed affair; Syrus says to Ctesipho (533 ff.):

> I understand his nature perfectly . . . he likes to hear you praised; I make a god of you in his mind; I tell him about your virtues.

Donatus comments on 535 that no father is so harsh that he does not become mild when his son is praised. In several plays the father himself engages in intrigue, e.g., Micio's tale about the stranger (*Ad.* 645 ff.),[56] and the attempt of Demipho and Chremes in the *Phormio* to separate Antipho from his wife. Chremes in the *Heauton* thinks that he is conspiring with Syrus to deceive Menedemus (who wishes to be tricked, cf. 494 ff.), not realizing that he himself is the dupe;[57] he says that Clinia's slave should have hatched some plot against Menedemus (cf. 532 ff.) and suggests trickery to Syrus (546 ff.; cf. 595 ff., 762 ff.). Simo in the *Andria* attempts to deceive his son by the trick of the pretended marriage; he is the best example in Terence of a *senex* who is so shrewd that he overreaches himself and continually draws the wrong conclusions. Always on his guard against Davus, he is difficult to deceive (cf. Davus' words in 211) but he fools himself by his unwillingness to accept the truth. Unlike the dupes in Plautus who consistently take falsehood as truth, Simo believes truth to be falsehood; he convinces himself that the birth of the baby is just a trick (468 ff., 490 ff.) and refuses to believe Davus' story about the arrival of Crito (855 ff.). Of the former passage Donatus says correctly that Simo is deceived by his own excessive *sagacitas* in a new fashion (*ad And.* 459).[58] This then is Terence's method: to make his *senes* far cleverer than those of Plautine comedy, have them engage in trickery, and let their cunning be responsible for their own undoing.[59]

(2) The nature of the deception. Since the *senex* is so often blind to the truth, the slave does not find it necessary to concoct an elaborate and fanciful scheme. A cunning mixture of truth and falsehood is usually sufficient. The slave lets his aged master deceive himself (as in the *Andria*) or he tells the truth and pretends it is a trick; cf. *Heaut.* 710 ff., where Syrus boasts of his plan:

---

[56] Donatus (*ad Ad.* 677) refers to Micio's story as a *fallacia*.

[57] This is not unlike Plautus' *Epidicus*, where Periphanes plots against his son but is himself the victim of the slave's trickery.

[58] Cf. also Donatus on 470: "The poet shows that a wary person is no less deceived than one who is stupid; for to him truth seems to be trickery, inasmuch as he is exceedingly keen and clever." Speaking of the soldier in the *Eunuchus*, Donatus says (*ad Eun.* 446) that there is no pleasure in having the dupe (*qui deluditur*) portrayed as utterly stupid.

[59] Terence's departures from tradition are sometimes exaggerated; to have Phaedria in *Phorm.* 1043 ff. the arbiter of his father's future is not quite "the unheard-of triumph" that Norwood implies (*The Art of Terence*, pp. 83 f.); cf. *Merc.* 991 ff., where Demipho is anxious to have his son appeased.

I have such depth and power of scheming that I shall deceive them both by telling them the truth; then when your father tells our old master that the girl is his son's mistress, he still won't believe it.

After telling Chremes the truth about the love affairs and maintaining that it is a lie to deceive Menedemus, Syrus persuades the *senex* to pay the money presumably owed to Bacchis.[60] So also Davus in the *Andria* (747 ff.) pretends for Chremes' benefit that the birth of the baby is a trick, knowing that Chremes will not believe him. Actually, deception of this type, although amusing, is sometimes pointless and ineffective, and the schemes of both Davus and Syrus have been criticized as contributing little to the solution of the plot which depends primarily upon the recognition scene. In the *Heauton*, Syrus' plan to get money from Chremes is possible only because Antiphila has been discovered to be Chremes' daughter, and in this play (as in the *Phormio*) Terence, in defiance of tradition, has placed the recognition early in the action. Whereas in Plautus deception was usually aimed at the *leno* (or *miles*) and only rarely at the *senex* (*Bacchides, Epidicus, Mostellaria*), the trickery in Terence, such as it is, leads invariably to the deluding (or self-deluding) of the aged parent, with the sole exception of the *Eunuchus*,[61] where the impersonation by Chaerea enables him to enter the home of Thais; cf. 383 ff., where Chaerea points out that it is much more proper to cheat courtesans than to play tricks upon one's father. Is Terence thus underlining the unconventional nature of the trickery in this play?

(3) The role of the slave. The greater importance of the *senex*, both as dupe and would-be trickster, means less emphasis on the slave, who ceases to be the cunning *architectus doli* of Plautine comedy (with the exception of the parasite Phormio). In Terence the slave often has a role very different from the traditional one assigned to such characters. Even when he takes an active part in the plot, he may be, like Davus in the *Andria*, a bungler whose suggestions and schemes confuse everyone but actually accomplish little.[62] Davus even admits that his advice

[60] There is a difficulty here. The scheme to get the money succeeds only because of the recognition scene, and Syrus apparently did not know of Antiphila's identity when he first mentioned Bacchis' demand for money (600 ff.). Or did Syrus really know, and has Terence suppressed this information in order to keep from the audience all foreknowledge of the recognition? This would explain Syrus' mysterious hints in 336 and 612, and remove what Norwood (*The Art of Terence*, pp. 47 f.) calls the "ragged edges" of the play. Kuiper assumes that there was a real debt in the Greek original; cf. *VAWA* 38 (1936), 2, pp. 254 f.

[61] There is no deception involved in Aeschinus' abduction of the music girl from the *leno* (*Ad.* 155 ff.). Sannio receives rough treatment but in the end is promised full payment; no *leno* in Plautus is treated so fairly with the possible exception of Labrax in the *Rudens*. Thraso, the soldier in the *Eunuchus*, is not the victim of trickery but he deceives himself about Chremes' relationship to Thais; this motivates the quarrel and the comic attack on her home to recover Pamphila.

[62] Norwood calls Davus "a fly on the wheel" (*The Art of Terence*, p. 33), "a fifth

to Pamphilus has been a failure and that he has been deceived (*And.* 669, 679 f.). Parmeno in *Eun.* 954 ff. is actually a dupe, for he believes the lies of Pythias about the treatment of Chaerea and reveals the truth to Chaerea's father—hardly the proper act of a *callidus seruus*. In another respect also Parmeno is decidedly unconventional; though considered by Pythias as responsible for the impersonation of the *eunuch* (718, 1013 f., 1021 f.) he mentions it to Chaerea only in jest, and attempts to dissuade his master from carrying out the scheme (378 ff.) ; he says (388) :

> Well, if you're determined to do it, all right. But don't lay the blame on me afterwards.

Geta in the *Phormio* also is far from the usual aider and abettor of the wayward and extravagant *adulescens*; he opposes the wishes of Antipho and Phaedria in an effort to be faithful to the *senes* (75 ff.) and objects when Antipho (in true Plautine fashion) hints that his father is the proper person to cheat to get money for Phaedria; cf. 546 f. :

> But is it a little thing that the old man is already angry at us all? Are we to arouse him still more, so that he'll never forgive us?

From such unconventional *serui* it is only a step to Parmeno in the *Hecyra* who is constantly ordered off the stage and prevented from taking part in the action (cf. 815), a slave who is amusing because he is never allowed to find out the truth; cf. his words in 879 f. :

> I've done more good today without realizing it than I ever did knowingly before.

Terence's desire to depart from the traditional themes and devices of ancient comedy—to write *novo modo*, in the words of Donatus—is nowhere better exemplified than in his handling of deception and, in particular, his treatment of the slave. Plautus had introduced into his plays trickery by *senes* and had occasionally permitted slaves to mingle truth with falsehood, but such was not his regular practice and the slaves of his comedies were regularly *callidi serui* who took delight in deceiving soldiers, slavedealers, and even their aged masters. What had been incidental in Plautus became far more prominent in Terence. Yet it is hardly correct to say with Norwood that the plays of Terence show a steady development away from the traditional role of the *seruus*;[63] the most unconventional slaves appear in Terence's earlier

---

wheel on the coach" (*Plautus and Terence*, p. 143). Cf. also Smith, *The Technique of Solution*, p. 23, n. 2.

[63] *The Art of Terence*, pp. 144 f. Norwood's argument is vitiated by the fact that he considers the *Hecyra* (in which appears the most unconventional slave of all) Terence's fifth play rather than his second, and then assumes that "his comedies, when arranged in chronological order, exhibit a steady advance in technical excellence" (*ibid.*, p. 6).

comedies, and in the two last plays the clever devices of Phormio and the lies of Syrus (*Adelphoe*) are handled in a more traditional manner. It looks as if Terence, as his technique matured, wished to prove that the more common methods of trickery could be woven into plays outstanding both for their psychology and their structural perfection.[64]

## Variety in Plautus and Terence

At the very heart of Roman comedy lie the misapprehensions and confusions which are produced either by mistaken identity and the working of chance, or by the deceitfulness and trickery of the characters themselves. The brief analysis of the twenty-six comedies, as given above, has revealed a surprising variety in their themes, in spite of a rather rigid fourfold classification. Terence favors the double love story and proportionately makes greater use of mistaken identity and recognition than does Plautus, to whom trickery is often an end in itself and who also, curiously enough, has many comedies in which deception plays no part. When we examine the dramas as a group, we find, as Kent states, "as great diversity of plot as in an equal number of plays or novels of the present time, analyzed in the same way, if allowance be made for the conditions of society and of scenic production."[65] Not only do the themes or plots have their essential differences but variety lies also in the treatment of the themes. It seems correct to say that the comedies of Plautus reveal far greater diversity of theme, whereas Terence was especially interested in handling a more traditional plot with subtle variations. This we have seen to be particularly true of his use of the recognition scene and the manner in which he departed from the more conventional methods of deception.

Terence's plays vary from the more farcical *Eunuchus* and *Phormio* to the serious *Hecyra* and the *Adelphoe*, a marvelous blend of humor

[64] Post (*AJPh* 59, 1938, p. 367) assumes that in the *Adelphoe* "the slave Syrus is almost pure Roman, and that the revelry which he encourages was not in the Greek play at all." My discussion of Terence's unconventional treatment of the *seruus* may now be supplemented by that of Amerasinghe in *G & R* 19 (1950), pp. 62-72. Amerasinghe believes that Terence consistently rebelled against the convention of the slave who manages the action, and says (p. 62): "I would even go so far as to suggest that his success as a dramatic artist is, to a large extent, dependent upon the way in which he solved the problem of the slave." Like Norwood, Amerasinghe looks upon the *Hecyra* as Terence's fifth play, and he thinks (p. 69) that "Parmeno is admitted only in order to show how unnecessary he is." In the earlier plays the slave had done little, or had lost his initiative to his master, or had had his role taken over by a parasite. In Amerasinghe's view, the *Adelphoe* represents a compromise between Terence's artistic ideals and comic convention; Syrus to Aeschinus is the servant but to Ctesipho he is the traditional slave who manages the master's affairs. Since he believes that the *Hecyra* shows promise of the development of a serious social drama, Amerasinghe wonders (p. 72) whether the *Adelphoe* "may not have to be regarded as a tragic event in the history of Roman literature." To this conception of the *Adelphoe* I am unable to subscribe.

[65] *PhQ* 2 (1923), p. 170.

and instruction, but we do not find in his works the wide range of Plautus—from quiet plays on more sober themes (*Captivi, Trinummus*), through romance (*Rudens*) and mythological travesty (*Amphitruo*) to plays of low farce productive of uproarious and vulgar laughter (e.g., *Asinaria, Casina, Persa*). In the musical structure of the plays there is likewise a striking difference between the two playwrights. Terence in general uses the regular meters of dialogue and *recitative* and has very few passages of lyric song, whereas song, either by individuals or by groups of characters, is an outstanding feature of Plautine comedy, and is especially prominent in his later plays. A consideration of the musical element in Plautus will be reserved for a later chapter but merits brief mention here, since the songs of Plautus, when combined with scenes of drinking, dancing, and general festivity (e.g., as in the *Mostellaria, Persa,* and *Stichus*) produce a type of drama so different from the average Roman comedy, as seen in Terence and the less farcical plays of Plautus, that they have sometimes been listed separately as musical comedies or comic operas.[66] These plays in theme and plot, however, fall into the regular categories but are added evidence of the richness and diversity of Plautine comedy.

It has been suggested that "the greater variety in the Plautine plays may indicate that Plautus showed better judgment in the selection of his sources, than did the more polished, but less lively Terence."[67] It is possible also that in the earlier period Plautus and his contemporaries had at their disposal a wider selection of Greek plays of more varied interest and that fewer plays were available at Rome in Terence's day. This, however, would hardly account for the differences between the productions of the two playwrights. Plautus obviously favored plays with a wider range of interest and remolded them, stressing the more boisterous humor of farcical deceptions and introducing the vivacity and gaiety of song and dance. Terence preferred comedies of a more uniform plot and structure but, by way of compensation, brought in variations and innovations that were both subtle and amusing. It is significant that the Plautine comedies based upon Menandrian originals (*Bacchides, Cistellaria, Stichus,* perhaps the *Aulularia* and the *Poenulus*) display much greater variety of theme and structure than do the four Menandrian plays of Terence.

[66] Cf. Lejay, *Plaute*, pp. 37 ff. (see above, n. 12); Little, *HSCPh* 49 (1938), pp. 219 ff., who sees in such festal plays of banqueting and dancing the influence of earlier Italian farces. Others, however, believe these elements are inherited from Greek comedy of the Old and Middle periods; cf. Prehn, *Quaestiones Plautinae*, pp. 8 ff.; Smith, *The Technique of Solution*, pp. 104, n. 2, 111. The origin of Plautus' lyrical and polymetrical *cantica* is a separate problem, for such *cantica* obviously do not derive from the metrical form of the Greek originals; see below, "The Origin of the Lyrical *Cantica*" in chap. 13.

[67] Kent, *PhQ* 2 (1923), p. 172.

# CHAPTER 7

## *METHODS OF COMPOSITION*

IN THE preceding chapter a classification of the twenty-six extant comedies with brief comments upon each was accompanied by remarks upon (1) the importance of *error* as an underlying motive of Roman comedy, (2) chance as a determining factor in plays of recognition, (3) deception as integral to a large number of the comedies although employed by Plautus and Terence in a surprisingly different manner, and (4) the variety of theme and treatment displayed by the extant comedies. We turn now to a somewhat more detailed analysis of certain features of plot-construction which again reveal outstanding dissimilarities in the approach of the two playwrights to their material, and show furthermore the nature of the difficulties which are encountered in the study of the plays.

Repetitions, digressions, contradictions, and improbabilities of every sort have long been grist to the scholarly mill in the interpretation of ancient authors beginning with Homer; the non-existence of the Greek originals of Roman comedy and the belief of many in the perfection of New Comedy make both Plautus and Terence especially susceptible to attack from those eager to reconstruct the Greek plays. One favorite method of explaining flaws, imaginary or real, has been the theory of *contaminatio*, to which reference has already been made; this is a highly technical and controversial problem which can be treated here only in the most general of terms. Contamination is a possible solution to many of the difficulties, but only one of several possibilities. In most instances we have no way of knowing what additions, omissions, or substitutions were made in the structure of the original Greek plays by the Roman playwrights. Countless conjectures have been made and undoubtedly will continue to be made, but we should always be conscious, in dealing with the writings of scholars and critics, that much is guesswork, sometimes based upon unsound premises, and we should attempt to distinguish between what is probable and what is merely possible.

## Unity and the Complex Plot

The plays of Roman comedy are in general well constructed; the basic problem which confronts the characters at the outset is developed through a series of amusing incidents and complications and is satisfactorily solved at the conclusion of the play. Only in the *Stichus* is there a completely episodic structure—a lack of organic relation between the exposition and the main action; this has been attributed to Plautine workmanship since many critics refuse to believe that Menander could be capable of such artless composition. Yet, as Prescott points out, given the exposition as we find it in the *Stichus*, it would be difficult for any playwright, Greek or Roman, to continue the play without developing inorganic characters and a series of loosely knit episodes.[1]

The *Stichus*, however, is exceptional. Unity of plot in a broad sense appears in twenty-five out of twenty-six extant comedies; the Roman playwrights, however great the changes they introduced into their originals, were careful to maintain a close organic relation between the exposition and the dramatic development. Even in a play like the *Aulularia*, devoted largely to the portrayal of Euclio's character, there is a simple but well-knit plot involving both Euclio and his daughter.[2] But, whereas the more intricate plots of Terence required careful attention to unity of action, several of Plautus' comedies display less regard for strict unity. In the *Truculentus*, which describes the adventures of three suitors for the hand of a brazen courtesan, there is a unifying thread but the interest shifts from one lover to another and the result is a loosely knit play which is more episodic than any other comedy, with the exception of the *Stichus*. Certain plays contain more than one deception (e.g., *Bacchides, Miles, Poenulus*), and the second intrigue brings about the final solution of the complications; this type of composition does not, strictly speaking, violate the unity of plot, but it too makes for a more rambling structure.

At times we have what may be termed a disregard for unity of personnel. In the *Mostellaria* a long and delightful exposition portrays the characters of Tranio, Philolaches, Philematium, the latter's aged nurse Scapha, as well as Callidamates and his sweetheart; with the return of Theopropides, the exigencies of the plot require the withdrawal of all these characters from the stage, with the exception of Tranio, who engineers the intrigue and dominates the later action; only Callidamates returns at the end to intercede for his friend. Here the characters of the exposition are removed from the later action as are the wives in the *Stichus*, but their disappearance is much more cleverly motivated and the plot of the play cannot be accused of lacking unity. There are many comedies, Terentian as well as Plautine, in which characters important in the exposition and the early action disappear later from the play and, conversely, others in which characters, for whose entrance there has usually been adequate preparation, enter later in the action— sometimes at the very end of the play—to aid in the solution of the difficulties. Characters thus loosely or mechanically attached to the action have in individual plays been used to bolster theories of composition and structural change, and it will be of value to note that such char-

[1] Cf. Prescott, *CPh* 11 (1916), pp. 136 ff.

[2] Cf., however, Prescott, *CPh* 15 (1920), p. 253, who speaks of "the poverty of incident in the presuppositions of the plot."

acters are not isolated phenomena but occur with considerable frequency in the comedies.[3]

Among the characters who are prominent in the early action and then disappear are (in addition to those of the *Mostellaria* and the *Stichus* already mentioned) Palinurus (*Curc.* 1 ff.), Callipho (*Pseud.* 415 ff.), Sceparnio (*Rud.* 83 ff., 414 ff.). I do not include in this group the purely protatic character (e.g., Thesprio in the *Epidicus*, Davus in the *Phormio*) who is introduced by Plautus and Terence alike to provide expository dialogue at the beginning of the play.[4] Palinurus in the *Curculio* has been considered a protatic character[5] but he is active on the stage as a confidential *seruus* throughout the first half of the play and disappears only when Curculio arrives to take over the role of intriguer. In the *Rudens*, Sceparnio—Daemones' pert and amusing slave in the early action—is replaced by Gripus who recovers the chest and solves the complications. Parmeno in *Ad.* 155 ff. deserves a brief mention; his part is limited to the scene taken from Diphilus' *Synapothnescontes*, and his presence in Terence's play is undoubtedly the result of *contaminatio*; it is probable that in Diphilus' play Parmeno was active throughout the action and had a function similar to that of Syrus in the *Adelphoe*. But Parmeno's role in the *Adelphoe* is very slight—he speaks only two words in 172—and quite unlike that of Sceparnio (*Rudens*) and Callipho (*Pseudolus*); to attribute the disappearance of these persons also to *contaminatio* seems unwise, especially since it is a regular feature of Roman comedy to present balanced pairs of characters—two brothers, two wives or sweethearts, two old men, two slaves. Such characters are used by Terence to excellent advantage in his dual structure but they are common also in Plautus; cf. the *Bacchides* (two fathers, two sons, two courtesans), the *Mostellaria* (two slaves, two young men, two sweethearts, two old men), the *Stichus* (two brothers, two wives, and at the conclusion two slaves drinking with Stephanium). So in the *Trinummus* Megaronides provides both a foil and later an assistant for Callicles, and in the *Pseudolus* a desire for contrast in character may be the dramatist's reason for introducing Callipho.[6]

Numerous characters are introduced into the middle of the action, often for only one scene, but they are usually incidental roles needed for a definite purpose and in no way disturb the unity of the action. Minor roles of this type are those of slaves, *pueri*, maids, cooks. Such charac-

---

[3] For a more complete discussion of these characters, see Prescott, *CPh* 15 (1920), pp. 250 ff.

[4] See above, pp. 108 f.

[5] Cf. Prescott, *CPh* 15 (1920), p. 251; Norwood, *Plautus and Terence*, p. 72.

[6] Cf. Prescott, *CPh* 15 (1920), pp. 255 f.; see, however, Hough, *The Composition of the Pseudolus*, pp. 65 ff., who considers the role of Callipho abnormal and believes that "Callipho's disappearance indicates definitely that some portion of a Greek original has been omitted" (p. 68).

ters often serve to entertain the audiences and fill time while a change of roles is being effected backstage, e.g., the *puer* in *Pseud.* 767 ff. Lurcio in *Mil.* 813 ff., a scene which has troubled many critics, may possibly be an incidental role of this type. The two slaves in *Most.* 859 ff. and 885 ff. provide time for Theopropides to inspect Simo's house but they are even more important in disclosing to Theopropides that he has been grievously tricked by Tranio. Professional types, e.g., the money-lender (cf. *Epid.* 620 ff., *Most.* 532 ff.), the doctor (*Men.* 889 ff.), the banker (*Curc.* 371 ff.), the soldier (*Bacch.* 842 ff., *Epid.* 437 ff.), and the parasite[7] are less episodic; they have an important function, are properly introduced and dismissed. Domestic types (*senex, matrona, adulescens*) are regularly organic but the part they play is sometimes temporary, e.g., the *senex* in *Men.* 753 ff., Hegio in *Ad.* 447 ff. In *Pseud.* 694 ff., Charinus supplies his friend with the necessary money and an assistant for the intrigue, and Antipho (*Eun.* 539 ff.) provides Chaerea with an attentive listener to whom the youth can unburden himself about his off-stage escapade.[8]

We have already seen, in our discussion of the long arm of coincidence, the Stalagmus (*Captivi*) and Crito (*Andria*) were mechanically introduced at the end of the play to resolve the ignorance of the other characters. The appearance of a character late in the action to aid in the discovery or the resolution of the plot is not at all rare in Roman comedy, but usually his entrance is much better motivated. Such a character is sometimes called a *homo ex machina*.[9] Diabolus appears in *Asin.* 746 with his parasite as a somewhat artificial device to effect the punishment of Demaenetus through Artemona; he is a typical *homo ex machina* unless, as some think, he should be substituted for Argyrippus in 127 ff.[10] But the role of Diabolus is not unlike that of Gripus in the *Rudens*; both are briefly mentioned shortly before their entrance (*Asin.* 634, *Rud.* 897 ff.) and each has an important part at the end of the play. The role of Gripus, whose discovery of the trunk achieves the

---

[7] There is great variation in the role of the parasite. Some (e.g., *Bacch.* 573 ff.) have a minor and mechanical part, others have more extended roles but remain somewhat inorganic (e.g., Peniculus in the *Menaechmi*, Ergasilus in the *Captivi*, Gelasimus in the *Stichus*). In the *Curculio* and the *Phormio* the parasite is the protagonist and engineers the deception.

[8] We know from Donatus, *ad Eun.* 539, that Antipho is Terence's invention, since in the Greek original Chaerea told of his adventures in a monologue; see Rand, *TAPhA* 63 (1932), pp. 63 ff. Prescott (*CPh* 15, 1920, p. 255) suggests that Plautus in the *Pseudolus* introduced Charinus to avoid narration of off-stage action in a monologue.

[9] Callidamates, who enters in *Most.* 1122 ff. to obtain pardon for Philolaches and Tranio, is almost a *homo ex machina* but he had earlier had an amusingly drunken role in the banquet scene.

[10] For discussion and bibliography, cf. Hough, *AJPh* 58 (1937), pp. 20 ff. Hough believes that the words of Argyrippus in 127-248 were originally spoken by an unknown *adulescens* in a second Greek model, in which Diabolus played a part. See, however, Smith, *The Technique of Solution*, pp. 126 f.

recognition of Palaestra, is more extended and the scenes in which he takes part are rich in characterization and humor. The late entrance and the feeble motivation of both characters have been used as arguments for contamination but equally abrupt introductions of characters late in the action are found in many other plays, e.g., Demipho (*Cist.* 774 ff.),[11] Syncerastus (*Poen.* 823 ff.), Callicles (*Truc.* 775 ff.), the father of Phaedria and Chaerea (*Eun.* 971 ff.) ; others who enter late are expected as a result of earlier announcements of the characters or statements in the prologue, e.g., Charmides (*Trin.* 820 ff.), Hanno (*Poen.* 930 ff.).

The illustrations given above prove that both Plautus and Terence were less concerned with unity of personnel than with unity of action. Characters could disappear from the action when they had fulfilled their function, or arrive late in the play as they were needed. When such entrances and withdrawals were properly explained and motivated, as was done in most instances, they did not affect the unity of the plot nor make it episodic.

Legrand in his discussion of the plots of Greek and Roman comedy[12] cites the *Asinaria, Captivi, Curculio, Epidicus, Pseudolus,* and *Trinummus* as plays in which there is a remarkable simplicity of plan; a single problem is presented and undergoes neither change nor complication in the course of the action; in the *Curculio,* for instance, Phaedromus is in an embarrassing situation from which he is rescued by the scheme of the parasite; danger arises with the arrival of the soldier but the recognition scene solves the difficulties. To produce plots of greater complexity the poet could increase the obstacles and the devices for overcoming them, as in the *Bacchides* and the *Heauton,* or he could multiply the objects of interest by showing the results of the main action on the lives of other characters, as in the *Mercator, Rudens,* and *Hecyra.*

Legrand's view of the simplicity of the comic plot is misleading; we can say with equal justification that almost no Roman comedy has a simple plot although many have single plots as opposed to double plots. Aristotle (*Poet.* 1452a) says of tragedy that all plots which involve discovery or reversal are complex. Since misapprehension is at the very basis of the plots of Roman comedy and the plays contain both discovery (of identity or unknown facts) and a solution of the difficulties leading to a happy ending, in the Aristotelian sense all the plots of the extant *palliata* may be said to be complex, again with the exception of the *Stichus,* to which should perhaps be added the *Truculentus* and the *Mercator.* The recognition scene in the *Truculentus* is of minor interest and the main action involves neither discovery nor reversal; in the *Mercator* the discovery of Pasicompsa's whereabouts is the inevitable

---

[11] The text of the *Cistellaria* is corrupt but there is no evidence that Demipho appeared in the earlier scenes.
[12] Cf. Legrand-Loeb, *The New Greek Comedy,* pp. 304 ff.

result of the earlier action, but the plot is unusually simple and straightforward.[13]

The *Mercator* best illustrates the simplicity of plan to which Legrand refers. Other comedies which, although complex in Aristotle's use of the term, seem far from intricate include the *Cistellaria* and the *Rudens* which have no deception and the *Asinaria* and the *Persa* which lack the recognition scene. Far more intricate are the *Captivi, Curculio,* and *Epidicus*, in which the discovery of trickery increases the difficulties, while the recognition of identity brings about the final solution. These have less simplicity of plan than Legrand implies, but they do not have a double plot (*duplex argumentum*), since both deception and recognition concern a single problem. The plot of the *Aulularia* may be termed double with more justification since the play deals not only with Euclio and his gold but with Euclio's daughter who has been seduced by Lyconides. The two themes are amusingly interwoven: Megadorus' plan to marry the daughter is responsible for the arrival of the cooks, and their presence in Euclio's house leads him to hide the gold elsewhere, whence it is stolen. When Euclio accuses Lyconides of the theft, the youth naturally assumes that he is being charged with seducing the daughter (744 f.):

EU.: Why against my will did you touch my dearest treasure?
LY.: I did it under the influence of wine and love.

Such an admission can only add to Euclio's pathetic confusion.

Plays containing two successive deceptions form a separate category, but here again we do not have the *duplex argumentum* in the true sense of the term, for both the problem and the solution are single. When the first deception is thwarted by a sudden turn in events, a second one is necessary to solve the same problem; in the *Bacchides*, Chrysalus' first trick is nullified by the misapprehension of Mnesilochus which leads him to return the money to his father; the intriguing slave of the *Epidicus* must devise a new plan when his master falls in love with a different girl.[14] The situation in the *Miles* and the *Poenulus* is somewhat different: in both comedies there are two separate intrigues and the second one is developed after the first has been brought to a satisfactory conclusion. In the *Miles*, Sceledrus is finally convinced that it was not Philocomasium but her twin sister whom he saw next door, and a new plan is then devised to provide satisfactorily for the escape

---

[13] Cf. Norwood, *Plautus and Terence*, p. 42: "The difficulty itself brings about its own solution. The *Mercator* is a small piece of machinery, but it is beautifully conceived."

[14] The *Heauton*, which does have a *duplex argumentum*, also contains two intrigues. Syrus' second trick is based upon the recognition of Antiphila's identity although he at first thought that the new turn of events had ruined his hopes; cf. 668 ff. His earlier plan concerning Bacchis and Antiphila is far from clear and is not developed; cf. 599 ff., and see Norwood, *The Art of Terence*, pp. 47 f.; cf. above, chap. 6, n. 60.

of Philocomasium and Palaestrio from the soldier's house, but the introduction of the second trick is awkward; cf. the words of Periplectomenus and Palaestrio:

PE.: I'll go back and join the senate; Palaestrio is now at my house, and Sceledrus is away; we can have a full session of the senate now. I'll go inside; I don't want a distribution of the parts to be made while I'm absent. (592 ff.)

PA.: I wish to know if we're to carry on with the same plan we considered inside. (612 f.)

PA.: I need your assistance, Periplectomenus; I've just thought of a splendid trick that will shear our long-haired soldier friend, and give Philocomasium's lover a chance to carry her off and keep her as his own. (766 ff.)

It seems probable that the earlier references to a plan are for purposes of foreshadowing—to hold the audience's attention during Periplectomenus' long discourse, until Palaestrio puts forward his plan of the pretended wife (766 ff., 790 ff.) which was apparently made on the spur of the moment and suggested by Periplectomenus' earlier references to his unmarried state.

In the *Poenulus* the first deception of Lycus succeeds and the *leno* will go to court the following day and be deprived of his property. But Milphio learns from Syncerastus that the two sisters are of free birth and concocts a new scheme whereby a newly arrived Carthaginian will claim the girls as his daughters—a more immediate and satisfactory means of freeing the sisters from the power of the slavedealer; cf. Milphio's instructions to Hanno in 1099 ff.:

MI.: Now this is the plan I'm preparing, the trick I have in mind—to get you to say that the girls are your daughters, kidnaped from Carthage when very young, and you're to bring suit to claim them as freeborn, just as if they were both your own daughters. Understand?

HA.: I assuredly do understand. For my two daughters *were* kidnaped from Carthage when very young in just this way, along with their nurse.

MI. (*thinking* HANNO *is pretending*): By Jove, that's a clever pretense! I like the way you're starting out.

The deception is of short duration, for Hanno proves in reality to be the father of the two girls.

Both the *Miles* and the *Poenulus* have been criticized because the successful completion of the first trick makes the second seem less necessary; as a result the two plays have been accused of *contaminatio*—of being constructed each from two Greek originals. We shall return to this problem later in the chapter but it will be noted that the second deception in each play has as its purpose a more complete and final rescue of the heroine. Philocomasium joins her lover and the soldier cannot claim her as he himself sent her away; Adelphasium in the *Poenulus* is not only free to join Agorastocles but is reunited with her father and, being of free birth, can marry her lover.

But in general the comedies of Plautus, even those which contain more than one deception as well as those which combine trickery and recognition, are far less intricate than those composed by the "duality-method" which is the outstanding feature of Terentian plot-construction.

## The Duality-Method

Contrasting pairs of characters appear with great frequency in the comedies of Plautus and Terence. I cited above instances from Plautus in which two *senes*, two young men, two sweethearts, or two slaves serve as foils to each other (*Bacchides, Mostellaria, Stichus*, etc.) and the list could be extended, e.g., *Asinaria* (Leonida and Libanus), *Casina* (Olympio and Chalinus, Lysidamus and Alcesimus), *Epidicus* (Epidicus and Thesprio, Stratippocles and Chaeribulus, Periphanes and Apoecides), *Mercator* (Demipho and Lysimachus, Charinus and Eutychus), and so on. The use of such balanced pairs is even more characteristic of Terence, especially in the case of *adulescentes*—Pamphilus and Charinus (*Andria*), Clitipho and Clinia (*Heauton*), Phaedria and Chaerea (*Eunuchus*), Antipho and Phaedria (*Phormio*), Aeschinus and Ctesipho (*Adelphoe*)—and of *senes*—Chremes and Menedemus (*Heauton*), Demipho and Chremes (*Phormio*), Laches and Phidippus (*Hecyra*), Micio and Demea (*Adelphoe*).[15] The extent to which the presentation of these roles in pairs contributes to and enriches Terence's delineation of character will be treated in a later chapter; our present concern is the value of these pairs for the structure of the plot and the development of greater complexity in the dramatic action.

As long as the characters, either singly or in pairs, devote themselves to the complications arising from a single problem (e.g., the difficulties of a lovesick youth who is prevented from possessing his loved one because of her status as a slave or foreigner or because he lacks sufficient funds) the plot is single, not double. When, however, the problem is twofold and the interest of the spectators is divided between two love affairs which are interwoven—an important requirement, for otherwise we should have two separate and parallel plots as is sometimes the case in Elizabethan drama, e.g., in Heywood's *The English Traveller*—we have the double plot or, as Norwood terms it, the "duality-method."[16]

---

[15] A third group of paired characters is that of the heroines; this is inevitable if the two *adulescentes* are each to have a love affair: Glycerium and Philumena (*Andria*), Bacchis and Antiphila (*Heauton*), Thais and Pamphila (*Eunuchus*), Phanium and Pamphila (*Phormio*), Pamphila and Bacchis (*Adelphoe*). Of these only Bacchis (*Heauton*), Antiphila, and Thais have speaking parts; Pamphila appears briefly as a mute character (*Eun.* 232 ff.), as does Bacchis (*Ad.* 155 ff.), while the other heroines remain off stage.

[16] It is, of course, possible to have a double plot with only one love affair. In the *Aulularia* the interest is divided between Euclio's gold and the fate of his daughter, but the two themes are neatly intertwined; see above, p. 182, and cf. Legrand-Loeb,

In Plautus' *Bacchides* two young men are in love with two courtesans
and the *Poenulus* has, in addition to the love affair of Agorastocles and
Adelphasium, the desire of a soldier for Adelphasium's sister Anteras-
tilis. But in both the *Bacchides* and the *Poenulus* the duality-method
appears in a somewhat embryonic or rudimentary form. Legrand has
pointed out the difficulties of the double plot: (1) one of the two problems or issues may appear insignificant in comparison with the other,
or (2) both may be so slightly related as to destroy the unity of the
play.[17] Plautus has not been able to avoid these difficulties in either play.
In the *Poenulus* the affair of the soldier is not only of secondary interest
but is poorly integrated in the action. The two love stories in the
*Bacchides* are combined with greater skill, for Pistoclerus' affection for
one sister complicates the action and renders the first deception ineffective when Mnesilochus, misunderstanding the situation, returns the
money to his father; in the conclusion the affairs of the two youths are
linked together when their fathers are won over by the courtesans;
cf. the words of Philoxenus in 1164 f.:

Why say more? I'm not angry at my son, and it's not right for you to be
angry at yours. If they're in love, they're acting wisely.

The interest throughout the play, however, remains centered upon
Chrysalus' cleverness and his desire to aid Mnesilochus in his difficulties, and the problem of Pistoclerus is definitely subordinate. Since
only two Plautine plays contain a double love-plot and these are not
handled with notable success, we can only conclude that Plautus did not
care particularly for dualism of structure and the intricate interweaving
of parallel problems; in each comedy one of the love stories provided
a basis for amusing intrigue and so Plautus devotes his attention primarily to the artful activity of Chrysalus and Milphio.

The situation is very different in the comedies of Terence, five of
which display the dramatist's desire to weave together two similar
problems or complications. Donatus in his commentary betrays a sound
realization of Terence's procedure when he says of the *Andria* that it
is composed of the dangers and delights of two *adulescentes* and comments that only the *Hecyra* is a comedy of one young man.[18] Norwood,
who correctly believes that the duality-method is a vital part of Terence's dramatic art, tries to find the same method at work in the *Hecyra*:
"whereas the other comedies exhibit two pairs of lovers and two love-

---

*The New Greek Comedy*, pp. 310 f. This type of double plot, however, is very rare
in Roman comedy and does not illustrate the real "duality-method."

[17] Legrand-Loeb, *The New Greek Comedy*, pp. 309 f. On the secondary plot of the
*Poenulus*, cf. Smith, *The Technique of Solution*, pp. 127 f.

[18] *Ad And.* 301; see also *ad And.* 977, *ad Phorm.*, Praef. 1, 9; cf Evanthius, *De fab.*
III, 9, who praises Terence for selecting richer plots drawn from double interests
(*ex duplicibus negotiis*) and likewise comments that the *Hecyra* in this respect
differs from the other five comedies.

difficulties entangled, here the two difficulties exist indeed but concern the same man and woman. The problems are Pamphilus' estrangement from his wife and Philumena's plight owing to the offence of an unknown man."[19] But assuredly we do not have here the type of *duplex argumentum* found in Terence's other comedies; Pamphilus' estrangement is the result of his wife's plight, and the two difficulties to which Norwood refers are in reality merely two different aspects of the same problem.

The other five plays reveal an ever increasing mastery of the dual plot. In the *Andria*, Pamphilus—passionately devoted to his mistress Glycerium—does not wish to marry Chremes' daughter, who is beloved by Charinus, and Pamphilus assures Charinus that he has nothing to fear (332):

I'm more eager to avoid that marriage than you are to contract it.

When Davus' plans go astray, Charinus' hopes are temporarily shattered but the recognition of Glycerium as Chremes' daughter solves the problems of both young men, and Charinus is now free to marry Philumena. Norwood defines the Terentian double plot as "the method of employing two problems or complications to solve each other,"[20] but in the *Andria* they do not solve each other; Pamphilus' situation has an effect upon Charinus' problem, but the difficulties of both young men are solved by the same external event, the arrival of Crito, the *homo ex machina*. Charinus' role is strictly subordinate and perhaps, as Donatus says (*ad And.* 301, cf. 957), he has been added primarily to effect a double happy ending lest Philumena be left scorned and without a husband while Pamphilus marries another. Charinus and his slave Byrria contribute little to the main action, and the double plot seems to be handled here with the same awkwardness which Plautus displayed in the *Bacchides*.[21]

The two love affairs are better blended in the *Heauton* and the *Eunuchus*. Clinia's love for Antiphila and Clitipho's infatuation with Bacchis are admirably interwoven when Bacchis poses as Clinia's sweetheart. The recognition of Antiphila almost wrecks the deception, but

---

[19] *Plautus and Terence*, p. 169.

[20] *The Art of Terence*, p. 146. Actually, this is not too accurate a statement of the method; two problems are so interwoven that they have a mutual effect upon each other, but in several instances the one love affair complicates the other, e.g., *Andria, Heauton, Adelphoe* (cf. also Plautus' *Bacchides*). The *Phormio* best illustrates the procedure of having one problem solve the other, although the solutions of the *Heauton* and the *Eunuchus* likewise depend upon the interplay of the two plots; cf. Harsh, *A Handbook of Classical Drama*, p. 377: "normally the two phases complicate each other, and the solution of the one may heighten the other's climax."

[21] Norwood (*The Art of Terence*, p. 31) admits that Charinus and Byrria are "dramatically useless"; their action "adds nothing and leads nowhere"; see also *Plautus and Terence*, pp. 144 f. Harsh (*A Handbook of Classical Drama*, p. 383) says that the *Andria* "has a plot that is essentially single."

the fact that Antiphila is Chremes' daughter provides the basis of Syrus' scheme to get money for Bacchis, and Chremes uses the betrothal of Clinia and Antiphila as a means of getting back at his wayward son (cf. 940 ff.). In this play only the love affair of Clinia ends happily, for Clitipho has to give up Bacchis and marry a girl who meets with the approval of his parents. Chaerea in the *Eunuchus* violates a maiden in the house of Thais, his brother's sweetheart; here the two love stories are perhaps less mutually dependent than in the *Heauton* but they are neatly brought together at the conclusion; Chaerea's misdeed brings his father to Thais and the older man's approval of the courtesan's character clears away all difficulties for Phaedria (1037 ff.). In both comedies the double strands are interwoven far more deftly than in the *Andria* where they are merely juxtaposed.[22]

Terence attains mastery of the duality-method in his last two plays. In the *Phormio*, Antipho—profiting by the machinations of the parasite—has married Phanium but fears he will lose her when his father returns; Phaedria has no money to procure his music girl. We have here an interesting contrast between the affairs of the youths and a neat variation on the usual situation of two young men in love. Although Legrand criticizes the adventures of the cousins for running parallel for too long a time without influencing each other,[23] the two problems are closely intertwined when Demipho and Chremes arrange with Phormio to break up Antipho's marriage; the money which Phormio receives as Phanium's dowry is paid to Dorio for Phaedria's sweetheart. The recognition of Phanium as Chremes' daughter by another wife not only solves Antipho's problem but puts Chremes in a position where he can no longer object to Phaedria's love affair.

In the *Adelphoe*, Aeschinus' difficulties are increased and numerous misapprehensions arise on all sides when he steals from Sannio the music girl whom Ctesipho loves. Demea's ultimate discovery of the truth concerning both *adulescentes* leads to an amusing yet serious conclusion in which the *senex* wins the approval of Aeschinus and confirms Ctesipho in the possession of his sweetheart. Since the comedy deals primarily with the problem of education and the delineation of character, much attention is inevitably bestowed upon contrasting the pairs of characters, Micio and Demea, Aeschinus and Ctesipho. The duality-

---

[22] In the *Eunuchus* the characters of Thraso and Gnatho form an additional subplot; they add to the action of the comedy and provide considerable merriment but actually have very little influence upon the fortunes of Thais and Phaedria, Pamphila and Chaerea. In this respect they resemble Charinus and Byrria in the *Andria*; cf. Norwood, *The Art of Terence*, pp. 64 ff., who refers to "the dramatic badness of the whole Thraso element," which he considers "distinctly Plautine." Rand finds much more inspiration and art in the scenes of parasite and soldier; cf. *TAPhA* 63 (1932), pp. 59 ff.

[23] Legrand-Loeb, *The New Greek Comedy*, p. 310. Another possible criticism is that Antipho's difficulty receives more attention than Phaedria's in the early part of the play.

method in the *Adelphoe* is, as Norwood says, "the poet's greatest achievement in construction."[24] But it is no longer merely a matter of plot-construction; dualism lies at the very heart of the drama. Actually, the dualism is itself double, for the love escapades of the two youths are subordinate to the conflict between the *senes* and the clash of two opposing educational systems. The final solution comes from the interaction of the two doctrines.[25] Terence in his final play has employed the duality-method with an expert hand; in no other comedy has he so successfully blended theme and structure and character, and one wonders to what greater heights of dramatic achievement he might have advanced, had his life been spared a few years longer.

Thus we find in Terence a dual construction and a complexity of plot quite unlike anything to be seen in the comedies of Plautus. Again we must ask the question: did this method originate with Terence, or did he merely adapt the plots as he found them in his Greek models? To what extent do we have here an indication of Terentian originality?

Two strong arguments in favor of Terentian originality are (1) the increasing skill displayed in the interweaving of the two themes or stories in the five comedies, and (2) the fact that Menander's *Andria* had only a single plot, the story of Charinus being added by Terence himself. Donatus says of Charinus and Byrria: "Terence has added these characters to the play, for they are not in Menander" (*ad And.* 301; cf. 977). Critics have been uncertain whether the characters are Terence's own invention or are taken from another Greek comedy (Menander's *Perinthia*?) but the former seems more probable;[26] in either case we have strong evidence of Terence's fondness for the double plot and a willingness to compose with the freedom necessary to attain this purpose.

Norwood says: "This duality-method is the centre, the focus of Terentian art and the Terentian spirit. . . . So far as can be learned, it is entirely his own—another, and the most impressive, proof of his originality not merely in play-conception but in play-construction also. For he actually recasts his 'original' in order to secure this dualism."[27] That Terence did so recast the Menandrian *Andria* is undoubtedly true. There is less certainty about the *Heauton*, where Norwood sees a strong proof of Terence's originality in line 6 of the prologue—a highly controversial reference to the *Heauton*:

> . . . duplex quae ex argumento facta est simplici.
> . . . which has been made double from a single plot.

[24] *The Art of Terence*, p. 127.
[25] See Norwood, *Plautus and Terence*, pp. 169 ff.
[26] On this cf. Beare, *Ha* 56 (1940), pp. 27 ff.; 71 (1948), pp. 72 ff. In the latter article, Beare states that Terence "nowhere mentions that he has added material out of his own invention; for this, though true, was precisely what he did not want the crowd to know" (p. 74). See also Beare, *The Roman Stage*, pp. 94 f.
[27] *Plautus and Terence*, p. 147.

This verse has been interpreted in various ways: (1) Terence has either invented one of the love stories or has taken it from a second Greek original. But verse 4 (*ex integra Graeca integram comoediam*) implies that the *Heauton* is not the result of *contaminatio* and, as Norwood himself admits, "it is extremely hard to imagine the action of this comedy with one of the love-affairs cut out."[28] (2) Terence may mean merely that he has closely translated the original and that there are now two versions of the same play.[29] Although this interpretation is a popular one, it seems very doubtful if *duplex fabula* or *duplex argumentum* can mean two plays—the Greek original and the Latin translation or adaptation. (3) Terence in verse 6 reinforces his statement in 4 that the play is free from contamination by saying that his comedy is double but nevertheless comes from one Greek play. This explanation requires interpreting *simplex argumentum* as "a single Greek play," but seems the most probable solution.[30] The two closely interwoven themes of the *Heauton* must have existed side by side in the Greek original.

Terence deserves great credit for his skillful handling of the double plots in the *Phormio* and the *Adelphoe*, but Norwood would not claim that in these plays Terence has introduced a secondary plot so as to make each play *duplex*. There is no reason to assume the non-existence of double plots in Greek comedy, and it is highly probable that the Menandrian originals of the *Heauton, Eunuchus*, and *Adelphoe* portrayed the love affairs of two young men. That Menander favored this type of plot is supported by the fact that the *Bacchides*—the one Plautine comedy which shows the duality-method in a rudimentary stage—is based upon a Menandrian original, as is possibly the *Poenulus* which also has a germ of a double plot.

It is therefore impossible to agree with Norwood that the duality-method was Terence's own invention. There can be no doubt that the principle of duality in unity appealed strongly to him and he made it a distinctive feature of his dramatic technique. For his first two plays, the *Andria* and the *Hecyra*, he chose models with a single plot; the other four were doubtless selected because they had the double plots which he desired and which, as his art matured, he could handle with increasing success. We must give credit where credit is due. However much Terence made the method his own, this type of plot could hardly

[28] *The Art of Terence*, p. 42; cf. *Plautus and Terence*, pp. 118 f. See also Webster, *Studies in Menander*, p. 83.

[29] This is the theory of Flickinger (*PhQ* 6, 1927, p. 252) who says that Terence "had made two plays to grow where there had been but one before"; cf. also Terzaghi, *Prolegomeni a Terenzio*, p. 78; Kuiper, *VAWA* 38 (1936), No. 2, pp. 52 f. This view is supported by Eugraphius (Wessner, III, p. 154): *ut simplex argumentum sit duplex, dum et Latina eadem et Graeca est*, but violates the normal interpretation of *duplex*.

[30] Cf. Koehler, *De Hautontimorumeni Terentianae compositione*, pp. 35 f. for bibliography and discussion; see also Arnaldi, *Da Plauto a Terenzio*, II, pp. 122 f., 187.

have been his own creation, and Harsh seems correct in stating that in Terence's later comedies "the minor phase of the plot is well fused with the major into an essential unity which seems to be the work of the Greek author."[31]

## Repetition and Digression

Terence's duality-method proved a successful means of enriching the dramatic action of his comedies; the blending of two love stories and two sets of characters provided numerous complications and left little space for extraneous matter. In comparison with the more intricate plays of Terence, many of Plautus' plots seem extremely thin and can be outlined with greater brevity and ease. The comedies of Terence are of a uniform length, varying from about one thousand to eleven hundred verses, with the exception of the *Hecyra* (880 verses) and this is the one comedy lacking a double plot. Six Plautine comedies[32] are shorter than the average Terentian play but the others range from about a thousand verses (*Captivi, Casina, Mercator*) to more than fourteen hundred (*Miles, Poenulus, Rudens*); although the opening of the *Bacchides* is lost, this play in its present form exceeds twelve hundred verses. The *Bacchides, Miles*, and *Poenulus* contain two successive intrigues and these would naturally be among the longest comedies. But others with single plots of relative simplicity are longer than any of Terence's comedies—the *Amphitruo, Menaechmi, Mostellaria, Pseudolus, Trinummus*. This suggests that the plays of Plautus contain material of a sort not to be found in Terence, that Plautus has used a different means of enriching his plays and filling out the action.

Plautus was far less interested in composing comedies with a closely knit dramatic structure than in arousing laughter; he excelled in rapid and vigorous dialogue and did not hesitate to insert scenes of lively discourse for the amusement and delight of his hearers. Such scenes were often not necessary to the plot and at times slowed up the action or even brought it almost to a stop. The gaiety and rapidity of the language, however, were such that the spectators doubtless never realized that the scenes were irrelevant and made no real contribution to the theme of the play. Repetitions, digressions, insertions and expansions of various kinds are all a regular part of Plautus' dramatic technique. The characters of Plautus are much less serious than those of Terence. The *senes* indulge in trivial jests and not-too-serious moralizing; the *adulescentes* recount their amours or relate the unhappy consequences of youthful love; parasites and slaves lament their unhappy

---

[31] *A Handbook of Classical Drama*, p. 377.

[32] The *Asinaria, Curculio, Epidicus, Persa, Stichus, Truculentus*. I do not include the *Aulularia* (831 verses), of which the ending is lost. The central portion of the *Cistellaria* is corrupt, and the length of the play, estimated from the Ambrosian Palimpsest, exceeded 1100 verses.

lot in lengthy monologues and discourse upon the conditions of the day; and the slaves abuse each other wholeheartedly and indulge in scenes of buffoonery.

The repetitions in the text of Plautus are of several kinds. (1) Some are real flaws which have crept into the text in the process of transmission or represent alternate versions probably going back to the period of *retractatio*. These are relatively rare and need not concern us here as they have nothing to do with Plautus' dramatic style. Fortunately, modern editors are far more conservative than those at the end of the nineteenth century (e.g., Leo) who bracketed as non-Plautine the passages which seemed to them unnecessarily repetitious.[33] Redundancy and repetition, however, are so characteristic of Plautus' style that deletions should not be made except in the case of verses which are obviously variants (e.g., *Epid.* 384 f., 419, *Poen.* 121 ff., 218) or longer alternative versions which seem clearly to be the work of a retractator (e.g., *Poen.* 923-929, *Stich.* 48-57, and the second ending of the *Poenulus*).[34]

(2) Repetitions of thought and expression abound in Plautus; these were conveniently collected by Langen more than a half-century ago,[35] and a few examples will suffice: for similarity of phraseology, cf. *Capt.* 959 and 968:

> si eris uerax, tua ex re facies—ex mala meliusculam.
> si eris uerax, e tuis rebus feceris meliusculas.

In *Rud.* 1133 a verse is repeated without change from 1109:

> cistellam isti inesse oportet caudeam in isto uidulo.

Whether such verbal repetitions occurred in the Greek originals cannot be determined; many modern critics ascribe this procedure to Plautus since they are convinced that no writer of Greek comedy would have used the same phrase or verse twice, but the presence of similar repetitions in Aristophanes and Euripides weakens the force of their arguments.[36] Repetition can be ascribed to Plautus with greater probability

[33] Nixon in his Loeb Library translations has relegated to the bottom of the page the verses which Leo bracketed. This gives the unfortunate impression that there is far more editorial agreement concerning these passages than actually exists. Lindsay and Ernout accept most such passages as Plautine.

[34] Leo, Goetz-Schoell, Lindsay, and Ernout all reject *Stich.* 48-57, but there is less agreement on *Poen.* 923-929 (bracketed by Leo and Lindsay, accepted by Goetz-Schoell and Ernout); cf. Coulter, *Retractatio in the Ambrosian and Palatine Recensions*, p. 55; Thierfelder, *De rationibus interpolationum Plautinarum*, p. 155. The difficulty in this passage is not merely that it is another version of 917-922 with repetitions (*di immortales*, 917 and 923, *ibo intro*, 920 and 929) but 929 wrongly locates Agorastocles in the forum. Goetz-Schoell, Lindsay, and Ernout consider *Poen.* 1372-1422 a substitute for the original ending, whereas Leo retains 1398-1422 and rejects 1355-1397; this is essentially the view of Langen, *Plautinische Studien*, pp. 343 ff., and Coulter, *ibid.*, p. 63.

[35] *Plautinische Studien*, pp. 1-88. See also Fenton, *Repetition of Thought in Plautus.*

[36] Cf. Harsh, *AJPh* 58 (1937), pp. 287 ff.

when the two similar phrases enclose a passage of jesting which appears to be a Plautine insertion; cf. *Capt.* 152 (*nunc habe bonum animum*) and 167 ( *habe modo bonum animum*) ; *Most.* 762 (*nunc hinc exemplum capere uolt*) and 772 (*at tamen inspicere uolt*).[37] Similarly, the repetition of the formula *numquid ceterum uoltis?* in *Pers.* 708 f. (cf. 692 f.) brings to an end a Plautine addition which has been inserted to provide an irrelevant but amusing conversation containing the long "contortuplicated" name of the Persian in 702 ff.

In many instances a sentence repeats essentially the thought of an earlier one; cf. the words of Menaechmus in *Men.* 855 f. and 858 f.:

You command me to take that staff of his and beat him to pieces, limb, bone, and joint.

I'll carry out your orders; I'll take a double axe and hack the old man's inwards to pieces, down to the very bone.

The pretended madness of Menaechmus makes such repetition amusingly effective. In *Epid.* 82 ff., the slave soliloquizes on the difficulty which his master's transfer of affection has created:

If you don't have some aid for yourself you're ruined. So much destruction overhangs your head.

If you don't find some firm support, you can't survive; such mountains of misery are toppling upon you.

Redundancy of this nature is characteristic of soliloquies, especially when, as here, they are composed in changing meters to be sung. One of the most striking instances of repetitious utterances is found at the beginning of Philolaches' song in *Most.* 84 ff. This introduction to the *canticum* fills fifteen verses and about all the young man says is: "I've decided that a man is like a new house and I want to tell you why." The loquacious nature of the lovesick youth and the lyric structure of the passage account satisfactorily for the redundancy (cf. also the monody of Lysiteles in *Trin.* 223 ff.) ;[38] there can be no doubt that such passages of song and dance had a great appeal for the spectators, who probably paid no more attention to the repetitions than does a modern audience to similar repetitions in the lyrics of a musical comedy.

[37] The repetition in *Stich.* 418 and 435 (*age abduce hasce intro*) is often cited as enclosing a Plautine insertion; if Plautus has added the intervening dialogue, which prepares for the slave banquet in Act v, we have an indication that the final action of the play comes from a different source; cf. Fraenkel, *Plautinisches im Plautus*, pp. 111 f.; Enk, *RPh* 64 (1938), pp. 290 f. But *Stich.* 435 ff. also refer to the later banquet; if Plautus has taken Act v from a second original or has composed a more festive ending to replace the reunion of husbands and wives, the entire passage (419-453) must be Plautine work; cf. Coulter, *Retractatio in the Ambrosian and Palatine Recensions*, pp. 84 ff. (who thinks that the *Stichus* comes from a single original but that the plot has been disturbed by omissions and additions). In any case, the repetition of 418 in 435 does not, as often, mark the end of a Plautine addition.

[38] The excessive zeal of critics to remove whatever seems logically unnecessary has led to the deletion of parts of both *cantica*; cf. Langen, *Plautinische Studien*, pp. 54 ff., 80 f. Langen points out that repetitions are frequently found in lyric passages.

(3) Repetition of the same word or phrase again and again for comic effect occurs in several passages. This type of verbal humor is characteristic of scenes which are obviously padded for the spectators' benefit and which do not advance the plot of the play. Many such scenes are extremely farcical, e.g., *Asin.* 920 ff., where Artemona discovers her husband dining with Argyrippus and Philaenium; her anger and disgust are rendered more vivid by the repetition of the phrase, *surge, amator, i domum*:

ART. (*to* PHILAENIUM): What business do you have entertaining my husband?
PH.: Heavens, he's almost killed me, he's such a nuisance.
ART. (*to* DEMAENETUS): Rise up, lover, come on home.
DE.: I'm done for.
ART.: You certainly are, don't deny it; you're the most worthless man alive. Look, the cuckoo's still sitting there. Rise up, lover, come on home.
DE.: Woe is me!
ART.: You're a true prophet. Rise up, lover, come on home.
DE.: Then you go a bit farther away.
ART.: Rise up, lover, come on home.

When Menaechmus I returns home he finds his wife and Peniculus lying in wait for him (*Men.* 620 ff.):

MEN.: Has one of the slaves done something wrong? The maids or the slaves have been talking back to you, I suppose. Tell me. It won't go unpunished.
WIFE: You're talking nonsense.
MEN.: She's really cross. I don't like this.
WIFE: You're talking nonsense.
MEN.: You're certainly angry at one of the servants.
WIFE: You're talking nonsense.
MEN.: At least, you're not angry at me, are you?
WIFE: Now you're not talking nonsense.
MEN.: I certainly haven't done anything wrong.
WIFE: There you go again; now you're talking nonsense.

This repetition of *nugas agis* reminds one of Gracie Allen: "There you go, George; now you're talking silly." Other examples of this type of verbal repetition are *aio* (*Most.* 975 ff.), *credo* (*Pers.* 482 ff.), *i modo* (*Merc.* 954 f., *Poen.* 428 ff., *Trin.* 583 ff.), *licet* (*Rud.* 1212 ff.), *censeo* (*Rud.* 1269 ff. ). The *censeo* and *licet* scenes in the *Rudens* are the longest of these repetitions. After eleven answers of *censeo* ("I reckon") to Plesidippus' questions, Trachalio concludes the series with three answers of *non censeo* ("I reckon not"). The *licet* scene extends for fifteen verses; Trachalio replies "Sure" (*licet*) six times to the commands of Daemones, then the latter amusingly turns the tables and makes the same answer the same number of times to the slave's requests; cf. Daemones' final comment (1225 f.):

The curse of Hercules on him and his sureness. He deafened me with his continual "sure" to everything I said.

(4) A somewhat different type of repetition is that of information or instruction. Plautus' purpose is to explain clearly for the spectators' benefit the basic situation in a play or the nature of a certain intrigue. Instructions concerning a trick are sometimes repeated to the participants several times; it is not that the characters are so slow to grasp the situation but rather that the playwright wants the audence to understand the details of the deception. Among the plays which have been criticized for their excessive detail are the *Amphitruo, Miles*, and *Poenulus*. Both Mercury and Jupiter explain the complicated nature of the impersonation to the audience and foreshadow the confusion of Amphitruo and the birth of the twins.[39] In the *Poenulus* the manner in which Collybiscus and the *aduocati* are to deceive the *leno* is described three times, once by Milphio to Agorastocles (170-187), once by the *aduocati* to prove to Agorastocles that they know their part (547-565), and again in a joint discussion of all the conspirators (591-603). There is far more variation and humor in these three passages, however, than is often believed. Palaestrio explains the trick to deceive Pyrgopolynices by means of the pretended wife in *Mil.* 766 ff., and the women when they enter have already learned the details from Periplectomenus (874 f., 903); Palaestrio motivates additional coaching with the words (904):

I desire to know how well trained you are; I fear you may make some mistake.

The instructions in 905 ff. are followed by additional instructions and discussion in 1143 ff. The intrigue in this play is complicated by the fact that Palaestrio has five assistants (cf. 1154 f.), and the audience must understand clearly the role of each; also, just as in the *Poenulus*, there is a strong comic element in the way the characters discuss their plans and coach each other, and the spectators would look forward with increased amusement to the completion of the anticipated deception.

Not all comedies of Plautus contain such repetitious passages of coaching and explanation; the trickery in the *Curculio, Persa*, and *Pseudolus* is no simpler than that of the *Poenulus*, yet the necessary information is given very briefly or merely hinted at. Hough has shown that the plays with little or no explanation are the ones usually believed to be late; the playwright may have considered the audience more capable

---

[39] Cf. *Amph.* 97 ff., 463 ff., 867 ff., 997 ff. The references to the later action in the *Amphitruo* are far more detailed than in most comedies, but the nature of the play is most unusual, both in its mythological theme which enabled omniscient gods to take part in the action and in the numerous errors arising from two sets of doubles. Plautus strives for clarity and avoids the confusion of which Shakespeare is guilty in *The Comedy of Errors*. I cannot quite agree with Hough (*AJPh* 60, 1939, p. 425) that "the explanations in this play are so ubiquitous as to be nauseating." On the repetition of information and explanation in the *Amphitruo* and the *Miles*, see also Legrand-Loeb, *The New Greek Comedy*, pp. 431 ff.

of understanding the course of the action, and he perhaps wished to make the plots of his plays more a matter of surprise.[40] Whatever the reason, it is significant that repetitions of this type are limited to a few plays, and those in general the earlier ones. In the later comedies Plautus employed a different method of expanding the action of his plays and padding the scenes.

In the comedies of Plautus are scenes of monologue or dialogue which were written primarily for their intrinsic interest rather than for the contribution which they make to the development of the plot; such scenes do not violate the unity of the play but they provide interludes, comic or otherwise, which do delay the action. Many monologues (and monodies) perform a function not unlike that of the chorus in fifth century tragedy and comedy—that of commenting upon the action and expressing hopes or fears about the future. These monologues, and even less those of exposition and announcement, are not digressions in the true sense of the word and occur frequently in Terence as well as in Plautus. But monologues for the purposes of moralizing, characterization, and comedy, very rare in Terence,[41] appear again and again in many of the comedies usually ascribed to Plautus' Middle and Late periods. It is interesting that early plays like the *Asinaria, Cistellaria, Miles,* and *Poenulus*—the very ones which are criticized for excessive repetition of information and explanation—have no or almost no monologues which interrupt the action; on the other hand, these same plays have long conversations which are no less digressions, for they contain moralizing (e.g., *Cist.* 22 ff., *Mil.* 637 ff.) and humorous banter and abuse between slave and slave (*Asin.* 297 ff., *Poen.* 851 ff.) or slave and master (*Asin.* 685 ff., *Poen.* 364 ff., 427 ff.).

Thus Plautus, unlike Terence, introduces into his comedies numerous digressions in both monologue and dialogue.[42] (1) Many of these are descriptive passages of a satiric nature—on the extravagance of women and their interest in dress (e.g., *Aul.* 505 ff., *Epid.* 225 ff.), on the double standard of morals (*Merc.* 817 ff.), on the disadvantages of marriage (*Mil.* 685 ff., *Most.* 690 ff.), on love, both youthful (*Trin.* 223 ff.) and aged (*Cas.* 217 ff.), on the discomforts of old age (*Men.* 753 ff.). Bankers, lawyers, and slavedealers are held up to ridicule

[40] Cf. Hough, *AJPh* 60 (1939), pp. 434 f. For the elements of suspense and surprise in Plautus, see below, "Devices to Arouse Suspense" and "Surprise in Plautus and Terence" in chap. 8.

[41] For passages of moralizing in Terence, cf. *And.* 625 ff., *Eun.* 923 ff., *Ad.* 26 ff., 855 ff., but these are closely related to the action and contain exposition or announcement. The one striking instance in Terence of moralizing for comic effect is the speech of Gnatho in *Eun.* 232 ff.—one of the scenes considered by Norwood (*The Art of Terence*, pp. 64 ff.) unnecessary and Plautine.

[42] I shall merely list the main types of digressions in this chapter; some of the passages will necessarily be considered later under other headings (e.g., delineation of character and the nature of Plautine humor). For additional examples of digressions, see Legrand-Loeb, *The New Greek Comedy*, pp. 300 ff.; Blancké, *The Dramatic Values in Plautus*, pp. 53 f.

(*Curc.* 371 ff., 494 ff., *Men.* 571 ff., *Poen.* 823 ff.) and Ballio in *Pseud.* 133 ff. gives an interesting, if unpleasant, picture of life in his establishment.

(2) Some digressions which contain moralizing are useful also for the delineation of character, e.g., slaves discourse at length on the value of loyalty to their masters (*Aul.* 587 ff., *Men.* 966 ff., *Most.* 858 ff.); in *Trin.* 279 ff. father and son are models of upright conduct and virtuous thought; as Philto says (299 f.):

If you carry out these injunctions of mine, many a good maxim will take root in your breast.

The words of Euclio in *Aul.* 105 ff., 371 ff., help us better to understand his character. A few scenes seem to have as their primary aim the creation of atmosphere, e.g., the song of the fishermen (*Rud.* 290 ff.); the elaborate exposition in the opening of the *Curculio* and the *Mostellaria* portrays the main characters and builds up a general atmosphere of dissipation prior to the return of a traveler, at which point the action of each play really begins.

(3) Many of the passages cited above contain incidental humor. Other digressions are introduced chiefly for the purpose of laughter; we find monologues and monodies by slaves, e.g., the drunken Pseudolus (*Pseud.* 1246 ff.) and the disappointed Sceparnio (*Rud.* 458 ff.),[43] by cooks (e.g., *Aul.* 406 ff.), and especially by parasites, of whom the audience apparently never tired.[44] Dialogue-scenes of jesting and buffoonery abound. Examples were cited above from the *Asinaria* and the *Poenulus*, and there are many more: the delightful scene of Mercury and Sosia is expanded to great length (*Amph.* 341 ff.); expository scenes often contain unnecessary repartee and abuse (*Epid.* 1 ff., *Most.* 1 ff., *Pers.* 1 ff.), and the action is hardly advanced by scenes of banter such as *Pers.* 272 ff. and the name-calling in *Pseud.* 357 ff., although there can be no doubt of the delight which the audience took in such loosely inserted episodes.[45]

Many of these digressions must have occurred in the Greek originals. Cooks and parasites were popular in New Comedy—in fact, judging from the fragments, the cook seems to have played a much greater part in Greek comedy than in the Latin *palliata*[46]—and these characters,

---

[43] Cf. also the monologues of the running slave or parasite (see above, pp. 106 f.); such speeches could be delivered with violent gestures and a frenzied pretense of haste.

[44] Cf. the speeches of Ergasilus (*Capt.* 461 ff.), Peniculus (*Men.* 77 ff.), Saturio (*Pers.* 53 ff.), Gelasimus (*Stich.* 155 ff.).

[45] Humorous but irrelevant jesting is often brought to an end when one of the characters says: "Enough of this"; "stop this idle talk"; e.g., *Asin.* 578: *iam omitte istaec; Capt.* 125: *sed satis uerborumst; Epid.* 39: *supersede istis rebus iam* (cf. *Poen.* 414); *Mil.* 737: *nunc istis rebus desisti decet; Most.* 897 f.: *quaeso hercle apstine iam sermonem de istis rebus.* Such statements are sometimes believed to mark the end of a Plautine insertion; cf. Fraenkel, *Plautinisches im Plautus*, p. 143.

[46] Cf. Legrand-Loeb, *The New Greek Comedy*, pp. 98 f., 302 ff.; Hough *The Composition of the Pseudolus*, pp. 85 f. and n. 71.

whose roles were predominantly laughter-provoking, could never have been very tightly joined to the action of the play. Likewise the large number of moral and philosophical maxims preserved in the fragments of New Comedy implies that moralizing was far from infrequent; many of the passages may have been longer and less well integrated in the action than is the case in Terentian comedy. It seems likely that Terence eliminated many loosely connected scenes of moralizing and comedy in the interests of his tightly woven, more complex plot-structure, whereas Plautus moved in the opposite direction, making additions and insertions which he knew would please his not-too-critical audience. As a result, his plays contain an abundance of laughter but are more susceptible to criticism from serious-minded scholars who believe that everything should fit neatly into its place and that loose structure is necessarily a sign of poor workmanship. Many of the Plautine repetitions and digressions may be detached from the plot, but much of the gaiety and the humor would disappear from the plays in the process. Plautus' truly comic spirit is perhaps seldom better displayed than in many of the passages which are not, strictly speaking, essential to the framework of the plot.

## Improbabilities and Contradictions

As we pass from repetitions and digressions to the neighboring region of structural difficulties, the way grows thorny indeed. The scholarly activity of the past century has accumulated an unwieldy mass of documentary material to prove that the Roman comedies are filled with logical inconsistencies, psychological improbabilities, structural flaws, instances of obscurity, neglect of minor details, lack of verisimilitude, and the like. Terence, a more painstaking craftsman, has fewer incongruous features of this sort than has Plautus but his comedies also have been subjected to a minute scrutiny in an effort to determine his originality and to establish as accurately as possible the nature of the supposedly more perfect Greek originals.

Only the general aspects of the problem can be sketched here. Fortunately, the task is simplified by three factors: (1) the more obvious and possibly more serious improbabilities and contradictions in Plautus have been collected by Langen,[47] who realized that in many cases Plautus was less interested in artistry and logic than in comic effect; Langen admitted that it was often difficult to determine whether the flaws derived from the Greek original or resulted from the activity of the Roman playwright. (2) Many of the difficulties adduced by scholars (including Langen) are not really flaws but are regular features of comic technique

[47] *Plautinische Studien*, pp. 89-232. Most of the verses and passages rejected by Langen in pp. 232-387 as the work of *retractatores* and interpolators are now accepted as Plautine.

appearing in Greek as well as in Roman comedy. The critics often fail to take into account the staging of the plays and the use of normal stage conventions. Furthermore, whereas scholars who devote themselves to the study of individual plays are able to find numerous flaws, others who have examined various irregularities of structure and technique in all the plays (e.g., Prescott, Wieand, Harsh) are much more sceptical about the value of these features for the interpretation of particular comedies. (3) Many of the so-called difficulties are a matter of subjective opinion; to one scholar a certain passage seems unnecessary or strikes a discordant note; therefore it cannot be good Attic style and must be crude Roman workmanship; to another the same passage is fine Attic technique, and therefore cannot possibly have been added by Plautus or Terence. One cannot avoid scepticism when scholars wax eloquent over the virtues of the non-existent Greek originals but fail to agree in their treatment of one and the same passage.[48]

It is my firm belief that most of the flaws and contradictions stressed by many scholars have far less significance than is usually ascribed to them. There has been far too much emphasis upon logic and art in discussing a form of drama where entertainment and amusement should be the main criteria; if the plot has unity and coherence, if the speeches of the characters are reasonably well fitted to the situation, if the action moves with rapidity and humor, have we the right to demand that the playwright must pay careful attention to every minor detail? Certainly the Roman audience did not expect it, nor would a modern audience (the nature of many comedies today, both stage and cinema, is sufficient proof of this!), and I doubt if the Greek spectators of the originals would be as critical as is often assumed. The more an audience is entertained, the less critical it is apt to be. Is it so improbable that many of the difficulties cited below never appeared in the plays of Menander and his contemporaries? The Greek and Roman comedies were never intended, as Miss Wieand says of Plautus, "to bear the microscopic analysis of literary criticism."[49]

The examples which follow will illustrate the general types of flaws which scholars have pointed out; I shall be brief here, as several improbabilities have already been mentioned in my discussion of stage conventions in Chapter 5[50] and in my comments upon the individual plays in Chapter 6.[51] Nor is it necessary to speak of the so-called "psy-

---

[48] Cf. the examples cited by Harsh, *Studies in Dramatic "Preparation,"* p. 87, n. 8; among the scholars most convinced of the perfection of Greek comedy are Jachmann and Kuiper; cf. Duckworth, *CPh* 30 (1935), p. 229; *CW* 41 (1947-48), pp. 83 f.

[49] *Deception in Plautus,* p. 144.

[50] E.g., the lack of dramatic fitness in monologue and asides, the surprising ignorance of characters concerning their neighbors, long silences on the stage, the disregard of time for off-stage action.

[51] Cf. especially on the *Stichus, Menaechmi, Captivi,* and *Pseudolus;* on the *Bacchides,* see chap. 6, n. 44; on the *Heauton,* chap. 6, note 60.

chological improbabilities"—the excessive gullibility of some characters (Theopropides in the *Mostellaria*, Demea in the *Adelphoe*), their stupidity (Menaechmus II), their willingness to put up with anything (Chremes in the *Heauton*); these are inherent in the nature of the plot and doubtless existed in the Greek models. Legrand says: "the cases in which the *dramatis personae* act in a way that violates psychological probability constitute a very small minority when we consider comic literature as a whole."[52] These "improbabilities" are part of the fun and do not constitute errors in the real sense of the term.

(1) Carelessness in regard to details. Characters at times seem ignorant of facts they would normally know; Pseudolus' lack of knowledge concerning his master's love affair has been condemned as most unlikely, since he is the confidant of Calidorus, but this ignorance motivates the exposition at the beginning of the play and seems no more improbable than that of Curculio or of Sosia (*Andria*), perhaps less so, since Pseudolus justifies his lack of information by saying that Calidorus hasn't let anyone share in his plans (*Pseud.* 11). On the other hand, characters have been criticized for discussing what they couldn't know. A case in point is *Poen.* 821: Milphio states that he sees Syncerastus returning from the shrine; how can he know where Syncerastus has been, since this is the latter's first appearance? There is no real difficulty here. Milphio knows that the *leno* has been sacrificing in the temple and when he sees the slave returning with the *uasa* it is a very natural assumption that he is coming from the shrine. Likewise in *Mil.* 145 ff. Palaestrio tells about his plan to deceive his fellow slave although he does not know until the next scene that Sceledrus has seen Philocomasium in the adjoining house. This may be considered a lapse in the dramatic illusion, but Palaestrio in 145 ff. is foretelling the action as a *prologus*, and I see no argument for the theory that Plautus is shifting to a second original at this point.[53] Certain passages are considered poorly motivated: the description of Casina's madness in *Cas.* 655 ff. is said to lack motive since it is not used in the solution of the plot.[54] There is no problem here if we realize that the passage does not prepare for the later appearance of Casina herself; the scene in general is valuable in frightening Lysidamus, and the important thing is the motif of the sword (660) which is used later with vulgar but hilarious results (907 ff.). Equally unconvincing is the problem of the soldier in the *Epidicus*; in 153 ff. the slave speaks of a Euboean soldier in love with Acropolistis but in 299 ff. calls the soldier a Rhodian; do we have here an example of Plautine carelessness, or is the discrepancy to be explained by *retractatio* or *contaminatio*, as many have assumed? But

[52] Legrand-Loeb, *The New Greek Comedy*, pp. 322 f.
[53] Cf. Duckworth, *CPh* 30 (1935), pp. 233 f.
[54] Wieand, *Deception in Plautus*, p. 82.

299 ff. is part of Epidicus' deception of the *senes*, and for the pretended *amica* of the intrigue a fictitious suitor seems most appropriate.[55]

(2) The non-fulfillment of expected events. If the poet prepares for a later action which does not occur, we are said to have an indication that the structure of the play has in some way been disrupted, either by the playwright's omissions or his clumsy use of two originals. Flaws of this type are frequently cited. The words of Callipho in *Pseud*. 552 ff. imply that he will witness the games of Pseudolus but he does not appear later in the action. We saw above that characters frequently disappear from the action when they are no longer needed and Callipho's interest in the outcome of the trickery may be merely a device for arousing the interest of the spectators.[56] In Terence's *Andria* Simo instructs Sosia to terrify Davus and to watch his son (168 ff.); Sosia promises to do so but he likewise disappears from the play. Also in the *Pseudolus*, as was pointed out in the preceding chapter, the phrasing of the wager in 535 ff. is thought to refer to a deception of Simo which is not found in the Plautine play and which is explained by the use of a second original. In the *Miles* several passages seem to refer to events which do not take place; 235 ff. and 246 ff. are thought to foreshadow a deception of the soldier by the trick of the twin sister; the references to purchasing provisions in 738 and 749 imply a later banquet, and 805 ff. contain instructions to Pleusicles which are not utilized later in the play. These passages have all been explained by *contaminatio* but there are other possibilities; in 235 ff. Palaestrio does not yet know the identity of the slave who has seen the lovers and so necessarily prepares for the possibility that the soldier may be told of the discovery (cf. 242 ff.); in 805 ff. Palaestrio warns Pleusicles that in the role he will play subsequently he must give to the supposed twin sister the name which she had in the deception of Sceledrus, and the later instructions mentioned in 810 are the ones he receives in 1175 ff.[57] As for 738 and 749, the abandoned dinner motif is found in several other plays and proves nothing about the structure of the *Miles*.[58]

A more serious difficulty appears in *Ad*. 193 f., where Syrus says to Sannio:

Nor do I believe she should be sold, since she is free; I formally declare her to be freeborn.

This passage implies that the music girl will be recognized as of free birth later in the play; this does not happen in the *Adelphoe*, but we know that this particular scene came from a comedy of Diphilus (cf.

[55] Cf. Duckworth, *T. Macci Plauti Epidicus*, pp. 196 f. The pretended Rhodian could remove the girl much farther from Athens than could the Euboean.

[56] So Harsh, *Studies in Dramatic "Preparation,"* p. 82, n. 2, who lists the passage as an example of false preparation (p. 93). See below, chap 8, n. 36.

[57] Cf. Duckworth, *CPh* 30 (1935), pp. 231 f.; Haywood, *AJPh* 65 (1944), pp. 383 f.

[58] Cf. Harsh, *Studies in Dramatic "Preparation,"* p. 97.

*Ad.* 6 ff.) where there was apparently such a recognition scene.[59] In their present context, however, Syrus' words may also be construed as an idle assertion designed to frighten the *leno*. In the *Poenulus*, the scene of which is laid in Calydon, Milphio says to Adelphasium, a girl of Punic birth (370 ff.) :

Don't be angry at my master; if you're not angry, I'll see that he pays a ninny for you and makes you a free Attic citizen.

This reference to Adelphasium as a free Attic citizen has been used as an argument for *contaminatio*.[60] But could the playwright be so careless as to forget that he was speaking of a Carthaginian maiden living in Calydon? It seems more likely that Plautus here was jesting upon the usual *anagnorisis*.

(3) Errors and Contradictions. In the *Miles* Sceledrus says in 582 that he will flee somewhere and hide for several days, but in 585 he declares his intention of going home. In 593 Periplectomenus states that the slave is now away from home (*foris*), but in 813 ff. (the Lurcio scene) Sceledrus is indoors in a drunken stupor, while in 1429 ff. he comes from the harbor with the news that Philocomasium has escaped with her lover. Here we have at first sight a horrible medley of contradictions and 585 has been considered an insertion to prepare for 813 ff., a scene perhaps added from another source. This theory seems hardly necessary; Sceledrus, changing his mind, may have spoken 585 in an aside which Periplectomenus did not overhear, in which case there is no inconsistency between 593 and 813 ff., and we cannot be sure that the slave in 1429 ff. is really Sceledrus; the best manuscripts do not give his name, and Leo assigns the speeches to a SERVVS. In the *Poenulus* the delineation of the sisters in 210 ff. is considered inconsistent with their character in 1174 ff., where they are *uirgines* who have not yet entered the profession; in the former passage they seem to be more experienced courtesans.[61] Of the *Trinummus* it is said that "Stasimus, the loyal slave grieved by his master's dissipation, changes by a miracle into a thieving rascal for a while."[62] The opening scenes of the *Pseudolus* are criticized not only for the surprising ignorance of the slave (mentioned above) but also because of the contradiction in the date set for the sale of the girl to the soldier—*cras* (60, 82), *hodie* (85, 373,

[59] Cf. Harsh, *Studies in Dramatic "Preparation,"* pp. 51 f. If Ctesipho's sweetheart was freeborn in Menander's *Adelphoe*, as Kuiper believes (*VAWA* 38, 1936, No. 2, pp. 131, 259), it would account for Micio's delight in 364 ff.; but Micio's attitude is equally well explained by his knowledge that Aeschinus was not acting for himself.

[60] Cf. Fraenkel, *Plautinisches im Plautus*, pp. 275 f.; Norwood, *Plautus and Terence*, pp. 89 f.

[61] See Langen, *Plautinische Studien*, pp. 182 ff.; Fraenkel, *Plautinisches im Plautus*, pp. 271 ff. Cf. Harsh, *Studies in Dramatic "Preparation,"* p. 50, n. 25, who comments upon the consistency of the characterization in the two passages.

[62] Norwood, *Plautus and Terence*, p. 86, who adds "*contaminatio* of course, but that is no excuse for Plautus."

cf. 622)—and the apparent surprise of Calidorus and Pseudolus when they hear from Ballio in 342 ff. that Phoenicium has been sold, although they learned this in 51 ff. The discrepancy in the date is curious, since Harpax actually does arrive *hodie* as expected.[63] The second difficulty is less serious; the audience already knows from the opening scene that master and slave are cognizant of the sale. The words of Ballio in 325 ff. have aroused Calidorus' hopes momentarily and the youth's angry surprise in 342 ff. is quite natural under the circumstances. There seems no inconsistency here and the passage can be paralleled by the attitude of Mysis in *And.* 236 ff.—her expressions of surprise at Pamphilus' fear of marriage although it is obvious from 268 f. that both she and Glycerium had earlier learned about the original wedding plans.[64]

Difficulties of the various types cited above can be found in almost every Roman play but they are especially numerous in the works of Plautus. I am unable to believe, however, that as structural flaws they are as serious as many scholars maintain, or that the majority of them is to be explained by the assumption of contamination. In most instances the significance attributed to them collapses when they are properly viewed in their context or compared with similar passages in other plays.

## The Problem of *Contaminatio*

In Homeric scholarship the Higher Critics have used repetitions and contradictions as a means of distinguishing Homeric passages from those which they believed to be earlier traditional material or later additions; so also in the study of Roman comedy scholars have attempted to separate the Roman elements from the Greek and have sought in repetitions and inconsistencies arguments to support various theories of composition. During the past half century they have endeavored particularly to prove that many of the plays of Plautus were composed by contamination, which they believe provides the most satisfactory explanation of the difficulties in the plays. I have had many occasions already to refer to *contaminatio*—the method of composition employed by Terence and assigned by him to Plautus. In the prologue to the *Andria* Terence states (13 ff.):

The poet admits that he has transferred from the *Perinthia* to the *Andria* such passages as suited him and has used them as his own. His enemies blame him for having done this and maintain that plays should not thus be contaminated. . . . When they accuse him, they are accusing Naevius, Plautus, and Ennius, whom our dramatist accepts as authorities, and whose

---

[63] The similarity of *haec dies praestitutast* in 58-59, 374, and 622 f. suggests that the day mentioned in the letter also is *hodie* and that *cras* refers to the *Dionysia* on the following day; but cf. Hough, *The Composition of the Pseudolus*, pp. 51 ff.

[64] For a discussion of *Pseud.* 342 ff. and additional parallels, see Fields, *The Technique of Exposition*, p. 13, n. 1.

carelessness (*neclegentia*) he desires to imitate rather than the obscure accuracy of his critics.

This passage is important for several reasons: it is one of the two passages—the other one being *Heaut.* 17—in which Terence applies the verb *contaminare* to his use of Greek originals; it is the only passage in Roman literature which ascribes to Plautus the same procedure; it is a passage which has perhaps been mistranslated and misinterpreted in the light of modern theory. Is it correct to translate *contaminari non decere fabulas* (*And.* 16) as Sargeaunt does: "two plays ought not thus to be combined into one"? There is need here for clarification both of the meaning of the word and the nature of the process.

As used by modern scholars, contamination signifies the joining or working together of material from two (or more) Greek originals to form one Latin play. Typical definitions are the following: "By *contaminatio* is meant the practice of inserting in a Latin translation of one Greek play a scene derived from another Greek play";[65] "*contaminatio* means the process of fusing two Greek originals together, or grafting a portion of one on the other, in order to produce one Latin play."[66] The second definition, it will be noted, refers to two different methods of composition: (1) the process of adding a small portion from a second original; this was the procedure of Terence who borrowed the opening scene for his *Andria* from Menander's *Perinthia* (cf. Donatus, *ad And.* 14), added to his *Eunuchus* from Menander's *Colax* the characters of the soldier and his parasite (*Eun.* 25 ff.; cf. Donatus, *ad Eun.* 228), and inserted in his *Adelphoe* a scene from Diphilus' *Synapothnescontes* (*Ad.* 6 ff.); (2) the process of combining two plots from two Greek originals into one Latin play. Plautine comedies which contain two deceptions (e.g., the *Miles* and the *Poenulus*) have been considered the result of such fusion or interweaving but there is no evidence in Terence that Plautus ever combined two Greek plays in this fashion.

The noun *contaminatio* occurs neither in Plautus nor in Terence but *contaminare*, although not in Plautus, is found in three passages in the younger playwright (*And.* 16, *Heaut.* 17, *Eun.* 552). The original meaning of *contaminare*, related etymologically to *tangere, contingere*, is "to touch," "to defile by contact," "to soil," "to pollute."[67] This is clearly the meaning of the verb in *Eun.* 552:

> . . . ne hoc gaudium contaminet uita aegritudine aliqua.
> . . . lest life pollute this pleasure with some distress.

---

[65] Clifford, *CJ* 26 (1930-31), p. 605.    [66] Beare, *CR* 51 (1937), p. 106.

[67] Cf. Beare, *RPh* 66 (1940), pp. 28 ff.; *The Roman Stage*, pp. 100 ff. For earlier discussions, see Schwering, *NJA* 37 (1916), pp. 167 ff.; Körte, *BPhW* 36 (1916), cols. 979 ff.; Hofmann, *IF* 53 (1935), pp. 187 ff.; Waltz, *REL* 16 (1938), pp. 269 ff. The attempt of Jachmann (*Plautinisches und Attisches*, pp. 142 ff.) to show that the verb meant in antiquity "to combine," "to work together," has not been favorably received.

The other two passages bear the same sense: Lanuvinus had accused Terence of soiling Greek plays by adding parts from a second orginal; in *And*. 13 ff. Terence admitted the procedure and appealed to the example of his predecessors; in *Heaut*. 16 ff. he referred again to the criticism that

> he has contaminated (i.e., spoiled) many Greek plays while writing a few Latin ones.

A Greek play was defiled (in the eyes of literal translators) if alien matter was added to it from another source; perhaps also the second original was spoiled for later adaptation if a part of it was inserted into another play. It should be noted that to speak of a Latin comedy as being "contaminated" is highly inaccurate; it was always the Greek play that suffered injury. This use of *contaminare* in Terence is supported by the commentary of Donatus (*ad And*. 16), who defines the verb as *manibus luto plenis aliquid attingere, polluere, foedare, maculare*. The added phrase, *ex multis unam non decere facere*, "that one ought not to make one play from many," is not a definition of *contaminare*, but an interpretation by the commentator which has been wrongly understood by modern scholars.[68]

There is thus little evidence that *contaminare* meant to Terence anything more than "soil" or "defile"; he was engaging in a method of composition which seemed to his critics to be injurious to the Greek originals; he did not deny the charge but claimed that others before him had done the same. If Terence is telling the truth, his words mean that contamination in Plautus was limited to insertions such as he himself had made; if Plautus had ever combined two Greek originals into one play— a much more thoroughgoing type of reworking—any indication of such a procedure must be found in the plays themselves. Beare goes even further in his attempt to discredit the external evidence for contamination in Plautus, slight as that evidence is; he believes that Terence is not telling the truth, or rather, that he is confusing his audience by giving them the false impression that his method of treating the Greek originals had been the practice of the earlier playwrights whereas actually it was something new.[69] Beare's argument in brief is this: to Lanuvinus, who favored close literal translation, Terence's insertion of material from a second source indicated a freedom in the use of the Greek originals; Plautus likewise had taken liberties with his models, adding and omitting in a somewhat careless fashion for the purpose of comic effect; thus, since *contaminare* meant "to stain" or "to soil" or "to change for the worse," both playwrights could be called contaminators and so Terence

---

[68] Cf. Körte, *BPhW* 36 (1916), cols. 980 f.; Waltz, *REL* 16 (1938), p. 274; Beare, *Ha* 71 (1948), p. 76.

[69] *CR* 51 (1937), pp. 108 f.; *RPh* 66 (1940), pp. 33 ff.; *Ha* 71 (1948), pp. 70 ff.; *The Roman Stage*, pp. 90 ff.

says (*And.* 20) that he would rather imitate the carelessness (*neclegentia*)[70] of his predecessors than the "obscure accuracy" of his critics; but both here and in *Heaut.* 20 f. he gives his audience the impression that the earlier playwrights had also inserted material from a second original.

Beare's theory is ingenious. It is not beyond the bounds of possibility that Terence defended his literary procedure by telling a direct lie and, if this is the case, we have no reliable testimony of any sort to connect Plautus with the process of contamination. On the other hand, if we accept Terence's statement at its face value, all we learn is that Plautus and others did occasionally add scenes from a second Greek model. The extent to which Plautus "contaminated" is still unknown. But in the absence of more definite external evidence scholars turn to a minute examination of the plays themselves; assuming the flawlessness of the lost originals, they list all the imperfections, repetitions, and contradictions which they can find, and point to these as proof of Plautus' clumsiness in combining the different parts of two or more Greek plays.

An immense amount of effort and ingenuity has been expended on the subject of contamination in Plautus (and, to a lesser degree, in Terence) during the past half century. Scholars, mostly German, have written dozens, even hundreds, of books, pamphlets, and articles on the composition of the various plays.[71] In 1920 Michaut pointed out that at one time or another every play of Plautus, with the exception of the *Asinaria, Cistellaria, Menaechmi,* and *Mostellaria,* had been believed to show traces of *contaminatio,*[72] but he argued strongly against the acceptance of these views. The plays more generally thought to derive from two or more originals include the *Amphitruo, Casina, Miles, Poenulus, Pseudolus,* and *Stichus,* but even here there has seldom been complete agreement among the proponents of contamination.[73] The structure of the *Amphitruo* does not necessarily imply that a play about Zeus' "long night" with Alcumena has been combined by Plautus with

---

[70] It should be noted (to support Beare's view) that Terence applies *neclegentia* to Plautus' omission of a scene from Diphilus, a passage *qui praeteritus neclegentiast* (*Ad.* 14).

[71] For a recent and useful collection of material on the individual plays of Plautus, see the bibliographies in Enk's *Handboek der Latijnse Letterkunde,* II, which follow his discussion of each play.

[72] *Plaute,* II, pp. 241 ff., especially 254 ff. More recently the *Asinaria* also has been considered the result of *contaminatio;* cf. Hough, *AJPh* 58 (1937), pp. 19 ff.

[73] Cf. Beare, *CR* 51 (1937), pp. 109 f. For analyses of these plays see, e.g., Leo, *Plautinische Forschungen,* pp. 167 ff.; *Geschichte der römischen Literatur,* pp. 125 ff.; Fraenkel, *Plautinisches im Plautus,* pp. 251 ff.; Jachmann, *Plautinisches und Attisches,* pp. 162 ff. Against contamination in these same plays, see Michaut, *Plaute,* II, pp. 261 ff., who says that the critics "se font de la contamination elle-même une idée fausse, contraire à la vraisemblance et contraire aux faits connus" (p. 276). Even for Terence, where definite statements exist in the prologues and in Donatus' commentary about his use of contamination, there is little agreement among scholars concerning the extent of his changes and the nature of the originals; e.g., on the *Eunuchus,* cf. Smith, *The Technique of Solution,* p. 76, n. 2; p. 119, n. 2.

another play dealing with the birth of Hercules.[74] The *Stichus* can hardly come from three different originals, as Leo assumes, if the first two sections of the play contain passages which resemble fragments from the same Menandrian original;[75] the conclusion of the comedy with its festal song and dance may be Greek, or Plautus may have developed it under the influence of Italian farce; so, too, the very farcical and ribald ending of the *Casina*: does it come from the original of Diphilus (Jachmann) or from a second Greek comedy (Fraenkel) or from Italian farce or mime (Leo)?[76] Does the *Pseudolus* come from two different sources, as Hough and others have assumed,[77] or has one deception, that of the *senex*, been omitted from the one original? Or is it not more likely that the wager with Simo in *Pseud.* 535 ff. anticipates just the sort of conclusion that we have in the play, the payment of the twenty minae by Simo when Ballio is successfully tricked?[78] The *Poenulus* with its double intrigue and possible minor flaws has been explained by Leo and Jachmann as resulting from the fusion of two originals but Fraenkel limited contamination in the play to the insertion of a single scene, and more recently it has been maintained that the first deception by Collybiscus and the *aduocati* is the invention of Plautus.[79] The *Miles* likewise has two deceptions, the second of which has wrongly been considered unnecessary; references to the twin sister are firmly embedded in the second part of the play and there is no evidence that the passageway through the wall was constructed for the purpose of escape; it is a far more satisfactory conclusion to have the soldier send Philocomasium away of his own volition and to give up Palaestrio at her request.[80] The play as it stands seems a much better comedy than either of the two originals postulated by Leo and others.

There are several basic weaknesses in the methods of the scholars favoring contamination: (1) they explain by *contaminatio* many features of the plays which are more properly attributed to the staging of plays with a limited cast, to conventions of ancient comedy, to the playwright's desire for clarity or humor; (2) they ascribe to Plautus or Terence all real or imagined weaknesses in the plays and assume that the originals were free from repetitions and inconsistencies—a most unlikely assumption; since, as Bowra says, "all authors contradict themselves, many contradict themselves violently";[81] (3) they believe that the Roman playwrights had little originality and no ability to com-

---

[74] Cf. Prescott, *CPh* 8 (1913), pp. 14 ff.

[75] Cf. Lucas, *PhW* 58 (1938), cols. 1101 ff.; see also Smith, *The Technique of Solution*, p. 104, n. 2.

[76] See chap. 6, n. 49.

[77] *The Composition of the Pseudolus*, pp. 103 f. For bibliography and discussion, cf. Hough, *ibid.*, pp. 13 ff.

[78] See above, pp. 162 f.

[79] Cf. Krysiniel, *Der plautinische Poenulus und sein attisches Vorbild*, pp. 12 ff.

[80] Cf. Duckworth, *CPh* 30 (1935), pp. 243 ff.

[81] C. M. Bowra, *Tradition and Design in the Iliad* (Oxford, 1930), p. 98.

pose scenes or episodes of any value, so that any additions or insertions must necessarily betray the crude and faulty workmanship of the Roman playwright; (4) above all, they fail to look upon the plays as comedy created for the amusement and delight of spectators. Even an audience far more critical and cultured than the Romans of the second century B.C. would fail to notice most of the minor flaws and difficulties which the modern scholar, poring over the text, discovers by a logical and unimaginative investigation of details.

In recent years more and more voices have been raised against this type of technical approach to comic drama. Harsh, after showing that many of the criteria are faulty and that inartistic features usually assigned to Roman playwrights occur in many Greek plays also, concludes: "the method of distinguishing Roman workmanship from Greek by means of logical analysis and theoretical standards of dramatic technique must definitely and finally be abandoned. The many years devoted to the problem by scholars have proved fruitful mainly in respect to the incidental results produced and to the stimulus given general studies in the field. Doubtless it would be advisable to relegate to the background consideration of contamination and Roman originality in future studies of Plautus and Terence."[82] Enk agrees that the theories of the scholars seem in general without foundation; he does not deny the existence of contamination in Plautus but limits it to the addition of single scenes, i.e., the method of Terence in the *Adelphoe*, and he finds only three instances in the plays where Plautus apparently made such insertions: *Mil.* 813 ff. (the Lurcio scene), *Pseud.* Act I, Scene 3, and *Stich.* Act v.[83] Beare considers none of these passages convincing. His view that modern scholars have been misled by Terence's statement in the *Andria*-prologue leads him to an extreme position: for solving the difficulties in the plays, "almost any proposed solution, however farfetched, lies nearer at hand than a theory of contamination. An *a posteriori* proof of contamination cannot be got out of the materials at our disposal; but for the statement of Terence, scholars would scarcely have wasted their time in spinning these cobwebs."[84]

Thus many of the conclusions of Leo, Fraenkel, Jachmann, and others have been discredited; the pendulum has swung in the opposite

---

[82] *AJPh* 58 (1937), p. 293.

[83] *RPh* 64 (1938), pp. 289 ff. Enk believes that Plautus prepared for the conclusion of the *Stichus* by an insertion between 418 and 435. But see above, n. 37.

[84] *RPh* 66 (1940), p. 42. Cf. also Beare's statement in *The Roman Stage*, p. 104: "The theory of contamination is that the Roman dramatists put together portions of Greek plays, adding a minimum of original work in order to fit the Greek material together. I think that the attempt to do this would inevitably involve the Latin translator in original work of a complicated character—and this is the negation of the contamination-theory, which denies to the Latin dramatists all powers of dramatic construction, while insisting that they made far-reaching changes in the structure of their originals. That such changes were made I do not believe; but if they were made, then the Latin dramatist himself must be given the credit for such unity as we are willing to concede to his play."

direction but, like most healthy reactions, it has perhaps gone too far. Most scholars today would hesitate to deny contamination to Plautus as completely as Beare does. Hough, for instance, has in recent years supported the use of a second original for both the *Asinaria* and the *Captivi*.[85] But the intricate combining and interweaving of two Greek plays cannot be definitely proved for any Plautine comedy. That the playwright made many insertions and additions is not to be doubted; if this new material came from a different Greek source, we have contamination in the Terentian sense; Plautus, however, may have added passages and scenes of his own invention. The older view that Plautus, though a comic genius and a master of Latin, was incapable of composing a scene of merry dialogue (e.g., the Lurcio scene in the *Miles*)[86] would claim few adherents today. If ever the sands of Egypt should deliver up to us the complete original of the *Miles* or the *Poenulus* or some other controversial play, the difficulties with which scholars have been struggling would be solved—but such a fortunate discovery seems at least highly improbable. Meanwhile, critics would do well to admit that the answers to many problems of structure and composition cannot be determined with any degree of certainty. There is no evidence that *contaminatio*, any more than *retractatio*, was ever as common in the second century B.C. as many scholars have believed.

[85] *AJPh* 58 (1937), pp. 19 ff., 63 (1942), pp. 26 ff. Hough's view of the *Asinaria* involves an elaborate interweaving of the two Greek plots; he believes that the Ergasilus scenes have been added to the *Captivi* from another source but have been much altered and expanded by Plautus.

[86] Miss Krysiniel (*Der plautinische Poenulus und sein attisches Vorbild*, p. 59) believes that Plautus himself composed the Lurcio scene; cf. also Beare, *RPh* 66 (1940), p. 41. See, however, Haywood, *AJPh* 65 (1944), pp. 382 ff., who argues that the scene fits perfectly into the structure of the play and sees no reason for viewing it as an addition or insertion. In a later work (on the *Miles*) Miss Krysiniel states that the hole in the wall and the twin-sister trick were directed against the soldier in the Greek original; Plautus substituted Sceledrus for the soldier and made the latter the butt of Acroteleutium's deception (cf. *Die Technik des plautinischen Miles Gloriosus*, pp. 5 ff., 38). This theory makes the greater part of the *Miles* Plautus' own invention. Miss Krysiniel, however, like Jachmann and Kuiper (see above, n. 48), is convinced both of the faultiness of Plautus' workmanship and of the perfection of the Greek originals; cf. her recent publication, *De quibusdam Plauti exemplaribus Graecis*.

# CHAPTER 8
## FORESHADOWING AND SUSPENSE

ONE of the most fundamental requirements in all drama is that of arousing and maintaining the interest of the audience. The spectator must be made attentive and absorbed in the action of the play, he must remain in a state of continued tension, if the dramatist is to succeed in his task. Dramatic interest or suspense may be of two different types: (1) suspense of anticipation; the spectator knows what is to happen, but not when or how; he follows the progress of the action and awaits with ever-increasing hope or fear the coming of the expected event; (2) suspense of uncertainty; the spectator does not know the outcome and remains in a state of ignorance and curiosity about the later action. The two forms of suspense are not incompatible, for ignorance of details may go hand in hand with a heightened anticipation of the main events, or the immediate action may be foreshadowed and the ultimate result left in uncertainty. Many critics, however, use "suspense" in the more limited sense of ignorance or curiosity; they maintain that foretelling or foreshadowing of the action (which is necessary if we are to have suspense of anticipation) eliminates suspense; actually, it eliminates only ignorance and uncertainty. But to avoid confusion in the discussion which follows I shall accept the narrower definition of suspense and shall refer to the other type of dramatic tension as "anticipation."

It is not often realized how much the Homeric epics resemble drama. Not only were they composed for oral presentation but even in the classical period they were delivered orally. One outstanding feature of both the *Iliad* and the *Odyssey* is the fact that much of the action is made known to the hearer in advance by the prophecies of the divine characters and the prophetic announcements of the poet. In other words, the epic bard did not keep his audience uncertain as to the later developments but built up anticipation of what was to come: not the "What?" but the "How?" and the "When?" were stressed. Some years ago I wrote of the Homeric poems as follows: "This knowledge of the later action does not remove the suspense experienced by the reader, however. He still feels a deep interest in the manner and time of the fulfillment of each foreshadowed event, an interest which the poet heightens by the repetition of the announcement and by the retardation of the expected event. The poet's insistence upon the ignorance of the characters does much to maintain the anticipation of the reader. At times the hopes and fears of the epic personages are so vividly portrayed that the reader, led to share the emotions of the characters, feels his faith wavering as to the inevitability of events which he has been informed are infallible."[1]

---

[1] *Foreshadowing and Suspense in the Epics of Homer, Apollonius, and Vergil,* p. 116.

Thus, even though anticipation rather than uncertainty was characteristic of the Homeric epics, the poems were eminently successful in holding the interest of the audience.

In Greek tragedy the general outline of many myths was known to the spectators in advance and this pre-knowledge which the characters did not possess made possible the tragic irony of which Sophocles was so great a master. On the other hand, different playwrights wrote on the same theme; the spectator would be uncertain as to the particular treatment he was about to witness and, by entering into the emotions of the characters, would share their hopes and fears; the result was a marvelous blend of anticipation and uncertainty. Furthermore, it may be doubted that the myths were as well known as many assume. Pratt admits that dramatic suspense in Greek tragedy is essentially anticipatory, but points out "in the first place, that this characteristic is the product of the dramatist's artistry and not the result of general familiarity with the myths, and, secondly, that there is opportunity in Greek tragedy for a greater medley of emotional reactions with a large admixture of uncertainty, unless this is dispelled by the dramatist, than is generally realized."[2] Pratt's statement is significant in that it seeks to combat the trend seen in many modern writers who look upon dramatic irony and suspense as mutually exclusive.

The famous fragment (191) of Antiphanes, a poet of Middle Comedy, is often cited to illustrate the difficulties which the comic playwright faced and to explain the lack of suspense and surprise in ancient comedy. Antiphanes says that the task of the tragic poet was easy, for he had only to mention the name of Oedipus and the spectators knew the rest, whereas the comic writer must invent everything—names, circumstances both past and present, the catastrophe, the point of attack; necessary information must be given by the characters in comedy but in tragedy characters like Peleus and Teucer did not need to do so. This fragment is interpreted by Frank to mean that in comedy an omniscient prologue "must present the whole situation and in addition he must give explicit hints of the solution, if the spectator was to have the same advantage as he had in tragedy where the solution was a matter of common knowledge. . . . The adoption of the same method of plot construction for comedy eliminated the use of tension and increased the employment of a kind of comic irony."[3] Such a view suggests a number of important questions: to what extent do Plautus and Terence arouse dramatic interest by the use of suspense and surprise? Are the plots revealed to the spectators in advance and, if so, does this necessarily eliminate suspense and make surprise impossible? Is it true, as many

---

[2] *Dramatic Suspense in Seneca and in His Greek Precursors*, p. 13. Cf. also Stuart, *SPhNC* 15 (1918), pp. 295 ff., who shows that Euripides arouses suspense by the use of both true and false foreshadowing.

[3] *Life and Literature in the Roman Republic*, pp. 108 f., 111.

now think, that the broad outlines of Plautus' plots are clear from the beginning and that Terence introduced suspense into ancient comedy and sacrificed dramatic irony in so doing? Finally, can we be so sure that suspense is impossible when irony is employed? These are questions of primary significance in our consideration of the two Roman playwrights.

## The Nature of the Plautine Prologue

Each of Terence's six comedies is prefaced by a prologue in which the playwright defended himself against the attacks of his critics[4] and appealed to the spectators for favor. The prologue was not a part of the comedy proper for it did not divulge any information about the dramatic situation at the beginning of the play, nor did it forecast or in any way allude to the later action of the drama. The Plautine prologue also was devoted in part to winning the attention and goodwill of the audience; we find appeals for favor (e.g., *Amph.* 13 ff., *Asin.* 1 ff., *Cas.* 1 ff., *Men.* 3 ff.), references to the actors and the spectators (e.g., *Amph.* 64 f., *Poen.* 1 ff.) and irrelevant jests (e.g., *Capt.* 10 ff., *Cas.* 75 ff.), all of which were doubtless designed to put the audience in a receptive mood. One jest in particular apparently delighted both playwright and public since it appears in almost the same form in two prologues:

If anyone wishes some business transacted for him there, he'll be a fool if he doesn't give me the money—but if he does give me the money, he'll be a much greater fool. (*Poen.* 79 ff., cf. *Men.* 49 ff.)

The primary purpose of most Plautine prologues, however, was to explain the *argumentum*—the complicated situation in which the characters find themselves at the beginning of the play. The audience could thus better understand the confusions arising from error and mistaken identity. Plautus in his use of the expository prologue (*prologus argumentativus*) was following the example of his Greek predecessors.

Before analyzing the nature of the material presented to the audience in the narrative prologue, I wish to stress the fact that several Plautine prologues contain no information about the plot of the play. The *prologus* of the *Asinaria*, after giving the author and title of the Greek original, says (13 f.):

This comedy is full of wit and mirth; the theme is a laughable one.

The two-verse prologue of the *Pseudolus* states merely:

You'd better get up and stretch your legs; a long play by Plautus is coming on the stage.

In the *Trinummus* the audience is warned not to expect the *argumentum* in the prologue since the *senes* who will appear will explain the situa-

4 Cf. "Terence and Lanuvinus" in chap. 3.

tion (16 f.),[5] and the fragmentary prologue of the *Vidularia*, if correctly restored, tells the spectators (11) that they will learn what the characters are doing when they do it. Such statements tend to arouse curiosity and heighten the expectation of the hearers. The prologues of these four plays are all short and Plautus obviously made no attempt in these comedies to give the audience preliminary information about the nature of the play. Both the *Asinaria* and the *Pseudolus* are plays of intrigue; the essential information is presented clearly in the opening scene or scenes,[6] and the spectator can follow the development of the action without difficulty; this is equally true of the *Trinummus* where, however, deception is less prominent. Several Plautine comedies—the *Curculio, Epidicus, Mostellaria, Persa*, and *Stichus*—have no prologue and the exposition in each instance is developed naturally by means of dialogue. We have thus a total of nine comedies (including the fragmentary *Vidularia*) which do not avail themselves of the *prologus argumentativus*. The beginning of the *Bacchides* is lost; there may have been a prologue but it need not have given the *argumentum* since the drama is not a recognition play and "all the facts necessary to the understanding of the play may be gathered from the early scenes of the play as it stands."[7] Our discussion of the expository prologue will therefore be limited to the remaining eleven comedies.

Much has been written on the nature and the variety of the Plautine prologue since Leo's classic treatment.[8] The prologue has often been considered superfluous and repetitious; much of the information which it supplies is found in the body of the play and therefore is, strictly speaking, unnecessary.[9] But perhaps such repetition is itself of value if the audience is to understand the situation clearly. Furthermore, in many plays essential facts could not be provided by the actors themselves. It is frequently stated that most of Plautus' comedies in which the speaker of the prologue[10] gives the presuppositions of the plot are plays which end with the recognition of identity. Since the true identity

---

[5] Cf. the similar phraseology in *Ad.* 22 ff. It is somewhat depressing to find the Plautine passage ignored and Terence's words cited as proof that the younger dramatist was using the prologue "for a new purpose"; cf. Andrewes, *G & R* 16 (1947), p. 34.

[6] Cf. Leo, *Plautinische Forschungen*, pp. 200 ff., 216 ff.; Leo believes that these plays (with the exception of the *Vidularia*) did not need a prologue, and he comments upon the Terentian nature of the prologues of the *Asinaria, Trinummus*, and *Vidularia*. See also Fields, *The Technique of Exposition*, pp. 4 ff., 11 ff.

[7] Fields, *The Technique of Exposition*, p. 19; for an attempt to arrange the fragments at the beginning of the play, see Law, *CPh* 24 (1929), pp. 197 ff.

[8] *Plautinische Forschungen*, pp. 188-247; see also Legrand-Loeb, *The New Greek Comedy*, pp. 393 ff.; Michaut, *Plaute*, II, pp. 116 ff.

[9] Cf. Legrand-Loeb, *The New Greek Comedy*, pp. 396 ff.

[10] The speaker of the prologue may be a god or an allegorical being, as in the *Aulularia, Casina, Cistellaria* (149 ff.), *Rudens*; an impersonal prologue (*Captivi, Menaechmi, Poenulus, Truculentus*); or a character in the play, as in the *Mercator* and the *Miles*; cf. also *Cist.* 120 ff. The prologue of the *Amphitruo* is given by the god Mercury who is an actor in the play.

of one or more of the characters is not known to the other actors, the audience, learning the facts of the case, can appreciate the irony inherent in the situation and can understand the errors of the characters. The existence of twins in the *Menaechmi*, of two pairs of doublets in the *Amphitruo*, must be made clear to the spectators at the outset; similarly, the real identity of Tyndarus (*Captivi*), Selenium (*Cistellaria*), the Carthaginian sisters (*Poenulus*), and Palaestra (*Rudens*) is an aid to understanding the complications and heightens the irony in the situation, e.g., Tyndarus a prisoner of his own father, Hanno pretending to be the father of his own daughters, and Daemones protecting his daughter from Labrax.

The expository prologue appears also in comedies which do not have recognition scenes (e.g., *Aulularia, Miles, Mercator*) and some plays with recognition scenes either have no prologues at all (*Curculio, Epidicus*) or have prologues which give no information concerning identity (*Truculentus, Vidularia*). Leo is willing to admit that Terence may have dispensed with the narrative prologue in order to create suspense but he does not allow the same for Plautus who, he believes, followed his Greek predecessors in composing prologues for the *Curculio* and the *Epidicus*; these prologues have been lost.[11] The *Truculentus* too, he thinks, should have information in the prologue preparing for the recognition of the baby but this prologue, altered by Plautus, has also been lost in part. The *Vidularia* was apparently unusual in that the prologue was a forerunner of the Terentian prologue and did not explain the situation leading to the *anagnorisis*.

Leo thus accepts as a definite principle of the technique of New Comedy that an expository prologue is necessary to give essential information to the audience if the characters themselves are not in possession of the facts. But it seems unwise to assume that the prologues of the Greek originals were lacking in variety and had to conform to a particular type;[12] it seems even more unwise to conclude on the basis of a preconceived theory that several Plautine prologues have disappeared. There is little difficulty in these plays since the presuppositions are made sufficiently clear in the opening scenes for the audience to follow the action with ease.[13] It is not impossible that Plautus may have varied

[11] *Plautinische Forschungen*, pp. 196 ff., 221. For the *Curculio* there is the added argument that, without a prologue, the audience does not know until 341 that the scene of the play is laid in Epidaurus.

[12] This is, of course, the method of Kuiper, who in his reconstructions of the Greek originals invariably assumes a prologue by a divinity at the end of Act 1 (i.e., deferred as in the *Cistellaria* and the *Miles*), a prologue which explains the complicated situations and makes intelligible the recognitions (usually of half-brother and half-sister) which he postulates for the conclusion of each Greek comedy. See above, chap. 6, n. 1 and n. 34.

[13] This is true of the *Curculio* and the *Truculentus*. On the *Epidicus*, where the exposition has been criticized as inadequate, see Duckworth, *T. Macci Plauti Epidicus*, pp. 97 ff., for bibliography and discussion.

his technique and at times let the recognition scene come more as a surprise to the spectators; this would be true of the *Curculio* and the *Epidicus*, if they had no prologue, and it seems likely that they did not since the opening scenes of dialogue present the expository material in a manner closely resembling the beginning of the *Asinaria*, the *Mostellaria*, the *Persa*, the *Pseudolus*—plays which either have no prologue or in which the prologue divulges no information concerning the plot. The *Curculio* and the *Epidicus* are, after all, primarily comedies of deception, and most plays of deception lack the narrative prologue.[14] It is possible also, as Hough suggests, that Plautus in his later plays eliminated dramatic preparation and increased the element of surprise.[15] This would explain why the playwright wished on occasion to have his audience discover the identity of the heroine simultaneously with the characters.

But is it permissible to speak of "surprise" in Plautus? Again and again critics remind us that the Plautine spectator is prepared for the plot in advance, that he not only must know the true facts of the situation but the solution as well, that in such circumstances there can be no suspense. Let me quote as typical of this point of view the words of Frank: "It has frequently been noticed that the writers of the New Comedy, including Plautus, were far more generous than present-day dramatists in 'preparing' their audiences for every turn in the plot and that they depended less for their effects upon the elements of 'suspense' and 'surprise.' . . . So in Plautus, wherever we have an intricate play that develops to a conclusion which could not be revealed by the character, the prologue, if it has survived, discloses the outcome to the audience."[16] These statements are half-truths, but they have been accepted uncritically by later writers who make broad and misleading generalizations about the plays. It is hardly accurate to say that Plautus prepares his audience "for every turn of the plot" nor is it true that the prologue "discloses the outcome to the audience" whenever we have a play with a conclusion which is unknown to the characters, i.e., a play ending with an *anagnorisis*. Let us examine briefly the eleven expository prologues to see if they support Frank's contention.

In the first place, almost half of the plays with expository prologues are not recognition plays. The *Casina* and the *Mercator* are comedies of intrigue in which a father tries without success to procure his son's sweetheart but in neither case is the action of the play outlined for the spectators; the prologue gives the basic exposition and in the *Casina* (63) states that the wife of the *senex* will continue to aid her absent

---

[14] Cf. Harsh, *A Handbook of Classical Drama*, p. 354, who argues against the existence of a prologue for the *Epidicus*.

[15] *AJPh* 60 (1939), pp. 422 ff.; cf. especially p. 429, n. 1.

[16] *Life and Literature in the Roman Republic*, pp. 106, 109.

son.[17] Charinus, speaking the prologue of the *Mercator*, is eager to keep his father from learning about the girl he has brought home with him (107). The story of his earlier love affair, which met with violent opposition from his father and resulted in his departure from home (40 ff.), gives the hearer the false impression that Demipho will disapprove also of the second love affair if he learns of the girl's arrival. There is thus no foreshadowing of the action of the play, and Demipho's violent passion for Pasicompsa (cf. 260 ff.) comes as a distinct surprise. The household god in the *Aulularia* gives the necessary exposition and then says (31 ff.) that the *senex* next door will propose marriage to Euclio's daughter and this will lead to her marriage with the young man who violated her. The prologue of the *Truculentus* refers to Phronesium's deception of the soldier by means of a pretended childbirth (18 f.). And Palaestrio in the deferred prologue of the *Miles* describes the chain of circumstances leading to his presence and that of Philocomasium in the soldier's house, explains Pleusicles' arrival next door and the passageway through the wall, and then (145 ff.) forecasts the deception of Sceledrus by means of the twin sister trick. In these three plays the prologue discloses the later action to the audience and in the *Aulularia* foretells part of the denouement. But what is not told is even more significant than what is revealed, and this is all too seldom mentioned in discussions of Plautus' prologues. As we saw above, the *Truculentus* contains a recognition scene of which there is no mention in the prologue as it now stands. The *Aulularia* is concerned primarily with the problem of Euclio and his gold but there is nothing in the prologue about his later difficulties with the money. The deception of Sceledrus in the *Miles* is subordinate to the tricking of Pyrgopolynices. Thus in all three plays Plautus foreshadows part of the plot but refrains from revealing the main action.

It is in the recognition plays, however, that the prologue is said to disclose the outcome to the audience. Frank cites the prologues of the *Poenulus, Rudens,* and *Amphitruo*; there are three other plays of this type—the *Captivi, Cistellaria,* and *Menaechmi.* In all six comedies the initial situation is explained in the prologue and the audience thus has foreknowledge concerning the true identity of characters which is denied to the actors themselves. But does this necessarily mean, as Legrand says, that the prologue "communicates the contents of the plot"?[18] Mercury describes how Jupiter has visited Alcumena in disguise and

---

[17] I do not include the announcement that Casina will be revealed as a freeborn Athenian (81 ff.) among the instances of foreshadowing the denouement since the discovery does not occur in the Latin play. Moreover, the fact that she will be recognized as the daughter of Alcesimus is mentioned only in the epilogue (1013). It is wrong to cite the *Casina,* as Frank does (*Life and Literature in the Roman Republic,* p. 110), among the illustrations to prove that the outcome of the play is disclosed to the audience.

[18] Legrand-Loeb, *The New Greek Comedy,* p. 393.

refers (140 ff.) to the imminent arrival of Amphitruo and Sosia but he foreshadows neither the misunderstandings nor the birth of Hercules at the end of the play.[19] There are no allusions to the dramatic action in the prologues of the *Cistellaria* and the *Menaechmi*, and all we learn from Arcturus about the plot of the *Rudens* is that Labrax's ship has been wrecked and that he and the girls will shortly arrive at the place where dwells Daemones, who is in reality Palaestra's father (72 ff.). This tells us little about the play itself, and Michaut seems far more accurate than most scholars when he says that Plautus in these four plays "laisse les spectateurs suivre l'action sans les prévenir ni de la manière dont elle se déroulera, ni du dénouement auquel elle doit aboutir."[20]

The remaining two comedies—the *Captivi* and the *Poenulus*—best illustrate the conventional belief about the Plautine prologue. The audience learns from the prologue of the *Captivi* not only the true identity of Tyndarus but the stratagem of exchanging roles; cf. 40 ff.:

> He will carry out this deception today in clever fashion and make his master a free man; at the same time he will unwittingly rescue his brother and enable him to return home to his father a free man.

The prologue of the *Poenulus*, after recounting the earlier events which brought both Agorastocles and the Carthaginian sisters to Calydon, describes Hanno's search for his daughter and then says (124 f.):

> The man who will arrive today will discover his daughters and his nephew.

In both prologues we have definite foreshadowing of the outcome. But it should be recalled that these two comedies combine mistaken identity and deception. It is rather significant that even here, where Plautus appears to give more advance information than in any other comedy, he still discloses the outcome only in part—in the *Captivi* he foretells the outcome of the deception but not the recognition of Tyndarus as Hegio's son (although Tyndarus' real identity is revealed); in the *Poenulus* he foretells the *anagnorisis* but gives no information concerning the tricking of the *leno* which comprises more than half the play. That Plautus was consciously endeavoring to combine suspense with foretelling is implied by *Poen.* 126 f.:

> I shall go, for I wish to become another person; as for what follows, others will follow to make it clear.

This statement resembles *Vid.* 11, included above among the passages designed to arouse curiosity and found in a prologue which, in spite of its corrupt state, Leo considered very Terentian in nature.

---

[19] The fact that the outcome of the play is foretold later in the course of the action (e.g., *Amph.* 463 ff., 867 ff.) is of course important for the amount of suspense and surprise in the plays but does not concern the problem of the expository prologue.

[20] *Plaute*, II, p. 119.

This then is the result of our investigations: of the twenty-one plays of Plautus (I include the *Vidularia*) six are without prologues (the beginning of the *Bacchides* being lost), although two (*Curculio, Epidicus*) have in addition to trickery recognition scenes and therefore, according to Leo and others, should each have a prologue; four more have brief prologues which make no attempt to give the *argumentum* although again one (*Vidularia*) is a play of recognition. Eleven comedies have expository prologues; four of these are recognition plays (*Amphitruo, Cistellaria, Menaechmi, Rudens*), but the prologue does not announce the recognition; two combine trickery and recognition and in one case (*Poenulus*) the prologue foretells the recognition, in the other (*Captivi*) the outcome of the intrigue. The *Miles* has two deceptions but only the minor one is foretold; in two other plays of deception (*Casina, Mercator*) there is no indication in the prologue of the action, and that of the *Mercator* actually gives the audience a false impression of what is to come. In the *Aulularia* and the *Truculentus* (both listed above as plays primarily of character) the prologue foretells part of the play but omits part, and in the *Truculentus* what is omitted is preparation for a recognition. Certainly there is far greater variety here in Plautus' use of the narrative prologue than is generally realized. If the audience learns from the prologue the denouement in only three instances (*Aulularia, Captivi, Poenulus*) and this only in part, it is highly erroneous to say that the prologue discloses the outcome or that "the broad outlines of Plautus' plots are generally clear from the beginning."[21]

The objection will probably be raised that I have been guilty of oversimplification in my analysis of the prologues and have ignored the possibility that the audience, as soon as it learns from the prologue the identity of a character, will naturally expect a denouement with a recognition. I am fully conscious that the recognition of a heroine as the daughter of free parents was a hackneyed theme in both Greek and Roman comedy and that any normal spectator familiar with the plays could assume that the *anagnorisis* would take place. I shall show below how both Plautus and Terence by subtle hints and allusions constantly prepared the audience during the action for such revelations of identity. The important point which needs to be stressed is that the recognition scene is not the play—it is the event which usually solves the complications and brings the comedy to its happy conclusion. Let us assume that the spectators of the *Menaechmi* or the *Rudens* foresee from the information given in the prologue that Menaechmus will meet his twin brother and that Palaestra will find her father; does this give them any idea of the plot of the comedy itself, the errors and confusions and difficulties into which the characters will be plunged? The audience can

---

[21] Dunkin, *Post-Aristophanic Comedy*, p. 135, n. 40.

anticipate that everything will turn out well in the end and can appreciate the irony in speech and situation; it seldom learns from the prologue the events of the play. As Harsh states, "the main function of the omniscient prologue, then, was not to foretell the recognition but to explain the secret identities in order to facilitate dramatic irony."[22] If the comedies of Plautus lack suspense, the reason must lie in the excessive amount of foretelling and foreshadowing during the action; certainly the details of the plot to be gleaned from the narrative prologue are far too meager and too general to eliminate dramatic tension.

## Dramatic Preparation and Foreshadowing

The primary purpose of the *prologus argumentativus* was to explain the situation at the beginning of the play and, on occasion, to reveal the secret identities and so prepare for the *anagnorisis*. But more than half of the extant Roman comedies do not have this type of prologue. To what extent did the existence or non-existence of the prologue affect the exposition of the essential facts within the play itself? How is the exposition handled in Terence's comedies, which lack expository prologues but contain discoveries and recognitions based upon mistaken identities? These questions concerning the preliminary facts in the plays must be answered before we consider the development of the plot and the manner in which the playwright either foreshadows or withholds the later action.

In general, there are two kinds of expository technique in the Roman comedies: (1) the dramatist explains the situation in full to the audience in the opening scene or scenes, or (2) he gives only the information that is necessary and withholds certain facts until they are dramatically more effective.[23] Exposition of the first type appears in plays of deception (e.g., *Asinaria, Miles, Mostellaria, Persa, Pseudolus*) and these are the very plays which have no expository prologue (with the exception of the *Mercator* and the *Miles*).[24] The situation at the opening is relatively simple, there are no hidden identities, and the audience can be put in possession of the necessary facts without delay. Plautus or his Greek predecessors apparently considered that most plays of trickery did not need a prologue. The remainder of Plautus' comedies and all of Terence's have gradual exposition of the second type; among the plays which best illustrate this method are Terence's *Hecyra* and *Adelphoe* and Plautus' *Rudens*. Most comedies in which the exposition is gradual are plays with recognition scenes, and the facts withheld from the spectators are usually those concerning the *anagnorisis*. But

---

[22] *A Handbook of Classical Drama*, p. 379.

[23] Cf. Fields, *The Technique of Exposition*, pp. 2 ff., 29 ff.

[24] It is worth noting that in both plays the prologue is spoken by a character rather than by a god or an omniscient *prologus*.

the effect of gradual exposition is very different when there has been a prologue (e.g., *Captivi, Poenulus, Rudens*) and when the play has no prologue and the discovery or recognition comes as a surprise (e.g., *Epidicus, Phormio, Hecyra*). In a play like the *Rudens* the essential facts may be revealed little by little but the information is only a repetition of what has already been given in the prologue; when the prologue is lacking, on the contrary, the audience may remain as much in the dark as the characters, but whether it actually does so depends upon the amount of foreshadowing prior to the revelation of the facts.

Both Plautus and Terence prepare for recognition scenes by alluding, sometimes openly, sometimes more subtly, to the true state of affairs. In the *Rudens*, for instance, there are numerous hints of Palaestra's real identity; cf. the words of Daemones:

I did have a daughter, but I lost her when she was young. (106)

O my daughter, when I look upon this young girl, how the memory of my loss makes me suffer! She was taken from me when only three years old, but if she lives she would now be like this girl, I know. (742 ff.)

There are even more obvious references to Palaestra's birth (217, 738 f., 1079, 1105; cf. 649, 714) and to the casket and trinkets which will enable her to find her parents (389 ff.; cf. 1078 ff., 1130 ff.). All such allusions heighten the anticipation of the spectators, who already know from the prologue that Palaestra is Daemones' daughter. Frequently, the preparation takes the form of more subtle references to a girl's chastity and good moral character or, if a courtesan (e.g., Selenium in the *Cistellaria*), to her devotion to one lover. It is interesting that most references to the heroine's purity occur in comedies that have no prologue; the spectator may not grasp the full significance of the passage at the time but certainly his curiosity would be aroused about the girl's identity. Among the examples of this type of preparation are the following:

As far as I'm concerned, she's just as chaste as if she were my own sister. (*Curc.* 51)

This girl is chaste and doesn't sleep with men yet. (*Curc.* 57)

Be sure to see that the girl's well treated. I've brought her up chastely and carefully at my house. (*Curc.* 517 f.)

I have never marred or scarred her innocence in any way. (*Epid.* 110)

The heroine is often described as a paragon of beauty and modesty, e.g., *Epid.* 43 (*forma lepida et liberali*), *Eun.* 132 (*forma honesta uirginem*), *Eun.* 230 (*facie honesta*); of especial interest are the references to Glycerium in *And.* 71 ff., 119 ff., 274, 288, and Donatus comments on the significance of her virtue and charm as preparation for the recognition and her later status as a *matrona*.[25] Glycerium, like

---

[25] *Ad And.* 71, 119, 274. For the extent to which Donatus was conscious of preparation and foreshadowing (*praeparatio, praestructio, παρασκευή, προπαρασκευή,* etc.) as

Selenium in the *Cistellaria*, is a *femina unius uiri* (cf. *And.* 293 f.).

In the passages cited above, the possibility that the heroine will be revealed as a freeborn citizen is held before the spectators, but there is no hint of her parentage (except in the *Rudens*). At times, however, the words of the characters reveal more than they themselves know. When Philippa in *Epid.* 532 and 562 states that her daughter was captured by the enemy, it would doubtless occur to the audience that the captive already purchased by Stratippocles will prove to be the daughter of Periphanes and Philippa. In the *Heauton* the "mother" of Antiphila was described as an old woman of Corinth (96 f., 600 ff.); Sostrata later reveals that she gave her baby girl to an old woman of Corinth (629 f.). The mention of the ring (614, 653 ff.) is hardly necessary to convince the audience that Antiphila is Sostrata's daughter. An unusually clever bit of foreshadowing is found in the *Andria*; Davus says to himself (220 ff.):

> Now they're concocting some scheme between them about her being an Athenian citizen. . . . Rubbish! It doesn't seem probable to me at all.

The fact that the slave here treats as unlikely what is actually the truth serves to instill a bit of uncertainty into the minds of the spectators; at least, it is a most unconventional instance of foreshadowing, which, as Donatus states (*ad And.* 220, 221), leaves room for error.[26]

The passages which prepare for or foreshadow the recognition deal primarily with the basic facts, the presuppositions of the play. This is the type of information given in the expository prologue when such prologues exist, but the foreshadowing gives little information about the plot itself. Whether the audience views the course of the drama with anticipation or uncertainty depends upon the extent to which the details of the plot are foretold. Vague foreshadowing of intrigue, for example, can arouse the interest of the spectators in what is to take place but they remain in a state of anxious tension through their ignorance of the nature of the trick to be unfolded. An excellent illustration of this type of foreshadowing is found in the *Mostellaria*, when Tranio says:

> Will you be satisfied if I arrange it so your father not only won't go into the house but will even flee far away? (389 f.)
> Tell him I'll fix things so his father won't even want to look at the house. He'll hide his head and fly off in fright. (422 ff.)

Tranio's words inform the audience of the purpose of his trickery but

---

an important feature of dramatic technique, cf. Harsh, *Studies in Dramatic "Preparation,"* pp. 4 ff. Preparation for and foreshadowing of the recognition of the heroine appear also in the fragmentary plays of Menander; see Harsh, *ibid.*, pp. 40 ff.

[26] But see Harsh, *Studies in Dramatic "Preparation,"* p. 37: "The mere mention of citizenship in such a case, however, probably constituted definite foreshadowing for a considerable part of the audience, since such mention occurs so frequently before a recognition." Cf. also Frank, *Life and Literature in the Roman Republic*, p. 118.

give no information concerning the method—an effective combination of anticipation and ignorance.

In their treatment of intrigue the playwrights range from preparation and vague foreshadowing to definite announcement of the trickery before it is put into effect. Many plays (e.g., *Asinaria, Miles, Poenulus*) have been criticized for the excessive amount of information given to the audience prior to the deception.[27] Such repetition of information and instruction enables the spectators to understand clearly the later action of the play but it also serves to heighten their anticipation and to increase their pleasure in seeing the expected events take place. Even in the *Miles*, however, where the intrigue seems to be completely foretold in advance, many details are added as the plan progresses. Among the elements mentioned late in the action are the escape of Palaestrio (first planned as flight in 1192 f., then arranged as a gift to Philocomasium in 1205) and the punishment of the soldier (prepared by Palaestrio's instructions to Acroteleutium in 1166 ff., and definitely foreshadowed by the words of the *puer* in 1388 ff.).

At the other end of the scale are the preparations and foreshadowing which increase the interest of the audience but give little or no real information. In plays of intrigue the lack of money is stressed again and again—the usual preliminary to a deception in which a slave procures the needed amount for his master.[28] The parasite's statement to Pyrgopolynices in *Mil.* 58 that all women love him prepares for the second deception of the play in which the soldier falls victim to his own conceit and lecherous desires. The longing of a loyal slave for his master's return foreshadows the arrival of the *senex* (*Most.* 78 ff., *Trin.* 617 ff.; cf. *Phorm.* 147 ff.) and in like manner the forebodings of a character suggest to the audience the subsequent events. In *Merc.* 586 f. Lysimachus fears that his wife will return and find the girl whom he is keeping for Demipho, and in *Phorm.* 585 Chremes is worried lest his wife will learn about his second marriage; the fears of both men are realized and scenes rich in comedy result. In *Ad.* 150 f. Micio refers to his hopes that Aeschinus was about to settle down; Donatus (*ad Ad.* 151) sees here an allusion to Aeschinus' affair with Pamphila and points out how neatly Terence can give the *argumentum* through the words of characters who themselves are ignorant of the truth.

In two instances, dreams of a very similar nature foreshadow the later action. The dream of Demipho in *Merc.* 225 ff. describes how he left a she goat in the keeping of an ape and how a kid led the goat away and then mocked him; the other, that of Daemones in *Rud.* 593 ff.,

[27] Cf. Hough, *AJPh* 60 (1939), pp. 422 ff., and see above, pp. 194 f.

[28] Cf. e.g., *Asin.* 55 f., *Bacch.* 46, 104, *Epid.* 52 ff., 114 ff., 141 ff., *Pers.* 5 f., 35 ff., *Pseud.* 45 ff., 80 ff., *Heaut.* 329, *Phorm.* 84, 93 f., 145 f.; Donatus comments on *Phorm.* 94 that *paupertas* is mentioned that there may be a reason for Phormio's trick (*fallacia*).

concerns the attempt of an ape to steal swallows from their nest. The audience would have little difficulty in fitting the animals to the characters and in seeing in the dreams a fairly accurate announcement of the development in each play. The dream in the *Mercator* outlines in a general way the entire plot; Demipho himself realizes that the she goat is the girl whom he loves but he does not yet know the identity of the ape and the kid (268 ff.); the parts of the dream which are not at first intelligible become clear as the action progresses.[29]

Occasionally the preparation for the later action is unusually subtle; in the *Casina* Lysidamus plans to spend the night with his "bride"; to his surprise (and that of the audience) he is anticipated by his assistant Olympio who first makes the disconcerting discovery that the bride is a male slave in disguise. But Olympio tells Cleustrata that he wouldn't give up Casina even to Jupiter (cf. 321 ff.); in 230 Lysidamus had said to his wife:

Look here, my dear Juno, you shouldn't be cross at your Jupiter.

In 331 Lysidamus again refers to himself as Jupiter, and in 405 ff. there is an amusing bit of slap-stick, as follows:

OL. (*hitting* CHALINUS) : There, take that!
CL. : What did you hit him for?
OL. : Because my Jupiter ordered me to.
CL. (*to* CHALINUS) : You hit him back, the same way. (CHALINUS *does so with relish.*)
OL. : Murder! I'm being punished with his fists, Jupiter.
LY. (*to* CHALINUS) : What did you hit him for?
CH. : Because my Juno (*pointing to* CLEUSTRATA) ordered it.

In the light of these passages, is it so surprising when Olympio refuses to give up Casina to Lysidamus (i.e., Jupiter)? In *Eun.* 230 f. Phaedria complains of the broken-down eunuch he is supposed to give to Thais; Donatus (on 231) comments that this is *praeparatio* for taking Chaerea in place of the eunuch. Certainly we have here preparation of the vaguest type and the audience would hardly realize the significance of the passage at the time.

To cite additional illustrations is unnecessary. Both Plautus and Terence are liberal in their use of preparation and foreshadowing, and it seems to make little difference whether the play has an expository prologue or not. Both dramatists obviously desire the interest of the spectators to derive in great part, at least, from their anticipation and expectation of events which have been foreshadowed vaguely or foretold

---

[29] Cf. Harsh, *Studies in Dramatic "Preparation,"* pp. 77 ff., who discusses also (p. 78, n. 23) the troublesome question of the origin of the dream in the *Mercator*; see also Beare, *CR* 42 (1928), pp. 214 f.; Enk, *T. Macci Plauti Mercator,* I, pp. 7 ff. Beare and Enk discuss the relationship of the two dreams and argue convincingly against the view of Marx and Fraenkel that the dream-scene in the *Mercator* was invented by Plautus and modeled upon that of the *Rudens.*

more definitely. Terence may have omitted the prologue to increase
suspense and surprise, but there is no indication that he eliminated
from the body of the play the preparation and foreshadowing which he
found in his originals.[30] The most detailed announcements concerning
intrigue occur in the earlier comedies of Plautus where the rehearsal
of instructions keeps the details of the deception clearly fixed in the
minds of the spectators. In Plautus' later comedies there is more uncertainty concerning the nature of the plot, and this is true also of
Terence's comedies. Both playwrights realize the value of dramatic
tension, and there are numerous passages which evince a deliberate
attempt to heighten the suspense and anxiety of the audience.

## Devices to Arouse Suspense

The methods employed by Plautus and Terence to maintain or create
suspense on the part of the audience fall into two broad but clearly defined categories: (1) when the spectators are ignorant or uncertain
about the events to be unfolded subsequently, their tension is increased
by stressing the ignorance or helplessness of the characters; (2) if the
spectators have been prepared for the later action either by foreshadowing or by more definite announcement, the playwright may counteract
the anticipation to a degree by portraying the fears and forebodings
of the characters that the expected happening will not occur or that
something will jeopardize the success of their plans.[31]

The passages which arouse the interest and maintain the uncertainty
of the audience include expressions of consternation and distress upon
hearing unexpected news: e.g., the many statements of Epidicus when
he learns about his master's new love affair:

Damn me for a poor fool! He's fixed me in fine style! (50)
Immortal gods! How royally I'm ruined! (56)
Ye gods! What a horrible mess this is! . . . When the old man finds all
this out, there's one ship here that will be an utter wreck. (72 ff.)[32]

Characters often feel themselves unable to cope with the difficulties
which confront them; a young man is despondent and depressed because
he has no money (e.g., *Asin.* 243 ff., *Pseud.* 80 ff., 299 f., *Phorm.*
162 ff., 534 ff.) or because his father may oppose his love affair (e.g.,
*Merc.* 588 ff., *Most.* 378 ff., *Phorm.* 153 ff.) and even force him to
marry a girl he does not love (e.g., *And.* 236 ff.). Even more frequently
a slave admits that he has no plan to aid his master. Typical of this type
of despair is the soliloquy of Pseudolus:

[30] Cf. Harsh, *Studies in Dramatic "Preparation,"* pp. 99 f.
[31] The devices which follow are an expansion of my suggestions in *CW* 35 (1941-42),
p. 196.
[32] Cf. also the fears of Tranio in *Most.* 348 ff., 541 ff., 660, 676 f.

He's gone now and you stand alone, Pseudolus. What are you going to do now, since you've been so generous with your promises to your young master? Where are the tricks? You haven't the ghost of a plan prepared, and not a bit of money, and not an idea what to do. You don't even know where to begin to start nor how to end the weaving of your web. . . . (*Pseud.* 394 ff.)

The effect of such a passage can only be the heightening of the dramatic tension, as the uncertainty of the slave and the ignorance of the spectators go hand in hand.

Later, the same character says (*Pseud.* 567 f.) that he doesn't know how he is going to carry out his plan but that it will be done; even when he boasts (574 ff.) about the mighty victory he will win over his enemy Ballio, whose house he will besiege with his legions, the audience still has no idea of the scheme, and perhaps Pseudolus likewise has none, for he abandons it gladly when the opportune arrival of Harpax suggests a new method of approach (600 ff.). Libanus (*Asin.* 249 ff.) and Epidicus (*Epid.* 81 ff.) talk about the need of devising some trick to aid their masters but they have as yet no idea how to go about procuring the money. In all such cases the audience remains in suspense and wonders how the action will develop. Sometimes a trick is attempted and fails; Davus (*And.* 599 ff.) and Syrus (*Heaut.* 668 ff.) lament that their plans have gone wrong and claim to be at a complete loss; although Davus promises to contrive some new scheme (*And.* 614 f., 622) and Syrus says he has a plan (*Heaut.* 677 f.), the audience does not learn until later the nature of their tricks. Earlier in the *Andria* Davus had himself been uncertain whether to aid Pamphilus or obey the *senex* (209 ff.), and Donatus comments (on 206) that such a deliberation stirred the audience with the expectation of things to come. But the suspense here would be uncertainty rather than anticipation.

Another means of arousing the spectators' interest is for a slave to postpone information or instructions. When Calidorus asks Pseudolus what he is planning to do, the slave replies (*Pseud.* 387 f.) :

I'll see that you learn in good time. I don't want to tell it twice.

In this instance, Pseudolus has as yet no plan, but that too is part of the playwright's attention to matters of suspense. Palaestrio refrains from explaining to Pleusicles why he should remember the name Dicea (*Mil.* 810) :

I'll tell you after a while when the occasion warrants it.

The fact that Dicea's name is not mentioned in the instructions when they are given (1175 ff.) has been considered a serious flaw, but it is possible that Plautus inserted *Mil.* 806 ff. to heighten the interest of the audience. In the *Heauton* Syrus keeps his questioners (and the spectators as well) in the dark by postponing information (273 f., 335 f., 612), and a delightful scene occurs in the *Andria* when Davus employs

Mysis as an assistant to deceive Chremes without revealing to her the purpose of the trick. Mysis obeys but doesn't know what is going on (cf. 737 ff.); when she complains later to Davus that he should have explained the situation to her beforehand, he says (794 f.):

Don't you think it makes a great difference whether you do a thing sincerely and naturally or with premeditation?

The most striking examples of the withholding of important information occur in scenes of running slaves. The function of the *seruus currens* is threefold: (1) there is a strong comic element in the manner in which he rushes on the stage eager to deliver his news and then indulges in idle jesting and buffoonery before he imparts his message; (2) the information which he brings marks a new stage in the development of the action; and (3) the delayed recognition of the character whom he is seeking and the retarded delivery of the important news create suspense both for his hearer and for the audience.[33] Since Frank and others state repeatedly that Plautus made little use of suspense and surprise, we might well expect that Terence would employ the running slave to arouse the interest of the audience to a greater degree than did Plautus. Actually, the reverse is the case, for in Terence the message brought by the slave is already known to the spectators (*And.* 338 ff., *Eun.* 643 ff., *Phorm.* 841 ff., *Ad.* 299 ff.) or is announced when the slave first appears (*Phorm.* 179 ff.), and the dramatic interest arises from the anticipation of the effect of the announcement upon the characters; comic irony is possible since the audience has a better understanding of the situation than do the characters. In Plautus, however, the spectators have no foreknowledge of the slave's message, and their ignorance and uncertainty are intensified by the retarding of the expected announcement. In *Asin.* 267 ff. Leonida rushes in with glad tidings for Libanus or Argyrippus, but over sixty-five verses of comic monologue and dialogue elapse before he delivers the information and during this interval the audience is as much in suspense as Libanus about the nature of the message. The interest here is especially keen after Libanus' helplessness in 249 ff. Tension is likewise maintained by the retarding of the slave's message in *Capt.* 768 ff., *Curc.* 280 ff., *Epid.* 1 ff., *Merc.* 111 ff., and *Stich.* 274 ff. We thus have another illustration of the difference between the dramatic technique of Plautus and Terence; in his use of the running slave Terence relies entirely upon anticipation and irony to hold the spectators' interest whereas Plautus makes the audience share the ignorance of the characters and uses comic delay to increase the dramatic tension.[34]

[33] Cf. Duckworth, "The Dramatic Function of the *servus currens*," pp. 93 ff., for bibliography and discussion.

[34] There are two scenes in Plautus where the running slave is treated in a Terentian manner. The information given by Stasimus in *Trin.* 1008 ff. was known to the spec-

The passages cited above serve to create or maintain suspense about happenings which have not yet been explained to the spectators. When, however, the nature and purpose of a deception have been foreshadowed or described in considerable detail, the dramatist often heightens the tension and creates suspense, temporarily at least, by instilling in the minds of the spectators some doubt about the success of the plan. When Hegio suggests sending someone else (*Capt.* 341 ff.), there is danger for the moment that the plan to provide for Philocrates' escape may collapse. In the *Casina* Cleustrata wants Olympio to give up Casina (269 f.) and Lysidamus fears she may succeed (304 f.). Tranio's deception of the *senex* almost fails when a noise is heard from inside the house; the slave says (*Most.* 510 ff.) :

I'm ruined! They'll wreck the whole plot. I'm scared stiff that he'll catch me red-handed.

Again and again slaves warn their assistants not to err and they express the fear that the intrigue will not succeed as planned:

I'm terribly afraid she'll make a muddle of it. (*Mil.* 526; cf. *Pers.* 624, 626)

Take care that she doesn't make any mistake. (*Heaut.* 361)

The comments of Pseudolus are more detailed (*Pseud.* 1024 ff.) :

Now I'm overwhelmed with fear for three reasons: I'm afraid this helper of mine will abandon me and go over to the enemy; I'm afraid that my master will return from the forum and the plunderers will be seized with the plunder they've seized; and I fear that the other Harpax will arrive before this Harpax gets away with the girl.

Such a soliloquy creates suspense, even though the tension is lessened when Simia appears with Phoenicium shortly after.

It is especially amusing when the intriguing slave or his assistant forgets a name and the completion of the deception is endangered, as in *Pseud.* 984 f. and *Phorm.* 385 ff.; suspense is increased as the audience watches with delight the manner in which the character extricates himself from the unexpected difficulty. Palaestrio warns Pleusicles against overconfidence in *Mil.* 1150 ff.; when the youth comes for Philocomasium in the guise of a ship-captain, his affectionate manner makes the soldier suspicious (1334 ff.) and the truth almost comes out; cf. the words of Palaestrio in 1348:

I'm fearfully afraid that this business will become too public.

Even this statement creates danger, for it is overheard by the soldier, but Palaestrio quick-wittedly gives it an innocent interpretation which lulls the soldier's suspicions. There is another tense moment soon after

---

tators early in the play. In *Most.* 348 ff. Tranio (like Geta in *Phorm.* 179 ff.) informs the audience almost immediately that his master has arrived from abroad.

when the slave overdoes his pretended reluctance to leave (1368). The *Miles* is one of the comedies in which the deception is announced and rehearsed in advance but it is rich in passages which introduce suspense. In general, the devices which counteract the audience's anticipation and arouse momentary uncertainty are more numerous in Plautus than in Terence.

The *adulescens* disappointed in love sometimes determines upon suicide but the plans are never fulfilled. Slaves express their fears for the future, e.g., *Epid.* 310 ff.:

> If the old man finds out the truth, I'm afraid he'll turn the elm switches into parasites and let them gnaw me to the bone.

Sosia (*Amphitruo*), Chrysalus (*Bacchides*), Epidicus, and Tranio (*Mostellaria*) are all threatened with punishment which never materializes.[35] The audience doubtless realized that the youths would not commit suicide and that the slaves would escape severe punishment, but such passages heighten the tension as the spectators share to a degree the misgivings and forebodings of the characters and wonder how the dreaded event will be avoided. There is another group of passages which deserves a brief mention in this connection; often a character states that he will perform some act but he is unable to carry out his intention, or a changed situation makes his action unnecessary, or the matter is ignored in the later action of the play. False foreshadowing of this type holds the interest of the spectators but the anticipated events do not transpire. Amphitruo says that he will bring Naucrates from the ship (*Amph.* 854) but he is unable to locate the man (1009 ff.). In *Truc.* 306 ff., the slave threatens to inform the *senex* of his young master's affair with Phronesium but when he next appears (669 ff.) he is no longer *truculentus* and nothing more is said about the threatened exposure. Similarly, Menaechmus says that he will ask the advice of his friends (*Men.* 700) though there is no mention of this later when he returns in 899 ff. (cf. also Antipho in *Stich.* 143).[36]

## Surprise in Plautus and Terence

Both Plautus and Terence, as we have seen, use foreshadowing to quicken the interest of the audience in what is to come and endeavor

[35] See Harsh, *Studies in Dramatic "Preparation,"* pp. 93 ff., who terms these passages "quasi-foreshadowing."

[36] Characters promise to take part later on in the action, but disappear from the play; e.g., Callipho (*Pseud.* 547 ff.) and Sosia (*And.* 168 ff.). There are references to marketing and dinners which never take place (e.g., *Mil.* 738 f., 749 f., *Most.* 66 f., 363, *Truc.* 127, 359 ff.); some scholars refuse to accept these passages as instances of false foreshadowing and look upon them as definite flaws; see above, pp. 200 f. On *Epid.* 166 ff. as possible foreshadowing of a marriage between Periphanes and Philippa, see Harsh, *Studies in Dramatic "Preparation,"* p. 87, n. 8; Duckworth, *T. Macci Plauti Epidicus,* pp. 394 ff. It is unlikely that the original ever contained the

also to arouse suspense either by keeping the spectators in uncertainty or by suggesting that the anticipated event may not occur and that something else may possibly happen. In general, foreshadowing and suspense in Roman comedy appear not to be affected by the existence of a narrative prologue. Both playwrights foreshadow recognition scenes with considerable subtlety, whereas trickery is foretold by the characters themselves. But in the works of neither playwright is the amount of foretelling and foreshadowing sufficient to preclude the use of surprise.

That Terence's complete omission of the narrative prologue increases the opportunities for surprise is of course obvious. The audience remains unaware of secrets and hidden identities at the beginning of the play, and Terence does not fail to exploit this ignorance. Whereas in Plautus, when the heroine's identity is known, vague references to her good moral character or her Attic birth heighten the anticipation and create irony, such allusions in Terence tend rather to arouse curiosity and foster suspense. In every play of Terence there are events which come to the spectator as a distinct surprise. Frank has pointed out the most significant of these,[37] but his treatment is far from adequate since he links surprise too closely to the revelation of a secret; there is far more surprise in Terence than he implies, as there is in Plautus, where the existence of an expository prologue blinds him to the possibility that surprise may exist in the many sudden turns of the plot, even though the identity of the heroine is known to the audience.

In the *Andria*, Davus refers to the story that Glycerium is an Attic citizen but rejects it as a fiction (220 ff., 779 ff.). Frank believes that Terence in his first play was giving a strong hint of the recognition. As I said above,[38] Terence's foreshadowing here is most unusual and it almost looks as if Terence wants Davus to mislead the audience. But if we assume with Frank that Davus' words gave the spectators a clue to the recognition, there is still no clear indication that Glycerium is an Athenian citizen until the words of Crito in 806, whose entrance (796) itself has come as a surprise. The information that she is Chremes' daughter first appears in 930 ff. In spite of the preparation in *Heaut.* 96 f., there is no evidence prior to 614 ff. that Antiphila is the daughter of Chremes and Sostrata. Frank says that "soon after the middle of the play (675 ff.) the spectators are admitted to the last important fact, namely, that Clinia's sweetheart is freeborn."[39] This is misleading, since Frank does not make clear that the recognition itself occurs at this point. Likewise in the *Phormio*, where the recognition occurs long before the conclusion of the comedy, the knowledge that Antipho's wife

---

marriage of the older couple, if Stratippocles did not marry his half-sister in the Greek play (see "Mistaken Identity and Deception: *Epidicus*" in chap. 6).

[37] *Life and Literature in the Roman Republic*, pp. 115 ff.
[38] See p. 220.    [39] *Life and Literature in the Roman Republic*, p. 121.

is actually Chremes' daughter comes in 755 although the first reference to a daughter by a second wife was made in 567 ff. Prior to that point the audience had no knowledge of Chremes' double life and no hint of Phanium's identity. The story concocted by Phormio that Antipho was Phanium's kinsman and therefore should marry her (124 ff.) proved later to be true but the audience had no knowledge of this at the time.

The *Adelphoe* and the *Hecyra* are said best to reveal Terence's desire for a suspended denouement. In the former play the spectators are led to believe that Aeschinus is stealing a music girl for himself; not until the appearance of Ctesipho in 254 ff. do they realize that Aeschinus has stolen the girl for his brother. In the *Hecyra* the secret is kept from the audience to the very end of the play. Parmeno, who himself does not know the truth, gives in 178 ff. the misleading impression that Philumena has quarreled with her mother-in-law and for that reason has returned to her mother's house.[40] The spectators learn from Pamphilus in 373 ff. why Philumena left the home of her mother-in-law, but not until 811 ff. do they discover that Pamphilus himself had violated her before their marriage and so was the father of her child. Frank attributes the double failure of the play to the fact that here, more than in any other Terentian comedy, the audience was kept in doubt and anxiety to the very end. "There is not one ancient play before the day of Terence, so far as we know, where an audience was left in such complete suspense before an accumulating mass of perplexities."[41]

The element of surprise in the passages cited above has concerned the revelation of a secret or a hidden identity. But surprise appears in Terence in connection with many sudden turns of the plot. A few examples will suffice. The audience has no knowledge of Charinus' love affair in the *Andria* prior to his appearance in 301, and in the *Adelphoe*, shortly after the audience learns the truth about the music girl—that Aeschinus has seized her for Ctesipho, not for himself, and therefore is less guilty than Demea believes—the revelation that Aeschinus has seduced Sostrata's daughter comes as a surprise (292 ff.). There is likewise no foreshadowing of the pretended conversion of Demea (855 ff.) which brings the comedy to its delightful and satisfying conclusion. Frank considers that the *Eunuchus* was composed in the Plautine manner since it depends largely on buffoonery, imposture, and ludicrous situations; another reason for his view is doubtless that the recognition of Pamphila is foreshadowed early in the play (108 ff., 144 ff., 202 ff.). But there is no lack of surprise in the *Eunuchus*. Chaerea impersonates the eunuch in order to be near the girl he loves

---

[40] Cf. Donatus, *ad Hec.* 178, 327.

[41] *Life and Literature in the Roman Republic*, p. 120. According to Frank, Terence "reserves the key-fact for line 829" (p. 119) but the reference to the ring in 811 f. provides a strong clue to the solution; cf. the words of Myrrhina in 574 and Donatus' comment on 574: "preparation for the ending, since the recognition will take place by means of a ring."

(372 ff., cf. 574 f.) ; there is no hint that he will rape the girl and the audience first learns of this when Chaerea describes his adventures to Antipho (cf. 604 ff.). Likewise the generosity of the *senex* which solves the problems of both Chaerea and Phaedria (1031 ff.) is not foreshadowed.

Terence is praised for his originality in omitting the expository prologue and introducing the elements of suspense and surprise into his plots. Whether the elimination of the *argumentum* was effected primarily for this purpose, as Frank and others maintain,[42] cannot be determined; it may have resulted from the poet's desire to devote the prologue entirely to a plea for favor and a defense against his adversaries and critics.[43] Whatever the motive, the plays are successful in maintaining the ignorance and uncertainty of the spectators through a very considerable part of the action, and dramatic suspense of a more modern type results. But we should not allow our admiration for Terence's skillful employment of suspense and surprise to blind us to the fact that it is less novel than it at first appears. Suspense and surprise exist in Plautus, and it is safer to view Terence's procedure as a continuation and development of a tendency perhaps begun by Plautus, possibly going back to the Greek originals. At least three plays of Plautus—the *Curculio, Epidicus*, and *Truculentus*—give no advance information concerning the *anagnorisis* except for the usual vague foreshadowing.[44] Are we to insist with Leo that the Plautine prologues of these three comedies have been lost, in whole or in part, or is it not more likely, as Hough assumes, that in these plays Plautus was giving more attention to matters of surprise?[45] The latter seems the more probable conclusion when we see how often, in spite of frequent foreshadowing and announcement, Plautus keeps his audience ignorant of many details of the plot.

Often in plays of intrigue the spectators have no idea what form the deception will take. This is true of Tranio's lies in the *Mostellaria*, and of Chrysalus' tricking of Nicobulus in the *Bacchides*; when the letter is composed (*Bacch.* 733 ff.), the audience is at first ignorant of the use to which it will be put. Curculio tells that he has stolen a ring from the soldier (*Curc.* 360 ff.) but how it will be used to trick the *leno* is not clear and there is of course no allusion to its significance for the *anag-*

---

[42] Frank, *Life and Literature in the Roman Republic*, pp. 115, 123; Rand, *TAPhA* 63 (1932), pp. 69 f.; Dunkin, *Post-Aristophanic Comedy*, pp. 135 f.; cf. Enk, *Mn* 13 (1947), p. 83. Kuiper (*VAWA*, 38, 1936, No. 2, p. 251 f.) cites several reasons why Terence may have omitted the prologue; e.g., his aversion to long monologues, his realization that the recognition had become banal and antiquated, his inability to relate the "secret" since in the Greek original the lovers proved at the end to be half-brother and half-sister. This last is of course pure hypothesis.

[43] Cf. Harsh, *CW* 28 (1934-35), p. 165.

[44] Cf. Harsh, *A Handbook of Classical Drama*, p. 354, who says of the *Epidicus* "nowhere in New Comedy, perhaps, is there a more startling surprise."

[45] See above, n. 15.

*norisis.* The *Casina* is full of sudden turns and surprises, as are the *Menaechmi* and the *Rudens,* although all three have expository prologues. Chalinus in *Cas.* 511 ff. alludes vaguely to a deception which will be prepared, but there is no indication that the male slave will be substituted for *Casina* until 769 ff., shortly before the appearance of the "bride." That Menaechmus II will be taken for his brother is to be expected, but that the brother will twice come upon the stage (571 ff., 899 ff.) and find himself in serious predicaments as a result of the confusion of identity could hardly be foreseen by the audience although the scenes which result are among the most laughable in the comedy. There is no advance information of the important role which Gripus will play in the *Rudens* prior to Daemones' foreshadowing of his entrance in 897 f. Although the deception of Dordalus has already been outlined in the *Persa* (147 ff.), the arrival of Sagaristio with money in 251 ff. is a complete surprise and makes possible the purchase of Toxilus' sweetheart before the tricking of the *leno.*

These illustrations (and many more might be cited) are sufficient to show that surprise is not as foreign to the comedies of Plautus as Frank and others imply. In reality, both playwrights achieve their effects partly by foreshadowing and anticipation, partly by uncertainty and suspense and surprise. We should give full credit to Terence for the extent to which he keeps his audience ignorant of many details of the plot and in particular for the manner in which he arouses tension by withholding secrets of identity. But, in so doing, we should not ignore the fact that most comedies of Plautus likewise exploit suspense and surprise far more effectively than is usually realized. The dramatic technique of Plautus and Terence differs in many striking respects, as I have shown above in connection with stage conventions, treatment of theme, and composition of plot, and additional dissimilarities will be apparent later. It is no service to the study and interpretation of Roman comedy, however, to attribute great originality to a later playwright and ignore evidences of the same technique in an earlier. Terence, by the elimination of the expository prologue, was able to handle suspense and surprise most successfully in a modern manner. But that Plautus was oblivious to the value of dramatic tension I am unable to believe, and that he did arouse both suspense and surprise, often in spite of the narrative prologue, has been shown by reference to the comedies themselves.

## Suspense and Irony

Comic irony is possible when the audience knows in advance more about the difficulties and confusions of the plot than do the characters; the spectators watch with amusement the attempts of the characters to extricate themselves from the situations created either by "innocent mistakes" or "guileful deceptions" and can enjoy to the full their words as they give expression to their false suspicions and wrong conceptions. Several omniscient prologues in Plautus give rise to dramatic irony; as Miss Wieand says, "where anagnorisis is approaching, the audience derives added enjoyment from the knowledge that the persons concerned are not aware of each other's identity—e.g., the recognition between Hegio and Tyndarus in the Captivi."[46] But what of Terence, where the audience discovers the *anagnorisis* simultaneously with the characters? Is irony possible in these plays?

Harsh states that "dramatic irony and suspense tend to be mutually exclusive, since the one often depends upon the superior knowledge of the audience and the other upon its ignorance."[47] What Harsh correctly considers to be a tendency has been taken by too many critics as a necessity. Miss Hamilton says of Plautus: "Irony is his chief source of dramatic interest and he is a master of it. . . . Suspense is automatically shut out when irony is used." Terence never used irony since he was interested in composing "a plot intricate enough to supply a full measure of suspense and surprise."[48] Similarly, Dunkin says of Terence: "If the result of his elimination of the prologue was the loss of dramatic irony, Terence as an artist may fairly be held to account for it."[49] Irony or suspense! In Plautus we have irony, therefore no suspense! In Terence suspense and surprise are found, therefore no irony! But this is not true of Plautus; we have had conclusive evidence that he did devote considerable attention to matters of suspense and surprise; as a master of comic technique, he was able to employ both irony and suspense—not, of course, at the same time but in the same play and often in the same scene. The scholars who so eagerly stress Terence's originality in introducing surprise into ancient comedy do him a disservice when they say, with unpardonable exaggeration, that he never used irony or blame him for the loss of dramatic irony. Frank can hardly be criticized for the extreme statements of later writers, as he is considerably more cautious; he says that Terence "does not entirely suppress dramatic irony, but he reduces its scope," and comments upon the *Adelphoe* as follows: "the audience, acquainted with a situation that Demea still fails to comprehend, can proceed for several scenes to enjoy the dramatic irony involved in this circumstance."[50]

There are two main sources of comic irony: (1) the foreknowledge which the audience acquires from the narrative prologue and (2) the

---

[46] *Deception in Plautus*, pp. 61 f. Miss Wieand says of the irony present in plots of trickery and impersonations, "the chief enjoyment comes from noting the perils and cleverness of the impostor while he plays his part."

[47] *A Handbook of Classical Drama*, p. 348; Harsh adds that Plautus' *Captivi* "combines both to a remarkable extent and with unusual subtlety."

[48] *The Roman Way*, pp. 58, 60 f.     [49] *Post-Aristophanic Comedy*, p. 135, n. 40.

[50] *Life and Literature in the Roman Republic*, pp. 115, 117. Cf. also p. 121, a reference to irony in the *Heauton*.

foreknowledge which comes more naturally from the exposition of the
plot and the development of the action within the play itself. Plautus
taps both sources in plays like the *Poenulus* and the *Rudens*. In the
former there is irony in Hanno's being asked to pose as the parent of
two Carthaginian maidens (1099 ff.) already known from the prologue
to be his daughters; there is likewise irony in Lycus' attempt to profit
from the supposed stranger (655 ff.) for the audience knows from the
earlier action that Lycus is about to walk into a trap. So also in the
*Rudens* the prologue enables the audience to appreciate fully Daemones'
references to his own lost daughter (e.g., 106) but Gripus' many conjectures about the contents of the trunk (926 ff.) are all the more
amusing because the audience suspects that this is the *leno's* trunk
containing Palaestra's trinkets (cf. 389 ff.). In fact, much of the
irony in Plautus derives not from prologue-information but from the
normal exposition of the plot. The *Epidicus* has no prologue, but
there is excellent irony when the pretended Acropolistis arrives and
Periphanes says (400 ff.):

Be sure you don't let her come in contact with my daughter, or even catch
sight of her. Do you understand? I want her shut off by herself in a small
room. There's a great difference between the character of a maiden and a
slut.

The spectators of course know what Periphanes does not—that the
"daughter" is really Acropolistis.

It is true that Terence lost one source of comic irony when he eliminated the narrative prologue. Pamphilus says in *And.* 247:

Is there no way I can escape marrying into Chremes' family?

Had the *Andria* begun with a prologue, the audience would undoubtedly have acquired information about Glycerium's parentage and would
have appreciated the irony in Pamphilus' statement. Geta in *Phorm.*
124 ff. tells how the parasite pretended that Antipho was Phanium's
relative. The spectators do not realize that this is true, as they do in
the case of Milphio's similar fiction in the *Poenulus*. When Demea
praises Ctesipho in *Ad.* 138 f., the audience has as yet no reason to
believe that the youth is other than his father wishes him to be.

In passages such as the above Terence, by keeping his spectators
in the dark, has deprived them of irony which would have been most
effective. But his comedies have no lack of comic irony which arises
from the development of the action. This type of irony, in Terence as
in Plautus, concerns usually the working out of intrigue, whereas the
irony which has its source in prologue-information deals more frequently with secrets of identity. There are many passages in Terence
which illustrate his ability to entertain the spectators by playing up the
greater ignorance of the characters. When Parmeno praises the eunuch
for his youthfulness and handsome appearance (*Eun.* 473) and says

that he is trained in everything that a well-born young gentleman should know (477 f.), the audience can appreciate his speech from their knowledge that the eunuch really is "a well-born young gentleman." Later in the *Eunuchus* Thais assures Chremes that his sister has been kept pure (748), little imagining what has already happened (which the audience has known since Chaerea's conversation with Antipho in 549 ff.). Here the irony is not comic, but pathetic, almost tragic.[51] Chremes' statements about the extravagance of Bacchis (*Heaut.* 449 ff., cf. 749 ff.) are highly amusing, for Chremes pities Menedemus, but the audience knows that Bacchis is the sweetheart of Clitipho, Chremes' son. The willingness of the *senex* to assist Syrus and his conviction that Menedemus is the object of the slave's trickery are effective comedy; the spectators realize that Chremes is himself the dupe. It is even more amusing when Simo (*And.* 471 f., 478 f.) deceives himself and takes as trickery what the spectators know to be the truth. In the *Adelphoe*, as soon as we learn that Aeschinus has stolen the music girl for his brother (cf. 256 ff.), we can enjoy the irony which resides in the wrong conclusions of Demea and Sostrata. Demea ascribes to Aeschinus the love affair of Ctesipho, whom he believes to be a model of virtue, but long remains ignorant of Aeschinus' own affair; cf. 546 ff.:

DE.: I'm the first to learn about our misfortunes, I'm the first to find out everything; I'm the first to bring bad news, and I'm the only one to suffer if anything is done wrong.

SY. (*aside*): I'm laughing at him; he says that he's the first to know, when he's the only one who doesn't know everything.

In the *Hecyra*, where, as Frank says, "there is no preparation, and the delay in relieving the tension of the spectator is carried to extreme lengths,"[52] we should expect to find, if anywhere in Terence, a complete absence of irony. Yet even here, suspense and irony go hand in hand; the audience knows more than the characters but not the whole truth. The childbirth comes as a complete surprise in 373 ff., but from this point on the spectators understand fully why Philumena left home and realize how incorrect the *senes* are in their interpretation of Pamphilus' attitude (cf. 536 ff., 675 ff.). There is excellent irony here and at the same time the audience is as ignorant as Pamphilus himself that he is the father of the child. That Terence can make such effective use of irony in the comedy which, above all others, stresses suspense and surprise proves how inaccurate many views of Terentian dramaturgy have been.

In conclusion, Terence lost some opportunities for comic irony by his elimination of the expository prologue but within the comedies them-

---

[51] Cf. Rand, *TAPhA* 63 (1932), p. 71; in note 61 Rand lists eight instances of dramatic irony in the *Eunuchus*.

[52] *Life and Literature in the Roman Republic*, pp. 118 f.

selves he so handled foreshadowing and foretelling that irony was frequently present. The use of the prologue in many recognition plays
made it easier for Plautus to present speeches and situations filled with
irony, though much of his irony came also from the development of the
action. Plautus was able, no less than Terence, to arouse suspense about
the outcome and to hold back information so that many events came to
the spectators as a surprise. The tendency of modern critics to deny
irony to Terence and to refuse to see suspense and surprise in Plautus
has led to one-sided and unsatisfactory views of both playwrights.
There is no justification for these views. The plays themselves provide
the best refutation.

# CHAPTER 9

## *CHARACTERS AND CHARACTERIZATION*

THERE are few Roman comedies which can properly be termed "comedies of character";[1] plays containing stereotyped plots which were motivated largely by coincidence or by deception hardly could be expected to display subtle delineation of character, and the playwrights themselves were conscious of the existence of numerous stock types. Plautus boasts in the prologue of the *Captivi* (57 f.) that this comedy does not contain characters such as the perjured slavedealer, the evil courtesan, or the braggart warrior (roles which appear frequently in his other comedies), and Terence likewise refers to certain stock characters of comedy—the running slave, the angry father, the hungry parasite, the impudent sycophant, the greedy slavedealer, the good wife, the evil courtesan (cf. *Heaut.* 35 ff., *Eun.* 35 ff.). Yet the characters of Roman comedy are far richer and more varied than such lists would indicate. There are numerous variations within each type, and the characters display a wide range of human virtue and frailty; characters downright evil and vicious are seldom found. The phrase "evil courtesan" may apply to Phronesium (*Truculentus*) and Bacchis (*Heauton*), but certainly not to Philematium (*Mostellaria*) and Bacchis (*Hecyra*).

The treatment of the characters in this chapter must necessarily be brief; earlier writers have devoted considerable attention to the topic,[2] and I have already shown, in discussing methods of trickery, how the roles of the slave and the aged master differ at the hands of the two Roman playwrights.[3] But an analysis of the more important roles will reveal additional distinctions in the interests and the techniques of Plautus and Terence and will help to show more clearly the manner in which character was delineated in ancient comedy. A later chapter will treat the attitudes of the characters—their ideas and their outlook upon life—and the effect of these attitudes upon the thought and the moral tone of Roman comedy in general.

In both Plautus and Terence the roles in numerical frequency fall into

[1] See "Portrayal of Character and Customs" in chap. 6.

[2] Cf. especially the discussion of the characters of Greek and Roman comedy in Legrand-Loeb, *The New Greek Comedy*, pp. 52-183; the characters of Plautus are treated extensively by Michaut, *Plaute*, I, pp. 199-307; II, pp. 1-97; for those of Terence, see Henry, *SPhNC* 12 (1915), pp. 57-98. Dunkin devotes a large part of his recent *Post-Aristophanic Comedy* to an analysis of the characters of Plautus and Terence but his work is vitiated by unwarranted assumptions and misleading conclusions; cf. Duckworth, *AJPh* 58 (1947), pp. 421 ff. Dunkin's division of the characters into Rich Men and Poor Men gives an entirely erroneous impression of Roman comedy.

[3] See "Methods of Trickery" in chap. 6.

three clearly defined groups: (1) the male members of the household: young man (*adulescens*), aged parent (*senex*), and slave (*seruus*); these characters form the backbone of the plot, so to speak, and naturally would appear in the comedies with the greatest frequency; (2) feminine roles; these include the heroine, a young girl (*uirgo*) or a courtesan (*meretrix*) who is beloved by the *adulescens*, the wife or mother (*matrona*), and the maidservant (*ancilla*); these characters, although numerically frequent, occasionally have minor and colorless parts to play and in some comedies hardly appear on the stage at all; on the other hand, some plays are rich in feminine roles, e.g., the *Cistellaria* has six, the *Epidicus* four, the *Hecyra* five; (3) roles rich in comic value, e.g., parasite (*parasitus*), slavedealer (*leno*), soldier (*miles*), banker or moneylender (*trapezita, danista*), doctor (*medicus*), cook (*cocus*); these characters, mostly professional types, are less numerous than those of the first two groups; many are inorganic, but others are essential to the action (e.g., Pyrgopolynices in the *Miles*, Ballio in the *Pseudolus*) and have roles even more prominent than those of the average *senex* or *adulescens*.

## *Adulescens*: the Youthful Lover

The *adulescens* of Roman comedy is presented in a sympathetic light; he is not caricatured and ridiculed as are so many characters, especially in the comedies of Plautus. Occasionally the *adulescens* is married, e.g., Menaechmus I, Antipho (*Phormio*), Pamphilus (*Hecyra*), but usually he is a young man whose love for a courtesan, a slave girl, or a girl of good family (whom he has earlier violated) motivates the action. Other young men often appear as friends and would-be helpers, e.g., Chaeribulus (*Epidicus*), Eutychus (*Mercator*), Charinus (*Pseudolus*); these characters serve as foils to the hero and point up his helplessness and distress.

The youthful lover, unable to procure his sweetheart or fearful that he will lose her, appears in fourteen Plautine comedies[4] and in all six Terentian plays where, with the exception of the *Hecyra*, there are two young lovers in each play—a natural result of Terence's fondness for the duality method. In several Plautine comedies the love story provides merely the basis for the complications of the plot and the *adulescens* plays a relatively minor role, e.g., Lyconides (*Aulularia*), Pleusicles (*Miles*), Pleusidippus (*Rudens*), or the love story is neglected in the latter part of the action (e.g., *Mostellaria, Pseudolus*). Terence, more interested in sentiment and less eager to make intrigue an end in itself,

---

[4] The exceptions are: *Amphitruo* (I am unable to accept Dunkin's view, in *Post-Aristophanic Comedy*, p. 100, that Jupiter is "the dashing Young Man"), *Captivi, Casina* (the son who also loves Casina does not appear in the comedy), *Menaechmi, Persa* (the slave Toxilus has the usual role of the *adulescens* in love), *Stichus*.

concentrates more upon the character and the emotions of the youthful hero.

Many of the lovers describe in lengthy monologues their unhappy plight and the evils of love; Alcesimarchus is tortured because he has been prevented by his father from seeing his sweetheart (*Cist.* 203 ff.); Charinus is in anguish lest another has bought his love (*Merc.* 588 ff.); Pamphilus fears that he will have to give up Glycerium and marry the daughter of Chremes (*And.* 236 ff.); Phaedria is miserable because he is penniless and Pamphila is about to be sold to another (*Phorm.* 509 ff.). Far from being rich, almost all the lovers suffer because they have no money; Calidorus says (*Pseud.* 299 f.) :

I'm in a wretched state; I can't find a cent anywhere, and I'm perishing from love and lack of money.

Just as a Wodehouse hero turns helplessly to his trusted valet and begs to be extricated from his difficulties, so the *adulescens* of comedy depends upon the machinations of his slave either to provide the needed money or to procure the girl. As Agorastocles says (*Poen.* 447 f.) :

Love compels a free man to obey his slave.

The young men have no illusions about the course of true love and are fully conscious of its disadvantages. Charinus enumerates these at length in *Merc.* 18 ff. (care, sorrow, insomnia, grief, misunderstanding, fear, flight, stupidity, folly, thoughtlessness, immoderation, impudence, lust, ill will, greed, laziness, poverty, abuse, extravagance, etc.), and the virtuous Lysiteles banishes love as follows (*Trin.* 256 ff.) :

When I think over in my mind how little a man's worth when he's in want—away with you, Love! I don't like you, I have no use for you. No matter how sweet it is to eat and drink, Love still provides bitterness, enough to make us wretched. The lover avoids the forum, avoids his relatives, avoids his own innermost thoughts, and people no longer wish to consider him their friend. In a thousand ways he must be shunned, O Love; he must be kept off and held off afar, for the man who has fallen in love has perished more completely than if he took a leap from a ledge. Away with you, Love; keep your own property for yourself, Love, and never be a friend of mine!

Philolaches, comparing the construction and destruction of a house to the careful rearing of a youth and his subsequent ruination from idleness and love (*Most.* 84 ff.), realizes that he has become worthless, that he is no longer a model of thrift and endurance (154 ff.), but his good resolutions vanish when he sees Philematium (161 ff.) :

O beauteous beauty! There she is, the storm that unroofed the modesty of my house! Then Love and Desire streamed like rain into my heart and now I'll never be able to make repairs. The ramparts of my breast are soaked, and my house is a total ruin.

At times the youth knows that the courtesan whom he loves is unworthy of his affection; Diniarchus admits that Phronesium is interested only in money (*Truc.* 77 ff.) and realizes that she and her maid cannot be trusted (178 f.) :

Your tongues and talk are steeped in honey; your deeds and your hearts are filled with gall and bitter vinegar.

He expresses clearly the doctrine that "lovers believe what they want to believe" (190 ff.) :

Our greatest fault, the thing that ruins us when we're in love, is this: if we're told what we want to hear, even when it's an obvious lie, we're fools enough to believe it's the truth.

Yet he succumbs to her endearments and yields to her requests; amusingly enough, he does not recall his earlier words when he praises her (439 f.) :

Now she's opened up her very soul to me. She'll never be faithless to me as long as she lives.

Phaedria admits (*Eun.* 70 ff.) that Thais is wicked and that he is disgusted with himself for loving her, but love her he does; in this instance the youth misinterprets the courtesan's motives and judges her unfairly.

Sometimes the frustrated lover in anger or despair threatens suicide; so Charinus in *Merc.* 471 ff. :

Why not die? What good is left for me in life? My mind's made up. I'll go to a doctor and end my life with poison, since the only reason for my existence has been taken from me.

In like manner, Calidorus wants to buy a rope with which to hang himself (*Pseud.* 85 ff.) and Phaedria declares his intention either to follow his sweetheart to the ends of the earth or to die (*Phorm.* 551 f.).[5] The determination of the *adulescens* to go into exile when he is deprived of his loved one is also found, e.g., *Merc.* 644, 658 ff., 830 f.[6] Such threats of suicide and exile serve to arouse the tension of the audience momentarily but they are even more effective in portraying the emotional reactions of the lovesick youth in comedy.[7]

The *adulescens* of Roman comedy has been accused of being weak and uninteresting, of being a stock character without personality. Dunkin believes this particularly true of Plautus' plays; convinced that the *adulescens* is a type of the rich man whom Plautus ridiculed in cruel caricatures, he describes him as follows: "slinking, whining,

---

[5] Cf. also *Asin.* 606 ff., 630 f., *Cist.* 639 ff., *Epid.* 148. In the *Casina* both slave and *senex* toy with the idea of suicide in case they are defeated in love (111 f., 307 f.).

[6] See also *Ad.* 274 f. Ctesipho in the Menandrian original was more violent and wished to die; cf. Donatus, *ad Ad.* 275.

[7] When the *adulescens* is successful in love, his emotions are equally extreme; he considers himself a god (*Curc.* 167, *And.* 959 ff., *Heaut.* 693).

sensual Spineless Young Man."[8] There are caricatures and grotesque personages in Plautus, but the *adulescens* seldom appears among them Plautus treats his youthful lovers with sympathy and humor; he sometimes portrays them as silly (as Calidorus says in *Pseud.* 238: "There's no fun unless a lover acts foolishly") but he does not make them disgusting. Dunkin approaches Roman comedy with a preconceived bias he looks upon Plautus as the spokesman of the poor man, always eager to attack and ridicule the rich, and he believes that Terence is the rich man's poet; hence the young man in Terence is necessarily less spineless than his Plautine counterpart. Actually, there is, in this respect little difference between the two dramatists; it would be difficult to find a more helpless youth in Roman comedy than Antipho (*Phormio*) or Ctesipho (*Adelphoe*); the latter is described by Norwood as "secretive weak, timid, hysterical, and self-indulgent."[9] Henry, speaking of the *adulescens* in Terence, says: "Thus the part assigned to these youths is very similar in the various plays: and as a rule their characters are very much alike. . . . They are resourceless, relying on their slave or good fortune to mend their troubles—but living in a sort of fools paradise. . . . They have not the courage and dash that make youth attractive. Sentimental, puny specimens of manhood, their whole interest in life begins and ends in a love intrigue."[10] Henry's words present almost as unkind an indictment of the Terentian *adulescens* as Dunkin's unreasonable denunciation of Plautus' youth. But Henry admits that Chaerea (*Eunuchus*) and Aeschinus (*Adelphoe*) possess qualities which win our interest and admiration and he states that most of the others have predominating traits that differentiate them from each other. This is equally true of the young men in Plautus' comedies; although not individualized to any marked degree, they are differentiated each has traits peculiarly his own, and as a group they are much less uniform and monotonous than is often believed: Lysiteles (*Trinummus*), a most virtuous youth who insists upon marrying Lesbonicus' sister without a dowry, is generous; Mnesilochus (*Bacchides*) is jealous, Alcesimarchus (*Cistellaria*) violent, Phaedromus (*Curculio*) sentimental, Calidorus (*Pseudolus*) melancholy, Stratippocles (*Epidicus*) fickle.[11]

To Plautus, however, love is a far less serious affair than to Terence, and the differing interests of the two playwrights are apparent in their treatment of the youthful hero. The more ridiculous aspects of the young man's passion are frequently stressed by Plautus in the dialogues

---

[8] *Post-Aristophanic Comedy*, p. 73.

[9] *The Art of Terence*, p. 114.

[10] *SPhNC* 12 (1915), pp. 69, 71; see also Post, *CW* 23 (1929-30), p. 125. But cf. Kraemer, *CJ* 23 (1927-28), p. 665: "His 'weak young men' are not merely characters drawn without accuracy or interest, but are the results of exact observation of youth in all the turmoil of transition from boyhood to manhood."

[11] On these and other Plautine *adulescentes*, cf. Michaut, *Plaute*, II, pp. 7 ff.

Plate V. Demea rushes in to find Ctesipho
*Ad.* 776-786 (MS O: folio 120)

Plate VI. Demea tries out his new affability

*Ad.* 889-895 (ms C: folio 63)

of master and slave, especially when the slave criticizes his master for being in love or makes fun of his sweetheart. Palinurus says (*Curc.* 175 ff.) :

I just can't keep from finding fault with my master. Sane love in moderation is all right; insane passion isn't good; and to go completely crazy with love—well, that's just what my master is doing.

Libanus and Leonida begin their ridicule of Argyrippus with the following jest (*Asin.* 619 f.) :

LE.: Is that woman whom you're embracing smoke?
ARG.: What do you mean?
LE.: Well, she's got into your eyes and made you weep.

Other slaves who tease their lovesick master are Milphio (*Poen.* 364 ff.) and Pseudolus (*Pseud.* 75 ff.). Plautus' procedure of contrasting the unhappy youth with the cynical and unsympathetic slave provides considerable merriment but it impairs the delineation of the youth's character and makes his distress seem a less tragic and heartrending affair. The situation is very different in Terence's comedies; the younger dramatist also works by contrast but he prefers to draw clearcut distinctions between the two lovers in the various comedies, e.g., Antipho and Phaedria (*Phormio*) or Aeschinus and Ctesipho (*Adelphoe*). The contrast is made by the speech of a third person (e.g., Demea in *Ad.* 88 ff.) or is implicit in the words and actions of the characters themselves; in the *Adelphoe* the frankness, self-reliance, and aggressiveness of Aeschinus makes the helplessness and timidity of Ctesipho all the more striking; Phaedria in the *Phormio* displays far more initiative than his cousin Antipho who, in spite of his good intentions, lacks the courage to face his father. The sympathy and cooperation of the slaves in Terence emphasize the pathetic plight of the youths.

In his portrayal of the *adulescens* (and this is typical of his treatment of the other characters as well) Terence uses greater restraint than Plautus. He makes his personages even more serious in their amatory endeavors but their relations to the other characters are usually more normal and decent. Pamphilus says (*And.* 260 ff.) :

So many cares draw me in different directions—my love and pity for Glycerium; then, too, the pressure put upon me to marry, and also my respect for my father, who has hitherto generously let me do whatever I pleased. How can I oppose him? Lord! I don't know what to do.

Later (897 f.) he promises to give up Glycerium if such is his father's command. Few Plautine youths would be so solicitous of their father's wishes (Calidorus is such a one, cf. *Pseud.* 290 f.). Ctesipho hopes that his father will be so tired that he will have to stay in bed for three whole days (*Ad.* 518 ff.), but no *adulescens* in Terence says, as does Philolaches in *Most.* 233 f., that he desires his father's death in order to

turn over the paternal estate to his sweetheart—even though this statement is hardly to be taken seriously as it occurs in a series of asides
whose chief purpose is to arouse laughter. But the youths of Terence
as a rule are more respectful and respectable than those of Plautus; they
are also less amusing and somewhat less colorful. The best portrayed
are Chaerea, the impulsive and likable young rascal in the *Eunuchus*,[12]
and Aeschinus, who openly steals a girl for his more timid brother but
lacks the courage to tell his adoptive father about his own love affair
(cf. *Ad.* 629 ff.) ; his sense of shame at the concealment and his respect
for Micio are shown by the well-known comment of the *senex* (643) :
"He blushes; all is well."[13]

The *adulescens* has an important role in most Roman comedies but
of all the major characters he is, in general, the least vivid and the least
interesting. Both Plautus and Terence present their other characters—
older men, slaves, wives, and courtesans—with richer and more varied
traits; whether we demand, with Plautus, brilliant but somewhat grotesque characterizations for the purpose of comedy, or prefer the more
subtle delineations of Terence, we must turn to roles other than that
of the *adulescens* for the most outstanding and memorable characters
of Roman comedy.

## *Senex*: Parent, Aged Lover, Helpful Friend

The role of the *senex*, like that of the *adulescens*, occurs in most extant
comedies; in only three comedies (*Amphitruo, Curculio, Persa*) is the
"old man" missing from the list of Personae, and in three others (*Menaechmi, Truculentus, Eunuchus*) he has a very incidental role; in each
of the remaining twenty plays, there is at least one *senex* who has a major
part in the action, often more (the *Trinummus* has four). Cicero (*De
amic.* 26, 100) says: "Even on the stage the silliest character is that of the
old man who lacks foresight and is easily deceived." But to look upon the
*senex* as a stock type of the curmudgeonly father, always harsh (*iratus,
saeuus, seuerus*)[14] and readily deceived (*credulus*), is far from accurate;

---

[12] On the character and actions of Chaerea, cf. Norwood, *The Art of Terence*,
pp. 60 ff.; Kraemer, *CJ* 23 (1927-28), pp. 662 ff. Rand (*TAPhA* 63, 1932, p 58) calls
him "one of the most charming scapegraces in all comedy . . . impulsive, passionate,
tender, resourceful, manly, pious, true, a Catullus in action, scandalously indecorous,
irresistibly lovable." See also Harsh, *A Handbook of Classical Drama*, p. 388.

[13] This is reminiscent of Antiphanes, fr. 261: "A youth of this age who still blushes
in the presence of his father cannot be bad." Norwood (*The Art of Terence*, p. 116)
is far too severe when he calls Aeschinus an "insolent, fastidious, elegant bully"; cf.
Siess, *WS* 29 (1907), pp. 103 ff.

[14] Donatus frequently refers to the *senex* in Terence as harsh and severe; the
*Andria* contains *seueri senes* (*ad. And.*, praef. I, 3), Laches in the *Hecyra* is *difficilis
et iratus* (*ad Hec.* 198), Demea in the *Adelphoe* is *saeuus* (*ad Ad.* praef. III, 6; 787) ;
on the other hand, Phidippus is *mitissimus*, a most lenient father (*ad Hec.* 243) and
Micio is *mitis* (*ad Ad.*, praef. III, 6; 787), as is Demea after his conversion (*ad Ad.*
789) although he still retains something of his former severity (*ad Ad.* 881).

as a parent the *senex* is often lenient and easy-going; as a husband he is less attractive: critical of his wife, often quarrelsome, he does not balk at infidelity; as a friend he is willing to undergo surprising risks to assist others in their difficulties. The all-inclusive term "old man" is very misleading. Other characters—professional roles such as the banker or slavedealer—may be as advanced in years but they are not listed as *senes*. Actually, the *senex* as a role refers merely to the older male members of the various households; as opposed to the *adulescentes* who are usually in their late teens or early twenties (cf. *Bacch.* 422), the *senes* are men somewhat past middle age, presumably in their fifties or early sixties; Micio in the *Adelphoe* (938) is in his sixty-fifth year; few seem as aged and decrepit as the father-in-law of Menaechmus I who complains that his strength has deserted him: his body is a burden and he can no longer move nimbly (*Men.* 756 ff.).

(1) The *senex* as parent. Here we find numerous gradations from the excessively indulgent and compliant father to the father who lacks sympathy and understanding and who, because of his harshness and severity, becomes the object of deception and ridicule. Many parents are lenient because they believe that it is characteristic of youth to be extravagant and to have love affairs. Micio says to Demea of the two youths in the *Adelphoe* (827 ff.):

I see that they are sensible, intelligent, high-minded and devoted to each other. You can tell that they are gentlemen in thought and disposition. Any day you wish you can bring them back in line. Perhaps you fear that they are too careless about money. My dear Demea, we grow wiser with age in all other respects, but one vice old age brings with it: we are all more interested in making money than we ought to be. Time will sharpen them enough in that respect.

Some parents refrain from criticizing their sons because they realize that they in their own youth committed the same faults. Philoxenus well expresses this point of view when he says (*Bacch.* 408 ff.):

The wisest course is to show moderation in severity. It's not strange for a youth of his age to do these things. It would be more surprising if he didn't. I did the very same things when I was young.[15]

Micio criticizes Demea for his angry condemnation of Aeschinus' actions (*Ad.* 103 ff.):

If you and I didn't do such things, it was because we didn't have the money. Do you now take credit for not having done what you couldn't afford to do? It's quite wrong, for if we had had the means, we would have done the same things.

[15] Perhaps Philoxenus here is merely trying to soothe Lydus' anger; the latter implies (420 ff.) that the rearing of Philoxenus had been very strict. Callipho reminds Simo (*Pseud.* 437 ff.) how he acted as an *adulescens* and points out that it's not surprising if Calidorus takes after his father; cf. Demaenetus (*Asin.* 64 ff.), who is eager to help his son's love affair because his father did the same for him when he was a young man.

But Micio is more deeply concerned about the welfare of his adopted
son than he is willing to admit to Demea (cf. *Ad.* 141 ff.) and he is
sincerely convinced that generosity and sympathy will be more effective
in the treatment of his son than fear (68 ff.).

Many parents are motivated by a desire for what they conceive to be
their sons' best interests, e.g., Simo (*Andria*), Chremes (*Heauton*),
Philto (*Trinummus*), although the latter's trite moralizing (259 ff.)
is hardly necessary since Lysiteles is a young man of exemplary character. There is no lack of paternal affection; witness the surprise and
delight evinced by *senes* when they discover a longlost son or daughter,
e.g., Hegio (*Capt.* 993 ff.), Hanno (*Poen.* 1262 f., 1274 ff.), Daemones
(*Rud.* 1172 ff.), or the anxiety evinced by a parent when his son fails
to return home at night (cf. *Ad.* 26 ff.). Euclio seems less concerned
about his daughter's welfare than in maintaining the secret of his
hidden treasure but he is a character *sui generis* and one of Plautus'
most brilliant delineations. The playwright is interested primarily in
portraying Euclio's fears and suspicions of his household and his neighbors as he endeavors without success to keep his riches from being discovered; hence Euclio insists upon his poverty and maintains that he
cannot give a dowry to his daughter (*Aul.* 190 ff., 238). Phidippus
seems unnecessarily harsh to his daughter (*Hec.* 623 f.) but it is wrong
to say, as does Gomme, that he "is absurdly indifferent to his daughter's
fate";[16] as a matter of fact, the solution of Philumena's problem results
from his suggestion (716 ff.) that Laches interview the courtesan.

As a rule the parents who are feared by their sons for their severity
are interested (even more than the lenient fathers) in the welfare of
their offspring. Chremes defends the former harshness of Menedemus:
naturally parents try to keep their sons from having love affairs with
courtesans and from squandering money; such severity is for their sons'
good (cf. *Heaut.* 204 ff.). To Menedemus himself Chremes had been
more critical (155 ff.):

You never revealed to him how much you loved him, nor did he dare to
confide in you as he should have done. If you had both acted differently,
these things would never have happened to you.

Menedemus regrets his former treatment of Clinia and, delighted with
his son's return, now swings over to a course of extreme leniency
(464 ff.):

Let him do whatever he likes; let him take my money, spend it, lose it.
I'm willing to endure anything if only I have him with me.

Chremes disapproves of both extremes (440 ff.) but he does not practice
what he preaches; actually, he is meddlesome, deceitful, and miserly,
and it is only fitting that he should be the victim of deception rather

[16] *Essays in Greek History and Literature*, p. 280.

than Menedemus, as he had expected. And when Chremes learns of his son's love affair, he is guilty of the same harshness which he had earlier criticized in Menedemus.

Terence's most outstanding portrayal of the "harsh father" is that of Demea in the *Adelphoe*: he was severe beyond all reason (64) in his rearing of Ctesipho and in his angry condemnation of Aeschinus; he was ridiculed by Syrus and long kept in the dark concerning Ctesipho's love affair; but he becomes pathetic and arouses our sympathy when he later realizes how little his sternness has profited him; cf. 870 ff.:

Now, at the end of my life this is the reward that I receive for my toil: hatred. My brother has the pleasures of a father without the labor; they love him, they flee from me; they entrust all their plans to him, they are devoted to him, they are both with him, and I am left alone.

Demea rejects his former severity but at the same time realizes that blind indulgence is equally harmful, and he succeeds in showing that the favor enjoyed by Micio has been the result of excessive leniency (cf. 986 ff.). Of Demea, Norwood says: "A splendid old man is this, who so late in life can learn such a lesson, announce his conversion without pettishness, and retain with dignity both the centre of the stage and the mastery of the moral situation," and he rightly points out that here the traditional function of the comic *senex* is "invested with breadth, freshness and humanity."[17]

But in Norwood's opinion the comic *senex* is an unattractive character, a "bad-tempered old imbecile whose one function is to be swindled out of the statutory forty minae."[18] Norwood is doubtless referring here to the Plautine parents who are deceived by their slaves, i.e., Nicobulus (*Bacchides*), Periphanes (*Epidicus*) and Theopropides (*Mostellaria*). Plautus exaggerates the credulity of these characters but fundamentally they are not bad-tempered; only when they discover the extent to which they have been tricked do they give vent to their rage and become grotesquely comical in their anger. Theopropides is perhaps the most striking instance of the *credulus* and *iratus* parent in Plautus, and in his case distress at his son's wayward life seems motivated primarily by financial considerations; at least, he is willing to forgive Philolaches when Callidamates offers to pay for his extravagances (*Most.* 1162 ff.). Nicobulus and Periphanes are more concerned about the welfare of their sons but the latter realizes that he is foolish to condemn his son for what he did in his own youth (*Epid.* 389 ff.). Stupid some of the *senes* may well be, especially in Plautus, but they are hardly "imbeciles," and the epithet "bad-tempered" is rarely apt. As a parent the *senex* of Roman comedy is more often easy-going and tolerant.

(2) The *senex* as lover. When an old man falls in love, his role as

[17] *The Art of Terence*, pp. 120, 117; cf. also Enk, *Mn* 13 (1947), pp. 89 f.; Webster, *Studies in Menander*, pp. 65 ff.
[18] *The Art of Terence*, p. 94.

husband and father is secondary to his laughable endeavors to win the favors of a young girl. There are few characters in Roman comedy more ridiculous than the aged lover and Plautus, fully cognizant of the farcical possibilities inherent in the role, usually presented such characters as grotesque caricatures. These *senes* may be married (in which case they attempt, usually without success, to deceive their wives) and sometimes they are rivals of their sons. In the *Phormio*, Chremes tries to conceal from his wife and son an earlier love affair and the existence of an illegitimate daughter but he is not a *senex amator* (cf. 1016 ff.), even though his situation is far from pleasant when Phormio reveals his secret to his wife. Terence's failure to introduce the amorous old man into his comedies is additional evidence of his dislike of coarse and vulgar farce.

The two most striking examples of aged love are found in the *Casina* and the *Mercator*. Demipho in the latter play sees the girl whom his son has brought to Athens; cf. 262 ff.:

> As soon as I saw her, I fell in love—not the way sane people do, but with a crazy kind of love. As a youth I was in love, to be sure, but never in the idiotic way I am now.

He tells his friend Lysimachus that he's a boy of seven, just starting school, but he's learned three letters, A-M-O (292, 303 ff.), and he seeks to justify his love affair:

> It's human to fall in love. (319)
> Only a short time of life is left for me, so I'll enliven it with wine, women, and fun. . . . When one reaches old age, he ought to take it easy and make love while he can. At my age it's pure profit to be alive at all. (547 ff.)

Lysidamus, who has fallen in love with Casina and hopes to spend the first night with her after she marries his slave Olympio, makes himself elegant with perfume (*Cas.* 225 ff.) thereby increasing the suspicions of his wife. The schemes of both old men come to naught but Demipho, who did not realize it was his son's sweetheart whom he had hidden away (*Merc.* 991 ff.), gets off easily and his wife never learns of the escapade. The fate of Lysidamus in the *Casina* is very different: the stratagem of the fake bride leads to a conclusion uproariously funny and unspeakably vulgar; Lysidamus begs his wife for forgiveness and promises never again to fall in love. In the *Asinaria*, Demaenetus helps his son procure Philaenium on condition that he be allowed to spend a night with her (735 f.); he is discovered by his wife as he is banqueting with Philaenium and his son and dragged home in disgrace to the refrain, "Rise up, lover, come on home" (921 ff.). These *senes* are stock types without individuality, and Plautus presents them as lecherous old reprobates whose amorous activities provide hilarious comedy. To make their conduct all the more unseemly, they are regularly described as gray-haired and decrepit old men (cf. *Asin.* 863, 934, *Cas.* 239 f., *Merc.* 291, 305, 314).

Other *senes*, less grotesque but amusingly amorous, are Antipho, the widower in the *Stichus* who attempts by his *"quasi ego"* fable to acquire for himself one of the music girls brought by his sons-in-law (538 ff.), and the father of Alcesimarchus, who suggests to Gymnasium that he would gladly keep her from being lonely and idle (*Cist.* 310 f.). The two fathers in the *Bacchides* are persuaded by the two courtesans to forgive their sons and join them at a banquet; it is misleading, however, to look upon these two *senes* as "interesting studies in the Ancient Gallant," even though they do "fall for the wiles of the painted women and enter their house to make merry."[19] The primary purpose of their weakening is the pardoning of their sons which brings about the "happy ending" and this, however improbable, does not differ essentially from the ending of other plays (*Epidicus, Mostellaria*) in which the youth or the intriguing slave is forgiven somewhat unrealistically. Nicobulus and Philoxenus are far removed from rascals like Lysidamus and Demipho, whose love affairs motivate the action of the *Casina* and the *Mercator*.

(3) The *senex* as helpful friend. The old men in this category, although seldom inorganic, are subordinate characters who have two chief functions in addition to their role as assistants in the intrigue: they serve as foils to point up the delineation of other characters, and they are useful for purposes of comedy, since they often find themselves in awkward and ridiculous situations as a result of their willingness to aid their friends. The instances of a *senex* assisting an *adulescens* are rare. Periplectomenus in the *Miles* makes his home available to Pleusicles and, to bring about the overthrow of the soldier, even takes to himself a fictitious wife; he is one of Plautus' most delightful creations, a *lepidus senex* who discourses at length on the advantages of bachelorhood (672 ff.). Callicles in the *Trinummus* concocts with Megaronides a scheme whereby Lesbonicus will receive money for his sister's dowry, but Callicles is primarily interested in the fortunes of the absent Charmides.[20]

Usually the helpful old men offer other *senes* useful advice (e.g., Callipho in the *Pseudolus*,[21] Megaronides in the *Trinummus*) or aid them in their schemes, sometimes to their sorrow; Apoecides is amusing when he returns exhausted after a fruitless search with Periphanes for the latter's slave (*Epid.* 667 ff.) and Charmides regrets his associa-

---

[19] Dunkin, *Post-Aristophanic Comedy*, p. 59.

[20] Simo (*Most.* 723 ff.) speaks with sympathy (and almost envy) of Philolaches' way of life during his father's absence; Tranio might have enlisted him as a helper in the tricking of Theopropides but preferred to deceive him also, so that he could boast of loading both old codgers with pack-saddles (778); thus Simo, like Theopropides, becomes a *senex deceptus* and the butt of Tranio's insolence (cf. 832 ff.).

[21] Callipho is an inorganic character whose disappearance from the action has been severely criticized; see above, p. 179 and n. 6.

tion with Labrax when they are shipwrecked and arrive on the stage
drenched and shivering; he is delightfully unsympathetic in a scene
rich in verbal humor, cf. *Rud.* 514 ff. :

> LA.: You're to blame because I'm a beggar; it comes from listening to your
> big lies.
> CH.: On the contrary, you owe me a debt of thanks; you were flat before
> and I've given you a dash of salt. . . .
> LA.: Was ever a mortal more wretched than I?
> CH.: Of course. I'm much more wretched than you.
> LA.: How so?
> CH.: Because you deserve it and I don't.

Perhaps the most generous of the friends are Alcesimus (*Casina*) and
Lysimachus (*Mercator*); although they disapprove heartily of the
amorous plans of Lysidamus and Demipho, each offers the use of his
house as a hideout for his friend's "sweetheart"; in the case of Lysimachus the results are unexpected and comic, for his wife returns and
naturally assumes that Pasicompsa is her husband's mistress.

These, then, are the *senes* of Roman comedy—parents, gay old
blades, helpful friends.[22] It would be more accurate to say that these
are the *senes* of Plautus, whose range is much wider than Terence's.
When Dunkin states that the old man in Plautus "is either an Ancient
Gallant or a tedious moralizer,"[23] he overlooks a large number of decent,
rather amiable and easy-going fathers in Plautus and concentrates on
the more disreputable and grotesque personages who have been introduced to arouse laughter. The *senes* of Terence are far less amusing
than those of Plautus; they take life and its problems more seriously;
they are more dignified and respectable, in other words, they are truer
to life and gain in verisimilitude what they lose in vigor. The younger
playwright was interested neither in gross caricature nor in frivolous
jesting, and so the "ancient gallant" had no place in his comedies. Also,
with the exception of Crito (*Andria*) and Hegio (*Adelphoe*), there
are no helpful friends; these are not needed, as in Plautus, for purposes
of contrast since Terence's duality method provides in most comedies
two *senes* of strikingly different characteristics, e.g., Chremes and
Menedemus (*Heauton*), Micio and Demea (*Adelphoe*).[24] Even in the
*Hecyra* where the plot is single there are two well-delineated fathers,
Laches and Phidippus.

The fact that almost all the *senes* of Terence were parents seriously
wrapped up in the problems of their children made more subtle delineation of character a prime necessity; otherwise the fathers would have

---

[22] On the *senex* as a husband, see "Love and Marriage" in chap. 10.

[23] *Post-Aristophanic Comedy*, p. 64. Cf., however, Perry, *Masters of Dramatic
Comedy*, p. 66: "Old men are, on the whole, the characters best depicted by Plautus."

[24] On these characters, see Henry, *SPhNC* 12 (1915), pp. 59 ff. Norwood's analysis
of Demea and Micio in *The Art of Terence*, pp. 117 ff., is especially good; cf. p. 120:
"Micio is beyond question Terence's greatest male character."

appeared colorless and monotonous. Plautus, with a larger variety of *senes* at his disposal, painted them with broader strokes. The *stultus, credulus* father was more foolish and more easily tricked, whereas his Terentian counterpart, being more sensible, often overreached himself when his shrewdness led to self-deception.[25] There are numerous parents in Plautus' comedies, some of whom are very well portrayed, e.g., Hegio in the *Captivi*,[26] but his most successful creations are Euclio (*Aulularia*) and Periplectomenus (*Miles*)—both *senes* of an unconventional sort; Euclio's role as father is clearly secondary to his problems which arise from his discovery of the treasure, and he dominates the action from beginning to end; Periplectomenus, whose role is less organic, is a delightful egoist whose praise of bachelorhood makes his character memorable among the *senes* of Plautus. On the other hand, Terence's greatest success occurred when he took the "harsh father" and the "lenient father" of earlier tradition and with unusual psychological insight created Demea and Micio, the two fathers whose conflict motivates and solves the problems of the *Adelphoe*. They are living personalities, human and likable, both partly right, but each mistaken in the value and the results of his method.

## *Seruus*: Clever Trickster and Faithful Servant

Every extant Roman comedy contains at least one slave and many have several (including incidental slaves, attendants, and *pueri* who have minor roles). Almost all the slaves have one characteristic in common—talkativeness; from this stems their boastfulness and self-glorification, their impudence and insolence, their inquisitiveness, indiscretion, and love of gossip, their fondness for moralizing. A free and easy attitude prevails in their dealing with others and they show little respect towards their elders and betters. They are often lazy and indifferent, fond of good food and drink, and they do not hesitate to lie, cheat, and steal when it seems necessary—usually for the benefit of their young master rather than for their own personal advantage, but not always. Even a slave like Stasimus, seemingly devoted to his master, jests as follows when Lesbonicus adds up his expenses (*Trin.* 413):

ST.: What about the money I cheated you of?
LE.: Ah! That's the biggest item of all.

And Cyamus, the slave of Diniarchus, says (*Truc.* 559 f.):

[25] See "Methods of Trickery" in chap. 6; cf. Perry, *Masters of Dramatic Comedy*, p. 78: "Plautus shows us old men who err by being too selfish, Terence shows us old men who err by being too blind; they unite in ridiculing old age as that period in life when a man's personality, having reached its fullest development, is at its most rigid and absurd."

[26] Cf. Harsh, *A Handbook of Classical Drama*, p. 350: "Hegio is not the stupid old man characteristic of comedy, although his figure has its amusing aspects; nor is he the stereotyped kindly old gentleman. He is thoroughly an individual."

Since he's so anxious to ruin himself, I'll give him a little aid on the sly and speed him on his progress to destruction.

The function of the *seruus* is twofold: (1) to provide humor, often of a farcical nature and, in Plautus, frequently descending to buffoonery or slapstick; (2) to supervise or assist in trickery and impersonation. The slaves most active in both capacities are the *serui callidi*, the cunning masters of intrigue, e.g., Chrysalus (*Bacchides*), Palaestrio (*Miles*), Toxilus (*Persa*), Milphio (*Poenulus*), and Pseudolus. Their schemes are ingenious and, despite moments of helplessness and despair, they carry their trickery through to a successful conclusion and boast of their achievements (the most striking of such exultant passages being the extended *canticum* of Chrysalus comparing his deeds with those of the Greeks before Troy, in *Bacch.* 925 ff.). Epidicus and Tranio (*Mostellaria*) are no less entertaining and clever but their tricks are of such a nature that discovery is inevitable; their insolence towards their elderly masters remains unabated, however, and Epidicus, profiting from the fortunate discovery of Telestis' parentage, even makes Periphanes beg his pardon and give him his liberty (*Epid.* 721 ff.). The schemes of the leading Terentian slaves—Davus (*Andria*), Syrus (*Heauton*), and Syrus (*Adelphoe*)—are also directed against a *senex*, but their deception, with its admixture of truth and falsehood, is less effective and, amusing as these slaves are, they lack the ingenuity and brilliance of the Plautine characters. That the slaves, especially in Plautus, take great delight in trickery cannot be doubted; Tranio boasts that he is doing immortal deeds equal to those of Alexander the Great and Agathocles (*Most.* 775 ff.). Our ignorance of Greek New Comedy is great, but the lack of deception in the extant fragments gives support to Gomme's conjecture that the Plautine slave, with his gaiety, cleverness, and unscrupulousness, is the creation of Roman comedy.[27]

Terence has been praised for his unconventional treatment of the intriguing slave of tradition[28] and there can be no doubt that he handles trickery in an interesting and unusual fashion.[29] But is it wise to stress the two Parmenos (*Eunuchus, Hecyra*) as proof of Terence's uncon-

---

[27] *Essays in Greek History and Literature*, p. 287; see also Post, *TAPhA* 69 (1938), p. 37. I am unable to understand how Dunkin, who looks upon the slave as the Poor Man of Roman comedy, can say that the Plautine slave is driven to cunning and vice by poverty and ill-treatment whereas the Terentian slave engages "in wanton and unscrupulous trickery, quite voluntarily and deliberately because, forsooth, the knave positively enjoys it" (*Post-Aristophanic Comedy*, p. 115, cf. p. 86); cf. Duckworth, *AJPh* 58 (1947), p. 425. Dunkin misunderstands the Plautine slave in his excessive zeal to prove an unsound thesis, that in the works of Plautus "may be seen the instinctive reaction of a vigorous poor man to an oppressive capitalistic system" (*ibid.*, p. 104). Miss Haight, however, quotes Dunkin's views with apparent approval (*The Symbolism of the House Door*, pp. 88 f.).

[28] Cf. Norwood, *The Art of Terence*, pp. 144 f.

[29] See "Methods of Trickery" in chap. 6, and especially n. 64.

ventional methods? Neither is a typical *seruus callidus*; in the *Eunuchus*, Parmeno not only does not engage in deception but he attempts to dissuade Chaerea from the impersonation and he is himself deceived later by Pythias; in the *Hecyra* the slave is useful only for purposes of exposition; there is no deception, and Parmeno, sent upon one errand after another, never does find out the truth. This is unusual, as Donatus points out on several occasions,[30] and Terence here is intentionally keeping Parmeno off the stage; the slave is amusing because he is prevented from being amusing, and his being kept in the dark at the end is, according to Norwood, "the exact negation of the *rôle* traditionally given to such characters."[31] But he should not be viewed as a new and negative type of intriguing slave; he and Parmeno (in the *Eunuchus*) are the result of Terence's desire to present comedies without the usual cunning *architectus doli*, and this is less exceptional than is often believed. Slaves are deceived in Plautus, e.g., Sosia (*Amphitruo*), Olympio (*Casina*), and Sceledrus (*Miles*), and all too frequently it is overlooked that at least half of Plautus' plays do not have, and do not need, slaves like Epidicus, Palaestrio, and Pseudolus.[32] In these comedies the slaves are witty, sometimes insolent, often vulgar, usually faithful, but not exceedingly clever. A slave like Parmeno in the *Hecyra* derives, not from the traditional intriguing slave, but from the loyal slave like Messenio (*Menaechmi*) whom Plautus brings on the stage only when needed.

It should be noted that even the cunning and unscrupulous slaves act out of faithfulness to their masters. Sometimes this faithfulness results from fear rather than devotion. Stratippocles threatens to "irrigate" Epidicus' back with blows and to send him to the mill if he doesn't produce forty minae (*Epid.* 121 ff.) and often the slave's duty to two masters—*senex* and *adulescens*—creates a serious dilemma; Pseudolus realizes that punishment is in store for him from Calidorus if he reveals the love affair, from Simo if he doesn't, and he chooses the more distant evil (*Pseud.* 497 ff.).[33] But such threats are primarily for humor and are seldom fulfilled; in general, the cunning slave, even though he ridicules the love affair of his youthful master, does everything in his power to help him. As Lesbonicus says of Stasimus (*Trin.* 527 f.):

[30] Cf. *ad Hec.* 799, 808, 809. On 851 Donatus says: "Terence cleverly arranges it so that the more inquisitive Parmeno is, the less he finds out what he is eager to learn." He describes Parmeno as *garrulus* and *curiosus* (*ad Hec.* 193, 799).

[31] *The Art of Terence*, p. 145.

[32] Actually, only eight of Plautus' twenty plays have intriguing slaves of this type; these are *Asinaria, Bacchides, Epidicus, Miles, Mostellaria, Persa, Poenulus, Pseudolus*. In the *Curculio*, as in Terence's *Phormio*, there is trickery, but it is engineered by a parasite. Master and slave indulge in deception in the *Captivi* but Tyndarus' role is very unlike that of the normal intriguing slave. It is noteworthy that the "master of intrigue" appears in Plautus' comedies in about the same proportion as in Terence's but the Plautine slaves, because of their cleverness and ingenuity, make a deeper impression upon the reader.

[33] Cf. the dilemmas of Sceledrus (*Mil.* 305 ff.) and Davus (*And.* 209 ff.).

He may be a rascal, but he's not unfaithful to me.

Most slaves of Roman comedy do not engage in trickery; among these are found many servants portrayed with considerable regard for realism. Messenio, who tries to keep Menaechmus out of trouble, has already been mentioned. Grumio, the rustic foil to the more corrupt Tranio, appears as a protatic character in the first scene of the *Mostellaria* but his character is clearly drawn; distressed at the extravagant and dissolute life of Philolaches, which he blames on Tranio, he prays for the return of his aged master before it is too late (78 ff.); he has much in common with Eumaeus, the loyal swineherd in the *Odyssey*.[34] Phaniscus in the same comedy moralizes upon the duties of a good slave (858 ff.; cf. the words of Messenio in *Men.* 966 ff.) and, accompanied by the less worthy Pinacium, later reveals to Theopropides that he has been deceived. One of the most serious and trustworthy slaves in all Roman comedy is Geta (*Ad.* 299 ff.) who, having the welfare of Sostrata and her daughter at heart, denounces vehemently what he believes to be Aeschinus' desertion. Geta in *Phorm.* 187 ff. states that only his compassion for Antipho keeps him from running away. Lampadio (*Cistellaria*) and Trachalio (*Rudens*) are active in their master's interests, as is the uncouth and surly Truculentus who condemns the wayward life of his master, at least until he is himself won over by Astaphium. He is one of the most interesting of Plautus' slaves, excelled perhaps only by Gripus, who has delusions of grandeur when he catches his "hamper-fish" (*Rud.* 906 ff.); the latter is delightful in his sullen and argumentative fashion as he attempts to retain his find against the claims of Trachalio and Labrax. Miss Wilner says that he "is a comic character, but the comedy does not rest on caricature; the character is drawn for its own sake."[35] The most noble and devoted slave in Roman comedy is undoubtedly Tyndarus in the *Captivi*, who risks his life in order that his master may be freed from captivity.

Such are the slaves of Plautus and Terence. As individuals they vary greatly—some are trustworthy and unselfish, others self-centered and unscrupulous; some are serious-minded and a bit stupid, others frivolous and witty. The most memorable creations are the brilliant *serui callidi* of Plautus; in spite of temporary setbacks they are never really at a loss and usually carry through their outrageous undertakings to an exultant and laughable conclusion. Yet these slaves, even more than the normal faithful servants, lack true individuality. They entertain us, they win our interest, but they do not gain our sympathy. Perhaps, by way of compensation, they have, as Arnaldi suggests,[36] a third dimension of

---

[34] Cf. Wilner, *CPh* 26 (1931), pp. 266 f., who points out that Grumio is characterized in more detail than Tranio, the protagonist of the play—an indication that the playwright is interested in characterization for its own sake.

[35] *CPh* 26 (1931), p. 278.

[36] *Da Plauto a Terenzio*, I, p. 143; cf. also Schild, *Die dramaturgische Rolle der Sklaven*, pp. 94 f.

comic or farcical delight, of rhythmical and linguistic agility, of tasty and expressive liveliness. But minor slaves such as Grumio, Messenio, Gripus, Truculentus in Plautus and Geta in Terence's *Adelphoe* have more real personality—at least they have as much as is discernible in any slave in Roman comedy. The slaves in general provide delightful comedy and several of them control much of the intrigue, but they are not as true to life as are many husbands, wives, and courtesans.

## Female Roles: *uirgo, ancilla, matrona, meretrix*

There are approximately seventy-five women who have speaking parts in the plays of Plautus and Terence; these fall into the following groups in descending order of numerical frequency: (1) maid, attendant, or nurse (*ancilla, anus, nutrix*), (2) courtesan (*meretrix*), (3) wife (*matrona*), and (4) young girl (*uirgo, puella*). In addition, there are incidental roles such as the old procuress (*lena*) in the *Asinaria* and the *Cistellaria*, the gracious and dignified priestess of Venus' shrine (*Rudens*), the music-girls of the *Epidicus*. Of the four main groups of woman characters, the least important to the development of the dramatic action are the first and the fourth. Maids regularly have inorganic roles, appearing often in only one or two scenes; the young girl seldom comes on the stage; those who do appear are usually girls of unknown parentage who are in the power of a slavedealer, e.g., Planesium (*Curculio*), Adelphasium and her sister (*Poenulus*), Palaestra (*Rudens*).

The only *uirgo* who appears on the stage in Terence[37] is Antiphila, whose presence in one short scene (*Heaut*. 381 ff.) sets in relief the character of Bacchis. Social convention and the rigidity of the stage setting (with its lack of interior scenes) alike made it difficult for young girls of good family to take part in the action. When the heroines of Roman comedy are girls of respectable parentage, they remain off-stage, e.g., Lesbonicus' sister (*Trinummus*), Philumena (*Andria*), Phaedria (*Aulularia*), Pamphila (*Adelphoe*)—the last two, like Glycerium (*Andria*), give birth to children behind the scenes. Most heroines, however, are either courtesans (to be discussed below) or girls like Planesium and Adelphasium who are saved from a courtesan's life by the discovery of their real identity. The most attractive girl in this group is undoubtedly Palaestra, forlorn and pathetic when she reaches land after the shipwreck and indignant that a virtuous life should be thus rewarded with suffering and distress (*Rud*. 185 ff.).[38] But greater troubles are in store for her before she finds her father; as she flees from the temple with Ampelisca, she says (664 ff.):

[37] With the exception of Pamphila who appears briefly as a mute character (*Eun.* 232 ff.); see chap. 7, n. 15.
[38] Cf. above, p. 104, where Palaestra's monologue is quoted in part.

Now we are utterly bereft of all aid and protection; we have neither safety nor hope of any safety, and we know not where to turn. What outrage and injury we have suffered from our wicked master! . . . In the midst of such misery it is better to die.

Although the role of the *uirgo* in Plautus is seldom active (and in Terence almost non-existent), the *Persa* provides an outstanding exception; the plot of the comedy requires that a free and unmarried woman act the part of a Persian captive; she is a parasite's daughter, hence from a lower social level but her character is delineated with unusual skill: modest, serious-minded, and idealistic (cf. 344 ff., 554 ff.), she carries out the deception with surprising wit and cleverness and carefully avoids outright falsehoods (630 ff.). Because of the abnormal features of her role, Prescott considers it possible that "Plautus expanded suggestions in his Greek original with a view to portraying a staid Roman virgin from his own environment."[39]

I have already said that the maid or nurse is loosely attached to the action, and examples come readily to mind, e.g., the unnamed *ancilla* of Erotium, who delivers a message to Menaechmus and begs him for earrings (*Men.* 524 ff.), or Syra, Dorippa's aged attendant, remembered chiefly for her remarks on a single standard of conduct for husbands and wives (*Merc.* 817 ff.). But characters of this type are useful in several ways. (1) At times, even when the role is mechanical and temporary, it aids in the development of the plot; the nurse or the maid may reveal essential information or assist in the discovery of another's identity, e.g., Bromia (*Amph.* 1053 ff.), Giddenis (*Poen.* 1120 ff.), Sophrona (*Phorm.* 728 ff.).[40] (2) Other maids, although equally inorganic, help to delineate more important characters. The scenes between Staphyla and Euclio in the *Aulularia* point up the disposition of her master, and the worldly advice of the aged Scapha (cf. *Most.* 188 ff.) reveals by contrast the loving and devoted nature of Philematium. (3) A third function of the maid—and this almost entirely Plautine—is to provide incidental humor, e.g., Leaena, the wine-bibbing *anus* of the *Curculio* (96 ff.), and Crocotium (*Stich.* 234 ff.); the extended dialogue of Sophoclidisca and Paegnium in *Pers.* 204 ff. is the type of comic interlude frequently introduced by Plautus to pad the plot with badinage and witticisms, and Stephanium makes a jolly third in the revelry at the conclusion of the *Stichus*.

In certain plays of Plautus the maid has a more extended part and all three functions are present. Milphidippa appears in four scenes of the *Miles*, assists in the deception of the soldier, and tells the story of Acrote-

[39] *CPh* 11 (1916), p. 135.
[40] Cf. Prescott, *CPh* 15 (1920), p. 277: "The casual appearance of a nurse to help establish the identity of a lost child is so short that we are not disturbed particularly by the rôle of Sophrona in the *Eunuchus* 910 ff. or of the *nutrix* in the *Heautontimorumenos* 614 ff." But in these two plays the role is unusually slight. No *ancilla* or *nutrix* in Plautus is treated so briefly.

leutium's supposed love with zest and humor; at the same time the delineation of Pyrgopolynices is continued from Act 1, Scene 1 in delightful fashion; cf. 1037 ff.:

MI.: Good day, handsome sir.
PY. (*aside*): She mentioned my surname. (*Aloud*) The gods give you whatever you wish.
MI.: That permission to spend a lifetime with you—
PY.: You're asking too much.
MI.: I don't mean for myself; it's my mistress that's dying with love for you.
PY. (*proudly*): Many other women want the same thing, but they don't have the opportunity.
MI.: Gracious me! I don't wonder that you set a high value on yourself—a man so priceless and preeminent in beauty and bravery! Was there ever a man more worthy of being a god?

Similarly, in the *Casina*, Pardalisca frightens Lysidamus with the fictitious tale of Casina and the sword (621 ff.), describes the deception planned off stage (759 ff.), and urges Olympio to tell about his adventure with the "bride" (892 ff.). Astaphium in the *Truculentus* is unique in having a more active role by far than does any other maid in Plautus. She is on the stage during almost two-thirds of the action and what she says about Phronesium and her suitors gives the play much of its cynical and satirical tone. She enters into the intrigue, such as it is, and is active in aiding Phronesium in the deception of the lovers, and there is much humor in the scenes (256 ff., 669 ff.) where she works her wiles upon the not-too-unwilling Truculentus.

There is nothing in Terence comparable to the roles of Milphidippa, Pardalisca, or Astaphium. In most cases the maids run errands or aid in the discovery of identity but the part they play in the action is usually very slight and they are seldom used either for characterization or humor; the only ones at all active are Mysis, Dorias, and Pythias. Mysis takes part in Davus' deception of Chremes without understanding the slave's purpose (*And.* 722 ff., cf. 789 ff.) and in the *Eunuchus* both Dorias and Pythias report off-stage action (615 ff., 643 ff.) and Pythias even deceives Parmeno, frightening him with false tales about the punishment in store for him and Chaerea (941 ff., 1002 ff.). But with the exception of these three characters the role of the maid in Terence is reduced to a bare mechanical minimum.

Let us turn now to the more important female roles—the *matronae* and the *meretrices*. Many wives in Roman comedy are presented in an unattractive light, as shrewish, hot-tempered, suspicious, extravagant.[41] But in many cases they have faithless husbands, e.g., Artemona (*Asinaria*), Cleustrata (*Casina*) and the unnamed wife of Menaechmus I, or husbands whom they wrongly suspect of unfaithfulness (Dorippa in

[41] See "Love and Marriage" in chap. 10.

the *Mercator*). These are the dowered wives (*uxores dotatae*) whom Michaut includes in his list of Plautine grotesques.[42] Menaechmus' wife says (*Men.* 559 ff.):

> How can I put up with marriage any longer, when my husband steals anything there is in the house and carries it off to his mistress?

But when she asks Peniculus how to treat Menaechmus on his return, the parasite replies (569):

> The usual way—rough treatment.

And even her father, when summoned to her aid, takes her husband's part (787 ff.). All this seems to justify Menaechmus' complaint earlier in the play (114 ff.):

> If I say I'm going out,
> You're on hand to ask about
> Where I'm going,
>     What to do,
> What's my business,
>     What's for you.
> I can't get out anywhere
> But you want me to declare
> All I've done and all I do.
> Customs officer—that's you!
> I've handled you with too much care;
> Listen what I'm going to do:
> Food I give you,
>     Maids, indeed,
> Money, dresses—
>     All you need;
> Now you'll keep your spying eyes
> Off your husband, if you're wise.[43]

But these wives usually reap a rich revenge upon their wayward husbands.

Other wives in Roman comedy are portrayed very differently. The two sisters of the *Stichus* are faithful and devoted to their absent husbands. The fact that the husbands may have become impoverished makes no difference; they married "for richer, for poorer"; Pamphila says (134):

> My mind is the same in poverty as it was formerly in wealth.

Plautus' outstanding portrayal of a wife is that of Alcumena, wrongly accused by Amphitruo of adultery during his absence. Her love for her husband is seen in her farewell to Jupiter, whom she believes to be

---

[42] *Plaute*, I, pp. 261 ff.

[43] Metrical translation by R. W. Hyde, in Duckworth, *The Complete Roman Drama*, I, p. 443. The translation of the *Menaechmi* by Weist and Hyde is unusually successful because of its colloquial nature and also because it presents in verse the more lyrical portions of the original.

Plate VII. Sostrata offers to withdraw to the country
*Hec.* 577-606 (MS C: folio 72 verso)

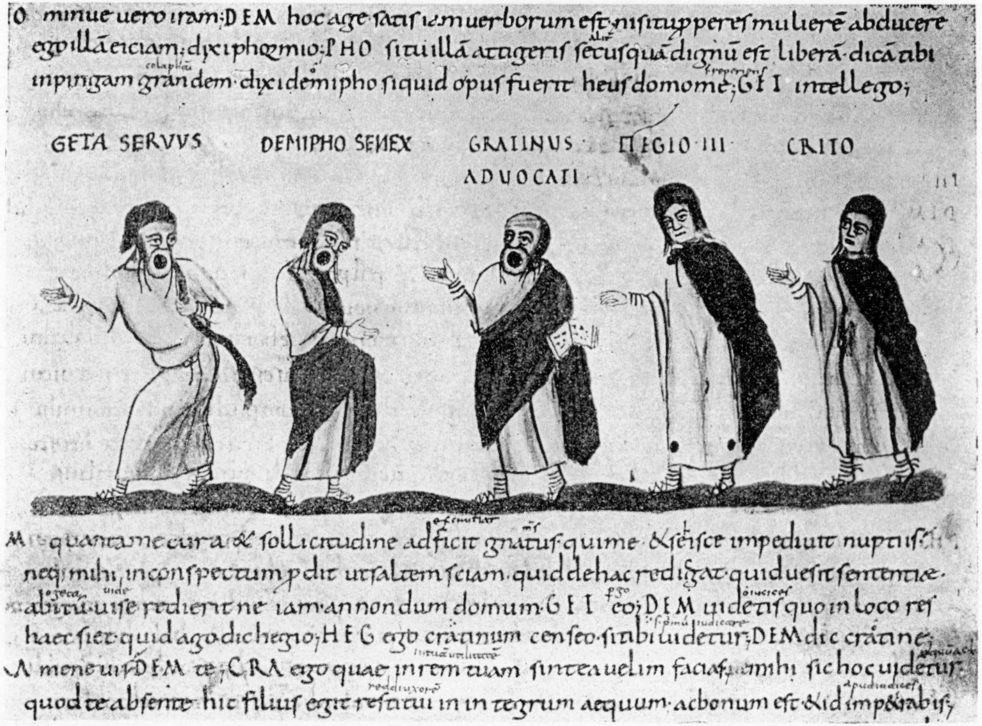

GETA SERVVS   DEMIPHO SENEX   GRATIINVS   LEGIO III   CRITO
ADVOCATI

Plate VIII. Demipho's friends are less than helpful
*Phorm.* 441-464 (MS C: folio 82 verso)

Amphitruo (529 ff.), and in her soliloquy after the god's departure; cf. 640 ff.:

> And now I am alone, since he is gone, the one I love above all others; the bitterness of his departure surpasses the pleasure I gained when he was here. . . . With courageous spirit I'll bear his absence to the very end, if only this reward I win—that he be victorious in the war. Valor is the best reward and comes before all else; by valor everything is preserved—liberty, health, life, property, our country and our parents. Valor possesses everything; to him who has valor all blessings come.

She stoutly defends her innocence to Amphitruo (839 ff.):

> Nor do I deem my dowry that which is usually thought a dowry; but rather purity and honor and self-control; fear of the gods, love of parents, and affection for my relatives; devoted to your interests, and generous and helpful in every way.

The chaste, noble, and patriotic sentiments of Alcumena sound thoroughly Roman, and as a character she is perhaps closer to real life than are most of the wives in Plautus.

Equally human and pathetic are the women who are eager to locate long-lost daughters, e.g., Phanostrata (*Cistellaria*) and Philippa (*Epidicus*), and those who are concerned about the happiness of their children, e.g., the three Terentian Sostratas (*Adelphoe, Heauton*, and *Hecyra*). Sostrata in *Ad.* 330 ff. is heartbroken at the thought that Aeschinus has deserted her daughter in her hour of need, and in the *Hecyra* Sostrata is willing to make any sacrifice for her son's happiness. Blamed by her husband for driving her daughter-in-law from the house (198 ff.), she maintains her innocence (208, 228, 274 ff.) and offers to withdraw to the country so that Philumena will return to Pamphilus (577 ff.); she says (595 ff.):

> All that I care for now is that my old age will not be a hindrance to my daughter-in-law and that she will not await my death. I see that I am disliked here through no fault of mine; it is time for me to go. By going, I think that I shall most effectively remove all grounds of complaint against me, clear myself of this suspicion, and please our neighbors. Please let me escape the common reproach of my sex.

On this passage Norwood comments: "Terence has often written more dazzling lines, but even he has never excelled this magnificent expression of unforced sad dignity, this voice of sheer goodness."[44] Just as Alcumena is Plautus' most noble woman character, so Sostrata is outstanding among Terence's *matronae* (all of whom are more realistically portrayed than the majority of wives in Plautus) and it is altogether fitting that the play "The Mother-in-law" was named after her. Donatus says that Terence is departing from usual dramatic practice in presenting on the stage a mother-in-law who is good (cf. *ad Hec.* 198, 774);

---

[44] *The Art of Terence*, p. 96; cf. *Plautus and Terence*, pp. 135 ff.

such a statement implies that mothers-in-law were portrayed in an unfavorable light in ancient comedy but there is no evidence for this in any of the extant plays.[45]

The courtesans of Plautus fall into two categories: (1) the ones who are clever and experienced but mercenary and unfeeling; (2) younger girls who, devoted to their lovers, have already become their mistresses or who are hoping to be purchased and freed. To those of the first group money rather than love is a determining factor in the bestowal of their favors. When Menaechmus I brings as a gift to Erotium a dress belonging to his wife, she says (*Men.* 192):

> You win out easily over the others who share my favors.

And Bacchis and her sister comment upon the money which they will make (*Bacch.* 102 ff.).[46] By far the most mercenary courtesan in Roman comedy is Phronesium, whose attitude towards her three lovers is well summarized in the words of Astaphium (*Truc.* 231 ff.):

> No one can ever be any good as a lover unless he hates his money. As long as he can pay he may love; when his money runs out he must seek another occupation; when he has nothing then he must be reasonable and yield his place to those who have.

And Phronesium says of the soldier (887):

> I love him better than my own soul—as long as I get from him what I want.[47]

Less cynical than Phronesium, and more amusing, is Acroteleutium, who boasts of her cleverness (*Mil.* 878 ff.) and carries out her part of the deception of Pyrgopolynices with great ingenuity.

The courtesans who are in love with youths are far more attractive and sympathetic even though Plautus for the sake of humor sometimes stresses their wit and cleverness rather than their emotional attachments; cf., e.g., Pasicompsa in *Merc.* 510 ff. The term "courtesan" is perhaps hardly justified since the girls are living with the men of their choice; Selenium says (*Cist.* 83 ff.):

> Since I didn't wish to be called a courtesan, my mother yielded to my request and permitted me to live with the man whom I love passionately.

This is very different from the life of Gymnasium as described by her mother—"marrying" a different man every day and every night, to keep the household from dying of hunger (cf. *Cist.* 43 ff.). Girls like

---

[45] Cf. Legrand-Loeb, *The New Greek Comedy*, pp. 138 f.

[46] Cf., however, 1184 f., in which Bacchis offers to return half the money to Nicobulus on condition that he pardon his son and Chrysalus.

[47] On Phronesium as a cold and unfeeling courtesan, cf. Legrand-Loeb, *The New Greek Comedy*, pp. 80 f., 87. It is an exaggeration to say, as does Dunkin (*Post-Aristophanic Comedy*, p. 89), that Erotium, the two Bacchises, and Philaenium (*Asinaria*) are "every bit as sensuous and greedy" as Phronesium.

Selenium, Philaenium (cf. *Asin.* 537, 542), and Philematium (*Most.* 214 f.) express their love and faithfulness to one man and resist the advice of older and more experienced women who urge them to be more mercenary (e.g., Scapha's words in *Most.* 194 ff.).

An examination of the role of the *meretrix* in Terence reveals far less variety. The younger playwright even here follows his general tendency of presenting his characters as decent and reputable persons, hence the more objectionable type of courtesan does not appear in his plays. Terence's only mercenary courtesan is Bacchis in the *Heauton*; extravagant and expensive, she arrives at Chremes' home with a retinue of servants (cf. 449 ff.) and proceeds to set the house in an uproar, Chremes meanwhile thinking that she is the sweetheart of Menedemus' son. When the truth is revealed, Clitipho is compelled to give her up. Still, in her words to Antiphila, Bacchis pays a sincere tribute to true love and marital devotion (381 ff.). Philotis, a protatic character, objects when Syra advises her to be mercenary and to treat all men alike (*Hec.* 63 ff.).

The two courtesans who have major roles in the plays of Terence, Thais (*Eunuchus*) and Bacchis (*Hecyra*), are unusually noble in every respect. Curiously enough, the impression which the audience gains of them indirectly is just the opposite of the character which they reveal in speech and action. Phaedria speaks of the insolence and wickedness of Thais (*Eun.* 46 ff., 71 ff.) and Parmeno mentions Bacchis' insults and tells how her character differs from that of Pamphilus' wife (*Hec.* 158 ff.). The audience might well expect from these statements that greedy and heartless Phronesium-like persons would appear on the stage; but when Thais and Bacchis enter they prove to be almost paragons of virtue and generosity. Thais wants her lover to retire temporarily in favor of a soldier but she is not mercenary (as is Phronesium in a similar situation); she is interested in the welfare of Pamphila and eager to determine the girl's identity. Bacchis is not only not angry at being deserted by Pamphilus but generously brings about the reconciliation of Pamphilus and his wife. Norwood speaks of the "sunny kindliness" of "this magnificent woman," and points out that Terence "loves to take some familiar *dramatis persona* and discover a new character beneath the traditional mask."[48] This is essentially what Donatus says of both Thais and Bacchis—that they are traditional characters presented in a new way; repeatedly he makes the point that Terence in the *Hecyra* departs from convention and portrays a *bona meretrix* who acts *contra officium meretricis*.[49]

Terence seems conscious that he is doing something new in his treatment of the courtesan. At least, the courtesans themselves realize

[48] *The Art of Terence*, pp. 97, 98, 99.
[49] *Ad Hec.* 840; cf. also praef. 1, 9; 58, 727, 756, 774, 776, 789; on Thais, see *ad Eun.* 198.

that they are acting as a *meretrix* is not supposed to act; Thais says (*Eun.* 197 f.) :

I suppose that he doesn't put much faith in me and judges me from the character of others.

And Bacchis declares in *Hec.* 756 f. (cf. 775 f., 833 f.) :

I'll do it, although I'm sure that no other woman of my profession would appear before a married woman about such a matter.

We have found in Plautus many courtesans who are *bonae meretrices* in a passive sense, who are tender and loving and eager to please their sweethearts. But there is no one in Plautus like Thais or Bacchis, women who are actively generous and anxious to help others and who boast of doing what no ordinary *meretrix* would do. Are they too self-righteous? Is Bacchis a great character, as Norwood maintains, or is she too noble to be true to life? Post calls her "an always unmoved, ever decorous example of goodness exempt from human frailty."[50]

Lana has recently made some interesting suggestions about Terence's characters and especially about his courtesans.[51] Convinced that Terence as a philhellene was consciously trying to make Greek life more acceptable to the Roman audience, he points out that the indirect description of courtesans like Thais and Bacchis (or of a *matrona* like Sostrata) does not agree with the characters when they appear. The less favorable, more conventional descriptions of courtesan and mother-in-law, he believes, reflect their delineation in the Greek originals, whereas the excessive nobility of Sostrata and Bacchis in their actions is Terence's own addition and represents a departure from the psychological truth of the originals. Terence has made his characters too good. It is very probable that Lana is correct to this extent—that just as Plautus portrayed many characters of his originals, even husbands and wives, as more grotesque and laughable, so Terence moved in the opposite direction and made them more refined and also less realistic than in the originals.[52] But Lana's argument from the difference between the indirect description of characters and the manner in which they act on the stage will hardly prove this theory of Terentian originality. In the first place, the contrast between what a character like

---

[50] *CW* 23 (1929-30), p. 125; cf. Gomme, *Essays in Greek History and Literature*, p. 281. De Lorenzi looks upon Bacchis as inferior to Selenium in Plautus' *Cistellaria*; he calls Selenium "la figura piú delicata, piú fine e piú soave del teatro plautino, forse di tutto il teatro comico classico" (*I Precedenti Greci*, p. 84).

[51] Cf. *RFC* 25 (1947), pp. 60 ff., 173 ff.

[52] Lana points out that Abrotonon in Menander's *Epitrepontes*, a less altruistic person, is portrayed with more regard for reality (*RFC* 25, 1947, pp. 65 ff.) ; cf. also Siess, *WS* 29 (1907), pp. 310 ff.; Post, *CW* 23 (1929-30), p. 126. See Croce, *Critica* 34 (1936), pp. 413 ff., for an interesting discussion of the Terentian *meretrix*, who, Croce believes, illustrates Terence's "senso di naturalità, d'indulgenza e di fondamentale bontà" (*ibid.*, p. 417).

Bacchis actually is and what she is thought to be is dramatically most effective and, second, such mistaken beliefs are inevitable in plays of misunderstanding like the *Hecyra*. In the *Amphitruo*, Alcumena as a person likewise differs from what her husband thinks of her.

## Professional Types: Characterization for Comedy

The characters discussed above have been chiefly family types (father, mother, son) or members of the household (slave, maidservant, nurse). Many young girls of questionable status (e.g., Planesium in the *Curculio*, Selenium in the *Cistellaria*, Glycerium in the *Andria*) join the family group in the end. We turn now to a number of so-called "professional" roles, all apparently inherited from New Comedy and all rich in comic possibilities. We have seen already that Plautus on occasion has developed both *senex* and *matrona* into grotesque roles—the amorous old man who falls in love with a young girl, and the wife who revenges herself upon her unfaithful husband; also the slave in Plautine comedy not only directs the intrigue, but in both monologue and dialogue provides merriment and coarse humor. Since in the plays of Terence the husbands and wives are regularly more decent and respectable, often almost pathetic in their attempts to solve their difficulties, and the slave has a less prominent and more subdued role, it is to be expected that comic characters such as the slavedealer, the parasite, the braggart warrior would also have little appeal for Terence.

Incidental roles of this type are the merchant (*Asin.* 381 ff.), the sycophant (*Pseud.* 913 ff., *Trin.* 843 ff.), the pilot (*Amph.* 1035 ff.), fishermen (*Rud.* 290 ff.), the doctor (*Men.* 889 ff.), an amusingly pompous practitioner, and *aduocati*, or counselors, who in *Poen.* 515 ff. aid in the deception of Lycus. Demipho in the *Phormio* seeks the advice of three *aduocati*, and their suggestions are less than helpful: Cratinus believes that Antipho's marriage should be annulled, Hegio recommends the opposite course, and Crito favors further deliberation on the matter. "You've done well," says Demipho, "and I'm much more uncertain now than I was before" (458 ff.). Terence's subtle humor is here most effective.

The more significant roles in this category will be treated in ascending order of importance. (1) The banker or moneylender (*trapezita, danista*). Lyco strikes an amusing (and familiar) note when he enters with the words (*Curc.* 371 ff.) :

I seem to be prospering; I've just done some reckoning to see how much money I have and how much I owe. I'm rich—if I don't pay my debts.

He is delighted when Curculio denounces slavedealers like Cappadox, less happy when the parasite turns upon bankers with equal vehemence (506 ff.; cf. the similar denunciation of bankers in *Pers.* 434 ff., *Pseud.* 296 ff.). The *danista* who arrives with Telestis (*Epid.* 620 ff.) and receives payment is a colorless character but Misargyrides, appropriately called "Hate-silver-son," is an ancient Shylock as he shouts to Tranio (*Most.* 598 ff.) :

But I'm not asking for the principal; it's the interest that must be paid to me first. . . . Give me my interest, pay me the interest, I want the interest! Give me the interest at once, won't you! Do I get my interest?

"Interest here, interest there," says Tranio in disgust, "he can't talk about anything but interest."

(2) The cooks (*coci*) are members of the household (*Curc.* 251 ff., *Men.* 219 ff., 273 ff., *Mil.* 1397 ff.) or hired as caterers for special occasions (*Aul.* 280 ff., *Cas.* 720 ff., *Merc.* 741 ff., *Pseud.* 790 ff.). A popular role in Greek Middle and New Comedy, the cook in Plautus is preeminently a character to create laughter, whether he boasts of his culinary skill, as in the *Pseudolus,* or interprets the dream of Cappadox (*Curculio*), or threatens a would-be adulterer with punishment (*Miles*). Cooks brought in from the outside were noted for their pilfering tendencies; cf. *Cas.* 720 ff. and the words of the *cocus* in *Pseud.* 851 f. :

Do you expect to find any cook who doesn't have the claws of a kite or an eagle?

It is altogether natural that Euclio in the *Aulularia* should suspect Anthrax and Congrio of coming to his house to steal his treasure.

(3) The *leno,* or slavedealer. These include Cappadox (*Curculio*), Dordalus (*Persa*), Lycus (*Poenulus*), Ballio (*Pseudolus*), Labrax (*Rudens*) and, in Terence, Sannio (*Adelphoe*) and Dorio (*Phormio*). The Plautine slavedealer, denounced as a class (cf. *Curc.* 494 ff.), is characterized by greed and accused of impiety, perjury, faithlessness, cruelty, and inhumanity.[53] Typical of the attitude towards the *leno* is Palinurus' reply to Phaedromus (*Curc.* 63 ff.) :

PH.: At one time he wants thirty minae for the girl, at another a whole talent; I can't get any fair and just treatment from him.
PA.: You're a fool to expect from him what no slavedealer has.

Boastful and confident, proud of his astuteness but actually credulous and stupid, the *leno* is a conventional type of grotesque comic character who is made the victim of deception and the butt of ridicule (cf. *Pers.* 777 ff.). As Labrax says (*Rud.* 1284 f.) :

The *leno* must be a true son of pleasure; he gives so much pleasure to everyone when he gets into trouble.

The slavedealer accepts abuse calmly, even complacently (*Pseud.* 359 ff.), and returns it in good measure (*Pers.* 417 ff.) ; occasionally he displays a sparkling wit (*Rud.* 485 ff.). The outstanding *leno* in Plautus is undoubtedly Ballio; his instructions to his household (*Pseud.*

[53] Cf. Stotz, *De lenonis in comoedia figura,* pp. 20 ff.

133 ff.), his treatment of Calidorus, his confidence that Pseudolus can be outwitted, and his final despair combine to make him a vivid and memorable character. When Simia comes hunting for "a scoundrel, a law-breaking, godless, perjured rascal" (974 f.), Ballio says proudly in an aside:

He's looking for me, for those are my surnames.

Ballio's popularity in later Roman times, attested by Cicero's allusion to him as *ille improbissimus et periurissimus leno (Pro Rosc. com.* 7, 20; cf. 17, 50 and *Phil.* II, 6, 15), seems well deserved.

We should recall, however, that many of the accusations hurled at the *leno* come from young lovers or their slaves, to whom the slave-dealer is harsh and unfeeling when no money is forthcoming (e.g., *Pseud.* 273 ff.). Also, we should remember that the *leno*, although viewed with hatred and contempt, was a business man engaged in a trade which, in an age which countenanced slavery, was legal even if lacking in respectability.[54] Hence the term "slavedealer" seems preferable to those often found in translations and discussions of the plays— "pimp," "pander," "procurer." Granted that they break their promises when they see an opportunity for greater profit (cf., e.g., *Rud.* 47 ff.)— this is true also of Dorio in *Phorm.* 523 ff.—they sometimes reveal, even in Plautus, a spark of decency surprising in characters that are little more than grotesque caricatures; cf. the desire of Cappadox that Planesium be well treated (*Curc.* 517), Lycus' frank admission that the girls are not his (*Poen.* 1347 ff.), and Labrax' expression of delight that Palaestra has found her father (*Rud.* 1365 ff.). It is perhaps exceptional for a *leno* to be invited to dinner (*Rud.* 1417) but it is hardly as shocking as Lejay considers it.[55]

Plautus has undoubtedly accentuated the greed and cruelty of these characters in order to make them more ridiculous. The two Terentian slavedealers are very different; they have minor parts and the element of abuse and invective is lacking (although Dorio is called *homo inhumanissimus* in *Phorm.* 509) ; neither is cheated of money nor taken to court; on the contrary, they are each paid in full for their girls. The farcical and grotesque note of Plautus is absent and as a result the two slavedealers become more worthy of respect. Sannio has been the victim of mistreatment (*Ad.* 196 ff., 244 f.) and is almost a sympathetic character; cf. his words to Aeschinus (188 f.) :

I am a *leno*, the ruination of young men, I admit; also a liar and a rascal. But I've never done you any wrong.

[54] Cf. Norwood, *The Art of Terence*, pp. 148 f., who suggests that the *leno* of comedy should be regarded, not as a modern *leno*, but rather as a modern money-lender.

[55] *Plaute*, p. 146; cf. also Norwood, *Plautus and Terence*, p. 87.

There seems little doubt that Terence intentionally portrayed the *leno* in a more subdued fashion than had Plautus, and both playwrights may well have departed from their originals, Plautus in the direction of unrealistic but laughable caricature, Terence in the direction of greater restraint.[56]

(4) The braggart warrior. The *miles* in Plautus, like the *leno*, is a caricature rather than a character, and his predominant trait is boastfulness, usually of his military exploits but sometimes of his ability to charm the opposite sex. His role in the play is always that of lover, and in most instances he appears as rival of the hero; the *Curculio* is unusual in that Therapontigonus is revealed as Planesium's brother and no longer proves an obstacle to Phaedromus' love affair. In three comedies (*Bacchides, Epidicus, Poenulus*) the soldier has a minor but interesting part. Cleomachus by his threats against Mnesilochus is a useful pawn in Chrysalus' deception (*Bacch.* 842 ff.); the unnamed soldier of the *Epidicus* is instrumental in revealing to Periphanes that he has been deceived and, what is more amusing, doesn't have a chance to recount his exploits (cf. 444 ff.); he says (453 f.):

I'm looking for a person to whom I can describe my battles, not one who wants to tell me about his.

Antamoenides in the *Poenulus* is more typical; he describes how he killed sixty thousand flying men in one day with his hands (470 ff.). Stratophanes in the *Truculentus* strikes an unusual note when he says that he doesn't want to boast of his military achievements; his deeds are made known by actions, not by words (482 ff.). But he blusters and threatens in the approved fashion when Phronesium appears to favor another lover (603 ff.). His best lines occur when Astaphium relates that Phronesium has borne him a son (507 ff.):

AS.: He's really the very image of you.
ST.: What, so big already? Has he joined the army yet? Brought back any spoils?
AS.: Now, now! He was born only five days ago.
ST.: What of it? After so many days he should have done something worthwhile. What business did he have to be born before he could go forth to battle?

Here speaks the true *miles*.

Plautus' most brilliant and delightful soldier is Pyrgopolynices; he is proud of his military exploits; cf. the dialogue with Artotrogus in *Mil.* 42 ff.:

PY.: What do you recall?
AR.: Let me see. I recall there were one hundred and fifty Cilicians, one hundred Scythobrigandians, thirty Sardians, sixty Macedonians—these were the men you killed in one day.

56 Cf. Stotz, *De lenonis in comoedia figura*, pp. 49 f.

PY.: What's the total of the men?
AR.: Seven thousand.
PY.: That's what it ought to be. Your calculation is quite correct.

But he is even more boastful about his supposed success with women;
cf. 58 ff.:

AR.: All the women love you and quite rightly, since you are so handsome. . . .
PY.: It's such a nuisance for a man to be so handsome.

Cf. his words in 1087:

My beauty is such a bother to me.

The soldier's conceit, his belief that all women are in love with him,
makes possible the deception of the pretended wife. His reaction to the
words of Milphidippa about her mistress (1038 ff., 1267 ff.) is delightful comedy, and he falls into the trap cleverly laid by Palaestrio
and his fellow-conspirators.

Terence presents the *miles* on the stage only once, in the *Eunuchus*.
Beare says of Thraso: "Terence's Captain is boastful, lecherous and
cowardly, like all other Captains."[57] But Thraso differs from the typical
Plautine *miles* in several respects: although stupid and conceited he
does not boast of his military exploits; rather, he prides himself upon
his wit and cleverness, and his victories are those of the word rather
than of the sword (cf. 412 ff., 422 ff.). He believes that he has an
especial gift—everything that he does wins him favor with other people
(395 f.). Nor does he rage and threaten as do Cleomachus and Stratophanes; even the famous attack of his "army" upon the house of
Thais is a relatively tame affair since he stations himself safely in the
rear (781 ff.) and favors negotiation rather than force (789 f.). Thraso
lacks the vigor and forcefulness of the usual *miles* even though he may
result from Terence's attempt to be amusing in a more farcical, Plautine
manner, as Norwood suggests.[58]

(5) The parasite is the "funny" man *par excellence* of Roman comedy. Living by his wits and always on the lookout for a free meal, he is
at times a professional jokester eager to amuse his prospective host, at
times a "handy man" anxious to win favor by running errands and
willing to accept both insult and abuse, at times a flatterer who points up
the stupidity of others by his cynical asides. The parasite had a long
tradition in the Greek theater, deriving ultimately from Epicharmus,
but it is very possible that Plautus developed and enriched the role,
making the parasite one of his most original creations.[59]

---

[57] *Ha* 71 (1948), p. 80.
[58] *The Art of Terence*, pp. 67 ff.; *Plautus and Terence*, pp. 152 ff. Cf. Henry,
*SPhNC* 12 (1915), pp. 78 ff. But Dunkin is unfair to Thraso when he calls him "a
heavily Bowdlerized specimen," "a mere puppet" (*Post-Aristophanic Comedy*, pp.
113 f.).
[59] Cf. D'Agostino, *MC* 7 Suppl. (1937), pp. 103 f.

Both the character of the parasite and the role he plays differ from comedy to comedy,[60] so that it is unwise to refer to him as a conventional type; but one characteristic all parasites display in common— love of good food and a desire for free meals.[61] Curculio suggests that Planesium be betrothed to Phaedromus and says that he will give the dowry—the privilege of being fed as long as he lives (*Curc.* 663 f.), and Saturio boasts that he is following the profession of his ancestors— eating at another's expense (*Pers.* 53 ff.). According to Ergasilus (*Capt.* 469 ff.) the true "art" of the parasite is to be a *ridiculus*, to entertain others with his jokes, and Saturio has his books of clever sayings—a suitable dowry for his daughter (*Pers.* 392 ff.). Gelasimus considers auctioning off his jokebooks (*Stich.* 221 ff.) but changes his mind when he learns that the two husbands have returned (383 ff.). Gelasimus is pure parasite; his only purpose in the play is to arouse laughter by his frantic but unsuccessful attempts to gain a meal. From his first appearance (155) when he says

My mother must have been Hunger herself, for never since I was born have I had enough to eat,

to his doleful words at his final departure (638 ff.)

No one will ever see me alive tomorrow, for I'll give my throat a dose of hempen rope. I won't let people say that I died of hunger,

he adds humor to the play, and the spectators could hardly be accused of being hard-hearted if they found him a laughable rather than a pathetic figure.[62]

Gelasimus is an exception, both in his role and in the treatment he receives. Peniculus in the *Menaechmi* fails to share in the hoped-for dinner (through no fault of his patron) but Ergasilus and Curculio are both well fed during the course of the action—the reward for their services. Although the primary function of the role is comedy (and many long monologues are designed for this purpose),[63] most parasites have an important part in the action, e.g., the parasite of the *Asinaria* reveals to the wife the truth about her husband, as do Peniculus and Phormio. Saturio aids in the deception by having his daughter impersonate a Persian captive. Both Ergasilus and Curculio are bearers

[60] See chap. 7, n. 7.

[61] Cf. *Asin.* 913 f., *Capt.* 69 ff., 461 ff., 845 ff., 901 ff., *Curc.* 317 ff., 366 ff., *Men.* 77 ff., *Mil.* 33 ff., *Pers.* 53 ff., 93 ff., 329 ff., *Stich.* 155 ff., *Eun.* 1058 ff., *Phorm.* 1053. Such passages account for the term *edax parasitus* (*Heaut.* 38, *Eun.* 38). See also Wilner, *CPh* 26 (1931), pp. 272 f.

[62] No other parasite so emphasizes his own hunger; yet Dunkin, speaking of the parasite as a class, describes him as "a pathetic figure which none but a social order so selfish as to be utterly hard-hearted, could possibly regard as amusing" (*Post-Aristophanic Comedy*, p. 86). But what of circus clowns today, or Charlie Chaplin in "The Gold Rush" devouring a boot?

[63] *Capt.* 69 ff., 461 ff., *Men.* 77 ff., *Pers.* 53 ff., *Stich.* 155 ff., *Eun.* 232 ff.

of important tidings (hence their appearance as "running slaves," *Capt.* 768 ff., *Curc.* 280 ff.), and Curculio plays the part of a *seruus callidus* by engineering the deception. Artotrogus, a protatic character, is a different type of parasite—one who wins favor by adulation.

There are two parasites in the comedies of Terence: Gnatho (*Eunuchus*) and Phormio. Gnatho boasts of his originality (*Eun.* 247 ff.):

> I've invented a new method. There's a class of men who want to be first in every thing but aren't. I attach myself to these. I don't aim to make them laugh at me, but I laugh with them and admire their ability. Whatever they say I praise, and if they say the opposite, I praise that too. . . . Just as schools of philosophy are named for their masters, so parasites should likewise be called Gnathonians.

Actually, however, Gnatho's method is not original, for his praise of Thraso and his cynical asides are very similar to Artotrogus' handling of Pyrgopolynices (cf. *Eun.* 397 ff. with *Mil.* 9 ff.). Phormio, like Curculio, has a major role; he controls the course of events from beginning to end with a masterful hand but, except for a jest about "doubtful food"—so delicious that you're in doubt what to eat first (*Phorm.* 342 f.)—and his final request for a meal (1053), he has none of the parasite's usual characteristics, neither the preoccupation with hunger and food nor the desire to win favor by jesting or flattery. Norwood calls him "far less a parasite than a συκοφάντης, a subtle and elegant blackmailer."[64] There is no lack of humor in the manner in which he outwits both Demipho and Chremes but neither he nor Gnatho has much in common with laughter-provoking characters such as Ergasilus, Peniculus, and Gelasimus.

These, then, are the various professional types who appear on the stage with the avowed purpose of arousing laughter. One or more of these characters is found in every Plautine comedy, with the exception of the *Cistellaria*, already mentioned as the most Menandrian of his plays.[65] Terence uses these roles less frequently and with more restraint; the soldier is less laughable, the parasite less clownish, the slavedealer more decent, but they do provide humor and somewhat more boisterous action (e.g., *Eun.* 771 ff., *Ad.* 155 ff.). It seems hardly accidental that Terence introduces these characters only in his last three plays. We have seen that in his use of stage conventions and in his handling of intrigue Terence departs from tradition more frequently in his earlier

---

[64] *The Art of Terence*, p. 76; but cf. Post, *CW* 23 (1929-30), p. 122. Siess considers Phormio an original character who combines the traits of parasite, sycophant, and true friend (*WS* 29, 1907, p. 293) and attributes the individuality of the character to Terence rather than to Menander (p. 302). On Phormio as a sycophant, see Lofberg, *CPh* 15 (1920), pp. 69 ff. Godsey (*CW* 22, 1928-29, pp. 65 ff.) considers Phormio a real friend of the *adulescentes*; but cf. Lofberg, *CW* 22 (1928-29), pp. 183 f.

[65] Several plays have only one such role (*Amphitruo, Aulularia, Captivi, Mercator, Mostellaria, Stichus, Trinummus, Truculentus*); the *Curculio* is unusually rich in characters of this type, having a slavedealer, cook, parasite, banker, and soldier.

comedies—the *Andria, Hecyra,* and *Heauton.* Likewise in his early plays he avoids the use of professional roles. Here again we have evidence that as he gained in experience he felt the need of more comic personages but he portrayed them with his usual restraint in an effort to avoid the farce and buffoonery of his predecessor.

## Character Portrayal in Plautus and Terence

I quite disagree with Juniper's statement that "because they had entirely different viewpoints no study of character portrayal in Plautus and Terence taken together can give very gratifying results."[66] On the contrary, a clear picture of the methods and aims of the two playwrights cannot clearly be discerned otherwise. There are two reasons for this: (1) the roles are, with minor exceptions, the same and it is important to see how Plautus delights in certain characters, magnifying and exaggerating their parts for purposes of farcical humor, whereas Terence is chiefly interested in portraying decent, serious-minded persons in situations more pathetic than comic; the contrast between the two playwrights in this respect is most enlightening; (2) the methods of character portrayal used by each dramatist are also identical. Since the preceding discussion has been devoted primarily to the numerous roles of comedy and the traits of the individual characters, a few remarks on the technique of characterization in Roman comedy will be in order.

Characters are revealed by their actions and by description. The description may be self-description in song or dialogue, or it may be pronounced by another character either in the absence of the subject (in which case it is most apt to be accurate) or in his presence, either to his face or within his hearing.[67] The songs of different individuals about love early in the action are helpful in revealing their true nature; compare, for instance, the *canticum* of the upright Lysiteles (*Trin.* 223 ff.) with that of the more dissolute Philolaches (*Most.* 84 ff.) or, better still, with that of the old reprobate Lysidamus (*Cas.* 217 ff.). The comic value of the long monologues in which the parasites describe themselves and their sorry existence has already been mentioned. Euclio reveals his true character in his monologues (*Aul.* 105 ff., 371 ff., 460 ff.) as does Micio at the beginning of the *Adelphoe.* Dialogues are even more effective for revealing character; witness the conversation of Scapha and Philematium (*Most.* 157 ff.) in which the traits of each are naturally introduced. The contrast here between the two women is unusually successful. Character description by another person is sometimes exaggerated (cf., e.g., *Aul.* 298 ff.) but normally is accurate and is

[66] *CJ* 31 (1935-36), p. 276.
[67] Cf. Wilner, *CPh* 33 (1938), pp. 22 ff., 31 ff. for a discussion of these descriptions. In several of Plautus' expository prologues (e.g., *Aulularia, Mercator, Miles*) the fundamental traits of the prominent characters are set forth, as is done also in Diniarchus' opening monologue in the *Truculentus.*

verified by the actions of the person described during the course of the action. When characterizations are erroneously given they result from the misapprehension of the speaker and are useful also for contrasting the false and the true traits of an individual. This, we have already seen, is particularly true of wives—Alcumena (*Amphitruo*) and Sostrata (*Hecyra*)—and courtesans—Thais (*Eunuchus*) and Bacchis (*Hecyra*).[68]

Two important devices of character portrayal, used by both playwrights, are contrast and repetition. In the plays of Terence where, as a result of the duality method, there are usually two *senes* or two *adulescentes*, contrast of the principal characters is easily achieved, e.g., Chremes and Menedemus (*Heauton*), Aeschinus and Ctesipho (*Adelphoe*). Micio compares his brother's way with his own (*Ad.* 34 ff.) as does Demea (855 ff.). There is direct contrast in each passage, and also between the two passages, in which the two men are seen from opposite points of view; neither view is complete or accurate but each corrects the other. Miss Wilner says that this is "the most sophisticated technique of character portrayal which we can find in the extant plays of Plautus and Terence."[69]

Although Plautus does not favor the duality method, he also makes great use of contrast. Fathers and sons are contrasted not only in the *Bacchides*[70] but in the *Mercator* and *Trinummus*; the *Casina* has contrasted pairs of wives, husbands, and slaves. The wives of the *Stichus*, the *senes* and the *adulescentes* of the *Epidicus*, the lovers of the *Truculentus* all form interesting pairs. Both Plautus and Terence occasionally contrast two persons by placing them in different scenes of a similar nature. The manner in which Laches and Phidippus both rebuke their wives reveals the basic difference between the two men (*Hec.* 198 ff., 523 ff.) and there is a decided contrast between the reactions of Sosia and those of Amphitruo to the same confusing situation of mistaken identity (*Amph.* 292 ff., 676 ff.).

The structure of many plays makes it possible for the playwright to portray character by repetition. The plot of the *Aulularia* consists of a series of repetitions as Euclio tries first to safeguard, then to regain, his treasure. Each episode serves to reveal his character more fully. In the *Mostellaria* there is a series of devices to keep Theopropides from learning the truth about his son; similarly the *Adelphoe* displays the reactions of Demea to successive reports about the actions, both good and bad, of his sons; later he retaliates with a series of "generous" deeds

---

[68] See above, pp. 260 ff. Other characters who are believed to be different from what they really are include Mnesilochus and Pistoclerus (*Bacch.* 457 ff., 489 ff.), Demipho (*Merc.* 61 ff.), Pamphilus (*And.* 88 ff.), Ctesipho (*Ad.* 138 f.). See Wilner, *CPh* 25 (1930), pp. 64 f.; 33 (1938), p. 32.

[69] *CPh* 33 (1938), p. 31; cf. *CPh* 25 (1930), pp. 59 f.

[70] This play, based upon a Menandrian original, displays the duality method in a somewhat rudimentary form; see above, p. 185.

at his brother's expense (*Ad.* 883 ff.). In all such cases the repetition of details, as well as the repetition of episodes, helps to delineate the characters.[71]

What then, in summary, can we say about the portrayal of character in Plautus and Terence? Both use the same methods to bring out the fundamental traits of their personages; that each is interested in the delineation of character is shown conclusively by the care with which they portray even minor and inorganic persons. In general, the characters are differentiated rather than individualized. They are far more than stock types, but they lack subtlety and complexity, and they do not grow or develop during the course of the play—with the possible exception of Demea in the *Adelphoe*.

Plautus favored characters that lent themselves to farcical treatment (e.g., clever and witty slaves, parasites, slavedealers, soldiers), and in his portrayal of ordinary types he stressed the weaknesses and peculiarities that would best entertain his audiences. With a few exceptions, notably the admirable Alcumena, his characters are hardly true to life, but they are vivid and amusing and well suited to the type of farce in which they appear. His outstanding characters (Euclio, Ballio, Pyrgopolynices) are imaginative and fantastic creations which in part perhaps stem (through Naevius) from earlier Roman farce; there is nothing comparable to such characters in the extant plays of New Comedy; the exaggerated treatment of these characters (and especially the development of the clever slave into a cunning master of intrigue) must be included among the Roman and Plautine features of ancient comedy.

The characters of Terence are more true to life and closer to the Greek originals but here too we undoubtedly have more than mere imitation. In his effort to lift his characters to a higher and more serious level Terence may well have distorted or lost the psychological truthfulness of his models. He avoids farcical roles, especially in his earlier comedies, and when they do appear they lack the boldness and imagination so characteristic of Plautus. Terence portrays normal, decent, well-meaning individuals—characters that are almost too good to be real, especially in the *Hecyra*, where we find his most unconventional characterization—and they are, in general, not only less amusing than those of Plautus but less interesting as well and almost monotonous in their goodness.[72] However, Terence does display an insight into the complexities of human nature that is entirely lacking in Plautus. Although

---

[71] For a fuller treatment of repetition in the portrayal of character, see Wilner, *CPh* 25 (1930), pp. 66 ff. Cf. also Juniper, *CJ* 31 (1935-36), pp. 282 f., who correctly states that "the function of repetition is more definitely to produce humor than to portray character."

[72] Cf. Henry, *SPhNC* 12 (1915), p. 94, who attributes this monotony to the monotony of the Terentian plot. On the greater variety to be found in Plautus' plots, see above, "Variety in Plautus and Terence" in chap. 6.

in his later plays he introduces more farcical roles and situations, the portrayal of character does not suffer. Nowhere in Roman comedy do we find characterization to surpass that of Micio and Demea in the *Adelphoe*.

# CHAPTER 10

## THOUGHT AND MORAL TONE

THE preceding chapter presented an analysis of the roles of Roman comedy and a brief description of the manner in which Plautus and Terence handled characterization in their plays. Even more important are the ideas of the characters, their attitudes towards various significant aspects of life—social, ethical, and religious. What do the characters themselves say about religion, education, money, marriage, and sex? What insight can we derive concerning the moral concepts of the playwrights and of the moral tone of Roman comedy in general?

It should be clearly understood that no historical picture of ancient life is here contemplated. To attempt to derive from the comedies of Plautus and Terence a clear and coherent account of Roman economic and social life is obviously unwise, for the plays are Greek in theme and setting; the lives of the characters and the ideas which they express reflect Greek far more than Roman conditions. Yet these ideas and conditions were by no means unintelligible to the Romans, for the plays, to achieve the popularity which they are known to have had, necessarily presented social and economic views which the spectators could understand and the humorous or farcical treatment of which they could appreciate and enjoy. The events of everyday life—financial dealings, the earning of a livelihood, love-affairs, marriage, the rearing and education of children, the position of slaves—all these were problems of Roman life as of Greek.

Plautus, however, made to his spectators many concessions which Terence was unwilling to make. The younger playwright, wishing to preserve the Greek atmosphere of his comedies, steadfastly refused to Romanize his productions and (except in his prologues) avoided all mention of Roman places and events. Plautus had less regard for the dramatic illusion; just as his characters joke about stage conventions or introduce allusions to persons, places, and events in Rome and Italy, so we find in his plays many allusions to military, political, and legal institutions and to details of social and private life which at first glance seem far more Roman than Greek. These passages have been collected and discussed at length elsewhere, some scholars maintaining that Plautus consistently refers to customs and institutions distinctly Roman, others believing that many such allusions are basically Greek rather than Roman.[1] In many instances it is impossible to determine with

---

[1] Cf. e.g., in the realm of legal phraseology the summary of earlier views in Schwind, *Ueber das Recht bei Terenz*, pp. 3 ff.; Berceanu, *La vente consensuelle*, pp. 7 ff.; see also Fredershausen, *De iure Plautino et Terentiano*, and the continuation in *H* 47 (1912), pp. 199 ff. For the historical allusions in the plays (many of them possible but hardly probable), see Buck, *A Chronology of the Plays of Plautus*, pp. 25 ff., and cf.

exactitude whether a given passage is Greek or Roman for we may have Greek customs presented in Roman terms for the purpose of greater intelligibility.

Also, we are dealing with comic drama and must, therefore, not overlook the probability that much in the plays is true of neither Greek nor Roman life but rather is presented in an exaggerated and fantastic guise for comic purposes. Even Terence, who avoids the grotesque and farcical elements so numerous in Plautus, does not portray life exactly as it was lived in Hellenistic Athens. Neither playwright is writing problem plays on social themes but inevitably, in the works of each, passages of serious thought occur and even the portrayal of characters in ludicrous situations may have an ethical function. The sight of moral disproportion on the stage may point a better way and laughter may enable the spectators to view moral issues more objectively.

## Wealth and Poverty

The characters of Roman comedy represent a well-to-do upper middle-class Greek society; they sometimes refer to their own wealth or to that of others (e.g., *Aul.* 166, *Mil.* 676 ff., *Ad.* 500 ff.), they own country estates as well as city houses, and they frequently go abroad on business trips. Yet the society portrayed is not necessarily one of extreme or even great wealth, and often the possession of a country home or a trip abroad on business is merely a useful device whereby the playwright can motivate the temporary absence of a character.[2] Everyone possesses slaves, but in a slave economy this means little; in nineteenth-century England even persons of relatively moderate means were dependent upon cooks, maids, governesses, gardeners. So Sostrata in the *Adelphoe* is in impoverished circumstances (cf. 302 f., 605 ff.) but has two slaves, Geta (who supports the household, cf. 481 f.) and Canthara; likewise in the *Aulularia* Euclio, a poor man (before the discovery of the treasure), owns a faithful and hard-working maid, Staphyla. Neither great wealth nor abject poverty is encountered in the comedies. There is occasional emphasis upon the poverty of the heroine (cf. *Heaut.* 274 ff., *Phorm.* 95 ff.) but the purpose of such passages is to arouse sympathy for the maiden's plight. The parasites are poor, but their hunger and desire for food are stressed by Plautus for the sake of

---

my review in *AJPh* 64 (1943), pp. 348 ff. Material on Roman social and private life has been collected, somewhat uncritically, by Westaway (*The Original Element in Plautus*, pp. 37 ff.) and Leffingwell (*Social and Private Life at Rome*). For bibliography, see Enk, *Handboek der Latijnse Letterkunde*, II, 1, 2, pp. 308 ff.

[2] E.g., Dorippa returns from the country in *Merc.* 667 ff., Phaedria goes to the country at Thais' request (*Eun.* 187 f.), and sons are wrongly assumed to be at the *villa* in *Most.* 928 ff., *Ad.* 400 ff. The return of leading characters from abroad during the course of the action is an essential feature of many plots; cf. *Amph.* 153, 551, *Bacch.* 385, *Capt.* 922, *Curc.* 280, *Epid.* 104, *Most.* 431, *Stich.* 402, *Trin.* 820, *Phorm.* 231, 567, *Hec.* 281. Cf. Knapp, *CPh* 2 (1907), pp. 19 ff., 281 ff.

274 THOUGHT AND MORAL TONE

comedy; they are funniest when they fail to gain the hoped-for meal (e.g., Peniculus in the *Menaechmi*, Gelasimus in the *Stichus*) and we are not justified in looking upon them as the victims of a hard-hearted and selfish social order. As for the slave, he lacks liberty, but in most instances he lives well and enjoys material comfort (provided, of course, that he behaves himself). Dunkin's statement[3] that "the Slave is the important Poor Man" gives an entirely erroneous impression of the position of the slave in Roman comedy.

Actually, in many plays the truly poor man is the *adulescens*; monetary considerations play a large part in many plots, for in order to consummate his love affair the youth must pay money either to the courtesan or to the slavedealer who has the girl in his possession. But the father has the money, not the youth, and the latter often complains of his penniless condition (e.g., *Pseud.* 80 ff., *Phorm.* 534 ff.). In *Pseud.* 286 ff. Ballio suggests three possibilities to the unhappy Calidorus: borrowing money, getting it from a moneylender at interest, stealing it from his father. All three methods appear in the comedies:

(1) The *adulescens* attempts to borrow from a friend; the usual response is that of Chaeribulus (*Epid.* 116), "I would promise it if I had it" (cf. 331, *Bacch.* 635; in *Pers.* 45 two slaves have the roles of impecunious youth and unhelpful friend). Lending to a friend was a thankless business, at best; Stasimus says (*Trin.* 1051 ff.):

If you give anyone a loan, it's lost and no longer your own; when you ask it back, you find that your kindness has turned a friend into an enemy. If you press him for the money, you have a choice of two things: either you lose your loan or your friend.

Occasionally a friend supplies the needed money, e.g., Charinus in *Pseud.* 734 (cf. *Pers.* 251 ff., 321) but in most instances the youth must get the money elsewhere.

(2) Demipho suggests (*Phorm.* 295 ff.) that Antipho, instead of marrying Phanium, should have given her a dowry and married her to someone else, borrowing the money at interest if necessary. In order to purchase the girls whom they loved, both Stratippocles (*Epid.* 52 ff.) and Philolaches (*Most.* 623 ff.) borrowed forty minae from moneylenders at a high rate of interest.[4] But often a youth could not borrow money from a banker or moneylender. He was considered a bad risk (cf. *Merc.* 51 f.); furthermore, contracts made by minors were not binding.[5]

---

[3] *Post-Aristophanic Comedy*, p. 102; cf. p. 136.

[4] The moneylender in *Most.* 592, 598 ff. insists upon his interest first but in the *Epidicus* the interest (four minae) is later ignored even though the rate seems exorbitant; cf. Duckworth, *T. Macci Plauti Epidicus*, p. 138.

[5] Cf. *Pseud.* 303 f., where Calidorus refers to the *lex quinavicenaria*; people were afraid to trust him because he was a minor under twenty-five. This is an allusion to a Roman law, the *lex Plaetoria*, which protected minors from the results of contracts which were not to their best interests. Athenian youths came of age at eighteen and

(3) The third possibility suggested by Ballio was stealing the money from the youth's father. Here it becomes the task of the young man's slave to aid his impecunious master. In several plays the slave does deceive the *senex* and procure money but the success of the intrigue is only temporary; sooner or later the youth's father realizes the extent to which he has been tricked (cf. *Bacch.* 1088 ff., *Epid.* 671 f., *Most.* 1032 ff., *Heaut.* 950 ff.).

A fourth and most likely possibility is for the helpful slave to deceive the *leno* himself; this was not mentioned by Ballio—one could hardly expect him to suggest it—but it is a type of intrigue which in Plautus' comedies is most amusing and always successful; cf. the tricking of Cappadox (*Curculio*), Dordalus (*Persa*), Lycus (*Poenulus*), and Ballio himself (*Pseudolus*). The *leno*, like the *miles*, is a character frequently despised and ridiculed and thus is eminently suitable to be an object of deception.

For the average *adulescens* of Roman comedy love was an expensive business; Beare seems correct in defining love in comedy as "that emotion which causes a man to forget, for the time being, how many minas there are in a talent."[6] The slave girls of comedy range in cost from twenty minae, e.g., Philaenium (*Asin.* 89, 230), Phoenicium (*Pseud.* 51 f., 344), Ctesipho's sweetheart (*Ad.* 191 f.), to forty minae (cf. *Epid.* 51 f.). Phaedria thinks his sweetheart cheap at thirty minae (*Phorm.* 558) and Philolaches pays thirty for Philematium (*Most.* 300), borrowing forty from the *danista* (623). If such a girl cost thirty minae, i.e., half a talent, or about $550, she was a very expensive luxury since an attractive town house could be bought for two talents (cf. *Most.* 644)—four times the amount—or even much less; in the *Trinummus* Lesbonicus sells his house to Callicles for forty minae (cf. 125 f., 403)—the cost of Stratippocles' captive in the *Epidicus.*

The greater purchasing power of money in Hellenistic times is indicated by the fact that Erotium in *Men.* 219 ff. gives the cook three *nummi* to buy food for a dinner for three (or ten, since Cylindrus says that Peniculus eats as much as eight men). The value of the amount, even if the *nummus* here equals a two-drachma piece, could hardly be more than $1.50 and was probably much less.[7] Skilled laborers worked in Hellenistic times for two drachmae a day yet a girl like Philematium cost three thousand drachmae. In view of the much greater purchasing power of ancient money, it seems safe to say that thirty minae spent for a girl would be the equivalent today, not of $500 or $600, but rather of

---

after that were able to make contracts of every kind. See also *Rud.* 1380 ff., where the aged Labrax impudently suggests that he is under twenty-five and therefore not bound by his contract with Gripus.

[6] *CR* 42 (1928), p. 110.

[7] At times the *nummus* seems equivalent to any small coin; cf. Frank, *AJPh* 54 (1933), pp. 369 ff.

$4,000 or $5,000. Perhaps we have here an indication of the excessive extravagance of young men like Philolaches. Are fathers who complain of the dissolute lives of their sons to be condemned as unduly miserly and unreasonable? We have also clear evidence that the cost of girls was grossly exaggerated for comic purposes.[8] The amount of the dowry which a father provided for his daughter was similarly exaggerated. One talent or less was considered an ample dowry in Hellenistic times, even for families of wealth,[9] but in *And.* 950 f. Chremes offers a dowry of ten talents (cf. also *Merc.* 703; in *Truc.* 845 Callicles deducts six talents to penalize Diniarchus for his rash behavior), and in *Cist.* 561 f. we hear of a dowry of twenty talents—an incredibly large sum. Comic exaggeration of this type was apparently inherited from the Greek plays; the passage quoted by Aulus Gellius (II, 23) from Menander's *Plocium* contains an allusion to a dowry of sixteen talents.

The sharp practices of moneylenders and slavedealers in their financial transactions were notorious; men like Ballio (*Pseudolus*) and Labrax (*Rudens*) and Dorio (*Phormio*) did not hesitate to break their word when they saw a chance for greater profit elsewhere, and such actions have their dramatic value in that the difficulties of the youth were immeasurably increased. Labrax swears a solemn oath to pay Gripus a talent for the hamper (*Rud.* 1332 ff.), but says later (1355) in words reminiscent of Euripides' Hippolytus (*Hipp.* 612):

My tongue may swear, but I still do as I please.

Still later, when he denies owing the money, Gripus protests (1372 ff.):

GR.: Didn't you just swear an oath?
LA.: I did, and I'll swear again, if it's my pleasure. Oaths were invented to save property, not to lose it.

When Ballio loses his wager with Simo, he tries to avoid payment by saying that it was all a joke (*per iocum, Pseud.* 1224) and he said earlier that even if he were sacrificing to Jupiter, he would walk out on the ceremony if a chance to make money turned up (265 ff.). Bankers also were held in bad repute; e.g., *Pers.* 435 f. (cf. 442 f.):

When money is entrusted to them, they flee from the forum more quickly than a hare when it is let out at the games.

It is amusing that both this passage and the denunciation of bankers in *Curc.* 679 ff. are spoken by slavedealers. But Lyco's own words (*Curc.*

---

[8] In the Greek world of the second century B.C. the normal manumission price of slaves seems to have varied from three to five minae; there were of course exceptions. Neaera, a famous courtesan of the fourth century B.C., cost twenty minae (cf. Demosthenes, *in Neaeram*, 32). The high price of girls in Greek and Roman comedy was a tribute to their beauty and charm and an indication of their desirability. Cf. Delcourt, *AC* 17 (1948), pp. 123 ff., who considers that the exceptional prices have a psychological basis in the devotion of the lovers.

[9] Cf. Ferguson, *Hellenistic Athens*, p. 68.

371 ff.) confirm the criticism of bankers, and Curculio puts the *leno* and the *trapezita* in the same class (506 ff.). All such statements are part of the conventional presentation of these characters as the comic "villains" of the plays.

The *senes* of Roman comedy are interested in business ventures and in making money, as are their wives. Ignorant of her husband's double life, Nausistrata complains about his carelessness in managing the farm which her father left him (*Phorm.* 788 ff., cf. 1013), and in the *Asinaria* Artemona apparently handles all the finances (cf. 84 ff., 94 f.). Different ways of making money (or, as in this case, of losing it) are mentioned by Philto in *Trin.* 330 ff.:

How did he lose it? Was he engaged in public contracts or maritime commerce? Was it by trading, or did he lose it dealing in slaves?[10]

The attitudes of the characters towards money seem sometimes far from praiseworthy. Philto points out to his son that to give food and drink to a beggar is a loss for it merely prolongs his life for further misery (339 f.)—a most inhumane attitude. He tells his son he should not pity others to such an extent that others will have to pity him (343); in other words, as Cicero was to say later (*De off.* 1, 14, 44), generosity should not exceed one's means. Philto's words, however, have as their chief purpose the portrayal by contrast of Lysiteles' generosity towards Lesbonicus and can hardly be used to prove the selfishness and meanness of the average Plautine *senex*. Theopropides too has often been criticized; he refuses to consider reselling the house which he thinks his son has just purchased (*Most.* 799 ff.):

If it had been a bad purchase, we wouldn't be permitted to sell it back. Whatever profit there is we ought to keep.

Such a sentiment undoubtedly appealed to many a Roman spectator. But Theopropides, unlike most *senes* of comedy, seems indifferent to everything but his financial welfare; the corrupt life of his son bothers him less than the money which has been squandered, and he is willing to pardon Philolaches when Callidamates offers to make full restitution (1160 f.).

Very different is Demea. When Micio explains that the two young brothers can use his money and that Demea therefore will not be affected by their extravagance (*Ad.* 815 ff.), the *senex* is still distressed: "It's not the money, it's their way of life." Micio may be correct in that the one vice of old age is excessive attention to monetary matters (cf. *Ad.* 831 ff.) but the comic *senex* as a rule is honest, even if shrewd and thrifty.[11] Daemones refuses to accept stolen property and wants no part

[10] Cf. Leffingwell, *Social and Private Life at Rome*, pp. 101 ff. for a discussion of the manner in which the methods listed in this passage reflect the business interests of the Romans.

[11] Dunkin (*Post-Aristophanic Comedy*, p. 61) curiously refers to "the Rich Man's

in wealth gained by deception (*Rud.* 1235 ff.) and Callicles faces unjust suspicion and abuse in order to protect the financial interests of his friend (cf. *Trin.* 153 ff.). In general, money and virtue are not equated in the comedies even though old Antipho maintains that money and friends go hand in hand (*Stich.* 520 ff.). That wealth brings responsibilities and obligations is clear from Hegio's words in *Ad.* 500 ff. and 605 ff.

Thus monetary considerations are prominent in the works of both playwrights but in their treatment of financial dealings no sharp distinction can be made between Plautus and Terence. I can see no evidence, therefore, for the view that "in the plays of Terence money is the motivating factor because it is the standard of respectability" or that "Terence's plays are highly artistic and philosophical studies of the gentleman of property trying to maintain his convention."[12] The characters of Terence's comedies are in general more respectable than many Plautine characters, not because they are richer but because they are portrayed as less ludicrous and grotesque; also, Terence uses less frequently and exploits less fully the more humorous roles—soldiers and slavedealers and parasites. The nature of the Plautine delineation derives from the playwright's conception of comedy, not from a desire to ridicule wealth or the rich man as such. There are in Plautus passages of a serious nature, as well as an abundance of fun, but that a Roman audience would find in his comedies "the Poor Man's complaint against ruthless exploitation"[13] is incredible. Such a view is an unwarranted ascription of modern socialistic beliefs to an ancient dramatist whose treatment of his characters for comic purposes lends no support to the theory.

On the contrary, the spectators of Roman comedy, being practical, business-minded persons, would follow with interest the financial transactions of the comedies, the various scenes of bargaining and sharp practices, and they would be delighted when greedy profit-seekers like Dordalus (*Persa*) and Lycus (*Poenulus*) were themselves outsmarted. Denunciations of extravagance and riotous living would appeal to them, as would complaints about the evils of dowered wives, but they hardly could fail to realize that all such discussions of monetary matters were exaggerated for comic effect. The convenience of the dramatist also must be considered; broken pledges and attempts at speedy profit were as useful dramatically to the playwrights as were business trips abroad

---

Golden Rule, 'Honesty is the best policy.'" Does he favor dishonesty for the poor man?

[12] Dunkin, *Post-Aristophanic Comedy*, pp. 107, 137. As an illustration of Dunkin's argument that Terence equates wealth and virtue, cf. p. 108, n. 4: Chremes (*Phormio*) is a scamp, but he has lost his money; "hence, the class of Good Rich Man is not disgraced"; p. 122: Hegio (*Adelphoe*) is a good man, therefore he is not really poor, merely "Stage-Poor." See Duckworth, *AJPh* 68 (1947), pp. 423 f.

[13] Cf. Dunkin, *Post-Aristophanic Comedy*, p. 140.

or the excessive extravagance of young wastrels. The conventional
social and financial background of the plays and the attitudes of the
characters towards poverty and wealth reflect closely neither Greek nor
Roman life, as the average citizen knew it, but rather they present a
blend of comic fantasy and reality—a reality which in Terence's comedies remains Greek. Plautus' admixture of Greek and Roman elements
and his far greater dependence upon improbable situation and grotesque
characterization heighten the sense of unreality in his comedies but do
not detract from their vigor and vividness. Certainly, from the evidence
of the plays, we are not justified in drawing conclusions about the attitude of either Roman playwright towards the wealthy citizens of
his day.

## Love and Marriage

Young men in their late teens and earlier twenties have always been
susceptible to feminine charms and wiles, and the *adulescens* of Roman
comedy was no exception. There are few plays in which love does not
have a prominent role although many of the comedies seem less concerned with love itself than with its consequences; that is, the love
affairs serve to motivate a deception which becomes the chief interest
of the playwright, or they create a series of misunderstandings which
are resolved by an *anagnorisis*. Both Plautus and Terence, however,
are interested in the joys and sorrows of young lovers and do not hesitate to describe their emotions in detail. Actually, there are few ardent
love scenes in Terence's comedies since his heroines so often do not
appear on the stage. The happy reunion of Antiphila and Clinia (*Heaut.*
403 ff.) pales by comparison with the more impassioned words of
Phaedromus and Planesium (*Curc.* 164 ff.), of Philolaches and Philematium (*Most.* 294 ff.). Plautus has seldom portrayed with more sentiment the devotion of lover and sweetheart than in the farewell scene of
Argyrippus and Philaenium (*Asin.* 591 ff.) :

AR.: Why do you hold me back?
PH.: Because I miss you when you're away.
AR.: Farewell!
PH.: I'd fare much better if you'd only remain.
AR.: Good-bye!
PH.: What's good in store for me, when your departure brings only sor-
row?...
AR.: Again farewell! I'll see you in the underworld, for I am determined to
depart this life as quickly as possible.
PH.: What? You desire to condemn me, an innocent, to death?
AR.: I? If I knew that you were dying, I'd gladly give my life to save you.
PH.: Why then do you threaten to kill yourself? For what do you think I'll
do if you carry out your threat? I'm resolved, if you die, to do the same.
AR.: O sweeter than sweet honey!
PH.: You are all my life to me.

But this sentimental scene degenerates into coarse farce when Libanus and Leonida begin to ridicule the two lovers.

There are various reasons why the young men of comedy fall in love.[14] Sometimes it is mere sexual gratification; a girl's beauty may arouse sensuous desire, and this is particularly true of youths like Lyconides and Aeschinus, whose love-affairs begin with the seduction of a girl. Lyconides says to Euclio (*Aul.* 794 f.) :

I admit that I wronged your daughter at Ceres' festival through wine and youthful impulse.

And Hegio says Aeschinus (*Ad.* 470 f.) :

He was aroused by darkness, passion, wine, youth. It's human nature.

*Nox, amor, uinum, adulescentia*—these were potent factors in initiating many of the love affairs of comedy (cf. also *Bacch.* 87 f.; in *Truc.* 829 ff. Callicles says that wine is not a sufficient excuse). But physical desire is only one of many reasons; the lover finds in his sweetheart qualities of mind and heart which attract him—tenderness, gratitude, fidelity; at times he feels a sense of duty to the girl who has entrusted herself and her love to his keeping (cf. *And.* 282 ff.), or love and pity are mingled (cf. *Phorm.* 91 ff.). As for the girls of comedy, they too have various reasons for falling in love—physical desire (cf. *Pseud.* 66 ff.), mutual affection, gratitude for being freed from slavery. Some women yield to their lovers for purely mercenary reasons, but these are hardened courtesans like Phronesium, whose true nature Diniarchus realizes when he sums up the dilemma of the lover (*Truc.* 49 f.) :

If the nights he spends with her are few, his peace of mind is ruined; if the nights are many, he is happy, but his money is gone.

So the angry Erotium tells Menaechmus that he shan't enjoy her favors again unless he brings money (*Men.* 694).

The restraints imposed upon young women of marriageable age in Hellenistic and Roman life are reflected in the love affairs of comedy. There were few opportunities for meeting socially the daughters of reputable citizens; hence the girls beloved by the *adulescentes* were usually either courtesans (e.g., Phronesium in the *Truculentus*, Bacchis in the *Heauton*), slave-girls in the power of a *leno* (e.g., Planesium in the *Curculio*, Palaestra in the *Rudens*), or girls in humble circumstances (often the supposed daughter or sister of a courtesan, e.g., Selenium in the *Cistellaria*, Glycerium in the *Andria*). Many of the heroines would have been doomed to a courtesan's life if they had not been freed from their owners or (as frequently happened) if they had not been discovered to be of respectable parentage. In some cases the

---

[14] For a more detailed treatment of this point, see Legrand-Loeb, *The New Greek Comedy*, pp. 142 ff.

girl remained a virgin and the youthful lover boasted of his self-restraint (cf. *Curc.* 51, *Epid.* 110); at times the girl had already become the mistress of the youth prior to the discovery of her identity; this was true of both Selenium and Glycerium. When the parentage of the heroine is revealed by a recognition scene, the obstacle to marriage is removed,[15] and it is significant that the youth welcomes the opportunity either to marry his loved one or to legalize a pre-existing union—an attitude which indicates that his passion was more than a mere passing fancy.

Not many youths in comedy fall in love with the daughters of their neighbors—girls of the same social status—and when they do the affair usually begins with an unfortunate episode of rape at a nocturnal religious festival. The marriage takes place but only after a long delay caused by the youth's indecision or his fear of parental disapproval. Meanwhile a child is born. In the case of Aeschinus, there can be no doubt of his love of Pamphila, but Micio's reproach seems well justified (*Ad.* 686 ff.):

You wronged a girl whom you had no right to touch. This was your first great sin, and a great one, and yet it is human nature. Many good men have often done the same thing. But tell me this: after it happened, did you ever show any realization of what was to be done? If you were ashamed to tell me the truth, how was I to learn about it? While you were hesitating, ten months passed by. As far as was in your power, you have betrayed yourself, the poor girl, and your son. Did you think the gods would do everything for you in your sleep and install her in your bedroom as your wife without any effort on your part?

In the *Aulularia* not only the birth of a child but also his uncle's desire to marry the girl spurs Lyconides to action. Diniarchus in the *Truculentus* seems too enamored of Phronesium to have much regard for Callicles' daughter, to whom he is betrothed; but he admits that he is the father of her child and begs to marry her. Callicles retorts (842 ff.):

Marry her? I think you decided that point long ago. You didn't wait for me to let you have her; you took her for yourself. Now that you've got her, you may keep her. But I'll penalize you with this big fine: I'll deduct six talents from her dowry because of this stupid act of yours.

There are two instances where love affairs between young people of the same social status do not involve pre-marital intercourse. Beare says of Charinus (*Andria*): "In the alterations which Terence introduced into his Greek originals we find something approaching a modern attitude in love and sex. Charinus is the first example in European literature of a youth pining with honourable affection for a maiden of equal station."[16] Beare perhaps claims too much for Terentian originality

---

[15] With the exception of the *Epidicus*, where Telestis proves to be Stratippocles' half-sister.

[16] *Ha* 56 (1940), pp. 35 f.

here. The attitude of Lysiteles towards Lesbonicus' sister in Plautus' *Trinummus* is equally honorable although his affection seems less intense, and he insists upon marriage without a dowry as a favor to his friend Lesbonicus (cf. 328, 333).

Marriage thus seems a highly desirable goal to the young men and women of Roman comedy. At times marriage is out of the question because of the girl's social status; in such cases the lover retains possession of his sweetheart in an extra-legal union; whenever marriage is possible the youth in almost every instance marries the girl of his choice.[17] One of the most attractive pictures of married love is given, surprisingly enough, by Bacchis in the *Heauton*, when she contrasts the life of a courtesan with that of a virtuous girl who looks forward to marriage; she says to Antiphila (388 ff.) :

> It's to your advantage to be good. The men with whom we deal won't let us be; our lovers cherish us because they are won over by our beauty; when that is gone they transfer their affections elsewhere and, unless we've provided for ourselves meanwhile, we're left forlorn. But when you women have decided to spend your life with one man whose character is as like your own as possible, you find husbands devoted to you, and you are both bound so closely by mutual love that no disaster can ever separate you.

But even for courtesans a good character is considered far more desirable than jewelry and beautiful clothing (cf. *Most.* 290 f., *Poen.* 301 ff.), and in the case of wives nobility of character is better than a dowry (cf. *Amph.* 839 ff., *Aul.* 239).

But what of the portrayal of married life in the comedies? Is the married state pictured as a happy and desirable one? With a few exceptions the answer must be in the negative. Alcumena is devoted to her husband and is genuinely distressed when he accuses her of adultery (cf. *Amph.* 882 ff.) and the two wives in the *Stichus* remain true to their absent husbands. In the *Phormio*, Antipho is made miserable by the thought that his bride may be taken from him. Pamphilus in the *Hecyra* loves his wife and grieves when he learns of her pre-marital misfortune, not realizing that he is the cause of her difficulties; he is torn between his love and what he conceives to be the honorable course to follow, now that, as he believes, she has given birth to the child of

---

[17] The exceptions are few: in *Trin.* 1183 f. Lesbonicus promises to marry a girl selected by his father. Clitipho in the *Heauton* is compelled to give up Bacchis and take a wife; he is allowed to choose the girl, however (1064 ff.). In the *Epidicus* the marriage is impossible; Stratippocles learns that the girl he loves is his half-sister and Epidicus then suggests (653) that he return to his former love. Copley (*AJPh* 70, 1949, p. 23) overstresses the ephemeral and physical nature of the ancient love affair when he says that it "had nothing whatever to do with marriage." The fact that so many love affairs of comedy end in marriage can hardly be dismissed as "quite accidental." Chaerea, after the seduction of Pamphila, is eager to marry her (*Eun.* 613 f.) and is delighted when his father approves of the marriage (1031 ff.). Harsh (*A Handbook of Classical Drama*, p. 388) seems correct when he says that Chaerea's desire to possess Pamphila in the future "is as natural to his character as it is necessary to the plot."

another man (403 ff.). But it should be noted that the marital devotion displayed in these cases is that of young persons. Married life among older people is consistently portrayed as unpleasant and disagreeable— a state to be endured rather than enjoyed. As Menander had said, "Marriage is an evil, but a necessary evil."[18]

Wives complain about the treatment they receive from their husbands—unjust criticism, indifference, infidelity, even the theft of their clothing,[19] and they themselves are described as stubborn, quarrelsome, vain, extravagant, ungrateful; the larger the dowry they bring to their husbands, the more domineering and disagreeable they are said to be. Periphanes agrees with Apoecides (*Epid.* 180):

A dowry is a wonderful thing to have—if it comes without a wife.

Women themselves do not hesitate to find fault with their own sex; Eunomia says (*Aul.* 139 f.):

It's impossible to find a good woman; each one is worse than the other.

And Myrrhina thinks Cleustrata is wrong to oppose her husband's will (*Cas.* 191 f., 198 ff.). But with all their faults, real or imaginary, there is one vice of which the wives in comedy are not guilty—infidelity. There are passing allusions to adultery (*Cas.* 200 f., *And.* 315 f.), and Acroteleutium poses as a faithless wife in the *Miles*, but neither Plautus nor Terence brought on the stage a wife guilty of adultery (Alcumena was of course the victim of deception). As Miss Leffingwell points out, the comedies satirize all classes of citizens, but "they never reflect in any way upon the virtue of the matron."[20]

Most of the criticisms of women are uttered by their husbands. What lecherous old men in love with young girls say about their wives (e.g., Lysidamus in *Cas.* 227: "My wife tortures me by being alive"; cf. *Asin.* 900 f., *Merc.* 556 f.) may be discounted but such complaints are far from infrequent.[21] Menaechmus accuses his wife of being stubborn, stupid, and suspicious (*Men.* 110 ff.), Daemones comments upon his wife's lack of trust when he brings home two shipwrecked maidens (*Rud.* 895 f., 1045 ff.), Chremes denounces Sostrata for her ignorance and folly (*Heaut.* 632 ff.), and Laches is extremely bitter about women

---

[18] Fr. 651. Many other fragments from Middle and New Comedy contain criticisms of women and marriage; see "Middle Comedy" in chap. 2, and cf. Legrand-Loeb, *The New Greek Comedy*, pp. 116 f.

[19] Cf. *Amph.* 882 ff., *Cas.* 185 ff., *Men.* 559 ff., *Merc.* 700 ff., *Phorm.* 1009 ff., *Hec.* 274 ff.

[20] *Social and Private Life at Rome*, p. 53.

[21] According to Aulus Gellius (II, 23), Caecilius in the *Plocium* has a husband speak as follows: "Should I wish long life to a woman who always tries to rob me of whatever gives me pleasure? While I am gaping expectantly for her death, I am a dead person among the living." The Menandrian original said merely: "Oh, that I ever married Crobyle with a dowry of sixteen talents and a nose a cubit long! Am I to put up with her insolence? No, by Olympian Zeus and Athena, not at all." The desire of the husband for his wife's death, so frequent in Plautus, is here a Roman addition.

in general (*Hec.* 198 ff.) and unjustly blames his wife for driving their daughter-in-law from the house (cf. 229 ff.). It is hardly surprising that elderly *senes* who have never married proclaim loudly the joys of bachelorhood and express reluctance at the thought of taking a wife (cf. *Aul.* 154 ff., 475 ff., *Mil.* 685 ff., *Ad.* 933 ff.).

Why is the picture of married life in Roman comedy so unpleasant? Primarily because marriage is a conventional theme for jesting and, as such, bears little relation to the realities of life. The joys and sorrows of youthful love as portrayed in ancient comedy may well present a fairly truthful picture of adolescent emotion but there is little in married happiness that lends itself to comic treatment; thus the delineation of older husbands and wives departs from real life and becomes a conventional means of arousing laughter; much that we find on marriage is not to be taken seriously.[22] In the *Trinummus* Callicles and Megaronides, otherwise decent and respectable *senes*, discuss their wives in a typical Plautine fashion (51 ff.):

CA.: How's your wife? Is she well?
ME.: Better than I want her to be.
CA.: I'm delighted that she's alive and well.
ME.: Damn it! I suppose you're happy whenever I have misfortune.
CA.: Well, I want my friends to have the luck I have.
ME.: Aha, you rogue! And how's your own wife?
CA.: Immortal. She's alive and will keep on living.
ME.: That's wonderful news. I pray the gods that she may successfully survive you.
CA.: My prayer exactly, by heaven—provided that she can be your wife.

And so on. This is perhaps the *locus classicus* in Plautus for the attitude of husbands towards their wives, but that the jest is purely conventional is shown decisively by verse 66:

Pay attention now and stop your nonsense.

This type of humor is reminiscent of the joke quoted by Cicero (*De orat.* II, 69, 278):

A certain man complained that his wife had hanged herself from a fig tree. "Please," said a friend, "give me some shoots from the same tree for me to plant."

And radio jokes today are similar:

Of course I had a good vacation. We went to the seashore and the very first day my wife drowned. It was wonderful.

---

[22] Cf. Michaut, *Plaute*, I, pp. 268 f. In Legrand-Loeb (*The New Greek Comedy*, p. 116) we read that "New Comedy is misogynous"; this is misleading unless we realize that much is said in jest; cf., however, a later (and sounder) statement: "People were not so simple as to imagine that these portrayals represented—or even pretended to represent—things as they actually were in family life as a rule" (*ibid.*, p. 458).

Certainly, from jests such as these no conclusions can be drawn about family life in either ancient or modern times. There is, however, a difference between Plautus and Terence in this respect. The more farcical plots and grotesque characterizations of the former make it impossible to take seriously his references to marriage and married life. But the quarrels of husband and wife in Terence, the bitter denunciations of women such as those by Chremes (*Heaut.* 632 ff.) and Laches (*Hec.* 198 ff.) strike a discordant note; they seem more unpleasant in tone since the saving grace of humor is lacking.[23] The conventional treatment of marriage in comedy was less appropriate when the *senes* and *matronae* were more serious and respectable and resembled more closely persons in real life.

## The Problem of Education

Roman comedy (and Greek New Comedy before it) seems to have been little interested in themes of political or social significance and in this respect differed strikingly from the fifth-century productions of Aristophanes. The one exception in the social area is the problem of education—a problem which inevitably makes its appearance in plays dealing largely with the relations of fathers and sons. There are numerous references to the desires of parents to provide a training for their sons that will enable them to be thrifty and intelligent citizens able to cope with the problems of life. Even the satiric picture in the *Truculentus* of a courtesan and her dealings with her lovers presents, as it were, the obverse side of the same problem, for it shows how the rearing of young men has failed to achieve the desired result.

Philolaches in the *Mostellaria*, although he admits that he has been unable to resist the onslaught of love, gives an interesting picture of the attitude of fathers in general and of his own boyhood in particular (118 ff., 149 ff.):

Now I want to tell you why you should think that men are like houses. First of all, parents are the builders of their children; they lay the foundations, raise them up and make them strong, and spare no expense that they may be useful and attractive both to the community and to themselves; at great expense and toil they have them instructed in literature and law. . . . I grieve at heart to think of what I am now and what I was. No other youth was more devoted to athletics, and I used to enjoy the discus, javelin, ball games, running, fencing, and horseback-riding. I was a model of thrift and endurance to the others, and all the best sought instruction from me. But now I'm worthless and I've found it out for myself.

The lovesick and extravagant youth of comedy is seldom so frank. The disappointment of parents when their sons fail to come up to expecta-

---

[23] Gomme (*Essays in Greek History and Literature*, p. 281) says of Sostrata in the *Hecyra*: "Her character too is marred, not so much by anything she says, as by the trite jests about husband and wife."

tions is well illustrated by Micio's words in *Ad.* 147 ff. Perhaps in this respect the most fortunate father in all Roman comedy is Philto, whose son is a youth of exemplary character. Lysiteles says (*Trin.* 301 f., 314 ff.) :

> From my earliest youth to my present age, father, I have always obeyed your injunctions and your precepts. . . . I have taken particular pains not to go to any den of iniquity, not to go roaming around at night, not to take from another person what is his, and not to cause you any anguish. I have always kept your instructions in good repair by my own correct conduct.

After such an effusion of virtue we can only applaud when Philto replies :

> Why make a fuss about it? The good you've done was done for yourself, not for me.

By Lysiteles is not a typical *adulescens*; most young men do not follow so closely the training and advice of their elders.

The three comedies in which the problem of education plays a prominent part are Plautus' *Bacchides*, and the *Heauton* and the *Adelphoe* of Terence, all three adapted from Menandrian originals[24]—an indication that Menander concerned himself with the proper methods of training young men to a greater degree than did Diphilus and Philemon.[25] In all three plays there is a marked contrast between two educational systems—the one more rigid and severe, the other characterized by leniency and understanding, the one presumably more old-fashioned, the other a more modern and progressive and enlightened way of handling youth. Lydus, the tutor of Pistoclerus, contrasts the two methods and laments the decay of the older discipline, when a pupil was whipped by his teacher if he missed a single syllable (*Bacch.* 432 ff.). But times have changed (440 ff.) :

> Now, before a boy is seven, if you lay your hand on him, he takes his slate and breaks his tutor's head. And if you complain to his father, he says to his son, "That's my fine boy! You know how to defend yourself." . . . How can a teacher exert any authority if he is beaten first?

But the attitudes and outlooks of the young men of Roman comedy are pretty much the same (always with the exception of the upright Lysiteles), and it seems to matter little how they have been reared. The

---

[24] The *Mercator*, adapted from Philemon, contains an interesting passage (61 ff.) in which Charinus describes his father's strict upbringing; but Demipho's later passion for Pasicompsa is hardly a good recommendation of his earlier training.

[25] Dunkin, without justification, places Menander's emphasis elsewhere; he believes that in all three originals "Menander seems to have shown how in a society which does not employ its wealth honorably young men and old are corrupted" (*Post-Aristophanic Comedy*, p. 22; cf. p. 34, where he suggests that the *Dis Exapaton*, the original of the *Bacchides*, "was a philosophical study of the reaction of the Rich Man to luxury").

educational problem is presented chiefly from the standpoint of the parents in the *Heauton* and the *Adelphoe*, the Menandrian originals of which have been called "Schools for Fathers."[26] Chremes in the *Heauton* criticizes Menedemus for his former severity and for the lack of confidence between him and his son (151 ff.) and, rather than reveal to Clinia the change in his father's attitude, favors a scheme whereby Menedemus consents to be swindled; as Norwood says, "theories of education have often led to wild results, but rarely to so quaint an outcome as this."[27] Chremes, however, is hardly a successful exponent of the newer educational method; in the words of Menedemus (922 f.), "he gives advice to others and is wise away from home, but is unable to help himself." And Clitipho, Chremes' son, says (213 ff.):

How unjustly fathers judge their sons! They expect us to turn at once from boys to old men and have nothing to do with the pleasures of youth. Parents govern us according to their present desires, not according to what their desires used to be. If I ever have a son, he will find me an easygoing father.

The innate harshness of Chremes appears when he discovers that he, rather than Menedemus, has been tricked.

The issue in the *Adelphoe* is more clearcut. Demea and Micio, as we have seen,[28] represent the two conflicting systems. Neither system is successful, as Demea proves when he gives up his severity and reveals by a *reductio ad absurdum* how Micio's character has been undermined by his own leniency. Neither Aeschinus nor Ctesipho lived up to his father's expectations. Terence favors neither extreme but a compromise that involves a reasonable amount of restraint and advice (cf. 992 ff.). If the scales seem tipped in favor of discipline, we should recall that throughout most of the comedy Micio is presented far more sympathetically than Demea, and also that Aeschinus proves to be a far more attractive and upright youth than Ctesipho; his regret for his misdeeds and his love and respect for his adoptive father (cf. 681 ff., 707 ff.) indicate that Micio's system (as outlined in 68 ff.) was, in spite of its disadvantages, preferable to Demea's harshness.

Had the dramatist played the part of a moralist rather than that of a comic writer, his own views about education might have been more evident; but it was effective drama as well as sound psychology to point up in a droll and surprising conclusion the basic flaw in Micio's method. This does not mean, however, that the system originally favored by the "harsh" father met with the playwright's approval.

26 Legrand-Loeb, *The New Greek Comedy*, p. 440. Legrand continues: "Nevertheless, considered as a whole, they are not didactic works, for neither of them clearly and unreservedly proposes a fixed system that is to serve as a model to the audience."
27 *The Art of Terence*, pp. 44 f.
28 See "Portrayal of Character and Customs: *Adelphoe*" in chap. 6; cf. also p. 245.

## Master and Slave

Slavery, however repugnant it may seem to twentieth-century readers (at least to those who believe in the classical traditions of liberty and the dignity of man), was accepted as a normal condition by both the Greeks and the Romans who, however, as civilized and humane persons, treated their slaves in most instances as human beings rather than as pieces of property. Yet it is hardly possible that in real life ancient slaves had as much freedom as the slaves of Roman comedy, nor could they have been as outspoken and as impudent. I have already shown how slaves ridicule the love affairs of their young masters, contrive elaborate deceptions against their older masters, and when caught in the act are insolent even as they are threatened with punishment (e.g., *Most.* 1114 ff.).

We have recently been informed that the Plautine slave is "a man driven to cunning by ill treatment,"[29] but there is little evidence in the plays for such an assertion. The cunning slaves are in a minority and the instances of ill-treatment are extremely few. Tyndarus in the *Captivi* is sent to the quarry; upon his release he says (998 ff.):

I've often seen paintings about the tortures of Hades, but in truth no place is so like Hades as where I was, in the quarries. That's the place where toil drives the tired feeling from a man's body.

But Tyndarus is not too exhausted to make a pun about the crow(bar) that was given to him for amusement. Also, it is important to recall that Tyndarus is not Hegio's own slave but has been purchased as a prisoner of war and has apparently ruined the old man's plans by his deception. Earlier, when the change of roles was discovered, Tyndarus had boasted of his loyalty to his master and his indifference to the threatened punishment (682 ff.):

I count it little, as long as I die for no wrongdoing; but if I die, and he does not return as he promised, yet this will be remembered of me when I am dead—that I freed my master from slavery and restored him to his native land and to his father, and that I preferred to risk my own head rather than that he should perish.

It is rather ironical that Tyndarus, the noblest slave of them all, is the one who suffers during the course of the action. The slaves who lie and cheat, on the other hand, do not actually undergo punishment. Of course, when the intrigue is directed against a pompous soldier or a rascally *leno*, the slave's machinations have the approval of the other characters and the sympathy of the spectators. Such trickery is successful and there is no question of punishment. It is different when the *senex* is the object of the deception. Then the slave is surrounded by threats—from the *adulescens*, if help is not forthcoming, from the aged

[29] Dunkin, *Post-Aristophanic Comedy*, p. 86; see above, chap. 9, n. 27.

father when the trick is disclosed. Stratippocles says of Epidicus (*Epid.* 121 ff.) :

> I'll irrigate his back with blows and send him off to the mill, if he doesn't produce forty minae for me this very day before I can say the last syllable of the sum.

And Theopropides is vehement when he discovers the extent of Tranio's falsehoods. When the slave seeks refuge at the altar, the *senex* shouts (*Most.* 1114, 1133) :

> I'll have you surrounded by firewood and flame, you jailbird.
> I'll have you taken to the cross, as you deserve.

Angry threats such as these are not to be taken seriously.[30] They are more useful in portraying the comic aspects of a young man's impatience or an old man's wrath than in throwing light upon the relation of master and slave in antiquity.

It is significant also that these slaves not only escape serious punishment but they are pardoned far too readily. Callidamates intercedes for Tranio, and Theopropides yields to his request, although with some reluctance. The case of Epidicus is unusual: he has twice deceived Periphanes, he has stolen from him, and made fun of him; surely, as Legrand says, "such misdeeds call for punishment."[31] Yet the fortunate discovery of Periphanes' daughter completely reverses the situation. Epidicus, whose hands have been fettered, is reluctant to be freed and agrees only on condition that he receive food, clothing, and his freedom —a happy ending for Epidicus that seems richly undeserved. Geta in *Phorm.* 140 ff. speaks somewhat sarcastically of going to a *precator*, who will plead in his behalf. Just as Terence on occasion expressed his dissatisfaction with many comic conventions,[32] so here he might seem to be ridiculing the conventional pardoning of slaves, were it not for the fact that he, even more than Plautus, ends his plays with unmerited forgiveness of wrongdoing. Simo (*And.* 955 f.) and Chremes (*Heaut.* 1066 f.) each pardons his slave upon his son's suggestion and, in the *Adelphoe*, Micio needs only the urging of Aeschinus to grant Syrus his freedom—although in this instance Syrus profits by the sudden generosity of Demea; cf. the ironical words of the latter (964 f.) :

> To buy food honestly, to bring a courtesan into the house, to prepare a feast in the middle of the day—these are not the accomplishments of an ordinary man.

[30] Cf. also *Epid.* 605 f., *Mil.* 156 f., 215 f., *Pseud.* 1099 f.; in *Amph.* 1029 f. we have an unusual situation when Amphitruo threatens Mercury, believing that he is Sosia. But instances of a *senex* threatening his slave are surprisingly few in number. Most of the passages cited by Dunkin (*Post-Aristophanic Comedy*, p. 82) to support his views are not threats but are expressions of fear (e.g., *Epid.* 310 f., *Pers.* 268 f., *Poen.* 885 ff.) or warnings uttered by another slave (*Mil.* 294 f.) or by a *senex* (*Most.* 742 f.).

[31] *The New Greek Comedy*, p. 455.

[32] See "Summary: Convention and Revolt" in chap. 5.

The freedom and insolence of the comic slaves, their immunity from serious punishment, their happy-go-lucky existence (cf. the festivities in the concluding scenes of the *Persa* and the *Stichus*) combine to paint a picture of slave life that bears little relation to reality. No respectable householder in Greece or Rome would have countenanced such activity and the spectators were well aware of the fact. Slaves guilty of lying, cheating, or stealing would have been whipped, or imprisoned, or condemned to hard labor.[33] It is very possible that a reflection of the true state of affairs may be found in some of the monologues which describe the nature of a faithful and industrious slave;[34] cf. the words of Messenio in *Men.* 966 ff.:

This is the proof of a good slave . . . one who watches over his master's business just as carefully when his master is absent as when he is present, or even more so. . . . Whippings, fetters, the mill, weariness, hunger, cold— these are the rewards of laziness. I fear misfortune, and that's why I've determined to be good rather than bad. I can endure tongue-lashings easily enough, but I hate whip-lashings, and I'd much rather eat the meal than turn the mill.

And Phaniscus says (*Most.* 872 f.):

A master is usually what his slaves want him to be; if they're good, he's good; if they're dishonest, he becomes a severe master.

But however much the slaves of comedy refer to whips and chains, to the mill and the quarry and the cross, they seldom experience them in the plays. The frequent use by slaves of epithets like *mastigia* (e.g., *Most.* 1, *Rud.* 1022), *furcifer* (e.g., *Amph.* 285, *Cas.* 139, *Most.* 69, *Rud.* 996), *uerbero* (e.g., *Amph.* 284, *Asin.* 416), *verbereum caput* (e.g., *Pers.* 184), as terms of banter or abuse does not mean that the slaves are necessarily referring to punishments which they or their fellow-slaves have themselves undergone. The blows which Milphio receives (*Poen.* 381 ff.) are part of an amusing scene in which the slave, pretending to assist Agorastocles in his love affair, utters a laughable series of endearing terms to his master's sweetheart (cf. 365 ff.), thereby incurring Agorastocles' wrath.

Thus far I have had reference to the slaves of decent citizens, of masters who were either hotheaded *adulescentes* or respectable, if somewhat irascible, *senes*. In exceptional cases the relation of master and slave seems far less pleasant. Staphyla suffers at the hands of Euclio (cf. *Aul.* 42), whose fears and suspicions prevent him from acting in

---

[33] Cf. Leffingwell, *Social and Private Life at Rome*, pp. 85 ff. for a discussion of the punishment of Roman slaves (a treatment which unfortunately draws too heavily upon the comedies themselves); see also Allen, *HSCPh* 7 (1896), pp. 37 ff.

[34] For such monologues, cf. *Aul.* 587 ff., *Men.* 966 ff., *Most.* 858 ff., *Pseud.* 1103 ff. Fields (*The Technique of Exposition*, p. 191, n. 2) observes that the monologue of the faithful slave is a conventional device for bringing on a character speaking, and that in each instance the slave gives the reason for his entrance.

a reasonable manner. When the owner of the slave is a *leno*, usually described as an inhuman and perjured scoundrel, even less can we expect his treatment of household servants to be normal. It should not come as a surprise, therefore, when Ballio cracks his whip and upbraids his slaves (*Pseud.* 133 ff.):

Out with you! Get a move on, you lazy bunch of bad bargains. Not a single one of you ever had a single idea of behaving properly. I can't get any work out of you unless I treat you like this. (*Beats a slave.*) I've never seen men more like mules; their sides are calloused with blows, and when you beat them it hurts you more than them. That's the nature of these whip-breaking rascals: they have one idea in mind; whenever the chance occurs, grab, steal, snatch, plunder, drink, eat, run away. . . . Now, then, if you don't pay attention to my proclamation and shake sleep and slothfulness out of your hearts and eyes, I'll make your backs so black and blue that they'll be more embroidered than a Campanian carpet or an Alexandrian tapestry.

Such a passage tells us much more about the character of Ballio than about the institution of slavery in antiquity.

Far more significant for an understanding of slavery is the devotion of slaves like Tyndarus (*Captivi*), Grumio (*Mostellaria*), Messenio (*Menaechmi*), Geta (*Adelphoe*) to their owners. If a slave served his master faithfully, he could look forward to obtaining his freedom but his motive does not seem a purely selfish one; in many instances there was real affection between master and slave. The *seruus callidus* of comedy with his cleverness and insolence was undoubtedly a rarity in real life. Nor did slaves, at least in Rome, have the freedom to make merry as they do on the stage, where such actions become conventional. Stichus says to the audience (*Stich.* 446 ff.):

You mustn't be amazed that slaves drink, make love, and arrange dinner parties. This sort of thing is permitted in Athens.

But, at best, slavery was a sorry business. What it meant in reality to become a slave is well expressed by the slave overseer in *Capt.* 195 ff.:

If the gods have willed that this trouble come upon you, you must endure it calmly; if you do, your load will be lighter. At home you were free men, I suppose; now that slavery has come upon you, you must accommodate yourselves to it and make it easy by obedience to your master's orders. Whatever he does, even if wrong, you must consider right.

Such a passage presents a portrait of the slave very different from that of the usual jesting and impudent *seruus* of Roman comedy.

## Vulgarity and Indecency

The love affairs of men and women played a large part in the plots of Roman comedy and it was inevitable that these should often be treated with considerable frankness. Girls of respectable parents were sometimes violated before the play began (*Aulularia, Truculentus, Hecyra, Adelphoe*) and, to account for the existence of daughters born out of wedlock, allusions were made to the earlier love affairs of men now *senes* (*Cistellaria, Epidicus, Phormio*). All such situations were an integral part of the exposition; the relationships were taken for granted by the ancients and there is little in them that would seem shocking or indecent today. Legrand even suggests that the prevalence of rape in the antecedents of many comedies results from a curious regard for propriety—no young girl of good family yields willingly; she must always suffer violence.[35] In this way the purity of young maidens is preserved.

On the other hand, certain episodes have been criticized as vulgar and disgusting; these include the rivalry of father and son for the same girl (*Asinaria, Casina, Mercator*) and the arrangement whereby two men will share the favors of the same *meretrix* (*Truc.* 958 ff., *Eun.* 1072 ff.).[36] Olympio's discovery that the "bride" was really a male in disguise (*Cas.* 879 ff.) is recounted in language reminiscent of a modern burlesque skit and doubtless familiar to the Roman audience from the mime or *fabula Atellana*. No plot of Roman comedy has a more vulgar conclusion, but the situation is frankly hilarious and ends with the complaint of Chalinus (1010 f.):

A terrible wrong has been done to me. I married two men, and neither treated me as a new bride should be treated.

The off-stage raping of Pamphila by Chaerea in the *Eunuchus*—also an integral part of the plot—is a more serious affair and lacks the saving grace of humor. Although Terence avoids all indecency of language in his handling of the episode, he seems to view sexual misconduct with sympathy and he portrays Chaerea as an impulsive and likable young man. Yet Chaerea's callous treatment of the girl he claimed to love and his justification of the deed by referring to the picture of Jupiter and Danaë[37] make the whole escapade somewhat more indecorous than usual. Elsewhere in the plays rape occurs only in the presuppositions of the dramatic action as a means of motivating hidden identity.

There are numerous incidental allusions of a vulgar and obscene nature in Roman comedy (and most of these are in Plautus). Among the least offensive are scenes of name-calling; slaves denounce each other in coarse language (e.g., *Asin.* 297 ff., *Most.* 1 ff.), or *leno* and slave heap abuse upon each other (e.g., *Pers.* 406 ff.). In *Pseud.* 357 ff.

---

[35] *The New Greek Comedy*, pp. 460 f.

[36] Norwood (*The Art of Terence*, p. 64) says of the *Eunuchus*, "The last scene remains an ugly blot upon the play." But cf. Rand, *TAPhA* 63 (1932), p. 70 and n. 59.

[37] Donatus (*ad Eun.* 584) rightly points out that Chaerea had assumed the disguise merely to see and be with Pamphila and that the picture suggested his misdeed; cf. Norwood, *The Art of Terence*, pp. 60 ff., who is rather too severe on what he calls the "detestable behaviour" of the youth. See above, chap. 9, n. 12.

Calidorus and his slave take turns in hurling harsh epithets at Ballio, who amusingly agrees that they are deserved. The more indecent and obscene references[38] may be roughly classified as follows:

(1) Coarse references to the body: malodorousness (e.g., *Cas.* 731, *Men.* 166 ff.), belching (e.g., *Pseud.* 1295), vomiting (e.g., *Curc.* 74, *Merc.* 576, *Pseud.* 952 f., *Rud.* 511), the excretory functions (e.g., *Curc.* 415 f., *Most.* 386, *Pers.* 98, *Pseud.* 1279). In this category belong jokes on the creaking door, e.g., *Poen.* 609 ff.:

This door just did a disgraceful thing . . . it made a loud noise.

(2) Allusions to love, sexual play, or sexual intercourse. In *Cist.* 43 f. an old woman says of her daughter:

Heavens, she marries a man every day, she's married one today and she'll soon marry again at night. I've never let her sleep alone.

References to love-making, to kissing and fondling, are found, e.g., *Bacch.* 480, *Cas.* 847 f., *Pseud.* 66 ff., 1259 ff., *Heaut.* 563 f.; for allusions to sexual activity, cf. *Asin.* 786 ff., 873 f., *Bacch.* 72, *Heaut.* 905 f. In the *Stichus* old Antipho talks about a *senex* "*quasi ego*" who would like a music girl. Pamphilippus says, somewhat brutally (572 f.):

He can have a girl to sing him to sleep at night, for I don't know what other use he would have for one.

And Palaestrio says (*Mil.* 682):

To beget children is a jolly business.

(3) Jests and allusions to handsome *pueri* and to homosexuality. Clearcut references to this form of sexual activity are rare. They usually appear in passages of name-calling and verbal abuse and bring forth the retort, "You be damned" or "Go to the devil" (e.g., *Pseud.* 1178 ff.). In *Mil.* 1111 ff., Pyrgopolynices asks if the ship-captain is a handsome fellow; Palaestrio replies:

Oh, get out, won't you! You're a fine stallion for the mares. You chase after the males as much as the females.[39]

(4) Puns and word-plays with sexual connotations, both heterosexual and homosexual. In *Aul.* 740 ff. Euclio accuses Lyconides of taking

---

[38] For a convenient list of passages in Plautus "indubitably coarse," see Hough, *TAPhA* 71 (1940), p. 187, n. 3. The topic is discussed at length by Gurlitt in his *Erotica Plautina*; Gurlitt is convinced (p. 31, cf. pp. 39, 96, 119) that all Plautine scholars have failed to see and understand the erotic coloring and the indecent allusions in the comedies but his own conclusions cannot be accepted. Gurlitt goes to amazing extremes in finding a sexual significance in many innocent statements of the characters. A few illustrations of his method will be cited below.

[39] Cf. also *Aul.* 285 f., *Capt.* 867, *Cas.* 449 ff., *Curc.* 691, *Most.* 895, *Pseud.* 1189 f., *Truc.* 150, *Ad.* 215, *Eun.* 479. The witty *puer delicatus* occasionally appears on the stage, e.g., Paegnium in *Pers.* 183 ff. Gurlitt believes that many *puer*-scenes were inserted only for their obscenity, e.g., *Mil.* 813 ff., *Pseud.* 767 ff. (cf. *Erotica Plautina*, pp. 119 ff); see also Delcourt, *AC* 17 (1948), pp. 130 f.

his gold and the youth naturally assumes that the *senex* is referring to his daughter whom he has seduced. The pun on *tangere* here occurs elsewhere (e.g., *Mil.* 1092), and *comprimere* likewise has a double meaning (e.g., *Rud.* 1073 ff.).[40] A would-be adulterer is allowed to go home *saluis testibus* (*Mil.* 1416 ff., cf. *Curc.* 31, 622). Puns of this type and other jests involving word-play in Latin are Plautine although in some instances indecent jests of a similar nature may have existed in the Greek originals.[41]

(5) Obscene gestures or suggestive acting on the stage. These are perhaps the most difficult of all to determine with certainty. The festal conclusion of several plays (*Asinaria, Persa, Stichus*) afforded opportunity for vulgarity of this type and incidental passages may be found, e.g., the words of Sceparnio to Ampelisca (*Rud.* 429):

> You can tell by looking at me what it is I want.

Gurlitt, who maintains that one does not understand Plautine comedy unless he sees obscene meanings and gestures everywhere in the plays, finds highly improper and indecent behavior on the stage in many scenes, e.g., *Asin.* 702 ff., *Cas.* 724 ff., *Most.* 718 ff., *Pers.* 765 ff.[42] The existence of indecency in these passages is undeniable but they are far less vulgar than Gurlitt believes; his interpretations are based upon highly improbable double meanings.

Plautus, like Aristophanes, introduced into his plays frank references to sex and bodily functions in order to provoke robust laughter. There are few gross allusions and indecent jests in the plays of Terence. Beare seems wrong when he attributes to the younger playwright a tendency to salaciousness: "Terence is at the opposite pole to Aristophanes; he is not indecent, he is seductive. What is dangerous in him is the association of refined and humane sentiment with lubricity. Typical of his art is the reference in the Eunuchus-scene to the picture hanging in the maiden's bedroom—it is a picture of Jupiter and Danae."[43] But Chaerea's escapade is hardly typical of Terence's art. There is nothing else like it in his plays and there is nothing in Terence to match the conclusion of the *Casina* or the threatened punishment of the soldier in the *Miles*. It is perhaps just as well. Vulgarities and obscene allusions which

---

[40] See chap. 12, n. 53. In addition to puns of the *tango, comprimo* variety, Gurlitt finds obscene meanings in a large variety of words, e.g., *anus, culpa, ius, uiscus, malum, res, rem tenere, facere, agere*; cf. *Erotica Plautina*, pp. 36, 47, 121. His explanations of many passages seem fantastic especially those in which he connects *oculus* and *Hercules* with *culus* (e.g., *Asin.* 908, *Men.* 156, *Pers.* 2, *Pseud.* 123, 510), and he finds allusions to the *membrum virile* in the most innocent statements (e.g., *Men.* 154, *Mil.* 1024, 1026, *Most.* 328, 858 f., *Poen.* 470 ff., *Pseud.* 770).

[41] On indelicate situations and indecent jests in New Comedy, cf. Prehn, *Quaestiones Plautinae*, pp. 71 ff.; Legrand-Loeb, *The New Greek Comedy*, pp. 485 f.; Harsh, *AJPh* 58 (1937), pp. 285 ff.

[42] On these passages, see *Erotica Plautina*, pp. 138, 149 ff., 115 ff., 155 f.

[43] *Ha* 56 (1940), p. 38.

in Plautus were laughable when spoken by characters themselves grotesque and comical would have seemed all the more indecent if uttered by the more restrained and reputable personages of Terentian comedy.

All in all, however, the obscenities of Plautus are fewer and less gross than we should expect for the age in which he lived. Much of what some moderns have considered shocking and abnormal would have seemed to the Roman spectator as a perfectly proper subject for ridicule and laughter. Their reactions were not hampered by centuries of Christian and Puritan morality. When we consider the bulk of Plautine drama, and when we think of the amazing frankness of other Roman writers such as Catullus, Martial, and Juvenal, we must agree with Hough that "the coarseness of Plautus' plays is not as great as is sometimes supposed, especially by casual readers and moralists."[44] Hough finds an average of only about four obscene allusions per play. This average is probably too low. Without accepting the extreme and improbable conclusions of Gurlitt, we might do well to admit that there were undoubtedly jests and indecencies intended by Plautus and understood by his audience which we do not comprehend. The acting may have been cruder and more vulgar than we realize but of this we have no actual proof. Certainly the Roman audience would have been more delighted than shocked at the fare provided by Plautus; most of the indecencies or coarse expressions were combined with humor or cloaked in ambiguities. It is interesting that the plays with the greatest number of obscene allusions are the *Casina, Curculio*, and *Pseudolus*, and these all date from the later period of his literary activity. Just as the playwright increased the amount of song and dance in his later plays, so he increased not only the quantity but also the vigor of his vulgarity. These facts, as Hough comments, "suit admirably, if in no too complimentary a fashion, the known requirements of the Roman audience of his day."[45]

## Religion and the Gods

In comedies of everyday life in which the characters are primarily concerned with love affairs, problems of education, the acquisition of wealth by fair means or foul, one would scarcely expect to find much opportunity for the expression of religious attitudes. In fact, religion plays a much larger part in Roman comedy than is often realized and, surprisingly enough, there are far more references to deities and religious rites in the plays of Plautus than in the more serious and philosophical productions of Terence. Here is another indication of the wide range of the older dramatist—just as he more frequently descends to

[44] *TAPhA* 71 (1940), p. 186; cf. also Beare, *CR* 42 (1928), pp. 109 f.; *The Roman Stage*, pp. 54 f.

[45] *TAPhA* 71 (1940), p. 191. Beare, however, says that "on the topic of sex the Romans were highly sensitive, and public taste imposed its own limits" (*The Roman Stage*, p. 55).

gross vulgarity and obscenity, so, on the other hand, he brings to his spectators a preoccupation with religious matters which could not fail to appeal to the audiences of his day.

The prologues of five Plautine comedies are spoken by gods who in each instance reveal the necessary background of the action: Mercury (*Amph.* 1 ff.), Lars Familiaris (*Aul.* 1 ff.), Fides (*Cas.* 1 ff.), Auxilium (*Cist.* 149 ff.), Arcturus (*Rud.* 1 ff.). These prologues differ little from those spoken by an impersonal Prologus (e.g., in the *Captivi*, *Menaechmi*, *Poenulus*) and there is little in them of religious value; Mercury says that mortals should reverence and fear Jupiter (*Amph.* 22 f.) and the Lar Familiaris implies (*Aul.* 16 ff.) that his refusal to reveal the treasure to Euclio's father resulted from the latter's failure to give due worship to the god. Arcturus is an exception; his words have a religious significance that is unique among the prologues (cf. *Rud.* 9 ff.). But in all these prologues the primary function of the deity is to explain the antecedent events and thus aid the spectators in their comprehension of the coming action. With the exception of Mercury, the gods do not enter into the play proper, although they sometimes claim credit for manipulating events before the action begins, e.g., the discovery of the treasure (*Aul.* 25 ff.) and the shipwreck (*Rud.* 67 ff.), the latter being a righteous punishment of Labrax for his perfidy. The elevated tone of the *Rudens* may in part result from the presence on the stage of the temple of Venus and from the entrance of the dignified priestess Ptolemocratia (259 ff.)[46] but only in part; the *Curculio* and the *Poenulus* in spite of their settings (Epidaurus and the temple of Aesculapius, Calydon during the festival of the *Aphrodisia*) do not have a religious tone comparable to that pervading the *Rudens*.

Epidicus refers to the twelve Olympian deities (*Epid.* 610, cf. 675), presumably the same twelve whom Ennius (*Ann.* 62 f. V.) ingeniously crowded into two lines of dactylic hexameter:

> Iuno, Vesta, Minerva, Ceres, Diana, Venus, Mars,
> Mercurius, Iovis, Neptunus, Vulcànus, Apollo.

The extent to which these twelve divinities are mentioned by Plautus stands in marked contrast to Terence's procedure.[47] Several of the gods (Vesta, Mars, Mercury, Vulcan) are not mentioned by the younger dramatist and none is named more than once or twice, with the exception of Jupiter.[48] Plautus, on the contrary, refers to all the Olympian deities, with the exception of Vesta, and to several of them (Neptune,

---

[46] Cf. Lejay, *Plaute*, p. 178: "Le temple de Vénus domine l'action, comme il domine le paysage."

[47] Cf. Hubrich, *De diis Plautinis Terentianisque*, pp. 130 ff.; Lejay, *Plaute*, pp. 187 ff.

[48] Jupiter is mentioned twenty-one times, but all but four instances are exclamations of the type *O Iuppiter! Pro Iuppiter!* The other Olympian deities appear in Terence only as follows: Juna Lucina (*And.* 473, *Ad.* 487), Apollo (*And.* 698), Diana (*Ad.* 582), Neptune (*Ad.* 790), Minerva (*Heaut.* 1036), Ceres and Venus (*Eun.* 732).

Apollo, Mars, Juno) many times. Two deities form a separate category, each being mentioned more than a hundred times: these are Venus and Jupiter.[49]

Love, as we have seen, plays an important part in Terence's comedies and is treated far more seriously than by Plautus, who often makes it a topic for jesting. Yet, surprisingly enough, Terence mentions Venus only once and then in a passage of metonymy (*Eun. 732*) :

> Venus isn't worth much without Ceres and Bacchus.[50]

So too, his allusions to Jupiter, exclusive of exclamations (*O Iuppiter! pro Iuppiter!*) are limited to two mythological references (*Heaut.* 1036, *Eun.* 584), one prayer (*Phorm.* 807), and one curse (*Ad.* 714). Terence in his use of entreaties, prayers, and imprecations—and these occur frequently in his comedies—refrains from mentioning the gods by name; the usual phrases are: *di bene uortant, ita me di ament, te di perdant*. Such general phrases are numerous in Plautus also, but the form *Iuppiter te dique perdant* (e.g., *Aul.* 658, *Capt.* 868, *Curc.* 317) or merely *Iuppiter te perdat* (e.g., *Amph.* 569, *Pseud.* 250, *Rud.* 569) is also common. Jupiter is invoked by the characters for assistance, as a witness to solemn oaths or agreements, and thanks are expressed to him and to other gods. There is nothing comparable to this in Terence. Similarly, Plautine characters refer to the aid, power, protection of Venus, thank her for favors, pray to her for assistance and guidance. Even if we exclude all references to the altar or temple of Venus, especially numerous in the *Rudens*, we find in Plautus an emphasis on Venus paralleled only by the frequent references to Jupiter.

The contrast in the methods of the two playwrights may be illustrated by Hegio's thanks to Jupiter and the other gods in *Capt.* 922 ff. and Demipho's thanks to "the gods" in *Phorm.* 894 f. Plautus' regular procedure is to mention one or more gods by name; cf. the expressions of gratitude to Neptune (*Most.* 431 ff., *Rud.* 906 ff., *Stich.* 402 ff., *Trin.* 820 ff.), and often he achieves a comic effect by the piling up of names; cf. *Bacch.* 892 ff., where the common formula *ita me di ament* becomes the following:

> ita me Iuppiter, Iuno, Ceres,
> Minerua, Lato, Spes, Opis, Virtus, Venus,
> Castor, Polluces, Mars, Mercurius, Hercules,
> Summanus, Sol, Saturnus, dique omnes ament.

[49] The references in the *Amphitruo* to Jupiter as a *dramatis persona* must, however, be excluded, as also those references in which Jupiter's name is humorously applied to a human character on the stage, e.g., *Capt.* 863, *Pers.* 99, *Pseud.* 326 ff.; on *Cas.* 230, 330 ff., 406 f., see above, p. 222. If we further eliminate from both Plautus and Terence exclamations of the *pro Iuppiter* type, we have a residue for Plautus of seventy references to Jupiter as against four for Terence—an amazing difference.

[50] Donatus (*ad loc.*) considers the passage a proverb; cf. Gourde, *CJ* 42 (1946-47), p. 433: "What a fitting motto for the doorplates of our modern night clubs!"

In this long list of divinities and abstractions we see Plautus introducing several specifically Roman personifications, and Virtus, Spes, Salus, Fides, Fortuna are mentioned as goddesses in many passages (e.g., *Amph.* 42, *Capt.* 529, *Merc.* 867, *Pseud.* 679, 709). Such abstract divinities are exceedingly rare in Terence,[51] but Plautus delights in enumerating them and in inventing new ones; cf. the dialogue of Lydus and Pistoclerus in *Bacch.* 114 ff.:

LY.: Who lives here?
PI.: Love, Delight, Venus, Charm, Joy, Jest, Sport, Chit-chat, Kissykissy.
LY.: What business have you with such deadly deities?
PI.: Men are bad who speak bad of the good. You blaspheme the gods and it's not right.
LY.: Is there any such god as Kissykissy?
PI.: Didn't you know? Why, Lydus, you *are* a barbarian. . . . So advanced in years, and you don't know the names of the gods.

Roman divinities such as Lares, Penates, Genius are likewise far more numerous in Plautus than in Terence.

Plautus has been accused of assailing religion and ridiculing the gods,[52] but there is little evidence for such a view; burlesque is inevitable in the *Amphitruo* when Jupiter and Mercury assume the guise of mortals, but this play is unique among the extant comedies. Slaves occasionally adopt an irreverent attitude; Sosia, commenting upon the length of the night, suggests that Sol has drunk too much and gone to sleep (*Amph.* 282), Libanus parodies the usual expression of gratitude when he gives thanks to Perfidy (*Asin.* 545 ff.), and Ergasilus suggests that Hegio now prepare a sacrifice to him as to a deity (*Capt.* 863 f.):

I'm your Most High Jupiter now, and I'm also Salvation, Fortune, Light, Gladness, Joy. Just fill me with food and you'll have a god well-disposed toward you.[53]

But in general Plautus' comedies do not display an attitude of irreverence. Periplectomenus says in *Mil.* 736:

A man is silly and stupid to criticize the gods and to find fault with their decisions.

The characters of Plautus seem convinced of the important role which the gods play in everyday life and the need of winning their favor. Plautus' treatment of the gods is Roman rather than Greek; it is another aspect of the Romanization and popularization of his Greek models, whereas Terence's failure to bring the gods into the speeches

[51] Cf. Salus in *Hec.* 338, *Ad.* 761, Fortuna in *Eun.* 1046, *Phorm.* 841, *Hec.* 406.
[52] Cf. Colin, *Rome et la Grèce*, pp. 343 f.; Dunkin, *Post-Aristophanic Comedy*, pp. 99 f. But see Leffingwell, *Social and Private Life at Rome*, pp. 123 ff.; Lejay, *Plaute*, pp. 196 f.
[53] Cf. also *Cas.* 348 f., *Pseud.* 326 ff.

of his characters undoubtedly reflects his desire to preserve the more philosophical nature of his Greek originals.

This distinction between the two playwrights is confirmed by the numerous references in Plautus to religious ceremony and ritual, to auguries, omens, and superstitions. These have been collected and discussed elsewhere,[54] and of the Roman nature of these passages there can be no doubt; Alcumena prays to the gods *manibus puris, capite operto* (*Amph.* 1094), and there are frequent allusions to favorable omens and birds on the left (e.g., *Epid.* 183 f., *Pseud.* 761 f.).[55] In Terence, on the contrary, there are almost no references to auguries and omens; here again we have clear evidence that the language and thought of Plautus is nearer the life and speech of the average Roman.

But superstitious fear and awe of the gods accompanied by a scrupulous adherence to correct ceremony and ritual do not necessarily breed true piety and reverence. On the contrary, the favor of the gods may be sought merely for selfish ends, and perhaps Periplectomenus has this in mind when he says (*Mil.* 675):

Whatever is spent on religious rites is pure profit.

Lejay thinks that Plautus lays too much stress upon the external forms of religion—a Roman trait, to be sure—and cites as confirmation Palaestra's assertion in *Rud.* 191 ff. that she has carefully avoided impiety towards the gods.[56] Lejay finds a completely different (and Greek) attitude in the words of Aeschinus (*Ad.* 704 f.):

Father, you pray to the gods rather than I, for as you are a much better man, so they will heed your prayers, I am sure.

But not all is ritual and ceremony in Plautus. Palaestra's reference to her *pietas* seems far less a matter of ritual than Lejay implies, and perhaps the best refutation of Lejay's criticism is found in the same play, in the famous speech of Arcturus, which sets the religious tone of the comedy (*Rud.* 9 ff.):

Jupiter, the ruler of gods and men, stations us here and there throughout the world to note the character and deeds of mortal men, their reverence, and their faith, and how each prospers. If any swear falsely to win their suit or perjure themselves for gain, we enter their names in Jupiter's account. . . . The virtuous citizens he has listed in another account. And the rascals who hope to appease Jupiter by gifts and sacrifices waste their time and money. He has no desire for offerings from perjurers; much more

---

[54] Cf. Gulick, *HSCPh* 7 (1896), pp. 235 ff.; Oliphant, *CJ* 7 (1911-12), pp. 165 ff.; Leffingwell, *Social and Private Life at Rome*, pp. 121 f. See also Riess, *CQ* 35 (1941), pp. 150 ff., who points out the Roman character of many passages dealing with religious matters.

[55] For discussion and bibliography on these and similar passages, see Duckworth, *T. Macci Plauti Epidicus*, pp. 220 f.

[56] *Plaute*, pp. 182 f. For a translation of part of Palaestra's monologue, see above, p. 104.

easily will the man of piety find his prayers answered by the gods than will the sinner. This is my advice to you who are good and who throughout your lives keep faith with men and show reverence to the gods: hold fast to your course that you may rejoice in your reward.

This passage, as Miss Leffingwell says, "presents Jupiter with a majesty almost monotheistic."[57] Nor are the words of Arcturus, a god, an isolated instance; Tyndarus in *Capt.* 313 ff. expresses the same idea of Jupiter as an omniscient deity who rewards the good and punishes evil-doers:

There is certainly a god who hears and sees all that we do; As you treat me here, so will he treat that son of yours. He will reward the deserving and repay the undeserving.

## The Moral Tone of Roman Comedy

The plays of Roman comedy are not "problem plays" in the modern sense, nor are they primarily didactic. The one comedy that comes nearest to being a play with a purpose is the *Adelphoe* with its preoccupation with the problem of education. There are, however, in both Plautus and Terence numerous passages in which the characters discourse upon social and ethical problems.

Many of these passages in Plautus take the form of monologues in which the moralizing has little connection with the plot of the play. Several digressions of this type have already been mentioned, e.g., those on the disadvantages of love, marriage, or old age, and on the nature of the good and devoted slave.[58] Others are more significant for their moral tone. Pseudolus soliloquizes upon the power of Fortuna and complains that mortals are too blind to know what is good for them (*Pseud.* 678 ff.), Syra comments upon the double standard of morality, maintaining that husbands should be bound by the same law as wives (*Merc.* 817 ff.), Megaronides in *Trin.* 23 ff. laments the growth of evil practices which have undermined sound morality; cf. 34 f.:

There's a group of men here who think that they get a lot farther by gaining the favor of a few than by considering what's advantageous to all.

Megaronides likewise inveighs against the evils of gossip (199 ff.).

In both Plautus and Terence are many scenes of dialogue in which one of the characters expounds moral precepts, sometimes at great length; Lydus condemns the laxity of modern methods of education

---

[57] *Social and Private Life at Rome*, p. 123. I see no evidence for the view of Miss Toliver, who says (*TAPhA* 80, 1949, p. 432): "An examination of Plautus' plays leads to the conclusion that the disrespect for the gods prominent in all of them except the *Captivi* would increase the skepticism which probably already existed among the people in some measure." She believes that Plautus by encouraging this rising skepticism "contributed to the gradual deterioration of the state cult and thereby to the social and political disintegration within the Republic."

[58] See above, pp. 196, 290.

(*Bacch.* 437 ff.), Periplectomenus in *Mil.* 685 ff. defends his bachelorhood and recounts the disadvantages of marriage, incidentally explaining how he profits from his relatives who hope to inherit his property
(he is perhaps a forerunner of Volpone, but a much more likable
person), and Daemones points out that the wise man will have no part
in stolen goods (*Rud.* 1235 ff.). Both Philto (*Trin.* 281 ff.) and
Saturio's daughter (*Pers.* 554 ff.) comment upon the evils of present
day society, Philto praising the good old standards, the *uirgo* suggesting
that ten deadly evils be driven from Athens; her list is imposing: treach-
ery, graft, greed, envy, political corruption, gossip, perjury, laziness,
fraud, wickedness.

At times the wise precepts of a *senex* are parodied by a slave; Terence affords two interesting illustrations: Demipho says (*Phorm.*
245 f.):

A man should be prepared for anything; whatever turns out better than
expected should be considered clear profit.

This calls forth from Geta the following aside to Phaedria:

Oh, Phaedria, it's wonderful how I surpass my master in wisdom. I've
already considered what might happen to me if he returned: the mill, beatings, fetters, toiling in the country. I'll be prepared for all of these. Whatever turns out better than expected I'll consider clear profit.

Similarly, when Demea in a famous scene (*Ad.* 412 ff.) tells Syrus how
he trains his son by bidding him to use other men as examples and to
look into their lives as into a mirror, the slave responds by describing
his methods with the other servants; cf. 428 f.:

I bid them look into the dishes as into a mirror, and I tell them what to do.

In the *Trinummus*, a comedy noted for its moralizing, Stasimus contributes his comments upon the evil practices of the day, and laments
the departure of the good old-fashioned ways (1028 ff.). His words
are an amusing echo of the earlier platitudes of Megaronides and
Philto.

We thus find that Roman comedy was full of sententious passages
which could convey moral instruction to the spectators. Most passages
of this sort contained little that was novel; the precepts were either
bits of commonplace wisdom known and accepted from time imme-
morial or doctrines already familiar from Greek philosophy.[59] One
should do one's duty, have mastery over one's desires, be temperate in
all things, live a simple life and be indifferent to wealth, endure one's
fate with courage and resignation, avoid evil companions, value character above wealth and social position—these are among the many

[59] Many precepts are expressed briefly in the form of proverbs or maxims; these
are very numerous in both Plautus and Terence; see below, pp. 337 ff.

lessons of the plays;[60] if they did not make the spectators better and
wiser, they did them no harm in thus restating precepts which they had
earlier learned.

Moderation, the golden mean, *ne quid nimis* in Sosia's words (*And.*
61), is praised highly; Sosia considers this "the most valuable rule of
life." The words of Panegyris (*Stich.* 124 f.),

> A woman who will keep her head when things are going well and will
> maintain her dignity after a reversal of fortune,

are an anticipation of Horace's classic treatment of the *aurea mediocritas*
(*Carm.* II, 10).[61] Hedonistic attitudes are naturally not infrequent
e.g., *Bacch.* 1193 ff.:

> Hasn't it occurred to you that, though you enjoy yourself while you live,
> your time is short and, if you pass by the chance today, when you're dead
> you'll never have another.

A similar expression of the *carpe diem* philosophy is found when Simo
advises Tranio in *Most.* 724 f.:

> Enjoy yourself. At the same time, remember how short life is.

In the light of the sound precepts spoken by the more serious characters, are the comedies of Rome to be praised for their high moral tone,
or must they be condemned for the hedonism which other characters,
especially love-smitten youths and courtesans, not only express but display in their actions? What of the other objectionable features of the
plays—the greed and heartlessness of most slavedealers and some courtesans, the ridiculous lust of a Lysidamus (*Casina*) or a Pyrgopolynices
(*Miles*), the low standards of supposedly decent citizens, e.g., the
brothers Menaechmus, of whom one profits by a confusion of identity
to enjoy the favors of Erotium (*Men.* 473 ff.), while the other is faithless to his wife (123 f., 130) and willing to accept money not his own
(1043 ff.),[62] the curious and rather sordid conclusions of the *Trucu-*

---

[60] Cf. the more extended list of precepts in Legrand-Loeb, *The New Greek Comedy*,
pp. 446 ff. (Legrand is speaking of New Comedy, but his illustrations are derived
primarily from Roman Comedy, as is his usual procedure.) See also Coleman-Norton,
*CPh* 31 (1936), pp. 320 ff., who believes that "through the medium of the stage the
Romans had become acquainted with the achievements of Greek philosophers before the
formal introduction of Greek philosophy into Rome" (p. 321). This is undoubtedly true
but Coleman-Norton includes in his list of philosophical passages some which fail to
support his conclusions; e.g., typical expressions of helplessness and despair (*Epid.*
610 f., *Ad.* 761 f.) hardly indicate an Epicurean belief in the impotence of the gods,
nor do the frequent appeals to the gods for assistance necessarily imply an adherence
to Stoic doctrine.

[61] Are we entering upon a new era when moderation is no longer desirable, when it
has become merely "the one virtue possible to weak and little men"? Such, at least, is
Dunkin's description of moderation (*Post-Aristophanic Comedy*, p. 127; see also,
pp. 56, 124).

[62] If a distinction on moral grounds is made between the twins, Menaechmus II
might be considered the better of the two. But I cannot agree with Thomson (*The*

*lentus* and the *Eunuchus* where an *adulescens* agrees to share a courtesan with a soldier? We have found also, chiefly in Plautus, a certain
number of vulgar and indecent expressions. Norwood says of Plautus:
"Not only do most of his works rest on sexual irregularity that is at
least condoned; some are utterly depraved in temper. Nevertheless,
verbal indecency is very rare."[63] The verbal indecency is perhaps less
rare than Norwood states but most of it is amusing and innocuous. But
is sexual irregularity condoned? Are some plays utterly depraved?

We must remember that much of the sexual irregularity, like the
exposure of children, was a conventional device used by the playwrights
to lay the foundation of the plot and it usually appeared in the antecedents of the action rather than in the action itself. Sexual irregularity
is condoned to a degree; *adulescentes* are forgiven by their parents,
just as slaves guilty of wrongdoing are readily pardoned. But the plots
are basically moral; the good are rewarded and villainous or lustful
characters (*leno, miles, senex amator*) are punished.[64] Witness the
manner in which Cappadox (*Curculio*), Dordalus (*Persa*), Lycus
(*Poenulus*), Ballio (*Pseudolus*) are overthrown and sometimes ridiculed in addition. Demaenetus (*Asinaria*) and Lysidamus (*Casina*)
pay a heavy penalty for their amatory excursions, the *Mercator* concludes with a decree (1015 ff.) that old men should behave themselves
and keep away from young girls, and the *Miles* ends with a warning
against adultery. All this is not very edifying, perhaps, but neither is it
harmful to the morals of the spectators. And the tone of several plays
(e.g., *Captivi, Trinummus*) is unusually high. Plautus' range is wide.
There is little in Terence to match either the more vulgar passages of
his predecessor or the moral and religious pronouncements found in
many of his plays.

There is no lack of humanity in Plautus but it is Terence who is justly
praised for his *humanitas*, for his understanding of and sympathy with
human nature.[65] Many of his *sententiae* are unusually apt and cling to
the memory; cf. the words of Micio in the *Adelphoe*:

It is a father's task to train a son to do the right thing from his own
choice rather than through fear of another. (74 f.)

There is no one more unjust than an ignorant person; he thinks nothing
is right except what he himself has done. (98 f.)

Life is like a game of chance; if the dice don't fall as you desire, you
have to make the best of the way they do fall. (739 ff.)

But Terence's love for mankind and his doctrine of human fellowship

---

*Classical Background of English Literature*, p. 186) that one of the twins is a good
young man, the other not.
[63] *Plautus and Terence*, pp. 65 f.
[64] Cf. Smith, *The Technique of Solution*, pp. 115 f., 120.
[65] Cf., e.g., Norwood, *The Art of Terence*, pp. 150 ff.

have been exaggerated. Both ancients (e.g., Seneca, *Epistles*, 95, 53) and moderns have found in the famous line of the *Heauton* (77),

I am a man; I think that nothing concerning man is foreign to me,

a statement of the doctrine of the world brotherhood of man. Too much has been read into the passage; as Cicero rightly saw (*De off.* 1, 9, 30), it is rather a justification for Chremes to concern himself in Menedemus' affairs.[66]

In general, however, there is a seriousness of thought and tone in Terence which seldom appears in Plautus, or rather in Plautus the serious ideas are obscured by the farce and buffoonery which so often surround them. Donatus on occasion comments upon the closeness of Terence's comedies to tragedy and the clever manner in which the playwright avoids crossing the boundary (cf. *ad Phorm.* 137, 750, *ad Hec.* 281, *ad Ad.* 288, 297), and observes also that Terence is satirizing the vices of individuals and the corrupt customs of the times (cf. *ad Eun.* Praef. 1, 9; 232, 244). But the moral intent of Terence is often overstressed; Cruttwell, for instance, maintains that "all the plays of Terence are written with a purpose."[67] Terence was not a moralist but, like Plautus, first and foremost a dramatist; it was Plautus, rather, who satirized and ridiculed corruption and vice. We should, of course, not take Plautus too seriously; that he himself was not convinced of the value of moral instruction in comedy is perhaps implied by the words of Gripus (*Rud.* 1249 ff.):

I've often gone to a play and heard talk like that, with the audience applauding the words of wisdom. But when we went back home, no one acted on the advice he had heard.

But if the spectators did not profit by the moral features of the plays, neither did they suffer from any immoral, or rather unmoral, elements. There is nothing in the plays of either dramatist that could be considered dangerous to the morals of the Roman audiences, or interpreted as an incentive to corrupt conduct. Legrand points out that vice in the comedies has fewer forms than in ancient tragedy or elegy.[68]

---

[66] But cf. Arnaldi, *Da Plauto a Terenzio*, II, p. 96, who considers *Heaut.* 77 the first and most characteristic expression of the *humanitas* of the Scipionic circle.

[67] *A History of Roman Literature*, p. 51. Cf. also Lana, *RFC* 25 (1947), pp. 52 f., 172 ff.; Lana looks upon Terence as a propagandist who supported philhellenism at Rome and endeavored to make Greek life more attractive to the Roman spectators by creating a "philosophical" comedy on social and educational themes. According to Dunkin also, Terence was a poet with a purpose; he "exalted the Rich Man with many a flattering touch" (*Post-Aristophanic Comedy*, p. 138). Such extreme views need no detailed refutation.

[68] *The New Greek Comedy*, pp. 461 f.

# CHAPTER 11

# THE COMIC SPIRIT IN CHARACTER AND SITUATION

NUMEROUS passages in the preceding chapters have touched upon the manner in which Plautus and Terence sought to amuse and delight their spectators, and we have already seen in their use of stage conventions, in their choice of theme and handling of plot, in their portrayal of character, some of the many devices which both utilized in order to provide entertainment for Roman audiences in a holiday mood. It will be instructive to make a cursory survey of what writers, both ancient and modern, have had to say about the nature of comedy, and then to subject the comic aspects of the plays to a brief examination; in other words, to what extent and by what means did Plautus and Terence endeavor to arouse laughter? How effective is their humor in the light of critical theory?

The present chapter is concerned with the fun inherent in character and situation, and such fun may or may not be closely related to the plot. This type of humor is in general preserved in translation, but comedy which derives from the use of words—puns, jests, word-play, and the like—usually disappears when translated into another tongue, unless the translator is very skillful. We have a distinction here, as Bergson says, "between the comic *expressed* and the comic *created* by language."[1] In the latter case, the language itself becomes comic. Fun of this type will be considered in the following chapter which will deal with the language and style of Roman comedy.

## Ancient and Modern Theories of Comedy

The essence of comedy and the nature of laughter—these have been discussed again and again since the days of Plato and Aristotle. Students of the drama, philosophers and, more recently, psychologists have devoted innumerable books and treatises to the stimulus and function of comic laughter, and there has been little agreement among their views. It has been truly said that "the student of laughter generally ends by becoming laughable himself."[2] Perhaps all too often each author has attempted to make his individual view the one and only explanation of what is comic, failing to realize that there are types of humor that demand a different, or possibly broader, theory. Even to attempt a short discussion of this much-debated topic is a hazardous undertaking and, at the risk of seeming superficial, I must limit the following treatment

---

[1] *Laughter*, p. 103. Cf. below, chap. 12, n. 63.
[2] Smith, *The Nature of Comedy*, p. 9.

to a summary of the more significant opinions of a few outstanding writers.

Even before the time of Plato ancient philosophers seem to have been occupied with the question of laughter. Anacharsis, the friend of Solon, is quoted by Aristotle (*Nic. Eth.* 1176b) as saying: "Be merry, that you may be serious"—an interesting anticipation of a later defense of comedy. Miss Grant says of the pre-Socratic philosophers: "A theory of the laughable is not definitely formulated, but there are suggestions which later find an important place in the theory, such as the necessity for relaxation and laughter as a preparation for serious pursuits, avoidance of excess in laughter, condemnation of laughter directed at the unfortunate, necessity for the reformer to be free from serious faults himself."[3]

Plato's views are scattered throughout his *Dialogues* and are mentioned incidentally in connection with other topics but his comments upon the subject initiate the history of the theory of comedy. Plato associates the ridiculous with what is morally or physically faulty and justifies laughter as a means of understanding serious things: he says (*Laws* 7, 816):

> For serious things can not be understood without laughable things, nor opposites at all without opposites, if a man is really to have intelligence of either. . . . And for this very reason he should learn them both, in order that he may not in ignorance do or say anything which is ridiculous and out of place.

His most significant remarks occur in the *Philebus* (48 ff.):

> And are you aware that even at a comedy the soul experiences a mixed feeling of pain and pleasure? . . .
> The ridiculous is in short the specific name which is used to describe the vicious form of a certain habit; and of vice in general it is that kind which is most at variance with the inscription at Delphi ["Know thyself"]. . . . The ignorant may fancy himself richer than he is. . . . And still more often he will fancy he is taller or fairer than he is, or that he has some other advantage of person which he really has not. . . . And yet surely by far the greatest number err about the goods of the mind; they imagine themselves to be much better men than they are. . . . Those of them who are weak and unable to revenge themselves, when they are laughed at, may be truly called ridiculous. . . .
> When we laugh at the folly of our friends, pleasure, in mingling with envy, mingles with pain, for envy has been acknowledged by us to be mental pain, and laughter is pleasant; and so we envy and laugh at the same instant.

Since the element of satire had been prominent in Old Comedy, Plato perhaps inevitably looked upon the essence of the comic as a kind of malicious pleasure afforded by the discomfiture of another. We find in his comments what modern writers have called the initial literary

---

[3] *The Ancient Rhetorical Theories of the Laughable*, p. 17.

expression of the derision or superiority theory, also a view of comedy as an intellectual affair, concerned with contradictions revealed in the form of the absence of power; the recognition by Plato that the comic is a mixture of pleasure and pain, although not fully developed, is a significant contribution.[4] And when he says that "we laugh at the folly of our friends," he makes clear that he is speaking of innocent, almost sympathetic, humor rather than personal satire and ill-natured ridicule.

Aristotle's comments upon comedy develop more fully the ideas of Plato. His famous dictum in the *Poetics* (1449a) is as follows:

Comedy is an imitation of characters of a lower type—not, however, in the full sense of the word bad, the ludicrous being merely a subdivision of the ugly. It consists in some mistake or deformity which is not painful or destructive.

Thus, for Aristotle also, the laughter of comedy is scornful laughter, the expression of an emotion of complacence. Some critics have seen in Aristotle's definition a contrast between actual deformity and normal wholeness but others maintain that it is merely a restatement and refinement of Plato's superiority theory.[5] But while Aristotle seems to recognize the feeling of superiority as the essential stimulus to laughter, he does have a perception of the contrast or incongruity between the actual and the ideal. The weaknesses and shortcomings of human beings point away from what is towards what ought to be, and comedy deals less with personal satire than with the more permanent flaws and imperfections of mankind. Aberrations from normal conduct are discussed in the *Nicomachean Ethics*, and certain of these characters are important for their appearance in comedy, especially the braggart who pretends to possess qualities which he does not have, the "ironical" person who disclaims the qualities which he does have, and the buffoon, or clownish person, who exceeds the proper limit in respect to the laughable (1108a, 1127ab).

Aristotle not only develops Plato's theory of derisive laughter but he has an inkling of another famous theory: that laughter is caused by the disappointment of the person who laughs. He speaks of the element of surprise when things turn out contrary to what one expects (*Rhet.* 1412a) and cites as an illustration a verse where the listener anticipates one thing and hears another:

He strode along, and under his feet were his—chilblains.

The anticipated word was "sandals." Aristotle in the same passage also refers to the pun of Isocrates on ἀρχή ("empire," "beginning") and

---

[4] Cf. Smith, *The Nature of Comedy*, pp. 33 f.; Feibleman, *In Praise of Comedy*, pp. 74 ff.; Eastman, *The Sense of Humor*, pp. 123 f. The passages in Plato's works dealing with comedy and laughter are conveniently collected by Cooper, *An Aristotelian Theory of Comedy*, pp. 104 ff.

[5] Cf. Smith, *The Nature of Comedy*, pp. 35 f. See also Atkins, *Literary Criticism in Antiquity*, I, pp. 101 f.

says that "the statement is unexpected, yet it is recognized as true." These examples belong more properly among the jests and puns to be discussed in the next chapter but are cited here to show that Aristotle understood the importance of the unexpected in arousing laughter. And he says elsewhere (*Probl.* 965a) that "laughter is a sort of surprise and deception."

Aristotle looked upon amusement not as an end in itself but merely as a relaxation, a means to a life of happiness; the happy life was the life that conformed with virtue, and such a life was serious—not one of amusement (*Nic. Eth.* 1177a). The extent to which Aristotle developed a theory of a comic catharsis is uncertain. References both in the *Rhetoric* (1372a, 1419b) and in the *Poetics* itself (1449b) indicate clearly that the *Poetics* once contained a discussion of comedy of considerable length and Cooper, drawing upon post-Aristotelian discussions and particularly upon the *Coislinian Tractate*, has attempted to reconstruct Aristotle's treatment of comedy.[6] The agreement among later writers who presumably used Aristotle's work makes Cooper's interesting and ingenious restoration plausible on many points even though his treatment of Aristotle is admittedly hypothetical.

The brief *Coislinian Tractate*, an anonymous condensation of a theory of comedy dating perhaps from the first century B.C., preserves the Aristotelian tradition and may even reproduce the substance of Aristotle's lost discussion of comedy. Cooper says that the *Tractate* "is by all odds the most important technical treatise on comedy that has come down to us from the ancients. And modern times give us nothing of comparable worth in its field."[7] The treatise defines comedy in Aristotelian terms and includes a doctrine of catharsis ("through pleasure and laughter effecting the purgation of the like emotions"); stating that laughter arises from two sources, diction ($\dot{\eta}$ $\lambda\acute{\epsilon}\xi\iota\varsigma$) and content or "things" ($\tau\grave{\alpha}$ $\pi\rho\acute{\alpha}\gamma\mu\alpha\tau\alpha$), the author gives seven categories of laughable diction (e.g., homonyms or ambiguities, synonyms, garrulity, diminutives) and nine categories of laughable things (e.g., assimilation towards the better or worse, deception, the impossible, the unexpected, the debasement of personages). The six constituent parts of comedy (iden-

---

[6] Cf. *An Aristotelian Theory of Comedy*, especially pp. 166 ff.; on the problem of Aristotle's comic catharsis, see Cooper, pp. 63 ff., 179 ff.; cf. also Post, *TAPhA* 69 (1938), pp. 24 f.; Fleming, *JPh* 38 (1939), pp. 545 ff.

[7] *An Aristotelian Theory of Comedy*, p. viii. For a translation of the *Tractate*, see Cooper, pp. 224 ff. (The Greek text may be read in G. Kaibel, *Comicorum Graecorum Fragmenta*, Berlin, 1899, pp. 50 ff.) The estimate of the *Tractate* by Feibleman (*In Praise of Comedy*, p. 84) is very different: "The *Tractatus* has no great value in itself. It proposes nothing new for comedy which could not have been equally well deduced by others from the general theories set forth by Aristotle in the *Poetics* and elsewhere." But Feibleman admits that the author of the *Tractate* was not guilty of the modern attempt to identify laughter and comedy and to analyze comedy as a physiological-psychological mechanism. For the author, as for Plato and Aristotle before him, "laughter was the psychological *effect* of comedy."

tical with those of tragedy given by Aristotle in *Poetics* 1450a) are briefly discussed and the characters of comedy are given as the buffoonish, the ironical, and those who are impostors.

Among Roman writers Cicero (*De orat.* II, 58, 235 ff.) and Quintilian (*Instit. orat.* VI, 3, 1 ff.) comment at considerable length upon the nature of the laughable especially as it relates to rhetorical theory and practice, and both reveal a dependence, direct or indirect, upon Plato and Aristotle. The two Roman writers make the distinction, already found in the *Coislinian Tractate*, between laughter arising from diction and laughter arising from things; they agree that the ridiculous stems from deformity and ugliness, i.e., from the moral vices of men (the superiority theory) and they realize also that the laughable is often caused by deceived expectations (the disappointment theory), i.e., words are meant to be taken in one way, and we take them in another. "These," says Quintilian (VI, 3, 84), "are the happiest of all." Cicero observes (*De orat.* II, 61, 250): "There is no kind of wit, in which severe and serious things may not be derived from the subject," thus implying that comedy indirectly affirms a greater truth than the errors which it ridicules and criticizes; hence it is not surprising that, according to *De comoedia* (v, 1), Cicero defined comedy as "an imitation of life, a mirror of custom, an image of truth." We find in the *De Oratore* also an emphasis upon good-natured laughter.[8] But both Cicero and Quintilian have an agnostic attitude towards laughter; they admit that they do not understand it and agree that those who pretend to explain it know little about it; "furthermore," says Quintilian (VI, 3, 7), "laughter is not habitually produced by a single cause." The two Romans thus anticipate the sceptical tendencies of many modern writers, such as Hume, Dugas, Croce, and others.[9]

Later Greek commentators (Iamblichus, Proclus, Tzetzes)[10] and Renaissance writers (e.g., Trissino, Castelvetro, Guarini)[11] follow closely the teachings of the classical critics. Again and again we find mention of scornful laughter at things ugly and deformed, of laughter at things that are contrary to expectation, of laughter at things incongruous and out of harmony with the existing order, and occasionally a realization that comedy emphasizes the ugly in order to demand a change for something better, that laughter purges men's minds of

[8] Cf. Grant, *The Ancient Rhetorical Theories of the Laughable*, pp. 130, 147 f. Upon the two types of wit described by Cicero as *dicax* and *facetus*, cf. Grant, pp. 103 ff.

[9] Cf. Eastman, *The Sense of Humor*, pp. 130 ff.; Smith, *The Nature of Comedy*, pp. 31 ff.

[10] Cf. Cooper, *An Aristotelian Theory of Comedy*, pp. 82 ff.; Feibleman, *In Praise of Comedy*, pp. 85 ff., 91 f.

[11] Cf. Smith, *The Nature of Comedy*, pp. 16 ff.; Herrick, *QJS* 35 (1949), pp. 1 ff. The more important Renaissance critics are conveniently reprinted in Gilbert, *Literary Criticism* (on comedy see, e.g., pp. 224 ff., 312 ff., 502 f., 513 f.). For a brief selection of Renaissance critics, see Clark, *European Theories of the Drama*, pp. 49 ff.

troublesome passions. In *The Defense of Poesie*, Sir Philip Sidney sums up much Renaissance thought on the subject of comedy: "Comedy is an imitation of the common errors of our life, which he representeth in the most ridiculous and scornful sort that may be, so as it is impossible that any beholder can be content to be such a one. . . . Laughter almost ever cometh of things most disproportioned to ourselves and nature. Delight hath a joy in it, either permanent or present. Laughter hath only a scornful tickling. . . . We laugh at deformed creatures, wherein certainly we cannot delight. . . . We shall, contrarily, laugh sometimes to find a matter quite mistaken. . . . But I speak to this purpose, that all the end of the comical part be not upon such scornful matters as stir laughter only, but mix with it that delightful teaching which is the end of poesy."[12]

The modern reader is deluged by theories of comedy—realistic, nominalistic, mechanical, subjective-metaphysical, subjective-literary, psychoanalytic, physiological, and the like[13] and to discuss the different views would require one more (and surely unnecessary) volume. The main attempts to explain the laughable must here be viewed far more broadly. Eastman says of the various theorists: "Their explanations divide themselves into three classes—those which seek the cause of laughter in some kind of disappointment, those which seek it in some kind of satisfaction, and those which seek it in a mixture of satisfaction with disappointment."[14] Similarly, Smith states: "The number of different theories is large, but almost all of them are reducible to one of two categories, which I shall call the superiority theory and the contrast theory. The former locates the cause of laughter in the heart; the latter, in the head."[15]

The ancient theory of scornful laughter, now known as the superiority, or derision, or degradation theory, is usually associated with the name of Hobbes, whose famous statement in the *Leviathan* (1, 6) is as follows: "*Sudden glory* is the passion which maketh these *grimaces* called LAUGHTER; and is caused either by some sudden act of their own, that pleaseth them; or by the apprehension of some deformed thing in another, by comparison whereof they suddenly applaud themselves." The opposing theory—called that of contrast, incongruity, or disappointment—stems from Kant's well-known observation that "Laughter is an affection arising from the sudden transformation of a strained

---

[12] Cf. Gilbert, *Literary Criticism*, pp. 431 f., 452; on p. 404 Gilbert calls Sidney's essay "the greatest of Renaissance works on its subject." See also Atkins, *English Literary Criticism: The Renascence*, pp. 130 f.

[13] Cf. Feibleman's classification and discussion in his *In Praise of Comedy*, especially pp. 123 ff. For brief historical summaries of theories relating to comedy and laughter, see Greig, *The Psychology of Laughter and Comedy*, pp. 225 ff.; Piddington, *The Psychology of Laughter*, pp. 152 ff.

[14] *The Sense of Humor*, p. 123. See also Sully, *An Essay on Laughter*, pp. 119 ff.

[15] *The Nature of Comedy*, p. 31.

expectation into nothing."[16] This was developed by Schopenhauer as follows: "The cause of laughter in every case is simply the sudden perception of the incongruity between a concept and the real objects which have been thought through it in some relation, and laughter itself is just the expression of this incongruity."[17] But this theory, as we have seen, is likewise not new, for in its essence it goes back through Quintilian and Cicero to Aristotle. Even Hobbes, considered the founder of the derision theory in modern times, is not completely untouched by the idea of the unexpected; this is implied by his use of the word "sudden."

Most later theories have developed from one or the other of these two views, or have resulted from a combination of the two. Among those who have attempted to bring together superiority and incongruity, satisfaction and disappointment, is Herbert Spencer with his theory of "descending incongruity." Smith considers that the famous theory of Bergson represents such a combination.[18] Bergson looks upon laughter as a purely intellectual affair which must have social significance; he conceives of comedy as arising from the rigidity and inelasticity of human beings and from their behavior as machines. But, as Eastman points out, "we do not only laugh when intelligent creatures behave like machines; we laugh also when machines behave like intelligent creatures; and we laugh oftener than that."[19] To Bergson, laughter is a corrective; it is intended to humiliate, to make a painful impression on the person against whom it is directed. Eastman seems correct, therefore, in considering Bergson an exponent of the derision theory, and he includes Meredith in the same category. Meredith, like Bergson, believes that the appeal of the comic is to the intellect and that its primary aim is the correction of folly. He says of the comic spirit that, whenever men "wax out of proportion, overblown, affected, pretentious, bombastical, hypocritical, pedantic, fantastically delicate; . . . whenever they offend sound reason, fair justice; are false in humility or mined with conceit, individually, or in the bulk; the Spirit overhead will look humanely malign, and cast an oblique light on them, followed by volleys of silvery laughter. That is the Comic Spirit."[20] But Meredith elevates

[16] I. Kant, *Critique of Judgement*, translated by J. H. Bernard (London, 2nd ed., 1914), p. 223.

[17] A. Schopenhauer, *The World as Will and Idea*, translated by R. B. Haldane and J. Kemp (London, 1883), I, p. 76.

[18] *The Nature of Comedy*, p. 49; cf. Nicoll, *The Theory of Drama*, p. 194.

[19] *The Sense of Humor*, p. 150. The criticism of Mathewson (*Bergson's Theory of the Comic*, p. 7) is similar; "It is true that we laugh at rigidity in the midst of life's flux; but we also laugh at spontaneous actions when a certain restraint is expected." For other criticisms of Bergson's theory, see Jensen, *CJ* 16 (1920-21), pp. 209 f.; Smith, *The Nature of Comedy*, pp. 49 ff.; Piddington, *The Psychology of Laughter*, pp. 33 ff.; Feibleman, *In Praise of Comedy*, pp. 123 ff.; Koestler, *Insight and Outlook*, pp. 74, 417 ff.

[20] *An Essay on Comedy*, p. 142.

comedy to a lofty spiritual plane and eliminates everything farcical. His belief that the test of true comedy is to awaken "thoughtful laughter" and that such comedy requires a select society of cultivated persons has been condemned as far too limited and narrow. Meredith admires Menander, Terence, Molière, but there is little room in his theory for Aristophanes, Plautus, or Shakespeare.

Some writers today are reverting to a type of agnosticism not unlike that expressed in antiquity by Cicero and Quintilian. For instance, Nicoll states: "The laughable may, and indeed generally does, depend not on one source of merriment, but on several, so closely intertwined that it is almost impossible to disentangle them and to analyse them separately."[21] And Perry observes that "one laughs intelligently at the wide gap which exists between promise and performance, between what is and what might be, between the animal and the divine elements in human life. A reasonable sense of humor adapts itself continually to changes in the physical conditions of existence, and one need never expect it to be exactly the same in any two individuals or in any two nations, at any two moments or in any two centuries."[22] Yet Perry's statement is itself a good expression of the incongruity theory, a theory which goes far to explain why people laugh. Often the social implications implied in such contrasts and incongruities are stressed, e.g., in the following statements: "A comedy is a play in which a moral flaw in individual character becomes ludicrous by its opposition to normal social exigencies."[23] "There is only one kind of comedy, namely, that which . . . consists in the indirect affirmation of the ideal logical order by means of the derogation of the limited orders of actuality."[24] Actually, these definitions combine incongruity with superiority, and Smith speaks of the feeling of superiority which comes from "the contrast between the ignorance of the characters and the knowledge of the spectator."[25] It is, however, wrong to think that comic laughter must be a social corrective; it may have a preservative effect upon established social conventions but such is not its primary function; Nicoll states: "It is the laughter we look for in comedy, not the sense of moral right or of moral wrong, not the purpose or the significance of the play."[26]

Many modern writers believe that superiority and incongruity do not tell the whole story. Perhaps we should make a greater allowance for sympathetic laughter, for the play instinct in mortals and their delight

[21] *The Theory of Drama*, p. 213; cf. p. 196: "Degradation, incongruity, automatism, and the sense of liberation are all sources of laughter, and these are by no means exhaustive. Of them all, however, undoubtedly the greatest is incongruity." See Godfrey, *Ha* 50 (1937), pp. 134 ff.
[22] *Masters of Dramatic Comedy*, pp. xiii f.
[23] Smith, *The Nature of Comedy*, p. 175.
[24] Feibleman, *In Praise of Comedy*, p. 203.
[25] *The Nature of Comedy*, p. 173.     [26] *The Theory of Drama*, p. 193.

in gaiety, for a holiday spirit with an absence of serious thought.[27] As Nicoll says: "we really do not laugh at the satirical as such; we laugh at the purely comic qualities with which it is accompanied or in which it is enclosed. The purest of comedy, however, usually rules satire in any form out of its province. The appeal of this pure comedy is solely to the laughing force within us."[28] The importance of the play instinct has recently been stressed by Fleming, who combines it with the superiority and incongruity theories to produce an unusually satisfying theory of comedy. His view deserves to be quoted at some length:

The comic spirit may, perhaps, be generally described as a playful attitude toward any kind of unpleasantness, confusion, disappointment, or incongruity. It represents a buoyant attitude which overrides misfortune in the expectation of ultimate or predominant good fortune, and since this expectation is not at all founded upon a sage and reasonable optimism, it delights in anything unexpected, irrational, or incongruous, for such things give the world an air of disarming inconsequentiality. . . . Many people are conscious in their laughter of feeling superior to the object that amuses them, and others perceive a kind of pathos in the ignobility of the comic person. Thus derision and pathos are aspects of comedy; for derision may be regarded as an exaggeration of the tendency to scorn the comic character, and pathos as a predominant tendency to sympathize with the comic character in his ignobility and misfortune rather than in his insolent successes.[29]

[27] Cf. Jensen, *CJ* 16 (1920-21), pp. 214 ff. On humor as an instinct, see Eastman, *The Sense of Humor*, pp. 224 ff. Against Eastman's view, cf. Smith, *The Nature of Comedy*, pp. 143 f.; Feibleman, *In Praise of Comedy*, pp. 135 ff.

[28] *The Theory of Drama*, p. 191. Eastman is convinced that the derision theory is incorrect; cf. *The Sense of Humor*, pp. 139 ff.; *Enjoyment of Laughter*, pp. 30 ff., 345 ff. Godfrey says (*Ha* 50, 1937, p. 136): "It seems that laughing at someone in order to humiliate is really an abuse of laughter. In laughter which is aesthetic we laugh with people and never merely at them."

[29] *JPh* 36 (1939), p. 551. The statements of professional humorists and comedians are interesting in the light of this definition; e.g., Groucho Marx says: "There are all kinds of humor. Some is derisive, some sympathetic, and some merely whimsical. That is just what makes comedy so much harder to create than serious drama; people laugh in many different ways, and they cry only in one" (quoted by Eastman, *Enjoyment of Laughter*, p. 336). The more recent theory of Koestler would eliminate pathos and sympathy as aspects of comedy; he maintains that the one quality whose presence is indispensable to the comic effect is "a very faint impulse of aggression or defence manifested as malice, derision, self-assertion, or merely as an absence of sympathy" (*Insight and Outlook*, p. 54). Although Koestler's emphasis (perhaps "overemphasis" is the correct term) upon aggressive-defensive self-assertion makes him a stout defender of the theory of superiority or degradation (cf. also pp. 56 f., 60, n. 5, 83), his explanation of the comic as the result of dual association or "bisociation"—a term referring to the clash of two normally incompatible contexts (cf. pp. 36 ff.)—depends strongly upon both surprise and incongruity and seems a marked improvement upon many earlier views, notably that of Bergson. See also Herrick, *QJS* 35 (1949), pp. 14 ff., who points out the importance of incongruity and surprise in modern theories of the laughable. The most recent trend, however, appears to be toward an acceptance of the superiority or derision theory as the *one* explanation of the comic; e.g., Capp (*AM* 185, 1950, p. 25) states that "all comedy is based on man's delight in man's inhumanity to man," and Rapp (*The Origins of Wit and Humor*, p. 21) says that "the single source from which all modern forms of wit and humor have developed is *the roar of triumph in an ancient jungle duel.*" Nevertheless, Rapp distinguishes between wit,

Here we have a generalization, it is true, but the statement does achieve a reasonable harmony between the two theories which, down through the ages, have been looked upon as conflicting. There can be no doubt that certain stimuli to laughter have played an important part in all comic theory both ancient and modern—superiority, degradation, surprise, incongruity, irrelevance, exaggeration. To what extent do these stimuli appear in Roman comedy, and do the two playwrights use them in the same manner? Let us turn now to a brief analysis and summary of the comic elements in Plautus and Terence.

## Superiority: Error and Comic Irony

The feeling of superiority mentioned by so many writers on comedy contributed materially to the enjoyment of the Roman spectators. This superiority is of two kinds, or at least derives from two sources: the nature of the characters, and the manner in which the situations are unfolded.

(1) Our analysis in Chapter 9 of the principal roles of Roman comedy has shown that many of the characters (especially those of Plautus) are, in the words of Aristotle, "characters of a lower type"; one of the methods of producing laughter mentioned by the author of the *Coislinian Tractate* was the debasing of personages, i.e., they are made somewhat worse than average, yet not painfully so. The comic *senes* often lose their dignity and common sense in their anger at their sons, or they are garrulous moralizers, or they become amusingly amorous in their old age and behave in an unseemly fashion; the young men are more extravagant and helpless than in real life. The professional characters—parasites, slavedealers, soldiers—are even more debased; their vices of gluttony, avarice, and boastfulness are accentuated and exaggerated in a ludicrous fashion. Usually they are foiled at every turn; Pyrgopolynices' exalted opinion of his charms leads to disaster in the *Miles*, and Dordalus' attempt in the *Persa* to drive a shrewd bargain fails. The lecherous *senex* is especially ludicrous, and no one suffers greater ignominy than Demaenetus (*Asinaria*) and Lysidamus (*Casina*).

In the case of such characters, the laughter of the audience naturally arises from a feeling of superiority and has in it an element of derision. But Roman comedy in general is remarkably free from bitter or satirical laughter. Even the rascals and the villains of the plays are portrayed as ridiculous rather than vicious; e.g., in *Rud.* 125 f., 316 ff., Labrax is described as a typical *leno*: a cheat, a perjurer, a rascal, a plague of gods and men, but when he first appears (485 ff.), wet and shivering, dejected by his misfortunes, he seems rather the clown and the buf-

---

which he describes as "often cruel, aggressive, and 'rapier-like,'" and humor, which "must be loving, tolerant, and understanding" (*ibid.*, pp. 92, 163).

foon.[30] His attempt later to drag the two girls (actually his own property) from the altar of Venus reveals his true character but this scene
too is made laughable by the threats and abuse that are heaped upon
him.

Plautus leans to caricature but there is little malice in his characterizations; the fun is too hearty and carefree and, as Miss Jensen comments,
Plautus "is a joyous participant, not a lofty observer."[31] His characters
are guilty of the fault described by Plato in the *Philebus* (48), that of
fancying they have some advantage, bravery, charm, or intelligence,
which in reality they do not possess, and the playwright stresses the
laughable results of their perverse desires and mistaken beliefs. The
characters of Terence, less grotesque and more normal persons than
Plautus' creations, are also ridiculous in the Platonic sense; they "err
about the goods of the mind" and "imagine themselves to be much
better men than they are"; so Demea in the *Adelphoe* is confident that
he alone knows all about the escapades of Aeschinus (544 ff.). The
great fault of the Terentian *senes* in general—the reason why the spectators can laugh at them so readily—is that they are all so sure that
their deductions and conclusions are correct. Simo (*Andria*), Chremes
(*Heauton*), Laches (*Hecyra*), and Demea (*Adelphoe*) well illustrate
Bergson's observation—itself a restatement of Plato's view—that "a
comic character is generally comic in proportion to his ignorance of
himself."[32]

(2) This blindness of the characters brings us to the second source
of the superiority enjoyed by the spectators. Misapprehension, comic
error, lies at the very core of the plays; many of the characters flounder
about in a maze of misunderstandings that have resulted either from
innocent mistakes (usually concerning identity) or from deliberate
trickery on the part of one or more wily rogues[33] and the audience knows
far more about the true situation than do the characters themselves. The
foreknowledge comes in part from information given in the prologue
(in several of Plautus' plays) but to a far greater degree it derives, as we

[30] Cf. De Saint-Denis, *Mélanges Ernout*, pp. 332 f. De Saint-Denis analyzes the
comic elements of the *Rudens*, a play which in theme is among the least humorous of
Plautus' compositions, and finds much in the comedy to support Bergson's theory of
mechanical rigidity; cf. pp. 339 f.: "La force comique de Plaute vient de ses arrangements mécaniques et de cet automatisme que nous voyons s'agencer et se détendre
dans le détail ou dans la structure du *Rudens*."

[31] *CJ* 16 (1920-21), p. 212. But Miss Jensen seems wrong in saying (p. 207) that
"Aristotle in his ex cathedra fashion condemns Plautus unborn." There is less emphasis
on derision and degradation in Aristotle than in Hobbes, Bain, and more modern adherents of the superiority theory.

[32] *Laughter*, p. 16; Bergson is less convincing when he says (p. 147): "Rigidity,
automatism, absentmindedness, and unsociability are all inextricably entwined; and all
serve as ingredients to the making up of the comic in character."

[33] See "The Importance of Being Mistaken" in chap. 6. The author of the *Coislinian
Tractate* lists deception as one of the sources of laughter; cf. Cooper, *An Aristotelian
Theory of Comedy*, pp. 243 f.

have already seen, from the dramatic preparation and foreshadowing which Plautus and Terence introduce in varying amounts into their comedies.[34]

Confusions and misunderstandings are thus one of the main sources of laughter in Roman comedy. The superior knowledge of the spectators enables them to appreciate the humor in the situation when one character is taken for another, as in the *Amphitruo* and the *Menaechmi*, or when impersonation leads to laughable results, e.g., Philocomasium in the *Miles* pretending to be her own twin sister, and Acroteleutium posing as the neighbor's wife. Often mistakes arise naturally from the development of the action and these are equally amusing; in *Merc.* 700 ff. Dorippa, returning unexpectedly from the country, wrongly concludes that the strange girl in the house is her husband's mistress and the tenseness of the situation is hardly relieved when the hired cook arrives, sees Dorippa, and comments (753 ff.):

Is this your mistress, the one you told me you were in love with, when you were buying food? . . . She's a fine figure of a woman, but a little old.

Dorippa is convinced that her husband hates her and the cook endeavors to be helpful (765 f.):

No, he didn't say he hated you, but his wife; and he did say his wife was in the country.

Many comic situations developed by the playwrights depend for their effectiveness upon the fact that the audience knows the secret. The more familiar of these include (a) misplaced confidence or credulity, often combined with suspicions at the wrong time, as in the case of Nicobulus (*Bacchides*), Theopropides (*Mostellaria*), and Simo (*Andria*); (b) perplexity when plans go astray (cf. the bewilderment of Periphanes in *Epid.* 475 ff., 570 ff. when neither girl proves to be the one he had supposed); (c) numerous expressions of hope or despair at variance with the true situation (e.g., the dupe, blinded by stupidity or conceit, often believes that the intriguing slave is working in his behalf and even thanks him for his services; cf. *Mil.* 1213 f., *Pers.* 719 ff.); (d) the many conversations at cross-purposes, as in *Aul.* 209 ff., when Megadorus wants to marry Euclio's daughter because she is poor and Euclio believes that Megadorus has learned about his wealth, or later (731 ff.) when Euclio charges Lyconides with the theft of his gold and the youth not unnaturally assumes that the *senex* is speaking of his daughter; (e) the laughable confusion of characters who are convinced that "white" is "black; so Sceledrus says (*Mil.* 402 f.):

Now, I don't know what to believe; I'm beginning to believe that I didn't see what I believe I did see.

[34] Cf. "Dramatic Preparation and Foreshadowing" in chap. 8.

In like manner, Sosia in *Amph.* 455 ff. laments the loss of his identity.

In all such passages the superior knowledge of the audience makes for excellent comic irony. The irony is especially rich in the *Captivi*, where the audience can appreciate the humor in the words of Tyndarus and Philocrates after their exchange of roles (e.g., 272 f., 346 ff., 417 f., 426 f., 444), but also knows that Tyndarus is the son of Hegio; thus in 310 and 316 Tyndarus' words provide a unique instance of triple irony.[35] Terence not only eliminates the expository prologue but apparently desires to keep his audience in the dark in the initial stages of the action. The spectators do not know at first the truth about the parentage of Glycerium (*Andria*), Antiphila (*Heauton*), or Phanium (*Phormio*); they assume that Aeschinus is in love with Bacchis (*Adelphoe*) and are at first as perplexed as the characters by Philumena's return home (*Hecyra*). Had Terence let the audience into the secrets earlier, more comic irony would have been possible; but there is still a surprisingly large quantity of irony in Terence's plays (even in the *Hecyra* where the secret is withheld until the very end), for Terence is skillful in his manipulation of the plots and much of the misapprehension of the characters is intelligible to the spectators.[36]

On the whole, the comedies of Plautus and Terence lend little support to a theory of comedy based upon derision or antagonism. The element of superiority is present. The characters are below average in their moral and intellectual attributes, and their blindness, their inability to see the truth already known to the spectators, makes them laughable and ridiculous. Some of the more grotesque creations of Plautus may arouse derisive laughter but usually they are presented in a spirit of boisterous fun. Plautus laughs with his characters, not at them; Terence seldom laughs at all, but rather smiles tolerantly and sympathetically at the follies and mistakes of human beings basically decent. Neither playwright reveals an intent to degrade or satirize with invective and bitterness.

## Contrast and Incongruity: the Unexpected

Contrast is invariably present in the laughter of superiority; when a character "of a lower type" is portrayed on the stage, that character is contrasted with a normal or average person, with whom the spectator identifies himself; also, when the audience knows the facts of a situation and can understand and enjoy the confusions on the stage, there is a contrast between the superior knowledge of the audience and the ignorance or blindness of the character. But when writers on comedy speak of a theory of contrast, incongruity, or disappointment, they use the

[35] See above, p. 152.
[36] For a discussion of irony in Plautus and Terence, see "Suspense and Irony" in chap. 8.

term "contrast" in a different sense—the contrast between what the audience expects and what it actually does see and hear. People laugh when things turn out contrary to expectation; they are surprised and in a sense disappointed; a certain situation or statement is anticipated, and something incongruous, or inconsequential, or impossible develops instead. These elements play a prominent part in both ancient and modern theories of comedy; among the causes of laughter listed in the *Coislinian Tractate* are the inconsequential, the impossible, the unexpected; and Fleming, among others, likewise speaks of disappointment, incongruity, inconsequentiality, irrationality, the unexpected. Yet not everything unexpected or incongruous is necessarily laughable and Fleming seems correct in defining the comic spirit as "a playful attitude toward any kind of unpleasantness, confusion, disappointment, or incongruity."[37]

Numerous features of Roman comedy mentioned in previous chapters illustrate the value of contrast and incongruity in arousing laughter. Incongruity of character is everywhere evident—but carried by Plautus to greater lengths than by Terence. The aged *paterfamilias* loses his dignity and becomes ridiculous when he is deceived, and the *matrona* is often portrayed as jealous, shrewish, and extravagant. Young men, who should be more resourceful as a result of their love affairs, are helpless instead, and (especially in Plautus) they become the object of ridicule rather than of sympathy. Incongruity of character is best exemplified by the comic slave. To the Roman audience, the concept of an intriguing, impertinent, domineering slave would clash violently with the realities of everyday life, and to have him boast of heroic achievements would strike them as highly incongruous, as in *Most.* 775 ff., where Tranio compares his trickery to the deeds of Alexander the Great and Agathocles. But when the *seruus callidus* becomes a fixed type in comedy, it is equally amusing to find the supposedly ingenious slave beset by doubts and uncertainties. Hence the comic *seruus* arouses laughter in every situation; like Chrysalus (*Bacchides*) and Palaestrio (*Miles*), he may override every obstacle or, like Epidicus and Tranio (*Mostellaria*), his ingenuity may be his own undoing.

When the slave himself was able to accomplish little (e.g., Davus in the *Andria*) or was deceived (e.g., Parmeno in the *Eunuchus*) or was prevented from taking an active part in the action (Parmeno in the *Hecyra*), his role may well have seemed unusual to the Roman spectators, and it is significant that the Terentian slaves are usually of this type—but they are also less laughter-producing than the cunning rascals

---

[37] *JPh* 36 (1939), p. 551. Bergson points out that contrast and surprise do not always make us laugh; cf. *Laughter*, pp. 39 f., 181 f. His solution is as follows: "Comic absurdity is of the same nature as that of dreams" (p. 186)—a view somewhat inconsistent with his theory that "we laugh every time a person gives us the impression of being a thing" (p. 58).

of Plautus. When a slave has encouraged his young master in his iniqui-
ties, it is likewise incongruous to find him uttering sound moral precepts
and longing for the return of the *senex*; this is the case with Stasimus
(*Trin.* 1028 ff., 617 ff.)—it is almost as if Tranio rather than Grumio
had desired the return of Theopropides in the *Mostellaria*. Donatus
comments (*ad Phorm.* 138) that serious statements are ridiculous when
uttered by slaves and are inserted for this reason. Another type of statement that is amusing because of the contrast with what both speaker
and audience know to be the truth occurs when a slave is praised for his
virtues; cf. e.g., *Ad.* 372, 964 ff.; Donatus says on *Ad.* 967: "all this is
spoken in seriousness that it may seem the more laughable."

Incongruous situations of every type abound. It hardly makes sense
when a Plautine running slave, eager to bring to his master news of
serious import, delays the delivery of his message with idle jests, but
the comic value of such scenes cannot be questioned.[38] The many digressions which we have noted in Plautus are in truth both incongruous
and irrelevant, and they would produce hearty laughter in an audience
which was in the proper playful and uncritical mood. So, too, with
repetitions. "Repetition," says Bergson, "is the favourite method of
classic comedy. It consists in so arranging events that a scene is reproduced either between the same characters under fresh circumstances or
between fresh characters under the same circumstances."[39] Thus in the
*Menaechmi*, Menaechmus II is confused with his brother again and
again (by Cylindrus, Erotium, Peniculus, the *ancilla*, the *matrona*, the
*senex*) and a misunderstanding occurs with "fresh characters" when
Menaechmus I is taken for Menaechmus II by Messenio. The *Aulularia*
presents a laughable series of repeated incidents as Euclio seeks to preserve his treasure. The effectiveness of Palaestrio's intrigue in the
*Miles* is shown by the two similar scenes in which the soldier meets first
the "maid" (991 ff.), then the "wife" (1137 ff.). Repetition of instructions, sometimes criticized as unnecessary,[40] has a definite comic value.

Many a scene in Plautus is extended beyond due proportion but
so exuberant are the characters and so rapid their repartee that the
delighted spectators would not object to the retardation of the action.
Terence, always more serious, concentrates upon the complications of
the plot and eliminates to a large extent both digression and repetition.
He is, however, particularly clever at reversing a situation; cf. the manner in which a character's words are used against him, e.g., *Ad.* 422 ff.,
Syrus' parody of Demea's words in 414 ff., and *Ad.* 952 ff., where
Demea hurls back at Micio the latter's belief (833 f.) that old men are
too interested in making money. Such humor is delightful and far more
subtle than much that we find in Plautus.

---

[38] On the value of such scenes for the creation of suspense, see above, pp. 106 f.,
225.
[39] *Laughter*, pp. 121 f.          [40] See above, pp. 194 f.

Many comic devices and conventions are amusing precisely because they are incongruous, irrational, or even impossible: improbable coincidences in plot, chance meetings on the stage, the failure of characters to hear speeches or asides, indiscreet revelations and excessive garrulity—all these are part of ancient comic technique and can hardly be condemned as unreal or absurd if we are willing to view them in the proper spirit of playfulness. The breaking of the dramatic illusion is, strictly speaking, highly illogical but it must be accepted in the same spirit; as Michaut says, "cette brusque rupture de l'illusion dramatique produit un effet de surprise et fait rire."[41]

The importance of surprise in Roman comedy can hardly be overestimated. It is the unexpected in character, in situation, in jest that proves so delightful, and many of the incongruities already cited are effective chiefly because they do come as a surprise. Cooper states: "Deception and surprise are, strictly considered, *the* sources of laughter *par excellence*, and underlie all others. Thus the irrelevant is unexpected, and similarly the impossible, since things normally follow one another in a 'probable' or 'necessary' sequence."[42] When the banker in *Curc.* 373 says,

> I'm rich—if I don't pay my debts,

a statement not unlike that attributed to Artemus Ward, that he was determined to live within his means even if he had to borrow money, we are amused because the statement makes good sense—but hardly the sense anticipated. In *Men.* 141, Menaechmus I asks the parasite: "Do you want to see a splendid piece of work?" Peniculus' reply ("What cook cooked it?") gives a somewhat unexpected insight into the speaker's thoughts. A soldier beaten at his own game of boasting (*Epid.* 453 f.) or a deceived *senex* begging for forgiveness (*Epid.* 728 f.) are unexpected departures from normal procedure, as is what Hough calls "the reverse comic foil"—jesting by a *senex* or *adulescens*, instead of the more usual joking by a character of lower social status (slave or parasite) ;[43] cf. Milphio's words in *Poen.* 296:

> Look here, master, you're getting me at my own game and cracking jokes.

It is unexpected, likewise, when a rascal like Labrax has the effrontery to insist that he has kept his promise (*Rud.* 863 ff.) :

[41] *Plaute*, ii, p. 197. For examples of *ex persona* speeches in Plautus, see above, "The Violation of the Dramatic Illusion" in chap. 5.

[42] *An Aristotelian Theory of Comedy*, p. 249. Cf. Starkie, *Ha* 42 (1920), p. 42: "In a sense 'surprise' may be considered the source of all laughter." Surprise plays an important part in Koestler's theory of "bisociation"; cf. *Insight and Outlook*, p. 27: "the sudden clash of two swift-flowing, independent association streams in the listener's mind . . . must have the impact of *surprise*"; see above, n. 29.

[43] Cf. *TAPhA* 73 (1942), pp. 108 ff. Hough points out that such jokes are more frequent in Plautus' later plays, that the quality of the humor improves, and that the jokes are employed with greater dramatic effect.

I tried to get the women away, but I wasn't able to, unfortunately. And I told you that I would be here at the shrine of Venus. I didn't break my word, did I? Aren't I here?

Perhaps the most surprising reversal in all Roman comedy is found at the end of the *Adelphoe* when Demea suddenly adopts his brother's theory; he sums up his method in 958:

> I'm cutting his throat with his own sword.

There are numerous events in the comedies of Plautus and Terence alike that come as a distinct surprise to the spectators. These have been discussed above[44] in connection with the playwrights' use of suspense and irony, and additional illustrations need not be cited. But it is significant that Plautus seems to have been the more successful in his mingling of anticipation and surprise. With Terence the spectator was too seldom let into the secret, and confusion rather than amusement was sometimes the result. His unexpected turns of plot lack the incongruities and irrelevancies which are so abundant in Plautus' plays. Terence's desire for a subtle humor that would appeal to a more sophisticated audience has been seen in his handling of stage conventions and in his treatment of deception; in each of these his departures from Plautus' procedure are readily apparent.[45] But the greater his striving for a restrained and realistic presentation of character and situation, the greater the loss of those elements which in Plautus' hands were productive of robust entertainment. That Terence himself realized this is indicated by the fact that laughter-provoking characters and farcical situations are more frequent in his later than in his earlier comedies.

## Comic Exaggeration: Buffoonery and Slapstick

Plautus' keen perception of comic effects and his ever-present desire to arouse laughter led him to the employment of devices upon which Terence frowned, devices which today we associate with lower forms of dramatic art such as musical comedy, farce, and vaudeville. These are the elements in his plays which doubtless had the greatest appeal for his spectators and he did not fail to exploit their possibilities in his treatment of both character and situation.

Chief among these devices is that of exaggeration. Exaggeration heightens the contrasts and incongruities described above and is an important factor in "debasing personages." It may also be considered one form of assimilation, mentioned in the *Coislinian Tractate* as a means of creating laughter. The exaggeration of defects in a character is assimilation from better to worse; but the attempt of a character to

[44] See "Surprise in Plautus and Terence" in chap. 8.
[45] See "Summary: Convention and Revolt" in chap. 5; "Methods of Trickery" in chap. 6.

magnify his achievements is assimilation from what is worse to what pretends to be better; this is equally ludicrous. Since persons usually make themselves out better than they are and only rarely does a person pretend to be worse than he is, the impostor and the braggart are far more frequent in comedy than the ironical person who feigns stupidity.[46]

Not all exaggeration is funny. Eastman says, "it is the *too* much—always and absolutely—not the *much*, that is funny . . . it is only when exaggeration goes beyond some humanly reasonable bounds that it makes you want to laugh."[47] Plautus far more than Terence makes his characters vivid and laughable by exaggerating their traits; the incongruities are pushed to an extreme. Hope, fear, rage, perplexity, stupidity, conceit, greed—all in excessive amounts—stalk across the Plautine stage in scene after scene. Examples come readily to mind: Gripus' hopes for fame and fortune as a result of his catch (*Rud.* 930 ff.), Lysidamus' fears when he accepts as true the trumped-up story about Casina's madness (*Cas.* 661 ff.), the desire of a moneylender or *leno* for payment (*Most.* 603 ff., *Pers.* 422 ff.), the amusing description of Euclio's avarice (*Aul.* 300 ff.), the desire of *senes* for the death of their wives.[48]

Exaggerated stupidity and rage are characteristic of many *senes*, even in Terence (e.g., Demea in the early scenes of the *Adelphoe*, perhaps so portrayed that the contrast is all the more striking when he finally gains the ascendancy over Micio), but they are even more evident when the Plautine *miles* appears; cf. the blustering threats of Cleomachus in *Bacch.* 845 ff., of Stratophanes in *Truc.* 603 ff., of Antamoenides in *Poen.* 1280 ff.; in the latter passage Agorastocles calls for slaves with clubs and the soldier becomes surprisingly meek (1320 f.):

Look here, don't take seriously anything I said in jest.

The braggart warrior has an exaggerated idea of his charm (*Mil.* 1074 ff.) or of his wit (*Eun.* 419 ff.) and his account of his military exploits soars to the realm of fantastic impossibility; cf. Antamoenides' story about killing sixty thousand flying men in one day; his method was unique (*Poen.* 477 ff.):

I gave birdlime and slings to my troops. . . . They put large balls of birdlime in their slings; I ordered them to open fire at the flying men. Why say more? The ones hit with the birdlime fell to the ground as thick as pears. As each one dropped, I straightway pierced him through the brain with one of his own feathers.

Curculio relates (*Curc.* 442 ff.) that the *miles* he represents, Therapontigonus Platagidorus by name, conquered singlehanded in twenty

---

[46] Cf. Cooper, *An Aristotelian Theory of Comedy*, pp. 262 ff.

[47] *Enjoyment of Laughter*, p. 150; he cites (p. 152) as an illustration Noel Coward's postcard from Paris with a picture of the Venus de Milo—"You see what will happen to you if you keep on biting your nails."

[48] Cf. "Love and Marriage" in chap. 10.

ays half the nations of the earth—including "the Persians, Paphla-
onians, Sinopians, Arabians, Carians, Cretans, Rhodes, Lycia, Eatonia
nd Tipplearia, Centaurfightiglia and Onenipplehostania, all the coast
f Libya, all Winepressbacchanalia." Lyco comments drily (452):

Damned if you don't come from him, for you jabber such nonsense.

.qually fantastic are the claims of the cook in *Pseud.* 829 ff. that his
oncoctions (ingredients specified!) enable mortals to live two hundred
ears.

The language of lower class characters—slaves, parasites, slave-
ealers—is rich in exaggerated jests and ridiculous boasts. The intri-
uing slave is often a mighty general about to lead forth his troops
o victory. Chrysalus, in an extended comparison of his intrigues to the
iege of Troy (*Bacch.* 925 ff.), considers himself a combination of
Agamemnon and Ulysses and says that he will take his master without
fleet, without an army, without such a host of men.[49] So, too, Pseu-
olus has his troops in readiness with "double and triple lines of tricks
nd double-dealing" (*Pseud.* 578 ff.). Great is the rejoicing when the
oe is vanquished and the victory won (cf. *Asin.* 545 ff., *Bacch.* 1068 ff.,
*Pers.* 753 ff.).[50]

Plautus seldom uses one phrase if three or six will be more effective.
When Agorastocles urges Milphio to win over his beloved Adelphasium
with endearing terms, the slave obeys (*Poen.* 365 ff.):

My darling, my delight, my life, my pleasure, apple of my eye, my little
Cupid's bow, my health, my kiss, my honey, my heart, my milk, my soft
ttle cheese.

The youth in anger beats Milphio and maintains that he should have
aid, "his darling, his delight," etc., whereupon the slave makes the
omewhat surprising appeal to Adelphasium (392 ff.):

I beseech you, his delight (*aside*) and my disgust—his buxom friend
(*aside*) and my brutal friend—apple of his eye, (*aside*) sore of my eye—
oney to him, (*aside*) poison to me.[51]

[49] On the Greek nature of this passage, cf. Legrand-Loeb, *The New Greek Comedy*,
. 469: "No comic author of the sixth century after the foundation of Rome would of
is own accord have conceived the idea of giving a detailed comparison between the
Trojan war and the rascality of a slave; for the greater part of his audience would not
ave been able to see the point." The passage may well be Greek in origin, but we
hould remember that early Roman tragedy had done much to familiarize the Romans
vith tales from the Trojan cycle. See below, chap. 12, n. 16.

[50] Dunkin (*Post-Aristophanic Comedy*, p. 97) makes a revealing comment on these
assages: "That he dared to utter such devastating ridicule against war to the face of
n extremely warlike race . . . shows at least an instinctive, if only partially conscious
eaction against war." Where in Plautus is the "devastating ridicule against war"? All
Dunkin proves here is that he, like many writers on comedy, lacks a sense of humor.
3ut need he assume that the Roman spectators were equally deficient?

[51] It seems impossible to bring out in translation the play upon *mel* and *fel*; Nixon
Plautus, IV, p. 41) translates "honey" and "henbane." On puns and word-plays in
eneral, see below, "Puns, Jests, and Double Meanings" in chap. 12.

Such scenes of ridicule at the expense of the young lover (cf. also *Asin.* 646 ff.—"a masterpiece of burlesque writing," according to Legrand[52] — and *Curc.* 166 ff.) are obviously inserted for the sake of laughter and bear little relevance to the theme of the play; this is true also of the numerous instances of threats and abuse, usually hurled by a slave at another slave (e.g., *Cas.* 89 ff., *Most.* 1 ff.) or at a *leno* (e.g., *Pers.* 406 ff., an interesting passage since Dordalus in 417 ff. hurls back at Toxilus insults of equal violence). The series of abusive terms which Calidorus and Pseudolus heap upon Ballio in *Pseud.* 357 ff. is all the more amusing when the *leno* welcomes and applauds their epithets. Pseudolus finally says in disgust (369):

It's like pouring water into a cracked pitcher; we're wasting our effort.

The threats and abusive language which occur in Terence (e.g., *Eun.* 668 ff., *Ad.* 168 ff.) seem mild by comparison. Plautus often resembles Rabelais in his fullness of expression, his heaping up of outrageous and laughable terms. But even Plautus cannot match the famous Frenchman in his use of exaggeration.[53]

Exaggerated and farcical action readily develops into extravagant scenes of buffoonery and slapstick. These scenes, mostly in Plautus, fall into sharply defined categories.[54] The following are noteworthy:

(1) Pounding on the door, e.g., *Bacch.* 577 ff., *Stich.* 308 ff. Plautus introduces an interesting variation in *Asin.* 384 ff., where Libanus accuses the *puer* of smashing the door before the latter has had an opportunity to knock.

(2) The excessive haste of the running slave and his insistence that bystanders get out of the way (parodied by Mercury in *Amph.* 984 ff.). The comic effect would be all the greater if, as Blancké assumes,[55] the actor made "a violent and frenzied pretense of running while scarcely moving from the spot. . . . Truly then his plea of exhaustion would not be without excuse!" For examples of the running slave overcome by exhaustion, cf. *Curc.* 309 ff., *Merc.* 123 ff.; in the former passage, the "running slave" is a parasite and naturally suffers even more from hunger (317 ff.):

---

[52] *The New Greek Comedy*, p. 491. Others have considered highly improper the conclusion of this scene (698 ff.) in which Libanus literally "plays horse" with his master.

[53] Cf., e.g., the abuse uttered by the cake-bakers against the shepherds in Book 1, Chapter 21. Eastman (*Enjoyment of Laughter*, pp. 153 f.) quotes the passage to illustrate his statement that "nobody ever equaled Rabelais in the humor of exaggeration, and nobody with a leash on ever will."

[54] Several illustrations of farcical extravagance have been given in earlier chapters but these elements are so prominent in Plautine comedy that a résumé seems advisable here. Cf. also the discussion of farce and buffoonery in Haile, *The Clown in Greek Literature*, pp. 5 ff.; Blancké, *The Dramatic Values in Plautus*, pp. 35 ff.; Michaut, *Plaute*, II, pp. 197 f.; Faider, *MB* 31 (1927), pp. 64 ff. Certain types treated by Haile and Blancké concern verbal humor and will be mentioned in the following chapter.

[55] *The Dramatic Values in Plautus*, p. 47.

I'm dead and gone! I can hardly see! My teeth are rheumatic, my jaws are bleary from starvation! My bowels are so lean and weary from lack of nourishment!

(3) Blows and beatings. In *Amph.* 374 ff., Mercury strikes Sosia in an attempt to persuade him that he is no longer Sosia; Olympio and Chalinus exchange blows at the command of master and mistress (*Cas.* 404 ff.). Labrax is threatened with clubs (*Rud.* 807 ff.) and in Terence's *Adelphoe* Sannio, already the victim of mistreatment (cf. 159), receives more blows than Aeschinus had intended (170 ff.).[56] One of the noisiest scenes in Plautine comedy is *Men.* 1007 ff., Messenio's spirited defense of Menaechmus I as the latter is being carried off by slaves to the doctor's house for treatment; Messenio of course thinks that the struggling Menaechmus is his master:

MEN.: I implore you, stranger, help me! Don't let this terrible outrage be done to me.
MES.: Of course not! I'll aid you and defend you and assist you assiduously. I'll never permit you to perish; it's better for me to perish. That fellow who has you by the shoulder, gouge out his eye, master, I beg of you. I'll make a garden of these fellows' faces and plant my fists there. (*To* SLAVES) You'll suffer plenty today for trying to kidnap him. Let him go!
MEN. (*hopefully*): I've got this fellow by the eye.
MES.: Knock it out of the socket. (*To* SLAVES) You villains! You robbers! You bandits!
SLAVES: Murder! Stop it, for God's sake!
MES.: Let go of him, then! (SLAVES *drop* MENAECHMUS I.)
MEN.: Take your hands off me! (*To* MESSENIO) Hoe 'em with your fists.
MES.: Come on, away with you! Get the devil out of here! There, take that! That's your reward for being last. (*To* MENAECHMUS I, *as* SLAVES *disappear*) I mapped out their faces in pretty good shape, I think! Well, master, I certainly came to your aid at the proper moment.

(4) Scenes of madness. No genuine madman is introduced on the stage in Roman comedy, but the unhappy lover in a frenzied mood considers himself a warrior arming for battle (*Cist.* 283 ff.) or a traveler on a long journey (*Merc.* 931 ff.). The latter scene, although praised highly by Norwood,[57] is less amusing than the feigned madness of Menaechmus II (*Men.* 828 ff.); pretending to receive commands from Apollo, he threatens to burn out the eyes of the *matrona* with blazing torches; then he turns to the *senex*, apparently still under Apollo's power:

I'll carry out your orders; I'll take a two-headed axe and hack this old fellow's inwards to mincemeat, down to the very bone.

[56] The recipient of blows is often a *leno* (cf. also *Pers.* 809 ff., *Eun.* 715 f.). In *Mil.* 1402 ff. the soldier considers himself fortunate to suffer nothing worse than a beating. It is interesting that slaves are seldom beaten by their masters; on Milphio, see above, p. 290.
[57] See chap. 6, n. 50.

When the twin brother returns (899 ff.) and meets his father-in-law and the doctor, his annoyance and anger at the doctor's queries convinces them of his insanity; a second scene rich in comic values results. In *Capt.* 547 ff., Tyndarus—in order to avoid discovery—attempts to convince Hegio that Aristophontes is insane; the latter's anger (592 ff.), like that of Menaechmus, is interpreted as proof of madness. O'Brien-Moore underestimates the comedy inherent in these scenes when he observes: "Madness is not introduced . . . for its own sake—as drunkenness, for example—as intrinsically funny, but for the comic effect of rhetorical exaggeration."[58]

(5) Drunkenness. Scenes of actual drunkenness are less common than one might expect. We meet the old woman eager for a bowl of wine (*Curc.* 96 ff.) or already tipsy and loquacious (*Cist.* 120 ff.). Syrus quietly indulges in a bit of wine off stage (*Ad.* 589 ff.) and is somewhat unsteady when he meets Demea in 763 ff.; Chremes claims to have drunk too much at Thraso's party (*Eun.* 727 ff.). The difference between Terentian restraint and Plautine exuberance and vulgarity becomes apparent when Syrus and Chremes are compared with Pseudolus, who staggers on the stage and describes how he has celebrated his victory (*Pseud.* 1246 ff.); he meets Simo and belches (1294 ff.):

SI. (*pushing him away*) : Go to the devil!
PS. : What are you shoving me for?
SI. : What the devil do you mean by belching in my face, you drunken fool?
PS. (*clinging to* SIMO *for support*) : Gently—please—hold me up; don't let me fall. Don't you see how sousedly soused I am?
SI. : The insolence of you! To go around drunk in the daytime with garlands on!
PS. (*belching again*) : I—urp!—like to.
SI. : You like to, eh? Are you going to keep on belching in my face?
PS. : It's a very pleasant belch. Just let me be, Simo.

Far more amusing is the famous scene in *Most.* 313 ff., when the already inebriated Callidamates arrives with Delphium to visit Philolaches. He stutters (319, 325, 331), is unable to stand without aid, forgets where he is going, falls asleep upon joining the party; when Tranio reports the imminent arrival of Theopropides, the others attempt to arouse Callidamates from his drunken stupor; cf. 373 ff.:

DE. : Callidamates, Callidamates! Wake up!
CA. (*starting up*) : I am awake. Give me a drink.
DE. : Wake up! Philolaches' father has arrived from abroad.
CA. : Farewell to his father.
PH. : He does fare well and I'm perished in a trice.
CA. : You're twice perished. How can that be?
PH. (*exasperated*) : Get up. I beg you. My father's here!

[58] *Madness in Ancient Literature*, pp. 53 f.

CA.: Your father's here? Tell him to go away again. What did he have to come back here for? . . .
TR. (*pointing to* CALLIDAMATES) : Just look at him! He's put down his head and gone to sleep again. Wake him up!
PH.: Wake up, won't you! My father will be here in a minute, I tell you.
CA. (*rousing to action*): Your father, huh? Give me my slippers, so I can take some weapons. Damn it, I'll murder that father of yours.
PH.: You're ruining everything.
DE.: Please be quiet, won't you?
PH. (*to* SLAVES) : Drag him into the house at once!
CA. (*as* SLAVES *take him inside*) : If you don't bring me a basin soon, I'll use you for one.

(6) Festal scenes of song and dance. The author of the *Coislinian Tractate* included clownish dancing among the causes of laughter, and Cooper amplifies this with the observation: "In pantomimic dancing and rhythmical dumb-show, the mechanical regularity imposed upon what is by nature irregular—like the motions of the drunken, or of men engaged in fisticuffs, or the like—is incongruous and is a source of laughter."[59] Two series of scenes stand out in Plautus for their wealth of song and dance; these are the conclusions of the *Persa* (753 ff.) and the *Stichus* (641 ff.). The celebration of Stichus and Sangarinus in the latter play might have been listed under the heading of drunkenness since the two slaves indulge in a ludicrous orgy of drinking and love-making almost unparalleled in Roman comedy. The celebration of Toxilus and his cronies in the *Persa* does have some relation to the plot in that it displays the final and complete overthrow of the *leno*. The complex of scenes in the *Stichus* forms a musical extravaganza composed for its own sake, and in this respect it is unique in Roman comedy.

In all the scenes of farcical buffoonery mentioned above, the modern reader must draw heavily upon his imagination and must attempt to visualize the stage-business, especially the exaggerated gesticulations which accompanied the dialogue. To both Greek and Roman actors gesticulation was of supreme importance; "even in Terence," Legrand says, "comic effects are occasionally accompanied by exaggerated gestures, brawls, grimaces and contortions."[60] But Terence indulged only rarely in farcical action; he permitted a tipsy slave, an occasional buffeting, but scenes of madness, drunkenness, vulgar song and dance do not appear. Exaggeration, extravagance, violent and boisterous action, allusions and jests of an indecent nature were foreign to his conception

[59] *An Aristotelian Theory of Comedy*, p. 253. Cooper's statement is interesting for its implied criticism and correction of Bergson's theory; we laugh, not primarily because of "something mechanical encrusted upon the living" (*Laughter*, p. 49) but because such an automatism strikes us as incongruous.
[60] *The New Greek Comedy*, p. 490. For a convenient collection of the references to gestures in Donatus' commentary on Terence, see Basore, *The Scholia on Hypokrisis*, pp. 11 ff.; cf. also Blancké, *The Dramatic Values in Plautus*, pp. 23 ff.

of comedy. In the scenes cited above, the Plautine actor must have indulged in gesticulation with energy and abandon. That the extravagances of the Atellan farces and mimes had a strong influence here can hardly be doubted.

Many of the costumes added to the ludicrous aspects of the plays. The descriptions of certain slaves (e.g., Leonidas in *Asin.* 400 f., Pseudolus in *Pseud.* 1218 ff.) and slavedealers (e.g., Cappadox in *Curc.* 230 f., Labrax in *Rud.* 317 f.) imply padded and grotesque figures which would heighten the merriment of the spectators.[61]

## The Comic in Plautus and Terence

"There exist," says Lange, "such things as *objects of universal laughter*, things which appeal to the sense of humor in every human intellect, which lightly upset the sense of propriety and order that is present in every human mind, and awaken laughter by their very suddenness."[62] He cites as the devices "which will be found in every comedian from Plautus to Molière to Shakespeare to George M. Cohan" the following: ludicrous characterization, unexpected situations, mistaken identity, the discernment of difficulty and clumsiness, relief from a great strain, the mechanical and the stupid, suggestiveness, loss of dignity, perception of incongruity, turning on masters, mimicry. The items in this list are of unequal value (e.g., "loss of dignity" is one aspect of "ludicrous characterization," and "turning upon masters" would seem to belong under either "perception of incongruity" or "unexpected situations") and the list as a whole adds little to the brief outline in the *Coislinian Tractate*.[63] But it is significant that the comic devices mentioned by Lange are all present in varying degrees in the extant Roman comedies. The differences between the two comic dramatists, however, are striking.

The fun of Plautus is characterized by haste and vigor;[64] he delights in incongruities and irrationalities, and his mastery of stagecraft has been summarized aptly by Duff: "He plays a whole gamut of comic effects, and manipulates to his liking the elements of comedy, farce, burlesque, operetta, pantomime, and extravaganza."[65] The greater restraint of Terence and his dislike of exaggeration and boisterous com-

---

[61] On the costumes of the actors, see "Costume and Mask" in chap. 4. That the costume sometimes included the representation of the phallus is possibly implied by *Rud.* 429. Padding and the phallus were characteristic of the actors of the *phlyakes* of southern Italy, as of Old Comedy at Athens.

[62] *CB* 9 (1932-33), p. 42.

[63] See above, p. 308. For a detailed analysis of the objects of laughter, see Sully, *An Essay on Laughter*, pp. 87 ff.

[64] Cf. Greig, *The Psychology of Laughter and Comedy*, p. 148, on the importance of haste and vigor; he says: "If the vicious characters go about their nefarious work with verve and enjoyment, they infect the spectators the more irresistibly."

[65] *A Literary History of Rome*, p. 193.

edy make for a more refined type of drama but he achieves subtlety at
the sacrifice of laughter. Post's observation that "a brief study of our
remains of Menander will show that the ridiculous is carefully subordinated to the serious"[66] applies also to Terence, especially in his earlier
plays, although in these same plays a compensatory striving for novelty
in character and situation is apparent. Of Plautus we may say that the
serious is subordinated with equal care to the ridiculous, for almost
everywhere a spirit of playfulness prevails.

Our analysis of the comic elements of Plautus and Terence in the
light of the main theories about the sources of comic laughter has revealed the strengths and weaknesses of each dramatist. To condemn
either playwright for not doing what the other did would be obviously
unwise and unfair. Plautus and Terence had different conceptions of
comedy and each used, or refrained from using, the elements of superiority, incongruity, contrast, surprise, exaggeration as it suited his
purpose.[67]

Or are we to assume that both playwrights were completely lacking
in originality and blindly followed the Greek originals at their disposal?
This is the position taken by many writers on ancient comedy. Legrand,
for instance, believes that many of the exaggerated features of Plautus'
technique were paralleled in New Comedy, and Prehn thinks that the
differences between Plautus and Terence can be explained only by the
differences in the Greek models which they used.[68] But there is another
solution if we do not blind ourselves to the possibility of Roman originality. Even those who assume the perfection of Greek comedy, and
are convinced that all possible contradictions and flaws are to be attributed to Plautus or Terence, make the two Roman dramatists less
imitative although the resultant conception of their originality is not
a happy one.

That many essential features of the Roman plays were inherited
from the Greeks cannot be denied. Yet Plautus' art is too vigorous and
spontaneous, too Italian in its essential nature, to be explained as resulting from a close imitation of Greek plays. Blancké overstresses the

[66] *TAPhA* 69 (1938), p. 25.

[67] My discussion in this chapter of the comic elements in Plautus and Terence may
now be supplemented by Miss Wilner's recent article in *CJ* 46 (1950-51), pp. 165 ff.;
she describes her analysis as follows (p. 176) : "I have classified four kinds of sustained comical scenes: incongruities of the social structure, especially in the humiliation
of masters; self-frustration; sustained bewilderment; and hilarity. Each is created out
of varying combinations of five types of the comical: incongruity, feelings of superiority, surprise reversal, buffoonery, and infectious gaiety."

[68] Legrand-Loeb, *The New Greek Comedy*, pp. 466 ff.; Prehn, *Quaestiones Plautinae*, pp. 70 f. Prehn assumes that Menander's earlier plays were more robust and
farcical; these were imitated by Plautus (*Bacchides* and *Stichus*) while Terence
adapted Menander's later and more refined comedies. The *Cistellaria*, according to
Prehn (*ibid.*, p. 62), was the one later play of Menander which Plautus imitated; it
was an experiment which he never repeated.

so-called "dramatic unrealities and absurdities" but he is correct when he says of Plautine comedy: "The minute we accept it as a consciously conceived medium for amusement only, we have a highly effective theatrical mechanism for the unlimited production of laughter."[69] Furthermore, the fact that the later comedies of both Plautus and Terence differ in many respects from their earlier plays[70] is a strong, almost a convincing, argument against those who believe that the two playwrights are uninspired imitators of Greek originals.

Our picture of the Roman comic spirit is still far from complete. An important aspect to be considered is comedy *in verbis*, verbal humor, and in this Plautus took far greater delight than did Terence. The following chapter will describe the more significant linguistic and stylistic devices that were used to arouse the Roman spectators to laughter at holiday time.

[69] *The Dramatic Values in Plautus*, p. 69.
[70] See "The Significance of Roman Comedy" in chap. 14.

# CHAPTER 12

## LANGUAGE AND STYLE

WHEN we speak of the language of Roman comedy we think primarily of the language of Plautus, which is both the delight of the reader and the despair of the translator. Highly colloquial in its nature, it is swift-moving, yet copious to the point of verbosity. Colorful and imaginative in its use of metaphor, it is rich in comic formations and characterized by alliteration and assonance. The Latin tongue of the second century B.C. differed considerably in its grammar, syntax, and vocabulary from that of the age of Cicero and Caesar, being in a much more fluid state. But the syntactical peculiarities of early Latin do not concern us here and have been adequately summarized elsewhere.[1] Far more significant for our present purpose are the many features of the language—vocabulary, phraseology, style, expression—which make for effective dramatic dialogue and add liveliness and humor to the plays.

Although the language of Roman comedy differs in many respects from that of the classical period and allows a greater variety of constructions, it is wrong to look upon it as vulgar Latin; in general it reflects faithfully the everyday talk of the educated Romans of the time. Plautus, born two generations before Terence, gives us a slightly earlier stage in the development of the language but the striking contrasts between the two playwrights are not to be explained merely upon a basis of years. Both writers used the colloquial speech of their day but Plautus' exuberance and fullness of expression, his desire for laughable effects, led him to write in a more popular and easygoing manner. The language of Terence, in spite of its colloquial nature, is characterized by a striving for elegance and grace and he avoided many of the features which, as we shall see, exist in Plautus in such abundance. Terence's diction is natural and straightforward but his characters have been criticized because they all talk "the same elegant, undifferentiated conversational Latin."[2] Plautus too could write with polish and refinement when the characters or the situations demanded smoothness and restraint; he could also put into the mouths of his characters, especially those of a lower type, expressions of gross abuse, obscene humor, laughable turns of phrase. Hence it is inevitable that the many features of verbal humor to be considered in the present chapter will be illustrated chiefly from the comedies of Plautus although, wherever possible, appropriate examples will be cited from the plays of Terence also.

[1] Cf. Bennett, *Syntax of Early Latin*; Lindsay, *Syntax of Plautus*; Allardice, *Syntax of Terence*.

[2] Post, *CW* 23 (1929-30), p. 122.

# The Language of Roman Comedy[3]

One aspect of the colloquial nature of the comic dialogue has already been noticed—the numerous expressions of greeting and farewell (*salue, quid agis, quid fit; uale, bene ambula, bene sit tibi*, etc.).[4] The greetings of slaves are often extended to include colloquial banter, e.g., *Pers.* 16 ff.:

TO.: O Sagaristio, the gods bless you!
SA.: O Toxilus, the gods will answer your prayers. How do you do?
TO.: The best I can.
SA.: How goes it?
TO.: I'm getting along.
SA.: Quite to your liking, eh?
TO.: Quite, if my wishes come true. . . .
SA.: Have you kept pretty well?
TO.: No, not very.
SA.: Then that's why you're pale.
TO.: I've been wounded in Venus' battle; Cupid has pierced my heart with his arrow.

The greetings of Epidicus and Thesprio (*Epid.* 6 ff.) are similar. Gelasimus in true parasitical fashion hopes to profit from the arrival of the brothers; cf. his greeting in *Stich.* 583 ff.:

O long-awaited Pamphilippus! O my hope, my life, my pleasure! I rejoice that you've returned home from abroad in safety.

His attempt to get a meal from Epignomus (465 ff.) is characterized by expressions equally fulsome, and he even professes to shed tears of joy at the sight of the newcomer.

Colloquial interjections abound in both Plautus and Terence. Among the many exclamations are those expressing laughter (*hahae, hahahae*), disgust or annoyance (*fu, uae*), grief (*ei, heu, papae, uae*), surprise, astonishment, embarrassment (*attat, attatae, ehem, hem, hui, papae, uah*), approval or delight (*eu, euge, eugepae*); others demand silence (*pax, st*) or attention (*eho, heus*). Plautus often creates a comic effect by his use of several interjections; e.g., *babae! . . . papae!* (*Cas.* 906), *heia! beia!* (*Pers.* 212), *babae! . . . bombax!* (*Pseud.* 365), *babae! tatae! papae! pax!* (*Stich.* 771). These exclamations are largely derived from Greek; many of them appear in Latin only in the dialogue of comedy, while others are found in later literature especially in the colloquial writings of Cicero and in Petronius' *Satyricon*.[5]

---

[3] In this and the following section I have limited my notes and bibliographical references as much as possible to the more general and more available works. Numerous monographs and articles have been written about the various topics discussed below, but they are usually of a very technical nature and of little interest to the general reader. These works may be found conveniently listed in Schanz-Hosius, *Geschichte der römischen Literatur*, I, pp. 81-83, 118, and (chiefly on Plautus) in Enk, *Handboek der Latijnse Letterkunde*, II, 1, 2, pp. 293-308.

[4] See "Entrance and Exit Announcements" in chap. 5.

[5] Interjections of this type, valuable for their emotional effect, are about three times

Exclamatory oaths are likewise numerous; *pol* and *edepol* are uttered by both men and women (*pol* chiefly by women in Terence), *hercule* and *mehercule* only by men (with the exception of *Cist.* 52), *ecastor* and *mecastor* only by women.[6] The frequent use of *malum* as an oath perhaps arose from an abbreviation of the formula *malum habebis* or *malum dabitur*; as an interjection it is regularly found in questions, e.g., *Cas.* 91: *quid tu, malum, me sequere?* "Why the devil are you following me"?[7] Characters in annoyance or anger often give vent to imprecations and curses which signify "Damn you!" "Go and be hanged!" "Go to the devil!" The commoner of these expressions are *omnes di te perdant! uae tibi! uae capiti tuo! i directe! i in malam crucem! i in malam rem!* More emphatic forms are *i in malam magnam crucem!* and *i directe in maxumam malam crucem!* These phrases, far more frequent in Plautus than in Terence, are often no more than expressions of disgust at a jesting or indecent remark (e.g., *Epid.* 23, *And.* 317),[8] sometimes merely an exaggerated exclamation of incredulity (*Capt.* 877). In *Poen.* 347, Milphio uses the *malam crucem* phrase in its strongest form (*i directe in maxumam malam crucem*) merely as a means of ridiculing his master's love affair:

Jove! What a beautiful little wench! Go straight to everlasting perdition! The more I look at her, the more worthless a bit of trash she seems.

Comic oaths and threats are combined in *Curc.* 574 ff.:

TH.: May my sword and my shield aid me well as I fight on the field; if the girl isn't restored to me, I'll make such mincemeat of you that the ants can carry you away from here bit by bit.

CA.: And may my tweezers, comb, mirror, curling iron, scissors, bath towel love me well; I don't give any more of a damn for your defiant words and dreadful threats than I do for the wench that cleans out my privy.

Equally exaggerated are the many colloquial expressions of abuse. The terms which Pseudolus and his master apply to Ballio give us an interesting insight into the richness of the Latin vocabulary in this respect; cf. *Pseud.* 360 ff.: *inpudice, sceleste, uerbero, bustirape, furcifer, sociofraude, parricida, sacrilege, peiiure, legerupa, permities adulescentium, fur, fugitiue, fraus populi, fraudulente, inpure, caenum.* Toxilus says that three hundred verses would be insufficient to recount the villainies of Dordalus—but he does extremely well in less than five (*Pers.*

---

as frequent in Terence as in Plautus; cf. Haffter, *Untersuchungen zur altlateinischen Dichtersprache*, pp. 127 ff.

[6] Cf. Duckworth, *T. Macci Plauti Epidicus*, pp. 122 f. For oaths and curses in Roman comedy, see also Echols, *CJ* 46 (1950-51), pp. 295, 297.

[7] For Plautus, cf. *Amph.* 403, 592, 604, 626, *Bacch.* 672, *Cas.* 262, 472, etc. Terence uses the expression sparingly; cf. *Heaut.* 318, 716, *Eun.* 780, *Phorm.* 723, 948, *Ad.* 544, 557.

[8] Cf. also *Asin.* 306, *Capt.* 868, 885, *Curc.* 317, *Epid.* 333, *Most.* 1002, *Poen.* 610, 863, 873, *Pseud.* 335, 846, 1182, *Rud.* 518, etc.

406 ff.; cf. the *leno*'s reply in 417 ff.). When Plautine slaves, in seriousness or in jest, heap abusive terms upon each other, they display an
earthiness and a vulgarity that one looks for in vain in the comedies of
Terence; cf. *Asin.* 297 ff., *Cas.* 89 ff., *Pers.* 275 ff. The opening scene
of the *Mostellaria* displays a rich variety of epithets—*mastigia* (1),
*erilis permities* (3), *frutex* (13), *urbanus scurra* (15), *germana in-
luuies, rusticus, hircus, hara suis* (40), *carnuficium cribrum* (55),
*furcifer* (69).[9]

Many other features of the language of the comedies must be passed
over with a brief mention; among the colloquial elements are the following: (1) Parataxis, or coordination of clauses, which makes for
simplicity and straightforwardness of sentence structure, e.g., *Epid.*
124: *spero seruabit fidem*, "He'll keep his word, I hope." (Any ele-
mentary student of Latin knows that the Romans should say *spero eum
fidem seruaturum esse*; the early Romans, however, and Cicero and
later writers as well, used in their everyday speech a diction more
flexible and natural.)[10]

(2) Pleonasm, the use of more words than necessary to express an
idea; e.g., *Curc.* 283: *subito, propere et celere; Most.* 476: *scelus, in-
quam, factum est iam diu, antiquom et uetus; Eun.* 246: *olim isti fuit
generi quondam quaestus apud saeclum prius.* Emphatic phrases like
*nil quicquam* and *nemo quisquam* are frequent and, as in colloquial
speech today, the double negative was sometimes used, e.g., *neque
nullus, neque numquam, neque haud.*[11]

(3) Ellipsis, the omission of a part of the sentence. Often the verb
(especially a verb of saying) is omitted, e.g., *Mil.* 375: *paucis uerbis
te uolo* (cf. *Curc.* 303, *Epid.* 460, *Trin.* 963, *And.* 29, 893). The omission of the verb is far more common in Terence than in Plautus—an
indication that the younger dramatist was striving for greater rapidity
and naturalness of dialogue.[12]

(4) Diminutives, used sometimes to denote smallness of size, e.g.,
*lunulam atque anellum aureolum* (*Epid.* 640), *sicilicula argenteola et
. . . maniculae et sucula* (*Rud.* 1169 f.), *pistrilla* (*Ad.* 584), but more

---

[9] On the frequency of these and other common terms of abuse (e.g., *carnufex,
uerbereum caput*), see Müller, *Ph* 72 (1913), pp. 492 ff.; Hofmann, *Lateinische Umgangssprache*, pp. 85 ff. Terence's epithets are less colorful than Plautus' but reveal a
surprising variety, including, among others, *asine, carcer, carnufex, fugitiue, furcifer,
ignaue, impurissume, mastigia, sceleste, scelus, sterculinum, stulte, uenefica, uerbero.*

[10] *Credo, scio,* and *faxo* are much more frequent in parataxis than *spero*; cf. e.g.,
*Epid.* 34, 156, 257, 535, and see Duckworth, *T. Macci Plauti Epidicus*, pp. 126 f., 179,
199 f.; Hofmann, *Lateinische Umgangssprache*, pp. 105 ff. Other verbs constantly
used in parataxis include *quaeso, obsecro,* and *amabo.* In this colloquial feature there
is little difference between Plautus' language and that of Terence.

[11] Cf. Lindsay, *Syntax of Plautus*, p. 131; Duckworth, *T. Macci Plauti Epidicus,*
p. 393.

[12] E.g., the verb of going is omitted in *And.* 361: *ego me continuo ad Chremem*; the
verb of seeing in *Ad.* 539: *siquid rogabit, nusquam tu me*; cf. Haffter, *Untersuchungen
zur altlateinischen Dichtersprache*, pp. 130 ff.

often expressing sympathy, tenderness, affection; cf. *animule, melilla, ocellos* (*Cas.* 134 ff.), *belliatula* (*Cas.* 854), *bellula* (*Mil.* 989), *puellulam* (*Phorm.* 81); the diminutive of proper names is similarly used: cf. Olympisce (*Cas.* 739), Stephaniscidium (*Stich.* 739), Syrisce (*Ad.* 763).[13] Plautus employs diminutives with far greater frequency than does Terence and often with little or no appreciable distinction in meaning between the diminutive and the regular noun or adjective.[14] Many of his diminutives seem especially coined for the purpose of humor; e.g., *ebriola persolla*, "you tipsy little fright" (*Curc.* 192), *meum corculum, melculum, uerculum,* "my little sweetheart, my darling honey, my springflower" (*Cas.* 837), *papillarum horridularum oppressiunculae,* "the playful squeezings of pouting breastlets" (*Pseud.* 68). The diminutive which, according to Aristotle (*Rhet.* 1405b), lessens the good or the bad in a descriptive term, is listed in the *Coislinian Tractate* as one of the sources of laughter arising from diction.[15]

Another feature of the comic diction may be mentioned at this time—the use of Greek words. This is not, strictly speaking, a colloquial characteristic of the language but rather a means of rhetorical embellishment that could be used for comic effect.[16] Both Plautus and Terence employed Latinized forms of Greek words to add a flavor of elegance or humor to their plays, but Plautus used such words to a far greater extent and he did not hesitate to introduce into his dialogue many words Greek in form, especially when he could achieve a ludicrous effect by so doing, e.g., *Capt.* 880 ff., *Cas.* 728 ff., *Pseud.* 712 (introduced for the word-play on Charinus). As his art developed, Plautus concentrated his Greek words for greater artistic and humorous effect and assigned them to more appropriate characters (to slaves and persons of low standing). Terence, using fewer Greek words, was more interested in

---

[13] Cf. Conrad, *Gl* 19 (1930-31), pp. 127 ff.; 20 (1930-31), pp. 74 ff.; Conrad believes that the diminutives in Plautus do not connote smallness; if they differ from the original word, they express affection or humor. In his first article (pp. 129 ff.) he lists more than three hundred Plautine diminutives; cf. also Cooper, *Word Formation in the Roman Sermo Plebeius*, pp. 173 ff., for lists of diminutives not only in Plautus and Terence but in the colloquial speech of later writers as well.

[14] Cf., e.g., *dicaculus* (*Cas.* 529) and *dicax* (*Truc.* 683); *occasiuncula* (*Trin.* 974) and *occasio* (*Bacch.* 673); *ratiuncula* (*Capt.* 192) and *ratio* (*Men.* 206).

[15] Cf. Cooper, *An Aristotelian Theory of Comedy*, pp. 235 f.; see below, n. 52.

[16] Although it does not occur frequently, a second means of rhetorical embellishment may be seen in the occasional parody of tragic style; e.g., *Bacch.* 933: *o Troia, o patria, o Pergamum, o Priame; Pseud.* 703: *io te, te, turanne, te, te; Ad.* 790: *o caelum, o terra, o maria Neptuni.* The extent to which other passages of a more serious or pathetic nature are to be viewed as tragic parodies cannot be determined with certainty, but cf. *Bacch.* 1053, *Men.* 330, 350, 402 ff., *Rud.* 268 f., 942, *Stich.* 365, and see Sedgwick, *CQ* 21 (1927), pp. 88 f. Allusions to specific tragedies (*Poen.* 1, *Rud.* 86) and references to the Trojan war (cf. chap. 11, n. 49) were not without meaning to the Roman spectators, who viewed tragedies as well as comedies at the games. Cf. Frank, *AJPh* 53 (1932), pp. 243 ff. It is very possible that the ravings of Menaechmus II in the famous scene of pretended madness (*Men.* 835 ff.) parodied a tragic performance which the Romans had recently seen; cf. Buck, *A Chronology of the Plays of Plautus,* pp. 71 f.

their rhetorical effect. Hough explains this difference in technique as
reflecting "the absence of such foreign elements from the ordinary
speech of the cultured (Terence) in contrast to the rougher language
of Plautus' characters. The latter more accurately represent the ver-
nacular of the lower classes, which was interspersed with foreign words
introduced through military service abroad."[17]

The importance of exaggeration as a comic device already has been
mentioned;[18] it is no less important as a characteristic of colloquial
language, which constantly seeks to gain emphasis by overstatement.
The striving for emphasis accounts for the many oaths and abusive
terms which the characters utter; it accounts also for the exaggerated
and grandiloquent statements of the characters, and in this respect also
Plautus shows less restraint than Terence.

Hyperbole is common: *perii, disperii, interii* ("I'm dead," "I've
perished") express despair when things go wrong and often are little
more than oaths or exclamations. If a character does something unusual,
or falls madly in love, he is "insane." Characters do not merely express
their wrath, they "vomit" it forth (cf. *Hec.* 515, *Ad.* 312, 510), and
*uomere argentum* is equivalent to our "cough up the money" (*Curc.*
688). Metaphor is frequently combined with hyperbole: instead of
eating food one "cuts it to bits" (*Most.* 65, *Stich.* 554); in place of the
usual phrase "get money" we have the exaggerated expression "coin
money" (*Merc.* 432, *Heaut.* 740); a character is not merely tricked
out of money, he is shorn (*Bacch.* 242, 1095), boned (*Pseud.* 382),
disemboweled (*Epid.* 672). A striking characteristic of metaphorical
hyperbole is its concreteness. Miss Glick says: "It is not enough to kill
someone but he is hewed limb from limb, cut to pieces, has his head
broken to bits, or he is made into sausage meat. It is always some
definite, specific type of treatment which he is to receive. . . . This concreteness is obvious also in the words used for tricking a person: he is
sheared, torn limb from limb, hewed down, planed off, boned, mangled,
torn out by the roots, or eaten up; his treatment is always something
definite and specific."[19]

It is natural that plays devoted largely to love affairs and to deception should have a rich colloquial vocabulary in these two areas. Specific
phrases for deceiving a person are numerous, e.g., *circumducere* ("lead
around"), *uerba dare* ("give words to"), *ludos facere* ("make game
of"), *os sublinere* ("smear one's face"), etc. Similarly, there are many
erotic expressions; in addition to terms of endearment such as *uita*
("life"), *animus* ("soul"), *uoluptas* ("darling"), *deliciae* ("delight"),

---

[17] *CW* 41 (1947-48), p. 18; cf. *AJPh* 55 (1934), pp. 362 ff. See also Cooper, *Word
Formation in the Roman Sermo Plebeius*, pp. 316 f. Examples of hybrid formations are
cited below; see "Comic Formations."
[18] See "Comic Exaggeration" in chap. 11.
[19] *Studies in Colloquial Exaggeration*, p. 137.

*ocellus* ("apple of my eye"), *rosa* ("rosebud"), *mel* ("honey"),[20] there are numerous verbs used with an erotic connotation, e.g., *tractare, contrectare, tangere, attingere* ("touch," "handle," "caress"), *ludere* ("dally amorously"), *cubare, cubitare* ("lie down with"), *quiescere, dormire* ("sleep with"), *uelle* ("be willing").[21]

Especially striking are the numerous similes and metaphors which allude to trickery and love. The planner of an intrigue is a shipbuilder (*Mil.* 915 ff.), a poet (*Pseud.* 401 ff.), a hunter seeking his prey (*Poen.* 647 f.), a statesman calling a meeting of the senate (*Epid.* 159, *Mil.* 592, 594, *Most.* 688, 1049 f.). Military metaphors are very frequent: the *seruus callidus* is the commander of troops (his allies or his tricks) who besieges and captures the enemy (e.g., *Bacch.* 709 ff., *Mil.* 219 ff., *Pers.* 753 ff., *Pseud.* 579 ff., *Heaut.* 669).[22] Comparisons of love with warfare are found more rarely (cf. *Men.* 184 ff., *Pers.* 24, *Trin.* 668); Astaphium says to Diniarchus (*Truc.* 170 f.):

A lover is like the city of the enemy. . . . It's best for his sweetheart to have him sacked as soon as possible.

Some of Plautus' most varied and colorful metaphors are lavished upon the *meretrix*: she is a swiftly flowing stream (*Bacch.* 85), a dangerous whirlpool (*Bacch.* 471); her house is a gymnasium where in place of helmet, spear, horse, and shield there await the cup, dice, couch, and harlot (*Bacch.* 66 ff.); she resembles a prosperous city—she can't get along without a lot of men (*Cist.* 80 f.); she is like a fisherman hauling in his net (*Truc.* 35 ff.), or a briar bush which causes pain to the men whom it touches (*Truc.* 227 f.).

Similes and metaphors of this type are relatively rare in Terence. But proverbs and maxims—always common in colloquial speech—occur in great profusion in the works of both dramatists. Terence is especially famed for the wealth of his quotable phrases, several of which have become a part of world literature:[23]

---

[20] Cf. the exaggerated piling up of such terms for comic effect in *Asin.* 664 ff., 691 ff., *Bacch.* fr. xii, *Cas.* 134 ff., *Poen.* 365 ff.; for a translation of the final passage, see above, p. 323. Callidamates' words of endearment in *Most.* 352 are rendered more amusing by his drunken stuttering.

[21] Cf. Preston, *Studies in the Diction of the Sermo Amatorius*, pp. 30 ff. Preston's work is a convenient storehouse of material on erotic diction in general. On the many expressions which denote trickery, see Brotherton, *The Vocabulary of Intrigue*; cf. also Glick, *Studies in Colloquial Exaggeration*, pp. 66 f., 78 ff.

[22] See Brotherton, *The Vocabulary of Intrigue*, pp. 64 ff., and cf. above, p. 323. Fraenkel (*Plautinisches im Plautus*, pp. 238 ff.) considers military figures such as these typical Plautine. The military expressions of Terence, fewer in number, are more literary and reflect less the language of the common soldier. Terence, for instance, does not use *adscriptiuus, aries, ballista, castra, catapulta, stipendium, uelitatio, uinea*; see Durry, *REL* 18 (1940), pp. 57 ff.

[23] These were frequently quoted or mentioned by Roman writers of the classical period, e.g., *And.* 126 (*hinc illae lacrumae*) reappears in Cicero, *Pro Cael.* 25, 61; Horace, *Epist.* i, 19, 41. With *Heaut.* 796 (*ius summum saepe summast malitia*), cf. Cic. *De off.* i, 10, 33. *Phorm.* 203 (*fortis fortuna adiuuat*) is likewise quoted by Cicero

Hence these tears. (*And*. 126)

I am a man; I think that nothing concerning man is foreign to me. (*Heaut*. 77)

The most law is often the greatest injustice. (*Heaut*. 796)

Venus is helpless without Ceres and Bacchus. (*Eun*. 732)

It's folly to kick against the pricks. (*Phorm*. 77 f.)

Fortune favors the brave. (*Phorm*. 203)

So many men, so many opinions. (*Phorm*. 454)

I've got the wolf by the ears; I can't hold him and I can't let go. (*Phorm*. 506 f.)

Friends have all things in common. (*Ad*. 804)

Many such Terentian expressions are undoubtedly Greek[24] and were taken over from the originals; others had already become a part of Latin colloquial speech before the time of Terence since they appear in earlier comedy at Rome as well, e.g.:

A hare yourself, do you hunt game? (Livius Andronicus, 8, *Eun*. 426)

You're looking for a knot in a bulrush. (*Men*. 247, *And*. 941)

A word to the wise is sufficient. (*Pers*. 729, *Phorm*. 541; cf. *Truc*. 644)

The wolf in the fable. (*Stich*. 577, *Ad*. 537)

Live as you can, since you can't as you wish. (Caecilius, 177; cf. *And*. 305 f., 805)[25]

Among the many Plautine proverbs the following also may be quoted:

Where there's smoke, there's fire. (*Curc*. 53)

As blows the wind, so turns the sail. (*Epid*. 49, *Poen*. 754)

It's a terrible thing to have to dig a well when you're thirsty. (*Most*. 379 f.)

It's not easy to blow and to swallow at the same time. (*Most*. 791)

In the country each one reaps for himself. (*Most*. 799, cf. *Merc*. 71)

---

(*Tusc. disp*. II, 4, 11) as an old proverb; cf. Verg. *Aen*. X, 284: *audentis Fortuna iuuat*. For *Phorm*. 454 (*quot homines tot sententiae*), cf. Cic. *De fin*. I, 5, 15; Horace, *Serm*. II, I, 27 f. Cicero alludes on several occasions to the famous *homo sum* passage (*Heaut*. 77); cf. *De fin*. III, 19, 63; *De leg*. I, 12, 33; that this Stoic sentiment is humorously used by Terence as an excuse for neighborly curiosity is implied by Cicero in *De off*. I, 9, 30; cf. also *De fin*. I, I, 3, and see above, p. 304.

[24] Donatus on *Phorm*. 506 (*auribus teneo lupum*, etc.) quotes the Greek form of the proverb; for other occurrences in Greek and Latin, see Dziatzko-Hauler, *Phormio, ad loc. Phorm*. 77 f. (*namque inscitiast aduorsum stimulum calces*) is a translation of a Greek proverb appearing in Aeschylus, *Agam*. 1624, Euripides, *Bacch*. 795, and elsewhere; cf. *Acts of the Apostles*, 26, 14. Cicero (*De off*. I, 16, 51) refers to *Ad*. 804 (*communia esse amicorum inter se omnia*) as a Greek proverb; the Greek phrase κοινὰ τὰ τῶν φίλων, appears not only in Menander's *Adelphoe* (fr. 9), but is quoted by Plato (*Lysis*, 207c) and Aristotle (*Nic. Eth*. 1159b), to each of whom it was already an old saying. Donatus (*ad Ad*. 804) ascribes the proverb to the Pythagoreans.

[25] Cf. Menander, fr. 50 (quoted above, p. 26). For other expressions taken by Terence from earlier Roman poets, see Terzaghi, *Prolegomeni a Terenzio*, pp. 92 f.

> You're trying to get water from pumice. (*Pers.* 41)
> You've hit the nail on the head, lit., "you've struck it with the needle." (*Rud.* 1306)
> One eye is better than ten ears. (*Truc.* 489)

Terence has been praised also for his aphorisms, for the maxims which "are so well thought out that they do not give a picture of Greek and Roman life only, but find easy application to life as lived by all men of all ages."[26] The following are often cited:

> Moderation is the most valuable rule of life. (*And.* 61)
> Complaisance makes friends, truthfulness enemies. (*And.* 68)
> Lovers' quarrels are a renewal of love. (*And.* 555)
> There's nothing so easy but that it becomes difficult if you have to do it against your will. (*Heaut.* 805 f.)
> Nothing is said now that has not been said before. (*Eun.* 41)
> A wise person should try every expedient before resorting to force. (*Eun.* 789)
> There's nothing that can't be made worse in the telling. (*Phorm.* 696 f.)

Plautus is equally rich in aphorisms—a fact that is seldom realized, perhaps because the farcical nature of his plays tends to obscure the value of many of his more sententious phrases (although, as we have already mentioned, there are many more passages of moralizing *per se* in Plautus than in Terence); the following are typical:

> Even if you have no modesty, you might at least assume a little. (*Amph.* 819) [27]
> A person free from sin should be bold and speak with confidence. (*Amph.* 836 f.)
> A contented mind is sufficient for life's enjoyment. (*Aul.* 187)
> A person prospers if he has a good reputation. (*Most.* 227; but cf. *Stich.* 520)
> A stout heart in misfortune is half the battle. (*Pseud.* 452; cf. *Rud.* 402)
> A man who criticizes another's faults should himself be spotless. (*Truc.* 160)[28]

If the plays of Plautus and Terence had been lost except for fragments containing maxims and aphorisms such as these (as is the case

---

[26] Gourde, *CJ* 42 (1946-47), p. 431.

[27] Cf. *Hamlet*, Act III, Sc. 4: "Assume a virtue, if you have it not." Similarly, the sentiment in Ben Jonson's *The Alchemist*, Act V, Sc. 2 ("Nothing's more wretched than a guilty conscience") is undoubtedly a translation of *Most.* 544.

[28] For additional aphorisms in Plautus and Terence, many in a serious vein, others of a more frivolous nature, cf. *Bacch.* 408, 816 f. (from Menander; cf. chap. 2, n. 15), *Epid.* 113, 425, *Merc.* 772, *Most.* 169, 190, 250, 273, 289, 291 (=*Poen.* 306), *Pers.* 346, *Poen.* 302, 304, 307, 328, *Rud.* 400, 939, 1114, *Stich.* 139, 178, *Trin.* 63, 363, *Truc.* 173, 494, 812, 885; *And.* 43 f., 77 f., 191, 309, 427, *Heaut.* 240, *Phorm.* 757 f.. *Hec.* 312, 608, *Ad.* 74 f., 98 f., 431, 739 f.; cf. "The Moral Tone of Roman Comedy" in chap. 10, and see Gourde, *CJ* 42 (1946-47), pp. 431 ff.; Beede, *CJ* 44 (1948-49), pp. 357 ff.

with the writers of Greek Middle and New Comedy with the exception of Menander), it would be difficult to tell from the fragments which playwright had written with the greater restraint and delicacy. Certainly there would be little indication from such passages of Plautus' emphasis upon colloquial exaggeration or his love for comic formations, puns, and word-plays, in short, all the devices which combine to make his language so effective in its spontaneity and humor, and so unlike the refined and precise speech of Terence.

## Stylistic Features

Alliteration, assonance, anaphora, asyndeton, and the like are marked characteristics of Latin writing and are found in other poetic forms (e.g., tragedy, epic, lyric) as well as in comedy. They were especially pronounced in early poetry.[29] Both comic playwrights loved to achieve interesting effects from the sound of words, and the repetition of the same or similar letters, syllables, and words undoubtedly delighted the ears of their spectators. Some of the more striking devices are the following:

(1) Asyndeton, the omission of connectives, which makes for the effective heaping up of nouns or verbs or adjectives. Eutychus in *Merc.* 845 ff. speaks of finding six comrades (*uitam, amicitiam, ciuitatem, laetitiam, ludum, iocum*) by means of which he has driven out numerous ills (*iram, inimicitiam, maerorem, lacrumas, exsilium, inopiam, solitudinem, stultitiam, exitium, pertinaciam*). Asyndeton is common in Terence; cf., e.g., *And.* 319 (*spem salutem auxilium consilium*), 334 ( *facite fingite inuenite efficite*), *Ad.* 856 (*res aetas usus*) 991 (*ecfundite, emite, facite*), and cf. particularly 863-876, but Terence does not use it in long and riotous lists of expressions such as are found in Plautus; these are especially characteristic of Plautus' monologues and monodies; cf. *Capt.* 770 f.:

> laudem lucrum, ludum, iocum, festiuitatem, ferias,
> pompam, penum, potationes, saturitatem, gaudium.[30]

Although colloquial speech is often full and redundant (particularly in Plautus), it may also be very brief and forceful; asyndeton helps, in a series of short disconnected sentences, to create a decidedly staccato effect, e.g., *Pers.* 310 f. (*adito. uidebitur. factum uolo. uenito. pro-*

---

[29] Cf. e.g., Ennius' *Alexander* (41, 47): *mater, optumarum multo mulier melior mulierum* and *men obesse, illos prodesse; me obstare, illos obsequi.* Ennius' fondness for alliteration may be illustrated equally well from the *Annales*; cf. 47 ff. V: *repente recessit, in conspectum corde cupitus, multa manus ad caeli caerula, uoce uocabam.* His metrical *tours-de-force* are famous, e.g., *Ann.* 109 V: *O Tite tute Tati tibi tanta tyranne tulisti*, and 621 V: *machina multa minax minitatur maxima muris.*

[30] Cf. also *Aul.* 508 ff., *Cist.* 206 ff. (translated above, p. 103), *Epid.* 230 ff., *Mil.* 189 ff., *Pers.* 406 ff., 418 ff., *Poen.* 365 ff., 387 ff., *Pseud.* 138 f., *Rud.* 408 f., *Stich.* 226 ff.

*moneto*.) and *Phorm*. 135 f. (*persuasumst homini. factumst. uentumst. uincimur. duxit*.) ; cf. also *And*. 284 f.

(2) Anaphora, or the repetition of a word at the beginning of successive phrases or clauses. This is a favorite device for making the words of the characters much more emphatic; cf. the following:

> ut subito, ut propere, ut ualide tonuit! (*Amph*. 1062)
> quid me adflictas? quid me raptas? qua me causa uerberas? (*Aul*. 632)
> doleo ab animo, doleo ab oculis, doleo ab aegritudine. (*Cist*. 60)
> uos scelesti, uos rapaces, uos praedones! (*Men*. 1015)
> scis amorem, scis laborem, scis egestatem meam. (*Pseud*. 695)[31]

(3) The examples of anaphora cited above illustrate also the frequency of asyndeton, but they display another stylistic feature in which both playwrights took great delight—triadic structure. Readers of Vergil's *Bucolics* will recall in VIII, 73 ff., the use of three as a magic number, and in literary expression the number three seems to have a force equally magical. Perhaps the best known triad in Roman literature —one that has asyndeton, alliteration, and assonance—is *ueni, uidi, uici*; one of the most famous in modern times is "Blood, sweat, and tears." The importance of the number three in Plautus appears in *Pseud*. 704 ff.:

> To thee I'll give blessings thrice three times three, thrice earned with triple arts in triple ways, three joys thrice swindled from three dupes through mischief, snares, and fraud.

Plautus' conscious use of the triad for comic effect is seen in *Truc*. 938:

sт.: What do you owe this fellow?
PH.: Three things.
sт.: What three things?
PH.: Perfume, kisses, a night together.

In *Poen*. 1401 *Antamoenides* says to the *leno*:

> You owe me three things now at once—gold, silver, and your neck.[32]

Triadic structure is one of the most frequently appearing stylistic devices in Roman comedy. In addition to the examples cited above, the following (usually with asyndeton, alliteration, and assonance) may be quoted as typical: with nouns, *seruitus, sudor, sitis* (*Merc*. 674), *inuentor inceptor perfector* (*Eun*. 1035);[33] *pernicies, . . . periurus, pestis* (*Ad*.

---

[31] Cf. also *Cas*. 595, *Cist*. 60, *Epid*. 680 f., *Men*. 997 f., *Mil*. 191 f., *Most*. 935 f., *Pseud*. 1243, *Rud*. 408, 413, *Truc*. 441 ff., *Heaut*. 793 f., *Ad*. 556, 799 f. See Hofmann, *Lateinische Umgangssprache*, pp. 61 ff.

[32] See also *Merc*. 118 f., *Pseud*. 691.

[33] Marouzeau (*Térence*, I, p. 218) says of Chaerea in the *Eunuchus*: "le bouillant Chéréa joue des mots et des sons avec une fantaisie quasi plautinienne"; cf. his triads in 574: *uiderem audirem essem*, 605: *tam brevem, tam optatam, tam insperatam*. Cf. also the alliteration in 613 f., cited below.

188 f.) ; with adjectives, *screanti, siccae, semisomnae* (*Curc.* 115), *indoctae, inmemori, insipienti* (*Pers.* 168), *procax, rapax, trahax* (*Pers.* 410, cf. 421*)* ; with adverbs, *indecore, inique, inmodeste* (*Rud.* 194); with verbs, *adiuuant, augent, amant* (*Epid.* 192, *Men.* 551), *retines, reuocas, rogitas* (*Men.* 114), *interemptust, interfectust, alienatust* (*Merc.* 833), *compellare et complecti et contrectare* (*Mil.* 1052), *supersit, suppetat, superstitet* (*Pers.* 331), *profundat perdat pereat* (*Ad.* 134), *ignotumst tacitumst creditumst* (*Ad.* 474). Sometimes a second triad follows immediately after the first, e.g., *Epid.* 222: *uestita, aurata, ornata ut lepide, ut concinne, ut noue!* (cf. *Epid.* 680 f., *Mil.* 191 f.).[34]

(4) Alliteration and initial assonance, the repetition of the same letter or sound at the beginning of words. Repetition of this type appears frequently in words grouped in pairs or triads, e.g., *multiloqua et multibiba* (*Cist.* 149), *constant, conferunt . . . opstant, opsistunt* (*Curc.* 290 f.), *lepida et liberali* (*Epid.* 43, *Mil.* 967, *Pers.* 130),[35] *uos uideo opportunitate ambo aduenire* (*Epid.* 203), *exspectando exedor miser atque exenteror* (*Epid.* 320), *optuma opportunitate ambo aduenistis* (*Merc.* 964), *facetis fabricis et doctis dolis* (*Mil.* 147), *praedam participes petunt* (*Most.* 312), *modice et modeste meliust uitam uiuere* (*Pers.* 346), *scio mea solide solum gauisurum gaudia* (*And.* 964), *in pecunia perspexeris, uerere uerba* (*Phorm.* 60 f.).[36] Two pairs and a triad appear in *Bacch.* 1088: *stulti, stolidi, fatui, fungi, bardi, blenni, buccones.* When the same letter or sound is repeated four or five times, it serves to produce a laughable effect, e.g., *Men.* 252: *non potuit paucis plura plane proloqui; Eun.* 613 f.: *quo pacto porro possim potiri; Most.* 352 f.: *ita mali maeroris montem maxumum ad portum modo conspicatus sum; Stich.* 120: *ex malis multis malum quod minimumst, id minimest malum.* The effect of the original can seldom be preserved in translation; *Most.* 352 f. may be rendered

I've just beheld at the harbor the mightiest mountain of monstrous misery.

For *Stich.* 120 we have Workman's happy version:

---

[34] For additional illustrations and a discussion of triads in general, see Leo, *Analecta Plautina*, III, pp. 10 ff.; Lejay, *Plaute*, pp. 229 ff.; Duckworth, *T. Macci Plauti Epidicus*, pp. 227, 241.

[35] Cf. *Rud.* 408: *ut lepide, ut liberaliter.* It is interesting that Terence prefers the combination *honesta et liberali*, thus avoiding alliteration; cf. *And.* 123, *Eun.* 682.

[36] For other striking examples of alliteration, cf. *Aul.* 279, *Rud.* 685 f., *Truc.* 484, *Ad.* 322. The repetition of the same letter or the same syllable at the beginning of each of the three words in a triad we have already seen to be very frequent, e.g., *supersit, suppetat, superstitet*. See Duckworth, *T. Macci Plauti Epidicus*, p. 175, on *Epid.* 118 (*differor, difflagitor*), where Plautus perhaps made a comic formation, repeating the preceding prefix, as if one should say "I am distressed, dis-troubled." A modern popular song has the title, "It's Delightful, It's Delicious, It's De-lovely" (a triad with asyndeton, anaphora, and alliteration).

Of many malignities, the minimum of malevolence makes the minimum of misery.[37]

(5) Terminal assonance, or similarity of sound at the end of words. A pleasing sound effect, sometimes of a comic nature, is produced by his means, and what we actually have at times is a kind of word jingle, almost a rhyme scheme within the verse. The words are grouped in pairs, asyndeton, anaphora, and alliteration are often present, and the internal rhyme is usually accentuated by the coincidence of meter and word accent. Cf. the following: *in medicinis, in tostrinis* (*Amph.* 1013, cf. *Epid.* 198), *compellare aut contrectare, conloquiue aut contui* (*Asin.* 523), *nec strategus nec tyrannus . . . nec demarchus nec comarchus* (*Curc.* 285 f.), *tunicam rallam, tunicam spissam* (*Epid.* 230), *cumatile aut plumatile, carinum aut cerinum* (*Epid.* 233),[38] *perdidisti et reperisti* (*Epid.* 652), *aetate et satietate* (*Most.* 196), *in labore atque in dolore* (*Pseud.* 686), *amentium, haud amantium* (*And.* 218), *sollicitando et pollicitando* (*And.* 912), *hortamentis . . . ornamentis* (*Heaut.* 336 f.), *ita cursando atque ambulando* (*Hec.* 815). We have a striking instance in *Amph.* 1062: *strepitus, crepitus, sonitus, tonitrus*, which may be rendered "clanging, banging, tumbling, rumbling." Plautus is unusually successful in grouping his words both by sound and by sense; e.g., *Epid.* 220: *fidemque remque seque teque properat perdere* (cf. *Truc.* 58) and *Merc.* 71: *tibi aras, tibi occas, tibi seris, tibi idem metis.*

(6) Etymological figure, the use of different words more or less closely related by etymology.[39] In its simplest form the figure results from the combination of two related words—noun and adjective (e.g., *pretio pretioso, miserruma miseria*), adjective and adverb (*scite scitus*), adverb and verb (e.g., *sapienter sapit*), verb and noun—very frequent in both Plautus and Terence—(e.g., *dicta dicere, facinus facere, gaudia gaudere, nomen nominare, pugnam pugnare, seruitutem seruire, uitam uiuere*). Plautus develops the etymological figure into a form of word-play designed primarily for comic effect. More typically Plautine are *machinabor machinam* (*Bacch.* 232), *opsonabo opsonium* (*Stich.* 440), *familiaris . . . familiariter* (*Amph.* 355, *Epid.* 2), *madide madeam* (*Pseud.* 1297), *suaui suauitate* (*Pseud.* 882). He weaves proper names into the figure: *Bacchis, Bacchas metuo et bacchanal tuom* (*Bacch.* 53), *o Salute mea salus salubrior* (*Cist.* 644), *Venerem uenerabor* (*Poen.* 278, cf. *Rud.* 305), *an Salutem te salutem?* (*Pseud.* 709). Laughable effects are created by his repeated use of the same word or related

---

[37] Duckworth, *The Complete Roman Drama*, II, p. 9.

[38] These two verses form part of a passage containing sixteen adjectives; see Whitsel, *Studies in the Grouping of Words*, p. 48: the series is composed of a triad followed by a succession of pairs, and "the climax of the series, *gerrae maxumae*, is a confession of his whimsical grouping."

[39] Cf. Leo, *Analecta Plautina*, II, pp. 4 ff.; Haffter, *Untersuchungen zur altlateinischen Dichtersprache*, pp. 10 ff.; Duckworth, *T. Macci Plauti Epidicus*, pp. 125, 177, 321.

words: *optumo optume optumam operam* (*Amph.* 278), *amoenitate amoena amoenus* (*Capt.* 774), *regum rex regalior* (*Capt.* 825), *mala malae male monstrat* (*Cas.* 826), *miseriarum quod miserescat, miser* (*Epid.* 526). Often the repetition is carried to extremes, as in *Epid.* 331 f.): *aliquid aliqua aliquo modo alicunde ab aliqui aliqua* (cf. also *Capt.* 255 f., *Pseud.* 940). Chaeribulus says in *Epid.* 331 f.:

I swear, if I had it, I'd promise it gladly. But somehow, some way, in some manner, from somewhere, from some one, there's some hope of your having good luck along with me.

Stratippocles replies (334 f.):

You keep jabbering to me about something, some way, from somewhere, from some one, and there isn't a thing anywhere.

Occasionally Plautus coins words to create the desired effect:

They're "countrifying it" in the country. (*ruri rurant, Capt.* 84)
I've been "homing it" at home. (*domi domitus sum, Men.* 105)
I have to 'ear him with my ears, so that my dental work can make dents in the food. (*auribus peraudienda sunt, ne dentes dentiant, Mil.* 33 f.)

(7) Another type of repetition is gemination, or the duplication of the same word; this serves less for comedy than for emphasis or for the arousing of sympathy; cf. *Cas.* 621: *nulla sum, nulla sum, tota, tota occidi.* It is especially frequent with imperatives, e.g., *age age* (*Asin.* 40, 327), *tene, tene* (*Aul.* 415, 713), *tace, tace* (*Curc.* 156, *Pers.* 591), and with vocatives, e.g., *o ciues, ciues* (*Curc.* 626), *Sceledre, Sceledre* (*Mil.* 313), *o Mysis Mysis* (*And.* 282), *o frater, frater* (*Ad.* 256). Triplication is less common but even more effective, e.g., *exi, exi, exi* (*Curc.* 276), *o Callicles, o Callicles, o Callicles* (*Trin.* 1094).

Terence has been praised, and justly, for the purity and the perfection of his language. Horace (*Epist.* II, I, 59) considered him outstanding in *ars*, but to understand *ars* in this context as rhetorical style, as does Terzaghi,[40] and to limit it to features like asyndeton, alliteration, and assonance produces too narrow an interpretation of Horace's estimate. That Terence in his use of stylistic devices followed to a degree the example of his predecessors Naevius, Plautus, and Caecilius cannot be doubted and this indicates that he translated his originals with a certain amount of freedom; in other words, his conception of translating *uerbum de uerbo* (cf. *Ad.* 11) can hardly be viewed as literal translation in the modern sense of the term. But Terence shows much greater restraint than does Plautus; he seldom permits the stylistic features to run riot as they do in the plays of the older dramatist. He uses them for emphasis, balance, contrast, rather than for laughable effects. Of the

---

[40] Cf. Terzaghi, *Prolegomeni a Terenzio*, pp. 95 ff. Terzaghi cites numerous instances of Terentian asyndeton, alliteration, etc.

stylistic grouping of longer lists of words, Miss Whitsel says: "Comedy is rich in word grouping, Plautus making it a very definite and recognizable feature of his style, Terence moving more cautiously, and more nearly approximating his Greek models. Plautus is actuated in his use of words by comic exuberance, and sometimes by an innate desire for elaborate arrangement, which Terence, if he felt it at all, carefully restrained."[41]

## Comic Formations

Another feature of Plautus' Latin which displays the popular nature of his diction and his desire for comic effects is seen in the freedom with which he coins words. In this respect also he differs from Terence, for the younger dramatist has little interest in laughable compounds or comic names. Plautus' fondness for Greek words was mentioned briefly earlier in the chapter, many of these are hybrids formed of Greek words and Latin terminations, e.g., adjectives like *elleborosus* (*Most.* 952, *Rud.* 1006), *hepatiarius* (*Curc.* 239), *thensaurarius* (*Aul.* 395); adverbs like *basilice* (*Epid.* 56, *Pers.* 29, etc.), *pugilice atque athletice* (*Epid.* 20, cf. *Bacch.* 248), *euscheme . . . et dulice et comoedice* (*Mil.* 213); verbs like *apolactizare* (*Epid.* 678), *atticissare, sicilicissitare* (*Men.* 12), *cyathissare* (*Men.* 303, 305), *patrissare* (*Most.* 639, *Pseud.* 442). More original and more amusing are hybrid epithets made up of Greek and Latin words, e.g., *ferritribax*, "iron-rubbed" (*Most.* 356), *flagritriba*, "whip-lashed" (*Pseud.* 137), *inanilogista*, "empty-handed windbag" (*Pseud.* 255), *pultifagus*, "porridge-eating" (*Most.* 828; cf. *Poen.* 54, where the Greek patronymic is added to form *pultiphagonides*), *ulmitriba*, "elm-rod-rubbed" (*Pers.* 279). Plautus is especially fond of comic patronymics, hybrid formations with the Greek patronymic added to a Latin word; cf. *plagipatida*, "buffet-bearer" or "scar-bearite" (*Capt.* 472, *Most.* 356), *glandionida, pernonida*, "the son of a glandule of pork, the son of a fattened ham" (*Men.* 210), *oculicrepidae, cruricrepidae*, "clatter-eyed and clatter-shinned" (*Trin.* 1021). Many of his laughable names (to be discussed below) are also formed with the patronymic. Cooper says that "such monstrous formations . . . were only possible in a semi-Greek play, addressed to a cosmopolitan audience, to whom such words were merely an absurd exaggeration of what was probably familiar to them in the slaves' dialect at Rome."[42]

Plautus is equally successful with coinages purely Latin; he forms superlatives not only of adjectives and participles but even of nouns and

---

[41] *Studies in the Grouping of Words*, p. 67. It should be noted that stylistic features (alliteration, assonance, etc.) appear far more frequently in Terence's prologues than in the body of the plays; cf. Fabia, *Les Prologues de Térence*, pp. 308 ff. Terence uses these features in his prologues as rhetorical devices in his desire to defend himself from criticism and to win the favor of his audience.

[42] *Word Formation in the Roman Sermo Plebeius*, pp. 323 f.

pronouns; cf. *perditissumus* (*Aul.* 722), *occisissumus* (*Cas.* 694), *uerberabilissume* (*Aul.* 633), *scelerum cumulatissume* (*Aul.* 825). When Menaechmus I finds himself shut out by Erotium as well as by his wife, he laments (*Men.* 698) that he is *exclusissumus*, "the shuttest-out of all men." In *Curc.* 15 ff., after Phaedromus has addressed his sweetheart's door as *oculissumum*, "closest to me," Palinurus ridicules his master and plays upon the word by calling it *occlusissumum*, "most closed"; Phaedromus undaunted terms it *bellissumum* and *taciturnissumum*, "most beautiful and most tactful of all doors." Sagaristio is *geminissumus*, "the twinniest twin there is" (*Pers.* 830) and Agorasto-cles addresses Hanno as *patrue patruissume*, "uncliest uncle" (*Poen.* 1197). Charmides, annoyed at the swindler's repeated questions (*ipsusne es*, "Are you he himself?"), replies (*Trin.* 988) *ipsissumus*, "his very selfest." This is an exact parallel to Aristophanes' comic superlative of αὐτός in *Plut.* 83 (αὐτότατος).

Striking compounds coined for the humor of the moment are numerous: gossiping neighbors call Callicles *turpilucricupidus*, "a filthy-lucre-grabber" (*Trin.* 100). Torturers who put chains on prisoners are termed *tintinnaculi*, "tinkle-tankle men" (*Truc.* 782). Ergasilus refers to the people who get in his way as *dentilegi*, "tooth-pickers" (*Capt.* 798), i.e., their teeth will be knocked out. Fists are *dentifrangibula*, "tooth-crackers," teeth are *nucifrangibula*, "nut-crackers"; Pistoclerus threatens the parasite in *Bacch.* 594 ff.:

PI.: Do you know how angry I am? Your face is damned near to disaster. These tooth-crackers in my hands are itching to be at it.
PA. (*aside*): As I understand his words, I'd better be on my guard that he doesn't knock out my nut-crackers.

In *Rud.* 422 Sceparnio makes an amusing slip of the tongue; intending to compliment Ampelisca upon her complexion he says, in place of *subaquilus* ("brownish"), *subuolturius* ("vulture-like"), i.e., he coins a word from the resemblance of *aquilus* to *aquila*, "eagle."[43]

When we turn to the names of Plautus' characters, we find a rich storehouse of comic material. The names of the Terentian characters are less colorful and consistently Greek; Terence did not necessarily preserve the Greek names of his originals, but he kept close to what may be termed a "Menandrian standard."[44] His plays suffer from the fact that the same names reappear in different plays, and it is particularly unfortunate when these characters have major roles; e.g., there are two *senes* and an *adulescens* named Chremes (*Andria, Heauton; Eu-*

---

[43] Such coinages are a test of the ingenuity of editors and translators; Chase renders: "A sweet confection—complexion, I mean" (in Duckworth, *The Complete Roman Drama*, I, p. 863); E. A. Sonnenschein in his edition of the *Rudens* (Oxford, 1901, p. 97) suggests: "*bruinettish*—I mean to say *brunettish*." Nixon (*Plautus*, IV, p. 329) translates: "A beauty, a real doughnut—no, no, I mean chestnut—beauty!"
[44] Cf. Ullman, *CPh* 11 (1916), p. 64.

*nuchus*) ; the slave girl in the *Adelphoe* is named Bacchis, and so are the courtesans—both important characters—in the *Heauton* and the *Hecyra*; the *matrona* is named Sostrata in three comedies (*Heauton, Hecyra, Adelphoe*).[45]

Various attempts have been made to show that the Terentian names are appropriate to the qualities and the actions of the various characters, and Austin concludes one such study as follows : "Terence consistently observed the rule of the significant name, employing it with individual significance if the elaboration of character or rôle permitted, and, if not, at least with type significance."[46] In most instances, however, the names have a type rather than an individual significance (cf. the difference between Bacchis in the *Heauton* and Bacchis in the *Hecyra*) and they provide little humor. The *Eunuchus*, more Plautine in plot, character, and language than the others, is an exception in this respect also. The name of the soldier, Thraso, signifies "boldness," and accordingly Thraso, in the comical advance upon the home of Thais, places himself in the rear. Gnatho comments (782) :

> That's true wisdom. He's drawn up his men in front and provided a safe place for himself.

There is considerable humor in Thraso's "army," composed of Gnatho, Syriscus, Simalio, Donax, Sanga, and Sannio. Austin translates the names in order as follows : General "Blunderbuss," Captain "Jawbone," Lieutenants "Rapscallion," "Pugnose," "Spindle-shanks," Corporal "Bloodsucker," and Sergeant "Wagtail."[47]

An examination of Plautus' use of Greek names reveals an amazingly wide range. Many names are derived, like those of Terence, from Greek New Comedy (e.g., Aeschinus, Antipho, Bacchis, Demipho, Hegio, Myrrhina, Sosia, Syrus). Several good Greek names occur when Artemona says of her husband (*Asin.* 864 ff.) :

> This is his reason for going out to dinner every day. He says that he's going to dine with Archidemus, Chaerea, Chaerestratus, Clinia, Chremes, Cratinus, Dinia, Demosthenes; all the time he is carousing and corrupting the youth at a harlot's house.

Most Plautine names, however, are chosen or coined for one or more of several reasons.

(1) They are significant or "tell-tale" names, i.e., the name is appropriate to the character as he appears in the comedy; e.g., Anthrax

---

[45] Other names which appear two or more times are the names of slaves (Davus, Dromo, Geta, Parmeno, Sosia, Syrus), of young men (Antipho, Pamphilus, Phaedria), of old men (Crito, Hegio). The *senex* in the *Eunuchus* (named Simo in the Menandrian original; cf. Donatus, *ad. Eun.* 971) is not named in the text of the play ; in the scene-headings of the manuscripts the name appears as Laches or Demea, each the name of an important *senex* in another play (*Hecyra, Adelphoe*).

[46] *The Significant Name in Terence*, p. 123.

[47] *The Significant Name in Terence*, p. 121.

("Charcoal"), Machaerio ("Knife") and Congrio ("Eel") are suitable
names for the cooks in the *Aulularia*; Phaniscus ("Revealer") betrays
Tranio's plot to Theopropides in the *Mostellaria*; Chaeribulus, the one
who "rejoices in giving counsel," is criticized by his friend because he
assists in word only, not in deed (*Epid.* 116 f.); Argyrippus ("Silver-
horse") is forced to play horse to his slave in order to procure money
(*Asin.* 698 ff.).[48] But significant names are even more effective in describing what the character is not: Demaenetus, "praised by the people,"
is ridiculed and dragged home by his wife at the conclusion of the
*Asinaria*; Nicobulus, "conquering in counsel" (*Bacchides*), Periphanes,
"notable" (*Epidicus*), and Theopropides, "son of prophecy" (*Mostellaria*) are ironical names for the three *senes* deceived by their slaves;
Charmides, "son of joy," may have had a pleasant ending to his troubles
in the *Trinummus*, but the character of the same name in the *Rudens*
is a most joyless person when he enters with Labrax after the shipwreck
(485 ff.); Stratippocles, whose name could signify "renown for horse-
manship in war," seems to have accomplished little beyond losing his
armor to the enemy (cf. *Epid.* 29 ff.).

(2) Many names provide Plautus with opportunities for jesting by
means of word-play. These too are tell-tale names, and sometimes we
have a play upon the sense of the word (with or without a play upon
the sound), sometimes upon the sound alone. To the first category
belong the plays upon Harpax as "plunderer" (*Pseud.* 653 f., 1010);
in 655 Harpax says: "I'm in the habit of snatching prisoners alive on
the battlefield; that's how I got my name." Lycus, "Wolf," an excellent name for a slavedealer, provides material for several jests (*Poen.*
91 f., 646 ff., 774 ff., 1382). Jests upon the meaning of names such as
Harpax and Lycus (cf. also Gelasimus in *Stich.* 174 ff., 630) obviously
derive from the Greek originals, but in other instances the jokes are
possible only in Latin. Peniculus, the parasite in the *Menaechmi*, is
appropriately called "little brush" because he sweeps the table clean
(77 f.); when the cook asks about the whereabouts of Peniculus, Messenio replies (286):

Why, I have the brush safe here in the bag.

Similarly, Menaechmus II asks Erotium (391):

What brush are you talking about? My shoe-brush?

---

[48] Cf. also Megadorus, "noted for generous gifts" (*Aulularia*), Callidamates, "tamer
of beauty" (*Mostellaria*). Telestis, "perfection" (cf. *Epid.* 623), Erotium, "little love"
(*Menaechmi*), Pasicompsa, "pretty in the eyes of all" (cf. *Merc.* 517), Acroteleutium,
"peak of perfection" (*Miles*), Philematium, "precious kiss" (*Mostellaria*) are names
highly appropriate for women characters. For other tell-tale names, see Mendelsohn,
*Studies in the Word-Play in Plautus*, pp. 47 ff. Mendelsohn seems correct (pp. 58 ff.)
in rejecting Fay's fanciful interpretation of Tranio, the name of the intriguing slave
in the *Mostellaria*, as "revealer," "piercer," "wood-pecker" (cf. *AJPh* 24, 1903,
pp. 248 ff.).

The pretended captive in the *Persa* is called Lucris, and this makes possible the various jests upon *lucrum*, "profit" (cf. 626 f., 668, 712 f.). Occasionally a Greek name provides an opportunity for a Latin as well as a Greek jest; in the *Pseudolus* there are two plays upon Charinus, the first Greek, one of both sense and sound (712), the other Latin and based upon the similarity of sound between Charinus and *careo* (726). Plautus retains the Greek jest upon Chrysalus (*Bacch.* 240): *opus est chryso Chrysalo*, "Chrysalus needs gold"; cf. 703 f.: "I'll give the gold; what's the advantage of having a name like Chrysalus if I don't make it good in deed?" In 362 he coins a name Crucisalus, "writhing on the cross," for its similarity of sound and contrast of meaning. Such plays upon sound are numerous: e.g., Ballio and *exballistabo* (*Pseud.* 585), Thales and *talento* (*Capt.* 274), Epidicus and *didici dixi* (*Epid.* 591 f.), Persas and *personas* (*Pers.* 783 f.), Sceledrus and *scelus, sceleste, scelerum caput* (*Mil.* 289, 330, 366, 494). In *Amph.* 384, Mercury finally makes Sosia admit that he is not Amphitruo's Sosia but Amphitruo's *socius*, "comrade." If we render *socius* as "associate," we have an instance—perhaps the only one in Roman comedy—where a Plautine word-play is more successful when translated into English.

(3) Many tell-tale names are manifestly coined by Plautus for their comic effect; among these perhaps should be included the three slaves in *Capt.* 657, Colaphus, Cordalio, and Corax, well rendered by Nixon as "Box! Buffum! Bangs!"[49] More definitely Plautine are Artotrogus, "Bread-muncher" (*Miles*) and Miccotrogus, "Crumb-eater" (*Stich.* 242). Comic patronymics are frequent, e.g., Misargyrides, "Hate-silver-son"—a fitting name for the moneylender in the *Mostellaria*. Philocrates (posing as his own slave) gives the name of his father (*Capt.* 285) as Thensaurochrysonicochrysides, literally "the son of gold surpassing treasures of gold." Hegio says, rather naïvely:

I suppose the name was given to him on account of his wealth.

Philocrates replies:

On the contrary, on account of his avarice and his greed.

Especially laughable are the names assigned to soldiers: Cleomachus, "renowned in battle" (*Bacchides*), Pyrgopolynices, "the taker of towers" (*Miles*), Stratophanes, "parader of armies" (*Truculentus*), Polymachaeroplagides, literally "son of many blows of the dagger" (*Pseud.* 988 ff.). Even more remarkable are the double names such as Therapontigonus Platagidorus, "Slave-son Rattle-gift" (*Curc.* 430) and Bumbomachides Clutomestoridysarchides, "Bumble-fighter-son Famous-adviser-hard to rule-son" (*Mil.* 14). These formations are surpassed only by the famous Latin coinages in *Pers.* 702 ff., hybrid forma-

---

[49] *Plautus*, I, p. 527. Similar are the names of the slaves (also *lorarii*) in *Rud.* 657: Turbalio and Sparax, "Disturber" and "Mangler."

tions invented on the analogy of Greek patronymics; when Dordalus asks his name, Sagaristio replies as follows:

Vaniloquides Virginesuendonides Nugiepiloquides Argentumextenebronides Tedigniloquides Nugides Palponides Quodsemelarripides Numquameripides.

SA.: Listen then, that you may know it: Blabberodorus Maidvendorovich Lightchatterson Cashscreweroutstein Ibn Saidwhatyoudeserve MacTrifle McBlarney Whatonceyougetyourhandson Neverpartwithitski! There you are!

DO.: Wow! Your name must be hard to write out.

SA.: That's the Persian custom; we have long, contortuplicated names.[50]

That Plautus himself made up many laughable names is obvious from Latin names such as Peniculus, Lucris, Crurifragius ("Broken-legs," cf. *Poen.* 886), from fictitious countries like Scytholatronia ("Scythobrigandia," *Mil.* 43) and Peredia and Perbibesia ("Eatonia and Tipplearia," *Curc.* 444), and especially from the "contortuplicated" name in *Pers.* 702 ff. Whether the comic coinages in Greek are also to be attributed to him is less certain. Many of his significant names may have been taken from the Greek originals, but there are no names in New Comedy like Argyrippus, Stratippocles, Acroteleutium and, above all, none like Polymachaeroplagides, Thensaurochrysonicochrysides, or Therapontigonus Platagidorus. Comic formations such as these are undoubtedly Plautus' own creations. They may have been suggested to him by the mimes and farces of southern Italy[51] but they, as well as the purely Latin names, seem additional evidence of his gaiety, spontaneous wit, and inventive genius.

## Puns, Jests, and Double Meanings

Many forms of verbal humor—colloquial exaggeration, the humorous use of stylistic devices, comic formations, laughable names—have already been considered. We turn now to the jests which are so numerous in Plautus, as they are in Aristophanes and Shakespeare. Here we find two basic types of verbal wit: (1) *equivoca*, or ambiguities: we expect a word to mean one thing and we suddenly discover that it means something else; (2) paronomasia, or word-play: we find, by the side of one word or in place of it, another word of similar sound used to produce a

---

[50] This is Murphy's translation in Duckworth, *The Complete Roman Drama*, I, p. 713. His rendering of Polymachaeroplagides in *Pseud.* 988 ff. as "MacSaberswipes" (p. 829) seems equally successful.

[51] Schmidt, *H* 37 (1902), pp. 624 ff.; cf. Leo, *Plautinische Forschungen*, pp. 109 f., who suggests that Plautus himself coined these Greek names with the comic abandon displayed by Aristophanes in Old Comedy. Legrand, however, assumes that the non-Latin names probably existed in the Greek plays adapted by Plautus (Legrand-Loeb, *The New Greek Comedy*, pp. 842 f.)—a view which receives no support from the extant fragments of New Comedy.

ludicrous contrast in meaning.⁵² Examples of both categories are usually termed "puns," since we have, in the one case, a different application of the same word and, in the other, two words of different meaning but of the same or similar sound.

Plautus' ambiguities are of various types: at times the second meaning is not intended by the speaker, but would be clear to the audience. When Tranio pretends to forget whose house Philolaches has purchased, Theopropides says, "Think it up" (*comminiscere, Most.* 662; cf. 668 and *Epid.* 281); the spectators would understand the word also in the sense (in this instance, the true meaning) of "invent," "make up." Usually the speaker intends to convey a double meaning: in *Merc.* 526 Lysimachus uses *tondere*, "shear," in the sense of "fleece," "cheat"; in the *Mostellaria* Tranio takes refuge at the altar, much to the disgust of Theopropides; cf. 1102 ff.:

TH.: Get up and come here. I want to ask your advice about something.
TR.: I can give my advice from here. I'm a lot wiser sitting down. Besides, you get better advice from holy places.

By "sitting down" (*sedens*) Tranio means both "sitting at the altar" and "presiding at court." The use of *res* for "matter in hand" and "money" appears in *Curc.* 600, *Epid.* 117, and *Most.* 653. The verb *habitare*, "to dwell," can also mean "to linger," "to spend time"; hence Milphio, after being beaten by his master, can say (*Poen.* 411 ff.):

You can sell your own house without the least disadvantage since you hang out around my jaw most of the time.

In many instances the second meaning of the word or phrase is brought out by the phraseology of the passage; cf. the play upon *carus*, "dear," in *Men.* 105 f.:

I've been at home with my dear ones; for everything I eat or buy is very dear.

*Tali* means both "ankle-bones" and "dice" in *Mil.* 164 f.:

⁵² The *Coislinian Tractate* lists as the causes of verbal humor (1) homonyms, (2) synonyms, (3) garrulity, (4) paronyms, (5) diminutives, (6) perversions, (7) grammar and syntax. The present section will deal almost entirely with double meanings (some of which are homonyms, i.e., separate words that happen to be identical in form) and word-plays (the latter seem to belong to the categories of both paronyms and perversions); paronyms, words created by the addition to or subtraction from the ordinary word, would include, strictly speaking, such comic compounds, superlatives, and character-names as have been described in the preceding section of this chapter; cf. Cooper, *An Aristotelian Theory of Comedy*, pp. 233 ff. Of the other categories mentioned in the *Tractate*, synonyms, i.e., calling things by better or worse names, have been illustrated above by the use of depreciatory epithets and colloquial metaphors; garrulity is seen everywhere in bombast, boastfulness, moralizing, repetition (cf. below, p. 357 and n. 65); on diminutives, a form of paronym, see above, pp. 334 f. An example in Plautus of humor from grammar and syntax is found in the faulty speech of Truculentus, e.g., *rabo* for *arrabo* (*Truc.* 688 ff.).

And, to keep them from breaking the Dicing-Law, be sure that they haven't any ankle-bones left when they give a party at home.

In *Most.* 427 f. *ludos facere* means both "make game of" and "provide funeral games for"; Tranio says:

I'll provide games for the old man today while he's alive, and that's more than will ever happen to him when he is dead.

The play upon *imago*, "appearance" and "mask," in *Amph.* 458 f. is similar. Sosia uses *dormire*, "to sleep," in the sense "to be knocked unconscious" in *Amph.* 297 f.:

Now, because my master made me stay awake, this fellow will put me to sleep with his fists.

The adjective *uorsutus* means "versatile," "shrewd," and Stratippocles plays upon the literal meaning of the word ("turnable") when he says to his slave (*Epid.* 371):

You've got more turns than a potter's wheel.[53]

A striking example of double meaning occurs when Tranio, deceiving two *senes* at once, ridicules them as well; cf. *Most.* 832 ff.:

TR.: Do you see the picture of a crow making fools of two old vultures?
TH.: No, I don't see it.
TR.: Well, I do. The crow stands between the vultures. Look, he's pulling pieces out of both. Look here in my direction, then you'll see the crow. Do you see it now?
TH.: No, I don't see any crow there at all.
TR.: Well, look toward yourselves, since you can't see the crow. Perhaps you can see the vultures.
TH.: I don't see any picture of a bird here at all.
TR.: Oh, well, let it go. I make allowances for you. You're old and can't see very well.

Often the second meaning is brought out only by means of dialogue; i.e., the second speaker intentionally or unwittingly takes in a different sense the word or phrase of the first speaker: when Agorastocles in *Poen.* 427 says *fugio* ("I'm hurrying off"), Milphio understands it in the sense of "run away" and replies: "That's more my job than yours." The twofold meaning of *seruare*, "protect" and "keep in custody," is brought out by Epidicus' reply to Stratippocles in *Epid.* 619:

ST.: I'll keep you safe.
EP.: Gad, they'll do a better job of that if they catch me.

[53] Many of the vulgar or obscene allusions in Plautus are ambiguities of the types illustrated above; verbs such as *tangere* (*Aul.* 740 f., cf. 754 f.), *conprimere* (*Amph.* 348 f., *Cas.* 362, *Rud.* 1073 ff., *Truc.* 262 ff.), and *cubare* (*Asin.* 937, *Most.* 701), adjectives like *consuetus* (*Asin.* 703, *Capt.* 867) and *morigerus* (*Capt.* 966, *Cas.* 463), nouns like *uas* (*Poen.* 862 f.), *saltus* (*Cas.* 476, 922, *Curc.* 56), *machaera* and *uagina* (*Pseud.* 1181) are all susceptible of a second and indecent significance; but see chap. 10, n. 40.

The verb *consuere* means both "patch up," "invent," and "sew together"; Mercury says to Sosia (*Amph.* 366 ff.) :

ME. : You've certainly come here to your sorrow today, you height of impudence, with your made-up falsehoods and patched-up tricks.
SO. : On the contrary, I come here with tunic patched up, not tricks.
ME. : Again you lie; you come here on your feet, not your tunic.[54]

The *Mostellaria* is rich in jests of this type, e.g., *bona fide*, "truly" and "in good faith," in 669 ff. :

TR. : Your son bought the house next door.
TH. : Honestly?
TR. : Yes, if you pay the money. But if you don't it won't be an honest transaction.

Later, when Theopropides asks about his son's character, Tranio pretends to misunderstand and takes *quoiusmodi* to refer to physical characteristics; cf. 1117 ff. :

TH. : Tell me, what kind of a son did I leave here when I went away?
TR. : One with feet, hands, fingers, ears, eyes, lips.
TH. : I'm asking you something different.
TR. : Well, I'm answering you something different.

Even Simo jests at poor old Theopropides; when the latter asks (999) if anything new happened (*processit*) at the forum, Simo interprets *processit* as "a procession passed along" and replies: "Yes, I saw a dead man carried out."[55]

The use of two words of similar sound is very frequent in Plautine jests. At times the two words are identical in sound and appearance. In *Curc.* 314 ff., we have a play upon *uentum*, (1) past participle of *uenire*, "to come," and (2) accusative of *uentus*, "wind." The weary and hungry parasite speaks:

CU. : Please make me happy to have come (*uentum*).
PA. : Certainly. (*He fans* CURCULIO *vigorously.*)
CU. : What are you doing, I'd like to know?
PA. : Giving you a good wind (*uentum*).

Such word-plays are nonsensical but for that very reason the spectators

---

[54] Mercury's final speech contains a second jest; he takes the ablative as one of means instead of ablative absolute. Another jest of a syntactical nature occurs in *Capt.* 866: Hegio says to the parasite: *essurire mihi uidere* ("You seem to me to be hungry") ; Ergasilus replies as if *mihi* belonged with *essurire: miquidem essurio, non tibi* ("I'm hungry for myself, not for you"). Lindsay says of this jest (*The Captivi of Plautus*, p. 315) : "It is impossible to imagine Terence tolerating a poor joke like this. . . . And yet one feels that in its setting here the reply of Ergasilus would provoke the laughter rather than the censure of any audience." Modern radio jokes are similar : "You're fond of men, I gather." "I'm not fond of the men you gather, but those I gather."

[55] Cf. also Simo's jest in 1006 f.; on this and other examples of intentional misinterpretations of greetings, see below under "The Surprise Turn."

were doubtless amused.[56] In *Poen.* 279, Agorastocles distorts Milphio'
*assum* (*adsum*, "Here I am") into *assum*, "roasted" and says, "I'
prefer to have you boiled." The play upon *cubito*, "elbow," and *cubitum*
"to go to bed" in *Cas.* 853 is almost untranslatable unless the passag
is expanded, e.g., as follows:

LY.: With her elbow she almost smashed my forehead.
OL.: That means she's ready for bed.

The word-plays of Messenio seem mild by comparison; cf. *Men.* 978 f.

I can stand a tongue-lashing (*uerba*), but I don't like a whip-lashing
(*uerbera*); and I'd rather eat the meal (*molitum*) than turn the mil
(*molitum*).

In most cases the words are similar only in their beginning or in thei
ending; the following are typical: *Bacch.* 943: *non in arcem, uerum i*
*arcam*, "not against the stronghold, but against the strongbox"; *Epid*
119: *amicos furno mersos quam foro*, "friends 'baked up' rather tha
bankrupt"; *Men.* 610: *palla pallorem incutit*, "the palla makes yo
pallid"; *Most.* 196: *te ille deseret aetate et satietate*, "he'll desert yo
with age and usage";[57] 654: *abeo: sat habeo si cras fero*, "I'm off. We
off—if I get it tomorrow." In 374 f. we have both a double meaning
of *ualere* and the play upon *disperire* and *bis perire*:

DE.: Wake up! Philolaches' father has arrived from abroad.
CA.: Farewell to his father.
PH.: He does fare well and I've perished in a trice.
CA.: You've twice perished? How can that be?

In *Truc.* 421 f. Plautus coins a word *accubuo* for its play upon *adsiduo*

PH.: After that, my darling, I'll be with you forever.
DI.: Jove! I'd prefer a bed with you forever.

Many such examples of paronomasia can hardly be rendered in trans
lation; e.g., *uolueram faciebatis . . . uotueram . . . fugiebatis* (*Asin*
211 ff.), *perdo pereo* (*Asin.* 637), *saeuiunt sapiunt* (*Bacch.* 408), *fe
. . . mel* (*Cas.* 223, cf. *Cist.* 69, *Poen.* 394, *Truc.* 178 f.), *ad cubituran
. . . ad cursuram* (*Cist.* 378 f.), *amoris . . . umorisque* (*Mil.* 639 f.)
Since these depend for their effect less upon humor than upon the pres
ence of alliteration, assonance, etymological figure, and the like, the
overlap with and should perhaps be included among the stylistic device
discussed earlier in this chapter.

The Punic words of Hanno (*Poen.* 995 ff.) provide an opportunit

---

[56] Radio performers apparently assume that modern audiences also are easily enter
tained; at least, the average Plautine jest is far superior to the following gem of th
air-waves: "My wife's in a huff—that's a metaphor." "I've always wondered wha
you met her for."
[57] The version of Nixon (*Plautus*, III, p. 307) is perhaps more proper but possibl
less Plautine: "he'll leave you when you're older and he's colder."

or an unusual series of amusing word-plays: Milphio, pretending to understand Carthaginian (cf. 991: "There isn't a Punicker Punic alive."), turns Hanno's words into Latin words of similar sound: e.g., *donni* (998) becomes *doni*, "a donation"; *meharbocca* (1002) is explained as *misera bucca*, "a pain in his back jaw"; *palumergadetha* (1017) is interpreted as *palas . . . mergas datas*, "spades and pitchforks given to him"; to keep the same play in English, perhaps we can render the phrase, "pails or garden tools."[58] Such plays upon sound must have delighted Plautus' hearers, many of whom probably had picked up from military service enough knowledge of Phoenician to know how inaccurate Milphio's versions were.

The ambiguities and jests cited in this section are merely a few examples of hundreds to be found in the pages of Plautus.[59] That these are Plautus' own inventions is of course obvious since such word-plays are possible only in Latin. The extent to which similar jests existed in the Greek originals cannot be determined. Certain passages in Plautus' comedies, more or less pointless in the Latin text, become effective as puns and word-plays when translated back into Greek. In *Men.* 59 ("He had no children except his wealth") the Greek word τόκος could mean both "child" and "interest (on money)." Olympio in *Cas.* 319 f. says to Lysidamus: "You're really a hunter—you spend your life day and night *cum cane*." A word-play was possible in the Greek original upon the similarity of κυνηγέτης and κύων. Many jokes upon proper names, e.g., Charinus (*Pseud.* 712), Chrysalus (*Bacch.* 240), Dicea (*Mil.* 438), Harpax (*Pseud.* 654), Lycus (*Poen.* 187, 647 f., 1333), Phoenicium (*Pseud.* 229), are clearly taken over from the Greek comedies.[60]

There is, however, no indication that New Comedy had the profusion of puns and verbal witticisms that are found in Plautus. There are, in fact, two arguments against such an assumption: (1) approximately forty per cent of the Plautine jests are assigned to slaves[61] and the Plautine slave with his cleverness and ingenuity seems largely a Roman

---

[58] Cf. also Milphio's not-too-happy attempts to explain Hanno's phrases in 1010, 1013, 1023. Whatever Hanno was saying (on this, cf. Gray, *AJSL* 39, 1922-23, pp. 10 ff.), we can be sure that Milphio's translations bore little relation to the real meaning.

[59] Mendelsohn (*Studies in the Word-Play in Plautus*, p. 138) includes over four hundred passages in his statistical summary, while Brinkhoff (*Woordspeling bij Plautus*) takes into consideration many types of paronomasia not treated by Mendelsohn. The reader is referred to these two works for additional illustrations of typically Plautine jests and for more deailed classifications. Word-plays upon proper names are frequent, e.g., the play upon Epidamnus and *damnum*, "loss," (*Men.* 263 f., cf. 267): "No one comes to Epidamnus without being damned." For word-plays upon the names of characters, see above, pp. 347 ff. Many Plautine jests and puns were perhaps lost in Roman times when the original spelling of certain words was modernized; cf. Postgate, *PBA* (1907-08), pp. 196 ff.

[60] Cf. Legrand-Loeb, *The New Greek Comedy*, pp. 476 ff.

[61] Cf. Mendelsohn, *Studies in the Word-Play in Plautus*, pp. 138 ff.

creation; (2) verbal humor of the Plautine type is extremely rare in Terence; the characters of his plays, even the slaves, were too seriously engaged in the dramatic problems—the serious complications and pathetic misunderstandings—to have time to indulge in jesting and pleasantries.[62] Terence seems to have been more hostile to this type of humor than were many dramatists of the New Comedy; in this respect also, as in his treatment of character and situation, he undoubtedly moved in the direction of restraint and refinement; even more surely Plautus gave full rein to his desire for laughable effects and, to the delight of his audiences, inserted puns and word-plays and obscene jests with an abandon not known to the ancient world since the days of Aristophanes. It is perhaps significant that the *Cistellaria* and the *Mercator*, two early comedies that are usually considered more faithful to the originals than most of Plautus' plays, have few passages of verbal humor.

## The Surprise Turn

Many of the jests and word-plays cited above depend for their comic effect not only upon their verbal features but also upon the element of the unexpected. We turn now to a type of humor, especially prominent in Plautus, in which the fun arises chiefly from surprise: a common phrase or colloquialism is given a new twist or is made the springboard for an unexpected turn in the dialogue: a character seems about to express a certain idea and then suddenly says the opposite, or introduces an incongruous or ludicrous thought. This latter is the true surprise turn, to which the technical term παρὰ προσδοκίαν, "contrary to expectation," is regularly applied.[63]

The colloquial greetings mentioned earlier in the chapter are sometimes amusingly reversed; instead of the usual "Farewell," "Good luck to you," we find "Fare ill," "Bad luck to you" (e.g., *Curc.* 554: *aegrote aetatem*; 588: *male uale, male sit tibi*; *Trin.* 996: *male uiue et uale*) Greetings are taken literally: *quid agis?* "How do you do?" can also mean "What are you doing?" Hence we have a response to *quid agis?*

---

[62] A few Terentian ambiguities are found, e.g., *And.* 955 (*recte*, "justly" and "securely"), *Eun.* 84 f. (*tremere* and *horrere*, "tremble" and "shiver" from love, also from cold), 403 (*mirum*, "wonderful" and "queer"), *Phorm.* 342 f. (*dubius*, "of doubtful quality" and "puzzling because of its excellence"), *Ad.* 427 (*sapientia*, "taste" and "wisdom"), *Ad.* 732 (*facere*, "react" and "do").

[63] In the *Tractate* παρὰ προσδοκίαν is a subdivision of laughter from "things," not from "words," but many of the passages from Aristophanes and Shakespeare cited as illustrations (cf. Starkie, *The Acharnians*, pp. lxvii f.; Cooper, *An Aristotelian Theory of Comedy*, pp. 249 f.) are surprise turns which are more appropriately listed as verbal humor. Language and thought are often so interdependent that it is difficult to distinguish between "words" and "things," but Cicero's distinction seems sound: if the matter is amusing, however it may be expressed, the humor is in "things"; on the other hand, the laughter comes from the diction if the humor vanishes when the words are changed (*De orat.* II, 62, 252).

such as the following: "I'm shaking hands with my best friend" (*Men.* 138, cf. *Most.* 719). The humor of these passages, such as it is, derives from the unexpected nature of the reply. The common formula of departure, *numquid uis?* ("Nothing else, is there?"), would normally be followed by *uale, bene uale, ut bene sit tibi,* etc., but Plautus and Terence both introduce an unexpected affirmative answer which either begins a new theme or provides humor by the sudden distortion of the convention, i.e., by taking the formula literally, as in the case of the *quid agis* greetings.[64] Among the answers of the latter type (for purposes of jesting only) are the following:

> Yes, that you die a horrible death and get out of here at once.
>   (*Epid.* 513, cf. *Men.* 328)
>       Yes, that you don't know me. (*Mil.* 575)
>     Yes, that I be no handsomer than I am. (*Mil.* 1086)
>       Yes, that you all have more sense. (*Ad.* 432)

Perhaps the repetition of the same word may be said to derive its humor from surprise, for a speaker does not normally in a conversation respond with the same word or phrase; e.g., "You're talking silly" (*nugas agis, Men.* 621 ff.), "Sure" (*licet, Rud.* 1212 ff.), "I reckon" (*censeo, Rud.* 1269 ff.); these repetitions illustrate well Bergson's theory of the mechanical as a source of laughter,[65] but such mechanical regularity may also be considered a form of incongruity which derives its effect chiefly from the unexpected.

The true surprise turn involves, not an unexpected response to another's speech, but a sudden shift in the sense of a speaker's words. Here again Plautus often uses a formula of greeting or of imprecation as a starting point. When a friend or neighbor returned safely from a trip overseas, the words of welcome would normally be followed by an invitation to dinner (cf. *Bacch.* 186 f., *Poen.* 1151) but Simo is less generous to the newly arrived Theopropides (*Most.* 1006 f.):

Tomorrow, if no one else invites—me, I'll dine at your house.

When Cappadox greets the soldier, one surprise turn is matched by another (*Curc.* 561 ff.):

CA.: Since you have arrived safely in Epidaurus, today here at my house—
  you'll never lick a grain of salt.
TH.: Thanks for the kind invitation, but I've made arrangements—for you
  to suffer plenty.

---

[64] Cf. Hough, *AJPh* 66 (1945), pp. 282 ff.

[65] Cf. Bergson, *Laughter*, pp. 72 ff. Cooper includes repetition of the same word over and over again under garrulity—one of the sources of verbal humor listed in the *Tractate*—and says that garrulity "embraces verbosity of every sort—bombast, triviality, learned nonsense, . . . the garrulity of age, of children and the childish, of the idle, of clowns, domestics, and the like" (*An Aristotelian Theory of Comedy*, p. 231). On verbal repetitions in Plautus, see above, p. 193.

In the case of imprecations (*di te perdant, i in malam crucem*) the meaning shifts in the direction of mildness; cf. *Men.* 328 f.:

ME.: Go to the devil!
CY.: Oh, better that you should go—inside and recline on the couch.

Similar are *Capt.* 868, *Cas.* 279 f., *Epid.* 23 f., *Mil.* 286.

More amusing are the examples of παρὰ προσδοκίαν which develop naturally in the course of a dialogue or monologue. For instances of the former, cf. the following:

> I'll punish you properly today, for I'll—make you my wife. (*Poen.* 1228)
> I love him better than my own soul while—I get from him what I want. (*Truc.* 887)
> While there's life there's hope that—we shall both be hungry enough. (*Heaut.* 981)

One type of surprise turn occurs in what may be called "semi-monologue," i.e., a character comes from his house and speaks to someone within, but the conclusion of the statement is not heard by the person inside; e.g., *Trin.* 40 ff.:

> Wife, pray to the Household God that our home may be happy, favorable, fortunate, and lucky for us—and that I may see you dead and gone as soon as possible.

(Cf. also *Epid.* 338; in *Most.* 529 Tranio concludes his speech after the departure of Theopropides.)

Often the surprise turn serves to add a touch of humor to a monologue spoken primarily for the benefit of the spectators; Euclio's gratitude to the raven leads to the suggestion that something good "be said" (*Aul.* 670 ff.); that something "be given" would hardly be in keeping with Euclio's character. It is fitting also for a parasite to say that he has been advised by his friends to cut his throat—"with hunger" (*Stich.* 581). Plautus sometimes places these passages at the end or close to the end of a monologue; in this way he brings a scene to an effective close with a laughter-provoking jest; cf. the following:

> I'll be his advocate so that by my assistance he'll be the more quickly—condemned. (*Rud.* 890 f.)
> Why don't I go in and hang myself—for a while, at least, until I feel better. (*Rud.* 1189 f.)
> I must summon my friends and determine by what statute I ought to—starve to death. (*Stich.* 503 f.)
> If a large and juicy legacy should come my way, . . . I would save it and live so thriftily that—within a few days I wouldn't have a cent left. (*Truc.* 344 ff.)

Although Terence favored the element of surprise in his handling of theme and situation,[66] there are almost no examples of παρὰ προσδοκίαν

---

[66] See "Surprise in Plautus and Terence" in chap. 8; cf. also "Methods of Trickery" in chap. 6.

in his comedies (cf. *Heaut.* 981, quoted above). Verbal humor for its
own sake did not appeal to him and it is hardly strange, therefore, that
he avoided the surprise turn, as he avoided also in large measure the
jests and word-plays which Plautus introduced so freely into his
comedies.

## Comedy *in verbis* in Plautus and Terence

The language of both playwrights was praised highly in antiquity by
numerous critics. Varro approves the statement of Aelius Stilo that the
Muses, if they wished to speak in Latin, would speak in the language of
Plautus (Quintilian, *Instit, orat.* x, 1, 99), and Aulus Gellius, an admirer of early Latin, calls Plautus "the glory of the Latin tongue."[67]
Both Cicero and Caesar appreciate the polish and refinement of Terence's style; Cicero refers to the grace and elegance of his diction and
Caesar speaks of him as a *puri sermonis amator*.[68] Pliny compares well-
written letters to "Plautus or Terence in prose" (*Epist.* 1, 16, 6). Each
playwright had his admirers and each well deserves the praise which
he has received.

Plautus' Latin is characterized by a wider range and a greater flexibility. His language has liveliness and color and also the charm of
novelty arising from picturesque phrases and ingenious coinages. Terence's diction has basically the same colloquialisms, the same stylistic
features, but everywhere present is a desire for restraint and refinement; he avoids colloquial exaggeration, comic formations, irrelevant
jests, and is extremely moderate in his use of such features as alliteration, assonance, and triadic structure. Although it may sound para-
doxical, the language of Plautus is both more natural and less natural
than that of the younger playwright: more natural in the sense that the
various speeches are appropriate to the characters (e.g., abusive epithets,
jests and witticisms, especially of a coarse nature, are regularly assigned
to slaves or to comic roles such as the parasite and the slavedealer); less
natural in that each speech seems composed as a separate unit, whereas
Terence's use of ellipsis makes for a more tightly knit, smoothly flowing
dialogue. This effect of compactness and smoothness is heightened by
the fact that Terence had little interest in verbal witticisms for their
own sake. His more subtle humor arises chiefly from character and

---

[67] *Noctes Atticae*, xix, 8, 6; cf. also 1, 7, 17: *verborum Latinorum elegantissimus*;
vi, 17, 4: *homo linguae atque elegantiae in verbis Latinae princeps.* On these and
similar statements (e.g., Cicero, *De orat.* iii, 12, 44 f., *De off.* 1, 29, 104), see Michaut,
*Plaute*, ii, pp. 200 ff. Most modern critics concur in these estimates. Even Norwood,
who unsympathetically refers to the verbal style of Plautus as "wretched" and speaks
of early Latin as "a dialect of creaks, grunts, and thuds" (*Plautus and Terence*,
p. 59), admits later in the same chapter (p. 99) that "Plautus is a master of Latin."
[68] *Vita Terenti*, 7. See below, chap. 14, n. 4.

situation, and the dialogue seldom strays far from the complications of the plot.[69]

Each playwright is thus a master of Latin style and phraseology and each uses colloquial dialogue to develop his conception of comic drama. The linguistic abilities of each are displayed also in the longer narrative speeches, e.g., Sosia's description of the battle (*Amph.* 203 ff.), Curculio's account of his adventures abroad (*Curc.* 329 ff.), Simo's story about the funeral of Chrysis (*And.* 106 ff.).[70] Such passages have liveliness and polish and are expressed in realistic language; both dramatists deserve praise for the perfection of their literary style. In such descriptive and narrative passages Plautus has the lighter touch, which Terence writes with greater warmth and sympathy—another indication of the *humanitas* for which he is so often praised.

---

[69] The most striking exceptions appear in the *Eunuchus*: the monologue of Gnatho in 232 ff., and the humorous dialogue between Thraso and Gnatho in 395 ff., which (like the somewhat similar scene in *Mil.* 1 ff.) does not advance the plot but serves primarily to characterize the *miles* and provide comedy for the spectators.

[70] Cf. also *Amph.* 1061 ff., *Epid.* 208 ff., *Rud.* 162 ff., *And.* 282 ff., *Heaut.* 96 ff., *Phorm.* 80 ff.

# CHAPTER 13

## *METER AND SONG*

THE comedies of Plautus and Terence, like all other extant dramas of ancient Greece and Rome,[1] were composed in verse. In his use of meters, however, Plautus differed from Terence, and there is nothing in the extant fragments of Greek New Comedy to provide us with models for his procedure. We know from the remains of Menander that the Greek playwright composed his comedies chiefly in iambic trimeters and that the chorus (indicated in the papyri by the word χοροῦ) sang songs—musical interludes—which had no connection with the action of the plays.[2] Plautus' comedies, on the contrary, contain numerous lyrical passages to be sung by one, two, or more actors, passages that are an integral part of the plot. The meters of these songs are often difficult and even today, after a century of intensive research, many verses are still imperfectly understood, sometimes wrongly scanned.[3]

The simpler meters of comedy, used by Plautus and Terence alike, had a flexibility and a freedom unknown to later Latin verse and, to the Romans of the classical period who did not understand the earlier systems, such meters must have seemed crude and formless. Quintilian (*Instit. orat.* x, 1, 99), although terming Terence's writings *elegantissima*, said that they would have won more favor if they had been limited to trimeters; in other words, Quintilian would have preferred a closer imitation of Menander's versification. It is hardly surprising, therefore, that Horace (*Epist.* ii, 3, 270 ff.) complains of the admiration and praise lavished by earlier generations upon Plautus' measures which have so much more variety than those of Terence. Aulus Gellius, a great admirer of Plautus, quotes (1, 24, 3) from Varro's *De poetis* an epigram which he ascribes to Plautus:

After the death of Plautus, Comedy mourned, the stage was deserted, and Laughter, Sport, Jest, and Countless Numbers all shed tears of sorrow.

Whether or not the epigram was composed by the playwright himself we do not know; at least, it stresses as one of Plautus' chief characteristics his "countless numbers" (*numeri innumeri*)—the variety of meters which makes his plays so different from those both of New Comedy and of Terence. It is this polymetry which provides the basis

---

[1] The one exception is the late *Querolus* (see above, p. 72), which is written in a kind of rhythmical prose, with numerous iambic and trochaic clausulae.

[2] See above, p. 29.

[3] Often the introduction into the text of unnecessary emendations has obscured the correct scansion; e.g., on *Epid.* 9-10, 25-26, 29-30, 57-58 (passages composed of two cretics followed by an iambic "run"), see Duckworth, *CPh* 32 (1937), pp. 63 ff.; 34 (1939), pp. 245 ff.; *T. Macci Plauti Epidicus*, pp. 106 f., 119 f., 122, 139 f.

for the elements of song and dance which are prominent in many of his comedies.

From what source did Plautus take the idea for his variety of meters? How did it happen that the lyrical element which in Greek comedy had been limited to choruses became in his hands an integral part of the play? These are among the most puzzling problems of Roman comedy. The differences between Plautus and Terence are nowhere displayed more clearly than in their use of meter, and if Terence (in spite of Quintilian's criticism) seems in this respect to reflect Menander and Greek comedy more closely, Plautus' use of song and dance may well be not merely a predominant feature of his plays but also an important element in his originality as a comic dramatist.

## Diuerbium and Canticum

The modern reader of Roman comedy is handicapped by his ignorance of the musical nature of the plays. Certain scenes were spoken, others were recited to the accompaniment of the flute, and still others (in Plautus) were sung but we have no knowledge of the melodies which accompanied the words of the actors. The ancient division of the scenes into *diuerbium* and *canticum* (reflected by the abbreviations DV and C in some medieval manuscripts of Plautus) makes a clear distinction between spoken dialogue and dialogue accompanied by music. The iambic senarius was the verse of ordinary speech (*diuerbium*) and the term *canticum* was used broadly to include all other meters. In a more limited sense the *canticum*-meters comprise long iambic and trochaic lines (septenarii and octonarii) and these *cantica*, long passages in the same meter, are known as "recitative" since they were recited to music. There are also in both Plautus and Terence numerous passages in a variety of meters and these are *cantica* in a special sense; Donatus calls them *mutatis modis cantica* ("cantica in changing measures");[4] all Plautine songs fall into this final group, although these songs are composed chiefly in lyric measures, whereas the *mutatis modis cantica* of Terence display the same basic meters found in the passages of recitative.

The two meters which appear most frequently in the comedies are the spoken iambic senarius and the trochaic septenarius, the most common of the recitative meters. In Terence senarii are more than twice as numerous (about 3,100 iambic senarii, 1,300 trochaic septenarii) but the proportion of these two meters in Plautus is very different (approximately 8,800 trochaic septenarii, 8,200 iambic senarii); in other words, Terence prefers the meter of quiet conversation and Plautus gives much greater scope to more animated speech accompanied by

---

[4] For the terms *diuerbia, cantica*, and *mutatis modis cantica*, cf. *De com.* VIII, 9; Donatus, Praefatio, I, 7 to each of the five comedies in his commentary; see also Schanz-Hosius, *Geschichte der römischen Literatur*, I, pp. 130 f., who favors spelling *diuerbia* rather than *deuerbia*.

music.[5] In several plays of Plautus the iambic senarii comprise only a third or even less of the comedy, e.g., *Captivi* (32%), *Truculentus* (30%), *Miles* (29%), *Mostellaria* (29%), *Asinaria* (22%), *Epidicus* (22%).

There has been considerable discussion about the delivery of *cantica* on the Roman stage. The story is told by both Livy and Valerius Maximus that Livius Andronicus, when as an actor he strained his voice from too many encores, initiated the practice of speaking the *diuerbia* only and leaving the *cantica* to a special singer brought on the stage for the purpose.[6] There is no other evidence for such a curious method of staging, it is contradicted for the period of the late Republic by Cicero's references to Roscius as a singer of *cantica*,[7] and it seems an impossible procedure for the comedies of Plautus and Terence. It is perhaps of some significance in this connection that Ballio in *Pseud.* 366 refers to Calidorus and Pseudolus as *cantores*. Since the non-*diuerbium*-scenes even in Terence amount to almost half the total number of verses, and the total for Plautus is almost two-thirds (62%) with some individual plays much higher (78%), are we to assume that the actors in all these non-*diuerbium*-monologues and dialogues acted in pantomime while the lines were recited or sung by non-acting vocalists? In the case of lyrical songs by two or more persons, was there a special singer for each actor?

Pseudolus is on the stage during three-quarters of the action, and the scenes in which he participates are about evenly divided (in total of verses) between *diuerbia, cantica,* and *mutatis modis cantica.* Is it conceivable that the only words he utters are in the *diuerbium*-scenes (*Pseud.* 1-132, 394-573a, 998-1051)? At 573a he withdraws from the stage momentarily, announcing that the flute-player will entertain the audience during his absence. Pseudolus has been on the stage steadily since the opening of the play and has had a prominent part in the action. The short rest at 573a is needed if he is to sing the song in 574-593 and

---

[5] If the other *canticum*-meters (iambic septenarii, iambic octonarii, trochaic octonarii) be added to the trochaic septenarii, the approximate results are, for Plautus: *diuerbia* 8,200, *cantica* 10,200; for Terence: *diuerbia* 3,100, *cantica* 2,900. These figures are misleading, however, as they include Terence's *mutatis modis cantica* (combinations of iambic and trochaic verses) which in a sense correspond to Plautus' lyric meters (except that they were recited rather than sung). If Plautus' lyrics are included in the above totals, the results for the *diuerbia* are as follows: 38% of Plautus' total verses, 52% of Terence's. The elder playwright's interest in livelier meters is apparent. Occasionally, however, the senarii seem as animated as the trochaic septenarii; cf. e.g., the senarii in *Men.* 701 ff., *And.* 740 ff., and see Nougaret, *Mémorial des Études Latines,* pp. 128 f.

[6] See "Horace and Livy on Early Drama" in chap. I.

[7] *De orat.* I, 60, 254, *De leg.* I, 4, 11. Cf. also Cicero, *Tusc. disp.* I, 44, 105 ff., *Pro Sest.* 56, 120 ff., for *cantica* and songs of tragedy uttered by actors to the sound of the flute. Horace (*Serm.* II, 3, 60 ff.) relates that the drunken actor Fufius, playing the part of the slumbering Ilione, really fell asleep and missed his cue. The passage quoted is part of a *canticum.*

participate in the *cantica* which follow (594-766). The festive conclusion of the *Stichus* (from 673 to the end) changes to iambic senarii at 762; the reason for the change is obvious: the flute-player drinks and then at 769 resumes the music. Any theory maintaining that only these seven verses were uttered by the two slaves is palpably false. As Beare says, "To suppose a distinction between actors and singers would render such scenes unstageable."[8]

The statements of Livy and Valerius Maximus concerning the delivery of *cantica* may refer to an early and temporary incident, or they may have arisen from confusion with the pantomime, a type of performance which became popular in the early Empire. To accept the theory seriously as referring to the *cantica* of Plautus and Terence would produce problems of staging unbelievably grotesque.[9]

## The Meters of Roman Comedy

The meters of Plautus and Terence are quantitative, not accentual, but both playwrights reveal a surprising regard for word accent; metrical rhythm and word accent often agree so closely that the verse can be read without difficulty. The following iambic senarii (*Men.* 7, 25; *Ad.* 739) illustrate almost perfect coincidence of rhythm and accent:

> atqu(e) hóc poétae fáciunt ín comoédiis.[10]
> oneráuit náuim mágnam múltis mércibús.
> ita uítast hóminum quási quom lúdas tésserís.

Other illustrations of harmony between the verse rhythm and the word accent will be noted below among the examples of the various meters. But not all the lines of Plautus and Terence read so easily; often there is a clash between rhythm and accent, in the case of the iambic senarius, to be found especially at the beginning or the end of the verse, e.g., *Men.* 28:

[8] *CR* 54 (1940), p. 71.

[9] Yet, strangely enough, some scholars accept the tradition; cf. Sedgwick, *CR* 39 (1925), pp. 55 f.; Lindsay, *Early Latin Verse*, p. 263, n. 1. Lindsay says: "We do not forget the Roman practice of having the vocal part of Cantica done by a professional singer behind the stage, while the actor undertook the movement." But Livy's phraseology in VII, 2 (*ante tibicinem, ad manum histrionibus*) clearly implies that he thought of the singer (or singers?) as being on the stage. How would Sedgwick and Lindsay stage *Most.* 313 ff., a song passage composed of solo, duet, and quartet?

[10] Most editors print the metrical ictus on the first, third, and fifth foot of the iambic senarius, which is misleading in that the meter thus appears to resemble the Greek trimeter more closely than is actually the case. On the existence of a metrical accent there has been much debate; cf. Abbott, *TAPhA* 75 (1944), pp. 127 ff. and Harsh, *Iambic Words*, pp. 7 ff. [27 ff.], who refer to the most significant earlier work on the subject. In this chapter, I use the accent-sign merely as a guide to the scansion of the various meters, as a metrical beat which may or may not coincide with the accent of the words; it is merely an indication of the quantitative rhythm, not a sign of a metrical stress accent. Harsh (*Iambic Words*, p. 108 [128]) favors the existence of "Metrical Stress."

illúm relíquit álter(um) ápŭd matrém domí

Other factors also sometimes make the scansion difficult: elision is extremely frequent; cf. *Men.* 16 and *Ad.* 42:

tant(um) ád narránd(um) argúment(um) ádĕst benígnitás
eg(o) hánc cleméntem uít(am) urbán(am) atqu(e) ótiúm

Also common are hiatus (absence of elision), especially after emphatic monosyllables, and synizesis (the running together of separate vowel sounds within a word to form a single syllable, e.g., *deos*).

The student must keep in mind also certain features of the speech accent of early Latin, e.g., that many quadrisyllabic words like *familia* were accented on the first syllable, and he must learn the principle of iambic shortening, known as the Brevis Brevians Law. Stated briefly, the law is as follows: a long syllable preceded by a short may itself be shortened if the word accent falls either on the preceding short syllable or on the following syllable (either long or short).[11] This law may apply to syllables long either by nature or by position, and it operates not only with words but with groups of words; e.g., *egŏ, benĕ* (but not *sanĕ*, since the first syllable is long and the word remains *sānē*), *egŏn te, uolŭptarii, uolŭptas mea* (the accent moving forward to the third syllable when *mea* is added as an enclitic; never *mea uolŭptas* since the accent then falls on the second syllable of the noun); in the verses quoted above, *apŭd* (*Men.* 28) and *adĕst* (*Men.* 16) are shortened by the working of the law, and *ego* (*Ad.* 42), being emphatic, should perhaps be scanned *egŏ hanc*, with shortening and hiatus. In *Epid.* 21, an eight-foot iambic verse (octonarius), there are three instances of such shortening:

uolŭptábilém mihĭ núntiúm tu(o) ăduént(u) adpórtas, Thésprió.

I have no desire to enter into the minutiae of either early Latin prosody or early Latin accentuation in a discussion which must remain general. The observations made above will, I trust, reveal some characteristics of the verse of Roman comedy, provide a foundation for a brief analysis of the meters, and indicate, above all, that the scansions of both Plautus and Terence echo the everyday pronunciation of Latin.

The Latin senarius, a six-foot iambic verse, differs from the more rigid Greek trimeter in that substitutions are allowed in the second and fourth feet as well as in the first, third, and fifth.[12] There is regularly

---

[11] For details about the Brevis Brevians Law, see Lindsay, *Early Latin Verse*, pp. 35 ff.; Laidlaw, *The Prosody of Terence*, pp. 16 ff. Some German scholars have maintained that iambic shortening is a metrical phenomenon, that the syllable is shortened when a metrical ictus precedes or follows, but such a theory would produce impossible pronunciations like *amŏrem* and *uenīre*; Lindsay (*ibid.*, p. 49) terms this "metrical" Law of Breves Breviantes "surely the silliest theory that ever led respectable scholars astray."

[12] For other differences between the senarius and the Greek trimeter, see Lindsay, *Early Latin Verse*, pp. 269 f.

a caesural pause in the third or fourth foot, and the final foot must be pure, i.e., an iambus ($\smile \_'$) or its equivalent, a tribrach ($\smile \smile' \smile$); in the other feet the following substitutions are permitted: spondee ($\_ \_'$), dactyl ($\_ \smile' \smile$); anapaest ($\smile \smile \_'$), and proceleusmatic ($\smile \smile \smile' \smile$). The trochee ($\_ \smile$) never occurs in an iambic rhythm and, conversely, the iambus never is found in the trochaic meters, where for the trochee ($\_' \smile$) and its equivalent ($\_' \smile \smile$) the following may be substituted in all feet with the exception of the final complete foot: the spondee ($\_' \_$), the dactyl ($\_' \smile \smile$), the anapaest ($\_' \smile \_$) and, rarely, the proceleusmatic ($\_' \smile \smile \smile$). The proceleusmatic is common in iambic rhythms since it echoes the rapidity of colloquial speech (*ĕgŏ nĕquĕ* is preferable to *ĕgŏ nĕc*). For examples of proceleusmatics in senarii, cf. *Capt.* 167 and *Most.* 513:

> hăbĕ mŏdŏ bon(um) ánimum, n(am) íllum cónfidó domúm
> fug(e), ópsecr(o) hércle. quó fŭgĭ(am)? ĕtĭam tú fugé.

The moneylender demands his interest in unusually excited senarii in *Most.* 603 ff.:

> DA.: cedo faénus, rédde faénus, faénus réddité.
> datúrin éstis faénus áctutúm mihí?
> datúr faenús mihi? TR.: faénus íllic, faénus híc!
> nescít quidém nisi faénus fábuláriér.

The statement has recently been made that the comedies of Plautus and Terence "are capable of being scanned, usually with a struggle; but only one line in fifty sounds like verse."[13] This is most misleading; elision and the Brevis Brevians Law are not difficult to learn, and with their aid the student does not have to struggle to scan either the iambic senarius or the trochaic septenarius; these two meters comprise over three-quarters of the total verses of the comedies. The situation is admittedly different with Plautus' lyrical *cantica*, where the rapidly changing rhythms combine with textual difficulties to make the scansion frequently very uncertain.

The trochaic septenarius is the easiest to read of all the comic meters, for in it accent and rhythm combine to produce a line that sounds natural to our ear; as Lindsay says, "ictus and accent fall into unison in Latin trochaics with no perceptible effort . . . and English readers find themselves on more familiar ground than with Virgil."[14] The septenarius is composed of seven and a half trochaic feet; the seventh foot is always pure (i.e., $\_' \smile$ or $\_' \smile \smile$), and the end of the fourth foot usually coincides with the ending of a word (diaeresis). The meter in an accentual form is found in English poetry, e.g., in Tennyson's *Locksley Hall*:

[13] Norwood, *UTQ* 13 (1943-44), p. 236.
[14] *Early Latin Verse*, p. 283.

In the Spring a livelier iris changes on the burnished dove;
In the Spring a young man's fancy lightly turns to thoughts of love.

Cf. the following (*Curc.* 286, *Men.* 859, 867) :

> néc demárchus néc comárchus / néc cum tánta glóriá
> ósse fíni dédolábo / ássulátim uíscerá
> cúrsu céleri fácit(e) infléxa / sít pedúm pernícitás

In lines such as these there is an amazing harmony of rhythm and accent. Often the presence of triads, with or without anaphora, facilitates scansion, e.g., *Men.* 1015, *Merc.* 833, *Pseud.* 695:

> uós scelésti, uós rapáces, / uós praedónes! périimús!
> interémptust, interféctust, / álienátust. óccidí!
> scís amórem, scís labórem, / scís egéstatém meám.

Elision is of course common, as in *Asin.* 526, *Epid.* 105, *Most.* 288:

> últr(o) amás, ultr(o) éxpetéssis, / últr(o) ad t(e) áccersí iubés.
> meórum maéror(um) átqu(e) amórum / súmm(am) edíctauí tibí.
> púrpur(a) aétat(i) óccultándaest, / aúrum túrpi múlierí.

For a typical Terentian scene in septenarii, cf. *Ad.* 855 ff., e.g., 872 f.:

> ill(um) amánt, me fúgitant; illi / crédunt cónsili(a) ómniá,
> illum díligúnt, apud íllum / súnt amb(o), égŏ desértus súm.

The trochaic septenarius is, as we saw above, Plautus' favorite rhythm; over forty per cent of his verses are in this meter, and if we add Terence's usage (22%) we have for the combined comedies of the two playwrights about thirty-seven per cent, i.e., over eighteen lines in every fifty; this is very different from Norwood's "one line in fifty." These septenarii may not be poetry but they do sound like verse.

The other important *canticum* measures are the following:

(1) trochaic octonarius—an eight-foot line allowing substitutions in all but the last foot; this is often a bustling meter of great excitement, but does not appear frequently (Plautus, about 150 verses; Terence, about 90 verses). Laidlaw says: "Neither poet uses the metre continuously; the pitch was clearly too high to be sustained."[15] Cf. *Aul.* 406 ff., when the cook dashes from the house shrieking:

> áttataé! ciués, populáres, / incol(ae), áccol(ae), áduen(ae) ómnes.

In *Pseud.* 143 ff., when Ballio threatens his slaves, two octonarii are followed by a septenarius:

> núnc ade(o) hánc edíctiónem / nís(i) anim(um) áduortétis ómnes,
> nísi somnúm socórdiámqu(e) ex / péctor(e) óculisqu(e) éxmouétis,
> it(a) ego uóstra látera lóris / fáci(am) ut uálide uária sínt.

15 *The Prosody of Terence*, p. 111.

(2) iambic septenarius, seven and a half feet, usually with diaeresis after the fourth foot; a rollicking rhythm, it appears about 1,300 times in Plautus, in Terence about 400 times—roughly the same average per playwright. Lindsay says that "the Septenarii of Plautus have an unretarded, lively movement that makes them very pleasant reading."[16] Cf. *Epid.* 347 f., *Hec.* 782:

decém minís plus áttulí / quam tú danístae débes.
dum tíb(i) ego pláce(am) atqu(e) ópsequár / meŭm térgum flócci fácio.
proféct(o) in hác re níl malíst / quod sít discídio dígnum.

(3) iambic octonarius, a line of eight feet; it is composed with somewhat less regard for diaeresis after the fourth foot, since the iambic nature of the line is stamped unmistakably on the line-ending (the final foot being a pure iambus). Plautus (who used this meter especially in soliloquies) wrote two types of octonarii: (a) a more conversational type which disregarded the break in the middle of the line, e.g., *Asin.* 830:

numquídnam tíbi moléstumst, gnáte mí, s(i) haec núnc mec(um) áccubát?

(b) those with diaeresis after the pattern of the iambic septenarii; cf. *Epid.* 20, *Pers.* 12:

quid erílis nóster fíliús? / ualĕt púgilic(e) átque athléticé.
quin m(i) ímperét, quin mé suís / negótiís praefúlciát.

Terence favors the former type, as in *Phorm.* 244:

aut fíli péccat(um) aút uxóris mórt(em) aut mórbum fíliaé.

It is interesting also that Terence uses this meter far more frequently than does Plautus. There are about 420 iambic octonarii in the twenty Plautine comedies, while Terence has about 870 in six plays—a ratio of approximately one to seven.

Terence's *mutatis modis cantica* are composed of long trochaic and iambic lines (both septenarii and octonarii) with a few shorter lines interspersed (iambic dimeter, cf. *And.* 244; trochaic dimeter, cf. *And.* 246). Plautus uses iambic and trochaic measures in his songs but combines them with a great variety of lyric measures based chiefly upon the anapaest ($\smile \smile \_$), the dactyl ($\_ \smile \smile$), the cretic ($\_ \smile \_$), and the bacchiac ($\smile \_ \_$). The songs produced by these metrical combinations will be discussed below but two points are worth noting in connection with the *canticum*-meters: (1) Terence has almost no lyrical meters; two short songs in the *Andria* (481-484 in bacchiacs, 626-638 in cretics) and one in the *Adelphoe* (610-617, chiefly in dactylo-trochaics)

[16] *Early Latin Verse*, p. 275. On Plautus' use of the iambic septenarius, cf. Arnaldi, *Da Plauto a Terenzio*, I, pp. 313 ff.

—a total of twenty-five verses in over six thousand; song is thus practically non-existent in Terence and his verses are about evenly divided between spoken dialogue and verses recited to a musical accompaniment. (2) Plautus made considerable use of long anapaestic lines; cf. *Men.* 602 (septenarius), *Pers.* 753 and *Pseud.* 134 (octonarii):

> quid aís? uirŏ mé malŏ mále nuptám. / satin aúdis qu(ae) íllic lóquitur?
> hostíbus uictís, ciuíbus saluís, / re plácida, pácibus pérfectís.[17]
> quorúm numquám quicquám quoiquám / uenit ín ment(em) út recté faciánt.

Latin anapaests of this type are characterized by a marked lack of harmony between the metrical rhythm and the word accent.[18] Terence apparently disliked the clash for he avoided anapaestic lines entirely. Lindsay suggests that he promoted the iambic octonarius to the place occupied by anapaestic meter in Plautus' plays.[19] This theory, however, hardly accounts for the striking difference between the two playwrights in their use of the iambic octonarius. The long anapaestic lines of Plautus number only about 500—an average of twenty-five a play. The iambic octonarii in Terence average 145 a play. Perhaps Terence looked upon this meter as a substitute not merely for the anapaests but for the lyric element in general.

## The Nature of Plautine Song

There are more than sixty songs in the comedies of Plautus—an average of about three a play; there is, however, a great diversity in the dramatist's procedure since several plays[20] have as many as five song passages, often of considerable length, and others have almost no song. The *Curculio* contains one song (96-157), the *Asinaria* has one short passage in cretics (127-137), and the *Miles* has no song at all, unless we include as song a passage (1011-93) in anapaestic septenarii (which seems rather to be recitative since there is no change of meter). At the other end of the scale are several plays in which the total amount of

---

[17] In the anapaestic meter the dactyl ($- \smile \smile$) and the spondee ($- -$) are frequently substituted for the anapaest. *Hostibus* and *ciuibus* are dactylic words since *s* does not make position in early Latin verse (Lindsay prints in his Oxford text *hostibu'*, *ciuibu'*, etc.). I again remind the reader that I use the ictus-symbol merely to show the quantitative rhythm; it does not indicate a stress accent on the second syllable of *hostibus* and *ciuibus*.

[18] Cf. Lindsay, *Early Latin Verse*, pp. 296 ff., who explains the clash by Plautus' desire to retain the diaeresis, a salient feature of Greek anapaestic meter. He adds (p. 297) that this is a useful reminder "that Plautus was a quantitative, not an accentual poet, and did *not* assign too high a place to the reconciliation of accent and ictus."

[19] *The Captivi of Plautus*, p. 80.

[20] These are the *Amphitruo, Captivi, Menaechmi, Mostellaria, Persa, Pseudolus*, and *Truculentus*.

song is between twenty and thirty per cent,[21] and one comedy, the *Casina*, is unique in that it is almost two-fifths song (38%). The songs in all comprise over three thousand verses, or approximately one-seventh of the Plautine total.

Conspicuous among Plautus' lyric meters are verses composed of the cretic ($\underline{\;}\; \cup\; \underline{\;}$) and the bacchiac foot ($\cup\; \underline{\;}\; \underline{\;}$). These two measures often appear by themselves, sometimes in combination with other meters.[22] The bacchiac and cretic verses in Plautus number each about four hundred. A typical song in bacchiac tetrameters is the lament of the *senex* in *Men.* 753 ff., beginning as follows:

> ut aétas meá (e)st atqu(e) ut hóc usus fácto (e)st
> gradúm proferám, progredíri properábo.
> sed íd quam mihí facile sít hau sum fálsus.

This meter, not only a favorite with Plautus but also, as Lindsay observes, "admirably suited to Roman 'gravitas,' "[23] is used for laments and expressions of sorrow (cf. *Amph.* 633 ff., *Capt.* 781 ff.). At times it expresses joy (cf. *Capt.* 498 ff., 922 ff.) but it is used in general for serious and dignified speech (cf. Eunomia's words in *Aul.* 120 ff., the moralizing on unworthy clients in *Men.* 571 ff., Ptolemocratia's greeting in *Rud.* 259 ff.).

Cretics too have a variety of uses, ranging from a battle description (*Amph.* 219 ff.)[24] to the portrayal of intoxication (*Pseud.* 1285 ff.);

---

[21] These percentages are: *Mostellaria* 20%, *Bacchides* 21%, *Truculentus* 21%, *Epidicus* 23%, *Pseudolus* 24%, *Persa* 27%. Law (*Studies in the Songs of Plautine Comedy*, p. 80) states that 20% of the *Amphitruo* is song; a more accurate figure would be 17%. Miss Law includes as song 984-1005, a passage in iambic octonarii which is more properly considered recitative. I am unable to understand how Sedgwick (*CQ* 24, 1930, p. 104) can list the *Amphitruo* as having only one lyric verse in nine, or 11%. But the lacunae is the *Amphitruo* and the *Cistellaria*, as well as the loss of both the conclusion of the *Aulularia* and the opening of the *Bacchides* make percentages for these four plays somewhat unreliable.

[22] These include not merely alternating iambic, trochaic, and anapaestic measures, but verses composed of ionics ($\cup\cup\underline{\;}\underline{\;}$) and choriambs ($\underline{\;}\cup\cup\underline{\;}$) and various trochaic, dactylic, and iambic combinations (cola), such as the ithyphallic ($\underline{\;}\cup\underline{\;}\cup\underline{\;}\underline{\;}$), the glyconic ($\underline{\;}\underline{\;}\underline{\;}\cup\cup\underline{\;}\cup\underline{\;}$), and the colon Reizianum ($\underline{\;}\underline{\;}\underline{\;}\cup\underline{\;}\underline{\;}$), cola which admitted of numerous variations; cf. Lindsay, *Early Latin Verse*, pp. 279 f., 286 f., 302 ff. I make no attempt here to analyze the complicated structure of a typical Plautine song; the reader is referred to the Schema Metrorum in Lindsay's Oxford text of Plautus.

[23] *Early Latin Verse*, p. 289. The bacchiac rhythm, it must be admitted, does not impress me as melodious, and Norwood (*Plautus and Terence*, p. 58) speaks of *Men.* 571 ff. "bumping against our ears." The addition of a musical accompaniment would have made it seem very different to a Roman audience.

[24] Fraenkel (*Plautinisches im Plautus*, pp. 349 f.) suggests that the original of this passage may have been a parody of a messenger's speech in tragedy but admits that in language and form it is entirely a Roman creation; he sees here the probable influence of Ennius. Cf. Sedgwick, *CQ* 24 (1930), p. 104: "It reads like a passage from a Roman annalist. The transformation of metre removes it still further from the New Comedy, while the humour is pure Plautus: not only is it unlike any conceivable Greek original, but probably no other Roman could have written it—certainly Terence could not."

expressions of emotion are frequent: joy (*Bacch.* 643 ff.), confidence
(*Pseud.* 926 ff.), suspicion (*Most.* 690 ff.), anger (*Asin.* 127 ff.,
*Bacch.* 1109 ff.), grief (*Cas.* 186 ff.), feigned terror (*Cas.* 621 ff.),
despair (*Rud.* 207 ff., 233 ff., 664 ff.). Cries of despair, e.g., *Rud.*
664 f.:

> núnc id est qu(om) ómnium cópiar(um) átqu(e) opum,
> aúxili, praésidi uíduitas nós tenet,

differ little in tone from the lamentations in cretics as they appear in
fragments of Roman tragedy; cf. Ennius' *Andromacha Aechmalotis*
(75 ff.):

> quíd petam praésid(i) aut éxsequar, quóue nunc
> aúxilio éxili aút fugae fréta sim?
> árc(e) et urb(e) órba sum. qu(o) áccidam? qu(o) ápplicem?

An unusual song in cretics is found in *Curc.* 147 ff.; this is Phaedromus' serenade to the closed door of his mistress—the earliest example in Roman literature of a paraclausithyron:

> péssul(i), heus péssuli, uós salutó lubens,
> uós amo, uós uolo, uós pet(o) atqu(e) ópsecro,
> gérit(e) amantí mihi mór(em), amoeníssumi,
> fíte caussá mea lúdii bárbari,
> sússilit(e), ópsecr(o), et míttit(e) istánc foras
> quaé mihi míser(o) amant(i) ébibit sánguinem.
> hóc uid(e) ut dórmiunt péssuli péssumi
> néc mea grátia cómmouent s(e) ócius!

This rhythm may perhaps be reproduced in English as follows:

> Bolts and bars, bolts and bars, gladly I greetings bring.
> Hear my love, hear my prayer; you I beg and entreat;
> Yield to me and be kind; favor me, charming bolts.
> Dancers be, for my sake;
> Spring apart, I beseech; open wide, send her out,
> She who drains all my blood. I am in such distress!
> But the bars stay asleep, villains all! And for me
> Not a move do they make.[25]

[25] Cf. Copley, *TAPhA* 73 (1942), pp. 96 ff., who points out that the intoxication of
the singer was a regular feature of the ancient paraclausithyron, and says (p. 99):
"Although in Plautus' *Curculio* Phaedromus seems to be saving his wine as a bribe
for Planesium's duenna, yet his maudlin song to the door-bolts suggests that he may
have sampled it rather liberally himself." Beare (*The Roman Stage*, p. 219) cites the
paraclausithyron in *Curc.* 147 ff. as "perhaps the most plausible example of song in
Plautus," but believes (*ibid.*, pp. 220 ff.) that the so-called "lyrics" were all spoken by
the actors and that "song" in our sense of the word did not exist. Beare's arguments are
not convincing; e.g., he says (*ibid.*, p. 224): "The normal action of the play is carried
on as freely in one metre as in another." This is not true of the many monodies which
are utilized especially for the expression of emotion or for moralizing. But even if the
numerous passages in "lyric" meters were spoken or chanted rather than sung, the
word "song" remains the most convenient term to distinguish the more lyrical portions
of Plautus' comedies from those composed in the regular *canticum*-measures. Cf. Sedgwick, *C & M* 10 (1949), p. 173, who maintains that the lyric meters were intended
to be sung.

Cretics and bacchiacs are combined in *Most.* 84 ff.—a passage in which rhythm and content go hand in hand to form a song of unusual artistry. Philolaches compares the building of a house and its subsequent destruction to the rearing of a young man and the ruin of his character from idleness and love; the song falls into four parts:

I A 84-104 (bacchiac-iambic): Introduction and building of the house;

I B 105-117 (cretic-trochaic): Destruction of the house from storms and neglect;

II A 118-132 (bacchiac-iambic): Building of the young man's character;

II B 133-156 (cretic-trochaic): Destruction of the young man's character; conclusion: Philolaches' despair at his own worthlessness.

It will be noted that the construction-theme in I A and II A is accompanied by a rising rhythm ($\cup \acute{\;} \_$ and $\cup \acute{\;}$), while the ruin of house and character in I B and II B is expressed in a falling rhythm ($\acute{\;} \cup \_$ and $\acute{\;} \cup$). Few songs in Plautus reveal such conscious regard for artistic structure. The chief flaw in the song is the unduly long and repetitious introduction, but repetition is a characteristic of many other monodies, e.g., *Cist.* 203 ff., *Rud.* 185 ff., *Trin.* 223 ff.; the repetitions in *Cas.* 621 ff. (a cretic song) are especially effective:

> núlla sum, núlla sum, tóta, tot(a) óccidi,
> cór metu mórtuomst, mémbra miseraé tremunt,
> nésci(o) und(e) aúxili, praésidi, pérfugi
> m(i) aút opum cópiam cómpar(em) aut éxpetam.

The Plautine songs do not have rhyme although a trace of a rhyme scheme appears in *Men.* 597 ff., a song in iambic dimeters:

> diém corrúpi óptumúm:
> iuss(i) ápparári prándiúm,
> amíc(a) exspéctat mé, sció.
> ubi prímum (e)st lícitum ílicó
> properáu(i) abíre dé foró.
> irátast, crédo, núnc mihí;
> placábit pálla quám dedí.

Also the songs lack in general any arrangement into strophes or stanzas, and few reveal the careful attention to structure discernible in *Most.* 84 ff. Attempts of scholars such as Crusius[26] to find elaborate strophic responsion in numerous songs have not been successful, and all too often such responsions have been achieved by alterations in text and meter. But that strophic responsions do exist in parts of several songs cannot be doubted. At the opening of the *Persa* Toxilus' six lines (1-6) cor-

[26] Cf. *Die Responsion in den plautinischen Cantica*, pp. 70 ff.

respond to Sagaristio's six lines (7-12), except in one small detail.[27] *Merc.* 356-363 may be considered as strophe (356-358) and antistrophe (359-361), each composed of a trochaic octonarius and two bacchiac tetrameters, followed by an epode (362-363) of two trochaic octonarii. We possibly have a similar division into strophe, antistrophe, and epode in *Epid.* 166-172, but the scansion of the passage is difficult and there has been little agreement concerning the meters.[28] *Epid.* 7-11 are best scanned as four iambic dimeters, two cretics followed by an iambic run of twelve feet, two trochaic dimeters; the same sequence of meters recurs in 27-31.[29] The opening scene of the *Epidicus* concludes with the monody of the slave and this falls into three parts: (1) four trochaic septenarii (81-84); (2) eight pairs of cretic monometers alternating with trochaic septenarii (85-99); (3) again four trochaic septenarii (100-103). The central portion, beginning with 85:

néqu(e) egŏ nunc
quó modo
m(e) éxpedít(um) ex ímpedíto / fáciam, cónsilíúm placét.
égŏ miser
pérpuli
méĭs dolís sen(em) út censéret / súăm ses(e) émere fíliám,

is divided by Crusius into strophe (86-91) and antistrophe (92-99),[30] but this seems unnecessary. Even without such strophic arrangement the monody displays a well-balanced and symmetrical structure.

Plautus' regard for symmetry is seen also in his manner of distributing song throughout the plays. Almost all songs, whether monodies or sung by two or more actors, are "entering songs," i.e., the song begins with the entrance of one or more persons on the stage.[31] Seldom, however, does a play begin with song; there are only four instances: the *Epidicus, Persa,* and *Stichus* begin with duets and the *Cistellaria* with a trio; the other sixteen plays open with a *diuerbium*—the regular meter for exposition, just as the final scene of each play is almost always composed in trochaic septenarii (there are three exceptions, the *Persa, Pseudolus,* and *Stichus* concluding with passages of song).

Roman comedies without song alternate between *diuerbia* and *cantica* (i.e., recitative meters); if we indicate *diuerbia* by the letter *d*, recitative by *r*, the metrical structure of such a play (e.g., *Miles, Hecyra*) may be expressed as follows: *dr dr dr dr dr dr*. Plautus prefers certain meters to others before and after song passages. The usual meter before song

---

[27] Cf. Lindsay, *Early Latin Verse*, p. 313. See also Crusius, *Die Responsion in den plautinischen Cantica*, pp. 2 f.

[28] Cf. Duckworth, *T. Macci Plauti Epidicus*, pp. 209 ff.

[29] Cf. Crusius, *Die Responsion in den plautinischen Cantica*, pp. 102 f.; Duckworth, *CPh* 32 (1937), pp. 64 f.; 34 (1939), pp. 247 ff.; *T. Macci Plauti Epidicus*, pp. 104 ff., 121 ff. Lindsay wrongly scans both 9-10 and 29-30 as trochaic.

[30] *Die Responsion in den plautinischen Cantica*, pp. 87 f.

[31] There are four exceptions: one monody (*Truc.* 209 ff.) and three short duets (*Capt.* 833-837, *Most.* 783-803, *Stich.* 769-775).

is iambic senarius (forty-three song passages preceded by iambic senarii, seventeen by trochaic septenarii, one by iambic septenarii).[32] Just as the *diuerbium* more frequently precedes the songs, so we find *canticum*-measures, and especially the trochaic septenarius, following song (seven song passages followed by iambic senarii, nine by iambic septenarii, forty-six by trochaic septenarii). Plautus' regular procedure is thus a sequence of *diuerbium*, song, recitative. Since songs are almost always sung by entering characters, the abrupt change of meter seems less harsh with the introduction of a new chapter of the action, and after the song we find a gradual transition from song to recitative to *diuerbium*. If we indicate song by the letter *s*, the normal sequence becomes *dsr* and we find a striking symmetry of structure in many of the plays, e.g.,

> *Aulularia:* d s r d s r d r d s r
> *Menaechmi:* d s r d s r d s r d s r d r s r
> *Poenulus:* d s r d r d r d s r d r
> *Pseudolus:* d s r d s r d s r d s r s
> *Trinummus:* d s r d r d s r d r d s r

The *Epidicus*, which begins with song, has no *dr* combination but still reveals a balanced arrangement: s r s r d s r d s r.

This somewhat technical analysis proves clearly that one important function of Plautine song was to vary the manner of delivery and thus add liveliness and gaiety to the productions.[33] Another valuable function of song was touched upon in the discussion of cretic and bacchiac passages—their use to express joy, grief, anger, despair, and the like. Songs in general are employed for the expression of emotion, but the emotional content is most conspicuous in the monodies. It is less easy to give expression to emotion when two or more singers are on the stage; some duets deal more closely with the plot of the play and others seem designed primarily for comic effect.[34] Miss Law sums up the function of song in Plautus thus: "The value of song as song in the plays

---

[32] See Law, *Studies in the Songs of Plautine Comedy*, pp. 7 ff.; cf. pp. 103 f. for an analysis of the metrical structure of the plays. Miss Law indicates *diverbia* by the letter *a*, recitative by *b*, and song by *c*.

[33] The alternation between *cantica* and *mutatis modis cantica* in Terence's comedies likewise varied the manner of delivery to a degree but the similarity of meter made the variation less striking. If we denote the *mutatis modis cantica* by the letter *s* the sequence *dsr* in Terence is frequent, but we find also *sdr* and *drs*. Terence shifts from *mutatis modis cantica* to *diuerbia* almost as often as to stichic passages in *canticum*-meters; only rarely did iambic senarii follow song in Plautus. But the comparison proves little since Terence's *cantica* and his *mutatis modis cantica* were both recitative and a shift to senarii did not involve an abrupt break as in Plautus.

[34] Duets important for the action of the play include *Bacch.* 979 ff., *Cas.* 630 ff., 892 ff., *Pers.* 482 ff., and especially those duets beginning a song sequence, e.g., *Aul.* 120 ff., *Epid.* 1 ff., *Most.* 783 ff., *Stich.* 1 ff. For songs by two or more characters which seem designed for comic effect, cf. *Cas.* 229 ff., *Most.* 717 ff., 885 ff. *Pers.* 272 ff., *Pseud.* 230 ff., 913 ff., 1285 ff., *Stich.* 315 ff.

seems to be three fold; first and most important, it enhances the force of the emotion expressed, whether grief, fear, or joy; less often, it heightens the atmosphere of dissipation and frivolity; in all cases, it varies the manner of delivery at more or less regular intervals."[35] Song may thus increase the note of pathos or tragedy (e.g., *Amphitruo, Rudens*) or it may provide a light humorous touch (e.g., *Mostellaria, Pseudolus*). Above all, the songs and lively dance movements which in many instances accompanied them provided for Plautus' audiences a form of musical comedy which helped to hold their attention by its gaiety and vivacity.

The metrical structure of the comedies is complicated and at times highly artistic, but is this a sufficient reason for saying that Plautus' creative genius was not equal to the task? Many modern scholars have been too ready to accept Horace's statement (*Epist.* II, I, 175 f.) about Plautus' careless and hasty workmanship—but Horace neither admired nor understood early Latin poetry. We have no reason for believing that Plautus found such songs in his originals. All the evidence points in the opposite direction. Quintilian, as we saw above, implies (x, 1, 99) that Terence did not follow the Greek models in his use of meter. Among the fragments of Greek comedy are two passages from Apollodorus' *Hecyra*; these fragments (10, 11) are in trimeters, while Terence's versions (*Hec.* 286 f., 380) are in trochaic septenarii; the Roman dramatist has transferred these passages from *diuerbium* to recitative. The polymetric song which Aulus Gellius (II, 23) quotes from Caecilius' *Plocium* was in the Menandrian original a passage in iambic trimeters. Plautus' procedure we assume to have been similar. Was he an innovator in the development of comic song or was he following in the footsteps of his Roman predecessors?

## The Origin of the Lyrical *Cantica*

One of the best-known explanations of Plautine song is the theory advanced by Leo:[36] the *Miles* and the *Asinaria*, he believes, reflect closely the metrical form of the Greek originals, and no play of New Comedy had the rich lyrical content to be found in most of Plautus' works. Songs such as *Most.* 84 ff. were the product of the Roman poet. Plautus differed from the writers of New Comedy in having no chorus and in providing songs for individual actors. The subject matter of the songs came in most instances from the Greek original, but Plautus amplified

---

[35] *Studies in the Songs of Plautine Comedy*, p. 106. See also Moulton, *The Ancient Classical Drama*, pp. 402 ff.; Moulton discusses at some length metrical variation in Plautus and Terence, for which he seeks to establish certain laws: the law of variety and contrast, and the law of persistence. Beare (*The Roman Stage*, pp. 217 f.) describes briefly "the dramatic uses to which the different meters are put."

[36] *Die plautinischen Cantica und die hellenistische Lyrik*, pp. 3 f., 76 ff., 111 ff.; cf. also *Geschichte der römischen Literatur*, I, pp. 121 ff.

and elaborated the themes, expressing them in a polymetric form very different from the simple meters of his model. The metrical structure of these monodies and duets was taken by Plautus from the contemporary Hellenistic music hall songs of southern Italy. We know something about the nature of such Hellenistic songs from a song discovered in Egypt in 1896 and published by Grenfell under the title, *An Alexandrian Erotic Fragment*. This song, dated in the second century B.C., is composed in a succession of dochmiacs, a meter used occasionally by Plautus but never in this particular way. Yet Leo believes that this song resembles Plautine lyric more closely than do any other extant remains of Greek literature, and he traces the metrical structure of Hellenistic songs of this type back to the lyrics of Euripides' latest plays.

Leo's view remained popular until 1922, in which year appeared both Miss Law's *Studies in the Songs of Plautine Comedy* and Fraenkel's *Plautinisches im Plautus*.

Miss Law does not present a new theory as such, but rather suggests a sceptical attitude toward the problem. She argues against too ready an acceptance of Leo's theory:[37] we know too little about Greek comedy to assert that, among the hundreds of plays composed, there may not have been many with a polymetric structure similar to that found in Plautus; Menander may have used song less than the other playwrights and this would explain the lack of lyrical passages in Terence; if the lyrics of Euripides influenced later Hellenistic music hall songs, it is very possible that they had a similar influence upon New Comedy. Miss Law insists that Leo weakens his own position when he says that certain songs (e.g., *Most.* 313 ff. and the conclusions of the *Persa* and the *Stichus*) have an atmosphere wholly Greek and were probably not invented by Plautus. If these songs are Greek in origin, the possibility that other songs also may be Greek should not be disregarded. She believes, furthermore, that the highly artistic structure of many Plautine songs is more in consonance with Greek genius than with Plautus' cruder workmanship and that, without such songs to relieve the monotonous use of trimeter and occasional tetrameter, the Greek comedies would have been less successful in portraying emotional crises. Miss Law thus rejects Leo's view and says: "It seems more natural to think that he [Plautus] followed the metrical arrangement before him in his Greek original, with certain variations, than that he laboriously adopted Greek meters from an entirely different branch of literature. . . . It is doubtful whether the question can ever be satisfactorily answered unless a considerably larger amount of New Comedy is discovered, an amount large enough and varied enough in authorship to be really conclusive."[38]

[37] *Studies in the Songs of Plautine Comedy*, pp. 108 ff.
[38] *Studies in the Songs of Plautine Comedy*, pp. 115 f. Cf. also Marx, *Plautus Rudens*, pp. 254 ff. On the basis of lyric meters found in the fragments of Antiphanes, Eubulus, and others, Marx is convinced (*ibid.*, p. 261) that we need not look beyond

Miss Law's theory is rather negative and unsatisfying. There is truth in her contention about our extreme ignorance of New Comedy but her point of view would have been more convincing prior to 1905, the year of the Menander finds. Our increased knowledge of Menander accentuated the difference between the metrical structure of New Comedy and that of Plautus, but proved the existence for Menander of non-organic choruses which could relieve "the monotonous use of trimeter." We still know little about the other Greek playwrights but the presence of numerous songs in the *Bacchides, Cistellaria,* and *Stichus*—plays adapted from Menander—weakens the theory that Plautus "followed the metrical arrangement before him in his Greek original." Miss Law holds an erroneous view of Plautus' creative power; whatever his faults as a dramatist, there can be no doubt of his control over a large variety of meters and his ability to handle them with ease, just as there is no doubt of his absolute mastery of the Latin tongue.

A more successful attack on Leo's position came from Fraenkel who advanced as an alternative a new and interesting theory.[39] Leo missed the main point at issue, Fraenkel maintains, for he did not answer the important question: "How did Plautus come to replace the dialogue of the original by song?" The question which Leo did attempt to answer ("From what source did Plautus get his polymetric songs?") was, according to Fraenkel, answered wrongly. The Grenfell song can certainly not be the bridge from tragic arias to Plautine *cantica,* for it is composed of dochmiacs and there is no such series of dochmiacs in Plautus. Furthermore, its structure is simple and it lacks the figures of speech and the rhetorical style of Plautine song. Fraenkel points out also that these Hellenistic songs were far less dramatic than Leo implied; they were delivered by a single speaker and dramatic action in the true sense of the word was impossible.

Fraenkel's own theory is an attempt to answer the basic question: "How is the change from dialogue in the Greek original to song in Plautus to be explained?" The solution to the problem has been obscured, he believes, by the fact that attention has been centered on Plautus' songs, while the fragments of the other early dramatists of Rome have been neglected. The fragments of Ennius' tragedies, when compared with their Greek originals, show that Ennius changed Greek choral lyrics to dialogue, but he also changed Greek dialogue to song; and, more important, both he and Plautus used cretic and bacchiac

---

Greek comedy for the models of Plautine song. But almost all the passages cited by Marx come from Middle Comedy, which still retained something of the polymetry of Old Comedy. That the lyric meters used by Plautus were Greek no one denies; the important question is, why did he introduce them into the monologues and dialogues of his plays?

[39] *Plautinisches im Plautus,* pp. 321 ff.

tetrameters. This leads Fraenkel to his main point: both Ennius and Plautus inherited from earlier Roman dramatists the principle of substituting song for the dialogue of the original. The innovation was made by a playwright who composed both tragedy and comedy, i.e., either Livius Andronicus or Naevius; Fraenkel admits that no decision can be made between the two possibilities but he rather favors the former.[40] In any case, the development of song in comedy was secondary and was possible only in connection with its development in tragedy. The poet introduced song into comedy to avoid the monotony of a dialogue drama of the Menandrian type. Such a play would have been wearisome to the average Roman playgoer[41] who took delight in scenes of song and dance.

Fraenkel's theory, as outlined above, was favorably received by many scholars. Flickinger, in a review of Miss Law's work, said: "Until such a time as new evidence of a substantial sort may become available, it seems to me that Fraenkel's theory must be given the right of way as best explaining the known facts."[42] But has Fraenkel really solved the problem? He says that Plautus in comedy and Ennius in tragedy followed their Roman predecessors in introducing song into their dramas. This explanation seems far from satisfactory. There are no lyrical meters in the few fragments extant of pre-Plautine comedy, and even if Naevius or Livius Andronicus did make the innovation, Fraenkel's solution merely pushes the problem back to the very beginnings of formal Roman drama. Why was the dialogue verse of Greek comedy changed to song? Why did the Roman spectators prefer song and dance to straight dialogue? Why their desire for so many scenes recited to the accompaniment of the flute? Perhaps something in their background, something in the pre-literary dramatic tradition had accustomed them to such songs as an integral part of dramatic performances. The weaving together of song and dance into an unbroken unity seems rather to have been an inheritance from the pre-literary Italian farces which had combined song and dance and dramatic action.[43]

The trend since the appearance of Fraenkel's book has been in the direction of these pre-literary forms. According to Lejay, whose criticisms of Leo resemble Fraenkel's, the forerunner of Plautine song was

[40] Cf. the fragment of the *Equos Troianus* (20 ff.). Livius Andronicus here writes in cretic dimeters (*dá mihi hásce opes, | quás peto, quás precor: | pórrige, opítula*). Fraenkel (*Plautinisches im Plautus*, p. 345, n. 3) compares *Curc.* 148: *uós amo, uós uolo, Men.* 116: *quíd petam, quíd feram, Rud.* 208: *néc cibo néc loco, Cas.* 194: *quaé mea* (*e*)*st, quaé meo.*

[41] Cf. the first two failures of Terence's *Hecyra*. But various other factors also were doubtless responsible for the rejection of this play by the spectators, e.g., its unusually serious theme and Terence's unconventional treatment of plot and character.

[42] *CW* 19 (1925-26), p. 96. Cf. also Sonnenburg, *RE* 27 (1928), cols. 117 f. The view of Immisch (*SHAW* 14, 1923, Abh. 7, pp. 3 ff.) is somewhat a combination of the views of Leo and Fraenkel.

[43] See "The Influence of Pre-literary Comedy" in chap. 1.

the dramatic *satura—impletas modis saturas* (Livy, VII, 2). The songs of the *satura* were accompanied by a *tibicen*. Lejay believes that Livius Andronicus retained the *tibicen* but reduced the variety of meters, while Plautus again developed the musical element.[44] The song and dance of Plautus are considered by Drexler an "etruskisches Erbe," an inheritance from Etruria.[45] Sedgwick says: "It is not at all unlikely that pre-literary Roman drama, the minor dramatic forms of *Magna Graecia*, and the Hellenistic music-hall, may all have contributed to the finished product."[46] In a more recent discussion of Plautus' relation to the early popular drama, Little observes that Plautus' polymetry is "shared by Old Comedy, the Mime, the *Phlyax*, the Atellan farce, and the *Satura*. Popular also in Old Comedy were the festal ending and the lively dancing or *saltatio*."[47] Little's conclusion seems of sufficient interest to justify quotation at some length: "Thus in the works of Plautus has been preserved a contrast of an upper-class comedy imposing its criteria from without and a native comedy vigorously resisting from within the intrusion of foreign standards. Both these comedies have a Greek inspiration, the New Comedy that of Hellenistic Athens, the popular comedy that of Hellenistic South Italy. The proof of this thesis is not possible without taking into consideration the archaeological evidence, by means of which can be traced two lines of heritage, the ancestry of New Comedy which produces Terence by Menander out of Euripides,[48] and the ancestry of Roman popular comedy, which produces Plautus by folk-drama, the *Satura*, by the Atellan farce, by South Italian and Sicilian drama, out of Dorian Comedy in the West. . . . To be understood, Plautus must be compared with Aristophanes, with Epicharmus, with Sophron, with the later forms of Roman comedy. When such a comparison is made, a unifying thread is visible in a popular continuity."[49]

Where, in all this discussion of the antecedents of Plautine song, does Plautus himself figure as an original playwright? Of the various writers who have discussed the problem, Sedgwick's contribution is perhaps

[44] *Plaute*, pp. 28 ff. See also Boyancé, *REA* 34 (1932), p. 24.

[45] *Plautinische Akzentstudien*, II, pp. 363 ff. This theory also is based upon Livy, VII, 2. See above, "Horace and Livy on Early Drama" in chap. I, and cf. the allusion to *ludii barbari* in *Curc.* 150.

[46] *CR* 39 (1925), p. 58; cf. n. I: "Fraenkel's assumed influence of Roman tragedy seems unlikely; the considerable fragments extant show no trace of the Plautine metrical variety as the long fragment of Caecilius does." Cf. also Giganti, *PP* 2 (1947), pp. 300 ff., who believes that Plautus was influenced both by the native *satura* and by Hellenistic song.

[47] *HSCPh* 49 (1938), p. 226.

[48] On the supposed influence of Euripides upon New Comedy, see "The Problem of Euripidean Influence" in chap. 2.

[49] *HSCPh* 49 (1938), pp. 227 f. Law (*Studies in the Songs of Plautine Comedy*, p. 114) points out similarities between Plautus and Aristophanes but uses such similarities as an argument that Plautus followed closely his Greek originals.

the most significant. Pointing out that the earliest plays (*Miles, Asinaria, Mercator, Poenulus*) have also the smallest lyric element and that the plays usually considered late (e.g., *Persa, Pseudolus, Casina*) have the largest percentage of song, he concludes that the plays of Plautus show "(1) an early period of apprentice work, while the artist is gaining full mastery over his material; (2) a middle period of technical perfection; and (3) a late period of more daring experiment."[50] The important fact here is that Plautus first produced plays reflecting more closely the simple metrical structure of his originals and then gradually transformed the spirit of his comedies so that his later works contained a far greater amount of song and dance. We can, therefore, hardly assume on his part too great an indebtedness to his predecessors. Naevius or even Livius Andronicus may have introduced song and dance into comedy and if they did so it was doubtless under the influence of earlier Italian farce. But if Plautus himself was an actor in Atellan farces, as seems highly probable,[51] he knew well the sort of comedy that had the greatest appeal to the average Roman spectator and developed it with increasing effectiveness.

The festival conclusions of several plays (*Asinaria, Bacchides, Persa, Pseudolus, Stichus*) seem definitely a popular feature, especially when they are accompanied by polymetric song and dance (*Persa, Pseudolus,* and *Stichus*). We must remember that the early Italian farces were not free from Greek elements which go back ultimately to the beginnings of comedy in Greece. In one sense, therefore, the polymetry of Aristophanes is not entirely unrelated to the lyrical structure of Plautus. The later Greek comedy simplified the meters as it lessened the importance of the choral element; Plautus, an original genius gifted with outstanding linguistic and metrical ability, reversed the process and, by adding to his Greek models the features of song and dance which he had found in the earlier Italian popular farces, he brought to the Roman audiences an effective combination of comedy and musical farce. The great popularity that Plautus attained in his own day is undoubtedly due in part to the musical element which is so firmly embedded in the structure of his later plays.

## Festal Song and Dance in Plautus

The three lyrical songs of Terence (*And.* 481-484, 626-638, *Ad.* 610-617) give us a total of twenty-five verses. If Plautus had used song

---

[50] *CQ* 24 (1930), p. 105; cf. *CR* 39 (1925), pp. 57 f. On the chronology of the plays and the value of the lyrical element as a guide to the dating of plays that are uncertain (e.g., *Menaechmi*), see above, pp. 54 f. In a more recent article, Sedgwick points out that Plautus' period of lyric development begins only at the death of Naevius and says: "That Plautus was able to constantly increase the number and variety of his lyrics was due not only to his own increasing skill, but to the increasing number and skill of actors at Rome" (*C & M*, 10, 1949, pp. 180 f.).

[51] Cf. above, pp. 50 f.

to the same extent, we should expect to find in his twenty plays eighty-three lines of song; actually we have over three thousand. Here is an amazing difference between the two playwrights. Terence undoubtedly looked upon song and dance as popular elements unsuitable for the more serious type of comedy he wished to compose and so avoided them, as he avoided ludicrous characterization, farcical action, and verbal jesting. But this hardly explains the almost complete lack of song in Terence, for song is as effective for the portrayal of emotional crises as for the introduction of scenes of gaiety and festivity. Cf. the song of Charinus beginning at *And.* 626:

Is it believable, is it conceivable that anyone's heart could be so unreasonably spiteful that he should take a delight in the sufferings of others and reap advantages from their misfortunes?

Some songs in Plautus are more serious than this; cf. Alcumena's lament in *Amph.* 633 ff. and that of Palaestra in *Rud.* 185 ff.[52] Perhaps Terence chose to follow more closely the metrical structure of his Greek originals; yet his use of *mutatis modis cantica* reveals a desire to vary the manner of delivery and avoid the monotony of long passages in the same iambic or trochaic rhythm. The conclusion seems inescapable that Terence had little or no gift for writing song and sought to compensate for the lack by the variation of his recitative measures. But even had Terence possessed the ability to compose song, he undoubtedly would have used it with restraint and chiefly for the portrayal of emotion.

The wide range of Plautine song is seen when we pass from serious laments such as those mentioned above, through lively duets filled with witticisms and jesting (*Epid.* 1 ff., *Most.* 718 ff., etc.), to scenes of festivity, where the popular features of pre-literary Italian farce have had their greatest influence upon Plautus' technique. Typical of a festal conclusion of song and dance is that of the *Persa*; cf. the passage beginning at 753:[53]

> (*Enter* TOXILUS *from his house.*)
> TO. (*singing triumphantly*):
>> The battle o'er, the foe subdued,
>> The citizens saved, the state secure,
>>> Peace firmly ratified,
>> The fires of war are quenched at last,
>> Success today our effort crowns,
>>> No losses in our ranks:
> For this, O Lord and all ye heavenly powers above,
> And for your aid, receive my gratitude and thanks,
> Since I have well avenged myself upon my foe.

[52] See above, pp. 103 f. In discussing the function of the monologue, I did not distinguish between monologue and monody, and quoted in that connection Palaestra's song in part and also Aeschinus' song of despair from Terence's *Adelphoe* (610 ff.). But Plautus' lighter touch is seen in the passage from *Cist.* 203 ff.

[53] The translation is by C. T. Murphy, in Duckworth, *The Complete Roman Drama*, I, pp. 716 f.

And now I'm going to divide and share the booty with my partners.
(*Calling into the house*) Come on out! I want to entertain my mates here
before the door.

(*Enter* LEMNISELENIS, SAGARISTIO, PAEGNIUM, *and several other slaves
from the house.*)

Set up the couches here, arrange here all that's customary. I want to hold
court here and make everybody happy, joyful, and sportive—everybody
whose assistance made it easy for me to accomplish what I wanted. For a
man's a knave who knows how to receive a favor but not how to return it.

LE.: Toxilus dear, why am I alone? Why aren't you with me?

TO.: Come then: approach and give me a hug.

LE. (*embracing him*): There you are.

TO.: Oh, there's nothing sweeter than this. Please, my darling, let's stretch
out on the couch right now.

LE.: All your wishes are mine.

TO.: That goes for me, too. Come on then! Come, come! Sagaristio, you
take the place at the head of the table.

SA.: I don't care about that. Just give me the partner I bargained for.

TO.: All in good time.

SA.: That "all in good time" is too late for me.

TO.: To business! Take your place. Let's spend this day in pleasant revelry;
it's my birthday. Here slaves! Pour water on our hands and set the table.
(*To* LEMNISELENIS) Here's a garland of flowers for you, my little
flower. You'll be our toastmistress.

LE. (*to* PAEGNIUM): Come, boy! Begin the game at the head of the table
there with two-quart mugs all around. Get moving there! Hurry up!

TO.: Paegnium, you're too slow with the drinks. Give me one (*Taking a
drink*) Good health to me, good health to you, good health to my mistress!
The gods have granted me this day I longed for; now, my dearest, I can
embrace you as a free woman.

LE.: Thanks to you, dear.

TO. (*raising his cup again*): Here's to all of us. My hand presents your
hand with this cup, as is proper for lovers.

LE.: Give it to me.

TO.: Take it.

LE.: Here's to the man who envies me, and here's to one who rejoices with
me.

Dordalus enters complaining that he has been cheated and damning
"that Persian, and all Persians, and all persons too" (783). He is
ridiculed and beaten. The festivity continues, with drinking, dancing,
and jesting, to the end of the play.

In *Stich.* 769 ff., after the flute-player has finished drinking with
Stichus and Sangarinus and has resumed his music, the comedy concludes in a whirlwind of activity, well brought out by the stage directions of the translator:[54]

SA.: What Ionian dancer or acrobat could equal this? (*He flies through the
air in a great leap.*)

ST. (*recovering from a similar gymnastic gyration*): Well, what if you did
beat me that time. Dare me again!

[54] J. R. Workman, in Duckworth, *The Complete Roman Drama*, II, p. 37.

SA.: Come on, try this one. (*He turns a tremendous tailspin.*)
ST.: You—you, try this one! (*He takes a gigantic jump.*)
SA.: Hippity!
ST.: Skippity!
SA.: Rippity!
ST.: Whew!
SA.: Now, both together—calling all dancers, calling all dancers! We can't get along without this any more than a mushroom can without rain!
ST. (*exhausted*): Come on, let's go inside. We've danced enough for our wine! And you, good spectators, give us your applause and then have a party of your own at home.

In scenes such as these Plautus has utilized song and dance to create a form of musical extravaganza that bears little relation to either New Comedy or the more sober and serious productions of Terence. But prose translations of such passages fail to give a true idea of the effect of the original. Wright seems correct when he says: "In the actual conditions of its representation with songs and music a Plautine comedy has more resemblance to *The Beggar's Opera* or *The Gondoliers* than to *The Way of the World* or *The School for Scandal*,"[55] and he endeavors to make this fact evident in his own translation of the *Rudens*; cf. his version of 222-228, Ampelisca's monody in anapaestic tetrameters:[56]

> There is nothing, I see, that is better for me
> than to just put an end to existing;
> For my life is a curse and it could not be worse,
> and my troubles are always persisting.
> I don't care a jot if I give up the lot,
> for I am completely despited:
> I can't find my friend, though I've tried without end
> with eyes, ears, and voice all united.
> There is not a soul here; it's a desert, I fear;
> not a person to tell me about her.
> But if she's alive, I will not cease to strive;
> for I really cannot live without her.

[55] *Three Plays of Plautus*, p. 53. On Plautus and *The Beggar's Opera*, cf. Lindsay, *CR* 37 (1923), p. 67. But cf. Beare, *The Roman Stage*, pp. 222 ff., and see above, n. 25.
[56] *Three Plays of Plautus*, p. 68.

# CHAPTER 14

## THE ORIGINALITY OF ROMAN COMEDY: A RECAPITULATION

### The Problem

FEW fields of Roman literature have received more attention in recent years than that of comedy, and in particular the problem of the originality of the two Roman playwrights. For more than half a century classical scholars, both here and abroad, have sought to determine the relation of Plautus and Terence to their Greek models and new and often conflicting theories are constantly being propounded. Far too often the emphasis has shifted from what we have of Roman comedy to a discussion of the non-existent Greek comedy, to a laudable but often mistaken attempt to reconstruct the Greek originals of the Roman plays. If this could be done with any degree of certainty, the results would be most helpful. It is difficult to discuss the creative ability of Plautus and Terence when their models have not survived, or to talk about the originality of Roman comedy as a whole when all we have of Greek New Comedy is a total of four or five fragmentary plays. Such a procedure involves "a comparison of the known with the unknown"[1]—a dangerous and almost futile undertaking.

The problem is complicated by another loss, that of scores of Roman comedies. Of the many plays written by Naevius, Plautus, Caecilius, Terence, and others—and the *fabulae togatae*, plays on Roman themes by Afranius, Titinius, and Atta, should be included[2]—we have only the twenty-six comedies of Plautus and Terence. The fact that the surviving plays are all *palliatae* gives in itself a false idea of Roman originality, since it emphasizes Roman dependence upon Greek plots, settings, themes, and characters. But the two dramatists, in adapting Greek originals of the same general type, have produced plays amazingly unlike in many respects. It is important to recall that the comedies of Plautus are those of a mature and experienced playwright, those by Terence the work of a young writer at the very beginning of his career. But is this sufficient to explain the differences between the achievements of the two men? That two dramatists, separated only by a generation, could have such contrasting ideals of dramatic art, is in itself an important point in our consideration of the richness and the variety of Roman comedy and not without effect upon our estimate of Roman originality.

Critical estimates of the originality of Plautus vary widely. Some scholars (e.g., Leo, Fraenkel, and Jachmann) subject his plays to a

---

[1] Cf. Harsh, *A Handbook of Classical Drama*, p. 336.
[2] See "The Decline of the Palliata" in chap. 3.

minute analysis and debate, usually without agreement, whether a certain passage reflects the Greek original or has been added from a second
(or even third) Greek comedy. Plautus can insert Latin puns and
Roman allusions, he can "contaminate," i.e., join together, more or
less awkwardly, parts of two or three originals, but he is almost incapable of composing one or more scenes of lively dialogue of his own;
in other words, Plautus is a master of Latin phraseology and his plays
are rich in comic values but he is little more than a translator. Far more
convincing are the views held by Sedgwick, Little, Hough, and others:
Plautus was an original artist whose technique developed and matured
in his later work; he made the Greek plots more farcical and the characters more laughable and grotesque; he gradually increased the amount
of song and dance, making the plays almost musical comedies with
gay and festal conclusions; he added Roman references and did not
hesitate to break the dramatic illusion; he increased the quantity and
vulgarity of his jests; and, by eliminating a certain amount of exposition and repetition of information, he sought to introduce more suspense
and surprise into his plays. Sedgwick says: "Plautus' originality lies
deeper than the mere expansion of dialogue and the scattering of puns
and Roman allusions—it consists in the complete transformation of the
spirit of a play."[3]

The range of views concerning Terence is equally great. The older
and more conventional theory is represented by Flickinger and Post:
Terence's plays have a certain elegance and charm but they display
neither the truthfulness and humanity of Menander on the one hand,
nor the variety and gay humor of Plautus on the other; the plots are
monotonous and the characters are alike. Terence translated closely
and his plays lack the vigor and forcefulness of the Greek originals.[4]

[3] *CQ* 24 (1930), p. 104. Similarly, Knapp (*CW* 19, 1925-26, p. 197) speaks of Plautus
as "a forceful and original genius, a man who, in his sphere, could do what Vergil did
in so very different a sphere, and what Shakespeare did in his, i.e. borrow widely only
to make the borrowings his own, to transform and transmute them into something
new." For Beare's view of the originality of Plautus, see *The Roman Stage*, pp. 53 ff.

[4] This is essentially the criticism attributed to Caesar by Suetonius; cf. *Vita Terenti*,
7. Caesar calls Terence *dimidiate Menander*, a "half-Menander," or, perhaps preferably,
"the other half of Menander," i.e., "Menander's double" (see Flickinger, *PhQ* 6, 1927,
pp. 252 ff.; Harsh, *A Handbook of Classical Drama*, p. 490, n. 21), but regrets that
he lacks *vis* (or *vis comica*, depending upon the punctuation, but this is rejected by
most scholars today; see Ferrarino, *SIFC* 16, 1939-40, pp. 59 ff.). On the nature of
the *vis* ("vigor," "force," "energy") which Caesar misses in Terence, see Radford,
*PAPhA* 32 (1901), pp. xxxix ff.; Norwood, *The Art of Terence*, pp. 140 f.; Post,
*CW* 23 (1929-30), pp. 121 f. Post says (*TAPhA* 62, 1931, p. 224): "I conclude that
Caesar meant by 'vis' the magic touch of genius that enthralls the reader or hearer";
but cf. Flickinger, *CJ* 26 (1930-31)," pp. 686 ff.; 28 (1932-33), pp. 518 ff.; Flickinger
prefers to take *vis* as referring to "distinction or elevation of style." Both Cicero and
Caesar refer to Terence's restraint and refinement; cf. Cicero: *sedatis motibus* (*vocibus*, MSS.); Caesar: *lenibus scriptis*; see Harsh, *loc. cit.*, who considers both epigrams
highly complimentary (cf. also Wright, *Cicero and the Theater*, pp. 65 f.). Some
modern scholars believe that the "dimidiate Menander" epigram is wrongly ascribed

Flickinger says that "his normal practice was such an adherence to his originals as could not be paralleled by any other Roman playwright of standing."[5] Other writers (e.g., Norwood, Frank, Beare, Kuiper) hold a very different conception of Terence's craftsmanship and originality. Norwood maintains that the six plays reveal a steady advance in technical excellence; Terence becomes more proficient in the use of the double plot and his characters develop in psychology and structural value—all evidence that he is not a translator but an innovator of outstanding originality. According to Frank (and to many who have accepted his theory), Terence was the first to introduce suspense into ancient drama, which he did by eliminating the expository prologue. Beare considers that the great secret of Terence was his originality, which he tried to conceal from his Roman audiences by stressing his close relation to his Greek models. Kuiper goes even further in his view of Terence's structural innovations; assuming for the originals of both Plautus and Terence a fixed structure which included a deferred prologue and marriages between half-brother and half-sister, he reconstructs the plots of the Greek comedies and points out the numerous (and often unfortunate) changes which the Roman playwrights made. Enk, like Norwood, looks upon Terence as a composer of high comedy; he accepts many of the theories mentioned above and attempts to show how Terence has improved upon the technique of both Menander and Plautus.[6] The tide of Terentian originality is running high at present, but the views just cited cannot be substantiated by the evidence of the plays themselves.[7] I do not, however, subscribe to the view of Flickinger that Terence was merely a close translator of Greek comedy. Terence introduces striking innovations, his treatment of comic themes is often unorthodox, and there is every reason to assume that he too departs in many respects from his originals, but his conception of comic drama is very unlike that of Plautus.

Other recent works point out differences between Plautus and Terence which, if sound, are of importance for the problem of Roman originality. Dunkin believes that Plautus was the poet of the poor and downtrodden classes and voiced their complaint against ruthless exploitation by ridiculing the rich men of his plays, whereas Terence, exalting the rich man, was the spokesman of the men of property. Somewhat similar is the view of Lana: Plautus supported the anti-Greek reaction of his day and sought to make Greek life ridiculous by criticism and caricature while Terence, as one of the leaders of the philhellenic movement of the following generation, sought to portray Greek life

---

to Caesar and is actually a part of Cicero's epigram; for bibliography and discussion, see Ferrarino, *ibid.*, pp. 51 ff.; Arnaldi, *Da Plauto a Terenzio*, II, pp. 225 f.; De Lorenzi, *Quaderni Filologici*, II. *Dimidiatus Menander.*

[5] *PhQ* 7 (1928), p. 114.     [6] *Mn* 13 (1947), pp. 82 f.

[7] See above, pp. 188 ff., 204 f., and 230 f.

sympathetically and subordinated to this purpose his ideals as a dramatic artist. Theories such as these may be questioned because they look upon the dramatists primarily as propagandists rather than as playwrights. These critics agree in ascribing great originality to Plautus for his departures from the tone and spirit of the Greek models, and to this extent they seem correct; but the reason lies, I am convinced, in Plautus' conception of effective comedy and in his realization of the value of caricature and good-natured ridicule.[8]

Two ever-recurring topics run through much of the scholarly work dealing with the originality of Plautus and Terence; these are the "contamination hypothesis" and a more recent development which may be termed the "half-sister fallacy." Both rest upon the unfounded assumption of the perfection of Attic comedy and upon the accompanying theory of the faultiness of Roman workmanship, but the "half-sister fallacy" ascribes greater independence to the Roman playwrights than does the theory of contamination. A few comments upon each by way of summary may not be inappropriate.

(1) The "contamination hypothesis."[9] We know from Terence's prologues (*And.* 13 f., *Eun.* 25 ff., *Ad.* 6 ff.) that he inserted characters and scenes from a second original, and we know also that, when he was criticized for contaminating the Greek plays, he defended his procedure by saying that Naevius, Plautus, and Ennius had done the same. This passage (*And.* 18 ff.) is the only evidence which we have for contamination by Plautus. It might support a theory of workmanship whereby Plautus made similar use of a second original; it does not prove any such method of interweaving or fusion of two plots as has been postulated for plays like the *Miles, Poenulus,* and *Pseudolus*; more and more in recent years this type of detailed analysis, based upon imagined rather than real flaws and contradictions, has been strongly condemned.[10] Contamination, either in the sense of interweaving two plots or of adding a small part from a second play cannot be proved for Plautus. Terence claimed to have done it in the latter sense in three instances. The procedure of contamination might well be considered a sign of Roman originality, but to far too many classical scholars it has become a cause for reproach, an indication that the Roman playwrights were unable to create characters or develop situations without finding a model somewhere in a Greek comedy. And yet there is nothing basically wrong with the procedure. The later dramatists of Italy, France, and England on numerous occasions "contaminated" by combining plots from two or more Plautine or Terentian comedies; cf., e.g., Shakespeare's *The Comedy of Errors*, adapted from the *Menaechmi* with

---

[8] On the basic flaws in the theories of Dunkin and Lana, see above, pp. 239 f., 260 f., and 278; cf. also chap. 9, n. 27.

[9] See "The Problem of *Contaminatio*" in chap. 7.

[10] Especially by Harsh, Enk, and Beare; see above, pp. 207 f.

additions from the *Amphitruo*, and Ben Jonson's *The Case Is Altered*, which results from the interweaving of two Plautine plays, the *Aulularia* and the *Captivi*.[11]

(2) The "half-sister fallacy." Kuiper has attempted in recent years to reconstruct the originals of many Roman comedies.[12] He assumes a mechanical structure for the Greek models, points out the many innovations which he believes the Roman playwrights to have made, and then seeks to show the superiority of the hypothetical reconstructions over the extant Roman comedies. If Kuiper is correct, both Plautus and Terence have displayed amazing and commendable originality in recasting the plots of the Greek plays. His conclusions, however, would be more acceptable if we could believe that so many Greek comedies had the same monotonous plot and ended so frequently with marriages of half-brother and half-sister, but the only Roman play which could possibly support this "plague of half-sisters" is the *Epidicus*, and Keyes has shown that even here it is doubtful that such a marriage occurred in the Greek version of the *Epidicus*.[13]

If, then, we reject both the "contamination hypothesis" and the "half-sister fallacy," how are we to compare the Roman plays with their lost models? If we abandon the effort to compare the known with the allegedly flawless unknown, can we discuss with any assurance the originality of Roman comedy? The fragmentary plays of Menander help a little, for they lack many of the elements of Terence's comedies, and Menander and Plautus are worlds apart. Are the characteristic features of Plautus and Terence to be ascribed to the Greek comedies which they adapted and imitated or to their own craftsmanship? The productions of the two Roman playwrights differ in a most striking fashion. Was one a close translator and the other an independent creator, or do the comedies of Plautus and Terence reflect the conception of comedy which each had and display the innovations which each desired to make? In order to clarify our conception of Roman comedy and enable us to accept or reject the numerous theories now in circulation, I have in the preceding chapters attempted to place side by side the chief features of the two dramatists and to point out the similarities and differences in their plays; in other words, I have tried to compare the known with the known. This is in essence the procedure suggested by Prescott more than thirty years ago when he said: "Twenty-six plays constitute a considerable mass of material. Should it not be possible, disregarding all theories, to analyze these plays, placing side by side like features, discriminating the unlike, and thereby ultimately obtaining a helpful

---

[11] See "Shakespeare and Ben Jonson" in chap. 15. If the originals of these two English comedies were lost and scholars attempted to restore the Plautine comedies utilized by Shakespeare and Jonson, how closely, one wonders, would their reconstructions resemble the actual Roman models?

[12] See chap. 6, n. 1.        [13] See chap. 6, n. 34.

synthesis which might lead to sounder constructive interpretation?"[14]
It is my sincere hope that this study has provided such a "helpful synthesis." A brief résumé of the more important conclusions follows.

# A Summary

*Stage Conventions.* Both playwrights take over from Greek comedy
the same conventions; criticisms of Plautus for his use of the protatic
character, the running slave, the creaking door, or the opportune meeting are easily refuted, for the same devices occur in Terence. But—and
this is all too often overlooked—Plautus with his hearty sense of fun
and his keen knowledge of good theater takes the conventions in his
stride and puts them to work; the protatic character, for instance, is
useful not merely for exposition but for humor and characterization, the
running slave for humor and suspense. Terence has little interest in
comic effect (cf. his monologues, especially those of the running slave);
he is less at ease with the various conventions and he uses them more
mechanically (e.g., the protatic character); he is bothered about their
lack of verisimilitude and hence avoids bringing on the stage many
scenes which add gaiety to Plautus' plays. He likewise avoids breaking
the dramatic allusion, and he is careful not to introduce Roman allusions. At times his characters express their disapproval of the accepted
conventions, e.g., off-stage births (*And.* 474 f.), conversations with
people indoors (*And.* 490 ff.), the revelation of secrets on the stage
(*Phorm.* 818, *Hec.* 866 ff.). Plautus accepted the conventions without
question and developed their comic possibilities, but Terence, less interested in their humorous aspects, rather sought for new variations
on old themes, and sometimes put to an unconventional use the very
conventions which he himself employed elsewhere without comment.

*The themes of the plays.* The misunderstandings and complications
of the plots arise in most comedies either from mistaken identity or deception, or from a combination of the two, but there is little evidence
that deception played such a prominent part in the plots of the Greek
originals. The Roman fondness for trickery and impersonation seems
rather an inheritance from the earlier farces of Italy. The comedies of
Plautus reveal a great diversity of theme and include quiet plays
(*Captivi, Trinummus*), sentimental comedy (*Cistellaria*), romance
(*Rudens*), mythological travesty (*Amphitruo*), coarse farce (*Asinaria,
Casina*). The plots of Terence are more uniform, but he does not subordinate the love element as Plautus does, and he handles the traditional
plot with subtle variations. In two instances he uses the *anagnorisis*, not
to bring about the final solution, but to provide additional complications
(*Heauton, Phormio*) and his treatment of deception is especially noteworthy: the fantastic falsehoods and ingenious impersonations of the

[14] *CPh* 14 (1919), p. 135.

Plautine slave disappear as do the grotesque portrayals of the gullible *senex*. In Terence the father is a more reasonable person and often, instead of being deceived, he fools himself by his unwillingness to accept the truth (cf. *And.* 468 ff., 490 ff., 855 ff.). The slave sometimes tells the truth and pretends that it is a trick (cf. *And.* 747 ff., *Heaut.* 709 ff.), and his role is very different from that of the Plautine intriguing slave. He is a bungler (cf. Davus in the *Andria*), or he tries to keep the *adulescens* from wrongdoing (cf. *Eun.* 378 ff., *Phorm.* 75 ff.), or he is ordered off the stage and prevented from taking part in the action (Parmeno in the *Hecyra*). It is interesting to note that the most unconventional treatment of deception occurs in Terence's first three comedies.

*Plot-Structure.* Plautus' comedies have in most instances a single plot with one problem and one set of characters, even when, as in the *Miles* and the *Poenulus*, there are two deceptions. Terence's plays, with the exception of the *Hecyra*, have a double plot—two love affairs more or less closely integrated, two young men, two sweethearts, usually two contrasted fathers. That Terence added the characters of Charinus and his slave Byrria to the *Andria* is known, and it is obvious that the duality-method appealed to him. But it does not follow that this method is Terence's own invention, as Norwood maintains. The two love affairs in the other plays, especially in the *Phormio* and the *Adelphoe*, are too closely interwoven to be separated and must have existed side by side in one and the same Greek original. Whereas Terence favored the *argumentum duplex* as a means of increasing the intricacy of his plots, Plautus filled out the simpler plots of his comedies with digressions and repetitions of a comic nature, again revealing his desire to write for the entertainment of his spectators. Humorous passages loosely connected with the plot did not appeal to Terence, hence there are fewer passages in his plays which can be criticized as flaws or contradictions, but improbabilities, carelessness in details, the non-fulfillment of expected events appear in the works of both dramatists and are not convincing arguments to support theories of contamination in regard to individual plays.

*Suspense and Irony.* One of Terence's most original features is his complete elimination of the expository prologue; he is said, therefore, to have introduced suspense and surprise into ancient comedy but to have lost comic irony in so doing. Plautus, on the other hand, is believed by his use of the prologue to prepare his audience for every turn of the plot. Actually, expository prologues appear in only about half of Plautus' comedies and in most instances reveal little about the outcome of the plot. In only three plays (*Aulularia, Captivi, Poenulus*) is the denouement foretold and then only in part. Furthermore, the foreshadowing of the recognition gives little information about the action within the play. The effect of the expository prologue upon suspense has been overstressed. Both Plautus and Terence make liberal use of preparation and foreshadowing during the course of the action and the interest of the spectators derives in part from the anticipation of events which are already known or hinted at. The most detailed preparation for later events occurs in Plautus' earlier plays. Both playwrights realize the value of dramatic tension and deliberately attempt to heighten the suspense of the audience by stressing the ignorance or the helplessness of the characters. Numerous events come as a surprise. This is especially true of Terence who, by omitting the narrative prologue, keeps the audience in ignorance of secrets of identity, e.g., that Phanium is the daughter of Chremes (*Phormio*). But there are unexpected developments and surprises in many of Plautus' plays, not only the *Epidicus* and the *Curculio*, which lack prologues, but in those with prologues as well (e.g., *Casina, Menaechmi, Rudens*). Also, the presence of surprise is not incompatible with the effective development of comic irony. Foreknowledge acquired from a narrative prologue is one source of irony but the main source is the information which comes naturally from the action within the play proper. Even in Terence's *Hecyra*, where the ignorance of the spectators is carried to extreme lengths, there is excellent irony when the spectators understand why Philumena left her husband's home and realize how incorrect the *senes* are in their interpretation of Pamphilus' attitude. The tendency of modern critics to deny irony to Terence and to refuse to see suspense and surprise in Plautus is not justified.

*Portrayal of Character.* The roles in the plays of Plautus and Terence are in general those of Greek comedy. Most frequent are the family types—husbands and wives, sons and daughters. Slaves are numerous, and the *meretrix* plays a prominent part, since daughters of respectable parents seldom appear on the stage. Many *senes* are portrayed by Plautus as ludicrous—both those deceived by their slaves, i.e., Nicobulus (*Bacchides*), Periphanes (*Epidicus*), Theopropides (*Mostellaria*) and, to a much greater degree, those unfaithful to their wives, i.e., Demaenetus (*Asinaria*), Lysidamus (*Casina*), Demipho (*Mercator*). Terence portrays his family types as more decent and respectable; there is only one husband guilty of an extra-marital affair and he does not escape detection (cf. *Phorm.* 1016 ff.). The adulterous wife is found neither in Plautus nor in Terence; Alcumena (*Amphitruo*) is guilty only in a technical sense, for she is devoted to her husband and is the victim of impersonation. The love affairs of young men are presented by Terence in a serious manner but Plautus, by having the slave ridicule both his young master and the youth's sweetheart (*Asinaria, Curculio, Poenulus, Pseudolus*), makes love more often a matter of comedy than of sentiment. Plautus develops the slave into a brilliant master of intrigue (e.g., Chrysalus, Palaestrio, Pseudolus) and among his most laughable creations are the roles rich in comic possibilities—parasites (e.g., Ergasilus, Gelasimus), slavedealers (e.g., Lycus, Ballio), and soldiers (e.g., Pyrgopolynices). The last two roles are more often the victim of deception and the butt of ridicule than are the fathers. The parasite, the slavedealer, and the soldier appear rarely in Terence's comedies and only in his last three plays; even then they are less exaggerated and more respectable than such characters in Plautus. Plautus' most successful delineations represent unusual types—Alcumena, the faithful wife accused of adultery (*Amphitruo*), and Euclio, a poor man overwhelmed with anxiety for his newly discovered treasure (*Aulularia*). Terence's outstanding creations are Demea and Micio, excellent psychological studies of the stern and the lenient father (*Adelphoe*), and the noble mother-in-law and the goodhearted *meretrix* of the *Hecyra*. These last two characters have been considered almost too good to be realistic, and Terence's delineations in general have been accused of monotony and lack of truthfulness. He avoids farcical and grotesque roles and seeks to represent his characters as well-meaning and decent citizens; they lack the vividness and color of Plautus' characters but are admirably adapted to comedies designed to arouse "thoughtful laughter." Also, they seem to reproduce the moral and philosophical conceptions of the Greek originals more faithfully than do Plautus' characters, who in their comic denunciations of love and marriage, their use of vulgar and indecent expressions, and their frequent allusions to the gods and to religious rites, omens, and auguries are more typically Roman and would have a far greater appeal to the average Roman spectator.

*Comic Devices, Language, and Meter.* Plautus not only develops the more grotesque aspects of many characters but he pads his plots with scenes of a farcical nature which have little to do with the action but which are most successful in creating laughter, e.g., humorous monologues by parasites and running slaves, comic asides, references to the dramatic machinery, and scenes of repetitious moralizing. Improbable situations, unexpected and laughable developments, ludicrous contrasts —these are his stock in trade. Terence avoids comic scenes not closely integrated with the action (the monologue of Gnatho in *Eun.* 232 ff. is an exception), hence his comedies are shorter than many Plautine plays in spite of their more intricate plots. There are many humorous situations in Terence, especially in the later plays, but he almost never introduces comic situations for their own sake. Both playwrights arouse laughter by means of incongruity, surprise, and exaggeration, but Plautus often descends to buffoonery and slapstick, whereas Terence shows great restraint in his use of comic devices and tends to subordinate the ridiculous to the serious. In language also Terence is far more restrained than Plautus and lacks the exuberance and extravagance of his predecessor. Puns, plays upon words, alliteration and assonance, comic formations (e.g., Thensaurochrysonicochrysides, *Capt.* 285), jokes often vulgar and coarse but always effective, verbal repetitions (e.g., *nugas agis, Men.* 621 ff.; *licet, Rud.* 1212 ff.; *censeo, Rud.* 1269 ff.), and surprise turns abound in Plautus but appear in Terence rarely, if at all. Plautus can be elegant and restrained in language when the situation demands an elevation of tone; Terence is almost always elevated, and his language is well suited to the more decent and respectable characters whom he presents on the stage, but the range and versatility of Plautus are lacking. The same is true of the musical element. Whereas Plautus' comedies are rich in polymetric effects and innumerable scenes are enlivened by song and dance—elements especially prominent in his later plays and undoubtedly developed by him under the influence of earlier pre-literary farces and songs—Terence makes almost no use of the lyrical *canticum* and avoids such scenes of gay festivity as are found in the concluding portions of the *Persa* and the *Stichus.*

## The Significance of Roman Comedy

The differences between Plautus and Terence are far too great to be explained by the nature of the Greek plays which they adapted. The choice of the Greek original was doubtless determined by each playwright's desire to produce a certain type of drama but there is no convincing evidence that either dramatist was a close translator. Everything that we know and can surmise of Greek New Comedy indicates that Plautus was interested in creating for the amusement and delight of his spectators a very different and more effective type of comedy. The originality of Terence is less striking but no less obvious; his innovations were in the direction of greater naturalness and artistry, a more subtle portrayal of character, a more elegant and refined type of comedy. His technical improvements include the substitution of dialogue for monologue, omission of the omniscient prologue, a greater use of surprise, and increased skill in the use of the double plot. But some of the extravagant claims for Terentian originality cannot stand: Frank's conviction that Terence first introduced suspense into ancient drama, Norwood's belief that Terence invented the duality-method of plot construction, and Kuiper's theory of the elimination of numerous recognition scenes must all be discarded. Plautus at times becomes more serious and Terence occasionally indulges in farce, but in general the tone and technique of their plays are very dissimilar, and neither should be condemned for not doing what the other did. And yet it is all too easy to exaggerate the differences between the two playwrights. Perhaps the farce of Plautus obscures his artistry, just as the restraint and elegance of Terence detract from a proper understanding of his subtle but often excellent humor.

What conclusions are we justified in drawing about Roman comedy as a whole? Perhaps its originality may be said to lie in the very fact that a Greek dramatic form, the extant fragments of which all agree to be social drama rather than comedy,[15] could be adapted by the Romans and developed in divergent directions, so that in essence we have two very different types of comedy.

(1) Of the one Plautus is the sole surviving exponent (although the fragments of Naevius and, to a lesser degree, of Caecilius indicate that they belong to the same tradition); this is a comedy of farce, robust humor, song and dance, gay and improbable plots, amusing and often grotesque characters, all richly embellished with jokes and puns and word-play. Hough and others have shown that many of these features were less prominent in the earlier plays but were developed by him and used with far greater frequency in his latest comedies.[16] There seems every justification for the conclusion that the chief ingredients of Plautine comedy were three in number: the Greek originals, the pre-literary dramatic forms of central and southern Italy,[17] and Plautus' own contributions to the genre. This third ingredient should not be underestimated. Plautus was a comic genius, whose expert knowledge of stagecraft was equaled by his mastery of language and style; he was a playwright who, as Oldfather says, "deserves to be named with Aristophanes and Shakespeare."[18]

(2) The other development, that by Terence, was in the direction of subtlety and artistry. There is little coarse humor, few scenes composed primarily for laughter, more intricate plots and greater suspense, characters more dignified and respectable, a greater emphasis upon sentiment and the more serious aspects of family life. Terence's more striking innovations, his most unorthodox treatment of stage conventions, plot, and character appear, surprisingly enough, in his earliest plays. The last three plays (*Eunuchus, Phormio, Adelphoe*)[19] are distinguished not only for their excellent integration of plot and character but also for more effective humor. Characters like Gnatho and Thraso (*Eunuchus*) and Phormio seem almost Plautine, as does Syrus (*Adelphoe*), who

[15] See above, p. 32. I realize, of course, that the lost plays of Diphilus and Philemon may have contained far more comedy than do the extant plays of Menander; see above, p. 28.

[16] See above, pp. 54 f. and especially the bibliography cited in notes 38 and 41; cf. also pp. 379 f. The exact chronology of the plays cannot be determined but there is general agreement concerning the relative order of many of the plays.

[17] On the nature of the *satura*, the *fabula Atellana*, and the mime, see chap. 1; cf. also "The Origin of the Lyrical *Cantica*" in chap. 13. Terence's failure to utilize the metrical and the farcical elements of these early dramatic forms doubtless explains many of the features of his plays and accounts in part for his closer adherence to his Greek models. But Terence obviously had little interest in this type of comedy.

[18] *CW* 7 (1913-14), p. 219. Cf. Wright, *Three Roman Poets*, p. 89: "Taken all in all, there is no playwright in any language ancient or modern, save Aristophanes, who for sheer humour can be matched with him"; Enk. *Mn* 13 (1947), p. 81: "Plautus is a Grand-Master of laughter."

[19] The *Hecyra* is Terence's second play. Norwood's theory of Terence's dramatic development is faulty, since he considers the *Hecyra* as the fifth play; see above, chap. 6, n. 63.

is far more the traditional *seruus callidus* than Davus (*Andria*) or Parmeno (*Hecyra*). Terence in his later plays seems to have discovered by experience how to compose more effective comedy.[20] When we contemplate the excellent blend of serious thought and subtle humor in the *Adelphoe*, his final comedy, and at the same time realize that Terence died almost at the beginning of his career, one is tempted to speculate upon the even more successful union of Plautine and Terentian elements which he might have achieved, had a long life as a dramatist been granted to him.

In the creation and development of these two divergent trends reside the true significance and originality of Roman comedy. The richness and variety in these twenty-six plays provided later comedy with a treasure-house of humorous and farcical situations and characters upon which it was able to draw. Can one imagine Molière or the Elizabethan dramatists if they had been dependent upon either Plautus or Terence alone, or if instead of the Roman plays a few comedies of Menander had survived to later times? Modern comic drama owes to the two Roman playwrights a far greater debt than is often realized. The final chapter will summarize the nature of this indebtedness.

[20] See Perry, *Masters of Dramatic Comedy*, pp. 76 f., who says that Terence's early plays are hardly comedies at all. He thinks that the dramatist gradually developed an increased sense of gaiety. According to Perry, there is hardly enough relief in Plautus' plays from the continuous merriment, while Terence erred in the opposite direction.

# CHAPTER 15

## *THE INFLUENCE OF PLAUTUS AND TERENCE UPON ENGLISH COMEDY*

NO TREATMENT of the two comic playwrights of Rome would be complete without some account, however brief, of the tremendous influence which they exerted upon European comedy in the Renaissance and later. The primary purpose of this chapter is to show something of the importance of Plautus and Terence to English comedy from its beginnings in the sixteenth century. The English dramatists derived their classical material in part directly from the Roman plays, in part indirectly through Italian, German, or French comedies which, in turn, were indebted to the Roman. A consideration of the revival of comedy in continental Europe must therefore necessarily precede the discussion of English comedy. The subject is an enormous one and can be treated here only in the most cursory fashion.[1] It is hoped that this brief sketch, and the bibliographical items mentioned in the notes, will be of value for those who wish to explore more fully the extent to which European comedy, both in form and content, is derived from that of ancient Rome.

In the later centuries of the Roman Empire, the comedies of Plautus and Terence, although no longer produced on the stage, continued to be read and admired; among those who praised the works of Plautus were St. Jerome, Eusebius, and Sidonius.[2] During the Middle Ages, however, Terence was far more popular than Plautus. The purity of his Latinity and the moral excellence of his verses, many of which were quoted as epigrams, made him a favorite, while Plautus was neglected, being considered both difficult and morally objectionable.

By some even the comedies of Terence were considered improper. In the tenth century Hrotsvitha (or Roswitha), the learned nun of Gandersheim, wrote in Latin prose six moral comedies in imitation of Terence with the avowed purpose of celebrating the virtue of Christian

---

[1] Reinhardstoettner in his *Plautus* devotes almost 800 pages to a consideration of the influence of Plautus upon later European comedy. I am indebted to this comprehensive work for many important details, also to the following brief but useful accounts: Wallace, *The Birthe of Hercules*, pp. 20 ff.; Bond, *Early Plays*, pp. xv ff.; Kennard, *The Italian Theatre*, I, pp. 78 ff., 105 ff.; Grismer, *The Influence of Plautus*, pp. 57 ff.; and Parrott, *Shakespearean Comedy*, pp. 37 ff. Norwood gives in an appendix to his *Plautus and Terence* (pp. 181 ff.) a convenient list of the Roman comedies, arranged alphabetically, with many English comedies indebted to each and brief statements concerning the nature of the indebtedness. I do not treat in this chapter eighteenth-century continental dramatists such as Lessing and Lenz in Germany, and Holberg in Denmark; on these see Reinhardstoettner, *Plautus*, pp. 82 f., 99 f.; Perry, *Masters of Dramatic Comedy*, pp. 219, 290 f.

[2] Reinhardstoettner, *Plautus*, pp. 14 f. On editions and commentaries composed in the late Empire, see above, p. 72.

virgins; they are religious dramas which portray the victory of chastity over lust and of Christianity over paganism. Each play was composed in a series of scenes, with many changes in time and place; they were intended to be read, not acted. Harrington says that these plays "are quite unique in our extant product of the Middle Ages, and thus fill a gap between the Roman classical drama and the miracle and mystery plays of the church."[3]

Plautus seems to have been best known throughout the Middle Ages, curiously enough, as the author of the *Querolus*, an anonymous Roman comedy composed perhaps in the fifth century A.D.[4] In the twelfth century Vital de Blois made an adaptation of the *Querolus* in elegiac verse with the title *Aulularia* and composed, also in elegiacs, a second play, the *Geta*, which dealt with the story of Amphitruo but which was apparently indebted to Plautus only indirectly, the main source being a story or drama of the early Christian era. At some period in the later Middle Ages the last twelve plays of Plautus were lost, and only the first eight were known to Petrarch and other scholars at the beginning of the Renaissance.[5]

## The Revival of Comedy in Italy

The influence of Plautus and Terence upon Renaissance Italy falls into three clearly defined stages: (1) comedies in Latin, modeled, at least in part, upon the ancient Roman plays; (2) performances of Plautus and Terence on the stage; and (3), latest and by far the most important, the numerous Italian comedies based on Roman models.

Among the many Latin comedies composed by the early Italian humanists were Petrarch's *Philologia*, now lost, the *Paulus* of Vergerio (c. 1390), Aretino's *Polyxena* (or *Poliscena*), the *Philodoxios* of Alberti (c. 1426), Ugolino's *Philogenia* (before 1437), and Piccolomini's *Chrysis* (1444). These plays, written principally to be read, combined the influence of ancient Rome and the late Middle Ages. The sentiments and manners were often those of the fourteenth century and reflected Italian university life; this was especially true of the *Paulus*. Some were conspicuous for their obscenity, being inspired by stories from Boccaccio's *Decameron*. Others, such as the *Philodoxios*, were filled with allegory, with characters representing abstract concepts such as glory, fame, wisdom, and time; yet this same comedy "is thoroughly saturated with Plautine influence, as may be seen from the

---

[3] *Mediaeval Latin*, p. 209; for a summary and discussion of the plays, see Coulter, *CJ* 24 (1928-29), pp. 515 ff., who says (p. 526): "There is little in these six plays which, from our point of view, can justly be called Terentian." The Terentian elements include the theme of love, the roles of courtesans, the use of disguise, occasional humor, and a few verbal similarities.

[4] See above, p. 72.

[5] On Petrarch's knowledge of Plautus, cf. Foresti, *Ath.*, N.S. 1 (1923), pp. 7 ff.

tone of the prologue, the nature of the setting, the names of the players, the characteristics of the principal figures, and the incidents of the plot."⁶ The classical tone is even more pronounced in the *Polyxena* and the *Chrysis*. The former is a tale of love and seduction, in which the youthful lover is aided by his servant Gurgulione, whose name comes from Plautus' *Curculio*, and who differs little from the slaves of Roman comedy. The *Polyxena* was written in prose without act-divisions but the *Chrysis* was composed in iambics in imitation of the iambic senarii of Plautus and Terence. The characters and even the speeches of the latter play resemble those of Plautine comedy; e.g., Criside is almost a second Gymnasium (cf. *Cist.* 43 ff.) when she says:

> With every new sun I procure new lovers.⁷

By the end of the fifteenth century the new Latin comedies had become rigorously classical and, as Kennard says, "subject-matter, situations, characters, language, style, structure, are all in direct imitation of the Roman theatre."⁸ The most noted of these productions were the *Epirota* of Medio, in which Clitifone marries his beloved Antifile in spite of the designs of his uncle who has fallen in love with her himself; the *Stephanium* of Harmonius Marsus, based on Plautus' *Aulularia*; and Zamberti's *Dolotechne*, which has two pairs of lovers in the Terentian manner, a complicated situation, and a recognition scene to solve the difficulties of the lovers.

This increased use of ancient situations and characters in the new Latin comedies of the Italian humanists was accompanied by a more widespread knowledge of Plautus and Terence through stage productions of their own plays. To understand the greater popularity of Plautus and Terence at this time, we must go back to the year 1429—a memorable date in the history of the Plautine text. In this year Nicolaus Cusanus (Niccolò di Treviri) brought to Rome a manuscript containing sixteen comedies of Plautus, twelve of which had been lost for centuries. Wallace states: "This event—one of the most important and remarkable in the whole history of the Humanistic movement—gave a strong impulse to classical study, especially to that of Plautus. Study and text-criticism of his works became general throughout Italy, and scholars earned reputations for their knowledge of Plautus alone, and for their ingenuity in supplying the numerous and extensive *lacunae* in the plays."⁹ The invention of printing made possible the wide circulation of the plays for reading; the *editio princeps* of Terence in 1470

---

⁶ Grismer, *The Influence of Plautus*, p. 58.
⁷ See Kennard, *The Italian Theatre*, I, p. 87, who refers also to the use of expressions from the *Asinaria* and the *Curculio*.
⁸ *The Italian Theatre*, I, pp. 88 f.
⁹ *The Birthe of Hercules*, p. 21. The missing portion of the *Amphitruo* was supplied by Hermolaus Barbarus, and the lost conclusion of the *Aulularia* by Codrus Urceus.

and that of Plautus in 1472 were soon followed by printed translations of the comedies.

At Rome performances of the plays of Plautus were revived by Pomponius Laetus (1425-1498) and the members of his Academy. At first the comedies were presented in the palaces of cardinals; in 1484 the *Aulularia* was presented on the Quirinal.[10] At Ferrara, under the encouragement of Ercole I, numerous poets made translations for production at the court; the comedies presented included the *Menaechmi* in 1486 (repeated in 1488 and 1493), the *Amphitruo* in 1487, the *Trinummus* and the *Poenulus* in 1499, the *Mercator, Captivi,* and *Asinaria* on three successive days in 1501. The great enthusiasm for Plautus at this time is likewise attested by the performance of five comedies[11] on five successive days at the wedding festivities of Lucrezia Borgia at Ferrara in 1502. In this same year, at Rome, the *Menaechmi* was played in the Vatican before the Pope.

The lively interest in Roman comedy at the end of the fifteenth century led to the composition of new Italian plays based upon those of Plautus and Terence. This new comedy, known as the *commedia erudita,* reigned supreme over the Italian stage for almost a century, after which it was supplanted in popularity by the comedy of improvisation, the *commedia dell' arte,* itself perhaps descended from ancient sources.[12]

Lodovico Ariosto (1474-1533), considered "the true founder of the modern European stage"[13] produced the first Italian comedy, *La Cassaria,* in 1508, and *I Suppositi* the following year; both were written in prose, verse-forms of the same comedies being made about 1529.[14] Each comedy reproduces in an Italian setting the form and spirit of the Roman originals; *La Cassaria* is indebted to situations from the *Mostellaria, Poenulus,* and *Rudens,* and *I Suppositi* to the *Captivi* and Ter-

[10] Grismer (*The Influence of Plautus,* p. 62) calls this production "the first stage performance of a Latin comedy during the Renaissance."

[11] The comedies were the *Epidicus, Bacchides, Miles, Asinaria,* and *Casina.*

[12] Some suggest that the characters of the *commedia dell' arte* have come, directly or indirectly, from those of Plautus; see Fletcher, *Literature of the Italian Renaissance,* pp. 289 f.; Highet, *The Classical Tradition,* pp. 140 f. The rise to prominence of the *commedia dell' arte* about 1550, a half century after the development of Italian adaptations of Roman comedies, supports this theory. It would be attractive to look upon the *commedia dell' arte* as a survival and elaboration of the ancient Roman *fabula Atellana,* but the *Atellanae* seem to have died out in the late Roman Empire, being absorbed by the mime (see "The Decline of the *Palliata*" in chap. 3), which persisted throughout the Middle Ages. Nicoll does not entirely reject the derivation of the *commedia dell' arte* from the ancient mime; he says (*Masks Mimes and Miracles,* p. 348) : "we may justifiably postulate the continuance of a largely improvisatorial comic tradition, utilizing stock types as its means of expression, and usually having laughter only as its end." See Lea, *Italian Popular Comedy,* I, pp. 223 ff.

[13] Bond, *Early Plays,* p. xvii; cf. Kennard, *The Italian Theatre,* I, p. 109.

[14] These are the generally accepted dates; cf., however, Grismer, *The Influence of Plautus,* p. 66, who dates the prose version of *La Cassaria* in 1498 and that in verse in 1508. Highet (*The Classical Tradition,* p. 136) says that *La Cassaria* was written in 1498 and produced in 1508.

ence's *Eunuchus*. The latter play is especially important in that it provided the model for *The Supposes* of George Gascoigne, the first prose comedy of English literature (1566). Wallace says that Ariosto's *I Suppositi* "may be taken as a representative of the perfect adaptation of Latin comedy to the portrayal of contemporary Italian life, and furnishes us in its English version a good example of the strongly classical influence which Italian dramatic literature was exercising on that of England."[15]

Other important comedies of the period were *La Calandria* of Cardinal da Bibbiena, in which the twin-brother motif of the *Menaechmi* was complicated by having the twins a brother and a sister who at times assume the garb of the opposite sex—the first of many comedies on the theme, another being *Gl' Ingannati* by the members of the Sienese Academy, a play which was very influential on Spanish, French, and English comedy; Machiavelli's *La Clizia*, a close imitation of Plautus' *Casina*; the same author's *La Mandragola*; and Ariosto's *La Lena* and *Il Negromante*. The last three comedies, being less indebted to classical models, give a vivid portrayal of Italian life, and in both *La Mandragola* and *Il Negromante* magic and sorcery play an important part.[16]

Many Italian comedies were more closely modeled upon Plautine originals. Of the hundreds of comedies written and produced in Italy during the sixteenth century,[17] only a few can be cited, e.g., those of Dolce and Cecchi. The plays of Lodovico Dolce (1508-1568) include *Il Marito* (based upon the *Amphitruo*), *Il Capitano* (*Miles Gloriosus*), *Il Ragazzo* (*Casina*), and *Il Ruffiano* (*Rudens*); those of Giovanni Maria Cecchi (1518-1587), the most prolific writer of comedy in the sixteenth century, include *I Dissimili* (from Terence's *Adelphoe*), *La Majana* (*Heauton*), *Il Martello* (Plautus' *Asinaria*), *Gl' Incantesimi* (*Cistellaria*), *La Moglie* (*Menaechmi*), *La Stiava* (*Mercator*), and *La Dote* (*Trinummus*). Others that were almost slavish imitations of the originals were Trissino's *I Simillimi* and Firenzuola's *I Lucidi*

---

[15] Wallace, *The Birthe of Hercules*, p. 64. For an analysis of the plot of Ariosto's comedy, see Wallace, *ibid.*, pp. 64 ff.; its indebtedness to the *Captivi*, the *Eunuchus*, and other Roman plays is treated briefly by Bond, *Early Plays*, pp. liii ff. On Gascoigne's *Supposes*, see below, "Early English Imitations and Adaptations."

[16] Kennard (*The Italian Theatre*, I, p. 113) considers *La Mandragola* "the most important comedy written in Italy in the sixteenth century" (cf. Perry, *Masters of Dramatic Comedy*, p. 239), but Bond (*Early Plays*, p. xviii) believes that it is "far surpassed in vigour and variety, in ease and naturalness of conduct, and in humour, both by *La Cassaria* and *I Suppositi*." Stuart (*The Development of Dramatic Art*, p. 287) says that "the *Mandragola* is more a highly developed medieval farce in situation, tone, and conclusion than a Latin comedy." Yet no comedy of the sixteenth century did more to reveal the vices of the day, and it "was accepted by Machiavelli's contemporaries as a vigorous and satirical representation of the Florentine and Italian society of the *cinquecento*" (Kennard, *op. cit.*, I, p. 117).

[17] See Reinhardstoettner, *Plautus*, pp. 56 ff.; Grismer, *The Influence of Plautus*, pp. 73 ff.

(both from the *Menaechmi*) and Gelli's *La Sporta* (from the *Aulularia*).

In each of these comedies the scene is laid in modern Italy, and the writers make frequent allusions to contemporary life and events. New characters appear—the priest, the teacher, the elderly suitor,[18] the astrologer, and the sorcerer;[19] even the regular characters of the Roman plays, such as military braggarts,[20] stern-minded parents, lovesick sons, and unscrupulous servants, reflect actual conditions in Italy. Yet these plays are basically Roman in plot and structure, and most of the typical conventions favored by Plautus and Terence are reproduced by the Italian dramatists: these include entrance announcements, addresses to persons indoors, monologues, eavesdropping and asides, the creaking of a door to announce a character's entrance, servants and parasites bringing good news, and servants denouncing each other in abusive language.[21] Even the romantic treatment of love, usually considered an Italian addition, stems in part from the serious portrayal of love affairs in Terence.[22]

Italian comedy thus came into existence at the beginning of the sixteenth century under the direct stimulus of the two Roman playwrights. Plautus was the great master; the enthusiasm for his works was unbounded, and the *commedia erudita* reproduced with new characters and situations the form and spirit and even the technical devices of his comedies. Since the new Italian comedy was influential upon the comic drama of Spain, France, and England, comedy in these countries in-

[18] The only instance of an elderly suitor of this type in Roman comedy is Megadorus in the *Aulularia*. This role is very unlike that of the married man who makes himself ridiculous by falling in love with his son's sweetheart (Lysidamus in the *Casina*, Demipho in the *Mercator*) ; see *"Senex"* in chap. 9.

[19] Bond (*Early Plays*, p. xxxi) says that the pretended sorcerer is "the most distinct expression of the modern element" and explains the popularity of the role by the interest of fifteenth-century Italy in magic and astrology. But one should not overlook the possible influence of Mandrogerus, the self-styled magician and astrologer in the *Querolus*.

[20] See Boughner, *PMLA* 58 (1943), pp. 48 ff., for a thorough discussion of the role of the braggart warrior in Italian comedy; he says (p. 48) : "The Greek soldier of New Comedy has given way to the haughty Spaniard billeted on unwilling Italian citizens or to the vile Italian mercenaries to whom the citizens entrusted their defense"; cf. p. 51: "The method of the Italians was the method of Roman comedy, to provoke laughter by the ridiculous incongruity between the soldier's pretensions and the stark reality, between his boasted valor and his actual poltroonery, between his vaunted power over women and the ease with which they dupe and deride him, and between his claims to social grace and acceptability and his despised boorishness." On the braggart warriors in Plautus and Terence (discussed also by Boughner, *ibid.*, pp. 42 ff.), see above, "Professional Types" in chap. 9.

[21] For a discussion of these conventions in Roman comedy, see above, chapter 5; Bond (*Early Plays*, pp. xlvi ff.) describes the use of these same devices in Italian and early English comedy.

[22] Parrott and Ball (*A Short View of Elizabethan Drama*, p. 44) say of the theme of love that "classical comedy was inclined to treat it with a certain Latin cynicism." This is true of Plautus, but not of Terence; see above, pp. 240 f.

evitably displayed many of the characteristics and themes of the Roman plays. Had there been no direct imitation of Plautus and Terence elsewhere, it would still have been impossible for comic writers, drawing their inspiration from the Italian dramatists of the Renaissance, to have developed a comic drama untouched by the influence of the two Roman playwrights. But, as we shall see below, many dramatists in France and England went directly to the Roman comedies themselves for their inspiration.

## Roman Comedy in Spain, Germany, Holland, and France

The comedy of Spain was influenced by Plautus during the sixteenth century, but far less than had been the case in Italy. The plays of both Plautus and Terence were read and studied in the universities, and performances of their comedies were given on various festival days. Numerous Latin plays were composed for presentation, some of which had plots and characters very similar to those of Roman comedy, while others were translations or reworkings of contemporary Italian plays, e.g., Ariosto's *I Suppositi*, and *Gl' Ingannati*, the anonymous comedy on the theme of twin brother and sister. In 1574 the presentation of a new Latin comedy at the University of Salamanca aroused the ire of the authorities and it was then decided that no comedies except those of Plautus and Terence should henceforth be performed at the university.

Juan del Encina (born c. 1468), who is considered the father of Spanish drama, studied at the University of Salamanca and made several visits to Rome but he seems to have been relatively untouched by either Roman or Italian comedy. His dramatic work consisted of fourteen *églogas*, dialogues between shepherds on pastoral or religious themes. His successor, Torres Naharro, used characters and themes of Roman comedy and imitated scenes from the *Asinaria* and the *Mostellaria*. Lope de Rueda composed several comedies, the plots of which he borrowed from Italian comedies or from Roman plays, the latter probably being known to him through Italian or Spanish adaptations of Plautus;[23] in *Los Engañados* (or *Los Engaños*) he made a Spanish version of the famous Italian comedy, *Gl' Ingannati*,[24] and his *Medora*, based on *La Cingana* of Giancarli, presents another variation of the theme of the *Menaechmi*. There is no evidence that Lope de Rueda knew Plautus in the original, but through translations and Italian

---

[23] Cf. Grismer, *The Influence of Plautus*, pp. 168 f.: "There was a large school of Plautine imitators in Seville, probably due to the Italian companies which played there."

[24] Cf. Gassner, *Masters of the Drama*, p. 179: "*Los engaños* bears a strong resemblance to Shakespeare's *Twelfth Night* and is derived from the same Italian source."

adaptations he acquired knowledge of the usual Plautine characters and comic devices.[25] The influence of Plautus is still more marked in the comedies of Juan de Timoneda; he wrote the *Amphitrion* and *Los Menemnos*, both based upon Spanish translations of the Plautine originals, and his *Cornelia* and *Trapaçera* were imitations of Ariosto's *Il Negromante* and *La Lena*.

The great dramatist of Spain, Lope de Vega (1562-1635), whose comedies are numbered by the hundreds, knew the plays of Plautus and Terence but professed to disregard them as unsuitable for his audience. He says in *The New Art of Making Comedies*: "When I have to write a play I lock the rules away with six keys; I remove Terence and Plautus from my study that they may not cry out at me, for the truth in silent books is wont to scream, and I write in the manner of those devisers who aspired to the acclaim of the crowd; for since it is the crowd that pays, it is proper to speak to it stupidly in order to please."[26]

Yet the characteristics of his plays[27]—aristocrats in disguise, children lost in infancy, two pairs of lovers usually reunited at the end, frequent misunderstandings and cross-purposes, impersonations and pretended madness, the clown (*gracioso*) who helps his master in his love affair and provides incidental humor by his satirical comments, general talkativeness, and desire for food—are similar to the themes and devices of Roman comedy. Stuart says: "In complexity of plot the Spanish dramatist far surpassed the French. . . . Love at cross purposes, abductions, disguises, duels, sudden encounters, all that is melodramatic is poured indiscriminately, sometimes to the point of confusion, into the plots of their plays. . . . Spanish plays offered a rich mine for French dramatists who were seeking relatively complicated plots developing through melodramatic events and situations."[28]

In Germany and Holland in the sixteenth century numerous Latin comedies were composed in the style of Plautus and Terence, as had been done in Italy a century earlier. That the Latin drama of Italy had some influence in Germany can hardly be doubted, since three plays— Aretino's *Polyxena*, Zamberti's *Dolotechne*, and Ugolino's *Philogenia* —were reprinted or translated in Germany between 1508 and 1520. Two Latin comedies of note had already appeared in Germany before

---

[25] Cf. Grismer, *The Influence of Plautus*, pp. 175 ff.

[26] Translated by O. M. Perlzweig, in Gilbert, *Literary Criticism*, p. 542.

[27] I am indebted here to Perry, *Masters of Dramatic Comedy*, pp. 118 ff.

[28] *The Development of Dramatic Art*, pp. 384 f. Gassner (*Masters of the Drama*, p. 186) points out that Lope's colleagues and successors were numerous; "to his incredibly large output, they added so many plays that by 1700, according to one account, the Spanish drama reached the staggering total of thirty thousand works. . . . It is not surprising that the Spanish stage should have wielded such an influence on later continental and English writers. It was at least numerically too overwhelming to be disregarded."

1508: Reuchlin's *Henno* (1498) and Chilian's *Dorothea* (1507); the former, adapted from the French farce of *Pathelin*, is a play of cheating in which "certain characters and incidents have a Terentian or Plautine colouring";[29] the latter is a religious play, resembling the *Dulcicius* of Hrotsvitha,[30] whose writings had been edited in 1501.

The influence of Reuchlin upon later writers, especially those of Holland, was very great. Dutch schoolmasters, eager both to instruct their youth in sound morality and to acquaint them with the colloquial Latin of Plautus and Terence, developed what is known as the education-drama, or the "Christian Terence"—a combination of Roman comedy and Biblical tales. Especially influential among the Latin plays of this type were the *Asotus* of Macropedius (printed in 1537 but acted probably about 1510), the *Acolastus* of Gnaphaeus (1529), and Crocus' *Joseph* (1535). Both the *Asotus* and the *Acolastus* deal with the parable of the prodigal son, the favorite theme of the education-drama; the *Acolastus* is called "the most famous and the finest, though not the first, Latin drama upon the Prodigal Son."[31] In the *Rebelles* (1535) and the *Petriscus* (1536) Macropedius adapted the prodigal-story to contemporary school life, while the *Studentes* (1552) presented a similar picture of university life. The humanists of Germany also produced many Latin plays, among others, the *Judith* and the *Susanna* of Birck, and Burmeister's *Mater Virgo*, a paraphrase of Plautus' *Amphitruo*, in which Alcumena is replaced by the mother of Christ.[32] The influence of the "Christian Terence" spread to England, where, as we shall see below, the best examples are the *Misogonus* and Gascoigne's *The Glasse of Government*.

The education-drama of Germany and Holland was closely connected with Roman comedy "in the relations of fathers and sons, the contrasts of character in young men, the conflict of educational ideals, and the opposition of good and bad servants."[33] The term "Christian Terence" is misleading, for the plays, especially those on the theme of the prodigal son, draw as much material from Plautus as from Terence, and in fact often resemble the older playwright more closely in their spontaneous and sometimes coarse humor.

[29] Herford, *Studies in the Literary Relations*, p. 82; cf. pp. 80 f.: "It showed how a modern comedy-subject fresh and dramatic and at the same time perfectly healthy, might be effectively made the base of a Latin play."

[30] Cf. above, pp. 396 f.

[31] Herford, *Studies in the Literary Relations*, p. 85; for brief summaries of the *Asotus* and the *Acolastus*, see Bond, *Early Plays*, pp. xcv ff.

[32] The slave Sosia is retained; the other characters are Gabriel (as Prologue), Joseph, Maria, Asmodes, Flamen Judaicus, *Obstetrix*, and *Pastores tres*; see Reinhardstoettner, *Plautus*, pp. 208 ff.; Lumley, *The Influence of Plautus*, pp. 35 f.

[33] Bond, *Early Plays*, p. ciii. The Roman comedies most deeply concerned with parental methods are Plautus' *Bacchides*, and Terence's *Heauton* and *Adelphoe*; see above, "The Problem of Education" in chap. 10.

The comic playwrights of France at first drew upon Roman comedy only indirectly through their imitations of the plays of sixteenth-century Italian dramatists. By 1550 the Italian comedies translated or produced in France included *Gl' Ingannati*, Ariosto's *I Suppositi*, Bibbiena's *La Calandria*, and Firenzuola's *I Lucidi*. The first original French comedy, Jodelle's *Eugene* (1552), was a farce in five acts but the theme of adultery was medieval rather than classical. The author says in the prologue that he will not tell the plot as the audience will learn the necessary facts from the opening scene.[34] Jean de la Taille in the prologue of *Les Corrivaux* (1562) stated that he was following Plautus, Terence, and the Italians, thus being "the first playwright in France to proclaim the imitation of Italian comedy as the basis of his art."[35] He first introduced into French comedy the use of prose for dramatic dialogue. *Les Corrivaux* had a double plot with two heroes and two heroines in the Terentian manner, and the complications involved intrigue, hidden identity, and recognition, with one lover proving to be the brother of his sweetheart, as in Plautus' *Epidicus*.

Numerous French comedies were written in the latter part of the sixteenth century. Baïf turned directly to the Roman plays, using Plautus' *Miles* as the basis for *Le Brave* and Terence's *Eunuchus* for *L'Eunuque*. The most famous writer of the period was Pierre de Larivey (c. 1550-1612); *Les Jaloux* was drawn from Terence's *Andria* and *Eunuchus*; *Le Laquais* was indebted to Plautus' *Aulularia* and *Casina* through Dolce's *Il Ragazzo*; and *Les Esprits*, considered his best work, was an adaptation of the *Aridosio* of Lorenzino de' Medici, which contained elements from the *Aulularia*, the *Mostellaria*, and Terence's *Adelphoe*.[36] In the early seventeenth century French dramatists derived their plays not only from Italian sources but also from the more complex and romantic plots of Spanish comedy. The latter influence is seen in Pierre Corneille's tragicomedy, *Le Cid*, his *Le Menteur*, "the greatest comedy yet written in France,"[37] and Scarron's *Jodelet*, whose principal character comes ultimately from the clever slave of Roman comedy and anticipates the many valets of later French comedy, such as Mascarille and Scapin. Corneille's *L'Illusion Comique* (1638) had as its chief character the captain Matamore, another in the long list of braggart warriors stemming from Pyrgopolynices and Thraso. Shortly after (1640) appeared *Le Capitan Fanfaron* of Mareschal, more closely adapted from Plautus' *Miles*.[38] Rotrou, rated as a writer of tragedy

---

[34] Cf. Plautus, *Trin.* 16 f., Terence, *Ad.* 22 ff. (see above, p. 61).

[35] Stuart, *The Development of Dramatic Art*, p. 305.

[36] *Les Esprits* was thus a forerunner of Molière's *L'Avare* (1668), based upon the *Aulularia*, and of Montfleury's *La Comédien Poète* (1674) and Regnard's *Le Retour Imprévu* (1700), both indebted to the *Mostellaria*. Another of Regnard's comedies, also closely modeled upon Plautus, was produced in 1705: *Les Ménechmes, ou Les Jumeaux*.

[37] Wright, *A History of French Literature*, p. 314.

[38] A later French comedy, also indebted to the *Miles*, was Cailhava's *Le Tuteur Dupé*, produced in 1765.

next to Corneille and Racine, reworked three of Plautus' comedies—
*Les Ménechmes* (1636), *Les Captifs* (1638), and *Les Sosies* (1638),
the last almost a verse translation of the *Amphitruo*. Quinault in
*L'Amant Indiscret ou le Maitre Étourdi* (1654) returned to an Italian
model, probably Barbieri's *L'Inavvertito*, in which the schemes of the
intriguing slave are upset by the stupidity of the master, a theme not
unlike that found in Plautus' *Bacchides* and *Epidicus*.

Molière, the most famous playwright of France and the master of
"thoughtful laughter," excelled in such diverse forms as pure farce,
comedy of manners, and comedy of character. He utilized the plots
and characters of earlier dramatists, as did his contemporaries, but he
was also a creative artist who blended his comic material into a new
and more perfect product. Stuart says: "One place where he found dramatic material had been overlooked by his fellow playwrights. He delved
into human character and society, and he drew from these unfailing
sources of humor the highest forms of comedy."[39]

Although it is often difficult to decide from what sources Molière
derived his material, there is no doubt that several of his plays were
modeled upon Roman comedies. The following are regularly cited as
illustrating his dependence upon Plautus and Terence:

*L'Étourdi ou les Contretemps* (1653)—distinctly related to Plautus
(*Bacchides*?) through Barbieri's *L'Inavvertito*. Mascarille, like the
cunning slave of Roman comedy, devises numerous schemes to enable
his master Lélie to win the girl he loves and each time the blundering
master spoils the trick, but finally wins the heroine through the discovery of her real identity.[40]

*L'École des Maris* (1661)—adapted chiefly from Terence's *Adelphoe*.
As in the Roman comedy there are two brothers of different character
and different theories of education, but entrusted to the care of each
is a young girl. Molière has thus complicated the situation by giving to
the two men the concern of lovers as well as that of fathers. This play
best displays the kinship between Molière and Terence in their conception of character and their attitude toward life.[41]

*Amphitryon* (1668)—modeled upon Plautus' comedy, which Rotrou

---

[39] *The Development of Dramatic Art*, p. 331. Similarly, Chapman states (*The Spirit
of Molière*, p. 240): "His comedy is more a comedy of character than a comedy of
manners, more a picture of universal humanity than a picture of contemporary society."

[40] Cf. Perry, *Masters of Dramatic Comedy*, p. 154: "The one serious charge that can
be brought against Lélie is that he never learns from experience. He blunders no less
than fourteen times in the five acts of the play." This of course adds immeasurably to
the humor of the action. In both the *Bacchides* and the *Epidicus* of Plautus, the action
of the master makes a second trick necessary, but in neither case is the master a
blunderer. Chatfield-Taylor (*Molière*, p. 62) calls *L'Étourdi* "little more than a French
adaptation of an Italian farce filched from classic sources."

[41] Cf. Wheatley, *Molière and Terence*, pp. 97, 118. Perry (*Masters of Dramatic
Comedy*, p. 159) says: "The background is always that of the happy mean, against
which the eccentricities of human nature are to be portrayed."

had already imitated in *Les Sosies*. Molière added the character of Cléanthis, Sosie's virtuous but unattractive wife, who provides an excellent foil for Alcmène. Jupiter wants Alcmène to love him for himself alone.

*L'Avare* (1668)—a reworking of the theme of Plautus' *Aulularia*, with additional material from other comedies (especially Ariosto's *I Suppositi* and Larivey's *Les Esprits*). Unlike Plautus' Euclio, a poor man until he found a pot of gold, Harpagon lived in comparative elegance, which made his avarice and meanness all the more effective by contrast. Also, Harpagon, unlike Euclio, was in love and desired the girl beloved by his son. Harpagon's anguish when his money is stolen resembles Euclio's famous monologue.[42] But *L'Avare* is a more serious and satirical comedy than Plautus' *Aulularia*; it is usually considered a study of character on a higher plane and is called one of Molière's "most valuable social dramas."[43]

*Les Fourberies de Scapin* (1671)—based upon the *Phormio*, one of the liveliest of Terence's comedies, but with numerous additions, either from other sources or of his own invention.[44] Like Phormio, Scapin plays a series of tricks upon the two fathers in order that the two young men may be successful in their love affairs, but the comedy is much more farcical than the *Phormio*.

Molière is usually considered Terentian in spirit rather than Plautine, and rightly so; but, as he excelled Terence in the delineation of character, so he surpassed him in his use of farcical situations and devices, and in these the French dramatist's close relationship to Plautus becomes apparent. Pounding on doors (e.g., *Le Dépit Amoureux*, Act III, Sc. II; *L'École des Femmes*, Act I, Sc. II), abusive language (e.g., *Le Bourgeois Gentilhomme*, Act II, Sc. IV), the use of repetition (e.g., *Monsieur de Pourceaugnac*, Act I, Sc. III; *Le Malade Imaginaire*, Act III, Sc. XIV) are thoroughly Plautine in their effect. Of incidental parallels the following are striking: *Monsieur de Pourceaugnac*, Act I, Sc. XI (the scene with the physicians) and *Men.* 910 ff.; *L'École des Femmes*, Act III, Sc. II (the maxims of marriage) and *Asin.* 756 ff.; *Le Bourgeois Gentilhomme*, Act IV, Sc. II (Mme. Jourdain's discovery of her husband) and *Asin.* 876 ff.; *Les Fourberies de Scapin*, Act II, Sc. X (Scapin's pretended reluctance to accept money from Argante) and *Bacch.* 1059 ff. Matthews believes that Molière, although originally preferring Terence, realized that he was not a practical man of the theater; "Molière's later experience must have disclosed to him that

---

[42] Cf. *L'Avare*, IV, vii with *Aul.* 713 ff.; the latter passage is translated in part above, p. 135.

[43] Matthews, *Molière*, p. 252. Perry is more severe in his estimate of the French play; in *Masters of Dramatic Comedy*, p. 183, he speaks of "the central subject of avarice, which Molière did not handle with much greater skill than Plautus had already shown."

[44] Cf. Wheatley, *Molière and Terence*, pp. 35 ff.

Plautus is a born playwright, a realistic humorist, able to present comic characters entangled in comic situations."[45]

## Early English Imitations and Adaptations

Comedy in England began under the influence of Plautus and Terence. Boas says that it was from the classical revival and the neo-Latin drama which followed in its wake that English comedy sprang.[46] Actually, there were four channels through which the classical influence came into English literature: (1) the study of Roman drama in the schools; (2) the presentation in schools of Roman comedies and English plays modeled upon them; (3) the influence of the new Latin plays written by the German and Dutch humanists; and (4) the translation or adaptation of Italian plays which were derived from classical comedy.

By 1520 both Plautus and Terence had become important authors in the English schools and universities, and in this same year one of Plautus' plays was presented, presumably in Latin, to entertain French hostages then in England. The *Menaechmi* of Plautus was performed by the boys of St. Paul's School in 1527, as was Terence's *Phormio* in the following year. That the presentation of plays was a regular activity in the universities is implied by the rule established a few years later (1546) that a student who refused to act in a tragedy or a comedy would be expelled; the same penalty was prescribed for those who failed to attend the performance. Just as Seneca was considered the master of tragedy, so Plautus became the master of comedy. Parrott says: "The lively action and boisterous mirth of Plautus were more in accordance with the English taste for drama than the simpler stories and more polished dialogue of Terence."[47]

The production of Roman plays led to the composition and performance of new Latin comedies (e.g., the *Piscator* by John Hoker of Oxford, in 1535) and of English plays in imitation of classical comedy. The most important of the schoolmasters who adapted Roman comedy for use in the schools was Nicholas Udall. About 1534 he published an anthology of Terentian phrases, *Floures for Latine spekynge selected and gathered oute of Terence and the same translated into English*; of his several comedies the only one extant is *Ralph Roister Doister*, apparently written about 1552.[48]

*Ralph Roister Doister*, the first real English comedy, is derived from

---

[45] *Molière*, pp. 234 f.     [46] *CHEL*, v, pp. 100 f.
[47] *Shakespearean Comedy*, p. 38. By "simpler stories" he must mean "more natural," "less exaggerated," for the Terentian plots were in general far more intricate than those in Plautus' plays; see above, "The Duality-Method" in chap. 7.
[48] There is some uncertainty, however, about the date of the comedy; Wallace (*The Birthe of Hercules*, p. 40) believes that it was composed when Udall was headmaster at Eton, i.e., between 1534 and 1541; cf. also E. Flügel, in Gayley, *Representative English Comedies*, I, pp. 95 ff.; Schelling, *Elizabethan Drama*, I, p. 87.

Plautus' *Miles Gloriosus*, with additional material taken from Terence's *Eunuchus*. Unlike the earlier morality plays and interludes,[49] Udall's comedy has a closely knit plot with complications and solution, and is divided into five acts, each having several scenes; the play is written in rhymed couplets, with occasional passages of song. The setting is English and the classical characters are transformed to suit English conditions; the courtesan of the *Miles* becomes a virtuous English widow in love with the master of a trading ship. Several minor characters have a purely native origin. But Ralph Roister Doister is an excellent Pyrgopolynices; he asks in Act I, Sc. II:

> Why did God make me such a goodly person?

Later in the same scene the speeches of Matthew Merrygreek, for instance:

> But such is your beauty, and such are your acts,
> Such is your personage, and such are your facts,
> That all women, fair and foul, more or less,
> They eye you, they lub you, they talk of you, doubtless,

resemble the words of Artotrogus in *Mil.* 56 ff. Merrygreek himself combines the roles of the parasite Artotrogus and Palaestrio, the intriguing slave, and, like Palaestrio, he pretends to further the braggart's aims, but actually works against him, e.g., by his delightful misreading of the love letter in Act III, Sc. IV. The amusing battle before the house of Dame Custance (Act IV, Sc. VII f.) is reminiscent of Thraso's abortive attack on Thais' home in *Eun.* 771 ff.[50]

Numerous other plays, influenced by classical comedy, were written in the next quarter century, and these, like *Ralph Roister Doister*, enriched

---

[49] Two of these interludes deserve a brief mention: (1) *Calisto and Melibea* (c. 1530) was adapted from the Spanish dramatic novel *Celestina*, and the latter work shows in its characters and situations numerous borrowings from Plautus and Terence (cf. Grismer, *The Influence of Plautus*, pp. 101 ff.); (2) *Thersites* (1537), adapted from a French neo-Latin comedy, portrays a braggart warrior even more vainglorious and ridiculous than Ralph Roister Doister. But we need not assume direct Plautine influence here; the *Thersites* is merely a series of loosely connected scenes, the parasite is lacking, and the characterization is weak; Wallace (*The Birthe of Hercules*, p. 32) states: "I have been unable to find any distinctly Plautine characteristics in the piece, and in spite of its classical setting I think we should regard it as a natural development of the comic elements in the earlier Mystery Plays. It is not difficult to conceive of the author of *Thersites* as a man who had never read a single Latin comedy." Yet Gayley (*Representative English Comedies*, I, p. lxxii) says that "the influence of Plautus is evident." Perhaps the Roman influence in *Thersites* comes through the original by Ravisius Textor, "the first of continental humanist playwrights . . . to influence the English stage" (Boas, *CHEL*, v, p. 107).

[50] See Maulsby, *ES* 38 (1907), pp. 251 ff., for an analysis of Udall's indebtedness to Plautus and Terence; Maulsby concludes (p. 277) that "*Roister Doister* is, after all, a comedy of English life and English manners, suggested in part by the classical reading of its author, but with substantial claim to an originality as genuine as one often meets in this imitative world." Cf. also Highet, *The Classical Tradition*, pp. 138 and 600, n. 30.

English drama with a sense of plot-structure, a variety of amusing characters, and a feeling for word-play, witty repartee, and literary style in
general.

*Jacke Jugeler* (c. 1553), a school drama, was a series of comic situations rather than an organically constructed comedy. The prologue
states that the play was adapted from Plautus' *Amphitruo*, but the imitation extends only to *Amph*. 632 (end of Act II, Sc. 1). The main theme
of Plautus' comedy—Jupiter's impersonation of Amphitruo in order to
make love to Alcumena, and the resultant complications—does not appear in the English play. We have here, however, the first instance in
English comedy of the use of doubles and also the first victim of confused identity. Jacke Jugeler disguises himself as Jenkin Careaway and,
like Mercury in the *Amphitruo*, convinces the unhappy servant that he
has lost his identity.[51]

*Gammer Gurton's Needle* (c. 1559-60), a combination of farce, moral
interlude, and classical school play, was produced on the stage at Christ's
College, Cambridge, and is the earliest university play which has survived. The drama is divided into the conventional five acts of the Roman
comedies and the plot, based on the loss of a highly valued needle, is
extremely complicated and farcical, the mischievous Diccon playing
the role of the intriguing slave of Plautus. Gassner comments: "No
comedy could be more remote from the midnight oil of scholarship."[52]

Of the comedies adapted from the sixteenth-century education-drama
of Holland and Germany,[53] the *Misogonus* (1560) is the most famous.
The play enables us, says Boas, "to claim for England the credit of
having produced one of the most elaborate and original comedies on the
prodigal son"; it is "the finest extant comedy that had yet appeared in
England."[54] Based upon the *Acolastus* of Gnapheus, the *Misogonus*
combines the characteristics of Plautus and the "Christian Terence"
with episodes from the native English farce; the play has a unified plot,
comic situations, misunderstandings, and a denouement with a recognition scene. It is very possible that the influence of Roman comedy may
have operated directly. Misogonus, the prodigal son, resembles the
*adulescens* by keeping a *meretrix* at home and by being forgiven by his
father after the identity of his twin, the virtuous elder brother, is
revealed.[55]

---

[51] Cf. Wallace, *The Birthe of Hercules*, pp. 32 ff., who quotes passages of dialogue
almost literally translated from the famous scene between Mercury and Sosia.

[52] *Masters of the Drama*, p. 198. Scholars disagree on the amount of classical material in the comedy; Stuart (*The Development of Dramatic Art*, p. 197) says: "In
*Gammer Gurton's Needle*, there is naught of classical comedy save the division into
acts." Cf., however, Parrott and Ball. *A Short View of Elizabethan Drama*, p. 33: "It
could never have been written except by an admiring student, though no slavish imi-
tator, of classical comedy." See also Parrott, *Shakespearean Comedy*, p. 40.

[53] See above, "Roman Comedy in Spain, Germany, Holland, and France."

[54] *CHEL*, v, pp. 110, 111.

[55] For other examples of its indebtedness to Roman comedy, see Bond, *Early Plays*,

Gascoigne's *The Glasse of Government*, printed in 1575, is said by Wallace to be "of all English plays perhaps the most representative of the complete adaptation of the Prodigal Son motif to the general form of Roman comedy."[56] Two citizens of Antwerp each have two sons, the two older boys being rascals and the two younger models of virtue. Each pair receives a fitting reward.

Romantic love and romantic adventure came into English comedy from the Italian plays which were modeled upon classical comedy. Among the earliest English plays of this type are *The Buggbears* and *Damon and Pithias*, both about 1564.[57] The two plays were written in the verse forms of the period. The former was adapted from Grazzini's *La Spiritata*, with additions from *Gl' Ingannati* and Terence's *Andria*. *Damon and Pithias*, although less classical in its external structure and anticipating the new romantic drama which was to combine both comic and tragic elements, shows the influence of classical types and methods.

Far more significant, however, is *The Supposes*, which was acted in 1566 by the students of Gray's Inn and presented later (1582) at Trinity College, Oxford. This play, the first English comedy to be written in prose, is a translation by George Gascoigne of one of the earliest and most famous of Italian comedies, *I Suppositi* of Ariosto, which was based upon two Roman plays: a master and a servant, Erostrato and Dulipo, exchange names and garb (as in Plautus' *Captivi*) in order that Erostrato, disguised as the servant, may gain access to the girl whom he loves (as in Terence's *Eunuchus*). Numerous complications, such as the desire of an elderly suitor Cleander to win the girl, an attempt to impersonate Erostrato's father, the arrival of the true father, the detection of the false Erostrato, are all solved by the discovery of the real identity of the servant (again as in the *Captivi*) who proves to be the son of Cleander. Erostrato marries his sweetheart, and Cleander gives up all claims to the girl, rejoicing that he has found his longlost son. Mistaken identity and trickery are thus combined in true classical fashion.

*The Supposes* is deservedly famous. Parrott says: "Students of the classics will recognize the indebtedness of the Italian play and of Gascoigne's version to Plautine comedy, particularly in the clever handling of the intrigue, the mistaken identity business, and the discovery of the lost child. Readers of Shakespeare, on the other hand, will at once note the likeness of the action to the minor plot of *The*

---

pp. ciii f.; cf. also Wallace, *The Birthe of Hercules*, pp. 56 f. Stuart (*The Development of Dramatic Art*, p. 196) endeavors to minimize the classical features of the play.

[56] *The Birthe of Hercules*, p. 57. On the indebtedness of Gascoigne's play to the *Acolastus*, the *Studentes*, and the *Rebelles*, see Herford, *Studies in the Literary Relations*, pp. 160 ff.

[57] On the date of *The Buggbears*, see Bond, *Early Plays*, pp. 81 ff. Parrott (*Shakespearean Comedy*, p. 51) dates it after 1566.

*Taming of the Shrew*."[58] The success of *The Supposes*, with its blending of classical and romantic elements, set the fashion for the translation and adaptation of Italian comedies for the English stage.

The combination of Italian and Roman elements is seen also in numerous Latin comedies produced at Oxford and Cambridge in the latter part of the sixteenth century. Romantic love affairs, complicated intrigues with disguises and impersonations, and stock characters (braggarts, parasites, pedants, would-be astrologers) abound. One of the most important of these new Latin plays is the anonymous *Laelia* (1590), based upon *Gl' Ingannati*; the heroine, who disguises herself as a youth and takes service with her lover, is mistaken for her twin brother—a situation very similar to that in Shakespeare's *Twelfth Night*. Other Latin plays of the period are *Leander, Labyrinthus*, and *Zelotypus*. In *Pedantius* (c. 1581) the themes and characters of Plautine comedy were applied to English university life, and the lovesick pedant became a caricature of Gabriel Harvey.

The comedies of Plautus and Terence continues to be presented in Latin; the *Andria* was produced at Oxford in 1559, and the *Aulularia* was staged before Queen Elizabeth at Cambridge in 1564. Translations of Roman comedies, however, were surprisingly few. Selections from Terence had been published in the late fifteenth century and Udall's *Floures for Latine spekynge* appeared about 1534; the *Andria* as a whole was translated and printed before 1530, a second translation of the same play being made in 1588. Only two English translations of Plautus in the sixteenth century are known: that of the *Amphitruo* by E. Courtney, dated in 1562-63,[59] and that of the *Menaechmi*, printed in 1595, and ascribed to W. W. (William Warner?). Unless Shakespeare had seen W. W.'s translation in manuscript, there was no translation of Plautus' *Menaechmi* available when he wrote *The Comedy of Errors*.

## Shakespeare and Ben Jonson

The writers and dramatists of the sixteenth century believed that, as Seneca was the master to be followed in tragedy, so Plautus was the

[58] *Shakespearean Comedy*, p. 50. On the indebtedness of *The Supposes* to Roman comedy, see above, n. 15. Wallace (*The Birthe of Hercules*, p. 66), speaking of the recognition scene, says: "The discovery of the long-lost child by the inevitable mole on the left shoulder is frequently met with in Plautus." Wallace is incorrect here; the means of identification in Roman comedy is almost always a token or ring. In *Poen.* 1072 ff. a physical peculiarity—a scar on the left hand—serves to identify Agorastocles as Hanno's nephew.

[59] Cf. Conley, *The First English Translators of the Classics*, p. 143. *The Birthe of Hercules*, a translation of the *Amphitruo* with considerable new material added (including a second servant, Dromio) is dated after 1600; cf. Wallace, *The Birthe of Hercules*, pp. 167 f. The name of Dromio for the second slave of Amphitruo seems to have been taken either from Shakespeare's *The Comedy of Errors* or from Lyly's *Mother Bombie*, a play so filled with typical situations of Roman comedy that it seems almost "a transcript of some lost comedy of Plautus" (Wallace, *ibid.*, p. 75).

model for comedy. That this conviction was shared by William Shakespeare is implied by the words of Polonius in *Hamlet* (Act II, Sc. II, 419 f.):

> Seneca cannot be too heavy nor Plautus too light.

The problem of Shakespeare's indebtedness to Roman comedy is part of the much larger question of his knowledge and use of classical authors —a question which has been needlessly complicated and confused by the theory that he was unable to read Latin.

The most striking instance of Plautine imitation is of course *The Comedy of Errors* (composed about 1591), which is based upon the *Menaechmi*, with additional material from the *Amphitruo*. Many scholars have believed that Shakespeare was unable to read the *Menaechmi* in the original and either must have seen the translation of W. W. in manuscript form or must have used *The Historie of Error*, which they assume to have been an adaptation of the *Menaechmi*. This view is accepted by Wallace, who says: "A third possibility is that Shakspere read Plautus at first hand, but this would seem the least plausible way of accounting for the facts, since we have direct evidence of his 'small Latin.' "[60] But Ben Jonson's famous phrase, "small Latine and lesse Greeke," written at a time when Latin was still well-nigh a universal tongue, did not mean what many today think of as "small Latin." Also, the attempt to prove that Shakespeare must have known the *Menaechmi* in translation seems especially futile; there is no evidence that Courtney's translation of the *Amphitruo* was used by Shakespeare as the second source of *The Comedy of Errors*,[61] and also, as we shall see below, several other Plautine plays bear marked resemblances to scenes and episodes in several Shakespearean comedies; how is his knowledge of these plays to be explained?

Baldwin's comprehensive analysis of the educational system in England when Shakespeare was a boy has shown clearly both that Plautus and Terence were a regular part of the curricula of the schools and that all the Latin authors used by Shakespeare were the authors read by

---

[60] *The Birthe of Hercules*, pp. 86 f.

[61] Courtney's translation of the *Amphitruo* seems to have been overlooked by many scholars; e.g., Whibley says of sixteenth-century translations (*CHEL*, IV, p. 4): "Plautus fared not much better: we have no more than the *Menaechmi* of William Warner (1595)." Highet writes as follows (*The Classical Tradition*, p. 624, n. 89): "The question whether Shakespeare used a translation of Plautus when writing *The Comedy of Errors* has been much vexed. It seems to me to have been given more importance than it deserves: for if Shakespeare could read *Amphitruo* in Latin, he could surely read *Menaechmi*, and no one has undertaken to show that a translation of *Amphitruo* was available." Yet, curiously enough, Highet himself mentions (p. 121) Courtney's translation of the *Amphitruo*, but later (p. 763) deletes the reference. For details concerning Shakespeare's use of the *Menaechmi* and the *Amphitruo* in *The Comedy of Errors*, see below, pp. 417 f. and n. 80.

students in the grammar schools of his day.[62] That Shakespeare read the *Menaechmi* and other Plautine plays in school seems highly probable. Furthermore, there is good evidence that Shakespeare read the *Menaechmi* in the standard edition of Lambinus, first published in 1576, for many details in *The Comedy of Errors* are best explained by his use of Lambinus' Latin commentary.[63]

There is thus no reason to deny to Shakespeare the knowledge of Greek and Latin authors that would be available at Stratford to any schoolboy between the ages of seven and fifteen. As this instruction included exercises in Latin conversation and Latin composition, it seems likely, as Parrott says, "that any boy except a hopeless dullard would acquire a mastery of Latin that would amaze most graduates of an American college. . . . It would, in fact, be hard to see where Shakespeare could have acquired the Greek, which Jonson's dictum . . . allows him, had he not spent a year or more in the upper forms of the King's School."[64] For us the important facts are that he did know both Plautus and Terence and that this knowledge is reflected in several of his comedies.

Literal translations of passages from Roman comedy are relatively infrequent, but there are several striking instances. Hamlet's denunciation of his mother's faithlessness (Act. III, Sc. IV, 160) includes the precept:

> Assume a virtue, if you have it not.

These are almost the exact words with which Amphitruo addresses Alcumena (*Amph.* 819) when he accuses her of adultery. In *The Taming of the Shrew* (Act I, Sc. I, 158) Tranio quotes to his master a passage from Terence's *Eunuchus* (74 f.):

> If love have touched you, nought remains but so;
> Redime te captum, quam queas minimo.

The Latin sentence has here the form in which it appeared in the Latin grammar of Colet and Lily, the grammar which Shakespeare seems to have used in school.[65] Also in *The Taming of the Shrew* (Act V, Sc. I, 114) Lucentio begs for the forgiveness of Tranio in almost the same words used by Callidamates in *Most.* 1159. The words of Ferdinand in *The Tempest* (Act III, Sc. I, 4 ff.):

[62] See *William Shakspere's Small Latine and Lesse Greeke*, I, pp. 7, 325 f., 641 f.; II, pp. 561, 673 ff.

[63] See Baldwin, *The Comedy of Errors*, pp. 119 ff.; *Shakspere's Five-Act Structure*, pp. 666 ff., 676 ff., 691 ff. Parrott says (*Shakespeare*, p. 103): "He had, no doubt, read Plautus at school; he had even, perhaps, taught Plautus himself, and seen a Plautine comedy presented by school-boys."

[64] *Shakespearean Comedy*, pp. 92 f. On Shakespeare's knowledge of Latin, see also Enk, *Neoph* 5 (1919-20), pp. 359 ff.; Gill, *BUTSE* 10 (1930), pp. 17 ff.; Highet, *The Classical Tradition*, pp. 200 f., 214 ff.

[65] See the delightful parody of Latin grammar in *The Merry Wives of Windsor*, Act IV, Sc. I, and cf. Baldwin, *Shakspere's Small Latine and Lesse Greeke*, I, pp. 561 ff.

> This my mean task
> Would be as heavy to me as odious, but
> The mistress which I serve quickens what's dead,
> And makes my labours pleasures,

resemble those of Sceparnio in *Rud.* 458 ff.

Other verbal similarities of this type might be added,[66] but far more significant are the presence in Shakespeare's comedies of the situations, characters, and comic devices which are regularly found in the Roman plays.[67] Here the threads of the classical tradition are so interwoven that it is practically impossible to separate the direct borrowings from those which come indirectly through Italian comedy and the German education-drama. The familiar conventions are present—the announcement of characters, running slaves, knocking on doors, horseplay and abuse, humorous asides, repetition for comic effect; Plautus' use of Greek words is paralleled by the French and Italian phrases in Shakespeare's plays and, as Miss Coulter says, "the Boy's interpretation of the French captive's plea (*Henry V* IV, 4) must have made the same humorous appeal as Milphio's attempt to translate Punic greetings into Latin (*Poen.* 995-1028)."[68] The plots of many Shakespearean comedies, which involve impersonation, exchange of dress, double love affairs, longlost children, recognition by means of rings or other tokens, would hardly seem strange, in spite of their more romantic coloring, to the ancient audiences of Plautus and Terence. Although the Shakespearean heroine differs from the ancient *meretrix*, the hero in love is not unlike the Roman *adulescens*, and "we can still recognize traits of the classical *senex* in the stern decrees of Antonio (*Two Gentlemen* I, 3) and Baptista (*Taming of the Shrew* I, 1), in Capulet's reminiscences of by-gone days (*Romeo and Juliet* I, 5), and in the 'wise saws' of Polonius to Laertes (*Hamlet* I, 3)."[69] The English clown, developed in part from the resourceful servant of Italian comedy who in turn is derived from the *seruus* of Roman comedy, no longer controls the plot by his trickery but retains many of the characteristics of the Plautine slave, being fond of soliloquies, clever retorts, abuse of other servants, and comic exaggerations.

The braggart warrior, always a popular character in Renaissance comedy, appears in Shakespeare in various guises—as Don Armado, Parolles, Bardolph, Pistol, and others, but especially in the role of Falstaff, who is a failure both as a soldier and as a lover. Falstaff, who is considered Shakespeare's greatest comic creation, is a most complex

---

[66] E.g., there are echoes of the *Captivi* in *The Comedy of Errors*; see Enk, *Neoph* 5 (1919-20), pp. 362 f.

[67] For a fuller treatment of these topics, see Coulter, *JEGPh* 19 (1920), pp. 70 ff.

[68] *JEGPh* 19 (1920), p. 82. See above, pp. 354 f.

[69] Coulter, *JEGPh* 19 (1920), p. 78.

character; he comes in part from Elizabethan life and from English history; in part he derives from Roman comedy and from Renaissance plays based upon that comedy. Many of his traits are those of the typical *miles gloriosus* but other characteristics, notably his love of good food, the cleverness of his wit, his flattery of others, and his willingness to live at another's expense, have been explained as coming from the parasite of Roman comedy; in other words, Shakespeare has combined in this famous and beloved character the two roles, *miles* and *parasitus*, which in classical comedy were always distinct.[70]

The Falstaff of *The Merry Wives of Windsor* seems quite different from the Falstaff of the historical plays and is, according to some, closer to the stock character of the *miles gloriosus*.[71] Parrott comments on the inconsistency of characterization: "In action Falstaff is almost always the butt and dupe, a very different character from the domineering Falstaff of *King Henry IV Part II*."[72] Pyrgopolynices (*Miles*) and Thraso (*Eunuchus*) are likewise butts and dupes but it is possible that Falstaff in this play has absorbed another role of Roman comedy, the lecherous *senex*. Forsythe finds in both the main plot and the subplot of *The Merry Wives of Windsor* a close relationship to the plot of Plautus' *Casina* and explains Falstaff as being influenced by the character of Lysidamus. "From the ready and resourceful old rascal of the historical plays he has become a gull—easily hoodwinked and falling into trap after trap, exactly the same kind of character as Lysidamus."[73]

A striking verbal similarity between the *Rudens* of Plautus and *The Tempest* has already been cited, and it seems probable that Shakespeare knew this Roman comedy also. The similarity of the setting, therefore—storm and shipwreck on a lonely coast—as well as certain likenesses between the exile Daemones and the exile Prospero, and the presence

---

[70] See Draper, *CJ* 33 (1937-38), pp. 390 ff.; on p. 401 he points out that the combination of soldier and parasite made for realism in an age when "the decay of feudalism and the military changes that gunnery imposed threw out of employment the older sort of soldier and reduced him to thief or parasite; and therefore Falstaff, in combining two major elements of his character, is not classical or medieval, or Italian, but above all contemporary Elizabethan English." For a thorough discussion of the character of Falstaff, see Stoll, *Shakespeare Studies*, pp. 403 ff., who sees in Falstaff not only the braggart and the coward, but also (p. 424) "the satyr, lecher, and parasite."

[71] Cf. Coulter, *JEGPh* 19 (1920), p. 80, n. 42; Stoll, *Shakespeare Studies*, pp. 455 f.

[72] *Shakespearean Comedy*, p. 260.

[73] Forsythe, *MPh* 18 (1920-21), p. 409; cf. pp. 404 ff. for a detailed comparison of the two comedies; other sources of *The Merry Wives of Windsor* he believes to have been *The Two Lovers of Pisa* and *Philenio*, but he shows that at least fourteen scenes of Shakespeare's comedy present striking resemblances to sixteen scenes of the *Casina* (cf. p. 419). Miss Coulter, therefore (*JEGPh* 19, 1920, p. 75) seems wrong in finding only "faint reminiscences" of the *Casina* in *The Merry Wives of Windsor*. The reviewer of Reinhardstoettner's *Plautus* in *QR* 173 (1891) p. 47, and Lumley, *The Influence of Plautus*, pp. 45 f., reflect the older view that Shakespeare's play is indebted to the *Miles*. Parrott apparently rejects or disregards Forsythe's theory when he says (*Shakespearean Comedy*, p. 254): "There is no known source for *The Merry Wives*."

in both plays of "an all-powerful and benevolent Providence,"[74] may not be entirely accidental, however much Shakespeare was influenced by the wreck of the *Sea Venture* off one of the Bermuda islands in 1609 and by the tales of shipwrecks found in Italian comedies.[75] That Shakespeare was acquainted with Plautus' *Mostellaria* is generally believed, for he apparently used this play in *The Taming of the Shrew*. Shakespeare's comedy was indebted to an earlier play, *The Taming of a Shrew*, which had a subplot clumsily adapted from Gascoigne's *The Supposes*. But the names of the two servants, Tranio and Grumio, seem to have come directly from Plautus; in Shakespeare's comedy as in the *Mostellaria*, Tranio is the tempter of his young master, the relation of master and servant is similar, as is the indignation of the old master at Tranio and also the request for pardon in the concluding scene; in Act I, Sc. I, Lucentio stands aside and beholds Bianca much as Philolaches admires Philematium in *Most*. 157 ff.[76] The scene (Act V, Sc. I) in which the pedant, disguised as Vincentio, meets the true Vincentio bears a certain resemblance to the *Trinummus* (870 ff.), where the sycophant pretends to be Charmides and encounters the real Charmides.

We turn now to *The Comedy of Errors*, the most famous instance of Shakespeare's imitation of Plautus.[77] The model was the *Menaechmi*, with its theme of identical twins and the numerous confusions which resulted when one twin was taken for the other. Shakespeare added a second pair of twins, having found this situation in the *Amphitruo*, where Jupiter and Mercury are disguised as Amphitruo and Sosia, and he borrowed also from the *Amphitruo* the idea for the scene in which Antipholus and Dromio of Ephesus are kept from their house while Antipholus and Dromio of Syracuse dine within (Act III, Sc. I). Shakespeare made numerous other changes: he added Luciana to provide a foil for Adriana and a love interest for Antipholus of Syracuse; he substituted Dr. Pinch for the *medicus* of Plautus' play; he transferred the scene to Ephesus, thereby introducing the theme of magic and witchcraft; and he enclosed the farce in a romantic, but somber, framework

---

[74] Parrott, *Shakespeare*, p. 1055. For the passage on Providence in *Rud.* 9 ff., see above, pp. 299 f.

[75] See Parrott, *Shakespearean Comedy*, pp. 391 ff.

[76] On the resemblances between the *Mostellaria* and *The Taming of the Shrew*, see Fay, *AJPh* 24 (1903), pp. 254 ff.; Enk, *Neoph* 5 (1919-20), pp. 363 f. Schelling (*Elizabethan Drama*, I, p. 457) considers *The Taming of the Shrew* "a comedy of character and intrigue ultimately derivable in conduct and spirit from Latin comedy."

[77] I pass over other suggestions of Plautine influence, e.g., that of the reviewer of Reinhardstoettner's *Plautus*, who says (*QR* 173, 1891, pp. 57 f.): "Mr. Reinhardstoettner has omitted all notice of the fact, of which we cannot doubt, that Shakespeare when he drew Shylock had heard or read of Euclio. Both misers lose a daughter and are robbed of their money: both lament their loss in terms which are purposely made as agitated and exaggerated as possible. . . . The spirit, not the words, is so like as to convince us that there is imitation here."

dealing with the fortunes of Aegeon and Aemilia, the parents of the twin Antipholuses—a framework which makes possible numerous reconciliations at the conclusion of the comedy.[78]

Scholars disagree about the relative merits of the two plays. The presence of two sets of twins in *The Comedy of Errors* greatly increases the possible number of farcical complications but makes the play more confusing and heightens the improbability of the situation, as was not the case in the *Amphitruo*, where the two pairs of doublets were created by divine *fiat*.[79] The entrances and exits of Antipholus and Dromio of Syracuse at times lack motivation and the conclusion of the comedy is complicated by an excessive number of recognitions. Plautus' comedy has a unity and a compactness lacking in Shakespeare's play; it is pure farce, while *The Comedy of Errors* has far greater variety and is thoroughly Elizabethan in its combination of farce, romance, and pathos. The characters are drawn with more delicacy and feeling than are the somewhat coarser personages of the *Menaechmi* but at the same time they lack the reality and the vividness of Plautus' creations. Parrott says: "Of all the many adaptations of the *Menaechmi, The Comedy of Errors* is by far the freest and the most original." "It is the best plotted of Shakespeare's early comedies, due, no doubt, to the fact that he had the play of Plautus as a model and preserved the Plautine unities."[80] One point should be emphasized: *The Comedy of Errors* is not a combination of scenes from two Plautine comedies but a completely new play, in which the classical material and the newer, more pathetic, elements have been blended to create an organic whole—an excellent fusion of romantic spirit and classical restraint in which pathos and farce exist side by side.

Ben Jonson, considered by some critics a more influential dramatist in the Elizabethan period than William Shakespeare,[81] had an excellent

---

[78] Perry (*Masters of Dramatic Comedy*, p. xv) says that the romantic framework of *The Comedy of Errors* "causes one to ponder on the mysterious ways of Providence." Aegeon, however, is not entirely original, having been suggested by the heart-broken father of the twins in the *Menaechmi* (cf. 24 ff.) ; his wanderings are based in part on those of Menaechmus Sosicles (*Men.* 235 ff.) ; see Baldwin, *The Comedy of Errors*, pp. xxiv f., 114 f. Baldwin suggests also (*Shakspere's Five-Act Structure*, pp. 675 ff., 684) that the transfer of the scene to Ephesus may be explained by the combined influence of St. Paul (Acts XIX) and Plautus (*Miles*, the scene of which is laid in Ephesus).

[79] But cf. Boas, *Shakspere and His Predecessors*, p. 170: "Shakspere . . . saw rightly, on this and later occasions, that two improbabilities buttress each other and have a greater plausibility than one."

[80] *Shakespearean Comedy*, pp. 103, 105. Parrott (pp. 101 ff.) gives a detailed comparison of the two plays; see also Connely, *CJ* 19 (1923-24), pp. 303 ff.; Watt, *CJ* 20 (1924-25), pp. 401 ff.; Gill, *BUTSE* 5 (1925), pp. 79 ff.; 10 (1930), pp. 13 ff. See especially Baldwin, *Shakspere's Five-Act Structure*, chapters XXVIII and XXIX (pp. 665-718).

[81] See Parrott and Ball, *A Short View of Elizabethan Drama*, p. 126. Schelling

knowledge of classical literature and he sought to combat the romantic tendencies of contemporary comedy by reverting to the structure and content of Roman comedy. Interested primarily in a realistic presentation of life, Jonson found realistic themes and characters in Plautine comedy and, adapting this material to the English stage, created a new type of satiric comedy with an emphasis on the portrayal of character and especially upon the exposition of individual eccentricities and abnormalities, or "humours," such as vanity, greed, jealousy, and affectation. Jonson himself defines "humour" in the Induction to *Every Man out of His Humour*:

> As when some one peculiar quality
> Doth so possess a man, that it doth draw
> All his effects, his spirits, and his powers,
> In their confluctions, all to run one way,
> This may be truly said to be a humour.

In thus taking over the exaggerated and sometimes ridiculous characters of Plautine comedy and developing them in accordance with his theory of "humours," Jonson was able to present a vivid picture of the foibles and the follies of the age, and his realistic and satirical comedies of "humours" had a decisive influence upon the later course of Elizabethan drama. Perry points out that Jonson never lost sight of Plautus and Terence as models, but he never limited himself to their narrow range of observation; "his particular gift was the ability to adapt classical precedents to the variety and profusion of life in Elizabethan England."[82]

One of Jonson's earliest extant plays, *The Case is Altered* (c. 1597),[83] is adapted from two comedies of Plautus, the *Captivi* and the *Aulularia*. It is a curious fact that this play, basically Roman in so many respects, should be Jonson's most romantic comedy. The *Captivi* has no love interest but, with its serious theme of friendship, exchange of roles, and mistaken identity, contains elements of romance, and the plot taken from the *Aulularia* has been made more romantic by having Rachel (= Phaedria), the supposed daughter of the miser Jacques de Prie (= Euclio), prove to be the longlost sister of Chamont (= Philocrates). Perry says: "The case is never so much altered from Plautus as when the story of the miser's gold is crowded off the stage by attention to his

---

(*English Drama*, p. 148) says: "Barring Shakespeare, Jonson is by far the most significant literary figure of his time."

[82] Perry, *Masters of Dramatic Comedy*, p. 81. Schelling (*Elizabethan Drama*, I, p. 538) says: "The Roman comedians are everywhere present in Jonsonian comedy from their general method to the suggestion of specific situations, personages, and passages."

[83] Cf. Parrott and Ball, *A Short View of Elizabethan Drama*, p. 132: "It was not included in any contemporary collection of his works. Yet internal evidence of the strongest kind points to Jonson, and no modern scholar doubts his authorship." See also Selin, *The Case is Altered*, pp. xi ff. (The passages cited below are taken from Hart's edition, from which Selin's arrangement into acts and scenes often differs.)

daughter's fate."[84] Phaedria in the *Aulularia* had only two suitors, but Rachel has five; upon the discovery of her real identity, she is wedded to Paulo (= Philopolemus), the son of Count Ferneze (= Hegio). In this ingenious manner the two plots are woven together. The comic antics of Onion and Juniper likewise bind together the threads of the action; they have the role of the slave of Lyconides, who in the *Aulularia* steals Euclio's gold.

The two characters who most resemble their Plautine counterparts are Count Ferneze and Jacques de Prie. Count Ferneze, like Hegio, has lost two sons (Act III, Sc. I, 163 ff.) :

> O, in what tempests do my fortunes sail ! . . .
> First in Vicenza lost I my first son, . . .
> And now my Paulo prisoner to the French.

In the final scene he is about to punish Gasper (= Tyndarus) when Paulo returns and Gasper is revealed as the longlost son Camillo. The miserly Jacques, who has stolen both the gold and the daughter of Lord Chamont, resembles Euclio in many respects; cf. with *Aul.* 89 ff. the following passage from Act II, Sc. I, (53 ff.) :

> Lock thyself in, but yet take out the key;
> That whosoever peeps in at the keyhole
> May yet imagine there is none at home. . . .
> Put out the fire, kill the chimney's heart,
> That it may breathe no more than a dead man;
> The more we spare, my child, the more we gain.

Jacques insists in Act III, Sc. I, 52 ff., that he has no dowry to give with his daughter (cf. *Aul.* 238 ff.) and in Act IV, Sc. IV, 96 ff., he questions Juniper in much the same manner in which Euclio examines the slave of Lyconides in *Aul.* 628 ff.[85]

*The Case is Altered*, in spite of its Italian setting and its romantic treatment of love, is largely Plautine in plot. In Jonson's other comedies, scenes, episodes, and direct quotations from Plautus are found but the plots are Jonson's own invention. He is praised for his observance of the unities of time and place though it is to be noted that Jonson's conception of unity of place differed from that of Plautus and Terence, in whose plays the scene remained unchanged throughout; Jonson kept

---

[84] *Masters of Dramatic Comedy*, p. 82.

[85] For a detailed comparison of *The Case is Altered* with its Plautine originals, see Lumley, *The Influence of Plautus*, pp. 74 ff. The *Aulularia* had been performed in 1564, but Jonson's play, produced about 1597, seems to have been the first English imitation of the Roman comedy. Shakespeare's *The Merchant of Venice*, presented about the same time, bears certain similarities to the *Aulularia* (see above, n. 77) ; striking resemblances to the *Aulularia* appear in the anonymous *Timon of Athens* (c. 1600), in which the miser Philargarus is a direct reproduction of Euclio; see Wallace, *The Birthe of Hercules*, pp. 93 f. In *The Devil is an Ass* (1616) Jonson again borrowed from the *Aulularia*; cf. with the speech of Euclio to Staphyla (*Aul.* 89 ff.) the words of Fitzdottrel in Act I, Sc. II, beginning "Lock the street-doors fast, and let no one in."

the setting in one and the same city but allowed frequent changes of scene from street to street and from house to house.

*Every Man in His Humour* (1598), the first of the plays to develop Jonson's theory of "humours," is one of his best known comedies. The scene was originally laid in Florence but in the revised version Jonson transferred the setting to London thereby increasing the realism of the comedy. The characters are vividly drawn even though developed largely from Plautine roles: Old Knowell recalls the classical *senex* in his attitude toward youth's follies, and Young Knowell is the gay *adulescens*. Bobadill as the *miles gloriosus* is one of Jonson's greatest creations, while Brainworm, the wily servant, engages in trickery both to gain money and for sheer love of amusement.[86] Kitely, the jealous husband, is included by some scholars among "the characteristic types of Roman comedy,"[87] but wrongly so, for nowhere in Roman comedy except in the *Amphitruo* (by no means a typical play) does a husband have cause for jealousy.

*Volpone, or The Fox* (1606), a play which attacks vice rather than folly, well illustrates the manner in which Jonson weaves the usual Plautine cheaters and dupes into an excellent plot of his own making. The drama gives a vivid presentation of the evils of legacy-hunting. Both Volpone, whose avarice and love of power are brilliantly depicted as he attempts to overreach his fellow-mortals, and Mosca, the intriguing parasite who finally turns against his master, end in ignominious disaster. An excellent satire on the love of money and its corrupting influence, the play has little humor and defies the rules of comic procedure in blending elements of comedy, satire, and tragedy. Rhys says: "It is a great comedy because it is a great tragedy; it is the last attainder of the sensual world that lives for gold and luxury, and denies the spirit of God."[88]

*Epicoene, or The Silent Woman* (1609) is a gay and farcical "comedy of humours." Morose, whose abnormality is his hatred of sound, was derived from the Greek sophist Libanius, who in his *Sixth Declamation* had portrayed with vividness the unhappy husband of a talkative wife. Morose marries a "silent woman" who proves to be a boy—

---

[86] Perry (*Masters of Dramatic Comedy*, p. 87) says: "This secondary element, delight in mischief-making for its own sake, is a contribution of popular drama to the comic tradition." But the intriguing slaves of Roman comedy, such as Chrysalus, Epidicus, Tranio, and Pseudolus, certainly delight in trickery for its own sake; see above, "*Seruus*" in chap. 9.

[87] Herford, in Gayley, *Representative English Comedies*, II, p. 6. It is the wife, not the husband, who in Roman comedy is sometimes jealous, and not infrequently her suspicions are justified; see above, pp. 255 f.

[88] *Ben Jonson*, p. 16. Cf. Perry, *Masters of Dramatic Comedy*, p. 99: "The play is enough of a comedy to have the servant triumph over the master, but it is tragic in depicting the ruin of an aspiring parasite. It does not purge the audience either by emotion or laughter; its appeal is to horror at the bestial impulses that lurk beneath the surface of human nature."

the same stratagem which was used against the *senex* in Plautus' *Casina*. We cannot be certain that Jonson adapted the theme of the "boy bride" directly from Plautus, for several earlier English plays had introduced a boy disguised as a girl, among them, Shakespeare's *The Merry Wives of Windsor*.[89] In the *Epicoene* Jonson keeps his audience as much in the dark as his characters until the end of the play,[90] thus destroying the possibilities for the comic irony that was so effective in the *Casina*, and introducing the element of surprise much as Terence had done in his *Hecyra*, where the basic secret—the identity of the baby's father—is withheld from the spectators until the conclusion of the play. Jonson's comedy, however, was very popular, unlike the more serious and somewhat unconventional *Hecyra*, which twice failed before it was successfully produced.[91]

In *The Alchemist* (1610), usually considered Jonson's comic masterpiece, love of wealth again provides the basic theme, and the plot is concerned with the contemporary interest in alchemy and with the trickery and deceit of characters in the London underworld. In this, perhaps his most ingenious comedy, Jonson has drawn upon Plautus for several details, especially at the beginning and the end, where the resemblances to the *Mostellaria* are striking. The quarrel of Face and Subtle in Act I, Sc. I, echoes that of Tranio and Grumio in *Most*. 1 ff., and in Act v, Sc. II and III, Face attempts to keep Lovewit from his house by the story of a plague, much as Tranio in *Most*. 447 ff. forces Theopropides to flee by means of his ghost story. In both comedies the voice heard from within the house is attributed to a spirit. In Act I, Sc. II, 47, Face says:

Nothing's more wretched than a guilty conscience.

These are the words of Tranio in *Most*. 544.[92]

[89] See Freeburg, *Disguise Plots*, pp. 101 f.; he says (p. 114): "The truth of the matter is, it seems to me, not that Plautus was the direct source of Jonson's play, but that Plautus was the ultimate source of a number of Italian plays, which inspired a number of English plays, which established a certain tradition, which culminated in *Epicoene*." But cf. Henry's edition of *Epicoene* in *YSE* 31 (1906), pp. xxxiv f.; Miss Henry points out that, in addition to the contribution of the *Casina* to the plot of Jonson's comedy, there are three instances of verbal parallels to passages in other Plautine comedies (*Bacchides, Aulularia*, and *Menaechmi*).

[90] Cf. Gayley, *Representative English Comedies*, II, pp. 117 ff., who considers the surprise element a vice, not a dramatic virtue.

[91] Cf. "Innocent Mistakes: *Hecyra*" in chap. 6. On the element of surprise in the *Hecyra*, see above, p. 229.

[92] Cf. Lumley, *The Influence of Plautus*, pp. 64 ff. Miss Lumley also suggests (p. 69) that the visions of wealth of Sir Epicure Mammon (Act II, Sc. I) are similar to those of Gripus in *Rud*. 930 ff. Smithson says (Gayley, *Representative English Comedies*, II, p. 255): "Finally, the device of having Surly speak a language [in Act IV, Scenes III and IV] which is not understood by the others is the same as that used by Plautus for the character of Hanno in the *Poenulus*, but the trick had become a stage property among the Elizabethans."

The influence of Roman comedy extends beyond Jonson's adaptation of plots, situations, and characters. Just as acrostic arguments were prefixed in Roman times to the Plautine comedies, so we find acrostic arguments at the beginning of *Volpone* and *The Alchemist*. Monologues and asides are used after the fashion of the classical models. Jonson's coinage of significant names is reminiscent of Plautus' effective use of "tell-tale" names.[93] Among his many amusing and meaningful names are Brainworm, Kitely, Downright, and Wellbred in *Every Man in His Humour*; Morose, Truewit, Cutbeard, and Sir Amorous La-Foole in *Epicoene*; and in *The Alchemist*, Sir Epicure Mammon, Pertinax Surly, and Tribulation Wholesome. One of his most delightful names is Sir Diaphanous Silkworm, in *The Magnetic Lady*. The Italian names in *Volpone* are equally significant: Volpone, the Fox; Mosca, the Fly; Voltore, the Vulture; Corbaccio, the Crow; and Corvino, the Raven. Since Jonson's theory of "humours" induced him to portray types rather than individuals, the tell-tale names were as appropriate for his characters as they had been for those of Plautus. Jonson, as a master of comic and satiric characterization, had an important influence upon later writers, not only dramatists but novelists as well. Thorndike says of Jonson's comedies: "Fielding and Smollett were conscious of their incentive, and . . . Dickens' comic invention and characterisation are often strikingly Jonsonian in method and effect."[94]

## The Seventeenth and Eighteenth Centuries

Our account of the influence of Roman comedy upon the contemporaries and successors of Shakespeare and Jonson must necessarily be brief. Intrigue, disguise, and mistaken identity continue to be popular. Schelling says: "Later comedies, which hark back to the ancients, show the classical influence in degrees which vary from a certain mannerism in the drawing of character or in the ordering of incident to the borrowing of whole personages and plots."[95] The indebtedness of the plots, situations, and characters of Plautus and Terence in many instances is indirect through the works of Ben Jonson and later, in Restoration Comedy, through the influence of Molière. The dramatic output in England during these two centuries was very great; for instance, in the half century between 1590 and the closing of the theaters in 1642

[93] See "Comic Formations" in chap. 12 for a discussion of the significant name in Plautus and Terence. Parrott and Ball (*A Short View of Elizabethan Drama*, p. 135) say that the names in the revised edition of *Every Man in His Humour* "have an allegorical significance, a new trait in Jonson which emphasizes the didactic strain and connects him with the native tradition of the Morals." But it seems very likely that Jonson, who derived so much else from Plautus, was influenced also by the many significant and laughable names to be found in Plautus' comedies.

[94] *CHEL* VI, p. 28. It may be added that Dickens is also strikingly Plautine in many of his effects; see below, "Modern Survivals."

[95] *Elizabethan Drama*, I, pp. 456 f.

about four hundred and fifty comedies were produced on the stage;[96] obviously it is impossible, for this period as well as for the Restoration and the eighteenth century, to do more than mention briefly certain striking imitations and adaptations of the Roman plays.

George Chapman, best known for his translation of Homer, was also a distinguished Elizabethan playwright, whose "idea of comedy, even more strictly than Jonson's, was that of Plautus and Terence."[97] *All Fools* (1599), considered his masterpiece, is an adaptation of Terence's *Heauton*, with additional borrowings from the *Adelphoe*. The wife of Gostanzo's son pretends to be the wife of Fortunio, son of Gostanzo's neighbor, and Rinaldo, Fortunio's younger brother, has the role of the wily intriguer, whose "fortune is to winne renowne by Gulling" (Act v, Sc. 1). Schelling calls the play "the best example of an English comedy conceived and carried out on the lines of Roman comedy."[98] *May Day* (1601), also a comedy of intrigue in the Roman manner, has in Quintiliano a *miles gloriosus* of the type already represented by Ralph Roister Doister, Pistol, Falstaff, and Captain Bobadill.

Another addition to this long list of warriors is Bessus, in Beaumont and Fletcher's *A King and No King* (1611), the delightful braggart and coward who admits (Act III, Sc. II) that his "reputation came principally by thinking to run away." The play has a serious plot of mistaken identity and recognition; King Arbaces' love for his sister Panthea ends happily upon the discovery that he is neither king nor brother— a situation just the opposite of that in Plautus' *Epidicus*, where the youth gives up his sweetheart when he discovers that she is his half-sister. *The Scornful Lady* (c. 1610), also by Beaumont and Fletcher, is often said to be indebted to Terence's *Adelphoe* but the resemblance is not striking; the competing systems of discipline are lacking, as is the relationship between fathers and sons; there are two contrasted brothers, and the sudden conversion of Morecraft, the usurer, in Act v, Sc. III, may be derived from Demea's professed change of heart in *Ad.* 855 ff. In its intrigue, and especially in the use of disguises, the play is rather more Plautine than Terentian.

John Marston's *What You Will* (1601), a farcical play infused with satire, is essentially a comedy of errors. Francisco's impersonation of the supposedly dead Albano makes it difficult for the real Albano to establish his identity since everyone pretends to take him for Francisco or for a second impostor—an interesting variation of the Mercury-Sosia theme of Plautus' *Amphitruo*. Marston's *Parasitaster, or The Fawn*

---

[96] Cf. Gayley, *Representative English Comedies*, III, pp. xciv ff., who gives a total of 250 comedies for the years 1590-1625, exclusive of Shakespeare's comedies, and for the years 1625-42 a total of 185. The number of plays produced between 1558, the accession of Queen Elizabeth, and 1642, the closing of the theaters, is estimated at 2,000, with about 900 extant; see Schelling, *Elizabethan Drama*, II, pp. 371 ff.

[97] Schelling, *English Drama*, p. 168.    [98] *English Drama*, p. 168.

(c. 1605) is frequently said to be modeled upon Terence's *Adelphoe*, but there is no real similarity between the two plays. *No Wit, No Help Like a Woman's* (1613), by Thomas Middleton, has two plots, and "the main plot dealing with the troubles of the Twilight family is essentially a Plautine comedy transplanted to Elizabethan London."[99] The secret wife of Philip Twilight pretends to be Grace, the daughter of Sir Oliver Twilight, but is really Jane, Sunset's daughter, while the supposed Jane is actually Grace. The situation is thus an adaptation to female characters of the exchange of roles in Plautus' *Captivi*, but also resembles the situation in the *Epidicus*, where Stratippocles' sweetheart pretends to be the longlost daughter of Periphanes, while a music girl poses as the sweetheart. *A New Way to Pay Old Debts* (1625), the most successful play of Philip Massinger, is a more serious play of intrigue which resembles Jonson's *Volpone* in that the villain, Sir Giles Overreach, is the victim of his own greed and self-confidence. The numerous asides and overheard conversations are Elizabethan conventions which go back to those of Roman comedy; especially interesting are the significant names: Overreach, Welborne, Alworth, Greedy, Furnace, and Tapwell, which Massinger has adopted in imitation of Ben Jonson's use of such names in his comedies of "humours."

The direct influence of Roman comedy upon the minor Elizabethan dramatists is best seen in the works of Thomas Heywood, who drew heavily upon Plautus for three of his comedies. *The Silver Age* (c. 1612), one of a series of plays presenting all classical myth and legend from the birth of Jupiter to the fall of Troy, contains as its second act an adaptation of the *Amphitruo*. Several scenes of the Plautine original are omitted, others are shortened, and some new material is added, e.g., Jupiter's opening soliloquy and the ensuing dialogue with Ganymede who, like Mercury in Plautus' comedy, disguises himself as Sosia. Ganymede later convinces Sosia that he has lost his identity; and the latter says:

I am gone, I am gone, somebody for charity sake either lend me or give me a name, for this I have lost by the way; . . . as he hath got my name, he hath got my shape, countenance, stature, and everything so right, that he can be no other than I my own self.

The confusion between Amphitruo and Jupiter leads Amphitruo to doubt his identity also. As master and slave sleep, Juno and Iris descend from heaven, thunder and lightning follow, and the act closes with Jupiter's explanation, as at the end of Plautus' comedy.[100]

[99] Parrott and Ball, *A Short View of Elizabethan Drama*, p. 164.
[100] The full title of Heywood's play is *The Silver Age, including The love of Jupiter to Alcmena, The birth of Hercules, and The Rape of Proserpine, concluding With the Arraignement of the Moone*. For the variations from Plautus' *Amphitruo*, see Wallace, *The Birthe of Hercules*, pp. 91 f. On Heywood's indebtedness to Plautus in general, see Gilbert, *JEGPh* 12 (1913), pp. 593 ff.

Both *The Captives, or The Lost Recovered* (1624) and *The English Traveller* (after 1625) have two plots, one of which in each play is derived from Plautus. The two plots are not integrated, as are the dual themes in Terence's comedies, but are presented in alternating scenes, with only a superficial connection between the two sets of characters. The main plot of *The Captives* is that of Plautus' *Rudens*,[101] which Heywood adapts to English life but follows closely scene by scene in both character and action. The transfer of the setting from the temple of Venus to a monastery at Marseilles enables him to introduce a minor plot on the immoral life of the monks. At the end of the play the two captive girls, Palestra and Scribonia, are discovered to be the daughter and the niece respectively of John Ashburne; they acquire English husbands and set sail for their home in England. Ashburne, who corresponds to Daemones, has a greater dignity and nobility of character than his Roman counterpart.[102] The minor plot of *The English Traveller* is that of the *Mostellaria*, and Heywood compresses into six scenes almost the entire action of the Roman comedy, from the abusive words of Reignald (= Tranio) and Robin (= Grumio) to the final forgiveness of Reignald by Old Lionel (= Theoproprides). Certain innovations are found; e.g., Young Lionel ( = Philolaches) appears at the end and asks his father to pardon him, but in general the plot follows its Plautine model with amazing fidelity, especially in Young Lionel's comparison of a young man to a house, the father's arrival from abroad, Reignald's tale of the haunted house, the entrance of the Usurer, and the pretended purchase of the house of the neighbor, Ricott (= Simo). Phaniscus and Pinacium, who in Plautus' play reveal the deception, are replaced by the Clown from the major plot and by Robin who is not a protatic character as was Grumio.

Latin plays were still written and staged in the first half of the seventeenth century. George Ruggle's *Ignoramus*, produced at Cambridge in 1615, was particularly successful, for King James twice journeyed from London to Cambridge to see it acted; it was a coarse but witty comedy adapted from Della Porta's *La Trappolaria*, which in turn was indebted to the *Pseudolus* of Plautus. Ruggle, however, deserves credit for considerable originality; he has added several new characters and has introduced into his play many satirical passages directed chiefly

---

[101] Schelling (*Elizabethan Drama*, I, p. 457) wrongly states that the major plot of Heywood's comedy comes from the *Captivi* of Plautus.

[102] Cf. Judson, *The Captives*, p. 17. Judson points out (p. 14 n.) that everyone of the important characters in the *Rudens* finds a counterpart in Heywood's *Captives*: Daemones = Ashburne; Plesidippus = Raphael, in love with Palestra; Sceparnio = Godfrey, servant of Ashburne; Gripus = the Fisherman (also called Gripus) ; Trachalio = the Clown; Labrax = Mildew; Charmides = Sarleboys; and Palaestra and Ampelisca = Palestra and Scribonia, young women in the possession of Mildew. The Abbot of the monastery has the role of Ptolemocratia, priestess of the temple of Venus.

against lawyers, Puritans, and Jesuits.[103] Equally famous was the *Naufragium Joculare* ("The Laughable Shipwreck"), by Abraham Cowley, a comedy of intrigue and mistaken identity in the Plautine manner, which was presented at Trinity College, Cambridge, about 1638. The plot is borrowed in part from Plautus' *Captivi* and *Mostellaria* and the play has all the familiar devices—puns and word-play, the "creaking door," the use of Greek words, occasional passages of song. Beers says: "The stock characters of the Latin theatre are present in force: the pedagogue, the *servus* and *ancilla*, the merchant father, the lost heir and supposititious son, the male and female captive with their master, the 'Thraso' or 'Miles Gloriosus'—in this instance named Bombardomachides,"[104] apparently an expansion of the name Bumbomachides (*Mil.* 14) under the influence of *bombarda* or "bombadier." The play is also of interest both for its numerous quotations from—and jesting allusions to—Cicero, Horace, Vergil, and other classical writers, and for its satirical references to contemporary education.

The work of Cowley provides an admirable transition to Restoration Comedy. His satirical English play, *The Guardian*, also a reproduction of Plautine situations and characters, was acted at Trinity College in 1642, and was produced publicly in 1661 in a revised form, under the title *Cutter of Coleman Street*. The plot is the usual one of disguise and substitution, impersonation and counter-impersonation, and Cutter and Worm, who have more prominent parts in the revised version of the comedy, are new variations of the *miles gloriosus*. *The Projectors* (1664), by John Wilson, is a typically Jonsonian comedy influenced in part by Plautus' *Aulularia*; the usurer is named Suckdry, his servant is Leanchops, and the victim who is gulled is Sir Gudgeon Credulous. Two well-known plays by John Dryden, *Sir Martin Mar-all* (1667) and *Amphitryon* (1690), are related to Plautus, the former indirectly through Molière's *L'Étourdi* and Quinault's *L'Amant Indiscret*, the latter chiefly through Molière's *Amphitryon*, but Dryden also used Plautus directly, since certain passages are closer to the Roman play than to Molière's version.[105]

Other plays related indirectly to Plautus include Thomas Shadwell's

---

[103] See Van Gundy, *Ignoramus*, pp. 13 ff., 23 ff.

[104] Beers, in Gayley and Thaler, *Representative English Comedies*, IV, p. 5, who adds that the Latin play "was freely translated into English by Charles Johnson in 1705 under the title *Fortune in Her Wits*."

[105] See Allen, *The Sources of John Dryden's Comedies*, pp. 273 ff. Estimates concerning Dryden's *Amphitryon* vary widely: Schelling (*English Drama*, p. 241) believes that Dryden has bettered his ancient and French models, while Palmer (*T. Macci Plauti Amphitruo*, pp. xvi f.) says of Plautus' play: "It is sufficient to contrast it with Molière's *Amphitryon* to show the immeasurable superiority of Plautus; it would be an insult to Plautus to compare it with Dryden's. . . . Neither Molière nor Dryden for one instant arrived at the conception of the loving husband and faithful wife which Plautus places before us."

*The Miser* (1671), adapted from Molière's *L'Avare,* and Edward Ravenscroft's *The English Lawyer* (1678), based upon Ruggle's *Ignoramus.* From the beginnings of English comedy to the end of the Elizabethan period the robust humor of Plautus had been preferred to the more sentimental comedies of Terence, but the Restoration comedy of manners favored the latter playwright. William Congreve, in his dedication of *The Way of the World,* spoke of Terence as "the most correct writer in the world"; it is not surprising, therefore, that Congreve "regarded himself as the legitimate heir of Terence and Menander, and claimed with perfect justice to paint the world in which he lived."[106] Both *The Cheats of Scapin* (1677), by Thomas Otway, and Ravenscroft's *Scaramouch a Philosopher* (1677) are imitations of Molière's *Les Fourberies de Scapin* and are thus indirectly indebted to Terence's *Phormio.*

Shadwell's very popular comedy, *The Squire of Alsatia* (1688), for all its local color of Whitefriars, is a close adaptation of Terence's *Adelphoe;* Sir William Belfond, who lives in the country and is stern, morose, obstinate, and covetous, is the Demea of the comedy, while his brother, Sir Edward, corresponds to Micio; Sir Edward is unmarried and lives a cultured life of ease in the city, being gentle and compassionate toward all. Sir William has two sons; the elder (= Ctesipho) has been reared with severity but has rebelled and is indulging in a life of vice; the younger son (= Aeschinus), who has been adopted by Sir Edward and reared with kindness and generosity, is by contrast a gentleman and a man of honor. Sir William considers his own son a model of conduct and reproves his brother for his laxity. The close relationship to Terence is apparent in such passages as the following (Act I, Sc. I):

SIR WILL.: . . . No, he's a good youth, the comfort of my age! I weep for joy to think of him. Good sir, learn to be a father of him that is one; I have a natural care of him you have adopted.

SIR EDW.: You are his father by nature, I by choice; I took him when he was a child, and bred him up with gentleness, and that kind of conversation that has made him my friend. He conceals nothing from me, or denies nothing to me. Rigour makes nothing but hypocrites.[107]

Sir William for a long time refuses to admit that his own son is engaged in lewd conduct, but finally the truth is forced upon him (Act v, Sc. I [III?]):

SIR WILL.: That I should live to this unhappy age! to see the fruit of all my hopes thus blasted. . . . Brother! I am ashamed to look on you, my disappointment is so great. Oh, this most wicked recreant! this perverse and infamous son!

106 Whibley, *CHEL* VIII, p. 155.
107 Cf. *Ad.* 125 f., 47-50.

SIR EDW.: Brother, a wise man is never disappointed. Man's life is like a game at tables; if any time the cast you most shall need does not come up, let that which comes instead of it be mended by your play.

SIR WILL.: How different have been our fates! I left the pleasures of the town to marry, which was no small bondage; had children, which brought more care upon me. For their sakes I lived a rustic, painful, hard, severe, and melancholy life: morose, inhospitable, sparing even necessaries; tenacious, even to griping, for their good. My neighbours shunned me, my friends neglected me, my children hate me, and wish my death.[108]

Sir William forgives his son and declares that he too will come to London and feast and revel, a more complete conversion than that of Demea in the *Adelphoe*, and he admits at the end that his brother's more tolerant methods are correct; it is Sir Edward who has the final word:

You, that would breed your children well, by kindness and liberality endear 'em to you: and teach 'em by example.
> Severity spoils ten, for one it mends:
> If you'd not have your sons desire your ends,
> By gentleness and bounty make those sons your friends.

Even closer to its Terentian model is *Bellamira, or The Mistress* (1687), by Sir Charles Sedley. Although it "presents a lively, if coarsely realistic, picture of the reckless pursuit of pleasure of Sedley's day,"[109] it is in both plot and character a faithful adaptation of Terence's *Eunuchus*. Sedley says in his Prologue:

> Our play old virtuous Rome the Eunuch nam'd
> But modest London the lewd title damn'd,
> Our author try'd his own and cou'd not hit:
> He now presents you with some foreign wit.

Keepwell (= Phaedria) loves Bellamira (= Thais) and has as a present for her a eunuch, but Lionel (= Chaerea), in love with Isabella (= Pamphila), impersonates the eunuch at the suggestion of Merryman (= Parmeno). The result is as in Terence, and Lionel says (near the end of Act III; cf. *Eun.* 605 f.):

Should I have slip'd so fair, so wish'd, so unexpected an opportunity, I must have been that eunuch that I seem'd.

Lionel and Isabella had earlier met and loved in Spain. The Terentian soldier and parasite, Thraso and Gnatho, appear in Sedley's comedy as Dangerfield and Smoothly; they assault Bellamira's house with their cronies, Culverin, Wildfire, and Hackum, but Bellamira and Eustace (= Chremes) refuse to give up Isabella, who has meanwhile been discovered to be Eustace's sister. At the end Dangerfield is accepted as Keepwell's rival, as in Terence, but Smoothly says:

---

[108] Cf. *Ad.* 739-741, 866-874. Norwood (*Plautus and Terence*, p. 182) does less than justice to the Terentian elements in the play when he says merely, "Two brothers contrasted."

[109] Whibley, *CHEL* VIII, p. 139.

You need not fear any woman should like him, he has been impotent these seven years: When you are weary of him you may kick him out of doors. . . . Now, gentlemen, take me into your protection, and then eat, drink upon, and laugh at the fool my master.[110]

Nicoll says: "During the early part of the eighteenth century far greater attention seems to have been paid to Greek and Roman comedy than in the period 1660-1700."[111] Terence as a model continued to be favored over Plautus. The Plautine imitations are relatively few and usually indirect, e.g., Henry Fielding's *The Intriguing Chambermaid* (1733), indebted to the *Mostellaria* through Regnard's *Le Retour Imprévu; The Miser* (1732), also by Fielding, who said that the comedy was "taken from Plautus and Molière"; and John Hawkesworth's *Amphitryon, or The Two Socias* (1756), which was "altered from Dryden."[112]

Adaptations from Terence were numerous. Thomas Cooke's *The Eunuch, or The Darby Captain* (printed in 1736) was taken from Terence's *Eunuchus*, with a few additions from Plautus' *Miles*, and George Coleman the Elder combined Plautus' *Trinummus* and Terence's *Phormio* in *The Man of Business* (1774). Ballentine lists also two plays, both published in 1778 but never acted: H. Brooke's *Charitable Association*, based upon the *Hecyra*, and Edmund Ball's *The Beautiful Armenia, or The Energy and Force of Love*, a "close imitation of the *Eunuchus* without any acknowledgement of the source of the play."[113] The two most popular Terentian comedies, however, were the *Andria* and the *Adelphoe*.

New versions of the *Andria* include *The Conscious Lovers* (1722), by Sir Richard Steele, and *The Perjured Devotee, or The Force of Love* (1739), by Daniel Bellamy; *The Foundling* (1748), by Edward Moore, incorporates certain features of the *Andria* in its plot, but the resemblance is not striking. *The Conscious Lovers*, on the other hand, follows the Terentian plot closely, especially in Acts I and II. Sir John Bevil (= Simo) wishes his son, Bevil Junior (= Pamphilus) to marry Lucinda (= Philumena), the daughter of Sealand (= Chremes). Lucinda is beloved by Myrtle (= Charinus), but Bevil Junior loves Indiana (= Glycerium), who proves in the end to be Sealand's daughter by his first wife. Nicoll is hardly correct in saying that Terence's *Andria* has been "sentimentalized out of all recognition," but it is true that "love in the comedy is tender and pure; the air is positively thick with sympathy and pity

---

[110] Cf. *Eun.* 1080, 1086 f. Gnatho in Terence's comedy does not state that Thraso is impotent. On Terence's *Eunuchus*, see "Mistaken Identity and Deception" in chap. 6.

[111] *A History of Early Eighteenth Century Drama*, p. 143.

[112] John Oxenford's farce, *I and My Double* (1835), was a still later play based upon Dryden's *Amphitryon*. Both Hawkesworth and Oxenford give us a much diluted Plautus, through Dryden's version of Molière's adaptation of the original Roman comedy.

[113] Ballentine, *Hauton Timorumenos*, p. xviii.

and emotion."[114] *The Perjured Devotee* is an attempt to present "Terentian Humour, join'd with Cowley's wit," part of the plot being an imitation of Cowley's *Naufragium Joculare*, while the remainder follows closely the *Andria*. Valentine (= Pamphilus) is secretly married to Silvia (= Glycerium), who had formerly lived in a monastery. Worthy has the role of Charinus, Olivia that of Philumena, and Sir Toby Testy that of Simo. Bellamy states in the preface that he wrote the play some years before *The Conscious Lovers*.

The comedies indebted to the *Adelphoe* include the following: (1) Steele's *The Tender Husband, or The Accomplished Fools* (1705), in which the contrast is between a son reared with too great restraint and a wife treated with excessive leniency. Clerimont Senior says in his concluding speech:

> You've seen th' extremes of the domestic life,
> A son too much confined—too free a wife.

(2) *The Jealous Wife* (1761), by George Coleman the Elder, the most popular comedy of its day. The play is based in part upon the *Adelphoe* but is largely a dramatization of *Tom Jones*. (3) *The Choleric Man* (1774), by Sir Richard Cumberland, whom Oliver Goldsmith called "the Terence of England."[115] Cumberland admitted his debt to Terence and denied use of Shadwell's *The Squire of Alsatia* but many critics considered his play to be more indebted to Shadwell's comedy than to its Terentian original.[116] (4) Fielding's *The Fathers, or The Good-Natured Man*, published in 1778 some years after the author's death. Again we find the contrast between two different systems of discipline. Sir George Boncour denounces the conduct of his nephew to the youth's father, Boncour (= Micio), much as Demea criticizes Aeschinus, but it is Valence, with his strict theories of rearing his son and daughter, who corresponds to Demea. Again it is the more liberal system that is victorious, the compromise of the Terentian original being rejected by the dramatists of the eighteenth century.

## Modern Survivals

We approach the end of our survey. That the comic playwrights of ancient Rome made a deep impression upon the dramatic literature of western Europe has become apparent and perhaps, as Miss Lumley observes, "no ancient writer has thus served as a model so generally, or has had so many successful imitators among poets as Plautus."[117] It is hardly an overstatement to say that European comedy was essentially a development from that of Rome. Today, however, both Plautus and

[114] Nicoll, *A History of Early Eighteenth Century Drama*, pp. 192 f.
[115] Cf. Schelling, *English Drama*, p. 310.
[116] See Williams, *Richard Cumberland*, pp. 112 f.
[117] *The Influence of Plautus*, p. 1.

Terence are little known and often underrated. In colleges and universities their plays are still read with enjoyment and frequently staged, in Latin or in English, with spectacular success, but to the world of the theater they are little more than names. Never again will Plautus and Terence be the masters of comedy that they were to the playwrights of the Renaissance; the position which they held then as classics has been taken by Shakespeare and Molière, by Shaw and other modern writers.

Occasionally a successful stage production recalls the plot of a Roman comedy; two outstanding examples in recent years are *Amphitryon 38*, by Jean Giraudoux,[118] and the Rodgers and Hart musical comedy, *The Boys from Syracuse*, which, as adapted by George Abbott from *The Comedy of Errors*, regains much of the spirit of Plautus by its emphasis on farcical situations and by its use of song and dance. The trickery and deception and impersonation in which Plautus delighted appear again and again in comedies in the nineteenth and twentieth centuries.[119]

In fiction also, the farcical situations and laughable characters of Roman comedy may be found, even though the writer is not conscious of any imitation. Such accidental resemblances prove that the essential nature of humor differs little from one age to another. Two such dissimilar writers as Charles Dickens and P. G. Wodehouse often remind the reader of Plautus. The reviewer of Reinhardstoettner's *Plautus* said of Plautus and Dickens: "Plautus popularized, vulgarized if you like, the sentimental comedy of Greece; and he became the national dramatist of Rome, and the father of the modern drama, if any one individual can claim to have originated it. Charles Dickens popularized, many will have it vulgarized, the English novel; but he vulgarized it in such sort that he is the undisputed favourite of the English race all over the globe. And it is in the writings of Dickens that we find the best parallels to the *importunae uxores* of Plautus. . . .

"When Samuel Weller is assisting Mr. Winkle to elope with his beloved Arabella, Dickens is unconsciously treading in the beaten track of the Latin comedy. When he makes Sam Weller rescue Mr. Pickwick from the Pound, he is also, without knowing it, narrating over again the rescue of Menaechmus of Epidamnus by Messenio. The promptness of Mr. Weller's action, and his exultation in his own success, are both reflected in the conduct and words of Messenio."[120]

In the case of Wodehouse, the resemblances to the plots and characters of Plautus are even more striking. The helpless young man (= *adu-*

[118] The Cole Porter musical comedy, *Out of This World*, presents a new version of the Amphitryon legend, in which Jupiter spends the night with an American bride in the guise of her husband.

[119] See Mrs. Cole, *CJ* 16 (1920-21), pp. 399 ff., who observes (p. 401) that "Plautus is as up-to-date as Pinero is antique."

[120] *QR* 173 (1891), pp. 56, 62.

*lescens*), in love with a fair maiden, depends upon the clever valet (= *seruus*) to extricate him from his difficulties, financial or otherwise, and enable him to wed his love. The hardhearted "bookie" is the modern counterpart of the *periurissimus leno*, and on occasion a military man is the jealous rival. The plots are stereotyped, the complications are farcical, and the ending is always happy. Even the long and laughable names, such as Augustus Fink-Nottle and Sir Masterman Petherick-Soames, recall Plautus' happy creations. McCracken says: "The finest name in all his works is . . . Stanley Featherstonehaugh Ukridge."[121] A very different sort of fictional survival is provided by Thornton Wilder's novel, *The Woman of Andros* (1930), the first part of which is based upon Terence's *Andria*.

Today, light farce, musical comedy, vaudeville, the movies, radio and television comedies—all the various forms of popular entertainment— provide much the same amusement that delighted Roman audiences in the days of Plautus and Terence. Adams seems correct in saying: "The humour of Plautus is still with us—on the vaudeville stage, for example, or in the broad farce, the burlesque, the minstrel show, the less grotesque movie comedies, or the superior varieties of comic strip."[122] Disguise, impersonation, mistaken identity, even the twin-sister motif, continue to provide stock themes for the movies, and the jests and puns of present-day movie and radio comedians are often far more in the Plautine spirit and manner than is realized. The most popular means of creating laughter today bear less resemblance to the delicacy and restraint of Terence than to the favorite devices of the more versatile and exuberant Plautus.

[121] *CJ* 29 (1933-34), p. 614.
[122] *UTQ* 7 (1937-38), p. 517; see also Skiles, *CJ* 37 (1941-42), pp. 534 f., for Plautine motifs in the motion pictures.

# APPENDIX

# A NOTE ON THE MANUSCRIPTS
## AND EDITIONS OF PLAUTUS
## AND TERENCE

THE modern reader usually has little conception of the enormous amount of labor which has been expended by editors and textual critics in their endeavors to establish the text of an ancient author. Errors and omissions in MSS, variant readings, erroneous conjectures, and problems of syntax and orthography (and, in the case of a poet, of meter) combine to make the determination of the exact words of the ancient writers a most difficult procedure. This brief note is appended, therefore, to give the reader of the comedies of Plautus and Terence a general idea of the MS tradition of the plays and to show how generations of scholars have made it possible for us to read the plays in their present form.

The extant MSS of the comedies of both playwrights fall into three periods: late Roman, medieval, and Renaissance. Each dramatist is represented by one ancient and very valuable MS of approximately the fourth century, written in rustic capitals. Numerous MSS are preserved from the Middle Ages; these, dated from the ninth to the twelfth century, are all in minuscule script; although they display great variation in their readings, they too are extremely important for the establishment of the text, and especially so where the two early MSS have omissions or cannot be deciphered. The late MSS of the fourteenth and fifteenth centuries are inferior copies of the medieval MSS and are generally ignored as being of little worth; these, however, were the MSS which were used by editors and printers for the earliest printed editions of each playwright.

The one ancient MS of Terence is the Codex Bembinus (Vaticanus 3226), known as A. This unfortunately is not complete; certain portions are lost (*And.* 1-786, *Hec.* 1-37) and others (*And.* 787-888, *Ad.* 915-997) cannot be deciphered. Yet, as Ashmore states, "notwithstanding its mutilated condition, the Bembine is our most trustworthy authority for determining the Terentian text."[1]

The medieval MSS of Terence are numerous. Editors today list twenty or more, exclusive of fragments. These MSS all go back to one original, probably of the fifth century; the text of this original was revised or altered by a grammarian named Calliopius, hence the later MSS are all considered representatives of the Calliopian recension; they fall, how-

---

[1] *The Comedies of Terence*, p. 60. Ashmore's readable account of the MSS of Terence is incomplete since additional medieval MSS have been collated and discussed by more recent editors; cf. Kauer and Lindsay, *P. Terenti Afri Comoediae*, Praefatio; Marouzeau, *Térence*, I, pp. 68 ff. Marouzeau's description of the MSS and his history of the Terentian text are accompanied by numerous bibliographical notes.

ever, into two main groups, known as δ and γ, with an additional group
called μ (or "mixti"). The traditional view that the δ family was decidedly superior to the γ family has been rejected by many scholars.[2] A
striking feature of the MSS of the γ family is the use of miniatures, most
of them colored, to illustrate each scene of each play. The four MSS
most important for their miniatures are C (Vaticanus 3868) and P
(Parisinus 7899), both of the ninth century, F (Ambrosianus H 75
inf.) of the tenth century, and O (Bodleianus, Auct. F. 2, 13, formerly
Dunelmensis) of the twelfth century.[3] Not only is almost every scene
illustrated, but portrayed at the beginning of each comedy is a little
temple, or *aedicula*, containing the masks used in the play.[4] The brightly
colored miniatures of C are by far the best, and are believed to reproduce
most closely the drawings in the original of the γ family; this original
is usually dated in the fifth century and is believed by some to have
been influenced by a more ancient illustrated edition of Terence.[5]

For Plautus fewer MSS are extant but the problems of their relationship are almost equally complex. The one early MS is A, the famous
Ambrosian Palimpsest (Ambrosianus G 82, sup.). The MS, written in
capital letters probably in the fourth century, was used again in the
seventh or the eighth century when the original writing was erased and
over it was written a portion of the Old Testament. The MS was discovered by Cardinal Angelo Mai, who in 1815 first attempted to de-
cipher the original Plautine text which had not been entirely effaced.
This work was continued by Friedrich Ritschl and by Wilhelm Studemund, the latter preparing, at the cost of his eyesight, a complete
*Apographum* of the text of A.

The Palimpsest originally contained twenty-one plays, very probably
the same twenty-one which were accepted as genuine by the scholars of
Varro's day and which are known as the *fabulae Varronianae*.[6] Many
leaves of the MS have been lost (including the *Amphitruo, Asinaria,
Aulularia*, and *Curculio* in their entirety, and almost all of the *Captivi*
and the *Vidularia*) and many pages cannot be deciphered. But wherever
the text can be read, the MS is invaluable, for it is not only much older

---

[2] Cf. e.g., E. M. Pease, "On the Relative Value of the Mss. of Terence," *TAPhA* 18
(1887), pp. 30 ff.; H. R. Fairclough, "The Text of the Andria of Terence," *TAPhA*
30 (1899), pp. 5 ff. See Jones and Morey, *The Miniatures of the Manuscripts of Terence*, Text, pp. 8 ff.

[3] For the illustrations of MSS CPFO see Weston, *HSCPh* 14 (1903), Plates 1-96,
and especially Jones and Morey, *The Miniatures of the Manuscripts of Terence*, who
reproduce also illustrations from nine other MSS. A few representative miniatures
appear in this volume; see Table of Contents.

[4] See Plate II.

[5] But see Jones and Morey, *The Miniatures of the Manuscripts of Terence*, Text,
pp. 200 ff., who argue that "the cycle of illustrations with which γ was furnished
originated as an embellishment of the edition of Calliopius and was not merely a copy
of a series of miniatures handed down along with the text of Terence, from a far more
remote antiquity" (p. 201; cf. p. 211).

[6] See above, p. 52.

but much better than the other extant MSS. Even when only a few letters in a verse can be deciphered, the Palimpsest may give a clue to the correct reading or to the metrical arrangement, especially of the lyrical *cantica*.

The other extant Plautine MSS, known as the "Palatine" family, are descended from a lost original in minuscule script, probably of the eighth century, which was itself a copy of a MS in capitals of about the fifth century. A fragmentary copy of this early archetype existed in the sixteenth century and was used by the French scholar Adrien Turnèbe, but seems to have been destroyed soon after. Our information concerning this MS, known as T (Codex Turnebi), is derived from Turnèbe's own references to it and from a collation of its text for a few plays which has been preserved on the margins of a sixteenth century edition of Plautus.[7]

At some date the text of Plautus' plays was separated into two parts, one containing the first eight plays, the other the last twelve. This division resulted in the neglect of the last twelve plays[8] and their disappearance in the later Middle Ages. The rediscovery of these lost plays by Nicolaus Cusanus in 1429 was one of the great events of the Renaissance, one which had a profound influence upon the revival of classical studies in Italy.[9]

The twenty extant plays of Plautus are preserved in the medieval MSS as follows: the last twelve plays are found only in three MSS of the tenth and eleventh centuries: B, the Codex Vetus Camerarii (Palatinus Vaticanus 1615), C, the Codex Decurtatus (Palatinus Heidelbergensis 1613), and D, the Codex Ursinianus (Vaticanus 3870). It was the discovery of MS D which restored these twelve plays to the Renaissance humanists. The first eight plays are contained also in B, the best of the Plautine MSS after the Ambrosian Palimpsest, while D has the first three and about half of the *Captivi*. Three twelfth century MSS (E, V, and J) also provide texts of the first eight comedies. The relationship of these MSS is very complicated; e.g., B for the last twelve plays stands one stage nearer the archetype than do C and D, but for the first eight B and D are copies of the same original.[10]

The *editio princeps* of Terence appeared in 1470, that of Plautus two years later. Not only these first printed editions but later editions as well were based upon Renaissance MSS and presented a text that was highly inaccurate. These Renaissance MSS contained numerous errors and were inferior to the earlier MSS which were still unknown or as yet unused.[11]

---

[7] See W. M. Lindsay, *The Codex Turnebi of Plautus* (Oxford, 1898).

[8] Perhaps, as Lindsay suggests (*The Captivi of Plautus*, p. 3), this neglect is to be attributed to a defective title-page.

[9] See above, p. 398.

[10] See Lindsay, *The Captivi of Plautus*, pp. 2 ff.; Ernout, *Plaute*, I, pp. xxvi ff.

[11] For Plautus the Renaissance MSS of the last twelve plays were based upon D,

Consequently, editions of the Roman comedies available in 1500 differ greatly from those of today. Palaeographers, textual critics, and editors have labored tirelessly for centuries to improve the text of the plays by comparing all known MSS and determining which are the most reliable, by correcting the countless errors from which not even the best MSS are free, and by emending (not always judiciously) passages which seem hopelessly corrupt. Only a few of the most significant contributions can be mentioned here.

A great advance in the establishment of Terence's text was made when, in 1565, Gabriel Faërnus' posthumous edition of Terence appeared; Faërnus had examined the Codex Bembinus carefully and was the first to realize its great importance. In 1726 Richard Bentley published a famous edition of Terence with a valuable critical commentary, based upon an examination of several different MSS. The critical edition of Umpfenbach (1870), with its fairly complete *apparatus criticus*, and the text of Dziatzko (1884) both marked a great improvement upon earlier work and established the modern text of Terence. The evidence of the MSS has been supplemented by the citations of the ancient grammarians, especially of Aelius Donatus (fourth century A.D.), whose commentary for five comedies (all but the *Heauton*) has survived. Standard texts today are those of Kauer and Lindsay (Oxford, 1926) and Marouzeau (Paris, 1942-49).

The establishment of a more accurate text of Plautus' comedies was the work of nineteenth-century scholars, and especially of Ritschl, who was known as *sospitator Plauti*, "the preserver of Plautus." Joachim Camerarius in the sixteenth century had used MSS B and C as the basis for his edition of the plays, but the great advance in our knowledge of Plautus' text came with the discovery and deciphering of the Ambrosian Palimpsest. Ritschl's many important papers on Plautus, published in 1845 under the title of *Parerga*, and his critical editions of nine comedies (1849-54) laid the foundation of modern Plautine scholarship and rendered obsolete all earlier texts of the plays.[12]

Ritschl's epoch-making edition was continued, revised, and completed by three distinguished scholars who had been his students: Georg Goetz, Gustav Loewe, and Friedrich Schoell. Their editions of the twenty plays (1879-1902), known as the "triumvirate edition," provided the basic critical apparatus for all later work on the text of Plautus, as Umpfenbach's critical edition had done for that of Terence. Studemund's publication in 1889 of the Ambrosian Palimpsest made available the readings of this ancient and very important MS. The most serviceable complete

discovered in 1429; those of the first eight plays seem to have been derived from a "doctored text" similar to J.

[12] E.g., that of K. H. Weise, *M. Acci Plauti Comoediae* (2nd ed., 1847-48). The name of the playwright was correctly restored by Ritschl as T. Maccius Plautus; see above, p. 49.

texts of Plautus for the student today are those of Lindsay (Oxford, 2nd ed., 1910) and Ernout (Paris, 1932-40).

Yet, even today, after a century of intensive scholarship devoted to problems of language, meter, and style, the texts of Plautus and Terence are far from perfect.[13] Lacunae and corrupt passages are numerous, particularly in Plautus, and unless new MSS of great antiquity and reliability are discovered these flaws will never be removed from the text. But to the scholars of the past hundred years we must express our gratitude for their unceasing efforts and amazing achievements. They have enabled us to read the comedies of the two Roman playwrights in a far more accurate form than has been possible since the days of antiquity.

[13] Cf. L. W. Jones, "Ancient Texts of Terence," *CPh* 25 (1930), p. 318: "There is hardly an important Latin author whose text is in worse condition today than that of Terence." But in 1942 Marouzeau refers with greater optimism to the text of Terence as "assez solidement établi" (*Térence*, I, p. 100).

# ABBREVIATIONS

(The following abbreviations are used for references to periodicals and handbooks both in the Bibliography and in the notes to each chapter.)

A & A    Art and Archaeology
AC    Antiquité Classique
AM    Atlantic Monthly
AJPh    American Journal of Philology
AJSL    American Journal of Semitic Languages and Literatures
Ath    Athenaeum

BPhW    Berliner Philologische Wochenschrift
BRL    Bulletin of the John Rylands Library, Manchester
BUTSE    Bulletin of the University of Texas. Studies in English

C & M    Classica et Mediaevalia
CB    Classical Bulletin
CHEL    Cambridge History of English Literature
CJ    Classical Journal
CPh    Classical Philology
CQ    Classical Quarterly
CR    Classical Review
CW    Classical Weekly

ES    Englische Studien

G & R    Greece and Rome
Gl    Glotta. Zeitschrift für griechische und lateinische Sprache

H    Hermes. Zeitschrift für klassische Philologie
Ha    Hermathena
HSCPh    Harvard Studies in Classical Philology

IF    Indogermanische Forschungen

JEGPh    Journal of English and Germanic Philology
JPh    Journal of Philosophy
JRS    Journal of Roman Studies

MB    Musée Belge. Revue de philologie classique
MC    Mondo Classico
MLN    Modern Language Notes
Mn    Mnemosyne. Bibliotheca Classica Batava
MPh    Modern Philology

Neoph    Neophilologus
NJA    Neue Jahrbücher für das klassische Altertum

PAPhA    Proceedings of the American Philological Association
PBA    Proceedings of the British Academy
Ph    Philologus. Zeitschrift für das klassische Altertum
PhQ    Philological Quarterly
PhW    Philologische Wochenschrift
PMLA    Publications of the Modern Language Association of America
PP    Parola del Passato. Rivista di Studi Classici

QJS      Quarterly Journal of Speech
QR       Quarterly Review

RCC     Revue des Cours et Conférences
RE       Real-Encyclopädie der classischen Altertumswissenschaft
REA     Revue des Études Anciennes
REL     Revue des Études Latines
RFC     Rivista di Filologia Classica
RPh     Revue de Philologie, de Littérature et d'Histoire Anciennes

SHAW  Sitzungsberichte der Heidelberger Akademie der Wissenschaften
SIFC    Studi Italiani di Filologia Classica
SPhNC  Studies in Philology, University of North Carolina

TAPhA  Transactions of the American Philological Association

UCPPh  University of California Publications in Classical Philology
UTQ     University of Toronto Quarterly

VAWA  Verhandelingen der koninklijke Akademie van Wetenschappen te Amsterdam

WS      Wiener Studien. Zeitschrift für klassische Philologie

YSE     Yale Studies in English

# BIBLIOGRAPHY

# BIBLIOGRAPHY

This bibliography contains only a selection of the many books, pamphlets, and articles on Plautus and Terence. I have attempted to include the most recent and significant works on the various topics discussed and also older works to which I have had occasion to refer. The General Bibliography contains the authorities cited in more than one chapter.

## SELECTED EDITIONS, COMMENTARIES, AND TRANSLATIONS

### EDITIONS

A. Ernout, *Plaute. Comédies. Texte et Traduction* (Paris, 1932-40). 7 vols.
G. Goetz and F. Schoell, *T. Macci Plauti Comoediae* (Leipzig, 1893-96). 7 vols. (Vol. I, 2nd ed., 1909; Vol. II, 2nd ed., 1904).
R. Kauer and W. M. Lindsay, *P. Terenti Afri Comoediae* (Oxford, 1926).
F. Leo, *Plauti Comoediae* (Berlin, 1895-96). 2 vols.
W. M. Lindsay, *T. Macci Plauti Comoediae* (2nd ed., Oxford, 1910). 2 vols.
J. Marouzeau, *Térence. Comédies. Texte et Traduction* (Paris, 1942-49). 3 vols.

### EDITIONS WITH COMMENTARIES

S. G. Ashmore, *The Comedies of Terence* (New York, 1908).
G. E. Duckworth, *T. Macci Plauti Epidicus, Edited with Critical Apparatus and Commentary* (Princeton, 1940).
K. Dziatzko-E. Hauler, *Ausgewählte Komödien des P. Terentius Afer. I. Phormio* (4th ed., Leipzig, 1913).
P. J. Enk, *Plauti Mercator cum Prolegomenis, Notis Criticis, Commentario Exegetico* (Leiden, 1932). 2 vols.
W. M. Lindsay, *The Captivi of Plautus* (London, 1900).
F. Marx, *Plautus Rudens. Text und Commentar* (Leipzig, 1928). [=*Abhandlungen der philologisch-historischen Klasse der sächsischen Akademie der Wissenschaften*, Band 38, Nr. 5]

### TRANSLATIONS

G. E. Duckworth, *The Complete Roman Drama* (New York, 1942). 2 vols.
P. Nixon, *Plautus* (Loeb Classical Library, 1916-38). 5 vols.
J. Sargeaunt, *Terence* (Loeb Classical Library, 1912). 2 vols.
F. A. Wright and H. L. Rogers, *Three Plays of Plautus* (Broadway Translations, n.d.).

[For the French translations of Ernout and Marouzeau, see above under Editions.]

## GENERAL

S. M. Adams, "Roman Comedy," *UTQ* 7 (1937-38), pp. 514-531.
F. Arnaldi, *Da Plauto a Terenzio. I. Plauto. II. Terenzio* (Napoli, 1946-47). 2 vols.
T. W. Baldwin, *Shakspere's Five-Act Structure. Shakspere's Early Plays on the Background of Renaissance Theories of Five-Act Structure from 1470* (Urbana, 1947).

W. Beare, "Recent Work on the Roman Theatre," *CR* 51 (1937), pp. 105-111.

———, "The Secret of Terence," *Ha* 56 (1940), pp. 21-39.

———, "Contamination in Plautus and Terence," *RPh* 66 (1940), pp. 28-42.

———, "Terence, an Original Dramatist in Rome," *Ha* 71 (1948), pp. 64-82.

———, *The Roman Stage. A Short History of Latin Drama in the Time of the Republic* (London, 1950).

H. Bergson, *Le Rire. Essai sur la signification du comique* (Paris, 1901). Authorized translation into English by C. Brereton and F. Rothwell, with title: *Laughter. An Essay on the Meaning of the Comic* (New York, 1911).

M. Bieber, *The History of the Greek and Roman Theater* (Princeton, 1939).

E. Bignone, *Storia della Letteratura Latina*, Vol. 1 (2nd ed., Firenze, 1946).

W. W. Blancké, *The Dramatic Values in Plautus* (Geneva, N.Y., 1918).

P. Boyancé, "A propos de la 'Satura' dramatique," *REA* 34 (1932), pp. 11-25.

C. H. Buck, Jr., *A Chronology of the Plays of Plautus* (Baltimore, 1940).

H. R. Clifford, "Dramatic Technique and the Originality of Terence," *CJ* 26 (1930-31), pp. 605-618.

W. L. Collins, *Plautus and Terence* (Edinburgh, 1873).

L. Cooper, *An Aristotelian Theory of Comedy with an Adaptation of the Poetics and a Translation of the 'Tractatus Coislinianus'* (New York, 1922).

C. C. Coulter, *Retractatio in the Ambrosian and Palatine Recensions of Plautus* (Baltimore, 1911).

G. Curcio, *Storia della Letteratura Latina. I. Le origini e il periodo arcaico* (Napoli, 1920).

A. Dieterich, *Pulcinella. Pompejanische Wandbilder und Römische Satyrspiele* (Leipzig, 1897).

G. E. Duckworth, "The Dramatic Function of the *servus currens* in Roman Comedy," in *Classical Studies presented to Edward Capps* (Princeton, 1936), pp. 93-102.

———, "The Unnamed Characters in the Plays of Plautus," *CPh* 33 (1938), pp. 267-282.

———, Review of Buck, *A Chronology of the Plays of Plautus, AJPh* 64 (1943), pp. 348-352.

———, Review of Dunkin, *Post-Aristophanic Comedy, AJPh* 68 (1947), pp. 419-426.

———, "Plautus: The Other Nineteen Plays," *CW* 41 (1947-48), pp. 82-91.

J. W. Duff, *A Literary History of Rome From the Origins to the Close of the Golden Age* (London, 1909).

P. S. Dunkin, *Post-Aristophanic Comedy. Studies in the Social Outlook of Middle and New Comedy at Both Athens and Rome* (Urbana, 1946). [=*Illinois Studies in Language and Literature*, Vol. 31, Nos. 3-4]

P. J. Enk, *Handboek der Latijnse Letterkunde van de oudste tijden tot het opstreden van Cicero. Tweede Deel: Het Tijdvak van Letterkundige Ontwikkeling onder Invloed van het Hellenisme: 1. De Dichters Livius Andronicus, Naevius en Plautus* (Zutphen, 1937). 2 vols.

P. J. Enk, "Terence as an Adapter of Greek Comedies," *Mn* 13 (1947), pp. 81-93.

P. Fabia, *Les Prologues de Térence* (Paris, 1888).

E. W. Fay, "Further Notes on the Mostellaria of Plautus," *AJPh* 24 (1903), pp. 245-277.

W. S. Ferguson, *Hellenistic Athens. An Historical Essay* (London, 1911).

D. E. Fields, *The Technique of Exposition in Roman Comedy* (Chicago, 1938).

R. C. Flickinger, *The Greek Theater and its Drama* (3rd ed., Chicago, 1926).

———, "A Study of Terence's Prologues," *PhQ* 6 (1927), pp. 235-269.

———, "On the Originality of Terence," *PhQ* 7 (1928), pp. 97-114.

———, "Terence and Menander," *CJ* 26 (1930-31), pp. 676-694.

———, "Terence and Menander Once More," *CJ* 28 (1932-33), pp. 515-522.

E. Fraenkel, *Plautinisches im Plautus* (Berlin, 1922). [=*Philologische Untersuchungen*, Heft 28]

———, "Cn. Naevius," *RE* Supplementband 6 (Stuttgart, 1935), cols. 622-640.

T. Frank, *Life and Literature in the Roman Republic* (Berkeley, 1930). [=*Sather Classical Lectures*, Vol. 7]

———, "On the Date of Plautus' *Casina* and its Revival," *AJPh* 54 (1933), pp. 368-372.

A. H. Gilbert, *Literary Criticism. Plato to Dryden* (New York, 1940).

A. W. Gomme, "Menander," in *Essays in Greek History and Literature* (Oxford, 1937), pp. 249-295.

L. Gourde, *O.S.B.*, "Terence the Philosopher," *CJ* 42 (1946-47), pp. 431-433.

E. H. Haight, *The Symbolism of the House Door in Classical Poetry* (New York, 1950).

C. H. Haile, *The Clown in Greek Literature after Aristophanes* (Princeton, 1913).

E. Hamilton, *The Roman Way* (New York, 1932).

P. W. Harsh, "A Study of Dramatic Technique as a Means of Appreciating the Originality of Terence," *CW* 28 (1934-35), pp. 161-165.

———, *Studies in Dramatic "Preparation" in Roman Comedy* (Chicago, 1935).

———, "Certain Features of Technique Found in Both Greek and Roman Drama," *AJPh* 58 (1937), pp. 282-293.

———, *A Handbook of Classical Drama* (Stanford, 1944).

F. Hornstein, "Die Echtheitsfrage der Plautinischen Prologe," *WS* 36 (1914), pp. 104-121.

J. N. Hough, "The Use of Greek Words by Plautus," *AJPh* 55 (1934), pp. 346-364.

———, "The Development of Plautus' Art," *CPh* 30 (1935), pp. 43-57.

———, "The Structure of the *Asinaria*," *AJPh* 58 (1937), pp. 19-37.

———, "The Understanding of Intrigue: A Study in Plautine Chronology," *AJPh* 60 (1939), pp. 422-435.

———, "Link-Monologues and Plautine Chronology," *TAPhA* 70 (1939), pp. 231-241.

———, "Miscellanea Plautina: Vulgarity, Extra-Dramatic Speeches, Roman Allusions," *TAPhA* 71 (1940), pp. 186-198.

J. N. Hough, "The Reverse Comic Foil in Plautus," *TAPhA* 73 (1942), pp. 108-118.

——, "The Structure of the *Captivi*," *AJPh* 63 (1942), pp. 26-37.

——, "The *Numquid Vis* Formula in Roman Comedy," *AJPh* 66 (1945), pp. 282-302.

O. Immisch, "Zur Frage der Plautinischen Cantica," *SHAW* 14 (1923), Abh. 7, pp. 1-41.

G. Jachmann, *Plautinisches und Attisches* (Berlin, 1931). [=*Problemata*, Heft 3]

——, "P. Terentius Afer," *RE*, Zweite Reihe 9 (Stuttgart, 1934), cols. 598-650.

M. Johnston, *Exits and Entrances in Roman Comedy* (Geneva, N.Y., 1933).

L. W. Jones and C. R. Morey, *The Miniatures of the Manuscripts of Terence Prior to the Thirteenth Century* (Princeton, 1930-31). 2 vols.

C. Knapp, "Travel in Ancient Times as Seen in Plautus and Terence," *CPh* 2 (1907), pp. 1-24, 281-304.

——, "Notes on Plautus and Terence," *AJPh* 35 (1914), pp. 12-31.

M. Knorr, *Das griechische Vorbild der Mostellaria des Plautus* (Coburg, 1934).

W. C. Korfmacher, "Humorous Effect in Roman Comedy," *CB* 10 (1933-34), pp. 17-20.

W. E. J. Kuiper, "Grieksche Origineelen en Latijnsche Navolgingen. Zes Komedies van Menander bij Terentius en Plautus," *VAWA* 38 (1936), 2, pp. 1-294.

I. Lana, "Terenzio e il movimento filellenico in Roma," *RFC* 75, N.S. 25 (1947), pp. 44-80, 155-175.

P. Langen, *Plautinische Studien* (Berlin, 1886). [=*Berliner Studien für Classische Philologie und Archaeologie*, 5, 1]

G. W. Leffingwell, *Social and Private Life at Rome in the Time of Plautus and Terence* (New York, 1918). [=*Columbia University Studies in History, Economics and Public Law*, Vol. 81, 1]

P. E. Legrand, *Daos. Tableau de la comédie grecque pendant la période dite nouvelle* (Paris, 1910). Translated into English by J. Loeb with the title *The New Greek Comedy* (London, 1917). See above, chap. 2, n. 13.

P. Lejay, *Histoire de la littérature latine des origines à Plautue* (Paris, 1923).

——, *Plaute* (Paris, 1925).

F. Leo, *Plautinische Forschungen zur Kritik und Geschichte der Komödie* (2nd ed., Berlin, 1912).

——, *Geschichte der römischen Literatur. I. Die archaische Literatur* (Berlin, 1913).

A. M. G. Little, "Plautus and Popular Drama," *HSCPh* 49 (1938), pp. 205-228.

C. W. Mendell, *Our Seneca* (New Haven, 1941).

G. Michaut, *Sur les tréteaux latins* (Paris, 1912).

——, *Plaute* (Paris, 1920). 2 vols.

C. R. Morey (see under L. W. Jones).

R. G. Moulton, *The Ancient Classical Drama. A Study in Literary Evolution* (2nd ed., Oxford, 1898).

A. Nicoll, *Masks Mimes and Miracles. Studies in the Popular Theatre* (London, 1931).

G. Norwood, *The Art of Terence* (Oxford, 1923).

―――, *Plautus and Terence* (New York, 1932).

―――, Review of Duckworth, *The Complete Roman Drama, UTQ* 13 (1943-44), pp. 235-241.

W. A. Oldfather, "Roman Comedy," *CW* 7 (1913-14), pp. 217-222.

H. T. Perry, *Masters of Dramatic Comedy and their Social Themes* (Cambridge, Mass., 1939.).

L. A. Post, "The Art of Terence," *CW* 23 (1929-30), pp. 121-128.

―――, "The 'Vis' of Menander," *TAPhA* 62 (1931), pp. 203-234.

―――, "Menander and Terence," *CW* 26 (1932-33), pp. 33-36.

―――, "Aristotle and Menander," *TAPhA* 69 (1938), pp. 1-42.

B. Prehn, *Quaestiones Plautinae* (Breslau, 1916).

H. W. Prescott, "The *Amphitruo* of Plautus," *CPh* 8 (1913), pp. 14-22.

―――, "The Interpretation of Roman Comedy," *CPh* 11 (1916), pp. 125-147.

―――, "The Antecedents of Hellenistic Comedy," *CPh* 12 (1917), pp. 405-425; 13 (1918), pp. 113-137; 14 (1919), pp. 108-135.

―――, "Inorganic Rôles in Roman Comedy," *CPh* 15 (1920), pp. 245-281.

―――, "Criteria of Originality in Plautus," *TAPhA* 63 (1932), pp. 103-125.

―――, "Silent Rôles in Roman Comedy," *CPh* 31 (1936), pp. 97-119; 32 (1937), pp. 193-209.

―――, "Link Monologues in Roman Comedy," *CPh* 34 (1939), pp. 1-23, 116-126.

―――, "Exit Monologues in Roman Comedy, *CPh* 37 (1942), pp. 1-21.

E. K. Rand, "The Art of Terence's *Eunuchus*," *TAPhA* 63 (1932), pp. 54-72.

―――, "Térence et l'esprit comique," *RCC* 36 (1934-35), pp. 385-397.

M. Schanz, *Geschichte der römischen Literatur*, I, 4th ed. by C. Hosius (München, 1927).

W. B. Sedgwick, "The *Cantica* of Plautus," *CR* 39 (1925), pp. 55-58.

―――, "The Composition of the *Stichus*," *CR* 39 (1925), pp. 59-60.

―――, "The Dating of Plautus' Plays," *CQ* 24 (1930), pp. 102-105.

W. Y. Sellar, *The Roman Poets of the Republic* (3rd ed., Oxford, 1889).

M. F. Smith, *The Technique of Solution in Roman Comedy* (Chicago, 1940).

P. E. Sonnenburg, "T. Maccius Plautus," *RE* 27 Halbband (Stuttgart, 1928), cols. 95-126.

W. J. M. Starkie, "An Aristotelian Analysis of 'the Comic,' illustrated from Aristophanes, Rabelais, Shakespeare, and Molière," *Ha* 42 (1920), pp. 26-51.

D. C. Stuart, *The Development of Dramatic Art* (New York, 1928).

N. Terzaghi, *Prolegomeni a Terenzio* (Torino, 1931).

A. Thierfelder, *De rationibus interpolationum Plautinarum* (Leipzig, 1929).

J. A. K. Thomson, *The Classical Background of English Literature* (London, 1948).

T. B. L. Webster, "Forethoughts on Later Greek Comedy," *BRL* 29 (1945-46), pp. 143-159.

―――, *Studies in Menander* (Manchester, 1950).

K. M. Westaway, *The Original Element in Plautus* (Cambridge, 1917).

K. F. Weston, "The Illustrated Terence Manuscripts," *HSCPh* 14 (1903), pp. 37-54 and Plates 1-96.

A. L. Wheeler, "The Plot of the Epidicus," *AJPh* 38 (1917), pp. 237-264.
H. E. Wieand, *Deception in Plautus. A Study in the Technique of Roman Comedy* (Boston, 1920).
F. A. Wright, *Three Roman Poets. Plautus, Catullus, Ovid. Their Times and Works* (New York, 1938).
F. W. Wright, *Cicero and the Theater* (Northampton, 1931). [=*Smith College Classical Studies*, No. 11]

### CHAPTER 1. Early Italian Popular Comedy

W. Beare, "Plautus and the *Fabula Atellana*," *CR* 44 (1930), pp. 165-168.
————, "Quintilian VI. iii. 47 and the *Fabula Atellana*," *CR* 51 (1937), pp. 213-215.
————, "The Italian Origins of Latin Drama," *Ha* 54 (1939), pp. 30-53.
T. Frank, "The Status of Actors at Rome," *CPh* 26 (1931), pp. 11-20.
W. M. Green, "The Status of Actors at Rome," *CPh* 28 (1933), pp. 301-304.
G. L. Hendrickson, "The Dramatic Satura and the Old Comedy at Rome," *AJPh* 15 (1894), pp. 1-30.
————, "A Pre-Varronian Chapter of Roman Literary History," *AJPh* 19 (1898), pp. 285-311.
C. Knapp, "The Dramatic Satura among the Romans, *PAPhA* 40 (1909), pp. lii-lvi.
————, "The Sceptical Assault on the Roman Tradition Concerning the Dramatic Satura," *AJPh* 33 (1912), pp. 125-148.
————, "Horace, *Epistles*, II, I, 139 ff., and Livy, VII, 2," *TAPhA* 43 (1912), pp. 125-142.
F. Leo, "Livius und Horaz über die Vorgeschichte des römischen Dramas," *H* 39 (1904), pp. 63-77.
H. Reich, *Der Mimus* (Berlin, 1903).
R. W. Reynolds, "Verrius Flaccus and the Early Mime at Rome," *Ha* 61 (1943), pp. 56-62.
————, "The Adultery Mime," *CQ* 40 (1946), pp. 77-84.
B. L. Ullman, "Satura and Satire," *CPh* 8 (1913), pp. 172-194.
————, "Dramatic 'Satura,'" *CPh* 9 (1914), pp. 1-23.
————, "The Present Status of the Satura Question," *SPhNC* 17 (1920), pp. 379-401.
R. H. Webb, "On the Origin of Roman Satire," *CPh* 7 (1912), pp. 177-189.

### CHAPTER 2. Greek Comedy

#### GREEK COMEDY IN GENERAL

P. W. Harsh, *A Handbook of Classical Drama* (Stanford, 1944), pp. 257-327.
G. Norwood, *Greek Comedy* (London, 1931).
D. L. Page, *Greek Literary Papyri* (Loeb Classical Library, 1942), Vol. 1, pp. 193-325.
A. W. Pickard-Cambridge, *Dithyramb Tragedy and Comedy* (Oxford, 1927), pp. 225-415.
H. J. Rose, *A Handbook of Greek Literature* (London, 1934), pp. 214-252.

#### ARISTOPHANES

M. Croiset, *Aristophanes and the Political Parties at Athens* (English translation by J. Loeb, London, 1909).

V. Ehrenberg, *The People of Aristophanes: A Sociology of Old Attic Comedy* (Oxford, 1943).
L. E. Lord, *Aristophanes: His Plays and his Influence* (New York, 1925).
G. Murray, *Aristophanes: A Study* (Oxford, 1933).
W. J. Oates and E. O'Neill, Jr., *The Complete Greek Drama* (New York, 1938), Vol. II, pp. 421-1116.
B. B. Rogers, *Aristophanes, with the English translation of B. B. Rogers* (Loeb Classical Library, 1924). 3 vols.

## MENANDER AND NEW COMEDY

F. G. Allinson, *Menander: The Principal Fragments* (Loeb Classical Library, 1921).
M. Andrewes "Euripides and Menander," *CQ* 18 (1924), pp. 1-10.
A. Kolár, "Der Zusammenhang der neuen Komödie mit der alten," *PhW* 41 (1921), cols. 688-696.
T. W. Lumb, "The New Menander, and other new Fragments of the New Comedy," in J. U. Powell and E. A. Barber, *New Chapters in the History of Greek Literature* (Oxford, 1921), pp. 66-98.
G. Murray, "Menander," in J. U. Powell and E. A. Barber, *New Chapters in the History of Greek Literature*, Second Series (Oxford, 1929), pp. 9-34. In revised form in Murray, *Aristophanes*, pp. 221-263.
————, *Two Plays of Menander* (New York, 1945).
C. R. Post, "The Dramatic Art of Menander," *HSCPh* 24 (1913), pp. 111-145.
L. A. Post, *Menander: Three Plays* (Broadway Translations, 1929). In revised form in Oates and O'Neill, *The Complete Greek Drama*. Vol. II, pp. 1117-1199.
————, "Menander in Current Criticism," *TAPhA* 65 (1934), pp. 13-34.

[For Menander see also General Bibliography under Ferguson, Gomme, Legrand, Post, Prescott, and Webster.]

## CHAPTER 3. The Golden Age of Drama at Rome

F. F. Abbott, "The Theatre as a Factor in Roman Politics under the Republic," *TAPhA* 38 (1908), pp. 49-56.
R. Argenio, "Il 'Plocium' di Cecilio Stazio," *MC* 7 (1937), pp. 359-368.
W. Beare, "The Date of the *Casina*," *CR* 48 (1934), pp. 123-124.
————, "Titus Maccus Plautus," *CR* 53 (1939), pp. 115-116.
————, "*Crepidata, Palliata, Tabernaria, Togata*," *CR* 53 (1939), pp. 166-168 [=*The Roman Stage*, pp. 256-258].
————, "The Fabula Togata," *Ha* 55 (1940), pp. 35-55.
————, "When Did Livius Andronicus Come to Rome?" *CQ* 34 (1940), pp. 11-19.
————, "The Life of Terence," *Ha* 59 (1942), pp. 20-29.
————, "Plays for Performance and Plays for Recitation: a Roman Contrast," *Ha* 65 (1945), pp. 8-19.
R. Blum, "Studi Terenziani: II. Didascalie e prologhi," *SIFC* 13 (1936), pp. 106-116.
R. M. Brown, *A Study of the Scipionic Circle* (Scottsdale, 1934). [=Iowa Studies in Classical Philology, No. 1]
G. Coppola, *Il Teatro Tragico in Roma Republicana* (Bologna, 1940).
E. H. Clift, *Latin Pseudepigrapha. A Study in Literary Attributions* (Baltimore, 1945).

P. Faider, "Le poète comique Cécilius, sa vie et son oeuvre," *MB* 12 (1908), pp. 269-341; 13 (1909), pp. 5-35.

C. A. Forbes, "Plautus 'in operis artificum scaenicorum,' " *CW* 39 (1945-46), pp. 44-45.

T. Frank, "The Decline of Roman Tragedy," *CJ* 12 (1916-17), pp. 176-187.

———, "Naevius and Free Speech," *AJPh* 48 (1927), pp. 105-110.

———, "On Suetonius' Life of Terence," *AJPh* 54 (1933), pp. 269-273.

———, "Notes on Plautus," *AJPh* 58 (1937), pp. 345-349.

L. Gestri, "Studi Terenziani: 1. La cronologia," *SIFC* 13 (1936), pp. 61-105.

G. K. G. Henry, "Roman Actors," *SPhNC* 16 (1919), pp. 334-382.

T. Hermann, "La tragédie nationale chez les Romains," *C & M* 9 (1948), pp. 141-154.

D. P. Lockwood, "The Plot of the *Querolus* and the Folk-tales of Disguised Treasure," *TAPhA* 44 (1913), pp. 215-232.

H. Mattingly and E. S. G. Robinson, "The Prologue to the *Casina* of Plautus," *CR* 47 (1933), pp. 52-54.

———, "Nummus," *AJPh* 56 (1935), pp. 225-231.

E. L. Minar, Jr., "Terence and the Poets' Guild," *PAPhA* 76 (1945), pp. xxxvi f.

H. Oppermann, "Zur Entwicklung der Fabula Palliata," *H* 74 (1939), pp. 113-129.

M. L. Pasculli, *Studio sulla Fabula Praetexta* (Palermo, 1921).

R. W. Reynolds, "Criticism of Individuals in Roman Popular Comedy," *CQ* 37 (1943), pp. 37-45.

L. Robinson, "Censorship in Republican Drama," *CJ* 42 (1946-47), pp. 147-150.

D. O. Robson, "The Nationality of the Poet Caecilius Statius," *AJPh* 59 (1938), pp. 301-308.

E. M. Sanford, "The Tragedies of Livius Andronicus," *CJ* 18 (1922-23), pp. 274-285.

W. B. Sedgwick, "Plautine Chronology," *AJPh* 70 (1949), pp. 376-383.

E. G. Sihler, "The Collegium Poetarum at Rome," *AJPh* 26 (1905), pp. 1-21.

F. Skutsch, "Caecilius Statius," *RE* 5 Halbband (Stuttgart, 1897), cols. 1189-1192.

E. M. Steuart, "Some Notes on Roman Tragedy," *AJPh* 47 (1926), pp. 272-278.

D. R. Stuart, "Author's Lives as Revealed in their Works: A Critical Résumé," in *Classical Studies in honor of John C. Rolfe* (ed. G. D. Hadzsits, Philadelphia, 1931), pp. 285-304.

A. F. West, "On a Patriotic Passage in the *Miles Gloriosus* of Plautus," *AJPh* 8 (1887), pp. 15-33.

*CHAPTER 4. Presentation and Staging*

F. Bauer, *Quaestiones scaenicae Plautinae* (Strassburg, 1902).

W. Beare, "Side-Entrances and ΠΕΡΙΑΚΤΟΙ in the Hellenistic Theatre," *CQ* 32 (1938), pp. 205-210 [=*The Roman Stage*, pp. 240-247].

———, "Seats in the Greek and Roman Theatres," *CR* 53 (1939), pp. 51-55 [=*The Roman Stage*, pp. 233-239].

W. Beare, "The *Angiportum* and Roman Drama," *Ha* 53 (1939), pp. 88-89 [=*The Roman Stage*, pp. 248-255].

———, "Masks on the Roman Stage," *CQ* 33 (1939), pp. 139-146.

———, Review of Weissinger, *A Study of Act Divisions in Classical Drama, Ha* 55 (1940), pp. 114-116.

———, "The Roman Stage Curtain," *Ha* 58 (1941), pp. 104-115 [=*The Roman Stage*, pp. 259-266].

———, "Horace, Donatus, and the Five-Act Law," *Ha* 67 (1946), pp. 52-59.

———, "The Roman Origin of the Five-Act Law," *Ha* 72 (1948), pp. 44-70.

———, "Χοροῦ in the *Heautontimorumenos* and the *Plutus*," *Ha* 74 (1949), pp. 26-38.

———, "Slave Costume in New Comedy," *CQ* 43 (1949), pp. 30-31.

C. C. Conrad, *The Technique of Continuous Action in Roman Comedy* (Menasha, 1915).

C. O. Dalman, *De aedibus scaenicis comoediae novae* (Leipzig, 1929). [=*Klassisch-Philologische Studien*, Heft 3]

P. Fabia, "Les théâtres de Rome au temps de Plaute et de Térence," *RPh* 21 (1897), pp. 11-25.

R. C. Flickinger, "ΧΟΡΟΥ in Terence's *Heauton*, the Shifting of Choral Rôles in Menander, and Agathon's ʼΕΜΒΟΛΙΜΑ," *CPh* 7 (1912), pp. 24-34.

———, Review of Conrad, *The Technique of Continuous Action in Roman Comedy, CW* 10 (1916-17), pp. 147-151.

A. Freté, "Essai sur la structure dramatique des comédies de Plaute," *REL* 7 (1929), pp. 282-294; 8 (1930), pp. 36-81.

A. S. F. Gow, "On the Use of Masks in Roman Comedy," *JRS* 2 (1912), pp. 65-77.

W. M. Green, "The Ritual Validity of the Ludi Scaenici," *CW* 26 (1932-33), pp. 156-157.

P. W. Harsh, "*Angiportum, Platea*, and *Vicus*," *CPh* 32 (1937), pp. 44-58.

H. M. Kemble, "A Study of the Significance of the Wing-Entrances from the Point of View of an Amateur Play-Director," *PAPhA* 61 (1930), p. xl.

C. Knapp, "The Roman Theater," *A & A* 1 (1915), pp. 137-152, 187-204.

C. M. Kurrelmeyer, *The Economy of Actors in Plautus* (Graz, 1932).

H. W. Prescott, "Three *Puer*-Scenes in Plautus, and the Distribution of Rôles," *HSCPh* 21 (1910), pp. 31-50.

———, "The Doubling of Rôles in Roman Comedy," *CPh* 18 (1923), pp. 23-34.

———, Review of Kurrelmeyer, *The Economy of Actors in Plautus, CPh* 29 (1934), pp. 350-351.

———, Review of Duckworth, *T. Macci Plauti Epidicus, CPh* 36 (1941), pp. 281-285.

E. F. Rambo, "The Significance of the Wing-Entrances in Roman Comedy," *CPh* 10 (1915), pp. 411-431.

K. Rees, *The So-Called Rule of Three Actors in the Classical Greek Drama* (Chicago, 1908).

———, "The Three Actor Rule in Menander," *CPh* 5 (1910), pp. 291-302.

C. Saunders, *Costume in Roman Comedy* (New York, 1909).

———, "The Introduction of Masks on the Roman Stage," *AJPh* 32 (1911), pp. 58-73.

C. Saunders, "Altars on the Roman Comic Stage," *TAPhA* 42 (1911), pp. 91-103.
——, "The Site of Dramatic Performances at Rome in the Times of Plautus and Terence," *TAPhA* 44 (1913), pp. 87-97.
L. R. Taylor, "The Opportunities for Dramatic Performances in the Time of Plautus and Terence," *TAPhA* 68 (1937), pp. 284-304.
J. C. Watson, "The Relation of the Scene-Headings to the Miniatures in Manuscripts of Terence," *HSCPh* 14 (1903), pp. 55-172.
R. T. Weissinger, *A Study of Act Divisions in Classical Drama* (Scottdale, 1940). [=*Iowa Studies in Classical Philology*, No. 9]

## CHAPTER 5. Stage Conventions and Techniques

K. S. Bennett, *The Motivation of Exits in Greek and Latin Comedy* (Ann Arbor, 1932).
J. D. Bickford, *Soliloquy in Ancient Comedy* (Princeton, 1922).
C. C. Conrad, "On Terence, Adelphoe 511-516," *UCPPh* 2 (1916), pp. 291-303.
R. C. Flickinger, "The Factual Basis for Representing Indoor Scenes *al Fresco* in Roman Comedy," *CJ* 34 (1938-39), pp. 538-540.
V. E. Hiatt, *Eavesdropping in Roman Comedy* (Chicago, 1946).
J. N. Hough, "Continuity of Time in Plautus," *CPh* 31 (1936), pp. 244-252.
——, "Plautine Technique in Delayed Exits," *CPh* 35 (1940), pp. 39-48.
D. M. Key, *The Introduction of Characters by Name in Greek and Roman Comedy* (Chicago, 1923).
C. Knapp, "References in Plautus and Terence to Plays, Players, and Playwrights," *CPh* 14 (1919), pp. 35-55.
W. Kraus, "*Ad spectatores* in der römischen Komödie," *WS* 52 (1934), pp. 66-83.
E. T. M(errill), "Plautus, *Amph.* 551 ff. and Simultaneous Action in Roman Comedy," *CPh* 11 (1916), pp. 340-341.
W. W. Mooney, *The House-Door on the Ancient Stage* (Baltimore, 1914).
K. Rees, "The Function of the Πρόθυρον in the Production of Greek Plays," *CPh* 10 (1915), pp. 117-138.
E. Riedel, "The Dramatic Structure of Terence's *Phormio*," *CW* 11 (1917-18), pp. 25-28.

## CHAPTER 6. Theme and Treatment

M. E. Agnew, "Lessing's Critical Opinion of the *Captivi* of Plautus," *CW* 39 (1945-46), pp. 66-70.
C. W. Amerasinghe, "The Part of the Slave in Terence's Drama," *G & R* 19 (1950), pp. 62-72.
B. Brotherton, "The Plot of the *Miles Gloriosus*," *TAPhA* 55 (1924), pp. 128-136.
G. E. Duckworth, Review of Kuiper, *Het origineel van Plautus' Epidicus,* *CPh* 35 (1940), pp. 86-90.
——, Review of Kuiper, *Two Comedies by Apollodorus of Carystus,* *CPh* 35 (1940), pp. 201-205.
——, Review of Kuiper, *Diphilus' Doel en Deel in de Rudens van Plautus, CPh* 35 (1940), pp. 201-205.
——, Review of Kuiper, *The Greek Aulularia, CW* 34 (1940-41), pp. 260-261.

J. N. Hough, Review of Kuiper, *Two Comedies by Apollodorus of Carystus*, AJPh 62 (1941), pp. 237-239.

R. G. Kent, "Variety and Monotony in Plautine Plots," PhQ 2 (1923), pp. 164-172, 315.

C. W. Keyes, "Half-Sister Marriage in New Comedy and the *Epidicus*," TAPhA 71 (1940), pp. 217-229.

W. E. J. Kuiper, *Two Comedies by Apollodorus of Carystus. Terence's Hecyra and Phormio* (Leiden, 1938). [=*Mn*, Suppl. 1]

———, *Het origineel van Plautus' Epidicus* (Amsterdam, 1938). [=*Attische Familiekomodies van omstreeks 300 v. Chr.*, 1]

———, *Diphilus' doel en deel in de Rudens van Plautus* (Amsterdam, 1938). [=*Attische Familiekomodies van omstreeks 300 v. Chr.*, 11]

———, *The Greek Aulularia. A Study of the Original of Plautus' Masterpiece* (Leiden, 1940). [=*Mn*, Suppl. 11]

R. A. Pack, "Errors as Subjects of Comic Mirth," CPh 33 (1938), pp. 405-410.

H. W. Prescott, "The Comedy of Errors," CPh 24 (1929), pp. 32-41.

L. A. Post, Review of Kuiper, *Grieksche Origineelen en Latijnsche Navolgingen*, AJPh 59 (1938), pp. 367-369.

F. Wehrli, *Motivstudien zur griechischen Komödie* (Zurich, 1936).

## CHAPTER 7. Methods of Composition

C. C. Coulter, "The Composition of the *Rudens* of Plautus," CPh 8 (1913), pp. 57-64.

G. E. Duckworth, "The Structure of the *Miles Gloriosus*," CPh 30 (1935), pp. 228-246.

P. J. Enk, "Quelques observations sur la manière dont Plaute s'est comporté envers ses originaux," RPh 64 (1938), pp. 289-294.

D. H. Fenton, *Repetition of Thought in Plautus* (New Haven, 1921).

R. M. Haywood, "On the Unity of the *Miles Gloriosus*," AJPh 65 (1944), pp. 382-386.

J. B. Hofmann, "*contaminare*," IF 53 (1935), pp. 187-195.

J. N. Hough, *The Composition of the Pseudolus of Plautus* (Lancaster, 1931).

O. Koehler, *De Hautontimorumeni Terentianae compositione* (Leipzig, 1908).

A. Körte, "Contaminare," BPhW 36 (1916), cols. 979-981.

B. Krysiniel, *Der plautinische Poenulus und sein attisches Vorbild* (Wilno, 1932).

———, *Die Technik des plautinischen Miles Gloriosus* (Wilno, 1938).

B. Krysiniel-Józefowicz, *De quibusdam Plauti exemplaribus Graecis. Philemo-Plautus* (Toruń, 1949).

H. Lucas, "Die ersten Adelphen des Menander," PhW 58 (1938), cols. 1101-1104.

W. Schwering, "Die sogenannte Kontamination in der lateinischen Komödie," NJA 37 (1916), pp. 167-185.

R. Waltz, "*Contaminare* chez Térence," REL 16 (1938), pp. 269-274.

## CHAPTER 8. Foreshadowing and Suspense

M. Andrewes, "Some Stage Conventions in the Classics," G & R 16 (1947), pp. 29-38.

W. Beare, "The Priority of the *Mercator*," CR 42 (1928), pp. 214-215.

G. E. Duckworth, *Foreshadowing and Suspense in the Epics of Homer, Apollonius, and Vergil* (Princeton, 1933).

———, "Dramatic Suspense in Plautus," *CW* 35 (1941-42), p. 196.

H. Law, "The Metrical Arrangement of the Fragments of the *Bacchides*," *CPh* 24 (1929), pp. 197-201.

N. T. Pratt, Jr., *Dramatic Suspense in Seneca and in His Greek Precursors* (Princeton, 1939).

D. C. Stuart, "Foreshadowing and Suspense in the Euripidean Prolog," *SPhNC* 15 (1918), pp. 295-306.

## CHAPTER 9. Characters and Characterization

V. D'Agostino, "La figura del parassito in Plauto," *MC* 7 (1937), Suppl., pp. 90-110.

B. Croce, "Studi su poesie antiche e moderne, 1. Intorno alle commedie di Terenzio," *La Critica* 34 (1936), pp. 401-423. [Reprinted with minor changes in *Poesia Antica e Moderna* (2nd ed., Bari, 1943), pp. 1-30.]

E. R. Godsey, "Phormio the Magnificent," *CW* 22 (1928-29), pp. 65-67.

G. K. G. Henry, "The Characters of Terence," *SPhNC* 12 (1915), pp. 55-98.

W. H. Juniper, "Character Portrayal in Plautus," *CJ* 31 (1935-36), pp. 276-288.

C. J. Kraemer, Jr., "In Defence of Chaerea in the *Eunuch* of Terence," *CJ* 23 (1927-28), pp. 662-667.

J. O. Lofberg, "The Sycophant-Parasite," *CPh* 15 (1920), pp. 61-72.

———, "Phormio and 'Art for Art's Sake,'" *CW* 22 (1928-29), pp. 183-184.

A. de Lorenzi, *I precedenti Greci della commedia Romana* (Napoli, 1946).

E. Schild, *Die dramaturgische Rolle der Sklaven bei Plautus und Terenz* (Basel, 1917).

H. Siess, "Über die Charakterzeichnung in den Komödien des Terenz," *WS* 28 (1906), pp. 229-262; 29 (1907), pp. 81-109, 289-320.

O. Stotz, *De lenonis in comoedia figura* (Darmstadt, 1920).

O. L. Wilner, "Contrast and Repetition as Devices in the Technique of Character Portrayal in Roman Comedy," *CPh* 25 (1930), pp. 56-71.

———, "The Character Treatment of Inorganic Rôles in Roman Comedy," *CPh* 26 (1931), pp. 264-283.

———, "The Technical Device of Direct Description of Character in Roman Comedy," *CPh* 33 (1938), pp. 20-36.

## CHAPTER 10. Thought and Moral Tone

F. D. Allen, "On 'os columnatum' (Plaut. M. G. 211) and Ancient Instruments of Confinement," *HSCPh* 7 (1896), pp. 37-64.

W. Beare, "Plautus and his Public," *CR* 42 (1928), pp. 106-111.

M. Berceanu, *La vente consensuelle dans les comédies de Plaute* (Paris, 1907).

P. R. Coleman-Norton, "Philosophical Aspects of Early Roman Drama," *CPh* 31 (1936), pp. 320-337.

G. Colin, *Rome et la Grèce de 200 à 146 avant Jésus Christ* (Paris, 1905). [=*Bibliothèque des écoles françaises d'Athènes et de Rome*, 94]

F. O. Copley, "Emotional Conflict and its Significance in the Lesbia-Poems of Catullus," *AJPh* 70 (1949), pp. 22-40.

C. T. Cruttwell, *A History of Roman Literature* (London, 1877).
M. Delcourt, "Le prix des esclaves dans les comédies latines," *AC* 17 (1948), pp. 123-132.
O. Fredershausen, *De iure Plautino et Terentiano* (Göttingen, 1906).
———, "Weitere Studien über das Recht bei Plautus und Terenz," *H* 47 (1912), pp. 199-249.
W. M. Green, "Greek and Roman Law in the *Trinummus* of Plautus," *CPh* 24 (1929), pp. 183-192.
C. B. Gulick, "Omens and Augury in Plautus," *HSCPh* 7 (1896), pp. 235-247.
L. Gurlitt, *Erotica Plautina. Eine Auswahl erotischer Szenen aus Plautus* (München, 1921).
T. Hubrich, *De diis Plautinis Terentianisque* (Königsberg, 1883).
D. R. Lee, *Child-Life, Adolescence and Marriage in Greek New Comedy and in the Comedies of Plautus* (Menasha, 1919).
S. G. Oliphant, "The Use of the Omen in Plautus and Terence," *CJ* 7 (1911-12), pp. 165-173.
E. Riess, "Notes on Plautus," *CQ* 35 (1941), pp. 150-162.
A. Schwind, *Über das Recht bei Terenz* (Wurzburg, 1901).
E. B. Stevens, "Topics of Pity in the Poetry of the Roman Republic," *AJPh* 62 (1941), pp. 426-440.
H. M. Toliver, "Roman Comedy and the State Cult," *TAPhA* 80 (1949), p. 432.

## CHAPTER 11. The Comic Spirit in Character and Situation

J. W. H. Atkins, *Literary Criticism in Antiquity. A Sketch of its Development* (Cambridge, 1934). 2 vols.
———, *English Literary Criticism: the Renascence* (London, 1947).
J. W. Basore, *The Scholia on Hypokrisis in the Commentary of Donatus* (Baltimore, 1908).
W. W. Blancké, "Plautus as an Acting Dramatist," *CW* 6 (1912-13) pp. 10-13, 18-20.
A. Capp, "The Comedy of Charlie Chaplin," *AM* 185 (1950), pp. 25-29.
B. H. Clark, *European Theories of the Drama* (New York, revised ed., 1947).
M. Eastman, *The Sense of Humor* (New York, 1922).
———, *Enjoyment of Laughter* (New York, 1936).
P. Faider, "Le comique de Plaute," *MB* 31 (1927), pp. 61-75.
J. Feibleman, *In Praise of Comedy. A Study of its Theory and Practice* (New York, 1939).
R. Fleming, "Of Contrast between Tragedy and Comedy," *JPh* 36 (1939), pp. 543-553.
F. La T. Godfrey, "The Aesthetics of Laughter," *Ha* 50 (1937), pp. 126-138.
M. A. Grant, *The Ancient Rhetorical Theories of the Laughable* (Madison, 1924). [=*University of Wisconsin Studies in Language and Literature*, No. 21]
J. Y. T. Grieg, *The Psychology of Laughter and Comedy* (New York, 1923).
M. T. Herrick, "The Theory of the Laughable in the Sixteenth Century," *QJS* 35 (1949), pp. 1-16.
R. Jensen, "Quid rides?" *CJ* 16 (1920-21), pp. 207-219.

A. Koestler, *Insight and Outlook. An Inquiry into the Common Foundations of Science, Art, and Social Ethics* (New York, 1949).

J. W. Lange, S.J., "How Plautus and Shakespeare Make Us Laugh," *CB* 9 (1932-33), pp. 41-43.

L. Mathewson, *Bergson's Theory of the Comic in the Light of English Comedy* (Lincoln, 1920). [=*University of Nebraska Studies in Language, Literature, and Criticism*, No. 5]

G. Meredith, *An Essay on Comedy and the Uses of the Comic Spirit.* Edited, with an Introduction and Notes by Lane Cooper (New York, 1918).

A. Nicoll, *The Theory of Drama* (London, 1931).

A. O'Brien-Moore, *Madness in Ancient Literature* (Weimar, 1924).

R. Piddington, *The Psychology of Laughter. A Study in Social Adaptation* (London, 1933).

A. Rapp, *The Origins of Wit and Humor* (New York, 1951).

E. de Saint-Denis, "La force comique de Plaute," *Mélanges de Philologie, de Littérature et d'Histoire anciennes offerts à Alfred Ernout* (Paris, 1940), pp. 331-344.

B. Sidis, *The Psychology of Laughter* (New York, 1913).

W. Smith, *The Nature of Comedy* (Boston, 1930).

W. Süss, "Das Problem des Komischen im Altertum," *NJA* 45 (1920), pp. 28-45.

J. Sully, *An Essay on Laughter, its Forms, its Causes, its Development and its Value* (London, 1907).

O. L. Wilner, "Some Comical Scenes from Plautus and Terence," *CJ* 46 (1950-51), pp. 165-170, 176.

## CHAPTER 12. Language and Style

J. T. Allardice, *Syntax of Terence* (London, 1929). [=*St. Andrews University Publications*, No. 27]

J. C. Austin, *The Significant Name in Terence* (Urbana, 1922). [=*University of Illinois Studies in Language and Literature*, Vol. VII, No. 4]

G. L. Beede, "Proverbial Expressions in Plautus," *CJ* 44 (1948-49), pp. 357-362.

C. E. Bennett, *Syntax of Early Latin* (Boston, 1910-14). 2 vols.

J. M. G. M. Brinkhoff, *Woordspeling bij Plautus* (Nijmegen, 1935).

B. Brotherton, *The Vocabulary of Intrigue in Roman Comedy* (Menasha, 1926).

F. Conrad, "Die Deminutiva im Altlatein. I Die Deminutiva bei Plautus," *Gl* 19 (1930-31), pp. 127-148; 20 (1931-32), pp. 74-84.

F. T. Cooper, *Word Formation in the Roman Sermo Plebeius* (New York, 1895).

M. Durry, "Le vocabulaire militaire dans le *Phormio*," *REL* 18 (1940), pp. 57-64.

E. C. Echols, "The Art of Classical Swearing," *CJ* 46 (1950-51), pp. 291-298.

T. Frank, "Two Notes on Plautus. I. Parody in Act V of Plautus' *Mercator*," *AJPh* 53 (1932), pp. 243-248.

M. K. Glick, *Studies in Colloquial Exaggeration in Roman Comedy* (Chicago, 1941).

L. H. Gray, "The Punic Passages in the 'Poenulus' of Plautus," *AJSL* 39 (1922-23), pp. 73-88.

H. Haffter, *Untersuchungen zur altlateinischen Dichtersprache* (Berlin, 1934). [=*Problemata*, Heft 10]

J. B. Hofmann, *Lateinische Umgangssprache* (Heidelberg, 2nd ed., 1936).

J. N. Hough, "Terence's Use of Greek Words," *CW* 41 (1947-48), pp. 18-21.

F. Leo, *Analecta Plautina. De figuris sermonis* (Göttingen, 1896, 1898, 1906). 3 parts.

W. M. Lindsay, *Syntax of Plautus* (Oxford, 1907).

C. J. Mendelsohn, *Studies in the Word-Play in Plautus* (Philadelphia, 1907). [=*Publications of the University of Pennsylvania. Series in Philology and Literature*, Vol. XII, No. 2]

A. Müller, "Die Schimpfwörter in der römischen Komödie," *Ph* 72 (1913), pp. 492-502.

J. P. Postgate, "Flaws in Classical Research," *PBA* (1907-08), pp. 161-211.

K. Preston, *Studies in the Diction of the Sermo Amatorius in Roman Comedy* (Chicago, 1916).

K. Schmidt, "Die griechischen Personennamen bei Plautus," *H* 37 (1902), pp. 173-211, 353-390, 608-626.

W. B. Sedgwick, "Parody in Plautus," *CQ* 21 (1927), pp. 88-89.

E. B. T. Spencer, *Adnominatio in the Plays of Plautus* (Rome, 1906).

W. J. M. Starkie, *The Acharnians of Aristophanes* (London, 1909). [cf. pp. xxxviii-lxxiv, "Aristotle on the Laughter in Comedy"]

B. L. Ullman, "Proper Names in Plautus, Terence, and Menander," *CPh* 11 (1916), pp. 61-64.

L. A. Whitsel, *Studies in the Grouping of Words in Roman Comedy* (Madison, 1932).

## *CHAPTER 13. Meter and Song*

K. M. Abbott, "Ictus, Accent, and Statistics in Latin Dramatic Verse," *TAPhA* 75 (1944), pp. 127-140.

W. Beare, "The Delivery of *Cantica* on the Roman Stage," *CR* 54 (1940), pp. 70-72.

F. O. Copley, "On the Origin of Certain Features of the Paraclausithyron," *TAPhA* 75 (1942), pp. 96-107.

F. Crusius, *Die Responsion in den plautinischen Cantica* (Leipzig, 1929). [=*Ph*, Supplbd. XXI, Heft 1]

H. Drexler, *Plautinische Akzentstudien* (Breslau, 1932-33). 3 vols. [=*Abhandlungen der Schlesischen Gesellschaft für vaterländische Cultur*, Hefts 6, 7, 9]

G. E. Duckworth, "The Verse Structure of *Epidicus* 25-26," *CPh* 32 (1937), pp. 63-67.

———, "Cretics in the First Scene of Plautus' *Epidicus*," *CPh* 34 (1939), pp. 245-251.

R. C. Flickinger, Review of Law, *Studies in the Songs of Plautine Comedy*, *CW* 19 (1925-26), pp. 94-96.

M. Giganti, "Il papiro di Grenfell e i 'Cantica' plautini," *PP* 2 (1947), pp. 300-308.

P. W. Harsh, *Iambic Words and Regard for Accent in Plautus* (Stanford, 1949). [=*Stanford University Publications. Language and Literature*, Vol. VII, No. 2]

W. A. Laidlaw, *The Prosody of Terence. A Relational Study* (London, 1938). [=*St. Andrews University Publications*, No. 40]

H. H. Law, *Studies in the Songs of Plautine Comedy* (Menasha, 1922).
F. Leo, *Die plautinische Cantica und die hellenistische Lyrik* (Berlin, 1897).
[=*Abhandlungen der königlichen Gesellschaft der Wissenschaften zu Göttingen*, Philol.-hist. Klasse, N.F., 1, no. 7]
W. M. Lindsay, *Early Latin Verse* (Oxford, 1922).
―――, "Plautus and *The Beggar's Opera*," *CR* 37 (1923), p. 67.
L. Nougaret, "La métrique de Plaute et de Térence," *Memorial des Études Latines offert a. J. Marouzeau* (Paris, 1943), pp. 123-148.
W. B. Sedgwick, "The Origin and Development of Roman Comic Metres," *C & M* 10 (1949), pp. 171-181.

*CHAPTER 14. The Originality of Roman Comedy:*
*A Recapitulation*

P. Ferrarino, "Il *Limon* di Cicerone," *SIFC* N.S. 16 (1939-40), pp. 51-68.
C. Knapp, Review of *The Broadway Translations, CW* 19 (1925-26), pp. 195-198.
A. de Lorenzi, *Quaderni filologici. II. Dimidiatus Menander alla luce della polemica antiatticista di Cicerone* (Napoli, 1948).
R. S. Radford, "The Judgment of Caesar upon the *Vis* of Terence," *PAPhA* 32 (1901), pp. xxxix-xli.

*CHAPTER 15. The Influence of Plautus and Terence*
*upon English Comedy*

(Anonymous), Review of Reinhardstoettner, *Plautus. Spätere Bearbeitungen plautinischer Lustspiele, QR* 173 (1891), pp. 37-69.
N. B. Allen, *The Sources of John Dryden's Comedies* (Ann Arbor, 1935).
[=*University of Michigan Publications. Language and Literature*, Vol. xvi]
T. W. Baldwin (editor), *The Comedy of Errors* (London, n.d.).
―――, *William Shakspere's Small Latine and Lesse Greeke* (Urbana, 1944). 2 vols.
F. G. Ballentine, "The Influence of Terence upon English Comedy," *P. Terenti Afri Hauton Timorumenos* (Boston, 1910), pp. vii-xviii; see also *PAPhA* 37 (1906), pp. xiii f.
F. S. Boas, *Shakspere and his Predecessors* (New York, n.d.).
―――, "Early English Comedy," *CHEL*, Vol. v (Cambridge, 1918), Chapter v, pp. 89-120.
―――, "University Plays," *CHEL*, Vol. vi (Cambridge, 1918), Chapter xii, pp. 293-327.
R. W. Bond, *Early Plays from the Italian* (Oxford, 1911).
D. C. Boughner, "The Braggart in Italian Renaissance Comedy," *PMLA* 58 (1943), pp. 42-83.
L. Bradner, "A Check-List of Original Neo-Latin Dramas by Continental Writers Printed Before 1650," *PMLA* 58 (1943), pp. 621-633.
P. A. Chapman, *The Spirit of Molière. An Interpretation* (Princeton, 1940).
H. C. Chatfield-Taylor, *Molière, a Biography* (New York, 1906).
Mrs. S. V. Cole, "Plautus Up-to-date," *CJ* 16 (1920-21), pp. 399-409.
C. H. Conley, *The First English Translators of the Classics* (New Haven, 1927).

W. Connely, "When Plautus is Greater than Shakspere," *CJ* 19 (1923-24), pp. 303-305.

C. C. Coulter, "The Plautine Tradition in Shakespeare," *JEGPh* 19 (1920), pp. 66-83.

———, "The 'Terentian' Comedies of a Tenth-Century Nun," *CJ* 24 (1928-29), pp. 515-529.

J. W. Draper, "Falstaff and the Plautine Parasite," *CJ* 33 (1937-38), pp. 390-401.

P. J. Enk, "Shakespeare's 'Small Latin,'" *Neoph* 5 (1919-20), pp. 359-365.

J. B. Fletcher, *Literature of the Italian Renaissance* (New York, 1934).

A. Foresti, "Quando il Petrarca conobbe Terenzio e Plauto," *Ath* N.S. 1 (1923), pp. 1-16.

R. B. Forsythe, "A Plautine Source of *The Merry Wives of Windsor*," *MPh* 18 (1920-21), pp. 401-421.

V. O. Freeburg, *Disguise Plots in Elizabethan Drama. A Study in Stage Tradition* (New York, 1915).

J. Gassner, *Masters of the Drama* (New York, 1940).

C. M. Gayley, *Representative English Comedies* (New York, 1903-1914). 3 vols.

C. M. Gayley and A. Thaler, *Representative English Comedies*, Vol. IV (New York, 1936).

A. H. Gilbert, "Thomas Heywood's Debt to Plautus," *JEGPh* 12 (1913), pp. 593-611.

E. Gill, "A Comparison of the Characters in *The Comedy of Errors* with those in the *Menaechmi*," *BUTSE* 5 (1925), pp. 79-95.

———, "The Plot-Structure of 'The Comedy of Errors' in Relation to its Sources," *BUTSE* 10 (1930), pp. 13-65.

R. L. Grismer, *The Influence of Plautus in Spain before Lope de Vega* (New York, 1944).

K. P. Harrington (editor), *Mediaeval Latin* (Boston, 1925).

H. C. Hart (editor), *The Works of Ben Jonson* (London, 1906).

A. Henry (editor), *Epicoene or the Silent Woman by Ben Jonson* (New York, 1906). [=Yale Studies in English, XXXI]

C. H. Herford, *Studies in the Literary Relations of England and Germany in the Sixteenth Century* (Cambridge, 1886).

G. Highet, *The Classical Tradition. Greek and Roman Influences on Western Literature* (New York, 1949).

A. C. Judson (editor), *The Captives; or, The Lost Recovered, Written by Thomas Heywood* (New Haven, 1921).

J. S. Kennard, *The Italian Theatre. I. From its Beginning to the Close of the Seventeenth Century* (New York, 1932).

K. M. Lea, *Italian Popular Comedy. A Study in the Commedia dell' Arte, 1560-1620, with special reference to the English stage* (Oxford, 1934). 2 vols.

E. P. Lumley, *The Influence of Plautus on the Comedies of Ben Jonson* (New York, 1901).

B. Matthews, *Molière. His Life and His Works* (New York, 1910).

D. L. Maulsby, "The Relation between Udall's *Roister Doister* and the Comedies of Plautus and Terence," *ES* 38 (1907), pp. 251-277.

G. McCracken, "Wodehouse and Latin Comedy," *CJ* 29 (1933-34), pp. 612-614.

G. H. Nettleton, *English Drama of the Restoration and Eighteenth Century (1642-1780)* (New York, 1914).

A. Nicoll, *A History of Early Eighteenth Century Drama 1700-1750* (Cambridge, 1925).

A. Palmer (editor), *T. Macci Plauti Amphitruo* (London, 1890).

T. M. Parrott (editor), *Shakespeare. Twenty-three Plays and the Sonnets* (New York, 1938).

———, *Shakespearean Comedy* (New York, 1949).

T. M. Parrott and R. H. Ball, *A Short View of Elizabethan Drama, Together with Some Account of its Principal Playwrights and the Conditions under which it was Produced* (New York, 1943).

K. von Reinhardstoettner, *Plautus. Spätere Bearbeitungen plautinischer Lustspiele* (Leipzig, 1886).

E. Rhys (editor), *Ben Jonson* (New York, 1915).

F. E. Schelling, *Elizabethan Drama 1558-1642* (Boston, 1908). 2 vols.

———, *English Drama* (London, 1914).

W. E. Selin (editor), *The Case is Altered, by Ben Jonson* (New Haven, 1917).

J. W. D. Skiles, "Plautine Motifs in the Motion Pictures," *CJ* 37 (1941-42), pp. 534-535.

P. S. Stapfer, *Shakespeare and Classical Antiquity. Greek and Latin Antiquity as presented in Shakespeare's Plays.* Translated by E. J. Carey (London, 1880).

E. E. Stoll, *Shakespeare Studies* (New York, 1927).

A. H. Thorndike, "Ben Jonson," *CHEL*, Vol. vi (Cambridge, 1919), Chapter i, pp. 1-28.

J. L. Van Gundy, "*Ignoramus*," *Comoedia Coram Regia Maiestate Jacobi Regis Angliae. An Examination of its Sources and Literary Influence with Special Reference to its Relation to Butler's "Hudibras"* (Lancaster, 1906).

M. W. Wallace, *The Birthe of Hercules with an Introduction on the Influence of Plautus on the Dramatic Literature of England in the Sixteenth Century* (Chicago, 1903).

H. A. Watt, "Plautus and Shakespeare—Further Comments on *Menaechmi* and *The Comedy of Errors*," *CJ* 20 (1924-25), pp. 401-407.

K. E. Wheatley, *Molière and Terence, a Study in Molière's Realism* (Austin, 1931).

C. Whibley, "Translators," *CHEL*, Vol. iv (Cambridge, 1919), Chapter i, pp. 1-25.

———, "The Restoration Drama, ii," *CHEL*, Vol. viii (Cambridge, 1920), Chapter vi, pp. 146-177.

S. T. Williams, *Richard Cumberland. His Life and Dramatic Works* (New Haven, 1917).

C. H. C. Wright, *A History of French Literature* (New York, 1912).

# INDEX

# INDEX

Modern scholars are cited when the reference contains a description or criticism of their views. References to important passages are in italics.

494 INDEX

*See also fabula palliata*; pre-literary
Italian farce; Roman tragedy
Roman law, *see* law, references to
Roman life, reflected in Roman comedy,
272, 279, 280, 284, 290
Roman tragedy, 39, 40, *43-46*, 70-71, 323n;
decline of, 70
Rome, customs of people in, 120
*Romeo and Juliet*, 415
*Romulus*, 41
Roscius, 70, 74, 92, 93
Roswitha, *see* Hrotsvitha
Rotrou, Jean de, 405-06, 406-07
*Rudens*, *148*; considered Plautus' masterpiece, 148; *contaminatio* in, 179; date
of, 55 and n; dream of Daemones in,
221-22, 222n; fishermen as a chorus in,
100, 261; foreshadowing of later events
in, 216, 221-22; Greek original of,
28n, 53; Gripus in, 104, 114, 148, 180-
81, 252; *homo ex machina* in, 180-81;
influence of *fabula Atellana* upon, 16n
  influence upon later dramatists: Ariosto, 399-400; Dolce, 400; Heywood,
426 and n; Shakespeare, 414-15, 416-17
  irony in, 233; Labrax as slavedealer,
148, 263, 276, 314-15; motivation of
entrance in, 114; number of vacant
stages in, 98; Palaestra's identity hinted
at, 219, 220; Palaestra's sufferings, 104,
253-54; religious tone of, 104, 296, 299-
300; repetition of off-stage conversation in, 124-25; romantic atmosphere of,
83, 148 and n, 176, 389; setting on
seacoast near Cyrene, 82, 83; setting
unlike that of other comedies, 83, 85,
148; song in, 383; suspense and surprise in, 217, 231; use of altar on stage,
83-84, 297, 315; wing-entrances in, 85,
86
Rueda, Lope de, 402-03
Ruggle, George, 426-27, 428
running slave, *106-07*, 137, 225, 392;
creates suspense, 107 and n, 111, 225,
392; haste of, 106, 324-25; incongruity
of, 319; increases irony, 107, 225; in
Shakespeare, 415; threefold function of,
106, 225

Saint-Denis, E. de, 315n
St. Jerome, 49, 58, 396
St. Paul, 26n
Salamanca, university of, 402
*Samia*, 27, 28, 29, 117n
Santra, 58
Sargeaunt, J., 121n, 203
Sarsina, 50, 51
satire: in digressions, 195-96; in English
comedy, 419, 421, 426-27; in Plautus

and Terence, 304; political, 21, 22, 30,
42; relation to comedy, 306-07, 313;
social in *Truculentus*, 144
*satura*, 5, 6, 7, *8-10*, 378-79; as a medley,
8, 10; existence of dramatic *satura*
denied, 8-9; influence upon Plautus,
16 and n, 379; musical nature of, 8,
10, 379
*Saturae*, 10, 43
*Saturio*, written in prison, 50, 52
Saturnian meter, 8, 11, 39, 43
*Satyricon*, 332
Satyrus, 34, 35
Saunders, C.: on costumes, 88n; on location of performances, 79; on masks,
92n, 93 and n
*scaena*, 79. *See also* stage
*Scaramouch a Philosopher*, 428
scarf, conventionalized form of *pallium
collectum*, 91
Scarron, Paul, 405
scene-divisions, 98
scene-headings, 98 and n, 347n
scenery, on Roman stage, 82-84, 121-22
Schanz, M., 94n
*Schedia*, original of Plautus' *Vidularia*,
53
Schelling, F. E., 417n, 418n, 419n, 423,
424, 427n
Schoell, F., 94n, 191n, 440
scholarly work: on *contaminatio*, 68, 197-
98, 205-08; on *retractatio*, 67 and n;
on Roman comedy, v-vi, viii, 440-41.
*See also* Beare; Duckworth; Dunkin;
Enk; Fraenkel; Frank; Harsh; Hough;
Jachmann; Kuiper; Legrand; Leo;
Lindsay; Michaut; Norwood; Pres-
cott; Ritschl; Sedgwick
*School for Scandal, The*, 383
schools, in England, 408
Schopenhauer, Arthur, 311
Scipio, possible reference to in *Asinaria*,
54
Scipio Aemilianus, 56, 57, 58 and n, 64
Scipio Nasica, 80
Scipionic circle, 56, 58
*Scornful Lady, The*, 424
Scylla, 102
seats: assigned to senators, 79; banned
by senate, 80; in early times, 79;
Ritschl's theory rejected, 80-81; used
in Plautus' day, 81
*Sea Venture*, 417
Sedgwick, W. B.: on *Amphitruo*, 370n;
on chronology of Plautus' comedies, 55
and n, 380n; on delivery of *cantica*,
364n, 371n; on origin of Plautine song,
379; on originality of Plautus, 385;